The Centennial Compilation
All of Emily Ruete, born Sayyida Salme, Princess of Oman and Zanzibar

By Andrea Emily Stumpf

To her great-great-great-grandson,

my dearest
Max Salme Stumpf

———•———

Copyright © 2024 Andrea E. Stumpf
First edition; published in the United States, 2024
Cover design: Andrea E. Stumpf
Copy Editor: Lauri Scherer, LSF Editorial
Graphic Designer: Joe Bernier, Bernier Graphics

Andrea E. Stumpf has asserted her right as copyright owner of this publication, including under the Copyright, Designs and Patents Act of 1988, to be identified as the author of this work, including as translator of the translated texts contained herein.

All rights reserved. No part of this book may be reproduced, translated, or transmitted in any form or by any means, electronic or hard copy, including by photocopying, recording, any storage or retrieval system, or otherwise, without prior written permission of the author, translator, and copyright owner. For permission, send a request with complete information to andrea@sayyidasalme.com.

www.sayyidasalme.com; www.emilyruete.com

ISBN 978-1-7323975-9-0

CONTENTS

Memoirs of an Arabian Princess:
An Accurate Translation of Her Authentic Voice

❦

Letters to the Homeland:
An Accurate Translation of an Intimate Voice

❦

The Centennial Collection:
More of Emily Ruete, born Sayyida Salme,
Princess of Oman and Zanzibar

1924–2024

To commemorate the centennial anniversary of Sayyida Salme's death in 1924, this book is presented in 2024 as a compilation of three previously published companion books:

Memoirs of an Arabian Princess:
An Accurate Translation of Her Authentic Voice (2022)

Letters to the Homeland:
An Accurate Translation of an Intimate Voice (2023)

The Centennial Collection:
More of Emily Ruete, born Sayyida Salme,
Princess of Oman and Zanzibar (2024)

Each of the three books appears here in full in its originally published form.

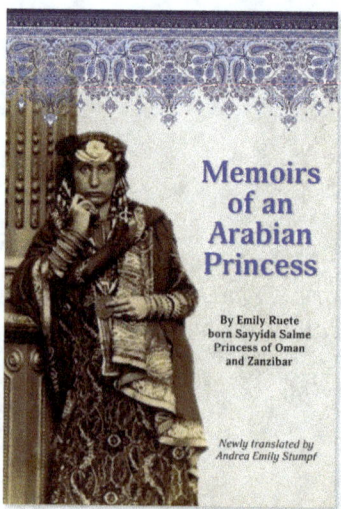

Memoirs of an Arabian Princess
An Accurate Translation of Her Authentic Voice

By Andrea Emily Stumpf

Translating the original 19th century
Memoiren einer arabischen Prinzessin
from her great-great-grandmother,

Emily Ruete,
born Sayyida Salme bint Said bin Sultan Al Bu Said,
Princess of Oman and Zanzibar

Copyright © 2022 Andrea E. Stumpf
First edition; published in the United States, 2022
Cover design: Andrea E. Stumpf
Copy Editor: Lauri Scherer, LSF Editorial
Graphic Designer: Joe Bernier, Bernier Graphics

Andrea E. Stumpf has asserted her right as copyright owner of this publication, including under the Copyright, Designs and Patents Act of 1988, to be identified as the Author of this work, including as Translator of the translated text contained herein. Max S. Stumpf is the copyright owner of the maps appearing on pages iv, v, and 215.

The original text that has been translated for this publication comes from the first and second volumes of *Memoiren einer arabischen Prinzessin*, published by the Friedrich Luckhardt publishing company of Berlin, Germany, in 1886 under the authorship of Emily Ruete, originally known as Sayyida Salme bint Said bin Sultan Al Bu Said, Princess of Oman and Zanzibar. The translated text incorporates subsequent edits from her marked copy provided by her son, Rudolph Said-Ruete, to the Oriental Institute in Leiden in 1937. The collection that included this marked copy was moved as a permanent loan to the Netherlands Institute for the Near East (NINO) in 1977 and became part of the Leiden University Libraries in 2018. The marked copy is available in the Leiden University Libraries' digital collection at NINO SR 613 a-b.

All rights reserved. No part of this book may be reproduced, translated, or transmitted in any form or by any means, electronic or hard copy, including photocopying, recording, by any storage or retrieval system, or otherwise, without prior written permission of the Author, Translator, and copyright owner. For permission, send a request with complete information to andrea@sayyidasalme.com.

www.sayyidasalme.com; www.emilyruete.com

ISBN 978-1-7323975-3-8

To Martin M. Stumpf

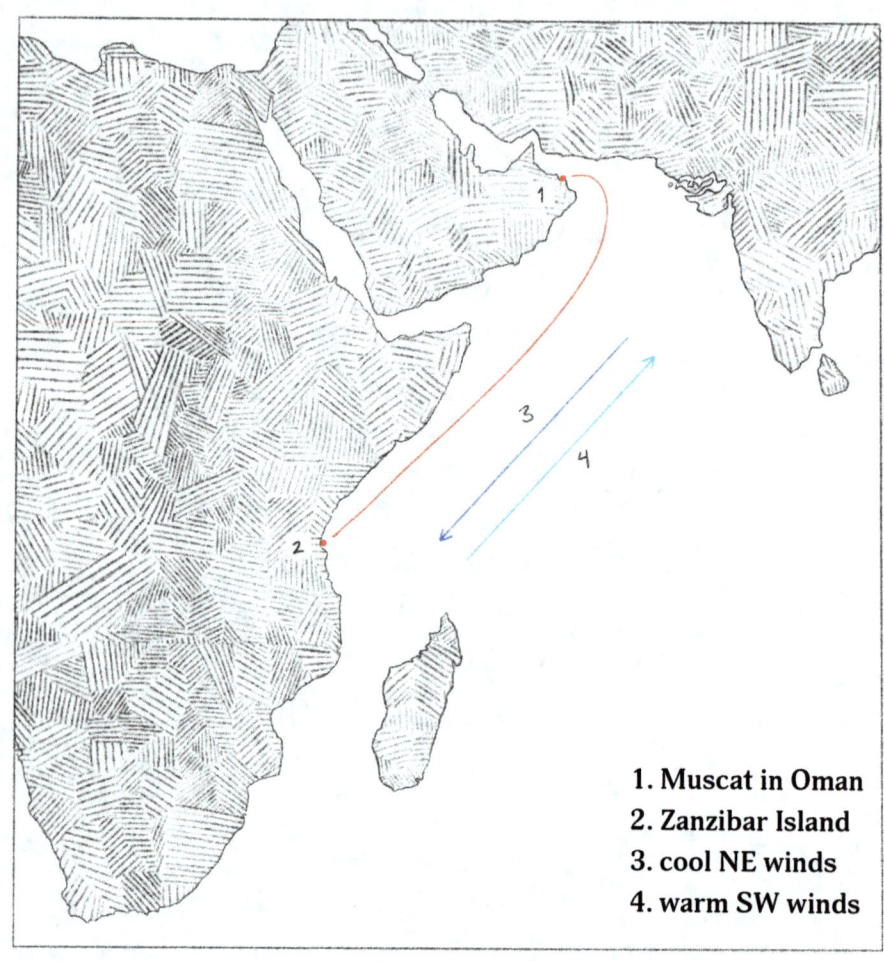

Indian Ocean monsoon trade winds

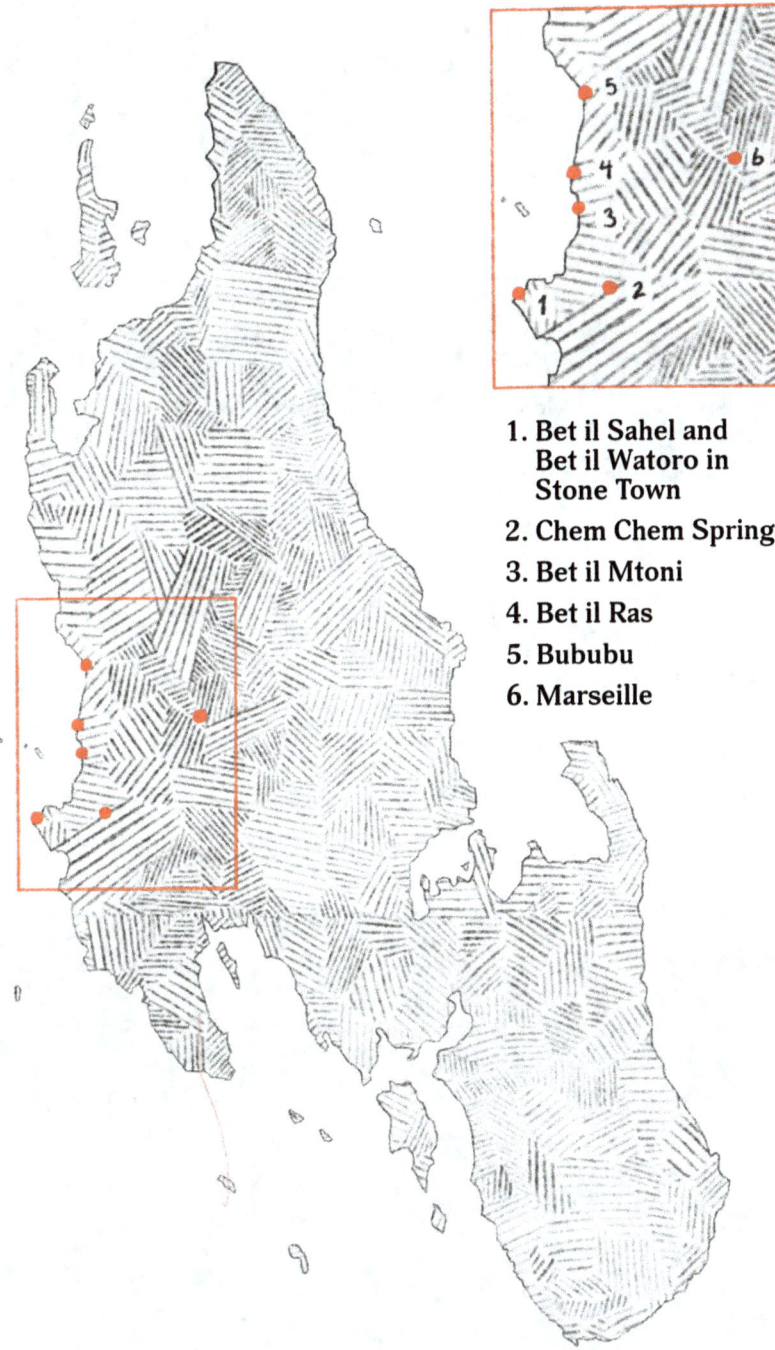

1. Bet il Sahel and Bet il Watoro in Stone Town
2. Chem Chem Spring
3. Bet il Mtoni
4. Bet il Ras
5. Bububu
6. Marseille

Zanzibar Island in the 19th century

CONTENTS

Introduction:

On Context and Content viii

Memoirs of an Arabian Princess

— see the detailed table of contents on the facing page —

From the translator:

On Contributions 232

On Family 235

On Fate 239

On Controversy 243

On Translating 252

List of Images 256

Memoirs of an Arabian Princess, translated from the original German:

Preface 1

Volume 1

1	Bet il Mtoni	3
2	Bet il Watoro	14
3	A Day at Bet il Sahel	21
4	Of Our Life at Bet il Watoro and Bet il Sahel	30
5	Relocating to Bet il Tani	34
6	Daily Life in Our House	37
7	Our Mealtimes	43
8	Birth and Early Years of a Prince or Princess	47
9	School in the Orient	55
10	Annual Provisions, Personal Care, and Fashion in Our House	61
11	On a Plantation	66
12	The Father's Voyage	73
13	News of a Death	80
14	Our Mourning	84
15	Personalities and Stories of My Siblings	89
16	Status of Women in the Orient	107

Volume 2

17	Arab Matrimony	123
18	Arab Visits Among the Ladies	128
19	The Audience; Interactions Among Men	133
20	The Time of Fasting	137
21	The Small Festival	142
22	The Big Festival	148
23	An Offering Festival at Chem Chem Spring	152
24	Diseases and Medical Care; the Possessed	158
25	Slavery	165
26	My Mother's Death; a Palace Revolution	170
27	Kizimbani and Bububu	189
28	My Last Stay in Zanzibar	196
29	Great Transformations	201
30	Sayyid Barghash in London	205
31	Returning to the Homeland After Nineteen Years	212

Afterword (original English) 229

ON CONTEXT AND CONTENT

Sayyida Salme—Princess Salme, Emily Ruete—surely knew, in her lifetime, that she was special. Born into the household and harem of the great Sayyid Said, venerated Sultan of Oman and ruler of Zanzibar, she grew up with the rank and privilege of royalty. But it was more than her station in life that made her stand out. Living forthrightly, she crossed color and culture lines, religious beliefs, country boundaries, and global hemispheres, all of which gave her exceptional insights and made her a remarkable resource.

To her great credit, she wrote about it and then decided to share it, her own story in her own words, written with care, perspective, and incisive commentary. She promised readers upfront that she would speak authentically, knowing they might not approve of all she had to say, but committing to accurate descriptions and frank observations, as best she could. In eloquent prose, she recounted her life growing up in Zanzibar as an unconventional daughter amidst scores of siblings and *sarari* (concubines), subject to all the rules and rituals of a Muslim household that became prone to political intrigue. And then she did the unthinkable, which set her on an extraordinary path from East to West.

When her *Memoiren einer arabischen Prinzessin* came out in Germany in 1886, she was—we believe—the first ever female Arab author of a commercially available book. The book immediately garnered great interest, was re-issued four times that year, and then quickly translated into English, with appearances in the United Kingdom and United States in 1888 to more popular acclaim. Today she remains an inspiration.

Sayyida Salme crossed a first boundary early on when she secretly taught herself to write, something young girls were not supposed to do. But her literary significance begins with her mother Djilfidan, who had also outdone her contemporaries, the other *sarari* in the harem, by learning how to read. Sayyida Salme describes how her mother's unusually early entry into the harem at age seven or eight let her learn to read with the young princes and princesses, unlike the others who arrived mature enough to have no interest in school classes for youngsters. An enduring image for Sayyida Salme was her mother going from room to room, with books in hand, to read religious verses to the sick. What a wonderful image, words on a page as a salve for the ill, nurturing the body and soul in times of need.

On Context and Content

Sayyida Salme was unique and unusual in many ways; indeed, special enough to still be among us today. Could she have imagined that her book and name would be so widely known all these many decades and generations later? Naturally, her *Memoirs* are a national treasure for Omanis and Zanzibaris, even many East Africans, whose cultures, conventions, and historical leaders are depicted in intimate detail. But the nineteenth-century story still fascinates and resonates far beyond those shores, even experiencing an uptick of interest in this post-modern age. Not only is her book still being read after more than 130 years, but it has generated a whole cottage industry of readily available reprints and reissues. Her detailed accounts are mined word-for-word and worldwide by scholars of history, sociology, anthropology, ethnography, semiotics, race relations, feminism, colonialism, Arab studies, African studies, and more.

Even her name signals something out of the ordinary. Born Salme, she later took the name Emily in a Christian baptism and Ruete in a Christian marriage, both on the same day. Thereafter she presented herself as Emily Ruete and signed the *Memoirs* Preface as "Emily Ruete, born Princess of Oman and Zanzibar." But she notably also placed her Arabic signature on the title page of her *Memoirs*, thus presenting her Arab self as the author. Over time, she kept both names close, one surely of necessity while living in Germany, the other intrinsic to her identity.

Beyond her double name that doubled her identity, we can see her in an array of other dualities. She was the consummate insider who became the observant outsider, the rare bird that flew the coop. She got caught in the currents of colonialism—first aided, then cornered, then jilted by the one power; useful, and then discarded by the other power. She changed her religion in good faith and remained a woman of great faith, even though she was condemned for giving up her Muslim faith. Split in two, she personified the bridge between East and West, but had to find strength in herself, as she lost her foothold on the one side and secured only weak moorings on the other. From young princess to young widow, she moved from a patriarchal dynasty to a patriarchal society—one box here, another box there—always finding her rights and agency curtailed. She was a pawn much of her life, driving her own destiny, but caught in the webs of other people and powers. And with that, she went from the height of privilege and prosperity to the edge of depression and poverty. Even so, she outlived every one of her many Sultanate siblings and lived vigorously to tell the tale.

The comparisons let Sayyida Salme see more clearly. Experiencing the West through the prism of the East, she perceived flaws and foibles of both Occident and Orient more directly. In this, she found a mission. Long before the technologies that now enable our extensive, pervasive, worldwide sharing, she sought to promote multicultural understanding. In her *Memoirs* lies a quest against disinformation, pushing back against caricatures and lockstep common wisdom. She was especially aware that her original culture and context were heavily shielded from the world. She also realized that cultures and customs tend to be self-validating when there is no awareness of alternatives.

Sayyida Salme handed us the intimate renderings of a most fantastical existence, one that reads like a fairy tale and a thriller, but in fact reflects a real life. And so, her story intrigues even as it engages. Her upbringing is out of this world, but still gives us mirrors and markers for our time. We see, for example, the unacceptable views of someone who grew up in a caste system and slave society, even as we continue our own struggles with questions of equality. Today's society has progressed, but there are still places where girls are not fully educated, and women cannot freely dress or vote; the list goes on. Then, too, Sayyida Salme reminds us that some challenges are nigh on eternal. There is no escaping hard choices when loving someone becomes a series of existential trade-offs, and we are all vulnerable to hard times when losing someone results in life-changing loss.

The value of Sayyida Salme's account lies in her dedication to fact, not fiction. She sought authenticity, not duplicity or publicity. She knew she was touching on sensitive subjects, but chose to speak her truth. As she wrote in the Afterword of her London edition from 1888, this was to be a "faithful recollection" and an "unvarnished reflection," which she saw as a way to contribute her share.

Against this backdrop, it is perhaps no wonder that I would step up, in my own small way, to offer a new translation, intended to replace prior inaccurate and archaic translations, so as to revive her true story as she told it. Could Sayyida Salme have imagined that a fourth-generation descendant would seek to restore and refresh her authentic voice? Could she have contemplated that her great-great-granddaughter, yet another continent over, would embark on a lifetime of lawyering, authoring, and love of language to prime herself for this project? I was born into German and English the way Sayyida Salme was born into privilege. Having both languages is a natural fit. Here, with this translation, I hope to make the most of it.

On Context and Content

Sayyida Salme originally wrote these *Memoirs* for her children, but offered them to us all:

And so, too, may my book travel into the world and find many friends, as I have been so blessed to do. (Memoirs, page 1)

The world was already getting smaller then. The importance of knowing and appreciating each other, across continents and cultures, was already on her mind. How now, that I can reach back into history to revive her revelatory voice, could she ever have suspected that these accurate and authentic *Memoirs* might be on your doorstep within two days, or immediately on your tablet! And in this way, may Sayyida Salme continue to find new friends throughout the world and into time.

Andrea Emily Stumpf
October 2022

This book is the first of two companion books, of which the second is *Letters to the Homeland: An Accurate Translation of an Intimate Voice*, also by Andrea Emily Stumpf, the author's great-great-granddaughter. The sequel contains a translation of the author's *Briefe nach der Heimat*, a handwritten manuscript that was found posthumously among her possessions.

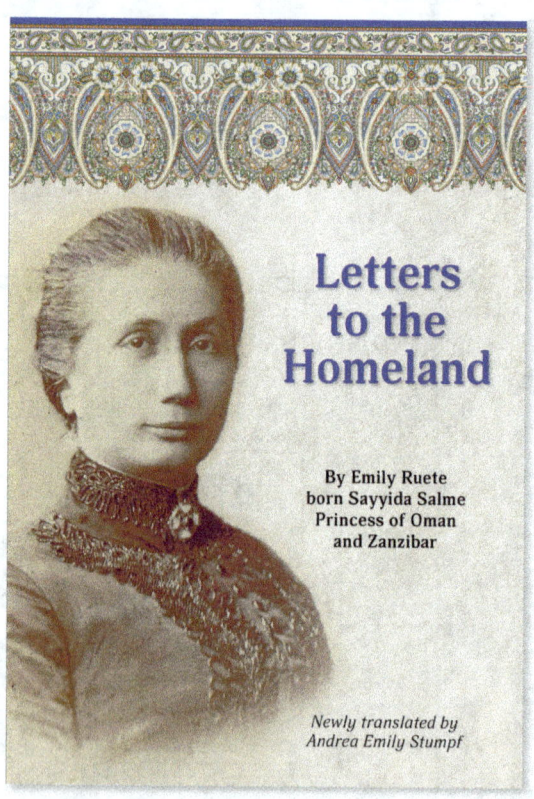

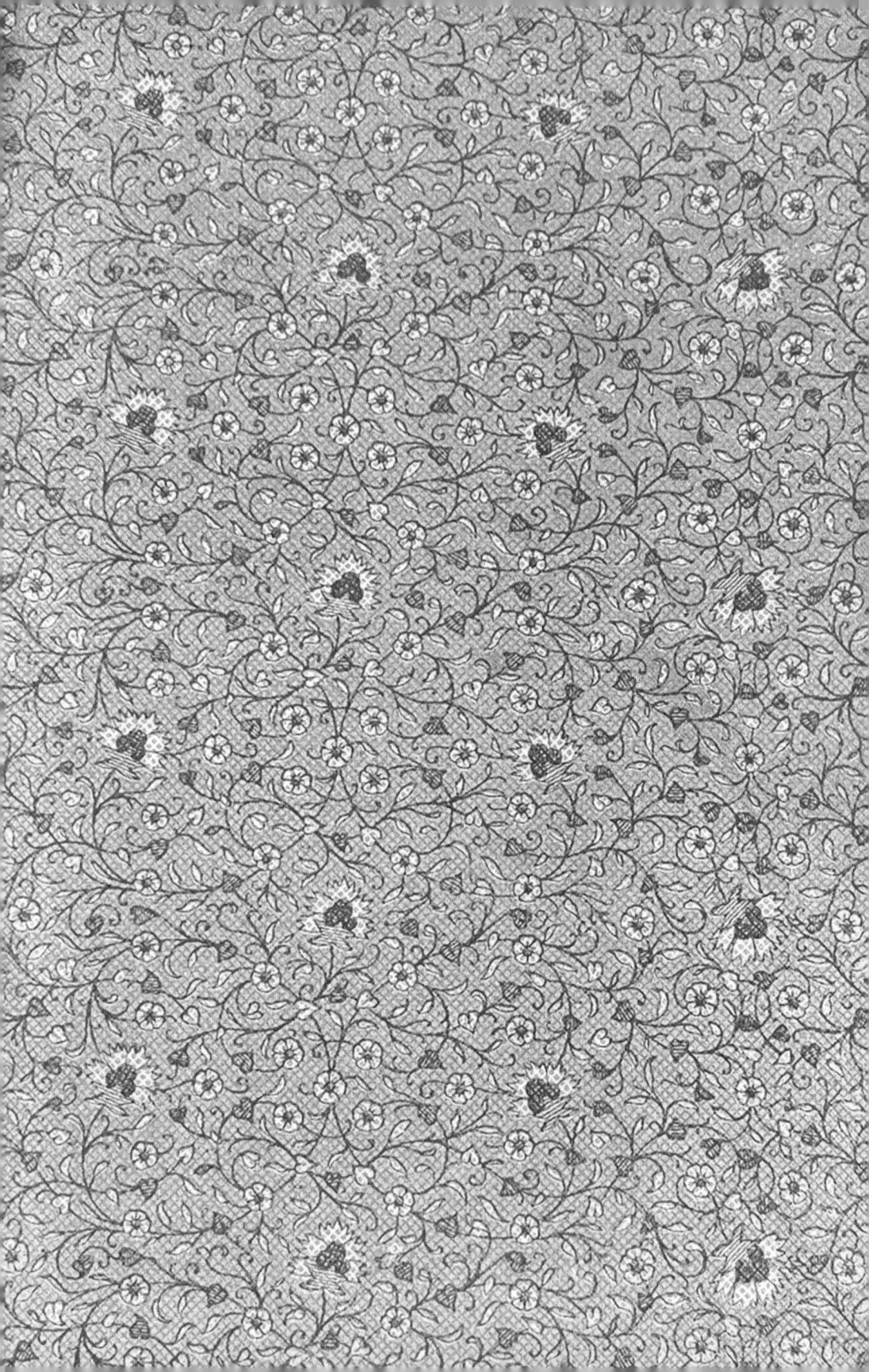

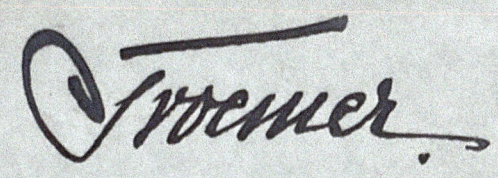

Memoiren
einer
arabischen Prinzessin.

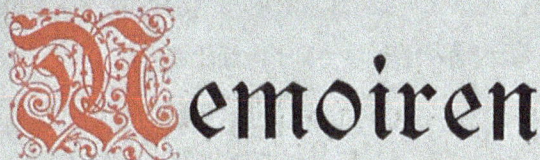

—❦— Erster Band. —❦—

Dritte Auflage.

Berlin.
Verlag von Friedrich Luckhardt.
1886.

Memoirs of an Arabian Princess

Volume 1

On the preceding pages, the end paper and title page are from an original edition of Volume 1 that belonged to either Rosa Troemer, the author's youngest daughter, or a member of her family. The bookplate on the previous page is from Emily Troemer, one of Rosa's two daughters and the translator's grandmother.

All footnotes in the following pages were added by the translator.

PREFACE

Nine years ago, I was inspired to recount some of my experiences for my children, who otherwise knew nothing about my past, except that I was Arab and came from Zanzibar. Physically and emotionally spent, I did not expect to last long enough to see them into adulthood to then tell them about my fateful journey and childhood memories. I therefore decided to write up my experiences and undertook the project with great love and dedication, knowing it was for my dear children, whose tenderness had comforted me during long and troubled years and whose deep empathy has sustained me through my trying times.

As such, my Memoirs were not originally written for the whole world, but as a testament of enduring love from a mother to her children. After much encouragement from others, I finally decided to have them published.

These pages were already completed years ago; only the last chapter was recently added. It describes the trip to Zanzibar, my old homeland, that my children and I were privileged to take last year. So, too, may my book travel into the world and find many friends, as I have been so blessed to do.

> Berlin, May 1886
> Emily Ruete
> born Princess of Oman and Zanzibar

Bet il Mtoni

CHAPTER ONE

Bet il Mtoni

It was in Bet il Mtoni, our oldest palace on the island of Zanzibar, that I was born in 1844 and lived until the age of seven.

Bet il Mtoni lies on the sea, about eight kilometers from the city of Zanzibar, in a most lovely setting, completely hidden away in a grove of majestic coconut palms, mango trees, and other tropical giants. The name of my birthplace, "Mtoni House," is from the little river Mtoni, which comes from the interior several hours away and streams through the whole palace in numerous basin-like extensions before emptying directly behind the palace walls into the wonderful, well-trafficked sea channel that separates the island from the African mainland.

A single, expansive courtyard fills the space between the various buildings that make up Bet il Mtoni. With a hodgepodge of structures that was built over time to meet the needs, and countless hallways and corridors that would merely confuse the uninitiated, the place is more ugly than pretty.

The rooms in our palace are also too many to count. Their layout slips my memory, though I clearly recall the spacious baths at Bet il Mtoni. Half a dozen bathhouses, all in a row, lay on the far side of the courtyard, so far off that when it rained, these beloved resorts could be reached only with the help of an umbrella. Off to the side was what we called the "Persian" bath, which was in fact a stand-alone Turkish steam bath whose masterful design was unmatched on the island.

Each bathhouse contained two basins about four meters long and three meters wide. The water level was set to reach chest-high for adults.

These bathhouses and their refreshing baths were very popular with all the residents. Most of them spent many hours a day there, praying, sleeping, working, reading—or even eating and drinking. From four in the morning until midnight, the traffic here never stopped. Day and night, people could be seen heading in and out.

At the entrances of these identical bathhouses, there were elevated resting areas on both sides immediately to the right and left, covered with the finest colorful mats, with verses woven into them, on which to pray or simply rest. No one is allowed to wear shoes on these elevated places, since that would be considered unholy. Rugs and all other luxury items are also banned from these rooms. To pray, Muslims (Mohammedans) are supposed to wear special, completely clean outfits intended only for this purpose and, if possible, all in white. Of course, this rather inconvenient religious prescription is strictly observed by only the most pious.

Narrow colonnades separate these resting areas from the bathing basins, which lie fully exposed under open skies. Steps on two arched stone bridges lead upwards from the basins to other completely segregated rooms.

Every bathhouse had its own designated occupants, and woe to anyone who failed to strictly observe these distinctions! Bet il Mtoni had a pronounced caste system that was impeccably followed by everyone, from high to low.

Bet il Mtoni

Orange trees as tall as the largest cherry trees here[1] bloomed in dense rows across the full expanse of the bathhouses. As young children, we often enough sought protection and refuge amidst their branches from our very strict teacher.

People and animals mingled quite comfortably throughout the immense courtyard, without bothering each other in the least. Peacocks, gazelles, guinea fowls, flamingos, geese, ducks, and ostriches roamed freely and were petted and fed by young and old alike. It was always a great delight for us youngsters to collect the many eggs here and there, especially the big ostrich eggs, and deliver them to the head cook, who would then reward us for our efforts with various treats.

Two times a day, early morning and evening, eunuchs gave children five years and older riding lessons in the courtyard, while our little zoo inhabitants kept undisturbed about their business. Upon completing enough basic training, we each received our own mounts from the father.[2] The boys could choose their horses from the royal stables, while the girls got large, snow-white donkeys from Muscat, which were often more valuable than the regular horses. These beautiful creatures were, of course, provided with the complete trappings. Virtually all the bridles consisted of heavy silver chains and other accessories.

Riding is a favorite pastime in family houses like these, since there are neither plays nor concerts to provide entertainment. Competitive races were often organized out in the open, although they unfortunately rather frequently ended in mishaps. Such a race even came close to costing my own life. Riding with complete zeal, so as not to let my brother Hamdan overtake me, I failed to see a mighty, oddly bent palm tree that suddenly blocked my way. Not until the trunk was directly in front of my forehead did I register the unexpected obstacle. In sudden alarm, I threw myself backwards and, as if by a miracle, escaped the looming danger.

An oddity of Bet il Mtoni was its many staircases, with steps of unrivalled steepness fit for a Goliath. Most of them headed straight up, without room to pause, turn, or pass, and practically the only way to reach the top was to grab onto rather primitive handrails. The stairwell traffic was so lively that these railings were in constant need of repair. I still remember the morning that residents in our wing were shocked to discover both handrails of our stone stairs, which were already so daunting, had collapsed in the middle of

---

1 "Here" in this case means Germany, where the author was living at the time.
2 "The father" was Sayyid Said bin Sultan, the Sultan of Oman and ruler of Zanzibar from 1806 to 1856.

the night. I marvel to this day that no one was hurt on these stairs, despite the enormous traffic at all hours.

Statistics being unknown in Zanzibar, no one really knew how many people actually lived in Bet il Mtoni. Were I to hazard a guess, all in all, I do not think a thousand inhabitants would overstate the case. To understand this, it is important to remember that in the Orient[3] one must occupy an extraordinary number of hands to be considered wealthy and well-off. Our father's other palace in the city, Bet il Sahel, also known as the "Beach House," had no fewer residents.

My father, Sayyid Said, the Imam of Muscat and Sultan of Zanzibar, along with his principal wife, a distant relative, resided in the wing of Bet il Mtoni that lay closest to the sea. He spent only four days a week here in the countryside, with the rest of the week spent in his city palace, Bet il Sahel. The title "Imam" is a religious honor that is very rarely bestowed on a ruler. We owe this distinction originally to my great-grandfather, Ahmed. Since then, this title has become hereditary for the whole family, and we are all entitled to add it to our signatures.

As one of my father's younger children, I only ever knew him with his venerable, snow-white beard. Somewhat taller than average, he had in his countenance something extraordinarily winsome and endearing, and yet his appearance commanded the utmost respect. Despite reveling in war and conquest, he was exemplary for all of us as the head of the family and ruler of his people. Nothing mattered more to him than justice, and he made no distinction between his own son and a simple slave when addressing possible transgressions. Above all, he was the definition of humility before God the Almighty. He had no trumped-up pride, unlike so many others of rank. Modest and with few needs for himself, he was charitable and generous toward others. He also appreciated when the people around him were well-dressed, cheerful, and in good spirits. I never saw him angry with anyone or heard him berate them. He had a good sense of humor and loved to put on a good joke. And yet, he was a great authority figure for young and old. If there was one thing he did not like, it was wastefulness. —If an ordinary slave that had gained his respect over many years of loyal service got married, it was not unusual for him to get his horse saddled, so he could ride out completely on his own to extend his personal congratulations to the young couple. —He always called me the "Old One" for my love of cold milk soup (Arabic *farni*), a dish favored by many of our toothless seniors.

---

3   The author places Zanzibar in the Orient relative to Germany in the Occident, the East relative to the West, and the South to the North. As understood in the nineteenth century, these geographical terms were laden with cultural and religious differences that also spawned no shortage of clichés and stereotypes.

My mother, a Circassian by birth, was torn from her homeland already at a young age. She had been living peacefully with her father, mother, and two siblings on the family farm. Then war broke out, marauding bands rampaged across the land, and the whole family fled to an underground location, per my mother's description. She apparently meant a cellar, something we did not have in Zanzibar. A wild horde penetrated even this refuge. They struck down the father and mother, and then three Arnauts[4] galloped off with the three siblings. The one with her older brother soon disappeared from view. The two others with my mother and her three-year-old sister, who could not stop crying for her mother, stayed together until nightfall when they, too, separated. My mother never heard anything more of her siblings.

My mother was still a child when she came into my father's possession, probably already at the tender age of seven or eight, since she lost her first tooth in our house. From the start, until maturity, she was paired as a playmate with two of my sisters[5] her age and raised and cared for the same as them. She also learned how to read with them, a skill that set her apart from those of her rank, many of whom had arrived at age sixteen to eighteen, if not older, and were naturally in no mood to join very young children on hard school mats. She was not that attractive, but tall and strong, with black eyes and black hair that reached to her knees. Gentle by nature, she derived her greatest pleasure from being able to help others and bring them joy. When someone got sick, she would be the first at their bedside and then care for them, as needed. I still see her before me, how she would go from one sick person to another, books in hand, to read them religious passages.

The father always had a special regard for her and never turned down her requests, which she usually made on behalf of others. He would regularly walk towards her when she came to him, a recognition that was very rare. With a good and pious disposition, she had a most self-effacing manner and was sincere and open in all things. Although not particularly gifted intellectually, she was very proficient in her needlework. She gave birth to only two children, namely a daughter who died at a very young age, in addition to myself. She was a tender, loving mother to me, although that never stopped her from punishing me vigorously when necessary.

---

4   "Arnauts" is an Ottoman exonym for Albanians, particularly soldiers, here apparently acting as mercenaries for Russian incursions.
5   The author refers to sisters and brothers who are, in fact, half-sisters and half-brothers, all sharing the same father, but with different *sarari* mothers. Since the author's mother joined the harem at an unusually young age, and the author was one of the youngest children of the Sultan, it makes sense that some of the author's siblings were her mother's age.

She had many friends in Bet il Mtoni, which is not the norm in an Arab harem. Her faith in God could not have been more steadfast and solid. I still remember a fire that broke out on a moonlit night in and around the adjacent royal stables when I was perhaps no more than five years old, while the father and his retinue were in the city. When a false alarm rang through our house that it, too, was in immediate danger of being engulfed by the fire, my good mother had nothing more urgent to do than take me under one arm and her large, handwritten Kurân (that is how we pronounce the word) under the other and rush out into the open. Nothing else had any particular value for her in this hour of peril.

As best I can recall, my father had but two wives equal to his rank in my time. The other wives[6] or *sarari* (singular *surie*), which numbered seventy-five at his death, were all purchased by him over time. His principal wife, Azze bint Sef, a born princess of Oman, was the absolute mistress of the house. Although very small in stature and outwardly very plain, she exerted unbelievable power over my father, such that he always acceded to her demands. As far as the other women and their children, she was exceedingly imperious, arrogant, and demanding. Fortunately for us, she had no children of her own, whose tyranny would have been unbearable. All my father's children—not more than thirty-six at his death—came from his concubines. We were therefore all equal amongst ourselves and had no need to dwell on the color of our blood.

Bibi (Swahili for lady-in-charge) Azze, whom everyone had to address as "Highness" (Arabic *Sayyida*), was feared by young and old, high and low, and loved by no one. Even today I remember her vividly, how she walked past us so stiffly, rarely addressing anyone in a friendly tone. How very different from my dear old father! He had something kind to say to everyone, regardless of rank. My superior stepmother knew only too well how to exert her entitled status, and no one dared come too close, unless they were invited to do so. I never saw her without her entourage, except when she went with the father to the private bathhouse that was exclusively for them. All who encountered her in the house were overcome with the same respect that a recruit pays a General in Europe.

Although we all felt the pressure she exerted from above, it was not enough to undermine the overall quality of life for the residents of Bet il Mtoni. Custom required that all my siblings, young and old, visit her at the start of each day to

---

6 Although the German word for *Frau* can mean either "woman" or "wife," Professor Abdul Sheriff, the widely respected Zanzibari historian and visionary promoter of local museums and archives, has clarified that *sarari* are considered wives—as he puts it, "secondary slave wives"—in contrast to Western-styled concubines, who have no such status. A. Sheriff, "*Suria*: Concubine or Secondary Slave Wife?—The Case of Zanzibar in the Nineteenth Century," in G. Campbell and E. Elbourne, *Sex, Power, and Slavery* (2014).

wish her a good morning. But everyone was so ill-disposed toward her that only rarely did anyone arrive before breakfast was delivered to her chambers, thereby denying her the pleasure of receiving the wholesale submission she demanded.

My oldest siblings lived in Bet il Mtoni. Some of them, like Shecha and Zuene, could have been my grandmothers. The latter already had a son, Ali bin Suud, whom I knew only with a speckled beard. She was a widow and had sought refuge in her parental home after her husband's passing.

In our family circle, we did not, as many here assume, favor sons over daughters. I do not know of a single case where the father or mother wanted a son over a daughter, or advantaged him just because he was a son. Nothing of the sort. Even though the law gives preference to boys over their sisters and affords them significant advantages—for example, in matters of inheritance where the sons get twice as much as the daughters—all children are nevertheless equally loved and cared for. That a particular child, both there in the South and here, whether boy or girl, might be a favorite, even if not overtly, is natural and certainly also human. And so it was with our father, except that his favorite children were clearly not sons, but two of his daughters, Sharife and Chole. Once, when I was about nine years old, my very rambunctious brother Hamdan, who was about my age, shot an arrow into my side, which fortunately caused no great harm. When the father learned of the incident, he told me: "Salme, go and get Hamdan for me." I had hardly arrived with my brother when he was subjected to a stream of invectives for being so reckless, words he would long remember. On this score, then, people here are very ill informed. Of course, it depends everywhere on the children themselves, and it would surely be very unfair to treat inconsiderate ones the same as considerate ones, without any noticeable difference between the two. —

The nicest spot at Bet il Mtoni was the *bendjle*, an immense, round balcony near the sea, in front of the main house, where one could have comfortably put on a grand ball, had such a thing been known to us or customary. The whole area was like a giant carousel, since even the ceiling, like the rest of the structure, was round. The entire framework, floor, and bannisters, as well as the tentlike ceiling, were made of painted wood. My dear father would spend hours here, pacing back and forth, head bent down, deep in thought. He limped a little. A bullet from the war, lodged in his thigh and a frequent source of pain, hindered the gait of this strong man.

Many cane chairs stood along the perimeter of the airy *bendjle*, surely several dozen, in addition to a powerful telescope for general use. But beyond that, nothing more. The view from this lofty balcony was breathtakingly beautiful.

VUE DE M'TONY.

Multiple times a day, the father, Azze bint Sef, and all his adult children would come for their coffee. Anyone seeking an undisturbed word with the father would look nowhere else but here, where he was mostly alone at certain hours.

All year round, the warship *Il Rahmani* lay at anchor across from the *bendjle*, with the sole purpose of sounding the cannon for us to wake up during the month of fasting and to man the many rowboats we needed. Signal flags were hoisted on a tall mast under the *bendjle* to order a larger or smaller number of boats and sailors to the shore.

As far as cooking is concerned, Bet il Mtoni, as well as Bet il Sahel, offered Persian and Turkish cuisine in addition to Arab cuisine. Indeed, the greatest diversity of races lived together in the two houses, amply reflecting the full range of looks from the most enchanting beauties to the complete opposite. But we were permitted to wear only Arab attire, and Africans only Swahili attire. Whenever a new Circassian showed up in her wide skirts, or an Abyssinian arrived in her fantastic robes, she had three days to put all that aside and start wearing her assigned Arab clothing.

Much in the same way that a hat and pair of gloves are indispensable for every proper woman here, the same is true for us with—jewelry. Jewelry is such a necessary part of a woman's presentation that even beggar women wear it when they beg. The father had his special coffers in both houses in Zanzibar, as well as his palace in Muscat in the kingdom of Oman, which were richly filled with large Spanish gold coins, British guineas, and French Louis d'ors. But they were also, and in greater part, filled with all sorts of women's accessories, from the plainest piece to a diamond-studded crown, all acquired to give as gifts. Whenever the family took on a new member, be it through the purchase of a *surie* or the frequent birth of a prince or princess, the door of the coffer would be opened to select a gift for the new arrival according to rank and station. When a child was born, the father would wait to visit the mother and child on the seventh day and then take along jewelry as a gift for the baby. A newly arrived *surie* would also receive the requisite items of jewelry right after being acquired, at the same time the head eunuch assigned her servants.

Although the father loved utter simplicity for himself, he was very particular about his overall environment. None of us, neither his children nor the youngest eunuch, were ever allowed to appear before him in anything less than our full attire. We little girls wore our hair braided into many thin plaits (often up to twenty). The ends from both sides were diagonally tied together in the center, and a heavy gold piece, often set with gemstones, was hung from the middle down the back. This hairpiece usually took the form of a crescent moon with a star set inside. Or sometimes a gold coin with holy verses was hung from each individual plait, which was a much more becoming look than the other one. At bedtime, nothing at all was removed except these specific jewelry pieces, which servants tied on again the next morning. We girls also wore bangs, exactly as one does here now, until the time we had to start masking daily. One morning, I ran undetected to the father without waiting for this hair adornment, so as to get the French candies he handed out to us children regularly at the start of every day. But instead of getting this much-desired treat, I was promptly sent back out because of my unfinished appearance, and a servant had to return me *nolens volens* from whence I had come. Ever after, I always took great care to never again show myself to him without being fully prepared.

My sister Zeyane and my stepmother Medine were among my mother's most intimate friends. Zeyane, the daughter of an Abyssinian, was practically the same age as my mother, and they loved each other indescribably dearly. My stepmother Medine was likewise a Circassian. This grounded the friendship, since she, my mother, and also Sara, another one of my stepmothers, all came from one and the same region. Sara's two children were my brother Madjid and my sister Chadudj (the ch is pronounced like the guttural German in *noch*, *doch*, etc.). The brother was a good bit younger than the sister. My mother had an understanding with her friend Sara that if Sara were to die first, my mother would care for Madjid and Chadudj as their second mother, and vice versa. But when Sara died, Chadudj and Madjid were already older and no longer needed my mother's help as long as they still lived in the paternal house. For us, which is to say my extended family, it was customary for the boys to remain with their mothers in the paternal house, entirely bound to the house rules, for some time after their boyhood. Once a prince reached the age of about eighteen to twenty, sooner or later depending on his good or bad conduct, the father would declare him of age. Then he could count himself among the adults, an honor he would have been awaiting with great impatience, there as here. At this time, every prince would then receive his own house, servants, horses, and all the rest, in addition to a sufficient monthly allowance.

My brother Madjid had now reached this point. He deserved the honor more for his overall character than his age. Madjid was the embodiment of modesty, and his kind and friendly manner won the hearts of everyone he encountered everywhere. Not a week went by that he did not ride out to us from the city (since he, like his mother before him, lived in Bet il Sahel, rather than Bet il Mtoni). Despite being about twelve years my senior, he still played with me as though we were one and the same age.

Thus he came to us one day, happy and excited, to let my mother know that the father had just declared him of age, set him on his own two feet, and given him his own house. Then he urgently entreated my mother that we, she and I, should now move into his new home to live with him and his sister there forever. Chadudj echoed the request. In response to this rousing appeal, my mother cautioned that she could not fulfill this wish without the father's permission, but would discuss the matter with him and then share the result. For her part, she was quite willing to live with them, if that was what they wanted. Madjid, however, offered to talk to the father himself, to spare my mother the effort. The next morning he returned with news that the father, who happened to be staying at Bet il Sahel, had approved Madjid's request. And with that, our move was decided. After lengthy consultations, my mother and Madjid agreed that we would move a few days later, so he and Chadudj could first settle somewhat into their new home.

RUINED PALACE OF SYED SAAID BEN SULTAN AT MTONY.

CHAPTER TWO

Bet il Watoro

My mother found it hard to follow through with the upcoming move. She was attached to Bet il Mtoni with heart and soul, having lived there since childhood. Her separation from my stepsister Zejane and my stepmother Medine was especially difficult. Nor did she relish change. But, as she told me later herself, the feeling that she might be of use to the children of her deceased friend outweighed any personal misgivings.

No sooner did my mother's decision to move into the city become known than she was accosted everywhere she showed her face with calls of "Djilfidan (that is the name of my dear mother), are you so heartless as to leave us forever?" "Oh friends," she would answer, "it is not my will that I would leave you; it is fate that I should go."

I believe some readers may read the word "fate" and feel some pity towards me, or if nothing else, shrug their shoulders. But one must not forget that the author was a Muslim and raised this way. And I am of course telling the story of an Arab life, an Arab household, that is, a real Arab home, in which two concepts in particular were as yet unfamiliar: the word "chance" and materialism. A Muslim not only recognizes his God as his creator and keeper, but also feels the presence of the Lord at all times. He is certain that it is not his will, but the will of the Lord that comes to pass, in all things, large and small.

A few days went by as we got our things together. Then we awaited Madjid's return, since he wanted to manage our trip himself. Three siblings, two sisters and a brother, all about my age, had been my playmates in Bet il Mtoni. I was

Bet il Watoro

very sorry to leave them, especially little Ralub, who had become quite attached to me. On the other hand, I was elated by the prospect of saying good-bye to our new and inhumanely strict teacher forever. —

With the coming separation from our many friends and acquaintances, our large room became a beehive. Everyone brought farewell gifts according to their means and degree of attachment. People take this custom very seriously. All true Arabs insist on presenting gifts to their friends, even if they have virtually nothing to give. This even applies to Africans. I still recall a case in point from when I was very young. We had taken an outing from Bet il Mtoni to our plantations and were in the process of boarding our many boats for the trip home. Suddenly I felt a tug from behind and saw a little old African lady beckoning to me. She gave me something wrapped in banana leaves with the words: "This token is for you, *bibi jangu* (my mistress), for your departure; it is the first ripe harvest from in front of my house." I quickly opened the leaves and found a single, freshly-picked—corncob. I did not know this little old African lady at all, but it later turned out that she was an old protégée of my dear mother. —

Madjid finally arrived and informed my mother that the captain of the *Rahmani* had orders to send a cutter the next evening for both of us, plus another boat for our belongings and the people bringing us to the city.

My father happened to be in Bet il Mtoni on the day of our departure, so my mother took me to see him to say good-bye. We found him walking back and forth on the *bendjle*. Upon seeing us, he immediately came towards my mother. They were soon engrossed in a lively conversation about our trip. He ordered a eunuch standing on the side to bring some sweets and sharbet (fruit juice) for me, probably to redirect my endless questions. I was, of course, very excited and curious about our new home and generally about everything having to do with life in the city. Up to this point, if I recall correctly, I had been in the city only once before and then only briefly. That is why I did not know all my siblings, nor all my many stepmothers.

After that we went to the chambers of my venerable stepmother to take our leave from her as well. Azze bint Sef accorded us a standing farewell, honoring us in her own way, as she otherwise always stayed seated when receiving or dismissing. My mother and I were both allowed to take her delicate hand to our lips, before turning our backs on her forever.

Then we traipsed up and down many more stairs to shake hands with all our friends, but found barely half of them in their rooms. So my mother decided to say farewell to them altogether at the next regular prayer hour, where everyone would be in attendance.

At seven in the evening, our cutter, a large one reserved only for special occasions, docked under the *bendjle*. It was manned by fourteen sailors as oarsmen and adorned at the front and back with large, blood-red flags, our flag, which has no further insignia. A large baldachin, with side curtains to shelter the women and ward off potential rain, was draped above the back end of the ship, under which ten to twelve people could sit on silk cushions.

Old Djohar, one of my father's loyal eunuchs, came to tell us everything was ready. He and another eunuch had been ordered by the father, who was watching our departure from the *bendjle*, to accompany us on the trip. Djohar, as usual, took the helm. Our tearful friends followed us to the front door, and the call *wedâ, wedâ*! "farewell, farewell!" still rings in my ears to this day.

Our beach is relatively flat without a jetty. As a result, we had three different ways to get onto boats. One was to sit in an armchair and be carried out by sturdy slaves; another was to simply ride on their backs; or we could instead walk to the boat on a plank extended out from the dry sand. My mother used this last, more comfortable approach to get on board, supported on both sides by eunuchs walking next to her in the wet sand. Another eunuch carried me to the boat in his arms and deposited me at the helm next to my mother and old Djohar. A few colorful lanterns in our cutter, together with the shining stars, spread a truly magical shimmer. As our boat launched into motion, the fourteen oarsmen broke into the rhythm of a melancholy Arab song.

We took the usual route along the coast, while I, half lying on my mother, half resting on my cushions, soon dozed off. Suddenly I was startled from my sleep by a cacophony of voices calling my name. Greatly alarmed and still only half awake, I eventually realized that we had reached our destination, meaning I had slept my way through the whole trip. We stopped directly under the windows of Bet il Sahel, which were all lit up and filled with countless heads. All these spectators were my stepsiblings and their mothers, mostly as of yet unknown to me. Many of the siblings were younger and no less curious to meet me than I was to meet them. They were the ones, my mother explained, who had started calling my name from a distance, as soon as our boat had come into view.

We disembarked the same way we had embarked, and my young brothers gave me a more than rousing welcome. They bid us come with them, but my mother of course declined, as Chadudj, who was already standing at the window of her house, would have had to wait for us that much longer. I was terribly sad not to be able to join my young siblings right away, having looked forward to that for days, but I knew my mother well enough to know whatever she said and wanted was final. Despite her incomparable, selfless love for me, she was always and in all things very firm and resolute. She consoled me with the prospect of spending the whole day together at Bet il Sahel as soon as the father returned there.

And so we passed Bet il Sahel and continued on to Bet il Watoro, Madjid's house. It lay directly beside Bet il Sahel and had the same unobstructed view of the sea. Upon entering, we found my sister Chadudj waiting for us at the foot of the stairs. She gave us a very hearty welcome and then took us straight up to their rooms, where her favorite eunuch Eman soon arrived with all sorts of refreshments. Madjid was in the parlor with his friends, but came up when he heard we were there. Oh, how happy he was, our dear, noble Madjid, to welcome us into his home!

Our own room was of a moderate size and looked directly onto a mosque next door. It was set up like most Arab rooms and left nothing wanting. We needed only one room. Since dress changes happen in the bathroom, and nightwear is the same as our washable daywear, no separate rooms are needed as in Europe. For people both high and low, the bedroom is in the living room.

The rooms of those who are rich and high society tend to have the following arrangement: Persian carpets or the very finest, soft mats cover the floor. Whitewashed walls, of considerable width, feature correspondingly deep recesses from floor to ceiling that are divided into multiple compartments. Green painted, wooden boards further divide these compartments into a kind of shelving. Symmetrically arranged on these shelves are the very finest and most precious glass and porcelain objects. Nothing is too expensive for Arabs when it comes to decorating their shelves—finely polished glass, a nicely painted plate, a stylish pitcher, no matter the price tag. If it looks pretty, it will be bought.

Efforts are made to cover even the bare and narrow wall spaces between the compartments. They are inlaid with large mirrors that reach from the top of the divan, just slightly above floor level, all the way up to the ceiling. These mirrors are always custom-ordered by height and width from Europe. Muslims generally disapprove of pictures as imitations of divine creation, although they are more recently tolerated now and again. By contrast, clocks are much beloved, and houses often have extensive collections, sometimes placed above the mirrors, or in pairs on either side. —In the gentlemen's rooms, the walls are adorned with all sorts of valuable trophy weapons from Arabia, Persia, and Turkey, the kind of ornamentation with which every Arab man prefers to decorate his home, according to his rank and riches.

The great double bed made of what is known as rosewood and covered with wonderfully skilled carvings, a product of East Indian craftsmanship, stands in one corner. White gauze or tulle drapes the entire bed from above. Arab beds have very high legs. To access them more comfortably, one first steps onto a chair, or uses the hand of a chambermaid as a more natural step. The ample space beneath the bed is then often used as a sleep station by others as well, such as wet nurses of small children or caretakers of the sick.

Tables are quite rare and then only with people of the highest rank, in contrast to chairs, which abound in all sorts of styles and colors. Cabinets, wardrobes, and the like are also missing. We instead used a kind of coffer or case that usually had two or three drawers, plus a secret internal compartment for money and jewelry. Every room tended to have several of these very large chests, which were made of rosewood and beautifully adorned with thousands of tiny yellow brass nail heads.

Windows, and by day also doors, stay open all year round, the former closed up at most briefly now and again for rain. And that is why the phrase "there's a draft in the air" is never heard in those parts. —

I completely disliked our new apartment at the start. I missed my young siblings too much and then also found Bet il Watoro oppressively small and confined in comparison to the enormity of Bet il Mtoni. Am I now supposed to live here forever?, I incessantly asked myself those first days. Where do you want to sail your boats now? In a washtub? There was, of course, no little river like the Mtoni here, and water had to be brought in from a well outside the house. And when my dear, good mother, who would have preferred to give everything she owned to others, advised me to take those pretty sailboats that I loved so much and give them to my siblings in Bet il Mtoni, I initially wanted to hear nothing of it. In short, for the first time in my life, I felt very unhappy and bitterly sad.

My mother, on the other hand, immediately settled in and stayed busy all day long, organizing and arranging things with Chadudj, so that she also had no time for me. Good-hearted Madjid took care of me the most. The very next morning, he took me by the hand and showed me his whole house from top to bottom. But I could not find happiness in anything. I was indifferent to everything and implored my mother to return with me to Bet il Mtoni, to my dear siblings, very soon. Of course, there was no chance of that, all the more because she really was a great help to both of them.

Fortunately, I discovered that Madjid was a big animal lover, with a large collection of all sorts of live creatures in his house. Among them were masses of white rabbits, who left the house in a complete mess, to the dismay of Chadudj and my mother. He also kept a large number of fighting cocks from all over the world. I have never again seen such a huge collection, not even in a zoo.

In visiting his pets, I soon became Madjid's constant companion, as he let me join in all his passions with endless goodwill. Through his generosity, it did not take long for me to accumulate a troop of fighting cocks, which did wonders to ease my loneliness in Bet il Watoro. Almost daily, we would both stand in front of our matadors, which servants had to carry on and off. A cockfight can really be quite interesting. It keeps the spectators riveted, and the whole thing presents an entertaining, often highly comical, picture.

Later he also taught me how to fence with sword, dagger, and lance, and when we went to the countryside together, he showed me how to shoot with rifle and pistol. In short, he made me half an Amazon, to the great consternation of my dear mother, who wanted to know absolutely nothing of fencing or shooting. Of course, my interest in embroidery flagged by comparison. I much preferred handling all sorts of weapons to spending quiet hours on the bobbins making lace.

All these new activities, coupled with my total freedom—they had not yet found a new teacher for me—livened me up in short order, and I overcame my initial displeasure with "lonely" Bet il Watoro. Nor did my horseback riding suffer. Eunuch Mesrur had to follow Madjid's orders to continue my training.

My mother was unable to pay much attention to me, as she was kept very busy by Chadudj. So I became increasingly attached to an experienced Abyssinian by the name of Nuren, who also taught me some of her language. Of course, by now that is all forgotten. —

We stayed in regular contact with Bet il Mtoni. Whenever my mother went there with me, we were warmly received and cared for by our friends. Beyond that, our contact was limited to oral dispatches through our respective slaves. In the Orient, no one really enjoys composing letters, even those who have learned to write. Anyone of wealth and standing owns several slaves that can run hard and fast, who are used exclusively for this purpose. All these runners have to cover a good number of miles every day, but they are also especially well-treated and cared for. The very well-being of their owners depends on their honesty and discretion, knowing they will be relaying the most confidential of messages! It is not uncommon for a friendship to be destroyed forever because of an act of revenge by such a messenger. And yet, despite all this hardship, very few are motivated to learn to write and make themselves self-sufficient in life. Nowhere else does the phrase "just take it easy" mean as much as it does for us.

My sister Chadudj loved to entertain. Rarely did a weekday go by that the house was not full of guests from six in the morning until midnight. Guests that came for the day, and arrived as early as six, were received by house servants and ushered into a specific room for this purpose, to be subsequently greeted by the mistress of the house at more like eight or nine. Until then, women that had arrived early tended to use this room to resume their interrupted sleep. I will take the opportunity later in a separate chapter to report more fully on such visits by the ladies.

While it took no time for me to become attached to dear Madjid, I did not have the same success with Chadudj. As strict and imperious as she was, I never found it in me to love her fully. The contrast between her and noble Madjid was too great. I was not alone in this assessment. Anyone who knew the two siblings, also clearly knew which of the two was kinder. She could be especially cool, even off-putting, towards strangers, and thus managed to make even more enemies. Despite her reputation as a hostess, she strongly resisted anything new and unfamiliar and was always very unenthused when a European woman came calling, even if such visits lasted at most half to three quarters of an hour.

Beyond that, she was, by our standards, extremely prudent and practical. She almost never sat still, and, when she had nothing else to do, sewed and embroidered the clothes of her married slaves' children as diligently as her brother's fine shirts. Among these children were three of the sweetest boys, whose father served as our building foreman. Selim, Abdallah, and Tani, as they were called, were a few years younger than me, but soon became my daily playmates for lack of other children my age, until I got to know my other siblings at Bet il Sahel.

CHAPTER THREE

A Day at Bet il Sahel

The day I had been waiting for with indescribable longing finally came, the day I would join my mother and Chadudj to be at Bet il Sahel from dawn to dusk. It was on a Friday, the Islamic Sunday, when we left the house early at five thirty, draped in our big black silk shawls with broad golden borders (called *shele*). We did not have far to go, as our destination lay only about one hundred steps away.

The loyal, but insufferable, grey-headed warden gave us an unfriendly welcome. He grumpily declared that he had been standing on his weak legs already over an hour just to receive the visiting ladies. Called Said il Nubi, the crotchety doorman was, as his name indicated, one of the father's Nubian slaves. His white beard—the only way I can put this, since it is an Arab custom to keep a clean-shaven head—had aged honorably in our service. The father valued him greatly, especially after the time the father was about to undertake a rash deed in a justifiable rage, and Said interceded by knocking the unsheathed sword out of the father's hand, thereby sparing his master pangs of conscience for the rest of his life.

As young children, however, we were not yet aware of Said's meritorious service, and our considerable rambunctiousness often led us to play the naughtiest tricks on our gruff, loyal servant. We were especially focused on his enormous keys, and I believe there is no place in all of Bet il Sahel where we did not hide them at least once. Particularly my brother Djemshid had an uncanny ability to cause them to vanish completely, without even us, his accomplices, suspecting their hiding place.

Upon reaching the residential floor, we found the house and inhabitants already in full swing. Only the especially devout were still in their morning prayers and totally invisible to the outside world. No one would dare disturb these worshippers, not even if the house were in flames. Our dear father was one of them, and so we were obliged to wait for him. Like many others, we had chosen this day to visit because he was present, to the aggravation of old Said.

The women that arrived were not all our acquaintances, much less friends. On the contrary, many were complete strangers in our house and unfamiliar to us. They mostly came from Oman, our original native country, for the sole purpose of requesting material support from the father, which he almost never denied. Both our home country and our tribal kin there are very poor, and our own prosperity dates back only to our father's conquest of rich Zanzibar.

Even though Islamic law generally prohibits a woman from interacting with male strangers, it nonetheless allows for two exceptions: She may appear before both ruler and judge. Because thousands upon thousands of women have no idea how to write, and therefore cannot submit written pleas, such needy supplicants have little alternative but to make their requests in person, even if it means taking the short trip from Asia to Africa in stride. Gifts were allocated on the basis of rank and position, without interrogating the hundred things Europeans try to draw out of their poor petitioners. Everyone received what they needed and what there was to give. There it is generally assumed that no respectable person would call on outside assistance for the mere pleasure of begging, and in many cases that is surely correct.

Siblings I knew and did not know received me very warmly, above all my unforgettable, beloved sister Chole. Having until then focused all my childhood love exclusively on my dear mother, I now also began to idolize this ray of light in our house from the fullness of my heart. My sister Chole soon became my ideal; she was also admired by many others and the father's favorite child. Whoever judged her fairly and without jealousy had to admit that she was an extraordinarily rare beauty. And is there anyone who is entirely unaffected by beauty? Not in our house. Chole was without equal in our whole extended family, and her beauty was the stuff of legend. Although it is well-known that beautiful eyes are no rarity in the Orient, everyone called her *nidjm il subh*, meaning "morning star." To wit, an Arab tribal leader was taking part in a popular mock sword fight in front of our house, as was customary during festivals, when his gaze was drawn by some invisible power to a particular window, causing him to completely ignore both the blood coming out of his foot and any pain that it caused, until one of my brothers snapped him to attention. It was our Chole who stood at that window. When this Omani's gaze fell upon the window and became so transfixed by Chole's beauty, he had, without realizing it, stabbed his own foot with his sharp, iron-shod lance. — After this incident, poor blameless Chole had to endure many years of teasing from the brothers.

Although Bet il Sahel is much smaller than Bet il Mtoni, it also lies directly by the sea. Its bright and cheerful atmosphere rubs off on its residents. All the rooms in the house offer the most splendid views of the sea with its boats, a sight that is deeply engrained in my soul. All the doors on the upper floor (where the residences are located) open onto a long and wide gallery. The gallery ceiling is carried by columns that reach all the way to the ground, and between them runs a tall guardrail, with many chairs along its length. The plentiful, colorful lanterns that hang from the ceiling set the house aglow with a magical shimmer when it gets dark.

Looking out over the railing, it would be hard to find a more colorful, lively, and noisy courtyard view. I was later reminded of this colorful commotion, albeit on a smaller scale, by the bustling market scenes in the operetta *The Beggar Student*.

Two large, completely freestanding stairs handle the traffic between the residential rooms on the second floor and the courtyard. An uninterrupted stream, traveling up and down, continues all day and night, at times so crowded at both ends that it can take several minutes just to wind one's way to the stairs themselves.

In one corner of the courtyard, large quantities of livestock are slaughtered and then skinned and cleaned in bulk, all just to feed our house, with every house here having to procure its own meat.

Off to the side, seated Africans are getting their heads shaved bald and bare. Next to them, numerous water carriers stretch out their tired, but likely also lounging, limbs and pay no heed to any calls for water, until one of the feared eunuchs comes over to remind them, at times a bit roughly, of their neglected duty. Upon spotting their strict supervisors, these men would often gallop off with their *mtungi* (water jugs) in such a rush that general laughter would ensue.

Not far from them, a dozen nannies are basking in the sun with their little ones and telling them all sorts of fables and stories.

The kitchen is situated in the open around one of the columns on the ground floor, where smoke merrily disperses upwards for lack of chimneys in these parts. Nearby, the greatest, sheer indescribable havoc is being wreaked. Untold numbers of kitchen staff are pitching endless quarrels and fights. Both male and female head cooks are uncommonly generous in distributing well-aimed slaps whenever their helpers are slower to react than they would like.

Here is where massive amounts of meat, always by the whole animal, would be cooked. Huge fish, so large they had to be carried by two stout Africans, could often be seen disappearing into the kitchen. Small fish were accepted only by the basket, and poultry only by the dozen. Flour, rice, and sugar, too, were counted only in bulk by the sack, and the butter, in liquid form from the north, especially from the island of Socotra, would be brought in by pitchers weighing about a hundred pounds. Only spices were measured at a different scale, namely by the *rattil* (a pound).

Almost more astonishing was the amount of fruit we consumed. Every day thirty to forty, even fifty porters came to the house bearing loads of fruit, in addition to the many small rowboats bringing deliveries from plantations abutting the sea. Without exaggeration, I would estimate the daily demand for fresh fruit at Bet il Sahel to equal the load of a two-axle railcar. Even so, there were days, like during the mango harvest, which we call *embe*, when we easily used up twice that amount. The massive transport of fruit was handled extremely carelessly. The slaves who had this task felt no compunction in letting the soft baskets filled with ripe fruit drop with all their might from their heads onto the ground, so that half of the contents ended up bruised and much was completely squashed.

The oranges of today mostly stay green on the outside, even when they are fully ripened. There are also two kinds of mandarins there, one the size of push buttons and the other like the usual Italian ones.

A long wall about two meters wide had been erected to protect the house from the sea. On the far side, a few of the best horses were tethered with long ropes every day at low tide, so they could roll around and frolic in the soft sand to their hearts' content. The father was extremely attached to the thoroughbred horses he had brought over from Oman. He visited them every day, and if one ever got sick, he would personally attend to its comfort in the stables. Indeed, here is an example of how gentle an Arab man can be with his favorite horse. My brother Madjid had a precious brown mare and wanted nothing more ardently than for it to have a foal. When the time came that his wish for "il Kehelle" (that was her name) was about to happen, he ordered the stable master to alert him immediately, whether day or night. And sure enough, one night in the wee hours between one and three, we were one and all roused abruptly from our beds for the happy event. The stable boy who had brought the glad tidings received a fifty-dollar reward from his overjoyed master. This is by no means an isolated case. The personal devotion to horses is said to be even more extreme in the Arabian interior.

When the prayer session ended and my father returned to his room, the three of us, my mother, Chadudj, and I, went to him. After a short while, he turned to me with his usual humor and asked: "Salme, tell me, how do you like it here? Do you want to return to Bet il Mtoni? Here, do they also serve your—milk soup?"

Between half past nine and ten, all my older brothers left their quarters to join the father for a communal breakfast. Not a single *surie* (purchased wife), not even the most favored, was ever allowed to eat with the father. Beyond us, his children and grandchildren, and then not before age seven, no one else sat at his table except his equal-status wife Azze bint Sef and his sister Aashe. The social stratification of people in the Orient is never more evident than at meals. Guests are treated with kindness and grace, often more so than their treatment by the upper ranks here in this country. At mealtimes, however, Oriental hosts courteously take their leave from their guests. This is such a deep-seated custom that no one takes personal offense.

The *sarari* have developed even further classifications amongst themselves. The pretty and pricey Circassians, who are quite aware of their own worth, do not want to eat with the coffee-brown Abyssinians. In this way, by some unwritten code, they all dine according to race. Of course, with the children, as noted above, this sorting by skin color has found little application.

Watching the activity at Bet il Sahel, I got the impression that people here were much happier and more playful than at Bet il Mtoni. Only later did I understand why. In Bet il Mtoni, Azze bint Sef ruled the day. She reigned over husband, stepchildren, and their mothers, in short, everything in her realm. Here by contrast, in Bet il Sahel, where Azze rarely appeared, everyone, my father included, felt totally free and could do whatever they pleased. There was no one to exert their authority, except the father, who could not have been kinder or milder. This feeling of being free and unencumbered makes people invigorated and inspired wherever they are in the world, whether they live in the North or the South. The father must have felt this as well. For years, he had not sent anyone permanently to Bet il Mtoni unless they had asked to stay there, even though the house still had ample space, and Bet il Sahel was filled to the brim. Bet il Sahel's overcrowding eventually became so dire that the father ingeniously had wooden pavilions built on the huge, aforementioned gallery to create more living space, and ultimately also needed to have a third house built, named Bet il Ras (Cape House). This one lay a few kilometers north of Bet il Mtoni, likewise by the sea, and was intended especially for the younger generation of Bet il Sahel.

Our gallery in Bet il Sahel would have presented ample material for any painter's brush. The continuous panorama of genre-pictures it offered was especially full of color and variety. Just the faces alone in the crowds that came and went presented complexions of at least eight to ten different shades, and an artist would have needed the most garish colors to faithfully reproduce all the colorful clothing. Equally pronounced was the noise from the gallery. Children of all ages scampered, quarreled, and skirmished in all corners. Mixed in were the sounds of loud calls and clapping hands, which the Orient uses in lieu of bells to summon the house help. And on top of all that came the clonking of women's wooden sandals, the *kabakib* (singular *kubkab*), pitched five to ten centimeters high and often very richly decorated with silver and gold.[7]

Our jumble of languages was especially delightful for the children. We were supposed to speak only Arabic, and that rule was strictly observed with the father. But the minute he turned his back on us, a kind of Babylonian bedlam took over. In addition to Arabic, there was a wholesale mix of Persian, Turkish, Circassian, Swahili, Nubian, and Abyssinian, not to mention all the various dialects.

And yet, no one was bothered by any of this noise, except an occasional sick person who might complain. Our dear father was entirely used to it and never showed any displeasure. —

On this day, all my adult sisters appeared on the gallery in their festive attire, partly because it was the Arab Sunday and partly to honor the father's visit. Our mothers came and stood in groups, where they conversed enthusiastically, laughing and joking in such high spirits that no one who did not know the context could have believed they were all wives of one and the same man. But from the stairs came the clanging of weapons carried by my many brothers and their sons, who also wanted to visit with the father and mostly, bar a few short interruptions, stayed with him the whole day.

Bet il Sahel was much more luxurious and extravagant than Bet il Mtoni. It also had many more of the beautiful and graceful Circassians than Bet il Mtoni, where my mother and her friend Medine were the only ones of this race. In fact, the great majority of the women in Bet il Sahel were Circassian, without

---

[7] As can be seen on the frontispiece of the author, page xviii.

a doubt much more distinguished in appearance than Abyssinians, although exceptional beauties are often found in the latter group as well. These natural advantages gave rise to much envy and resentment. A Circassian blessed with a courtly manner would mostly, through no fault of her own, be shunned and even despised by the chocolate-colored Abyssinians, merely because she looked so regal.

Under these circumstances, it was unavoidable that a kind of ludicrous "racial hatred" occasionally also reared its head among us siblings. An Abyssinian is by nature, despite her various virtues, often hot-headed and quick-tempered. Once enflamed, her passion seldom knows any bounds, much less a sense of decorum. Our Abyssinian siblings typically called us Circassian children "cats" because a few of us were unlucky enough to have—blue eyes. They also referred to us derisively as "Your Highness," further proof of their anger that we had been born into this world with lighter skin. They naturally never forgave our father the fact that his chosen favorites, Sharife and Chole, were of the detested cat race. Both had Circassian mothers and Sharife even had blue eyes. —

In Bet il Mtoni, the oppressive reign of Azze bint Sef had made for a kind of monastic living, while in Bet il Watoro, I felt even lonelier, and so in Bet il Sahel, I loved its cheerful lifestyle all the more. I soon linked up with the siblings of my same age. Two nieces my age, Shembua and Farshu, my brother Chalid's only children, were also part of this inner circle. They were sent from their home to Bet il Sahel every morning and picked up again every evening, so they could study together with their aunts and uncles and then join us in our games. Chalid's mother, Churshit, a born Circassian, was a very striking personality. As someone with a mighty build, she also exhibited exceptional willpower coupled with a high degree of natural sagacity. I have never in my life seen another woman like her. It was said that when Chalid stepped in for the father during his absence, she did the governing, with her son but her instrument. She gave indispensable advice to the whole family, and her opinion carried great weight in decision making. Her two eyes watched and immediately absorbed everything just as sharply as the hundred eyes of Argus. When it came to matters of importance, she always maintained a kind of Solomonic wisdom. As children, we found her disagreeable and pointedly tried to stay away from her. —

We were getting ready to return to Bet il Watoro that evening when, to my dismay, the father told my mother that I needed to resume my lessons and get back to reading. When my mother responded that we were still looking for a suitable teacher, he determined that I should, like my nieces, be brought to Bet il Sahel every morning and picked up every evening, so I could benefit from lessons with my siblings. This was very distressing news. I was much too wild to take any pleasure in sitting still, and besides, my last teacher had positively ruined my appetite for any learning. Only the thought that I could now spend every day, all day (except Fridays) with my siblings gave me some comfort, especially when my charming sister Chole assured my mother that she would take me under her wing and watch over me. And so she faithfully did, caring for me like a mother.

By contrast, my dear mother was very saddened to have to give me up six days a week. But she, too, had to live with the father's decision. Several times a day, though, she bid me to appear at a particular spot, so she could at least see me from Bet il Watoro and nod my way.

[Frontispiece] Portrait of Said bin Sultan

CHAPTER FOUR

Of Our Life in Bet il Watoro and Bet il Sahel

All I want to say about my new teacher is that I will forever owe thanks to the Almighty for also giving me such a faithful friend while I was still young! She was a strict, but fair teacher. I was often the only one with her, since my siblings disliked going into her dark sickroom and instead took advantage of her infirmity by staying away. I could not bear to see her, my poor, wretched teacher, ask something of me and then not fulfill her requests. Of course, my obedience brought me not only her satisfaction, but also much teasing from my absconded siblings, on top of the frequent beatings they made me endure.

I came to like Bet il Sahel more and more, where I could romp around far more than in Bet il Watoro. Nor did we forgo any chance to play a stupid prank. When it came to potential punishment, though, I usually fared the best, since my caretaker Chole was far too kindhearted to impose any consequences.

Here are just two examples of our pranking:

The house had a number of magnificent peacocks, including a very cantankerous one that had it out for us children. One day we were walking around, five of us, past the round dome of the Turkish bath that was connected to Bet il Sahel by one hanging bridge and to Bet il Tani, basically a side house of the first, by another. Suddenly this peacock raced toward my brother Djemshid in a foaming rage. Quick as a flash, we threw ourselves onto the beast and subdued it. Our anger, especially Djemshid's, was too great for us to simply let the animal go. We decided to exact gruesome revenge by plucking every one of his beautiful tail feathers. Oh, did that formerly feisty, color-spangled bird look pitiful now. We were lucky that the father happened to be in Bet il Mtoni just then, and the incident was fortunately hushed up by the time he returned.

In the meantime, two new Circassian women had joined us from Egypt, and it did not take long for us children to conclude that one of the two was rather arrogant and dismissive of us. That hurt our pride, so we tried to come up with an appropriate punishment. It was not easy to encounter her, since we never crossed paths and normally had nothing to do with her. That fed our grudge all the more, especially since she was but a few years older. It was in this spirit that we one day happened to walk past her room. Her door stood open as usual. The poor thing was sitting on an unusually frail Swahili bed, made of nothing more than a mat with four posts latched together by coconut rope, while belting out a merry national song. My sister Shewane was our ringleader this time. One look from her was all it took to secure our immediate, like-minded consensus. In no time, we had grabbed the bed ties, raised the bed with its inhabitant as high as we could, and then suddenly let it drop again, to this unsuspecting soul's great shock. It was a rather childish prank, but had the intended effect. Our victim was thereafter cured of her disregard for us. From then on she was kindness itself, and that was all we had wanted.

Full of mischief, I also played my own pranks. Once, shortly after moving to Bet il Watoro, I almost broke my neck. We had gone, as we often did, to enjoy some time at one of our many wonderful plantations. One morning, I managed to evade my chaperone and instantly climbed undetected up a tower-high coconut palm, agile as a cat, but without the *pingu*, the heavy cord that fastens to the feet, without which not even the most skilled climber would be persuaded to climb a palm. About midway up the tall trunk, in my total exuberance, I began to shout at unsuspecting passersby, loudly wishing them a very fine good morning.

What a fright! Immediately a whole throng of people gathered below me and pleaded that I carefully come down. Sending someone up would have been inadvisable. Climbers need both hands when scaling palm trees and cannot additionally carry a seven- or eight-year-old child. But I was having a great time up there. Not until my mother stood below me, desperately wringing her hands and promising me all sorts of treats, did I slowly slide down and land, happy and unharmed, back at the base. On this day, I was everyone's beloved child and received more than a few presents to mark my salvation, even though I had instead deserved an exemplary punishment.

We put on pranks like this daily, and no punishment was enough to deter us from new ones. There were seven of us, three boys and four girls, and we kept the whole house in a perpetual state of upheaval. And we also unfortunately often enough left our poor mothers with a range of inconveniences.

Now and again my dear mother would keep me at home in Bet il Watoro in addition to Fridays, and kind-hearted Madjid eagerly used those occasions to spoil me. It was on such a day that he gave us a huge scare. The poor man suffered from frequent seizures, and for that reason he was only rarely, and basically never, left alone without immediate help nearby. Even when he was in the bath, my mother and Chadudj, who did not entirely trust the slaves, would take turns keeping watch at the door, exchanging a few words with him from time to time, to which he liked to jokingly respond "I'm still alive." One day Chadudj was pacing up and down in front of the door to the bath when she suddenly heard a dull thud inside. Scared to death, she rushed in with others and found her beloved brother lying on the raised prayer area in the midst of a truly awful seizure. It was his worst one ever. A messenger on horseback was dispatched immediately to Bet il Mtoni to fetch the father.

Out of general medical ignorance, we were always beholden to wretched quackery. Now, after having gotten to know the natural and sensible way that doctors handle things here, I fear that many of our dead may have fallen victim to the barbaric treatments more than the disease. Were it not for the unwavering, rock-solid belief in our "destiny," I am not sure we could have endured the oh! so many deaths in our family and all around us with such resignation!

Poor Madjid, who lay unconscious with these dreadful spasms for hours, had to spend the time on his bed inhaling air that would have harmed even a healthy person. Although we have a great, natural preference for fresh, open air, at the very moment someone gets sick, specifically, as in this case, the moment the devil comes under suspicion, the room is hermetically sealed to the outside and massively fumigated, along with the whole house, through and through.

An hour later, to everyone's amazement, our dear father arrived in a *mtumbi*, a small, one-person boat, and rushed with rapid steps into the house. My father's relationship to his children was truly patriarchal. He loved each and every one equally, just as we all venerated him. More than forty children called the old man their own, and yet he was deeply shaken by the illness of even one.

Visible tears ran down his cheeks, as he stood by Madjid's sick bed. "Oh Lord, oh Lord, spare me my son!" he prayed incessantly, and his plea was heard by the Highest. Madjid was spared.

Later my mother asked him why he had come in such a miserably little dinghy. "When the messenger brought me the news," he said, "there was not a single boat on shore. I had no time to wait for one to be signaled over. Even getting a horse saddled would have taken too long. Then I happened to see a fisherman in a *mtumbi* under the *bendjle*, headed out to sea. I grabbed my weapons, called him to me, and as he got out, I immediately jumped in and rowed over." Now one has to know that such a *mtumbi* is a wretched vessel, consisting only of a hollowed-out tree trunk, seldom holding more than one person, and propelled forward with a double-shovel, rather than oars. Narrow, pointed in front, and relatively short, it is no comparison to our so-called Greenlanders here.[8]

For Western sensibilities, it must also seem quite odd that a father, who is concerned about the life of his child and recklessly sets aside all protocol, would still find time to remember his weapons. But here, too, the saying applies: Other countries, other customs. Just as Europeans cannot comprehend the unbounded love that true Arabs have for their weapons, there is much in turn about the North that Arabs find incomprehensible.

And so I attended school in Bet il Sahel daily, returning every evening to my mother in Bet il Watoro. Once I had finally learned about a third of the Koran by heart, at about age nine, I was considered to have outgrown school. After that, I only got to Bet il Sahel on Fridays with my mother and Chadudj, when the father was there.

---

[8] Large, reinforced whaling ships that sailed past Greenland and could push through ice in the Arctic Ocean.

CHAPTER FIVE

Relocating to Bet il Tani

We lived comfortably and peacefully together in Bet il Watoro for about two years. But times like these seldom last. The least expected, least anticipated events and circumstances are bound to come along. And thus it was for us as well. The disruption to our homelife could not have come from a dearer or kinder person. Aashe, a distant relative of ours, had only recently come to Zanzibar from our Omani homeland. It did not take long before she became Madjid's wife. We all loved her dearly and were glad for my brother's good fortune and happiness, save for his own sister Chadudj. It pains me deeply to admit that Chadudj treated Aashe utterly unfairly from beginning to end. The latter was, as mentioned, charming in every way, but still very young. Instead of being taught by Chadudj and respectfully mentored over time commensurate with her status, as it should have been, she was simply ignored by Chadudj, yes, even treated with hostility. Aashe should have become mistress of the house when she married Madjid, and yet, Chadudj lorded over poor, gentle Aashe so much that she often came to my mother, tears streaming down her face, to complain about the latest injustice.

My mother was caught between two fires, and her situation became increasingly fraught. Chadudj had no intention of giving up any of her perceived rights and continued to treat Aashe like an underage child. My mother tried in vain to impress upon Chadudj the proper rights and status of Madjid's wife. For naught did she ask her, for the love of Madjid, to refrain from anything that could cause him anger or annoyance. It was all to no avail. The once pleasant and happy conditions in Bet il Watoro deteriorated so much that my mother finally decided to leave the house she loved so dearly, to no longer bear witness to the perpetual strife.

Madjid and his wife would hear nothing of it, and especially Aashe, who even called my mother Umma (Mama), was inconsolable. Chadudj, by contrast, remained completely indifferent, which only strengthened my mother's resolve in her decision.

Eventually Aashe could no longer bear to live under Chadudj's rule and decided to divorce Madjid. The poor thing had, despite her youth, taken this bitter lesson so much to heart that she wanted nothing more to do with Zanzibar and its inhabitants. When the south winds started to blow, the ones that take our ships north, Aashe came to us to say good-bye. She wanted to go to Oman, to return to her old aunt near the capital Muscat. She was a poor orphan, with neither father, nor mother.

My mother and I had already left Bet il Watoro by then and moved to Bet il Tani. My sister Chole rejoiced, now that we lived in practically one and the same house. She had even obtained and furnished the new quarters for us.

With our houses already filled beyond capacity, individual rooms were very difficult to find. Sometimes rooms had to be shared by multiple residents, and not until someone died were room assignments rearranged. Over time, it became customary to console people with the prospect of someone's eventual death, much as with some of our asylums here. It was rather profane to watch how often one or the other person would take note of a neighbor's light coughing and immediately suspect the onset of a severe case of consumption,[9] thereupon conjuring up plans for a tasteful renovation of the soon-to-be-inherited space. Truly sinful thoughts, but the overcrowding was simply too great. We owed significant thanks to Chole that we got an attractive, spacious room in Bet il Tani right away, without first having to wait for someone to die.

After that, we seldom saw Chadudj. She felt offended by our departure and accused my mother of a lack of affection. How completely unjustified! My mother's sense of fairness simply could and would not allow her to watch such ugly treatment of a defenseless, inexperienced woman, especially because poor Aashe bore no fault other than having simply dared—to become Madjid's wife. Madjid, on the other hand, continued to visit us frequently and remained a good and loyal friend.

Bet il Tani stood right next to Bet il Sahel and was, as already mentioned, connected to the latter by a hanging bridge that stretched above the former joint Turkish bath that lay midway between the two houses. Only the

---

9   A medical condition whereby the body was "consumed" from within, usually a reference to tuberculosis, one of the major killers of the time.

remnants of Bet il Tani's original splendor were left. Many years ago, the upper floor of this palace had housed my father's second equally-ranked wife, a Persian princess, the delightfully charming Shesade. She was said to exalt in extravagance, but loved her stepchildren no less dearly. One hundred fifty horsemen, naturally all Persian, lived on the ground floor and made up her little entourage. She rode and hunted with them in broad daylight, which for Arab sensibilities went rather too far. For their physical training, Persian women enjoy a Spartanesque upbringing. They are free, much freer than Arab women, but also coarser in their thoughts and conduct.

Shesade's display of luxury was also said to have defied description. Her clothes (always worn in a Persian cut) were stitched with genuine pearls, literally from top to bottom. In the morning, when slaves rounded up a large number of fallen pearls during their morning cleaning of her chambers, the princess never wanted them back. She not only abused our father's coffers, but also overstepped some serious boundaries. She had married the dear father only for his rank and wealth, while her heart had long belonged to someone else, something she made no attempt to hide. Upon returning with her retinue one day from one of her outings, the father confronted her in open anger, and it was only the loyal Said il Nubi who singlehandedly kept him from committing a rash and ill-considered deed. Divorce was the only possible outcome after such a scene, and fortunately, Shesade had

not had any children. A number of years later, when my father led the Persian war and had enough good fortune to seize the fortress Bandar Abbas on the Persian Gulf, it is said that the lovely Shesade was spotted among the enemy troops, taking aim at members of our family.

Here, in the former house of this princess, I also began to teach myself to write, although in a very rudimentary fashion. Of course, I had to do this in secret, since women are never taught to write, nor may they let on if they can. I simply took the Koran as a guide and tried to replicate the letters faithfully on a kind of slate, using the bleached shoulder blade of a camel. It worked, and my courage grew. I needed but a few last pointers to get it right. So I entrusted one of our so-called learned servants with the rare honor of becoming my writing teacher. When word got out, I was denounced in the strongest terms, but not much bothered. Oh, how grateful I have been over the years for a decision that enabled me, however imperfectly, to correspond directly with my loyal friends in my distant homeland!

CHAPTER SIX

Daily Life in Our House

How endlessly often have I been asked, "Tell me please, how can your people possibly live without ways to occupy their time?" In the course of a single evening, I was afforded the pleasure of addressing this same topic between six and eight times at a large gathering, and naturally found this line of questioning altogether appealing and stimulating in the repetition. Clearly, the question is justified from the perspective of a Northerner, who cannot bear to imagine a life without work, while holding the firm conviction that an Oriental woman does nothing more than dream her days away in the confines of a harem, at most briefly livening up with some luxury item every once in a while.

Natural conditions vary everywhere, and they contribute to our differing perspectives, traditions, and customs. Northerners have to work to survive and then work even more for the pleasures in life. Blessed Southerners have an entirely different lot. Yes, I repeat the word "blessed" yet again because the contentedness of a population is one of its significant, invaluable features. Arabs, who are so often caricatured in books as indolent, in fact have a great degree of contentedness, comparable perhaps only to the Chinese. By virtue of their natural surroundings, Southerners *can* work, but Northerners *must* work. Northerners tend to think highly of themselves and look with pride and disdain upon their opposites, a trait that does not seem very praiseworthy. But this easily overlooks how essential Northern diligence and Northern hard work are if hundreds of thousands are not to perish. A Northerner must work, and there is no point in turning that necessity into an excessive virtue. Are not Italians, Spaniards, and Portuguese also less industrious than Germans and

Englishmen? And why? Well, simply because the latter have much more winter than summer, and accordingly more of a fight for their survival. The cold brings with it so many thousands of needs and wants that the day often flies by like a short dream, with daily tasks that are so crucial for life, but as to whose meaning, even existence, the Southerner has no clue.

Everywhere one goes, luxury is the same. Anyone with the requisite funds and corresponding inclinations will find ample opportunity to give their passions free rein, whether they live in the North or the South. We can therefore set this aspect aside and instead focus only on the really essential needs of people here and there.

Whereas here even a newborn child needs a hundred things to protect its frail life against the rigors of the variable weather, a brown-skinned, Southern baby can basically just lie there with next to nothing on and doze uninterrupted in the warm breeze. Here, a two-year-old child absolutely needs, among other things, shoes, stockings, pants, a dress, two skirts, mittens, an overcoat, a hat, a scarf, gaiters, a muff, and a fur cap, whether that child belongs to royalty or a tradesman—only the quality varies—but there as well, the wardrobe of every two-year-old son of a prince consists of only two items: a shirt and a little cap.

Should an Arab mother, who needs so precious little for herself and her child, work as much as a German housewife? She has no idea what it means to darn holey stockings and mittens or undertake all of the countless activities that are needed for a German mother to provide continuous care for her child. In particular, she knows nothing of the one major chore in every European household: the big laundry. There, clothes are washed daily, dried in less than half an hour, pressed flat (not ironed), and set aside. She also has no tiresome curtains like the ones that block every ray of sunshine here, whose care and cleaning take so much time. And the amount of clothes an Oriental woman might tear, may she be the finest of ladies, is unbelievably minuscule. That is easily explained by the fact that people move around less there and do not go out much.

All this and much more contributes to making the life of Oriental women, virtually without distinction across positions, more comfortable and bearable. But it takes being there, and living there for a "longer" time, to learn about all this household minutiae. Tourists with their temporary stays, who cannot penetrate such detail and are likely to glean their information from hotel staff, cannot be relied upon to know. As for any European women who actually may have been admitted to a harem, whether in Constantinople or Cairo, they still have not seen a real harem, but just its outward shine, as it were, the sanitized showrooms that are already heavily influenced by Western decor.

Moreover, the magnificent climate is so enjoyable and beneficial that no one practically ever needs to worry about the next day. I am not disputing that people there are generally quite relaxed by nature. But one need only recall the July and August days of a hot European summer, and it becomes evident what effect a tropical sun can have on people.

By disposition, Arabs have little inclination toward industry. They care far more for the art of war and agriculture. Only the smallest percentage takes up an artisanal trade. Arabs also do not figure prominently among merchants and exhibit virtually no Semitic business hustle, although they have to barter extensively. With their modest lifestyles, they can easily make do with very little, and, as a rule, their focus is day-to-day, especially since they are always mindful that their time may come at any moment. This constant anticipation of their last hours limits the impulse to craft any plans for the coming future. Only rarely do they plant things they cannot harvest for their own needs. Anyone who does is considered a foolish farmer (see Luke 12).[10] I also recall a case where a rather aged minister leased his plantations out for many years. He was accordingly considered a godless person for disposing of his land well beyond his expected lifetime.

Oriental life thus proceeds calmly without much work, something I needed to highlight and justify before going into details about daily life in Arabic households. But I also have to emphasize that I am referring only to Omani and Zanzibari conditions, which differ in many respects from other Oriental countries.

To an extent, every Muslim's day is governed by prayers. They happen five times a day, and when properly conducted with everything that goes along with them, like the mandated ablutions and change of clothes, all told, they take up at least three hours.

Those in the ranking class are woken for the first prayer between four and five thirty every morning, after which they go back to sleep. Especially pious individuals, however, choose to add a prayer at sunrise. For ordinary folk, daily work starts with the first prayer.

In our house, with its hundreds of residents, fixed rules were elusive, since everyone could and did follow their own tastes and convenience. Only the two main meals and regularly recurring prayers forced the community to live according to a specific, more established order.

---

10 This biblical reference to Luke 12:16-21 reflects the author's Christian faith at the time she wrote her *Memoirs*.

Most of the residents therefore slept on until about eight o'clock, at which time women and girls were woken by female slaves with gentle and indescribably pleasant massaging, before bathing and dressing for the day. Islamic law stipulates that bathing and cleansing of the body be done only with flowing water. Since there was no river in Bet il Tani, as there was in Bet il Mtoni, we made use of large masonry or brass containers, positioned at a certain height with large spigots and sprinklers, which streamed water onto the body, while the bathing individuals wore wooden sandals and stood on marble surfaces with built-in drainage. Already the previous night, the attending female slave had laid everything out that was needed to get dressed, including bestrewing the outfit with jasmine and orange blossoms and perfuming it with amber and musk.

It takes having lived in the Tropics to truly understand how blissful a cold bath can feel for the whole body. Such a bath greatly freshens and strengthens, and the fine aromas that are so expertly assembled liven up the spirit in the most pleasant way.

After the hour it usually took to get ready, everyone presented themselves to the father to wish him a good morning and soon thereafter settled down to breakfast, the first of our two main meals. Because everything had already been put out in advance, before the drum roll called us to the table, our mealtime, even in all its abundance, took much less time than it does here.

Now the actual day begins, and it is of course spent in various ways. Men arm themselves before heading to the official gathering room. Women, who have no need to work, seat themselves at the windows to watch the bustling street, especially any noteworthy arrivals for the gathering, perhaps even to catch a private greeting known only to the recipient. This diversion is highly entertaining and variable. A lady might easily be disturbed, pushed out of her spot, or even slyly displaced by a concerned mother or aunt. —

Two or three hours can fly by like this, with no notice of the passing time. Meanwhile, men reciprocate each other's visits and relay their oral messages to ladies about evening plans. Demure and decent women, who have no taste for such behavior, retire on their own or in groups to their airy rooms and busy themselves with handiwork, where they embroider their masks, shirts, or pants with gold, or even the batiste shirts of their husbands, brothers, or sons with red or white silk that requires special skill, or make lace with silk and gold lametta. Others read novels, visit healthy or sick people in their residences, and take care of their various private affairs.

And then it is already one o'clock. The slaves come to announce the second prayer. Now the hot sun is at its peak, and everyone is glad to take time after

Daily Life in Our House

praying to comfortably dream away some hours in cool and light attire on a lovely, soft mat, usually interwoven with holy verses. Between sleeping and chatting, and cakes and fruit to eat, this time, too, passes quickly.

At four o'clock, everyone conducts their third prayer and then throws on their more stylish afternoon attire. The father is once again sought out to wish him a good afternoon. The older siblings are allowed to call him "Father," while us young folk and our mothers address him only as "*Hbabi*" (Sir).

This was the liveliest time of the day for us. The main meal followed, when the whole, big family came together with the father for the second and last time.

At the end of the meal, the eunuchs carried European-style chairs into the open hall fronting the father's quarters, but naturally, only for the adults. The young children had to stand in deference to their elders, who likely receive more respect in the Orient than anywhere else. The sizeable family gathered around the usually rather earnest-looking father, while well-groomed, well-armed eunuchs stood in rank and file at a set distance along the gallery. Coffee was passed around, along with lots of the children's favorite fruit juice imported from southern France. A massive barrel organ played in the background, while conversations ranged. For an occasional change of pace, one of the large music boxes would play its melodies, or a blind Arab woman named Amra, who was gifted with a delightful voice, would be brought in to sing for us.

After about an hour and a half, the family split apart again, and everyone sought out activities and leisure according to their moods and inclinations. Betel chewing had a big part in this. As a Swahili custom, it is not popular with Arabs born in Arabia. However, those of us who came to this world on the east coast of Africa, who grew up with Africans and mulattoes, readily took to this custom despite being derided by our Asian siblings and relatives, so long as the father did not catch us in the act. As soon as we left him, the sinners among us succumbed to the betel nut, although in my case not until many years later.

With no shortage of pastimes, this interlude also passed quickly, until the gunshots and drum rolls of the Indian guard reminded us of sundown and our fourth prayer. Of all the daily prayers, none was conducted as quickly as this one. Anyone who did not plan to go out (we and our mothers always had to get special permission from our father or his deputy, although this was denied in only the rarest of cases), or anyone who was not expecting company from outside, invariably had someone to visit in the house or was visited by siblings, stepmothers, stepchildren, and secondary wives. We had coffee and lemonade, fruit and cake, joked and laughed heartily, read out loud, played cards (but never for money or any other winnings), sang, listened to native African music on the *sese*, sewed, stitched, and made lace, all depending on what anyone felt like doing.

It is therefore very mistaken to assume that women of rank in the Orient do absolutely nothing. That they do not draw, play musical instruments, or dance is, of course, well-known. But is this the only way to pass the time? People there are, without exception, easily contented and do not feverishly chase the perennially variable amusements and pleasures we pursue here. When judged on the basis of attitudes prevailing here, Oriental people may indeed appear to be Philistines. —

Male servants are let go in the evening, so they can return to their homes and families outside of the house. The eunuchs also have external lodgings.

The oil lamps in the rooms and corridors are mostly left to burn throughout the night, and only the candles are extinguished at bedtime. Young children above the age of two are no longer put to bed at a set time. They fall asleep whenever they feel like it. It was not unusual for children overcome with sleep to simply lie down wherever they might be and fall into a deep slumber. A few slaves would have to carefully pick up the sleepy heads and carry them to their cots, often across long distances, without them even noticing.

Bedtime for those who did not go out or who had received their guests usually came around ten o'clock. Many, however, love to stay up until midnight to stroll across the flat and well-maintained rooftops under the bright moonshine, a pleasure like no other.

The fifth and last prayer session is supposed to take place at about seven thirty. However, many in the house are busy with visits or other things right then. It was therefore determined that one could postpone this prayer time all the way to midnight. In that case, then, the last prayer is, as a rule, conducted just before bedtime.

When it is finally time to go to sleep, a well-to-do lady is waited upon by two female slaves, who are both tasked with easing the mistress into sleep and watching over her. One massages all the limbs, as in the morning, and the other swings the fans back and forth, until they can slip softly away. Members of the high-ranking and wealthy world also get their feet washed in eau de cologne and water beforehand, which is extraordinarily refreshing. That such women go to bed in their full attire, with all their jewelry on, has already been mentioned.

CHAPTER SEVEN

Our Mealtimes

As described, we had two mealtimes a day. Our brothers and nephews that lived outside the house, married or not, joined us for breakfast whenever the father was in the city with us. By contrast, I cannot recall a time when he would have eaten at his sons' places or anywhere else on the outside.

Our dishes were set up on the long *sefra*. It was much like a billiard table with short feet, except that ours was a lot longer, with a rim the breadth of a hand. The whole thing was no more than ten to fifteen centimeters off the ground. We do not have separate dining rooms, and so the *sefra* was simply placed on the gallery. Although we owned random pieces of European furniture, such as sofas, different types of tables and chairs, and the stray wardrobe (there was a lot of European furniture in the father's room, but more for show than actual use), we were consummate Orientals at mealtime and simply sat flat on the floor, which is to say, on rugs or mats.

The table order was strictly observed according to rank. The father always took his place at the head of the *sefra*. Next to him, on both his right and left, sat my oldest siblings. We little ones (only after turning seven) were last in line. We had no concept of mixed seating and no visitors at the table.

The food itself consisted of various dishes, often as many as fifteen. Every meal featured rice prepared in one of many different ways. Our favorite meat was lamb, our favorite fowl, chicken. Plus we had fish, Oriental breads, and plenty of cakes and sweets. The many eunuchs were usually lined up some distance from us, ready to respond to any special requests.

That included when the father really liked a certain dish. The eunuchs would often hand him plates that he would fill for the younger children who were not yet allowed to eat with him, or for individuals who were sick. He would always summon me to a specific corner in Bet il Mtoni where I would get such a filled plate. Even though we, of course, were served the same food as the adults, it was naturally much nicer to get it as a special selection from the father, and he, too, took much pleasure in it.

Upon taking their seats, everyone said grace softly but audibly: "In the name of Allah, the All-Merciful," and upon rising as well: "Thanks be to the Lord of the Universe," and so on. The father was always the first to be seated and the first to rise.

Unlike here, individuals do not get their own separate plates. Instead, all the various dishes (except the rice) were served on numerous small plates that were arranged in meticulous symmetry along the length of the *sefra*. We would then eat in pairs of two per plate. Rice enough for five to six people was served pyramid-shaped on a type of large platter, and everyone helped themselves with their fingers from where they sat. We rarely ate vegetables.

We never drank while eating. Sharbet and sugared water were available only after the meal was over. We also rarely spoke at meals, at most when the father explicitly addressed one of us. Otherwise, we kept quiet while we ate, which, not to be underappreciated, has its benefits. Fruit or flowers were also never placed on the *sefra*.

A few minutes before and after the two main meals, well-appointed male and female slaves stood near the table with water pitchers, soap, and hand towels at the ready, so we could wash our hands before and especially after we ate. Of course, we ate solely with our fingers. Knives and forks were superfluous and emerged from their hiding places only when we served Europeans. Meat and fish were already pre-cut by the kitchen into bite-sized pieces. Spoons were used only for whatever was not quite compact enough for cutting.

After the hands were washed, it was customary for people of refinement to perfume them as well, so as to remove any residual odor.

Fruit was never enjoyed right after mealtimes, but rather beforehand or somewhat later. Everyone would have a large quantity of fruit, corresponding to seasonal availability, brought to their rooms.

By contrast, eunuchs would regularly distribute genuine mocha in dainty Oriental cups that sat in gold or silver saucers, a quarter or half hour after mealtimes. The coffee is thick, boiled down to its essence, but then filtered completely clean. It is always consumed pure, without milk or sugar, and served without other food, except perhaps to enjoy a bit of finely-cut areca nut.

The coffee is always poured right when it is ready to be enjoyed. The act of pouring calls for very special dexterity, by which the slaves fill the little cups, much like beer poured with foam, in a long and rapid stream. This takes a quick motion of the spout downward as much as possible, followed by an equally quick return of the spout upwards, without spilling even so much as a drop. The coffeepot is made of tin with a brass coating. An assistant follows from behind the coffee pourer with a tray full of additional, empty cups and a large back-up coffeepot. If the group is still gathered, their duty is swiftly carried out. But if the group has already dispersed, they must pursue everyone individually, seeking them all out wherever they may be, to serve them all their precious drink.

Coffee, of course, as everyone knows, is cherished in the Orient and consequently handled with meticulous care. As proof, suffice to say that coffee is roasted, ground, and boiled only for immediate consumption, which means it is enjoyed completely fresh several times a day. Neither boiled coffee, nor roasted beans are ever stored. Any that are no longer fresh are thrown out or at most given to the lower house servants.

The second and last principal mealtime occurred punctually at four o'clock in the afternoon. It was in all respects like breakfast, so I am spared any further description. After that meal, it was rare to partake of anything other than coffee and fruit until the next morning at nine o'clock.

VUE DE LA VILLE DE ZANZIBAR
(Rade du Kouilligo.)

CHAPTER EIGHT

Birth and Early Years of a Prince or Princess

The birth of a prince or a princess may not have been greeted with thundering cannon shot, but was nonetheless an important event for us that caused much happiness and, unfortunately, much envy as well. The father and relevant mother were always elated about the birth of a newborn, and we young children always shared their joy wholeheartedly. That is because a newborn brother or sister had to go through many ceremonies, all of which became family festivities that catered especially to us youngsters. In our family circle, these birth celebrations happened about four to six times a year.

Muslims are not familiar with male obstetricians. Instead, they turn only to female midwives for advice, even though these midwives are paragons of ignorance. Most of them come from Hindustan and are much preferred to the native ones, although I could not say why, since a Hindustani midwife knows as little as an Arab or Swahili one. This much is clear, that when a brand new mother and her child stay healthy and alive, it is but thanks to God and her own solid health, rather than her extremely simple-minded midwives. I later heard much from my married friends about their extremely barbaric methods, which I must naturally refrain from recounting here.

After the newborn is thoroughly washed in warm water, a bandage is wrapped around its torso and a vegetable-based, heavily perfumed powder is spread on its neck and underarms. It is then dressed in a tiny shirt of pure cotton or muslin. With the little baby laid on its back, and hands and legs straightened out as much as possible, a broad cloth is used to wrap the baby from bottom to top, up to the shoulders, tightly bringing in both arms and legs. The child stays imprisoned like this day and night for forty days, with but a brief respite from bondage twice a day to be bathed and dried off. The goal of this bandaging is to ensure a flawlessly straight posture for life.

Despite the many servants, the mother always keeps watch directly and lovingly over the child. The spacious crib, skillfully carved out of the finest wood and imported from East India, is rocked non-stop by alternating slaves, often with gusto. Depending on the season, it may also be covered by a lace or gauze curtain as a mosquito net.

Only rarely does a mother nurse her child, and when she does now and again, then usually just to pass the time. Every child has one or two wet nurses at its full disposal until the age of two.

If the newborn is a girl, then right at the end of the first week, her ears are pierced with a sewing needle and red silk thread, usually six holes per ear. Within a few months, they are already bearing the heavy gold rings that stay on forever. Anyone not wearing earrings is mourning a loved one.

On the fortieth day of a child's life, a very special ceremony takes place: the shaving of the first hair. The chief eunuch does the shaving according to prescribed formalities, which are not complete without heavy doses of incense from a type of gum arabic (much like the incense in Catholic churches). These first hairs have a special status. They may not be burned or thrown in the trash, but are instead buried underground, thrown out to sea, or hidden in some crack in the wall. About twenty to thirty people attend this festive ceremony. It is the only time the chief eunuch serves as barber, which he does while in constant danger of negligently crushing the vulnerable soft spots on the little baby's head. After this precarious work, he, along with the rest of his numerous assistants, always receives an appropriate gift of honor from the father.

This is also the day the child is released from its body wrapping forever. Now the child is adorned with rings on the arms, feet, and ears, and dressed in a silken shirt and *kofije*, a little cap made of gold brocade, complete with ear cuffs. Not until then is the child ready for public viewing. Up to this point, only the parents, the most essential slaves, and the new mother's very closest and most devoted friends have been allowed to see it. This reflects the widespread belief in the evil eye and sorcery of all kinds. —

Indisputably, little Oriental children at this age look much prettier than European ones, if only because the latter are kept too much in white. I have now been in Germany for many years and still cannot conclude otherwise. Even my own children looked perfectly drab in their baby garb. The contrast was just too great whenever I thought of my younger siblings, nephews, and nieces in their winsome attire, while seeing my own children in their European outfits.

The heavy perfuming already starts with the smallest children. Everything that is theirs, clothing, bed sheets, bath towels, and diapers, is bestrewn for the night with wondrously fragrant jasmine (different from the one we have here), then freshly smoked before use with ambergris and musk, with a final sprinkle of rosewater. But it is worth remembering that doors and windows stay open practically year-round, all day and night, which has the fortuitous effect of circumventing any harm from this fondness for fragrance.

To protect children from the purported evil eye, they are draped with amulets from the fortieth day onwards. Called *hamaje* or *hafid*, they are especially common with the lower classes, who use all sorts of objects. An onion, for example, or a piece of garlic, small seashells, a piece of bone, and the like are worn by young children in leather pouches tied around their left upper arm. Instead of such amulets, the higher classes use selected verses from the Koran, which are engraved on gold or silver plates hung from matching chains around the neck. Boys keep these sayings only up to a certain age, whereas girls frequently keep them longer. The girls especially love the *hurs* (the guardian), a mini-book with very tiny print, about seven centimeters long and four to five centimeters wide, that is placed in an elegantly crafted gold or silver case and fastened to a necklace. Anyone wearing such an amulet, on which God's holy name is engraved, must never set foot in an unclean place, surely a testament to the boundless veneration devout Muslims have for their God and Maker! —

In addition to breast milk, it is not long before children are served milk soup several times a day, made of milk that is cooked with rice flour and some sugar for a very long time and then served from a cup with a long spout. Bottles were not yet in use in my time. But that is all children are given to eat until they get their teeth and can eat anything.

Children are seldom carried. They are preferably just placed on a rug-covered floor, where they can roll around to their hearts' delight.

When a child makes its first attempts to sit upright, it is time for another celebration, one that is geared exclusively to all the youngest siblings. To further encourage participation in the sitting party of our little brother or sister, something special was always baked or cooked that day.

Mother, nurses, and child come dressed in their absolute finest, wearing their most precious jewelry. The child is placed in a medium-sized, square wagon that sits on very low wheels and is filled with cloth and cushions. The celebrated child's legs are placed on either side of a small rod that rises perpendicularly from the axle. All the other little children gather around.

In the meantime, corn kernels have been roasted in a special manner until they open up to the size of a thimble and become as soft as wadding. This is mixed with lots of very small silver coins, and the mixture is then poured on the child's head. Immediately, all the siblings pile on to raid their little brother or sister. And yes, this can easily become life threatening. —Many other children in our circle between four and ten years of age were often invited to join these parties as well.

As long as children lack the strength to wear sandals (the wooden ones for girls and women are called *kubkab*, the leather ones for boys and men are *watje*), they simply run around barefoot. Since the *watje* are significantly easier to wear than the *kubkab*, very young girls are initially allowed to walk with *watje* until they have the skills to take on *kubkab* for the rest of their lives. —Neither young nor old, male or female, wears stockings. Only higher-ranked ladies need them now and again for horseback riding, since custom requires that they cover their ankles.

Already at the age of two to four months, the father presents a child with two or three attending slaves, in addition to its wet nurses, who from then on become the child's property. The older the child becomes, the more slaves it receives for personal service. If one of the slaves dies, the father finds a replacement or gifts a corresponding amount of money. —Up to a certain age, young girls wear boys' caps in the house as well.

Every prince stays in the house with the women until he turns seven, when he undergoes the Mosaic rite.[11] Naturally, ceremonies are also a big part of this process, culminating after the child's recovery in a special celebration open to all dignitaries and top officials. Whenever possible, this event takes place out in the countryside, with the father present. It also features food and entertainment for the public, usually lasting three days.

This is also the time every young boy gets his very own docile mare. His escorts can get their mounts from the stables, where a couple hundred Arab horses

---

11 Presumably a reference to circumcision, one of the rituals included in the Law of Moses that traces back to God's covenant with Abraham.

are always available. This way boys early on become very proficient riders, acquiring an amazing degree of agility and flexibility otherwise seen only among trained circus riders. Since we do not use regular saddles or stirrups, it takes much more skill to sit tight than here. And the father took an unconventional approach whenever his sons got in trouble on outings. Not only the sons, but also the escorts had to reckon with getting punished. The father assumed they must have been way too lenient with their princes, especially in light of the tight responsibility and strict instructions he had given them.

The fact is, none of us was ever spoiled in our upbringing. The father's great love of justice and his incomparably noble character came with equally firm consequences that knew no weakness. We had to obey all our teachers and caretakers. We knew any complaint that made it to him would no doubt leave us in shame, if not slinking away in tears. This strictness taught us due deference toward such individuals. As we grew older, we also became increasingly aware of our deep moral indebtedness to them.

The wet nurses, even if they served only briefly in that role, were especially revered and benefited from this special recognition their whole lives. They always start as slaves, but, as a rule, gain their freedom in recognition of their dedication and sacrifice. African nurses, in particular, usually excel in their extraordinary devotion and attachment. Even the most anxious mother can fully entrust her child to the nurse, who considers herself a second mother and steps up to that role. What a contrast with the lack of interest and heartlessness shown by nurses here! How often have I felt compelled to lecture some total stranger on a public walkway after watching her brutal treatment of the poor little creature in her care.

This contrast between the wet nurses here and there may be mostly explained by the poverty that forces the former to entrust their own beloved children, with considerable sacrifice, to utter strangers. These nurses serve their masters only for the money. They are not interested in whether the children in their care are called Saul or Paul. Their thoughts and feelings are naturally with their own children. And what mother could hold that against them!

How very differently an African wet nurse takes to the child entrusted by her mistress. She has already served her mistress for years and was perhaps even born in the same house. Not surprisingly, she has few personal interests, having always made her master's concerns her own. Add to this the most significant factor, that such a wet nurse only rarely, if ever, has to give up her own child, but can instead readily keep it with her. The nurse's child receives the same food as the little master or mistress, the same milk soup, some of the same chicken, and so on, and the same with the bath, and even the used clothes it inherits. And after the mother finishes as wet nurse, her child continues to be a playmate of her second care. Even when the child remains a slave, it is given preference over all other slaves, and only bad people would ever break the bond with their milk brother.

Yet there is also one very bad trait that African wet nurses have. They are known to tell young children three to five years old fantastical and often very harrowing stories and fairy tales, both to entertain them and to keep them quiet. Of course, the lion (*simba*), the leopard (*tshui*), the elephant (*tembo*), and the many witches (*watschawi*) feature prominently in these fables that are terrifying even for adults.

In general, there is no question that childcare is much easier in the South than here in the North. Notably, children there are spared the never-ending coughs and colds, and all that entails. Children there are also very self-reliant and resilient, despite all their comforts, partly because they are freer and less constrained (both in their settings and clothing) to naturally play and romp as they please. They may not know anything about regular gymnastic exercises, but it is not uncommon for a lad of ten to twelve years to launch into an ardent sprint and leap over one or even two horses. High jumps are generally very popular, and everyone does their best to outdo the others.

Swimming in the sea is practiced no less eagerly, with everyone basically self-taught. Shooting also starts very early and is exercised with much passion. Mock battles are especially popular. Hours are spent on them from youth onward. Even though young boys usually walk around armed to the teeth, carrying as much powder and lead as any adult, it is very rare to hear of any careless accidents. —

The young princes, as already mentioned above, lived in the paternal household only up to a certain age. After that, each young prince was assigned his own house to take care of himself and, as a rule, his mother, if she was still alive. The father granted him a fixed monthly allowance, designed to match the son's circumstances, with which he had to cover his needs. Additional amounts could be expected for a marriage or an addition to the family, as well as for exemplary conduct, but nothing more. Only when the father's ships arrived annually, with a new load of goods, did all the siblings that lived outside the father's house and their families show up to receive their allocated shares, whether needed or not. As to anyone who had the serious misfortune of letting their expenses exceed their allowance, it was never made easy for those debts to be repaid. The father hated nothing

Birth and Early Years of a Prince or Princess

more, and whosoever disgraced himself this way once took great care never to do it again.

If war broke out, as was unfortunately so often the case in Oman, then all the princes, even those that were still underage, had to head out and join the fighting, just like every common man.

The upbringing was strict overall, but that only increased the respect and reverence of the sons for the father. As a child, I sometimes watched with amazement as the older brothers rushed ahead of the slaves to straighten the sandals the father had slipped off before entering the room. The older brothers also appeared in the paternal household several times a day, as soon as the father himself was there, and then took part in the meals.

About the upbringing of a princess, there is little to say. The first years are basically the same as for her brothers, except that the sons have much greater latitude to leave the house after their seventh year. The only aspect worthy of note at the birth of a princess is the wide comb, usually of silver, that is placed, to suit the local fashion, under the back of the newborn's head to flatten it for later. —If a princess marries one of her cousins, of which there are, to be sure, many more in Oman than Zanzibar, then she naturally leaves her paternal home in exchange for her husband's. And yet her paternal home, the one true bulwark against all of life's hardships, always remains open to her as a place to live. Or if she prefers, she can move in with a brother. Every sister has a favorite brother and vice versa; the two stick together in both joy and woe and support each other with both advice and assistance. As laudable as this custom may have been, and as fortunate for those involved, it also frequently and understandably, given the size of our family circle, provoked jealousies among siblings. It can take a strong disposition to rise above it all.

Often it was up to a loving sister to intercede with the father about a favorite brother's mishap. The father tended to favor his daughters and rarely left their pleas unanswered. He was especially obliging with his older daughters. As a rule, he would walk towards them from far across the room and then let them sit beside him on the sofa, whereas the adult sons and the rest of us children had to stand respectfully before him.

View of Stone Town by Rosa Troemer

CHAPTER NINE

School in the Orient

School (*mdarse*) is of very scant importance to Orientals in general, and so it is for us. In Europe, school is at the center of the State and the Church, for royal and regular citizens alike. Educational resources have a major bearing on every individual, as to both character development and future prospects. In the Orient, by contrast, the *mdarse* is completely tangential. For many, it does not even exist. But before I allow myself further commentary, I want to report on some of what we called school in our house.

At the age of six to seven, all the siblings, both boys and girls, had to enter the *mdarse*. The girls only had to learn how to read, while the boys had to learn both reading and writing. Bet il Mtoni and Bet il Sahel each had only one female teacher to lead classes, whom the father had brought over from Oman. Whenever the teacher got sick and had to stay in bed, we were very happy. There was no available replacement, so we simply got time off.

There was no designated classroom. Class took place in an open gallery, with unhindered access by pigeons, parrots, peacocks, and bobolinks. From there, we could also comfortably look into the courtyard and greatly amuse ourselves with scenes of the lively activity down there. The schoolroom layout consisted of but a single, gigantic mat. School supplies were equally basic. We needed only a Koran on a stand (*marfa*), a little pot with homemade ink, a bamboo pen, and a well-bleached shoulder blade from a camel. The last item was in lieu of a blackboard. It is easy to write on it with ink, and nerves are spared the aggravating scratching sounds on slate. Our slaves usually took care of wiping off the blades.

First, just as here, we had to learn the very complicated Arabic ABCs. Then, in the absence of any other schoolbooks, we began to read the Koran, followed, as mentioned, by writing lessons for the boys. When students are still at a rudimentary level, they all read in unison and usually very loudly. But that is the extent of it, since what is read and learned is never explained. That is also why at most one student out of thousands understood enough to interpret, word for word, all the thoughts and directives in the Islamic holy text, even though eighty out of a hundred had learned half of it by heart. Reflections upon the holy text are actually considered irreverent and unauthorized. People are simply supposed to believe what they are taught, and this rule was strictly followed.

Bright and early at seven o'clock, after having enjoyed some fruit, we had to assemble on the mat that had been rolled together overnight and was now swept clean, to await our stern teacher. Before she showed up, we exalted in wrestling, boxing, jumping, risky acrobatics on the balustrade, and other childish antics. At the bend in the gallery, we put up a watchman, who would flag a sighting of our teacher from afar with a forced cough. In an instant, we seated ourselves on the mat, a picture of utmost innocence. When her steps got closer, we popped up like rubber balls to respectfully extend our hands and wish this dreaded person a good morning. She always held her despised bamboo cane in one hand and carried a large brass inkpot in the other. We stood in proper order before her until she took her seat, after which we could take ours. Encircling the teacher, we all sat together cross-legged on the mat.

Now she began to pray the opening surah of the Koran, considered the Muslim Lord's Prayer, whereupon we responded in a chorus, closing with the familiar *amin* (not *amen*). Then the lesson from the previous day was reviewed, followed by some new reading or writing. In this way, lessons would regularly go until nine o'clock and then, after finishing breakfast, again until noon, when it was time for the second prayer.

All of us were allowed to bring some of our slaves to school to let them participate in class. They sat at a distance behind us, while we grouped ourselves however we pleased. We had neither fixed seats, nor differentiated classes. We also did not have the feverish excitement that erupts here when grades are given a couple of times a year. If anyone made especially good or bad progress, or distinguished themselves through especially good or bad behavior, the relevant mothers and the father would be told about it directly. The teachers were under explicit instructions from the father himself to punish us quite thoroughly if there was ever cause to do so. Wild as we were, she did have ample need to resort to that nasty cane.

Beyond reading and writing, we learned only a bit of arithmetic, namely, up to one hundred in written form and one thousand orally; anything more was apparently harmful. Little effort was made to teach grammar and spelling. Only over time, with much reading, was it possible to figure out the rather difficult *ilnahu*[12] on one's own. Back home, I had never heard of any of the bodies of knowledge, like history, geography, science, math, and all the rest, much less learned them. Not until coming here did I have the pleasure of discovering all those academic subjects. But whether the modicum of added knowledge that I have painstakingly acquired here leaves me better off, compared to the others over there, remains an open question for me. One thing in any case is clear: I have never been so swindled and cheated as during the time when I was most informed. Oh, you happy folks back home! You cannot fathom, even in your dreams, all that is part and parcel of this holy civilization! —

As for the so-called home-work for school, which takes up so many hours here, that was naturally quite out of the question with our approach to schooling.

The teacher, no matter how dreaded she may be, is held in especially high esteem by all her students. They would never fail to grant her due respect, and they always approach her, even later in life, with utmost regard. It is not unusual for someone to call upon the teacher as a last resort to help mediate a dispute. This somewhat resembles the way devout Catholics relate to their priests.

Oriental school children have at least one thing in common with their European counterparts: the natural instinct to try to win over their teachers with gifts, basically to bribe them. When my children here frequently asked me for a few coins to buy a bouquet or a flowerpot for Miss So-and-So, I could not help but think back to my own school days. This behavior lies deep in mankind itself, not in a particular nation. Before I had even an inkling of Germany and all its school children, I together with my siblings carted all sorts of things, preferably all sorts of snacks, to our teacher to gain her precious favor. We laid the best French bonbons, which our father took care to give us every day, at her feet. But the recipient, who to our joy, I am sorry to say, often endured major tooth pain and had to let us run free, was not always thrilled with our gifts. She claimed we were simply out to make her sick and exacerbate her tooth torments. And to be honest, I am quite sure we never really wanted this poor lady to get any meaningful relief from her hollow teeth.

---

12 *Al-nahu*, literally "the way" in Arabic, defines the Arabic rules of syntax.

The duration of our schooling was never fixed. What there was to learn had, in any case, to be learned, whether it took a child one, two, or three years to get there. That depended entirely on the child's natural abilities.

Lessons in handiwork did not belong to the school curriculum, if I may put it this way. This task belonged to our mothers, who almost universally had a ready, in some cases exemplary, competence in sewing, embroidery, and lace making. As a result, in this area, too, we had a wide range of training experiences, with learning heavily dependent on interest and inclination. I have sisters, for example, who are so talented they would have no issue whatsoever if they ever had to earn their daily bread through their own handiwork, while others would find it impossible to sew even a single button. —

Public schools are also available, but only for the sons of poor parents. Anyone with even moderate means keeps a private teacher. If necessary, the master of the house could also enlist his clerk to teach the lessons, although for girls naturally only while they are still very young.

That is what little I know to report about our schools. It is, of course, a natural topic for me, this comparison between these schools and the German ones, between hypereducated European school children and ignorant Arab ones. I was born and raised there, so I can speak firsthand from experience. I have lived here for many years and sent my own children to school, with every opportunity to develop my own views. I may even have an edge over natives, who, being so accustomed to some things, may not see what a neutral observer coming from a different culture might notice right away. I have absolutely no desire to set myself up as a judge—and precisely for this reason, it may interest some to become acquainted with my thoughts.

In general, I find that Europeans set overly high demands on schools to the same extent that Arabs set overly low ones. No people has yet found the right middle road, and none will find it. These contrasts will endure, not to be overcome, as long as the world continues to exist.

There is hardly anything more that children can be taught beyond what they are already taught here, which they are taught in such abundance that their juvenile brains cannot possibly retain it all. Once children enter school, parents no longer have anything of them. In addition to school hours, children are so overloaded with their many homework assignments that there is often little prospect of a comfortable family life together, nor the ensuing regular influence on their character development. The whole blessed day is but a never-ending rush and push from assignment to assignment. And how many of these assignments have no enduring value for the children! How much of it requires laborious learning and yet appears designed to recede into obscurity again as soon as possible. To let such things steal time away from children when they could instead be spending it with their families is surely wrong.

Meanwhile, these poor beings are crammed together five and more hours a day in a cage-like room, a so-called classroom, filled with indescribable heat and pent-up air. Why is anyone here still surprised when a school child gets sick? Young ones are nurtured and cared for at home, as much as possible, and then the school air makes these efforts all moot. How do some of these school children look; it pains the heart to see these pitiable beings! Was our open-air gallery not better? And what good is the highest-level education when the body is destroyed by its acquisition?

Generally, respect for elders was practiced not only towards parents, but also teachers and caretakers, in a way that went well beyond what we consider common practice here.

In my opinion, academic learning is emphasized much too much here. Everyone wants to advance more and more through their education, until no one is left to be a worker. Priority is placed on learning and knowledge. When the majority of people attain such lofty educational goals, then their desires and their justified and unjustified demands in life are naturally also on the rise, which leads to a more challenged and aggravated ability to exist, with all its consequences. Yes, the mind may be extraordinarily educated, but meanwhile the heart is ignored and pushed aside.

I was truly shocked to come across a statistic about the mentally ill, which indicated that the vast majority of these unfortunate cases were former students at high schools or institutes of higher learning; presumably many fell victim to academic pressures. I could not help but reflect on my homeland, where we do not need insane asylums and where I only ever came across two cases of insanity, one an African woman and the other from Hindustan.

As already indicated: My intention is not to cast judgment on all European education, something I am in any case unable to do. I simply wanted to share a few of my observations that have convinced me that schools and education here also have their share of negative aspects. It will accordingly be no surprise that it has always been and remains an open question for me if it is in fact appropriate for Europeans to lament as yet "unenlightened" folk, and if they should even be allowed to use external force to instill their enlightenment in them. Some will scoff and shrug their shoulders, but regardless! I can state with great certainty that those who believe it is in the interests of such peoples to have education and enlightenment brought to them are sorely mistaken. As an Arab woman that was born and raised in what Europeans consider a totally backward sphere, I know best how little resonance the European educational approach would find in the Islamic Orient.

With peoples that have other beliefs, who actually desire European enlightenment, as with the Japanese, the matter is different. May they find their way in, as best they can. Muslims, however, face innumerable elements in the European upbringing that are absolutely antithetical to their strictly religious point of view. How often people here demean the half-cultured Turks, and yet, the Turks have endeavored, more than is good for them, to become civilized, if only to an extent. In so doing, they have merely weakened themselves, without reaching their goal, because European civilization conflicts with and runs counter to all their basic beliefs. Civilization simply cannot be compelled through force. One should in fairness allow other peoples the free and unencumbered right to continue to cultivate their national views and institutions, which have been developed over the course of centuries, undoubtedly through mature experience and practical wisdom. Above all, a pious Arab would be deeply violated by enlightenment attempts that start with the kind of scientific teachings that are at the core of European education. It would shock his whole being. Speaking to him of the laws of nature would cause him the most acute internal conflict when he sees in the whole of the universe, down to the minutest detail, with unshakeable faith, but one thing: the all-steering, all-overseeing hand of God!

Probing the deepest meaning of nature and all creation will surely always be an elusive quest for our limited human capacities. In my reading, I once came across quite an appealing reflection. Given our short duration on earth, humans were compared to dayflies that have seen the light of day in the Strasbourg Cathedral. In the same way that these little flies could not even begin to absorb this entire marvelous construct in all its details in the course of a single day, so, too, our short lifespans cannot come to know, much less understand, all the wonders of this world. May wise people continue to study and explore, but may we not fill the heads of our children with so much knowledge that they are then unable to comprehend. In seeking to keep the right balance here as well, may we above all, and I say it again and again, not forget the heart for the head.

CHAPTER TEN

Annual Provisions, Personal Care, and Fashion in Our House

Here in Europe, the paternal head of a household who provides a monthly or quarterly allowance to his wife and unmarried daughters is usually absolved from any further care for their upkeep. Things were quite different in my father's house. Zanzibar has no industry to speak of, and therefore also no factories. All clothing and all fabric for the entire population are acquired exclusively from abroad.

My father would thus undertake some amazing bartering to cover the massive needs of his houses. Every year several of his own big sailing vessels, as many as necessary, were loaded up with our local products (especially cloves) and sent to England, Marseille, Persia, East India, and China, where our local agents set about procuring whatever we needed in exchange. The captain in charge was always handed an endless shopping list, most of which invariably constituted items for our daily care.

The annual day of distribution for these items depended, of course, on the successful return of the ships. Our household naturally awaited these ships with increasing impatience. Their arrival signified the start of a new season for us, and our whole regime depended on their cargo for the entire subsequent year.

Even the younger children found these ships steeped in a special magic. They brought us all those wonderful toys from Europe. When on one such occasion, the first time the father gave me a finely dressed doll, which could cry and had front teeth, I was beside myself with joy.

Once the ships had successfully returned, a date was quickly set to distribute the contents to everyone in our house, old and young, high and low. Even before that date, the younger brothers beseeched and beset the captain of the ship to find out what special toys were on board. Twenty to thirty crates were always filled to the brim with toy horses, little wagons, dolls, whips, fish and ducks that followed magnets, music boxes in all sizes, harmonicas, flutes, trumpets, small guns, and more. If these items did not live up to our expectations, that was bad news for the captain. He was personally responsible for everything, had the broadest powers to act, and but one overarching order to follow: Always buy the best you can find and spare no costs.

When the distribution finally began in both Bet il Mtoni and Bet il Sahel, it always lasted three to four days, until every one of the hundreds of people had received their proper share. The eunuchs took care of the unpacking and sorting. My older siblings undertook the actual distribution. Envy, resentment, and jealousy were, unfortunately, never more evident in our house than during these days of delight.

The fabric for our clothes, whether luxurious or simple, was handed out in whole bolts, and it was up to everyone individually to exchange their excess with others. This took place on a large scale, often lasting a fortnight. Since we had no tables, cloth was cut while sitting on the floor, making it not uncommon for a lady to accidentally, in her zeal, cut into her own attire.

Also to be distributed were musk, ambergris, countless oriental fragrances, rose oil and rose water, saffron (which, in combination with other ingredients, is essential for women's hairstyles), silks in all colors, gold and silver threads (tinsel) for handiwork, and woven gold and silver buttons, in short, everything that belongs to an Arab lady's upkeep, plus a certain amount of Maria Teresa coins, naturally apportioned by rank and age, to cover the cost of other miscellany.

Now and again, a few fashion-addicted Oriental ladies will have spent more than their allotment over the course of the year and would thus have to ask the father or their husbands for special supplements. Such entreaties were presented only in the greatest secrecy, as Arab heads of households were not enamored of excessive waste, any more than here, and the petitioner was sure to get an unwelcome bonus lecture on top of any extra funds.

Annual Provisions, Personal Care, and Fashion in Our House

As is the case everywhere, our house featured not only wasteful characters, but also frugal ones. These held the laudable view that slaves were not just for luxury, as was normal for the noble and wealthy classes, but should instead become revenue generating. Their slaves were accordingly trained in a variety of crafts, like sewing, stitching, and lace making for young girls, or as a saddler, carpenter, or the like for older boys. Whoever took this course was naturally less likely to run out of pin money, whereas the others had to relinquish their cash to outsiders, making it hard to balance receipts and expenses. Slaves that had acquired special skills were also accorded greater status and would, in the event of a possible release, be better positioned to establish themselves. In Oman, where relatively few slaves are kept, it is the norm to teach them all a specific craft, so they can benefit both their masters and themselves. Slaves were thus often first sent from Zanzibar to Oman to, in effect, be raised and trained. They naturally became more valuable as a result.

If anyone happened to be visiting on distribution day, and the father heard of it, then this guest would also, according to rank, get a share of whatever was being distributed, even if it was just hard cash. Any leftover cargo was put in storage and intermittently distributed throughout the year to our kinfolk from Oman.

Since summer never ends below the equator, and the four seasons are known in name only, our yearly arrangements were considerably simplified. It would have gotten quite complex if we had had to take care of fall, winter, and spring at the same time. The monsoon, which lasts six to eight weeks and during which the temperature drops to about +18°R,[13] is the only winter we know there. In this time of year that was more wet than cold, we wore mostly velvet and other thick fabrics. We also tended not to wait until nine o'clock to enjoy some food, but took our tea and cakes earlier.

Every bit of our attire was prepared by hand. We knew nothing of sewing machines back then. Our apparel benefits from a simple cut that is the same for both men and women. The intolerably unhealthy practice of corseting has not yet affected Orientals, to the preservation of their precious organs. So it is not the cut, but the fabric and adornment that distinguishes the Oriental outfit. By contrast, people here are soon bored by sticking to one thing, although we need not settle whether lack of variety properly characterizes Oriental attire. One thing is certain, however, that "fashion" and its constant variability does

---

13 Noted using the Réamur temperature scale, where water freezes at 0 degrees and boils at 80 degrees. 18°R is the equivalent of 22.5°C and 72.5°F.

not enrich the economy. To the contrary! Everyone can see for themselves how much family stress, and how many domestic scenes, could be avoided if we were more measured in our need for fashion. This addiction to always dressing in the latest style has unfortunately become so widespread that everyone is forced to participate *nolens volens*, regardless of whether they can or care to.

I have absolutely no intention of reversing the unreasonable fashion practices here or recruiting enlightened Europeans to become Philistines. I simply want to state that in point of profligacy, European women far surpass their Arab counterparts. How much it takes to stay even somewhat fashionable here: a paletot or shawl for the spring and so-called summer, a raincoat for the winter, lots of dresses, lots of hats (plenty of ladies have a special hat for every dress), various umbrellas also matched to hats and dresses, and so on. How modest by comparison is the wardrobe of an Arab woman!

The clothes of an Arab woman, regardless of rank, consist of only one ankle-length garment, a pair of pants (no bloomers), and a head scarf, as can be seen on the frontispiece.[14] The fabric varies greatly. Rich people prefer gold brocade in the most diverse patterns, velvet and silk with ample adornment, and only plain, light calicos and muslins for hot days. The garment and pants never have the same pattern. And care is taken not to allow the length of the garment to cover the rich embroidery of the pants and the two golden ankle bracelets, one of which is adorned with numerous bell-like gold pieces that pleasantly chime with every step. The headband, which is wound around the forehead, features two long ribbons with large tassels that hang down the back or either side of the head. The actual silk head scarf reaches down to the ankles.

When an Arab lady wishes to go out, she throws on her *shele*, which serves as shawl, paletot, jacket, raincoat, and duster all combined. This is a large, black, silk scarf, fitted with gold or silk trim according to the wealth and taste of its bearer. An Oriental woman wears this one and only covering until it is completely worn out without ever going out of fashion. Even the fanciest and wealthiest women make it a point to never own more than one *shele*.

During the monsoon, the finer Arab ladies in the house also wear a *djocha*, a kind of paletot that reaches down to the ankles and is made of cloth richly adorned with gold or silver embroidery. The *djocha* is worn exactly like the paletots here, which is to say never on its own, but always over the other regular clothes. It is open in the front from top to bottom and held together only at

---

14 Page xviii.

Annual Provisions, Personal Care, and Fashion in Our House

the chest level with gold braiding. Older ladies prefer a thick and sumptuous Persian shawl to the *djocha*.

This is thus the only piece of clothing that has any association with winter. Beyond that, of course, we have scant need to protect ourselves from the cold, since it never goes below +18° in the wet season.

Apropos, worth mentioning here, we also kept a kind of heating apparatus, and a very comfortable one at that. A brass bowl, roughly twenty centimeters deep and thirty centimeters wide, seated on three legs, each fifteen centimeters high, would be filled with glowing coals and placed in the middle of the room. This coal fire disperses an extraordinarily mild and pleasant warmth that draws everyone to the *mankal*. The very popular corn harvest happens during the same season, when corn is prepared in many different ways. A favorite is to shuck the fresh cobs, which grow significantly larger than here, and lay them for roasting on the glowing coals of the *mankal*; just five minutes, and they are ready to eat. As the corn on the cob starts to get done, it emits a steady popping noise, which was always great fun for us children. —Windows and doors almost always stay open, even with this small-scale heater.

Bet il Ras by Rosa Troemer

CHAPTER ELEVEN

On a Plantation

I mentioned previously that my father owned forty-five plantations that were scattered across the whole island. Each one had about fifty to one hundred, on the big ones up to five hundred, slaves as workers, under an Arab manager. Only two of these plantations came with real palaces, while six to eight had larger cottages, and the rest contained only staff and farm buildings. Consequently, we had access only to the first ones for longer stays.

During times when my father was in the city, we were unable to take a plantation outing all together because a portion of his governing entourage always had to stay with him, and he personally was too caught up in his business affairs to accompany us. But for us children and adults, it was always great fun to visit a plantation. My older siblings gave the good-natured father no peace until he permitted some of us to ride over without him.

Preparations for these outings were always quite involved. It was no small matter to ensure the plentiful upkeep of such a throng of people on a plantation that was often one to two German miles hence, for which everything was carried on the heads of slaves. Already three days prior, several hundred slaves were engaged to transport what was needed. Much to the dismay of the cooks and chief eunuchs, who had to take care of the entire company, these transfers resulted in considerable loss of food and heavy spoilage along the way, so they always had to provision double of what was actually needed. The plantation managers at the other end got the greatest benefit, since they were allowed to keep any leftovers for their own use.

On a Plantation

Most participants remained sleepless with joyful anticipation the night before. Already that evening, they had inspected the snow-white passenger donkeys, whose tails were now colored red with a plant-based dye called *hinna*. Any of the ladies (namely, the *sarari*) who did not have their own donkeys would borrow from friends and acquaintances, or have them supplied by my brothers and the eunuchs. And yet, it was not unusual for someone to get left behind if she neglected to organize her transport on time. This was just something the father never concerned himself with; in this respect, everyone was on their own.

If the plantation we wanted to visit was on the coast, the matter was naturally much easier. In those cases, no one ever had to stay home for lack of transport. Our ships always put enough row boats at our disposal. Our provisions also benefited. Peacefully stowed in the boat, they naturally had a better chance of reaching their destination than when inconsiderately thrown back and forth by slaves at a large number of rest stops on country roads.

These outings seemed especially designed to bring out the ardor for all the extensive finery that Oriental women possess. Everything was mustered, everything was applied, lest there be any chance of lagging behind the others. And for any beauty facing the great misfortune of not having her new outfit ready on time, she would rather forgo the event entirely, lonely and alone.

As a rule, the departure time was set early at five thirty, directly after the first prayer. Leading up to this time, our courtyard was filled with such a confused and frenzied cacophony of voices and noises that anyone with weak nerves could have been brought to despair. Fortunately, people there are equipped with unusually robust nerves. The regular lifestyle, freedom from worry, and magnificent ocean air keep such nervous maladies from our shores.

The traffic on our two stairways backs up continuously. There are shouts down the stairs, shouts up the stairs, screams, and hefty pushes. Slaves exchange crude profanities and then resonant slaps in the face. The saddled animals, who have already been waiting an hour, are restless and start to add their pleasant donkey voices to the overall racket. All the while, they are earnestly endeavoring to indulge in their favorite activity, to roll around on the ground, never mind their rich adornment and charming tack. Their supervising slaves have their hands full just keeping them in check. And in the meantime, impatient travelers have already saddled up.

After everyone has inspected their animals in the courtyard, the animals are routed up over the elevated pitch to the street, where their owners mount. The weak and delicate eunuchs also ride along, while the stout African slaves must run the distance on foot. And thus begins the most amusing ride one could ever imagine. Great, but usually harmless, pranks are mixed in with cheerful joking, causing so much laughter that it can be hard to stay in the saddle.

The snow-white donkeys present a most picturesque sight, so richly decorated with little gold and silver plates that chime pleasantly with every step, and their lightly elevated saddles resting on fancy saddle pads. No less stunning are our foot runners with their exquisitely polished weapons and their clean, white attire. As the sun climbs higher, the more elegant ladies keep these African speed runners by their sides to be protected from the blazing heat with wide-reaching parasols that these runners carry as they stay apace. Other slaves trot along with small children straddling their shoulders. Somewhat older children, but not yet old enough to ride their own horses, are each assigned to ride with a eunuch.

We had to pass through the city while it was still twilight, and during this time, the whole company kept close together. But as soon as we were out in the open, all discipline came to an end, and everyone rode ahead at their own pace. Any efforts by the eunuchs to keep a closed caravan were in vain. Whoever felt themselves astride a fiery mount had little interest in holding back for the sake of the whole, and the eunuchs could call and shout in their delicate pitch however much they wanted. After having set out all together, as if by command in one big crowd, we reached our destination strung out in various larger and smaller groups.

There we were greeted by the first and oldest of our slaves at the plantation and, if the Arab manager was married, by his family. Being a man that adhered to custom, he himself was not allowed to be seen by any of us during our entire stay.

We always left for such outings on an empty stomach, and thus arrived with that much more appetite to enjoy the countless delicious fruits that had been set out for us. The first opulent main meal was served immediately afterwards, which the ensemble ate in our various groupings, as we did back home, according to rank. When the meal was done, everyone took off to do whatever they pleased. No one had to worry about spectators here, where only the dear cattle lowed under the magnificent trees. Here, everyone could be completely unrestrained and indulge to their hearts' delight. The group came back together as a whole only for mealtimes and prayers. All prayer requires cleansing, and since there was no water on parts of the island, that was reason enough to have to head home.

Over the course of the day, neighboring estates would send their invitations, and other neighboring ladies would announce their visits. Both invitations and visitors always applied to the whole family. In practice, though, outside guests were hosted exclusively by my older siblings, while invitations could be accepted by anyone who wanted to attend.

Our ability to live simply in the lovely South, since we hate to make a fuss, is evident in our mass outings. It would have been impossible to provide beds for all the many participants. Instead, everyone, whether of high or low rank, just lay down on their pile of saddle blankets and, in place of a pillow (ours always being round, much like the French), put their arms under their heads.

What we consumed on these occasions can hardly be described. I have already mentioned the extreme amounts of provisions brought over by hundreds of slaves over the course of many days. But that was not enough. Our kindly neighbors insisted on showing their good graces by sending daily shipments of massive amounts of cooked and uncooked food. As a rule, this was followed by various discomforts, much like the Christmas sicknesses here. —

Good old Ledda, the customs manager, was permitted to greet us, as a man of a different faith, even though Arab men were strictly forbidden to do so. He was unusually loyal and had a touching personal attachment to our whole house. Especially for us children, this grey-headed star worshipper took every opportunity to make us happy. On every one of his holidays, and ours as well, he made sure to share all sorts of delightful gifts from his Indian homeland, in particular many sweets and baskets of fireworks (*fetak*). As soon as he heard that we were planning a trip to the countryside, he made a special point of bringing such gifts. Every evening we then had fun burning the widest assortment of products made by talented Indian pyrotechnicians.

The evenings were otherwise filled with watching Africans play games and dance, which they did in the garden under the open sky. Native dancing is nowhere near as ugly and unpleasant as some travelers have claimed in their books. On the other hand, I, too, initially took a total dislike to European dancing. The eternally twirling pairs just made me dizzy, even when I was sitting still in my chair.

Hindustani dancers were also frequently brought out to the plantations to regale us in the evenings with their artistry. These dancers are extraordinarily talented and, even though they are not compensated as richly as in Europe, they quickly become very prosperous, regardless of their expenditures, and are able to return to their homeland with satisfaction. Even so, they get but minimal respect from us.

Such evenings in the Orient are truly romantic. Picture a large group, featuring an array of complexions, elegant, but very colorful and creatively dressed, gathered in a large circle, whether standing, sitting, or squatting, and filled with hearty laughter and harmless jokes in the relaxed manner of the South, and all that in lush greenery under the most magnificent trees, while bathed in the intense light that shines down from the tropical moon. You have to have experienced it to be able to imagine it. Not until late, very late in fact, would the gathering disperse, and the visiting ladies would mount their donkeys and ride home.

A whimsical little French girl by the name of Claire, along with her two wild brothers of fourteen or fifteen years of age, the children of a French consular doctor and very good at Swahili, were often included on these outings and knew how to liven things up with their songs. Claire precipitated general laughter one evening, on her first overnight with us, when she appeared—in her traditional European white nightgown.

For extended stays, our father might occasionally come out to visit us, but always returned to the city by evening. Horsemen then continuously circled back and forth to maintain a seamless connection between us and the city, as a kind of postal service.

Come harvest time, we preferred to avoid such outings because that would have disturbed the slaves too much in their work. The clove harvest comes upon us so suddenly and transpires so quickly that it is challenging to gather the whole bounty in good condition within the short time available. The rice harvest also has to be completed right away, whereas sugar cane, coconuts, sweet potatoes, and the other farm products could tolerate more of a delay. Cattle are never used for farming. Farm tools are practically nonexistent; we do not have even the most basic plow. Everything has to be done by hand. To turn the soil, we use spades. Rice ears are tediously cut by the bushel with standard small and straight knives. The master or mistress may even join the clove harvest, so as to motivate and energize their slaves. Africans are known to resist work, and they need very sharp and steady oversight to be productive.[15] That kind of ongoing control is, however, totally untenable for the clove harvest. A better method is to require a daily quota of cloves from each slave based on age and ability. Those who bring in more get extra wages; those who neglect their duties can expect commensurate consequences.

---

15 The author has been criticized for racist statements in her *Memoirs*. The translator provides some reflections in "On Controversy" on pages 243–51.

On a Plantation

Only the actual harvest requires effort. Little is needed leading up to the harvest. The soil is so incredibly rich that it needs no fertilizing. And the general practice of burning straw on the fields fortuitously keeps the soil from depleting. —

The father always set the exact length of our plantation stays. He would determine the day we were to be back in the city between six thirty and seven thirty in the evening, after nightfall. At our departure, the plantation manager's family would receive suitable gifts hand-selected by the father, and our nearest neighborhood women usually accompanied us a bit down the road. The father always sent out about one hundred to one hundred and fifty soldiers that ran alongside the long procession. Despite their heavy load of weapons (at all times bearing rifle, shield, lance, saber, and dagger), they still managed to keep up with our mounts.

Even on these trips, the mandatory six o'clock evening prayer was not to be missed. And so the whole company would stop somewhere, typically in Ngambo or Mnazi Mmoja (both towns lie just outside the city), and settle into prayer mode. Everyone carried a small mat that they kept especially clean, on which to pray under the open sky. If, as often happened through negligence of the servants, a mat went missing or was even left behind at home, a huge leaf from the *moz* (banana) tree would be sent for as a substitute. We are allowed to pray on plant material only.

Darkness would quickly descend. As we returned to our mounts, a great number of colossal lanterns were lit. We then rode in almost fairy-tale splendor back into the city.

Mackatè from the Harbour

CHAPTER TWELVE

The Father's Voyage

I was about nine years old when the time came for the father to go back to his old Omani empire, as he did every three to four years, to personally manage the situation there. Up to that point, my oldest brother Tueni (often called Sueni, but that is less correct) had represented him in Muscat, both as regent and head of the family.

This time my father had an especially urgent reason to travel to Oman. The Persians had made several incursions near Bandar Abbas on the Persian Gulf, which were not so significant on their own, but could have easily led to military entanglements. This small piece of land within Persia, with its controlling location at the entrance to the Persian Gulf, had given us nothing but trouble since its conquest and proved very costly for the father. It was taken from us again later, which was surely no bad fortune. Until then, the Persians gave us no peace, for which we could hardly blame them.

We had no steamboats back then, only sailing ships. We were thus very reliant on the wind and entirely dependent on its moods, which frequently delayed travel. Travel preparations took at least eight to ten weeks until everything was procured and in place. It took especially long to bake the so-called long-duration cakes that were needed to feed about a thousand heads over a ten-week period. Salt-cured meat was unknown to us, and food preserves, even if we had had them, were *haram* (unclean, contrary to the food laws) and not something we could enjoy. Instead, a colossal number of livestock had to be ferried along, including about a dozen milk cows. Incalculable quantities of fruit were added to the cargo. All forty-five of our plantations had to deliver fruit to the ships for days on end.

All the sons were allowed to participate in the trip, but only a few daughters, given the inconveniences that women generally cause. A couple of the *sarari* were taken along as well, but only the most favored ones.

In fact, not many of us wanted to go to Oman. The proud Omani women treat the Zanzibari women as an uneducated lot. This condescension even carried over to our siblings. Family members born in Oman deem themselves extraordinarily distinguished compared to us Africans. They believe that our upbringing among the natives has of necessity rubbed off on us. They consider our coarsest feature to be that we, how horrid! speak another language besides Arabic. —

As already mentioned several times, many of my siblings and many more of my relatives lived in Oman, most of whom were quite poor and depended on the support of our father. All of them expected presents when the father arrived, and so the travel load grew even larger.

At this time then, everyone's thoughts gravitated to their loved ones in far-off Asia, which caused the otherwise languishing correspondence to liven up. But this is where the inability to write would become a major obstacle. One had to witness the great predicaments that arose to truly appreciate the scale of the distress. Letters had to be written by someone else, and, at the other end, strangers would then have to read them to the recipients. My brothers and any literate male slaves were more than overloaded in this task, and when they were no longer able or willing (yes, that also happened), then this letter writing had to be outsourced, for better or worse, to complete outsiders. That these letters very seldom meet the mark goes without saying.

Here is an example: One of the beauties calls to her slave: "Feruz! Go to this-and-that *kadi* and tell him, he should write a sweet letter to my friend in Oman. Pay him whatever he charges for the letter." And then Feruz is loaded up with a host of details that the *kadi* should include in the letter. The *kadi*, however, is under time pressure with a dozen such letters to be written, and so it is no wonder when the various assignments get wildly mixed up. Triumphantly, Feruz returns to his lady: "Bibi, here are the letters!" To play it safe, this lady then goes to another literate person to have the letters from the *kadi* read back to her. She is soon astounded, and her dismay increases with every additional word. The letter is totally inaccurate. Where she wanted to offer condolences are congratulations, and vice versa, and so on. Every letter must therefore be written multiple times by multiple people until it is more or less in shape for mailing.

Everything was finally ready. The three-masted ship *Kitorie*, meaning "Victoria" (named for Her Majesty, the Queen of England), was assigned to the father and his family, and the other two or three were for the retinue, servants, and baggage. The number of travelers in relation to the total number of ships was thus very large. Notably, however, Orientals take up less space and do not require their own separate cabins. When night arrives, everyone looks for their own spot on the upper deck and lies down on the personal mats they brought along.

The retinue and servants embarked first. Then around five in the morning came the women and, toward midday, the father with his sons. My brothers Chalid and Madjid and the younger ones accompanied the travelers to the ship and stayed there until the anchor was raised. With a twenty-one gun salute, the father gave his last farewell to the country and family members that stayed behind. —

Right away our house fell into an unfamiliar quiet, even though the place was still overcrowded. We could tell the head of the family was missing, and a sort of solitude reigned despite the masses of people. My brother Chalid acted for the father, as the oldest son in Zanzibar. He stopped by our house multiple times a week to check on our well-being and went just as often to Bet il Mtoni to check on the inhabitants there, especially to take requests from our venerable stepmother.

As the leader of the family, Chalid was very strict, and we often had reason to complain about his harsh treatment. Here are two examples: A fire once broke out in Bet il Sahel, which, fortunately, was quickly extinguished. We understandably flew into a panic when it started and rushed toward the house doors, only to find them locked and tightly guarded by soldiers. Chalid had immediately ordered the doors closed, so there could be no chance that we might recklessly, in broad daylight, emerge to the eyes of the public.

Another time, he brusquely expelled a distant relative, who was very influential in Zanzibar, from a mosque because this man had had the temerity to ask him in that space for the hand of one of our sisters. For months thereafter, this poor suitor could not present himself at the daily official gatherings, nor in this mosque where Chalid tended to pray. Destiny, however, saw to it that this rejected fellow took another sister of ours home with him a few years later, after the father and Chalid had died.

To the chagrin of many, the father had appointed Chole to be the female head of household at Bet il Sahel and Bet il Tani during his absence. It was easy to understand why this bright light of our house found no joy in her leadership role. How could it be otherwise when this post engendered nothing but jealousy and lack of gratitude? Despite her good nature, there was no way to satisfy everyone; she was as human as the rest of us mortals. Impossible demands were made of her, and no one cared about the limits of her power. She could hardly help the fact that the father favored her, but the jealousy was simply too great and robbed any sense of perspective from those who thought ill of her. —

In the meantime, our three-masted ships often sailed back and forth between Oman and Zanzibar, bringing frequent news and gifts from the father. Whenever these ships docked, there was understandably much joy. The place would always be full of people rushing around, with lots of noise and lively gesticulating, the way only those in the South can.

Sadly, not long after the father's departure, our brother Chalid was called back to the Lord. The regency transitioned to Madjid, now the oldest son, who knew how to win over all the hearts with his kind nature.

Finally one day, a ship arrived from Muscat with the joyful news that the father was ready to leave Oman and return to Zanzibar. The news spread quickly and raised the spirits of the whole country. Our father had been gone for three years and was indeed missed at times. Even those who were not lovingly attached to him at least looked forward to the endless supply of gifts for young and old that he always made sure to bring back from Oman. The whole place was full of anticipation, and preparations worthy of our greatest celebrations were happening everywhere.

But the time passed in which the travelers could have readily reached Zanzibar, and still there was no ship in sight. The house and the country eventually became restless. Arabs love to probe the hidden future with so-called clairvoyants, and in Swahili lands, in Zanzibar, this custom is especially pronounced. Even Hungarian gypsies would have a lot to learn from their Swahili counterparts. What the latter practice in terms of lies and deceit is beyond description. On the other hand, gullibility knows no bounds.

The Father's Voyage

Understandably, no stone was left unturned in seeking any possible explanation for the three missing ships, and so these fortune tellers were trafficked in droves through our house. They were brought in from miles away, often from the furthest corners of the island, especially from the tribe of the *Wachadimu*. If the fortune tellers were elderly, they were seated on donkeys and triumphantly trotted in.

An unusually bizarre appearance came in the form of a woman, who, it was said, or more precisely her unborn child, could foretell the future. We had never seen such a monstrosity, so of course, she had to be called in for questioning. It was on an afternoon (the scene is forever indelibly marked in my memory) when this soothsayer, or seemingly sacred person, who was possessed of an unnaturally large circumference, strode past me. The child, which she had allegedly carried under her heart already for years, was virtually omniscient. It could report on everything, from what was happening high up in the mountains to what could be seen deep down in the oceans. Now it was going to tell us about the fate of the father and explain why his arrival was so delayed. With a distinct, but very squeaky voice, this enormous being recounted her vision, while the whole, sizeable assembly sat spellbound. From afar, it saw several three-masted ships on the high seas headed toward Zanzibar. It wanted to ascend the mast of the father's ship to see what was going on there. After a short while, it described in minute detail what each person was doing at that very moment. To conclude, it told us to bring copious offerings to ensure the continued good favor of the sea spirits, so as to guard and protect the travelers from harm. The instructions of this exceptional child were of course strictly followed in every detail. All the professional beggars, of which we have legions on our lovely island, were able to indulge for days on end in the abundant meat, chicken, and rice, not to mention clothing and cash, that we had distributed to them.

I was later ashamed to realize we had all simply fallen victim to a ventriloquist. At the time, we were all convinced that this amazing child had the ability to unveil the invisible world, all the secrets that were totally hidden from human perception. Whether this woman was indeed a fraud that fully intended to deceive us, I am not sure. No one had ever heard of a ventriloquist, and therefore no one could have come up with that explanation. Maybe this woman herself had no clear sense of the matter. Maybe she actually believed, when she heard those strange tones for the first time, that this was an unusually precocious and privileged child and then only gradually became a sophisticated swindler.

We do love all things mysterious in our parts; the more esoteric and opaque the matter appears, the more we buy into it. Everyone believes in invisible spirits, both good ones and bad. When someone dies, their room is thoroughly fumigated with incense for days in anticipation of the expected, frequent return of the pining soul of the deceased, which usually prefers the room where it died, where no one likes to enter, certainly under no circumstances at night.

And superstitions abound. For sickness, betrothal, pregnancy, and all manner of events, people seek the help of fortune tellers. They want to know if the sickness can be cured and how long it will take; if fortune will smile on the betrothed; if the expected child will be a boy or girl; and so on. If the opposite in fact occurs, which naturally happens time and time again, the soothsayer always has a plausible excuse at the ready. She says it must have been her unlucky star on that particular day—better luck next time. And people accept that. Whoever takes up this kind of business does not fare poorly and is soon a made man or more precisely, a made woman.

No 2.

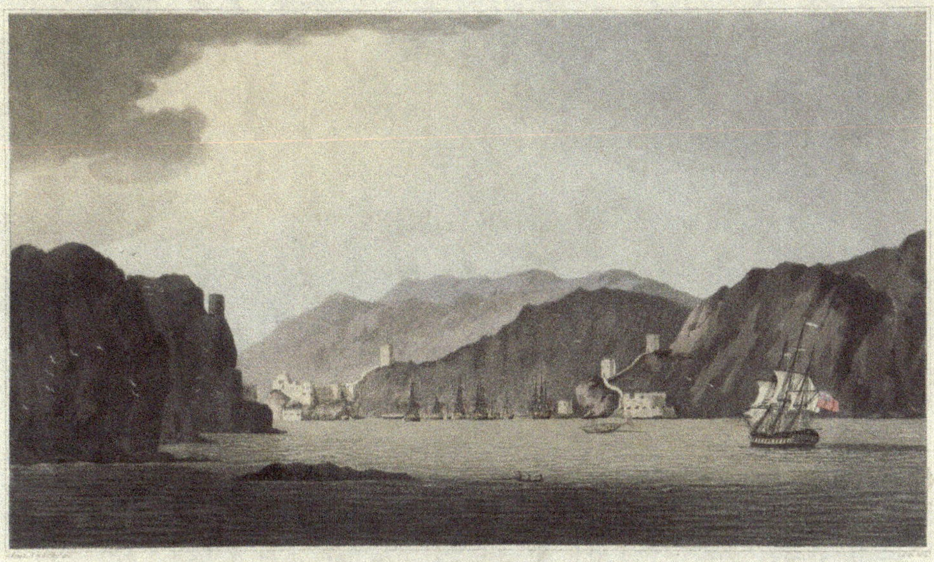

Muskat Har. &c.
from the Fisher man's Rock

No 4.

A View of Matra from the East

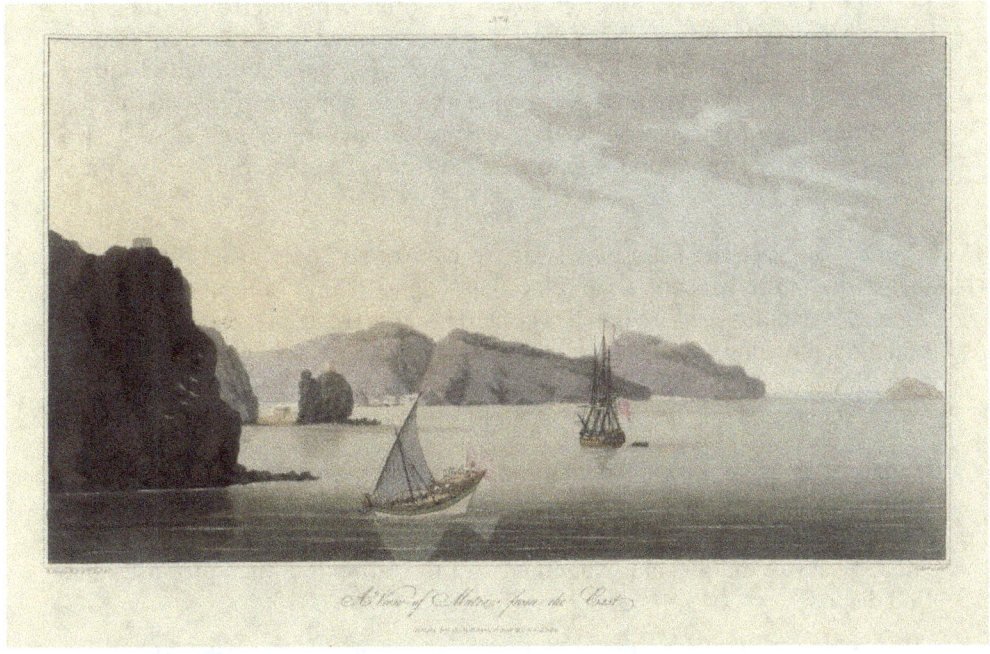

CHAPTER THIRTEEN

News of a Death

Time slipped away, day after day, week after week, with no sign of the father. The long wait was shortened only by the never-ending dealings with the soothsayers, so there was at least some good in that, even if their prophecies never came true. Finally one afternoon, while we were still at prayer, the happy news spread that a fisherman had seen several ships with our flags far out on the high seas, although stormy weather kept him from getting any closer. That could only be the father! Everyone rushed to put on their festive outfits that had been ready for weeks, to welcome the long-awaited father with the greatest joy. We always preened and adorned ourselves like this for loved ones returning from travel or even after victorious battle, while we wore decidedly simple and unadorned clothes to express our sorrow on a day of departure.

Even as we made the fisherman swear to us over and over again that he was telling the truth, we sent a mounted messenger to share the news with our venerable stepmother in Bet il Mtoni. The courtyard became active with slaughter, cooking, and baking, the chambers were richly perfumed, and everything was put in the best order. According to the fisherman, we could expect the ships to arrive within two to three hours.

Madjid rushed out with his retinue to reach the father. They set off in two cutters, fighting against a massive storm that threatened to obliterate them and their boats at any moment. They hoped to be back in our midst at the latest by seven that evening, together with the father. But man proposes and God disposes.

News of a Death

Time passed. Seven o'clock had long come and gone, and still there was no sign of the ships. An unusual disquiet gripped the whole city, but mostly our house. We sensed that something was amiss, although not quite what we were soon to learn. We feared that Madjid and his escorts could have lost their lives in the raging gale, and this horrible discovery naturally would have delayed the father's arrival. Eventually the view prevailed that all the ships, large and small, had gone under in the storm. Conjecture was heaped on conjecture. No one, not even the youngest children, wanted to go to bed before those we awaited had happily arrived.

And then a message suddenly spread that no one wanted to believe. The whole palace was said to be surrounded by several hundred soldiers keeping strict guard. Everyone rushed to the windows to see for themselves. The night was pitch black, and all we saw in all directions were the glowing fuses of soldiers' weapons, a sight that could only add to our already petrified spirits. And to make matters worse, we were informed that the soldiers were not letting anyone pass, neither in, nor out.

What has happened? Why are we locked in? Everyone wanted to know. Principally, though, we debated back and forth about who had issued the order. Madjid had, as much as anyone knew, not yet returned, and even his own house—where we could clearly see figures pacing restlessly back and forth in the bright lights—was also guarded by sinister figures, just like ours.

With the eunuchs and all the other male slaves sleeping outside the house, we were in especially dire straits. The whole building contained only women and helpless children. A few fearless women showed great courage and pushed forward to the front hall on the ground floor where only one more door separated them from the designated security room, where they could readily speak with the guards through the hall windows. But these men proved hard and heartless, as they kept to their orders and withheld all information. When the shrieks and queries of the slave women got to be too much, the guards swore high and holy that if they did not settle down, they would simply shoot them down.

We cried and hurled accusations at the invisible power, which clearly was an evil one. The children cried and screamed everywhere and could not be calmed. The pious prayed to the Almighty. It was a spectacle that defies description. Had anyone happened upon the dreadful disarray of this night of horror, they surely would have thought themselves in an insane asylum.

Morning was already dawning, and still we had no idea why we were being treated as hostages or where Madjid might be. Even with all our fear and agitation, we dispersed into groups at the appointed time for morning prayer duty. But alas, who can describe our utter dismay when we finally saw our fleet, clearly anchored before us with flags at half-mast. How unspeakable the lamentation when our gates opened in the early morning, and our brothers came to us without the father!

Only then did it become clear to us for whom the ships mourned, what irreparable loss we and our country were meant to endure. Our dear father is no longer! On this trip from Oman to Zanzibar, amidst but a few of his children and faithful followers, he had been called to meet the Lord, whom he had always served with the greatest humility! The gunshot wound to his leg, that had plagued him for so long, had finally put an end to his precious life.

This departed soul was not only the most caring head of his family, he was also the most conscientious ruler and true father of his people. How beloved he was could be seen in the widespread grief at his passing. Black flags waved from every house, and even the very poorest hut had set out a small black cloth.

We learned details of the father's illness and his last hours from Barghash, who was on the same ship and with him at his death. We also had Barghash to thank that the precious corpse had not been lowered into the bottomless sea, as required by Islam. Barghash had spoken forcefully in favor of taking the father back to Zanzibar, and even had him preserved in a coffin to enable the transit. His natural devotion to the dear father led him to do this, but in so doing, he violated our traditions and customs, our religion, even more. For us, coffins are completely unacceptable. Every one of us, from prince to pauper, all of us in the same way are to be returned directly to the lap of Mother Earth, back to that from which we came.

Now we also discovered why we had been so strictly guarded the night before. Madjid, with his retinue, had suffered greatly in the storm and feared they would go under. Their small vessels, which were designed only for coastal runs, had had to sail far out to sea to reach the ships. By the time they arrived, Barghash was gone. As the eldest son on the flotilla, Barghash had taken command and, with land in view, had ridden off quietly to take the body to shore and bury it secretly and unseen in our burial ground.

This maneuver arose from an old tradition that any disputes over the throne were to be handled in the presence of the body of the deceased father or brother, with the expectation that filial devotion would, as a rule, benefit the rightful heir. But Barghash wanted to win the lordship for himself. Knowing that such a formal rite would favor Madjid, he decided to thwart it altogether.

He opted instead for blatant force, above all hoping to blindside everyone while they were still reeling from news of the death.

He had therefore, immediately upon landing, ordered our house and Madjid's to be surrounded, with the goal of capturing Madjid there. And yet, his plan failed, since Madjid had already set out to sea. Barghash later sought to explain his measures as an attempt to forestall a potential revolution. —

And so Madjid, who, as already mentioned, had ruled Zanzibar as the acting head following Chalid's death, retained his position and proclaimed his status as ruler that same morning. But we still hung in the fearful uncertainty about whether he was truly our leader, or if our oldest brother Tueni, who continued to stay back in Oman, might not seek to wrest his entitlement by force.

altes arabisches Kriegsschiff

CHAPTER FOURTEEN

Our Mourning

Our mourning was full of rituals. For starters, all of us, young and old, had to remove our fine clothes and were allowed to dress in only the most common black cotton. Our richly embroidered face coverings were replaced by plain, black fabric. Creams and perfumes of any kind were strictly off-limits, and anyone who sprayed rose oil or even rose water just once onto their clothes was considered heartless, or at least decried by all as a coquette. All the adults refrained, at least initially, from sleeping on their beds. Like the father, who slumbered directly on the ground, so, too, his beloved, if they wished to express their devotion, had to deny themselves such comforts.

For a full fortnight, our house was like one of the largest hotels in the world. During this time, anyone and everyone could come and eat their fill, whether prince or pauper. In keeping with long-standing custom, especially the favorite dish of the deceased is always cooked and served to the poor in massive quantities.

All wives of the deceased man, without exception, from those of noble birth to purchased slaves, must observe a special religious mourning period that spans a full four months. These poor souls are obliged to grieve for their husband or master in a dark room. They cannot intentionally step into daylight, much less sunshine. If a *terike* (widow) ever has to leave her artificially darkened room and go through the open gallery, she must throw a dark, heavy scarf over her mask, covering herself to the point where she can barely find her way. During this time, the eyes become extremely sensitive to light and can only slowly resume direct exposure after the mourning period comes to an end.

Our Mourning

Right at the start, widows are formally tied to their status through specific ceremonial words uttered by the *kadi*, a kind of priest, to whom they of course appear fully covered. He then also has to expressly free them from this widow status with a special ceremony when the four months are over. There are other dark and superstitious rites that widows are subjected to on the day of their release. Above all, they must simultaneously undergo a complete cleansing, from head to foot, while each one is flanked from behind by a female slave that clangs two sword blades over the head of her mistress in a regular rhythm (poor people may have to use nails—the material must be iron). Given the number of widows the father left behind, there was no way to conduct the ceremony in the baths, which were too small for this purpose despite their great expanse. And thus, the cleansing of all these women was undertaken on the beach, making for a peculiarly animated and outlandish spectacle.

From then on, the widows wore different clothes. Only now could they contemplate remarriage. Although previous access to them had already been restricted to male family members and our personal slaves, this was even further restricted after the four months, so that no one but our brothers could see our mothers. —

In our first year of mourning, some of us went regularly on Thursday evenings, the eve of the Islamic Sunday, to visit the father's gravesite. It was a rectangular structure with a large dome, in which other siblings of mine also rested in peace. After reciting the first sura of the Koran (effectively the Islamic Lord's Prayer) and other verses, and pleading to the Almighty to show mercy to the departed and grant forgiveness for their sins, we would pour precious rose oil and rose water over the graves and waft smoked ambergris and musk, while wailing loudly about the painful loss.

Muslims maintain an unwavering belief in immortality, and accordingly also believe that the soul of the deceased is permitted, now and again on special occasions, to visit the former site of its own earlier being and its relatives, naturally unobserved. That is why we like to go to a beloved gravesite and share all our joy and pain with the immortal soul of the deceased, who still pays intimate attention to us in the afterlife. In short, we honor the dead in all ways. One can be confident that a decent Muslim, who swears by the head or the name of his deceased, would sooner perish than violate the sworn oath. —

As long as our mothers were in mourning, our houses kept to their usual routines. We, of course, could not conduct any business during this time. But we also had to first settle our affairs with our siblings in Oman. A ship was immediately dispatched to share the news of the misfortune that had hit us so hard. How would Tueni, who was the father's oldest son and by rights entitled to be his successor, react to all this? Would he come to an understanding with Madjid, or did we have a violent family quarrel looming on the horizon? Such questions were in daily discussion.

After quite a few months, our brother Muhammed arrived in Zanzibar as the representative of our siblings in Oman, primarily to participate in the distribution of the estate. And then he returned to Muscat as quickly as possible, the moment his task was done. Muhammed was considered the most religious of all our family members. From youth onwards, he had cared little for the world and worldly interests. As an enemy of all that glittered externally and all material goods, he had never embraced his status as prince. He put little stock in riches and never wore elaborate attire, in lieu of clothes that were very modest and plain. Since Omanis were not accustomed to much pomp, he found the Zanzibari opulence all the more off-putting. So much grandeur made him feel outright unhappy. Hence his great haste to be able to return without delay to the simpler conditions of our original Asiatic homeland.

The question of succession remained unaddressed. Madjid, who held the power in Zanzibar, made no issue about whether Tueni, who now took full control of Oman, was on board with his illegitimate position, and Tueni in turn never formally recognized him as the Sultan of Zanzibar. Later they came up with a sort of compromise, through British mediation, under which Madjid was to pay his older brother an annual sum. Madjid, however, kept to the agreement but a short while and soon stopped making payments, since they could easily be seen as a kind of tribute to, and he as a vassal of, Oman. Tueni could do nothing about it. He had battles of his own to fight in Oman, and his means were no match for the wealthy ruler of Zanzibar, should he have wanted to exert his rights by force. Lacking a formal, contractual basis, Oman and Zanzibar have ever since continued as two separate kingdoms, independent of each other.

By contrast, the siblings were able to agree on a distribution of the father's private estate with Muhammed's engagement. We have no nation-state in the European sense and therefore have nothing that stems from this label or concept. In particular, we have no concept of government income or expenditure. Whatever customs duties came in were simply private assets of the ruler, our father. With these and especially the profits from his plantations, considering that he was also the largest landowner on the island, he covered all costs and filled his treasury. In turn, at least in my time, we also had no income, property, business, or other taxes, unlike the many we have here.

All these private assets were distributed among the siblings. Even the military ships were handled this way and accrued to Tueni and Madjid as offsets from their shares under an agreed formula. Islamic law gives significant advantage to sons over daughters in matters of inheritance, under a justification that a man has a duty to maintain his entire family, which a woman does not. And so, we sisters received only half as much as our brothers.

Even I was declared of age, together with my brother Ralub, my former playmate in Bet il Mtoni, although we were both barely twelve years old. This was early even for our customs, but it was simply an unusual time for us all, and one upheaval followed another. We thus received our inheritance just like the others and were standing on our own two feet at twelve years of age. Our still younger siblings remained under Madjid's guardianship, who kept custody over their assets.

In his last will and testament, my father had instructed that any of his women without children should be cared for as long as they lived. By contrast, the mothers of his children received only a relatively small, one-time payout. He may well have assumed that we would care for our own mothers, but in this way, the mothers ended up entirely dependent on their children, the mother owning practically nothing, and the child everything. But the father had gauged his children correctly. I can, to the credit of all my siblings (we totaled thirty-six still living at the time of his death), gladly certify that not one disappointed his admirable trust in them. They all loved and respected their mothers as before; no one ever took advantage of their privileged position. Indeed, that would have been extremely damnable. A mother is always a mother, whether she is a born princess or a purchased slave. She needs neither rank nor riches to forever have a rightful claim to the greatest devotion from her child.

Not long after distribution of the inheritance was completed, our once-crowded house became empty and lonely, at least in comparison to earlier times. A number of my siblings, together with their mothers and personal slaves, moved out of the father's houses to establish their own homes. Chole, Shewane, Aashe, my mother, and I chose not to follow this example right away, and so I continued to live with them and my mother for some time at Bet il Tani.

Changes also took place at Bet il Mtoni, with Zemsem moving out to her new plantation where she stayed until her subsequent marriage, and Mettle also transferring a short time later to hers. It was, in fact, necessary that some of us leave the big houses, now that we were able to live independently and unrestrained, according to our own tastes. We needed to make room for our younger, underage siblings.

Having been collectively cared for out of an admittedly massive common pot during the father's lifetime, this now, of course, changed things. Everyone who had received their inheritance henceforth had to take care of themselves. Conditions were unchanged only for the underage siblings, alongside their mothers and slaves, and the women without children. Their care was now Madjid's responsibility, so that all their wealth and earnings were naturally at his disposal.

Sultan Madjid bin Said

CHAPTER FIFTEEN

Personalities and Stories of My Siblings

Over the course of my narrative, I have already spoken about my siblings, some more, some less. How many siblings I had overall, I do not know. Certainly, a large number had already passed away before the father died, and I do not believe I exaggerate when I put the total around one hundred. When the father died, we were thirty-six, eighteen sons and eighteen daughters. If I were to list each one and recount the personalities and fates of them all, European readers would hardly take interest. And yet, I cannot help but say a bit more about at least some of them, so as to highlight a series of characteristics and traits that illustrate the life, traditions, and customs of my homeland more clearly.

1. Sharife

Our father, who managed the government himself and personally oversaw everything, had little time for his younger children. He directed all the more loving attention to the adults. This raised considerable jealousy among the host of little ones, who, like the older brothers, had to stand before him as stiff as sentinels, while the older daughters were allowed to join him on the sofa. My childish jealousy found its target mostly in my sister Sharife, while for my brothers, it was Hilal.

Sharife, the daughter of a Circassian, was a blinding beauty with the complexion of a German blond. She also had a sharp mind, which made her a loyal advisor to the father. Whether in war or peace, he discussed everything with her, and, as I was later told, only rarely or almost never had cause to complain about her counsel. Certainly, proof again that Oriental women rate more than mere simpletons.

She had only one period of disagreement with the father. Following her heart, she married a cousin whose character the father deemed substandard for the husband of his favorite child. After that, she avoided the father's house until his disapproval finally subsided. She had chosen well and remained the exclusive wife of her husband. Her only child, Schnun, a most beautiful young boy that she loved passionately but raised very strictly, was my playmate. Every Friday, when he came with his mother, he would bring me a little something, especially when the monsoon (Arabic *mossem*) sent the ships from Muscat to us. Sharife had many connections there. She loved Muscat above all and lived out the end of her life there while accompanying the father on his last trip.

2. Chole

When I got to know Bet il Sahel, as I mentioned, Chole became my ideal. She was particularly close to the father, and her charming manner, effervescence, and grace totally won him over. Never again have I come across a woman that was as perfectly proportioned as Chole. She had excellent taste in how to dress, and everything looked good on her. Even when everyone showed up in their finest velvet from Lyon, she could wear a simple calico dress and stand out from all the rest, like a born ruler to her underlings. Her judgment in all aspects of fashion was considered as unerring as that of Empress Eugenie in her time for all of Europe.

Chole's mother, who was from Mesopotamia, had such excellent discretion and intelligence that the father gave her top oversight of the household in Bet il Sahel. Chole's own much older, proper sister Aashe always caused Chole much suffering, which she bore with touching fortitude. Whenever other sharp tongues sought to disparage Aashe to her, Chole always coolly brushed them off. Only I knew how deeply her sister's behavior pained her, for she divulged all her suffering to me, withholding no secrets from me, despite my young years. "Oh my God, Salme," she often exclaimed in tears, "what have I possibly done, how can I help it, that the father chooses to favor me? Do I not share everything I get from him with her? Am I to blame that the father constantly calls for my help?"

Sadly, many in the house showed her the same resentment. If people needed her to put in a good word with the father, they would flatter her. Then in no time, her loving support was forgotten. She assisted her mother in overseeing the household, and the father later transferred full responsibility to her. That was fodder for many new complaints. It was impossible to satisfy everyone

Personalities and Stories of My Siblings

in the overcrowded palace. If the extreme heat caused even one chicken, one piece of meat, one fish to spoil, if plantation fruits arrived late or were squashed, if goods procured for the residents did not meet their expectations, if Turkey had a bad rose harvest with insufficient rose water and rose oil for our huge consumption: Chole was to blame for it all. She was made responsible for everything.

What people resented even more was that the father took her into the treasury with him or even sent her there alone. Her enemies would have liked to search her at the exit every time, treating her just like the pearl divers in the Persian Gulf, to make absolutely sure she absconded with nothing for herself. So great was this spiteful jealousy and resentment. And then one day, these numerous adversaries were confronted with the appalling news that the father had given her a very pricey, opulent crown, ordered especially for her from Persia. This truly marvelous tiara consisted of many golden, diamond-laden palms, with one large palm in the center flanked on both sides by more palms that decreased in size all the way to the capstones at the ends. It was not suitable as actual headgear, but instead constituted a valuable asset for times of need. Considering how much every Oriental woman loves jewels, it is not hard to understand that such a magnificent gift only increased the number of Chole's enemies. Even the father was bitterly resented for this kind of preferential treatment, although he was clearly in no position to satisfy all the wishes of his large family.

And how did Chole handle this envy? That was her best quality: She always stayed equally gracious, equally accommodating toward everyone. She never had a single thought of revenge or retaliation. Her attitude was always: "If the father is satisfied with what I do, then that must suffice for me."

Chole cared faithfully for me as a child, and later became my dearest friend. When she moved from Bet il Sahel to Bet il Tani after the father died, our relationship grew especially close. We were always together. I ate at her place, or she at mine. We talked long into the night and sought our rest side by side. How much influence she won over me will become clear later. She kept her love for me all her life. In 1871, after the death of my husband, she commissioned a letter to me, as she was unable to write herself, saying I should send her one of my children for her to adopt. I was unable to take her up on it, as the child would have had to become Muslim.

Her generosity and gentleness became truly proverbial. Her subordinates were very well kept in her services. She forgave all their mistakes and always put in a good word for the slaves of others. I, for example, had a Nubian slave who had mastered the art of cooking while in a Persian household in Oman. As good as she was for my physical well-being, she soon became insufferable, since anything that came near her went missing. None of the many warnings and unmaskings made a difference, so I finally decided to sell this thief. When Zafrane, so the name of this fiend, found out, she ran in the dead of night to my Chole's plantation to plead for her benevolent help. As skilled as she was in garnering Chole's sympathy, I had no choice but to keep this dangerous person for the love of my sister.

After the father died, Chole (who received no more than the rest of us) used her inheritance to acquire one of our most beautiful plantations, which the father had frequented most often. Complete with a gorgeous palace and splendid furnishings, this cost her a hefty sum and brought little income. And yet, she paid no mind to such calculations in her devotion to the father, who had loved her like the apple of his eye. She gladly made the greatest sacrifices simply to own his favorite refuge. Every year, around the clove harvest, she would spend two to three months in Sebe, as the plantation was called. I have such unforgettable memories of those days, as I ambled with Chole, hand in hand, under the wonderfully fragrant trees in the garden, and as we conversed innocently and easily with the many slave children or sat in the deep window bank and watched people go about their day.

The sumptuously furnished room of the father was never used and only opened for distinguished guests upon special request.

Her hospitality was grandiose, and Sebe's beauty always drew many guests. The rarest of plants, otherwise unknown in Zanzibar, decorated the garden, and everything was carefully nurtured by the cherished caretaker, just like in the father's times.

A most charming stone building stood in front of the formidable wall that encircled the garden, in the shade of a marvelous tree, larger than the largest oaks we have here. It had only one room, with a marble floor, ceiling-high wall mirrors, masses of colorful lanterns, and scores of cane chairs. Whenever he spent time in Sebe, the father would drink the evening coffee here with his male associates. Now we could visit this beautiful and refreshing place undisturbed, to enjoy ourselves like children and remember our dear father.

The much beloved, much envied, and much despised Chole is no longer of this world. I had to lose her in the year 1875. She was said to be the victim of a treacherous poisoning, although the matter was never fully clarified. She remains close to me always!

3. Aashe

Seldom has nature been so capricious when endowing two proper sisters as in the case of Chole and Aashe. While Aashe had a small figure and dark skin, Chole was tall with light skin. Where Aashe was completely disfigured by smallpox, Chole was the perfect Oriental beauty. And while Aashe presented a formal, closed, yes, even cold manner, Chole was charming in her natural generosity and goodness, even if, on the other hand, Aashe did surpass her in intellect. The contrasts could not have been starker. Asian relatives coming for a visit could never believe that Aashe and Chole stood before them as two true sisters.

Poor Aashe was acutely aware how much her face bore the pockmarked scars of smallpox and therefore rarely appeared unmasked. She always stayed covered, even among her siblings and servants. Understandably, she cared little about her appearance. Relative to rank, she dressed very plainly and looked almost shabby next to other family members. A single Abyssinian slave, who was very adept at finery and hair care, served her simultaneously as hairdresser, milliner, and chamber maid.

By contrast, she was acknowledged far and wide as the top food connoisseur, and indeed, no one making the rounds would have encountered a cuisine as fine as what she offered. Others accordingly sought to place young people under her experienced kitchen staff to learn the many secrets of the proper art of cooking. Even my brother Madjid took up her services. Every day he had her staff prepare five to eight dishes, for which he paid a fixed monthly sum.

With her intelligence, she was often engaged to referee and always showed sound discretion with the right answer. This sharp mind especially did wonders for her finances. She conducted her business masterfully, a compliment that only few of us deserved. Her accounts were never in the red, not even prior to the harvest that was essential for replenishing our purses. Big spenders, on the other hand, were wont to call her stingy now and again. —

Her favorite brother was poor Hilal. She was unusually devoted to him and cared for his oldest son Suud in every possible, motherly way after his death.

4. Chadudj

Chadudj, Madjid's sister, is already familiar to the reader. Although preferred in our house to Aashe, she lived with Madjid, whom she loved above all else, and therefore had less contact with us.

In later years, she assumed the role of mother for our twice-orphaned, youngest brother Nasor. Weary of life after Madjid died, she headed with him to the final refuge of Muslims, to Mecca. There they were both, one after the other, soon called from this world.

5. Shewane

When I moved into Bet il Sahel, Shewane became my playmate. She was older than me, but closest in age of all my siblings. Gifted with a clever mind, strong build, and a look that would have subdued a lion, she was bound to play an important role in the house. She basically appointed me her errand boy. Every day I was made to feel her admonishing hand, and, as thanks for my service, I received at most a flattering: "You white monkey!" She was the daughter of an Abyssinian, a people known by us for both their heated temperament and intelligence. And I came from a "white" mother, which subjected me to various attacks by my darker siblings. But nothing like what my brother Djemshid had to endure, having inherited not only the hair, but also the blue eyes, from his blond mother.

Early on, not long after the father's death, Shewane also lost her mother and her only proper brother Ali, whose markedly different character had made him more popular than her. Half grown, she stood alone in a world that was so different from what she would have wished. She felt no warmth for any of the many brothers except perhaps Madjid, and then only out of her devotion to Ali, who had been his close friend.

Her truly majestic figure and the almost classical beauty of her face lent her a dignity that impressed everyone. Her main character trait was a well-developed sense of independence. She could never get herself to seek advice from anyone, and no one quite knew what she was about. Unable to write, she was taken advantage of by a cunning African slave, who thoroughly fleeced her. Despite her gruff approach, she was extraordinarily benevolent, and towards her subordinates, she was strict, but always fair.

She sought out the handsomest and choicest slaves and overloaded them with the most precious weapons and jewels. Everything around her radiated with the splendor and riches of fairy tales.

I was the only sister who managed to get along with her, more or less, despite all the rough treatment I had had to endure in my younger years. When I occasionally found an opportune moment to open up with her about how much others criticized her huge expenditures, specifically her extensive display of slaves, she would respond quite calmly that she was well aware that she did not have long to live and wanted to bestow some of her wealth on poor people during her lifetime, or use it up as quickly as possible herself, so there would be nothing left for us to inherit. She was rich, having taken on Ali's considerable fortune, in addition to her own share of the father's estate. But she still stayed on in the father's house, even into her later years, which was generally disfavored.

Shewane had no interest in the opinions of others. Even though she lived under the same roof with hundreds of people, she looked to no one and lived only for and among her many slaves. For this reason, we also did not learn of her grave illness until it was too late. Angered by Chole's and my alleged unkindness, she refused to receive any more visitors from that time on. No matter how much our hearts bled, we could not go against her will. She always got her way. And when she realized that her flourishing life was being undone by an unstoppable case of galloping consumption, she made all those around her promise high and holy that no one, other than the woman who washed her corpse, would ever see her dead body. Her command was strictly observed. As soon as Shewane passed away, her room was firmly locked. Only after the corpse had been washed, bestrewn with camphor, and wrapped in white linen seven times around, including her face, all as prescribed, only then were we allowed to go to her. Speechless, I knelt before her corpse and embraced her, not heeding the fearful individuals that warned me of contagion and sought to pull me away. In such moments, even if only briefly, our normally very controlling egoism relents.

Despite our considerable differences, I was devoted to Shewane with all my heart. I always defended her, and anyone who could see past her abrupt style and peculiarities was bound to love her. Her pride and ambition made her some enemies, especially among older people who chose not to tolerate them. And indeed, precisely this pride was one of her many riddles, considering that her soul was filled with a strong and deep faith.

Even on her deathbed, she still looked after her city slaves and the higher-ranked land slaves. She not only gave them freedom, but also gifted them all her costly weapons and jewels, in addition to an entire plantation for their livelihoods. All those who had taken such care of her should no longer need to earn their upkeep after her death.

6. Mettle

Mettle was, like Shewane, the daughter of an Abyssinian, but no one could tell because of her light complexion. During the time I lived in Bet il Mtoni, she and her brother Ralub were my playmates. Their mother was completely paralyzed from an illness and could do little to take care of her children. That, however, did them no damage, and they both became exemplary, upstanding people.

This poor suffering mother had to live on the ground floor that was otherwise used only for the major storerooms, a space that was hardly suited for an infirmary. Musty basement air filled the room in which my siblings grew up.

In front of this room, directly by the banks of the murmuring river Mtoni, a special resting place was set up, not quite a meter high and three to four meters square. Here the sick mother could sit or lie the whole day, while being attended to by her good children and slaves. Her stepchildren and their mothers enjoyed stopping by and checking in. My mother, in particular, sought to read to her from the Koran and other holy texts, since she was unable to read, like most other women that came to us as adults.

Mettle and Ralub were a rare pair of siblings, filled with the dearest childhood love for their mother and always seeking to make the poor woman happy. Mettle, who was a couple of years older than me, was especially good-natured. She always gave in to our wishes, the best playmate in the world. —

After the father's death, Mettle became my nearest neighbor in the countryside. We visited each other daily when we were on our plantations. Only merry Ralub loved to disrupt this peace by frequently surprising us together with his friends. That always created hapless confusion, since we were not supposed to be seen by strangers, but that was Ralub's whole point. —

Mettle lived the rest of the year in Bet il Mtoni, even after her mother's death, until she married a distant cousin in the city. Two sweet twin boys were her sole joy. I could stop by whenever I wanted, and she would always have a boy on the arm or both on her lap. No one was more unassuming or content in our house, and in this, she was the complete opposite of Shewane. But even that found the displeasure of some, who considered such modesty unbecoming of a princess. Then Mettle would declare firmly, she would always stay the same, whether interacting with a prince or a pauper; her nobility would remain undiminished in their eyes. "That I do not always run around in silks and velvet, that is my business. Does it make me any less worthy than my siblings? Am I not always still the daughter of my father?" I am ashamed to admit that I had absolutely no sense for this philosophy at the time. It was only later, after I had occasion to reflect on her wisdom, that I came to give it my full endorsement.

7. Zeyane

Zeyane and Zemzem are true sisters, the children of an Abyssinian mother. When we were still living in Bet il Mtoni, there was, as mentioned, a deep friendship between my mother and Zeyane. Zeyane in turn had a soft spot for me and spoiled me more than my mother considered beneficial. Our rooms were spaced far apart, so that I had to traverse two stairs and the whole courtyard to get to Zeyane and ZemZem. I accordingly always ended up staying there that much longer, often five to seven hours a day, which left my mother quite frustrated. Messenger after messenger would come to pick me up, all to no avail. At last my mother would come herself and then end up spending the afternoon or evening with the sisters as well.

I can thank Zeyane for introducing me to making lace. She had become very skilled in this. Either alone or together with my mother, she created the most beautiful designs, which no one was allowed to see until they were deemed a completed success.

Zeyane made friends everywhere through her benevolence. She never tired of caring for and consoling sick and helpless beings.

In Bet il Mtoni, the women could go out wherever they wanted during the daytime, as long as the father and his male retinue were not present. We often saw Zeyane head out in the company of one or two slaves bearing packages, on the way to this or that official's family, where she always left thankful hearts behind.

As the day of our move to Bet il Watoro neared, my mother and Zeyane shed many passionate tears. They were well aware that they would rarely see each other after this. Zeyane hated the city and could not often get herself to go there. My mother, on the other hand, would be too busy with her many duties to frequently visit Bet il Mtoni.

On the last day, I ran over to Zeyane very early while my mother was busy, so I could be with her as long as possible. She was overcome with tears, overloaded me with parting gifts, gave me boiled eggs the way I liked them, in short, tried to show me all her love. And she urged me to be well-behaved and devout and give my mother much joy.

It is impossible for me to describe this departure from her. It made that much more of an impression on my young sensibilities to go straight from Zeyane to our very rigid stepmother Azze bint Sef for last farewells with my mother.

8. ZemZem

Far more beautiful than Zeyane, ZemZem possessed all the good and noble qualities of her sister, who passed from us much too early. Only later when ZemZem and I became plantation neighbors did I get to know her better. She was by nature extraordinarily practical. Averse to any exaggerated displays of luxury, she preferred all that was pure and simple. Everything under her prospered to an extent rarely seen in an Arab household. On the whole, if I may put it this way, she came the closest to the German ideal of a *Hausfrau*.

She was very motherly to me, as I had been the favorite of her dearly beloved Zeyane. Whenever I did something wrong, which was unfortunately quite often, she would gaze at me for a long time, silently, with her big, soulful eyes. "Oh, what a pity," she would then say, "that your good mother had to leave you alone in this harsh world so soon. Yes, if Zeyane were still alive, she could have been your second mother, and you would have stayed a child much longer. Since that is of course what you still are, a child without a proper understanding." And she would soothingly finish with these words: "But do not be upset with me that I speak to you like this. I do it only for my love of Zeyane, who held you so dear. See, others do the same stupid things, but I would never think to reproach them for any of it."

She was especially helpful to me in agricultural matters. For hours, she would ride with me through the plantations and draw my attention to this or that good practice. Once she even turned to my *nakora* (a type of inspector): "Your mistress is simply still a child (*mtoto* in Swahili) and does not understand the first thing about these matters. That is why you need to make an even greater effort for her, and whatever you do not understand, you can always check with my *nakora*." That was hardly flattering for my conceited self-esteem, but since she meant so well, I could not be angry with her.

Not until relatively late did ZemZem end up marrying our distant cousin Humud. (We try to maintain the custom of marrying amongst ourselves to preserve the blue blood.) He was the one who, in the mosque, had dared ask Chalid for the hand of a different sister and had then been harshly rejected because of the affront. After Chalid's death, he tried his luck again with his chosen one directly, but without success. His aggrieved ambition had no desire to play the scorned suitor for long. He turned to ZemZem, and she accepted his overture. The wedding was celebrated without delay, plainly and absent any fanfare, since Humud was extraordinarily stingy despite being one of the richest people in Zanzibar. He did not even observe the basic standards of traditional Arab hospitality. And on top of that, he was fanatically orthodox and flaunted his strict piety for show, which most people saw as pure hypocrisy, since he was capable of the worst cruelty in response to the slightest cause. Naturally, no one loved him, and many despised him, even if everyone shied away from openly crossing this rich and influential man.

I seldom saw ZemZem after her marriage, but she seemed happy enough in her union with this much disliked man. Presumably, in her practical way, she also knew how to handle him well.

9. Nunu

I also want to share some details about a sister that nature treated very badly, who deserved our pity. Nunu was the daughter of a Circassian we called Tadj (meaning crown) because of her striking beauty. Tadj had been given special attention by the father, which caused much jealousy and resentment. When her child was born, with the same stunning beauty, but completely blind, many considered it just retribution for the mother's guilt in securing the father's favor. The poor mother suffered bitterly because of her child. Her grief was abated only by the firm belief that everything was as God willed it. But she also did not have to bear the sight of her blind child for long, as a case of dropsy soon snatched her away.

Poor, blind Nunu was then on her own. But here, too, it held true that God's help is closest when the need is greatest. An extremely dutiful Abyssinian slave made a sacred promise to the dying Tadj that she would diligently care for Nunu until the very end, never to desert her. She kept her promise in exemplary fashion and protected her little mistress from all the trials of life. She took instructions only from the father, who in his love naturally cared for the poor blind girl far more than all his other children. To be sure, this, too, generated all sorts of disparaging talk.

Nunu was the wildest, most misbehaved child I have ever seen. She was a horror for all mothers with small children. From the age of six to ten, she made a mission, as crazy as it sounds—of scratching out the eyes of all her younger siblings. As soon as she heard that a new brother or sister had been born, she would ask if it could see with healthy eyes. Eventually it was easier to lie, and then one could clearly see her joy in learning that others, too, would never see the sun and the moon. The most bitter envy filled her little heart.

Nunu had a better sense of her surroundings than one would ever expect of a blind person, and she moved around with great ease and speed. She ranged all over the place, and everywhere she went, she caused great mischief, like a dreadful little hurricane. Whatever she could get her hands on, porcelain, glass, especially our fine Asian water carafes, she shattered with great pleasure.

I must mention another one of Nunu's peculiarities. She wanted to be treated like someone with full eyesight. As soon as the cannon shot announced the sunset, she demanded that her room be lit. She wanted to choose the fabrics for her outfits and always stood in front of the mirror when her slaves dressed her. If she heard that one of us had nice hair, nice eyes, or nice eyebrows, then nothing was more urgent than to subject the relevant part of the head to an often very precarious examination, after which she would opine nonchalantly whether her expectations had been met or perhaps exceeded.

As time went by, to our general relief, Nunu became more reasonable and composed. She no longer needed to be constantly feared, but could instead be appreciated for her good sides and even come to be loved. The poor, unhappy being then also lost her loyal caretaker, after having lost both father and mother. Since she was in no position to live on her own and still needed some degree of guardianship, our sister Aashe took her in and kept a joint household.

10. Shembua and Farshu

Two of my nieces, Shembua and Farshu, who went to school with me, played with me, and later belonged to a political party with me, must also be mentioned. Back then, they lived across the street, and, since streets in Zanzibar tend to be narrow, we were able to have direct conversations from window to window, without having to resort to our well-developed sign language. We talked about personal care and household matters, and we even indulged to our hearts' content in—politics. Only with respect to the last topic did we take security measures by posting innocent-looking servants at the house corners, who could alert us to an approaching enemy by dropping a cane, coughing, or whistling softly. But of this exciting time, I will share more later.

Shembua and Farshu were my brother Chalid's only children. They had had such deep love for each other since childhood that they never wanted to be apart. This resulted in considerable conflict with their respective mothers, who bore deep-seated jealousies toward each other. Shembua, who was a good bit older than her sister, was by nature sweet and modest, while Farshu was the total opposite. Shembua was so very accommodating that she was practically a mother to the latter.

Personalities and Stories of My Siblings

Chalid, as one of the father's favorites, had received a sizeable fortune that his two only children inherited. In keeping with their deep attachment to each other, they resolved not to divide their inheritance, but hold it jointly throughout. This simply increased the jealousy of Farshu's mother, an Abyssinian, who ultimately demanded that her daughter give up this title in common. Farshu was by nature very stubborn and refused to comply, instead declaring firmly that as long as she and her sister remained unmarried, they would not divide their fortunes. With relations already on a razor's edge, this left her mother feeling deeply aggrieved, and without a word, she left the house and child forever, taking only a small pack and a few funds. At first no one knew where she had gone, but were consoled by the hope that she would return to Farshu once she calmed down. But this was never the offended's intention. Rather than see her daughter again, much less live off her mercy, she chose instead to earn her keep through needlework. I have already mentioned how a widow is almost entirely dependent on her children after the husband dies.

The unhappy mother kept totally out of sight, while her means lasted. Only when her last *pesa* was spent did she seek out my older sister Zuene, who had been close to Chalid, in Bet il Mtoni. There she remained under the condition that Zuene make no effort whatsoever to reunite her, as long as the daughter did not of her own free will acknowledge her injustice. Quite unbelievably, Farshu remained indifferent to this news and made no effort to reconcile with her mother, not even when her mother became sickly. It made no difference that she was widely rebuked, or that I repeatedly reminded her of her filial duty; Farshu stayed obstinate and unyielding. One would hardly have imagined such harshness in this delicate little being, and yet her gorgeous eyes betrayed the adamant resolve behind her decisions. Soon after my departure from Zanzibar, Farshu's life was snatched away by a bad case of consumption, and I never could find out whether she had reconciled with her mother before her death.

The most beautiful property owned by my nieces was the superbly magnificent plantation Marseille, a name that reflected Chalid's predilection for France and everything French. All the walls, except in the prayer rooms, were covered with mirrors that made for a glorious effect in the shimmering light. The floors in the chambers had inlaid black and white marble tiles, whose coolness in the South cannot be overstated. With an ornate clock, whose strokes upon the hour revealed figurines that danced and played musical instruments; round powder room mirrors that variously distorted their reflected images; large, round quicksilver spheres, like the ones we see on occasion in gardens here; and other works of art, Marseille Palace felt like a veritable museum, especially for simple folk that were little acquainted with civilization, meaning primarily our relatives from Oman. How often did I hear these words of wonder: "By God, these Christians are real devils!" Marseille and life there were ideally suited for conveying a true sense of the Orient to unfamiliar outsiders.

What wonderful days I spent there. With my nieces' love of emancipation and their well-known tolerant attitudes, this was a place where we could freely circulate, and the house was always full of guests. There was no end to the comings and goings. Non-stop we could hear forerunners and foreriders yelling *sumila! sumila!* (make room! make room! in Swahili) and slaves announcing new arrivals. Only cheerful guests, seemingly without a care, were to be found here. Those who thought to stay for three days were often rallied by the kind hostesses into staying a fortnight, which the fathers and husbands simply had to accept.

Each day was spent relishing the utmost informality. Everyone could do whatever they pleased without being considered impolite. That is true hospitality, when it poses no constraints, but offers full freedom. Only towards evening, as the sun went down, did the guests come together to spend time in the large rooms illuminated by countless shining candles and lanterns or in the park under the dazzling moonlight until one or two in the morning. When there was no moonlight, tall piles of wood, soaked in palm oil, were fired up at various locations, where we could avidly converse late into the night.

This place of radiance and joy was later destroyed. My brothers Barghash and Abd il Aziz entrenched themselves in the palace, despite our outrage, during our plot against Madjid. This is where the decisive battle took place. The entire property was ruined, and my nieces took a great loss. Even so, they had enough other wealth to absorb this downturn and resisted any further discussion; it was not worth the talk! —

11. Hilal

Of my brothers, I want to highlight two of them, Hilal and Tueni, both unhappy, one through his own fault, the other a victim of his own son.

Our religion is known to forbid Muslims the pleasure of all alcoholic drink, and our sect, which also forbids smoking, is much stricter on these points than, say, the Turks or Persians. Now, at one point, an ugly rumor spread in our family that our brother Hilal (meaning new moon) had been seduced by Christians, especially the French Consul at the time, to give in to drinking. He suddenly began to experience inexplicable fainting spells and soon the smell of wine became evident. The poor man could no longer rid himself of this evil spirit that had taken hold. Hilal was one of our father's favorite sons, and this caused the father bitter grief. To correct this wayward soul, he initially put Hilal under house arrest, but soon had to banish him entirely from the family.

Our sister Chadudj was especially close to Hilal and had the most to suffer for him. He continued to visit her often in the father's house, even after being banished. With much difficulty and at great risk, he would enter secretly and spend the night with her and his other loyal friends in a dark room, so that no light would betray his presence. No one ever had the heart to let the father know about these touching visits. Because the father kept him on very limited terms to make sure he had nothing left to spend on alcohol, Chadudj always gave him generous support, though hardly in his best interest.

Hilal succumbed increasingly to the effects of this harmful passion. He had fewer and fewer sober moments and soon death put an end to his sad state. Despite all that had happened, our father felt an unspeakable grief for his beloved son. He often locked himself away in his prayer room, and traces of his tears could later be found where he had knelt in prayer to his Lord. Indeed, he even expressed his pain in words, something he otherwise never did, and repeated over and over: "Oh my misfortune, oh my despair for you, Hilal!" —

Hilal left behind three sons, Suud, Fesal, and Muhammed. The youngest, Muhammed, was adopted by my otherwise childless stepmother, Azze bint Sef. I do not know what gave her the idea; perhaps she did it out of love for our father. Muhammed really knew how to win Bibi Azze over completely, a feat the rest of us never managed. Up to that point, she was known to be very exacting and frugal. No one could believe their eyes when Muhammed began to allow himself the greatest profligacy, naturally with her money. Although none of us had ever thought of owning dogs, Muhammed went ahead and ordered a whole pack from Europe, including some superb specimens we had never seen before. His entire life was consumed by the upkeep of these dogs, which of course were never tolerated in the house, along with several especially beautiful horses. These dear creatures naturally could not be expected to live off leftovers. A whole special cuisine, with no shortage of variety, was arranged for them. The plumpest chickens, the best cuts of meat, the biggest fish all wandered into the huge pots. Rumor had it that these dogs, as well as the horses, did not just drink cheap water, but rather—champagne. I do not know if that is true, but either way, Muhammed stirred up much negative talk borne of envy and resentment, after drawing many enemies through his extravagance and having but few friends.

Suud also projected in every way that he appreciated the lifestyle, customs, and practices of Europeans. He was the most like his father.

Hilal's third son, by contrast, was completely different. While Muhammed and Suud tended to luxury and the high life, sweet Fesal presented himself so modestly that one would have assumed him to be a normal citizen instead of a prince. He had a contemplative nature that was not drawn to material pleasures, and thus remained a mystery to his brothers. Later he bought a small plantation in my neighborhood and came to visit me often. He seldom went into the city without bringing me a little something, even if it was just a few packs of fireworks, of which I was especially fond.

Misunderstood by his brothers, the poor thing was deeply unhappy. He had a gentle, noble character, the sort that is so easily overlooked in this world. But those who got to know him were soon charmed by his friendly manner and kindness. Having lost his mother quite early, he had hardly ever known love. "That is why I am doubly depressed," he would confide in me, his much younger aunt, "even my brothers consider me totally superfluous and want nothing to do with me. I really do not care if I live or die; I am dispensable to everyone." How my heart bled to hear this good man, who deserved so much love, talk this way. Would such a tired soul, who has nothing left for this world, not find his best chance for peace in a cloister?

After I gave in to my brother Madjid's request to return to the city, no one was more deeply hurt than my poor Fesal. Over time he had gotten so used to sharing all his thoughts and concerns with me, as if I were truly such a sensible aunt, instead of what I actually still was at the time: a very wild and naïve young girl.

12. Tueni

Our oldest brother Tueni was born in Muscat and spent his whole life in Oman. He never visited Zanzibar, and his prejudice against the birthplace of most of his siblings was unshakable. Muslims are not allowed to have their portraits painted, and a deeply ingrained superstition reinforces this rule even more than others. There was also no photography back then. So Tueni remained, for those of us who had never been to Muscat, a completely unfamiliar personality. We only heard of his kindness to others, as well as his courage and determination in battle. His soldiers practically idolized him, and his mere presence instilled great confidence in them. Even as a youngster, he loved war, like our father, and he was the most competent soldier of all my brothers. He apparently spent most of his time out in the camps, thus causing much heartbreak for his wife

Ralie, who was our proper cousin of equal rank and gave him several children.

For all the time our father stayed in Zanzibar, Tueni was his representative in charge. But Tueni usually left the responsibility for domestic matters, meaning the actual governance, to our second oldest brother, the devout Muhammed, who, as mentioned, was filled with a similar dislike of Zanzibar. Tueni had enough to do with the external defense of the kingdom. There were Persians at Bandar Abbas to be fought, and incursions of nomadic tribes from inner Arabia to be defended against. These numerous tribes are all very poor, and many survive only on their pillage. Few desert Arabs own anything more than a camel, some indispensable weapons (gun, sword, dagger, lance, and shield), one or two iron cooking pots, a sack of dates, and, if fortunate, a milk-bearing goat. All the men, big and small, carry their guns into battle, while the wives and daughters follow on foot from afar, ready to restore their men after combat with cooling water, milk, and food. Every year these bands, sometimes stronger, sometimes weaker, would invade Oman and keep the country in eternal unrest. Only a determined and energized ruler could maintain his ground there.

That was the state of affairs when our father died on his return to Zanzibar. If death had reached him while still in Muscat, Tueni would have been in a position to secure his reign over Zanzibar, instead of having Madjid, as the fourth-oldest of our brothers, leverage the circumstances to proclaim himself Sultan of Zanzibar. I have already mentioned how Madjid agreed to make fixed annual payments to Tueni, but soon thereafter pulled back on this commitment. Madjid was widely rebuked for this, especially as Tueni's situation deteriorated from day to day.

The ongoing military runs devoured huge sums, and the missing payments from Zanzibar hit at exactly the worst time. Tueni had to get funding at any cost and found himself forced to levy taxes on various items. Fortunately, no one in Oman thought of taking on debt, which has been the current ruin of other Oriental states. But even these limited charges awakened the specter of discontent. Sadly, those who were displeased succeeded in gaining influence over Tueni's oldest son, Salum, pulling him tightly into their web, until he brought upon himself the darkest sin a man can commit.

One day Tueni returned from a meeting and threw himself exhausted onto the divan to get some rest. Suddenly, his son came forward and demanded the reversal of this tax decree so categorically that his father had to emphatically rebuke him. Salum flew into an extreme rage, pulled out a hidden revolver, and shot down his own unsuspecting father!

This bedazzled youngster did not enjoy the fruits of his bloody act for long. He, too, soon faced retaliation. He had barely installed himself as the ruler of Oman when his brother-in-law Azzan decided to dethrone him. Completely unexpected, Azzan struck the capital Muscat in the dead of night, filling it with plunder and carnage. The tremendous bitterness people felt towards the evil Salum greatly facilitated Azzan's endeavor. No right-thinking person would reach for his weapons to defend a father murderer. There was little resistance to the invading wild hordes, who dragged off anything that was portable and destroyed all the rest. Especially Salum's palace was heavily damaged. Under the most perilous conditions, he managed to flee with his family on one of his war ships, saving but his bare life.

Even his unhappy mother Ralie, along with her other children, barely managed to escape on a ship. She lost everything. And yet, a young Indian merchant, named Abd il Rab (meaning servant of the Lord), later succeeded in purchasing most of her valuable jewels from a Bedouin at a bargain price (said to be three hundred Maria Theresa thalers), and the good soul returned this lost property to the trial-tested princess simply as a gift! —

The invader Azzan was soon chased away by my third-oldest brother Turki, who then suffered the same fate by my younger brother Abd il Aziz (likewise servant of the Lord). This one, a foster child of Chole, had distinguished himself as intelligent, courageous, and energetic. Already at the age of twelve, he had joined us in the plot and battle against Madjid, thereafter spending time in Baluchistan, where we recruit our soldiers. Abd il Aziz succeeded in finally giving Oman a brief period of calm. But even he was unable to maintain his reign for long. Turki returned and empowered himself anew as the ruler, at which point Abd il Aziz sought refuge for a second time in Mekran in Baluchistan, where he remains to this day. —

Surely a sad spectacle, these family feuds, that can be understood only by those familiar with the inbred lust for power of Oriental princes and the passionate nature of Orientals generally. Even I was not to stay unaffected by such sad circumstances. Yes, I, too, had to find my way through it!

CHAPTER SIXTEEN

Status of Women in the Orient

Before I continue with the story of my personal experiences, I would like to bring in a few more chapters that address various aspects of Oriental life. It is not my intent to provide a comprehensive account of all the customs and practices. I do not wish to write an academic tome, but only try to give European readers a more accurate understanding of the more important attitudes and customs of the Orient. Some details will be less interesting, but I prefer not to leave them out, as they may be of interest to at least a few.

I will step right into the most important of all these questions: the status of women in the Orient. This is a rather difficult topic for me. As a native Oriental woman, I am certain I will be considered biased and therefore fail in thoroughly dispelling the distorted and incorrect views that prevail in Europe about the position of an Arab woman in relation to her husband. Despite easier connections, the Orient is still far too much of the old fantasy land, about which one can say just about anything with impunity. A tourist heads off for a few weeks to Constantinople, or Syria, Egypt, Tunisia, or Morocco, and then writes a ponderous book about the life, customs, and practices in the Orient. And yet he has never had a closer look inside real family life. So he contents himself with stories that are passed from mouth to mouth and become increasingly distorted, perhaps from a French or German waiter in his hotel, or that he hears from sailors or donkey drivers, which he records and then uses to pass judgment! There is not much to be learned this way. He simply lets his imagination run wild and then supplements at will. If his book then happens to be amusing and artfully written, it will certainly garner many more readers than the less spicy, more reality-based accounts, and accordingly shape the views of the broader public.

I, too, judged things in Europe for a long time only by their superficial sheen. When I first saw the beaming faces in society here, I naturally came to believe that the interaction between men and women in Europe was much more properly structured, and that marriages would therefore be much happier than in the Islamic Orient. Later, however, as my children got older and no longer required my constant oversight and care, my increasing engagement with the world led me to understand more and more that I had incorrectly assessed people and social relations and allowed myself to be dazzled by outer appearances. I have observed relationships that were called marriages, but whose sole purpose seemed to be for mutually shackled pairs to already enact the torments of hell in this world. I have seen too many unhappy marriages to believe that Christian marriages are really all that superior to Islamic ones, that its participants are so much happier. In my opinion, neither religion, nor current customs and attitudes determine *ab initio* whether marriages will be happier or unhappier. What matters everywhere is whether the married couple has a genuine understanding toward each other. It is on this basis that happiness and peace can arise, from which an inner harmony can ensue, to ultimately make the marriage into a true marriage.

Having learned from this experience, I will make an extra effort to avoid passing judgment, and instead seek to use the following pages simply to report on the position of women in the Orient, specifically in marriage. I only know the precise conditions in Zanzibar, and those in Oman about as well. Nonetheless, Muslim views are still the most authentic in Arabia and among Arabs, and these perspectives form the basis of other Oriental cultures. My descriptions may thus be considered relevant for the rest of the Islamic Orient, except of course for some deviations and off-shoots that have arisen most notably because of their close association with the Christian Occident.

It is definitely wrong to think that Oriental women have less social status than men. A woman of commensurate birth is equal to her male counterparts in all respects. She maintains her rank and the full scope of all emanating rights and entitlements. Only the position of *sarari* is a subordinated one.

What causes an Arab woman to appear more helpless and somewhat less entitled is simply the fact that she lives a withdrawn life. This is the custom for all Muslim (and also many non-Muslim) peoples of the Orient, and the higher a woman's social rank, the more stringently she must abide by these restrictions. She may be seen by only her father, son, uncle, nephew, and all her slaves. If she needs to appear before an unfamiliar man, or even speak with him, then the religion requires that she cover her head and body, especially part of her face, her chin and neck, and her ankles. As long as she obeys this rule, she is entirely free to move around during the day and can walk unrestricted on the streets.

However, since such coverings are so unpleasant and disfiguring, high-ranking women avoid going out by day and frequently enough envy the Bedouin women who forsake these requirements. If such a Bedouin woman is asked whether she is embarrassed to go out without the required coverings, she will respond: "Such rules are only for the rich, they were not created for poor women!"

Today I am quite willing to admit that these Oriental practices are excessive, but I am not yet ready to pronounce European customs superior. When a stately woman is seen here in her ball gown, one would be justified in deeming her paucity of clothing to be an even greater exaggeration.

Under certain circumstances, the seclusion of women can become quite burdensome, and this custom really does go too far. However, Oriental women need not be pitied as much as we love to do here.

The law allows a Muslim man to possess four lawful, official wives at a time, and if one dies or divorces, he can bring home a fifth. *Sarari*, or secondary wives, can be bought and sold again as often as the man wants and as much as he can afford. I have, however, never seen anyone that really had four primary wives side-by-side. A poor man can of course take only one. A rich man tends to set limits as well, possessing at most two and putting them in separate living quarters, where each can keep her own household.

Needless to say, there are also Oriental women who know to look after their independence. These women first check if a suitor already has another wife and then secure a formal promise in the marriage contract stipulating that he neither take on another wife, nor purchase a *surie*.

In practice then, monogamy mostly rules. However, in those cases where men take full advantage of what the law allows, unedifying dissension will readily arise among the wives. The practice naturally leads to all sorts of resentment and envy, which the hot temperament of Southerners can turn into raving jealousies.

Jealousy can make polygamy into the greatest torment, and that is a good thing. Many a rich and high-ranking man is put off by the thought of dealing with these daily dramas and therefore sticks with monogamy. And that then significantly limits this vile custom. The fact that there is really no justification or excuse whatsoever for polygamy must be evident to anyone who is right-thinking, and especially to every woman. But now a counterquestion: What is the situation with Christians, with civilized Europeans, on the subject of marriage? I will not even dwell on the fact that the Mormon sect, as self-described Christians, openly practices polygamy in a Christian state. But does civilized European society really consistently treat marriage as being so sacred? Is it not often pure illusion to speak of "one" wife? To be sure, a Christian is allowed to marry only one woman, and that is a major advantage of Christianity. On this subject, Christian precepts seek what is good and right, while Islam permits what is bad. But current practices and practical realities in the Orient significantly dampen the negative effects of the law—while here, despite the law, sin rather frequently gets the upper hand. I am tempted to say that the only difference between an Oriental wife and a European wife appears to be that the first has knowledge of the number, as well as the nature and character, of her rivals, while the other is kept in loving ignorance. —

Naturally, only a rich man can afford *sarari*. Born as slaves, *sarari* are considered free after they bear children. Only in the rarest of cases would a master resell his *surie* if a child dies, and then only if he is very mean-spirited, as a matter of necessity or ennui. If the man dies, then his remaining *sarari* are usually perfectly free; no master lords over them anymore. If one then marries a brother or other relative of the deceased master and liberator, she becomes a legitimate wife as a free person. —

It is a myth that Arab husbands treat their wives worse than here. Religion is a major factor in that it encourages male protection, as though for a helpless child. A faithful, god-fearing Muslim man is as humane as any refined and well-mannered European man. The former is perhaps even stricter with himself, always mindful of the ubiquity of the Lord, as the author of those commandments, and believing firmly until his dying breath in the just accounting for his good and bad deeds.

Of course, alongside its noble characters, Zanzibar also has its share of tyrants, just as we do here, who demonstrate neither the appropriate kindness nor respect that is due their better halves. And yet, I can in good conscience state that I have heard more here about gentle husbands beating their wives than in my homeland. It is different, though, with the Africans. On my plantations, I have often enough had to throw myself between a contentious couple to make peace.

A wife is, moreover, in no way subject to her husband's every whim. If she ever encounters behavior by her husband that she is unwilling to accept, she can always get protection from her relatives, or she has the right to take her complaint personally to the *kadi* if she has no one else to turn to. Often she helps herself.

One of my very dear lady friends was sixteen when she married her significantly older cousin, who was far from worthy of her. Ever the playboy, and believing she would put up with anything, he was rather surprised when he returned

Status of Women in the Orient

home one evening and found a harshly worded message instead of his wife. I had always visited this friend on her plantation unannounced because I knew this dear husband preferred to spend his time gallivanting around the city. One day, however, she came to inform me that I could no longer come without notice because her husband was now staying at home. Full of remorse, he had pursued her and fervently begged her forgiveness. Once he realized how resolute his little wife was, he made sure to never hurt her again. I could share many more such examples of independent Oriental wives.

Spouses greet by kissing each other's hands. They share meals with their children. The wife shows the husband a range of loving gestures, like handing him his weapons when he leaves the house and taking them from him when he returns, or offering him water to drink. In short, she attends to all the little details that make a life together warmer and dearer. These are purely voluntary acts, and she is in no way bound to perform them.

The whole household is the exclusive domain of the wife. She is the undisputed head of this terrain. There is no such thing as a household allowance by which the husband takes care of his wife, but rather both operate out of a single account, except when a man splits his income in two for two wives of equal rank, with separate homes and households.

Naturally, how far the wife's domain extends depends on the couple. Here is an example: I had invited a large group of ladies to one of my plantations. However, since my invitation had gone out rather late, potentially too late for some of them to get their transport animals from the countryside in time, I feared a number of invitees would decline. One of my female friends immediately offered up a whole host of Omani donkeys, complete with all their gear and even the necessary guides. When I suggested that she first speak with her husband to get his approval for such a generous offer, she promptly replied, not to worry, she was not in the habit of getting her husband's permission for such a trifle.

Another female acquaintance of mine in Zanzibar carried much broader responsibility for all the business and investment dealings. She alone managed her husband's large estates, along with his city houses. He was not even aware of how much income he had and seemed perfectly content to get whatever money he needed from her hands. Due to her care and competence, he in fact did quite well.

The job of raising children belongs entirely to the mother, whether as a wife of equal rank or a purchased slave. In this, she recognizes her greatest good fortune. Whereas in England, it is customary, and considered quite sufficient, for the mother to throw a quick glance into the nursery once every twenty-four hours, and in France, the mother sends her children to the countryside under the care of complete strangers, an Arab mother, by contrast, is highly attentive to her children, protecting and nurturing them with the greatest diligence, and hardly ever leaving them alone, for as long as they need motherly care. In return for her devotion, she earns the sincerest piety and deepest love. This relationship with her children more than compensates for the disadvantages of polygamy and makes her family life happy and contented.

It takes having seen the joy and outright exuberance of wives in the Orient to fully appreciate how little truth there is in all the tales of their oppressed, downtrodden status and thoughtless, degrading aimlessness. But visits that are arranged for only a few short moments cannot provide deeper insight into the essence of these conditions. And even when translations about this or that are more or less correct, they hardly amount to a real conversation, not one that goes beyond rudimentary exchanges.

As polite as they are, Arabs dislike having strangers delve into their personal affairs, especially when those strangers belong to different nations or religions. Whenever a European woman came to visit us, she would initially be subjected to intense staring at the colossal circumference of her fashionable crinoline, which would typically fill the breadth of the staircase. The very spare conversation on both sides would rarely go beyond the mysteries of our respective outfits. After being hosted in the usual fashion, perfumed with rose oil by the eunuchs, and then sent off with parting gifts, she would have left none the wiser than when she came. She would have entered the harem, seen the to-be-pitied Oriental women (to be sure, only behind masks), marveled at our outfits, our jewelry, and our flexibility at sitting on the floor, but that is all. She could never boast of seeing anything more than any other European women before her. Eunuchs would escort her up, serve her, and lead her back out, under constant surveillance. Rarely would she be shown anything other than the room in which she was received. Indeed, often she would not even be able to decipher the identity of the masked lady to whom she had spoken. In short, she would have had no opportunity whatsoever to get a good look at Oriental family life and the role of the women. —

One more point is important for a proper understanding of Oriental marriage. When a young woman weds, there is no change to her name or rank. The wife of a royal prince that comes from a common family would never consider herself equal to her husband. Despite the marriage, she remains the "daughter (*bint*) of N.N."[16] and is addressed this way. This also goes for the reverse in the frequent case when a prince or ruler allows his daughter or sister to marry one of his own slaves. He says to himself: My servant also remains her servant, and she therefore continues to be his superior. Although the husband loses his formal slave status upon marriage, he will naturally always refer to his wife as "Highness" or "Lady."

When a man refers to his wife in conversation with another man, something he generally prefers to avoid, he never says "my wife," but rather refers to her as the "daughter of N.N." Or at most he uses the expression *um ijali*, meaning "mother of my family," whether she has children or not. —

It is understandable that couples, who would not have known each other beforehand, often have trouble getting along. Difficult, distressing relations can arise, as happened between my father and Shesade and between Madjid and Aashe. For such cases, Islamic law has the undeniable advantage that divorce is made incredibly easy. It is clearly better that two married individuals with starkly opposing world views and character traits are able to separate in peace, rather than be forever bound in mutual torment, which so often leads to the most horrible crimes. At the separation, the wife gets back her complete assets, over which she also had free disposition during the marriage. If the husband requests the divorce, the wife also retains the gifts he gave her at the wedding, but if she seeks to divorce, she must return them.

I believe all these examples suffice to show that Oriental women are not quite as subjugated and repressed, or stripped of their rights, as is assumed here. How much power and influence some of them are able to wield is amply apparent from the characteristics of my stepmother, Azze bint Sef. She totally ruled over our father. Indeed, matters of court and state often turned on her highly variable moods. Although divided in most things, all of us stepchildren were united in seeking to weaken her influence, but no matter what we tried, it almost always failed. Should one of us want something from the father, it would regularly be deferred up the chain for Bibi Azze's prior endorsement, as there was no matter over which she could not lay some claim before the father could proceed. She knew how to maintain her power across the board until the day he died.

Another example: The daughter of a commanding officer of one of the fortresses in Oman came to Zanzibar with her husband. They were of average means and, as the wife herself told me, "fortunately" without children. By nature, she was

---
16 From the Latin *nomen nescio*, an unnamed person, used here as a generic reference.

sharp and witty (a trait that succeeds nowhere better than there), but truly unattractive. Nevertheless, her husband was completely devoted to her and bore her many moods with the patience of an angel. Whenever she wanted to go out, he had to escort her back and forth, like a slave, whether he wanted fresh air or not. He never had control of his own time, and from the moment he finished his morning prayers, his day was hers, whether his lady chose to stay with him or leave him alone the whole day. He was her complete slave.

I want to recognize one more member of our family, someone who especially belies the inferiority myths of Oriental women. My great aunt, the sister of my grandfather, is still today considered the model of a clever, courageous, and energetic woman. When the story of her life and deeds is told and retold, young and old listen with rapt attention.

When my grandfather Sultan Imam of Muscat in Oman died, he left behind three children, my father Said, my uncle Salum, and my aunt Aashe. As my father was only nine years old, this required the establishment of a regency. Against all custom, my great aunt declared categorically that she would run the government herself until her nephew came of age, and she forbade any opposition. The ministers, who had not anticipated such a decision, but had instead secretly looked forward to years of their own rule, had no choice but to obey. Every day, the new regent called on them to report and receive her orders and instructions. She watched over and kept up with everything. Nothing escaped her sharp gaze, to the anger of any who were disloyal and lazy.

For herself, she simply stripped the shackles of proper etiquette. When appearing in front of her ministers, she covered herself only in her *shele*, the outfit a lady wore to go out. Whether the world wished to carp about her approach made no difference, as she followed her own undeterred path with skill and verve.

Soon enough, she was put to the most serious test. She had barely taken up the reins of government when, as unfortunately happens often in Oman, a very treacherous war erupted. Our nearest tribal neighbors believed they could easily overthrow the female regency, and with it our house, to claim the reign for themselves. Burning and killing their way through the land with their hordes, they finally arrived at the gates of the capital city Muscat. Many thousands of people from the countryside had fled here from their ruined provinces, abandoning their land and belongings, to seek refuge and aid. Muscat is well-protected and can withstand a siege. But what good are the most fortified walls when supplies and munitions run out?

In this challenging time, my great aunt proved herself beyond measure and even won over the admiring respect of her enemies. At night, she always rode solo in male attire along the front lines. She managed her soldiers in the most dangerous locations, sometimes eluding an unexpected attack with only the speed of her steed. One evening she set out especially worried. She had learned that the enemy was going to try to bribe its way into the fortress under the cover of night for a total massacre. She therefore decided to test the loyalty of her troops. With utmost care, she rode up in disguise to one of the sentries, demanded to speak to the *akid* (a senior officer) and presented, in the name of the attackers, the most enticing offers. The outburst of anger that erupted from this dutiful sentry alleviated any concern about her soldiers' sentiments, even as it put her life at great risk. They immediately wanted to knock down this apparent spy, and she had to draw on her utmost skill to avoid being killed by her own people.

Muscat's situation became increasingly dire. Starvation was widespread, and hearts were filled with hopelessness. There was no chance for help from the outside. It was decided to try one last, desperate push, even if it meant going down with honor. They had just enough powder reserves for one more fight, but the deadly lead needed for guns and cannons was completely spent. The regent called on everyone to collect every last nail for the guns, and even to search for the right-sized pebbles to use instead of bullets. Whatever iron or brass they could find was smashed and loaded into the cannons. Her Highness even opened the doors of her treasury and had bullets poured from her Maria Theresa thalers. Everything was offered up, and lo and behold, this desperate effort paid off. The enemy was fortunately caught by surprise and scattered in every direction. More than half of their troops were left behind, dead or wounded. Muscat was saved. Freed from her heavy load, this courageous woman dropped to her knees and thanked the Almighty in ardent prayer for his merciful help.

After that, she reigned in peace and was then able to transfer the kingdom to her nephew, my father, in such good shape that he could focus on other, more distant goals, above all to conquer Zanzibar. That the acquisition of this second empire was even possible is in part thanks to her, my great aunt.

That, too, was an Oriental woman!

Froemel

Memoiren
einer
arabischen Prinzessin.

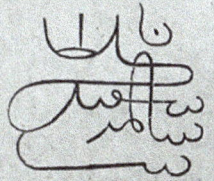

— Zweiter Band. —

Dritte Auflage.

Berlin.
Verlag von Friedrich Luckhardt.
1886.

Memoirs of an Arabian Princess
Volume 2

On the preceding pages, the end paper and title page are from an original edition of Volume 2 that belonged to either Rosa Troemer, the author's youngest daughter and the translator's great-grandmother, or a member of Rosa's family. The bookplate on the previous page is from Rudolph Said-Ruete, the author's son and Rosa's brother.

All footnotes in the following pages were added by the translator.

View of Stone Town by Heinrich Ruete

CHAPTER SEVENTEEN

Arab Matrimony

In general, in Arabia, the father or head of the family arranges the children's marriages. There is nothing unusual about that, and it also happens in Europe, where young men and young girls have the greatest freedom to interact. We have all heard about the irresponsible fathers here, who have plunged themselves so deep into debt that they have no way out but to hand over their pretty or genteel daughters to their creditors as sacrificial lambs; or how fun-loving mothers push their children into unhappy marriages simply because they would rather be rid of them at any price.

No less tyrannical parents can be found among Arabs as well, those who disregard the happiness of their marrying children and tune out any pangs of conscience. But it is not generally an abuse of power when parents there make choices for their children. The isolation of women makes this support necessary. No one disputes that, despite all the customs and laws, there may still be encounters with men from time to time that can lead to more interaction. But as a general rule, a young girl will neither see her prospective husband, except perhaps through a window, nor speak to him until the wedding night. And yet, he does not stay a complete stranger. His mother, sisters, and aunts practically compete to describe him as aptly as possible and fill her in on anything that could possibly be of interest.

Often the two already know each other from their childhood. Until their ninth year, girls can interact with boys of the same age and get to know them this way. And so it may happen that the former playmate later remembers his female friend and asks the father for her hand, having of course first sought her opinion through her mother or sister.

With virtually all candidates, the cautious father leads with the following question: "But where did you actually see my daughter?" "Oh," comes the response, "I have never yet had the privilege of seeing your honored (*mahshume*) daughter. But I have heard my family speak all the more of her virtues and charms."

Only when the candidate for marriage completely fails to meet the father's requirements does the suitor get an immediate rejection. As a rule, however, the father gives himself ample time to consider the matter and observe his daughter and her mother. Eventually, he mentions with studied indifference that he is thinking of inviting some men over in the next days, and when his wife or daughter ask whom he plans to invite, he proceeds to casually list out his friends. If he perceives a certain joy upon mentioning the name of the applicant, he can rest assured that there is full consensus between his family and theirs. Only then does he reveal to his daughter that N.N. has asked for her hand and solicits her opinion. Her yes or no is almost always dispositive. Only a despotic and callous father decides unilaterally, without first ascertaining his daughter's approval or disapproval.

In these questions, too, however, our father maintained his sense of justice and laid the fate of his children in their own hands. My older sister Zuene had just turned twelve when a distant cousin, Suud, came to him for her. The father was upset at receiving this request while she was still so young, but also could not bring himself to dismiss the bid out of hand without first having informed his daughter of it. Zuene had lost her mother, for whom there was really no adequate substitute at this crucial age. Still half a child, and lacking good advice, she found the thought of becoming a married woman so amusing that she insisted that Suud not be turned away, and the father let her prevail.

It is quite common for us that children in their earliest youth are already promised, and yes, even married. Two brothers, for instance, had made a solemn promise to have their children marry each other. As it turned out, each had only one child, one a boy and one a girl. As soon as the boy turned sixteen or seventeen, while the girl was still seven or eight, talk turned to the forthcoming wedding. The mother of the boy was my plantation neighbor. A very smart and prudent woman, she often complained to me about the harsh insistence by her husband and brother-in-law that she take in a young child that she would first have to care for and raise, instead of receiving a daughter-in-law. The mother of the young girl was no less dismayed that anyone would even think to tear her child away so soon. The combined efforts of the two mothers succeeded only in having the wedding postponed by all of two years. I left Zanzibar not long after and therefore cannot report what became of this relationship. —

The formal engagement is ceremoniously announced to all friends and acquaintances. Beautifully dressed female slaves, often as many as twenty, go from house to house bearing the announcement and invitation to the wedding celebration, for which they reap ample gifts.

At this point, the house of the bride's parents becomes unusually lively, with the wedding often taking place just a month later. Regardless, the engagement period never lasts long, and there is also little to prepare in the blessed South. People in the Orient would never dream of the many indispensable necessities that Northerners must have, and an Arab bride would be rendered speechless at the sight of a European trousseau. Why do people here love to burden themselves with so much ballast?

An Arab bride, by comparison, is sent off with relatively little. Depending on rank and wealth, her trousseau consists of precious clothes, jewelry, slaves, houses, plantations, and cash. She receives gifts not only from her own parents, but also from the parents of the groom and the groom himself. All of this becomes her own personal property. When her parents' estate is divided after they have died, this trousseau is never netted from her share.

Considerable effort goes into preparing the bride's clothing. An elegant lady must change her outfit two or three times a day in the week after the wedding. A specific bridal costume, like the white dress and white veil here, is not customary in the Orient. The only requirement is that the bride wear brand new things, from head to toe, while color choices are entirely up to her. Some may even dazzle with all the colors of the rainbow, and yet their attire is anything but tasteless and ugly.

In addition, special perfumes are prepared, as they play a major role in wedding celebrations. That includes *riha*, a very costly mixture of pulverized sandalwood, ground musk, saffron, and large amounts of rose oil that is rubbed into the hair, as well as a pleasantly aromatic incense mixed of the wood *oud* (a type of aloe resin), the finest amber, and much musk. An Oriental woman can never have enough perfume of any kind.

Add to that the baking, the production of all sorts of confections, the procuring of animals for slaughter. In short, all hands are fully occupied.

Meanwhile, the bride has to subject herself to various uncomfortable and burdensome customs. She must spend the entire last week in a dark room, where she refrains from all embellishments and finery. This is supposed to make her appear all the more beautiful and graceful on her wedding day.

She is a tormented being during this period, with one visitor after another. All the old women she has ever known, especially all her former nurses and nannies, whom she may not have seen in years, now seek her out, all with open hands. The chief eunuch who once shaved off her first hairs pays a call with special pride for this past honorable service, seeking her continued goodwill—and a token. He receives a precious shawl, a ring for the little finger of his left hand, a pocket watch, or some guineas.

The groom is spared from being cooped up in a dark room, but otherwise suffers no less. Anyone who once served either him or the bride comes to him as well, thereby carting off a double load of gifts.

During the last three days, the groom stays home and is seen only by his closest friends. Now the interaction between the two families becomes even more intense. There is no end to the exchange of greetings and gifts between the bride and bridegroom.

Finally, the big day arrives. The wedding ceremony normally takes place in the evening at the home of the bride, not in the mosque. A *kadi*, or if none is available, a man generally known to be devout, officiates the marriage. Strange as it may seem to Europeans, the bride herself, the principal person, is not present at the formal ceremony. She is represented by her father, brother, or some other male relation.

Only if she has absolutely no male relatives does she appear personally before the *kadi* to be bound to the bridegroom with the usual ceremonial words. In this case, she enters the empty room alone, mummified beyond recognition, after which the *kadi* enters, followed by the bridegroom and witnesses. After completion of the act, during which the voice of the bride is barely discernible, the men again exit first before the newly wedded wife rises and returns to her chambers.

The wedding ceremony is followed by a rich meal for all the men who are present, including the bridegroom, complete with heavy smoking of *oud* and perfuming with rose oil.

The handover of the bride takes place three days after the wedding. Countless hands are then busy preparing and bedecking her to the utmost. Towards nine or ten in the evening, she is then escorted by her female relatives to her new home, at which point the bridegroom immediately enters, accompanied by his male relatives. At the threshold to the private chambers, the men take their leave of the bridegroom, and the women take their leave of the bride, with profuse congratulations and blessings. The guests then head to the gender-segregated social rooms on the ground floor to begin the joyful celebration that carries on for days.

After the bridegroom enters the bridal chambers, the proceedings always follow certain rules of etiquette. If the woman ranks higher than the man, she stays seated when he enters and waits for him to address her. She continues to leave on her elegant mask, which jealously covers her face. To ask her to de-mask, and to show his love and respect, the young husband must place a gift worthy of his means at her feet. For poor people, a few pennies may suffice, while the rich give significant sums.

As mentioned, starting with this evening, the house of the young husband becomes a center of hospitality for the next three, seven, or fifteen days. Friends, acquaintances, and even non-acquaintances are welcome and may eat and drink to their hearts' delight. Of course, no wine or beer is served, and even tobacco smoking is forbidden by our Ibadi sect. Nonetheless, people are extraordinarily full of happiness and cheer. They eat, drink almond milk and lemonade, sing, perform war dances, and listen to passionate speeches. Eunuchs spread *oud* incense and besprinkle guests with delightful, cooling rose water from silver bowls, which regrettably wafts away so quickly.

The ladies linger together until about midnight, while the men may spend the entire night in this house of joy, until the breaking dawn calls them to their duty, to prayer. —

Honeymoons are, of course, unknown in the Orient. The young couple is much more likely to spend the first week or two at home with each other, hidden from the outside world. The young wife receives guests only after this period is over, and then her chamber overflows every evening between seven and midnight with friends and acquaintances bringing her all their best wishes.

CHAPTER EIGHTEEN

Arab Visits Among the Ladies

I have repeatedly referred to the many visits we made to our friends and acquaintances, and the many we hosted. It may well be of interest to learn more about such socializing among Arab ladies, how we interact, what we talk about.

If we wished to visit someone, we usually sent elegantly dressed female slaves to convey our intentions the same day. Only rarely did we dare show up unannounced on good luck. All city visits are made on foot; we only ride out to the countryside. We also dress in our finery for such occasions, not just to show respect to the friends we are visiting, but also to flaunt our clothes and jewels in the hopes of outshining the others. The same as here!

That said, an Arab woman may not show her face. It stays covered with a mask, often at home and always on outings. This is not like the Egyptian mask, which is ugly and hard for breathing. Our masks were very elegant, stylized in black satin and decorated with gorgeous lace made of colorful silk and gold and silver threads. They consisted of two main parts, connected by a thin support, one part covering the forehead and the other covering the nose and part of the cheeks. The eyes and lower part of the face were left completely open. The mask was fastened with either silk strings entwined with gold or meter-long gold or silver chains wrapped multiple times around the head, which also kept our headscarves in place.

Rainy days, uncommon as they are, dampen the mood because there is no chance to socialize outside the house, and we are stuck within our own four walls. Not everyone in the Orient has an umbrella, this indispensable companion in the North, and it is not always easy to borrow one when going out. The middle class, and Africans now and again, carry enormously large umbrellas imported from India, which are covered in yellow, green, or very occasionally black oilcloth.

I hardly need to mention again that Muslim ladies may not, as a rule, go out on public streets in broad daylight, but rather only in the early morning hours or evenings after the sun sets. There were no streetlights when I grew up in Zanzibar. We had to carry our own light in order to wind our way through the narrow, mostly crooked and dirty streets. Lanterns thus became objects of great luxury. The larger ones were one to two meters round. The prettiest ones had the form of a Russian church, with a large dome in the middle ringed by four turrets. In each tower, a bright candle threw its light through white, red, green, yellow, or dark blue panes onto the street. Every upper-class lady was preceded by two to six such lanterns, depending on her rank and means, all carried by escorts chosen from among the few slaves with enough strength to handle them. Regular citizens, by contrast, contented themselves with one lantern.

The train of every traveling lady additionally consisted of a whole host of armed slaves, who tended to look more battle-ready than they really were. These escorts always carried a high price tag. Their weapons, aside from the gun and revolver, were fully adorned with precious gold and silver and quite expensive. This did not, however, deter the rascals from selling them for a song, or pawning them off for a pittance to a usurer (these fine men are usually Hindus or Banyans),[17] only because the reckless knaves wanted to quench their thirst with *pombe* (palm wine). A mistress had no choice but to reclaim the weapons for ten times the price, or arrange a new outfit for the scoundrel, along with a well-deserved, exemplary punishment.

Ten to twenty armed slaves would thus proceed with their lanterns, two-by-two or in whatever combination of orderly rows, at the head of a high-ranking lady's train. Behind this distinguished lady, who was sometimes accompanied by an Arab woman, a group of well-dressed female slaves would form the end of the train.

If a bystander, whether of high or low rank, was encountered en route, the slaves would motion him out of the way or detour him into a side street, open door, or shop until the train went by. But this worked consistently only with the family

---

17 Among its mix of cultures, Zanzibar had a significant Indian population, known primarily as Banyans, both from the convenience of the alternating monsoon trade winds and the Sultan's preference for their business and administrative capabilities. Interesting details can be found in G. Dale, *The Peoples of Zanzibar: Their Customs and Religious Beliefs* (1920); located in the Leiden University Libraries at NINO SR 739a.

of the Sultanate. Other fine ladies did not always fare as well in securing clear passage, and the rougher street folk were especially disinclined to move aside.

The long procession of richly clothed pedestrians and the colorful sheen of lanterns in the dark and narrow streets made for an enchanting sight. Even though good behavior in the Orient also calls for keeping as calm and quiet as possible when moving around in public, our lively nature would invariably break through, as the group proceeded loudly and jokingly enough for curious onlookers and eavesdroppers to be drawn to their windows and doors or lured onto their low, flat roofs.

Frequently, I would happen upon a sister or encounter a friend that was on the way to visit me. At that point, we would continue together, causing the train to swell to double and sometimes triple its length.

Having arrived at our destination, we allowed our arrival to be announced according to local custom. To be sure, we did not wait around in a dark corridor or anteroom until the lady of the house had finished her toiletries, but rather followed directly on the heels of the person announcing our arrival. Visitors were then received inside or, on moonlit nights, up on the clean and flat, balustraded roof.

The hostess sits on her *medde*, a kind of horizontal cushion about ten centimeters high and made of the finest brocade, and leans against the *tekje*, a large, square cushion placed against the wall that is also made of brocade. It is not our custom for the hostess to step forward, whether warmly or politely, every time a guest comes in. She does so only to show her personal affection for the guest or out of respect for her guest's higher rank and status.

An Arab woman is generally very reserved with respect to complete strangers, whether the strangers are of high or low rank. That is in contrast to closer acquaintances. As soon as a close friendship is established, any difference of rank or birth disappears.

After the arriving guests have kissed the hostess's hand, head, or hem of the shawl (while those of equal rank simply shake hands), they take their rank-appropriate place. Only a lady of equal rank may seat herself unbidden on the *medde* and claim the comforts of the *tekje*, while those of lower rank take their place at a certain distance on the mat- or rug-covered floor.

The mask stays on, as does most everything else, including the thin, light *shele*. Only the shoes are removed. Instead of the wooden sandals (*kubkab*) that are

Arab Visits Among the Ladies

normally worn at home, we go out with elaborately stitched *kash*, a kind of slipper with a broad heel. These shoes are readily slipped off before entering the room, a custom that everyone, from ruler to slave, follows. It is then the unenviable task of the many slaves standing at the door to arrange the shoes in pairs, despite looking mostly the same, so the guests can immediately slip them back on for departure. Here, too, a strict protocol applies. The shoes of the highest-ranked guest are placed in the middle, with those of lower rank placed around them in a semi-circle.

Soon after a guest arrives, slaves pass around little cups of coffee, and this ritual is repeated every time a new guest arrives. Fresh fruit and confections are also enjoyed. Everyone can just take as much as they want.

The hostess is similarly spared the need to keep up the often rather forced conversation that counts as good etiquette here and takes the greatest effort. No, everyone is completely at ease and chats freely about whatever comes to mind. Without theatres, concerts, balls, or circuses, conversation topics are already rather limited, and no one there loves witty quips about the weather either. Instead, conversations are mostly about personal matters and agriculture, with all that pertains. Everyone with a higher rank is active in farming, perhaps not as experts, but with great interest.

Guests can freely indulge a good mood, and laugh and joke, without having to worry if their reputations might suffer as a result. In addition to all other advantages of the South, its residents are mostly cheerful, upbeat, and content. Why not, with nature, always sunny and bright, setting such a good example? Under a clear sky beaming with full sunlight, the melancholic spleen never gets the upper hand in the South. And nature is so bountiful, generous to excess, that people are guaranteed whatever they need to live, with nary a care.

The master of the house is not allowed to enter the rooms of his wife, daughter, or mother during visiting hours. Only the ruler and his immediate male relatives are exempt from this rule, except that the presence of an equally ranked female cousin would also bar any unannounced visits by my brothers and nephews.

This custom becomes very uncomfortable when a lady visits her friend for the whole day, say early from half past five in the morning until seven in the evening. The men in the house sometimes have considerable trouble staying out of the way. That is surely burdensome. But, in this case as with other special customs, Orientals do not feel put upon in the slightest. This is how they grew up, they know no other way and cannot compare, it all feels absolutely normal and right. Everywhere the force of habit and its penetrating influence! I do not deny that many things in the Orient may appear excessive or even exaggerated when considered more objectively. But is Europe the only place that is free from such lopsided perspectives and behaviors? Over there, the strictest restraints between men and women; over here, the most unbridled freedom. Over there, constant coverings and masking, despite the heat; over here in the cold north, full cleavage; and so on. These are certainly extreme contrasts, but we exaggerate here just as there. In my opinion, the happy middle has not yet been found anywhere.

Evening visits by the ladies can easily last three to four hours when filled with the liveliest conversation and gesticulation. And then finally, it is time. The slaves are roused from their deep sleep to form an orderly procession. Meanwhile the lanterns have been allowed to burn during the whole visit, completely unnecessarily, but such is the fashion.

After the hostess hands each visitor a parting gift, be it but a trifle, and everyone says good-bye, the train is set in motion to return home. If I end up leaving the house at the same time as a sister or friend, it always takes a while to disentangle the confusion of retinues on the street. Our path is still traceable long after we pass through, given the intensity and sustained fragrance of our heavy perfumes. We must all be home by midnight at the latest, since that is the deadline for the nighttime prayer. —

Arab women have another special advantage over European women. They are under no obligation to express thanks for the social occasion to which they were invited. They need not feign or pretend. Is it not bad enough to sit through a boring gathering without having to then also show gratitude for it? How often have I heard ladies give their most flattering compliments to the hostess for a lovely time and then stand outside the door and unload their biting critiques. What an abhorrent charade! Would we not stand closer to our merciful Creator if everyone tried especially hard to stay open and honest toward their fellow humans? Why the eternal masquerade?

CHAPTER NINETEEN

The Audience; Interactions Among Men

It is a long-standing custom that the ruler grants his male relatives, ministers, and other officials, as well as anyone else who wants to see or speak with him, open access two times a day, namely after breakfast and after the fourth prayer. The designated hall for this gathering (Arabic *barze*) was on the ground floor of our house, right by the sea, whose waves at high tide always splashed the base walls of this wing, and from whose expansive and lively setting the windows looked out onto a magnificent view. The hall was large, but often not large enough for all the visitors that came. The interior had the same simple character as every Arab room. Beyond rugs, floor-to-ceiling mirrors, clocks, and a large number of chairs along the walls, there were no other furnishings.

Because no high-ranking Arab ever travels unaccompanied, there was always a throng of several hundred attendants at the door. Anyone who could find room took a seat on the stone benches that ran the length of the house wall. The latecomers had to stand in the open palace courtyard to wait for their exiting masters or friends. Those were always interesting sights for us. For this audience, men always appeared in their full state regalia, with turban, tunic down to the ankles (*djocha*), and sash tied at the waist.

At home, Arab men wear white caps that are often nicely embroidered on heads that are clean shaven once a week. When they go out, they put on a turban (*amame*). Building a turban requires a certain dexterity. It takes some men half an hour to construct them properly. That is why removal is handled so very delicately, since even the smallest misstep can cause the whole thing to fall apart. But anyone who cares about his looks reconstructs a new turban every time he goes out. The cloth that is used for turbans is relatively plain and costs less than five to eight dollars. The fabrics used for sashes (*mahsem*) are much more expensive, with prices ranging from twenty to two hundred dollars. These are silk fabrics, richly interwoven with gold and silver threads. Someone of higher rank normally owns a whole series of sashes that are swapped out, much as men do with their neckties here. Older and devout people, who are less bound to fashion, just wear plain white or black silk *mahsems*.

An Arab man's outfit is naturally not complete without, as already often mentioned, his weapons. His wife, daughter, or son normally hands them to him when he is about to go out.

Before the men enter the gathering hall, they remove their shoes, which is when the different ranks become apparent. The lower-class men take off their *watje* at a distance, the higher class right at the door. But this is not the result of some despotic decree; the practice is completely traditional and voluntary. Arabs show their due respect at every opportunity, according to custom. Above all, they harbor pious, instinctively royalist sentiments toward their ruler and his whole house.

Once the gathering hall is full, the Sultan makes his way to greet the distinguished attendees. The official procession in my father's time always took the following order: First came an African guard unit, then a company of younger eunuchs, after them the chief eunuchs, and finally our father in advance of his sons, with the youngest at the very end. Downstairs at the door of the *barze*, the guard unit and eunuchs formed a lane through which the father and his sons entered the room. All rose to greet him, and the same ritual was then repeated when he left the gathering in the same orderly procession. Our father also showed due respect to all in return. When someone of high rank took his leave, the father would accompany him a few steps, while all others stood to rise.

Coffee was only rarely served to the morning audience, but always in the evenings. This audience was simultaneously also a legal proceeding in which my father handled the main matter quickly and efficiently, and knew how to resolve difficult questions with Solomonic wisdom. People were free to come and go, and this freedom of movement was in some ways contrary to the otherwise very ceremonial style of Arabs. Anyone could present a matter, request, or complaint and seek a response. Virtually everything was handled only orally, since business affairs were not settled in writing. Petitioners would

The Audience; Interactions Among Men

usually have to come and present their matters directly. Smaller matters were typically delegated for decision to the relevant ministers, *kadis* (the appointed judges), or chief eunuchs. The audience lasted about one and a half to three hours. Those who did not get their turn or came too late to push their way into the overflowing *barze* were summoned anew by the chief eunuchs, and their items then topped the agenda for the next day.

Between the ages of fourteen and sixteen, princes are permitted to attend the audience, after which attendance becomes mandatory. Similarly, every man of rank must show respect for his ruler by being present every day, unless deterred by something especially urgent. If someone goes missing several days in a row, slaves are sent to find out the reason for the absence. If this person is lying infirm, he can be certain that the ruler himself will soon pay a visit. Not even the most contagious diseases, like cholera or smallpox, are deterrents; God decides and ordains all! The female caretakers of the sick person, as well as the wife, mother, daughter, and sister, must of course vacate the room as long as male visitors are present. When, however, someone remains absent from the gatherings without justification, then resentment, even hostility, is presumed.

Every distinguished Arab has a *barze* on the ground floor of his house, set apart from the women's quarters, where he spends his time and receives his friends and acquaintances. The floor is usually laid out in black and white marble tiles from France. Rugs or mats are not used, so as not to diminish the pleasant coolness of the stones.

The men pay their visits during the same hours as the women, with evenings after seven being the favorite time. When Arabs go out, they must have a specific destination. They have no inkling that one could, or even should, take a walk for health reasons. Any European seen pacing back and forth on his roof is presumed to be praying in his peculiar Christian manner. —

I need not add anything about the social practices and interactions among men. They are just like those of women, except that men naturally discuss more of the general questions that affect the well-being of the city and country and take a keen interest in the events of the last audience with the Sultan, the various petitions, the many cases, that were decided. Europeans are readily able to attend male gatherings, especially the audiences with the Sultan, so that our patriarchal activity, with all its good and bad sides, is more familiar to the North than the sequestered lives of Oriental women.

ZANZIBAR FROM THE SEA.

CHAPTER TWENTY

The Time of Fasting

Everyone has probably heard that Muslims have to fast for a full month, every day, the whole day, as long as the sun can be seen in the sky. Islamic fasting is nothing like the Catholic version, which amounts to child's play by comparison. Fasting is obligatory for all Muslims, and children are expected to start when they reach twelve years of age. Because my mother was very devout, she had me practice the sacred month of *Rumdân* already in my ninth year. (We pronounced it *Rumdân,* not Ramadan, the way it is usually written here.)

It is certainly not easy for a nine-year-old child to spend a full fourteen and a half hours every day without being allowed to eat or drink. The hunger is not nearly as tortuous as the horrible, indescribable thirst that impacts someone living in the Tropics. At my age, I naturally had a weak grasp of religion, and so I am ashamed to admit that I initially snuck a little water here and there. Under my mother's penetrating questioning, I remorsefully confessed my sin and received her pardon on the condition that I would never again disobey the sacred religious commands. During the first days, I was so totally dazed that they let me sleep as long as I could to take off some of the pressure. The rules are applied extremely strictly. To be considered fully compliant, even intentionally swallowing one's own spit is not allowed. Thirst can drive people to insanity. My poor mother, who normally followed every commandment with the utmost strictness, was so extremely beset with thirst one day that she forgot herself and in a stupor emptied an entire earthen jug filled with water in a single draft, despite the father's resonating warning voice from on high. As a consequence, she had to fast an entire extra day.

At four in the morning, our ship sends out a cannon blast to signal the start of the fast. Anyone in the midst of eating must stop immediately. Even someone with a cup in hand, ready to take that last quenching sip for the next fourteen and a half hours, has to set it aside, untouched, the moment the cannon shot is heard. No healthy adult may from that time on eat or drink anything. People love to sleep away the day and then stay up late into a pleasure-filled night.

At six the sun sets. It is time for the evening prayer, after which fasting can be interrupted at six thirty. The loveliest fruits, and above all precious drinking water in cool, porous clay pots, have already been set out to offer languished individuals an initial respite. Soon the family gathers to enjoy a truly epicurean meal that amply rewards the harsh deprivations. Considering how contented Arabs usually are, and how simply they usually live, they become veritable gluttons and luxuriate in food and drink during *Rumdân*.

At this time, life is especially sociable, and everyone comes together in the evenings, or rather nights, for religious songs, rhetorical speeches, and storytelling, while eating and drinking throughout. At midnight, the first cannon shot resounds and wakes anyone who has to prepare the night meal (*suhur*). This is then served between three and four in the morning. Small children that were sent to bed at nine or ten are woken up for it. The *suhur* is rarely shared in a group, but rather eaten individually in each person's own room.

That is how the month goes by. At the start, there are plenty of fainting spells. One can almost watch people become trim and thin. But gradually, people get used to dealing with the privations, they do not sleep as much of the day away, and many who until now were seen only at meals and prayers again appear regularly on the gallery.

Everyone is supposed to adhere strictly to the fast, and masters are expected to order their slaves to comply as well. Those who provide household and personal services, who can be controlled, are held to this standard. On the other hand, the plantation slaves, who mostly have no religion, are free to decide if they want to fast or not.

Children and sick people are excused from fasting. However, once the sick get well, they still need to make up what they missed within the same year, by fasting the full number of missed days back-to-back. The same applies to those who have been on a difficult trip. And pregnant women facing imminent delivery may, if the conditions are challenging, postpone their fasting duty as well. Of course, they would rather avoid facing all the deprivations later alone,

The Time of Fasting

when it is so much harder. If a woman delivers during *Rumdân*, she must stop her fasting immediately and may not resume until at least two weeks have gone by. But the strictest rule always applies, that every missed day must be recouped later. Someone who is injured with loss of blood, or is suddenly indisposed without being sick, still has to fast for the rest of that day and also make up the lost time after the fasting period.

Of course, fasting is not merely an outward trial. During this time, devoted Muslims focus primarily on their inward contemplation. They seek to discover and improve their moral failings, to pray for forgiveness of their sins, much like when good Christians prepare themselves for holy communion in the Holy Week before Easter. Even dangerous animals are spared, and extra efforts are made to do as much good as possible. In this way, *Rumdân* is a heartwarming time. People become more conciliatory, kinder, even the ones who are hardened to the core. These long, drawn-out sacrifices undertaken in the service of the Lord bring them closer to Him. And so they are lifted and bettered, some admittedly perhaps only for a short while, but others for their whole lives.

Above all, the traditional hospitality of Arabs achieves a high point during this time, essentially becoming a religious duty. Every man with a family and household feeds strangers, as many as he can find, even people whose names he does not know. The prayer leader of the mosque that he frequents is often simply instructed to send him a set number of strangers every evening for a meal. These are not just poor people, but often men of higher birth and wealth who are foreign and miss their homeland now more than ever in this holy time. To fill in for such guests is always a pleasure for the truly hospitable Arab. No one considers it inappropriate to be served by someone who is poorer, and no one would dream of offering to compensate the host. That would be a severe insult. Truly, egoism cannot take root where such principles prevail, and blessed are those peoples for whom love of their fellow man or woman is an unassailable duty.

The month of *Rumdân* has its similarities to the weeks before Christmas here. We also have to come up with various presents that are distributed on the first day of the following month of *Shewal,* one of the two most sacred holidays of Islam. Handcrafted items are seldom given as presents and then only to the closest family and friends, never to those outside the inner circle. Just as here, such projects take a lot of time to complete. On occasion, I would even spot some lonely soul hiding away, plaguing herself, eager and afraid, trying to finish a delicate piece of work under the bright light of the African moon.

Most gifts are bought as finished products. For this, goldsmiths do the best business. This trade is totally in the hands of Hindus and Banyans, who are known for their cunning, lies, and deceit. Very skilled in their craft, they have managed to drive all Arab goldsmiths out of business. In the lead-up to the holidays, their business is booming. Orders come in one after another, and they take them all in. To ensure that our orders would be ready on time, we usually had to send a few armed slaves to the master smith's workshop to monitor his progress and keep him from working on other orders. That may sound very drastic. However, nothing short of this approach, devised by one of my sisters, proved effective against these Hindus and Banyans, who, as indicated, are the worst swindlers. Their word is not reliable, and they are extraordinarily craven.

Among the favorite gifts are weapons of all sorts. Europeans may consider it strange that an Arab woman would give expensive arms to her husband, brother, adult son, or to-be-betrothed. But such weapons are exactly where Arabs place their greatest extravagance. They are always on the lookout for beautifully crafted pieces and can never get enough of them. Price is never an issue when it comes to procuring a weapon.

Weapons and jewelry are thus at the top of the list for holiday gifts. But there is plenty more that can be given: regal horses, white travel donkeys, and—an atrocity for civilized Europeans—even slaves!

The month of *Rumdân* always passes quickly with all these pressures and purchases. In the last week and often earlier, baking and other household preparations for the imminent celebration begin. The closer the first day of *Shewal* comes, the more the excitement and expectations rise. Everyone is feverishly trying to get their presents and households ready on time.

The night before the 27th of *Rumdân*, the "Night of Value," in which Muhammad is said to have received the Koran from heaven, is considered especially sacred. Prayers that are raised to the Lord on this night can surely count on being granted.

Finally, the last day of *Rumdân* arrives, the 29th or 30th day. It is well-known that we measure by moon months of 29 or 30 days, so that each year amounts to only 355 days. Everyone is now eagerly trying to spot the rising moon. The new sliver of the crescent moon has to actually be seen before the fasting can end. What luck that Muslims almost always look up at the clear and bright sky of the South, which is rarely clouded over like in the bleary North.

The Time of Fasting

Anyone who owns a telescope or opera glass is much envied. The popular instrument is passed from hand to hand; friends and acquaintances from all around ask to borrow it briefly. Our father sends people with sharp eyes onto the roof of our fortress, which still stands from the days of Portuguese occupation, and to the tops of ship masts, to keep watch for the emerging moon from both land and sea.

In the evening of the 29th day of fasting, everyone is tense with anticipation. By the minute, one or the other person thinks they just heard the cannon shot announcing the happy discovery. Every little sound is taken to be the real thing, forgetting in our excitement that shots from ships directly in front of our house always give the palace such a shake that we not only hear, but also feel, the blast. Finally, the actual shot roars. Exultant cheers fill the whole city, and everyone wishes everyone *id mbarak* (blessed festival).

So much for the city. The matter is more complex in the countryside, where direct support of the ruler is missing, and no official signal tells everyone when to stop fasting. Those who live on distant plantations usually send riders into the city to await the cannon shot and then return with the official news that the new moon has in fact been seen. Others let slaves ascend the crowns of the highest coconut palms to watch the horizon from various locations on their properties. Occasionally such a look-out makes a mistake, believing he has spotted the narrow crescent moon when it was in fact just the delicate wisp of a rising cloud. Fasting is then immediately interrupted, only to later discover that fasting is still ongoing in the city, which is what counts. There is hardly a more bitter disappointment for Arabs than having to make up for lost fasting time when they were so ready to celebrate.

CHAPTER TWENTY-ONE

The Small Festival

Baking, as explained, has already been underway for a week. The last few days have also seen major purchases of animals for slaughter, like oxen, sheep, goats, gazelles, chicken, ducks, and doves (we do not eat veal, and Muslims are strictly prohibited from enjoying pork). The stalls are all full, and many of the animals that will be sacrificed for the feast have to be kept in the courtyard. Wealthy people are tasking their eunuchs with exchanging the Louis d'ors and guineas into Maria Theresa thalers to distribute to the needy during the celebration, especially all the poor and humble immigrants from Oman, who have never seen gold currency.

As soon as the cannon shot bursts out, the joyous news spreads far and wide that the next morning is indeed the day of the "small celebration." Life in Arab households becomes even more picturesque, exciting, and over-the-top. Hundreds of beaming folk forget their usual measured steps and run about urgently, here and there. Everyone wants to wish their loved ones all the best and many blessings. With such joyful religious excitement, it is not uncommon to see two enemies extend their hands in reconciliation because they hope to have attained this state with their all-merciful God in the time of introspection and examination. The giddy commotion, the hundred voices calling in many different languages, the agitated complaints of slaves overloaded with work, all this hardly lets anyone get any rest that night.

The service workers in particular get no rest. The slaughterers (slaves) hastily throw themselves onto their bellowing, shrieking, and squealing victims, ending their lives with the prescribed words "in the name of God, the All-

The Small Festival

Merciful." Following strict rituals, the throats of the cattle are slit, heads quickly removed, and slaughtered carcasses immediately skinned. Then it is off to the kitchen where they are prepared overnight for the next day's feast. On this evening, our slaughter yard looked like a sea of blood from all the butchered animals, and a humane vegetarian would have fled the scene in dismay. Our local vegetarians in Zanzibar, the Banyans, were horrified by our celebrations and made sure to stay far from our abattoirs. They are manufacturers, but, at the same time, they are loan sharks and the worst throat-slitters in the world. Hated bitterly by their victims, they are gruesomely mocked and derided on these occasions. Under the pretense of this or that lady still wishing to buy something for the celebration, it is a sport to lure these lower-class Banyans—who would never miss a chance to make a deal—into this bloody arena and make a mockery of them. It is a bitter taunt, for these star-worshippers have at least one good side, which is that they stay extraordinarily faithful to their religiously-prescribed vegetarian views.

The ladies, who already cannot sleep a wink with the rowdy noise from all the commotion, also have an array of important wardrobe concerns roiling in their heads. Three completely new outfits are commissioned for the three days of the festival.

An important part in the presentation of a fashion-minded Oriental lady, especially at major celebrations, is played by *hinna*,[18] which is made from the leaves of a mid-sized tree and creates a red coloring on the hands and feet of women and children. The poor *hinna* trees, which almost never get to enjoy their full leafy bounty, look much like dry rods during festival times. Every little leaf has been stripped off, and it takes six to eight weeks for new ones to appear. It is a sad sight to see those trees standing there, so bare against the ample foliage of the other trees.

Oriental women have two main uses for this entirely indispensable *hinna*: as a cure for bumps, heat blisters, itches, and the like, and as a beautifier. The small leaves alone, which are like myrtle leaves, are insufficient to produce either result. They first have to be dried, pulverized, and then supplemented with the juice of several limes, which are smaller than the lemons we have here, but much juicier, plus a bit of water. The mixture is kneaded together into a firm dough, placed in the sun for a few hours, probably to promote acidification, and then reworked with lime juice to soften the mix again.

---

18 *Lawsonia inermis*, also known as henna, of the Lythraceae family that includes crepe myrtles and pomegranates.

Now the beautification of the lady in question can begin. There she lies on her precious bed, ideally flat on her back, and may not move. First, the *hinna* paste is expertly applied flat on the feet about an inch high above the sole and on the toes, which, being undefiled by pinching boots, have retained their natural form. The top surface of the feet is not colored. Big, soft leaves are layered on the *hinna*, and then the whole thing is wrapped tightly in cloth. This is then repeated with the hands. Here, too, only the insides of the hands are covered in a half moon shape, plus the fingertips up to the first joint in a thimble shape, and then that is all wrapped up. And thus the proud beauty has to lie there, bound up the entire night and not allowed to move, or risk blemishes if the mixture shifts. Only the designated areas may be dyed red. If, say, the back of the hand or an additional finger joint picks up the color, that would be considered very unsightly.

Mosquitoes and flies, attracted to the bright lights, may descend in droves upon this helpless body, but no matter how much they plague her, she cannot defend herself. The situation is less severe for the higher-ranking ladies. Female slaves must keep watch and take turns to fan these vexing creatures away from their mistress until the break of dawn, after which the mixture is carefully washed off. The next night this trial begins anew. Three agonizing nights are needed for this part of a lady's regimen to achieve a very nice, dark red color, which then also tolerates all the washing to last up to four weeks.

I recall reading somewhere that it once was fashionable in France to get one's hair done by a particular, especially skilled hairdresser. For the large public holidays, this much sought-after coiffeur already had to start his work the day before to satisfy all his many customers. Those who were first in line then had the pleasure of spending the entire night stiff and stuck on their armchairs to avoid undoing their stylish hairstyles. This reminds me vividly of my own young years in the Orient, although our vanity tortures were even worse than the one described here.

Older ladies and younger children are spared these torments. For them, *hinna* is only used as a cooling wash in a more liquid form.

The day of the festival dawns. By four o'clock, everyone is up and about. They all take extra time during morning prayer to give special thanks to the almighty Creator and Guide of the world for everything he has granted us, all the blessings, and all the misfortunes, which he has imposed on us to test us.

Around five thirty, morning prayer is over. Decked-out ladies can already be seen here and there rushing across the gallery to show off their clothes and

The Small Festival

jewels to others, for in an hour the pomp and splendor will be so widespread that no one expects to stand out enough to be closely regarded and admired. The comparison to a full ballroom would be apt, except that outfits in the North predominate in so much pale and monotone white attire. In the Orient, only the liveliest color combinations get acclaim. It would surely strain the eyes of a fashionable European lady to see an upper-class Arab woman in her fashion regalia, wearing a shirt-like garment of red silk, featuring various patterns of interwoven gold threads and covered with lots and lots of gold and silver strands, paired with pants of bright green sateen! Quite naturally, she would find this rather too eccentric. The same thing happened to me, when I first saw people in Europe dressed mostly in gray on gray or black on black. This is what I am supposed to wear in the future? These civilized colors really grated on me, and it took a long time before I was able to subject myself to this purported fine fashion.

At six o'clock, a first shot resounds from our ships, punctuated thereafter by one shot after another, to celebrate the Festival of the Faithful. If foreign ships are in the harbor, they join in with their twenty-one gun salutes. All Arabs shoot their weapons in joyous celebration, sparing no powder on this day. A stranger would surely think the city is under bombardment. All ships are decorated, with flags waving on every mast and yardarm, both on our own ships and those from elsewhere.

An hour later, all the mosques are overflowing. On this day, every Arab shows up to say a special festival prayer to his Lord. Hundreds that no longer find room in the houses of worship pray in front of and beside them on the open streets. Muslim prayer involves significant bodily effort, as it requires a very deep and continuous bow, with the forehead down low, touching the flat earth, to honor the Almighty. Nothing, not even thunder and rain, is allowed to interrupt the prayers of a believer, and the duty to pray in or near a mosque is heightened during major festivals. Our father, too, took his place shortly before the hour in the nearby mosque to pray, accompanied by his numerous sons and an unending entourage.

Meanwhile, the already massive undertaking in our house escalates even more in preparation for the scores of well-wishers that will start arriving when the men return from the mosque. Repeated cannon shots announce the end of the prayer hour. From this point on, everyone can fully indulge in their long-denied daily pleasures. The fast thus continues even into the first hours of the first day of the new month, coming definitively to a complete stop only when the shared prayer in the mosque concludes.

We women waited in the father's chambers for his return. This location also gave us the best vantage point to watch the flood of people coming to see the father, all of whom could then confirm the culinary skills of our cooks while at it.

When the father entered the room, everyone rose and went toward him to wish him good fortune, one after another, and reverently kiss his benevolent hand. The distinguished upper-class hand, of both genders, has much to withstand on days like this in the Orient, and it is washed and perfumed until late into the night. Only people of the same rank kiss each other's hands. The middle class kisses people with higher rank on their lowered heads, or more properly on their headcloths. A common woman is allowed to press her lips only to the feet.

The time for distributing gifts was now approaching. The father went into the treasure chamber with my sister Chole and the giant chief of the eunuchs, Djohar, both of whom faced considerable envy for this proof of trust. Many highly-coveted items emerged from the vault: expensive, expertly crafted weapons with inlaid stones; Oriental jewelry of every kind from the most spare to the most ornate designs; the rarest of fabrics specially procured from Persia, Turkey, or China for this day; rose oil and other fragrant oils in large carafes, whose contents were sorted into smaller bottles; and lots of gleaming gold coins.

Distribution by the father naturally took place on a broad scale. There was no way he could remember all the jewelry pieces his women and children already owned and what they especially wanted. So he would usually check their wishes several days beforehand, to see if they might like this or that item. But people tended to turn to Chole as well, so she could remind him of their individual desires during the selection process.

Eunuchs sorted all the gifts in the presence of the father. Every item was noted with the name of the recipient on a strip of paper and then delivered by the eunuchs to each individual. Understandably, these items were subjected to careful examination immediately upon receipt, while the messenger was still present. Frequently, eunuchs had to relay gifts back to the father, along with discerning comments that this or that item was not quite useful, but some other item or two would be more desirable. And sure enough, recipients mostly got what they wanted. Our father was so extraordinarily good-natured and accommodating that no one who appealed to his generosity ever did so in vain.

The father gave and gifted with full hands, but never received in return. It is a nice and endearing custom in Germany that children, according to their ages

The Small Festival

and circumstances, give their parents gifts for Christmas and birthdays. The head of the family in the Orient fares poorly by comparison. Arab children, big and small, never give their fathers anything.

Up to this point, I have addressed only gifts from the father to our family, but his obligations hardly ended there. On this day, everyone expected something from him. He had to think of all the official Asian and African chiefs who were in Zanzibar at the time, all state officials, all soldiers and their officers, all sailors and their captains, the managers of his forty-five plantations, and finally all his slaves, which may have numbered more than six to eight thousand. Naturally, all these gifts reflected the ranks of the recipients. The slaves, for example, received simple fabric for clothes.

On top of that, there were the hundreds of humble poor, some of whom were still coming by for festival gifts two weeks later. Poor people did well everywhere, since wealthy people all made great efforts to care for them.

Similar activity as in the city also took place at Bet il Mtoni. Here, too, massive amounts of presents were handed out. To us, it was almost miraculous the way the treasure chamber never fell short of the sizeable demands that had to be met over the course of these three days, especially in terms of cash—evidence that our father also must have been an excellent businessman.

CHAPTER TWENTY-TWO

The Big Festival

Muslims celebrate only two major festivals annually, which must be rather unfathomable to Catholics with their many holidays. Two months lie between the small festival and the big festival, which is usually described in Europe and Turkey as the Great Bayram.

This celebration is like the earlier celebration, except more beautiful, more grandiose, and for the people, even more dignified and solemn. It is the time of the great pilgrimage to *Mekke* (the way we pronounce Mecca), which all devout Muslims aspire to undertake at least once in their lifetimes. The horrors of cholera and other plagues that often claim many thousands of pilgrims do not trouble the faithful. Every year countless droves set out anew to plead for full forgiveness of their sins in the holy city of the Prophet of the Almighty. The poor must traverse great distances on foot, and their travel by ship, where they practically lie on top of each other, is horrendous. But trusting in God, they set out with their lives in His hands. Truly, such confident faith, which eschews no effort, no discomfort, no danger in pursuit of a religious duty, may justify expectations that prayers will be answered.

This greatest Islamic festival occurs on the tenth day of the twelfth month of the year and lasts three to seven days. Many already start observing it on the first day of the month with a voluntary nine-day fast, exactly as the devout pilgrims in Mecca do.

Whoever can afford it gets a sheep, to be slaughtered on the first day and distributed to the poor. The law requires that this sacrificial sheep must be

The Big Festival

the best that can be found, indeed flawless. It should be correct in all aspects, without even a single missing tooth. A totally flawless sheep is of course hard to find, and we would send a few slaves on reconnaissance of the whole island already two weeks or more ahead of time. If they failed to find anything suitable, they would have to travel to the African mainland to try their luck in the interior, where there was more selection. In this way, expenses got quite high, and the actual purchase price would go even higher. Herd owners knew full well how much the Arab royals needed a model specimen, for which any sum would gladly be paid. Neither the person putting on the sacrifice, nor his family or slaves, were allowed to enjoy the meat of the sacrificed animal, not even the smallest piece. None of it stays in the house; all of it belongs to the poor.

The big festival is the most significant event of the year for the poor. It represents one of the best Islamic customs there is: a broad self-taxation to benefit the needy.

In the real Orient (excluding Turkey, Egypt, and Tunisia because of their mixed cultures), people have no concept of government bonds and securities. The phrase "investing money" has no meaning there. Assets are primarily held in tangible form, as in fully-paid plantations, houses, slaves, jewelry, and major coins. If there is anything left at the end of the year from the harvest, rental contracts on housing, or any other income, religious precept requires that a tenth of it must be paid to the poor.

At the same time, Arabs must have their entire fortunes in precious stones, gold, and silver appraised by experts, with a tenth of the total valuation also to be gifted to the poor every year. As such, a wealth tax with a voluntary self-assessment.

All of this happens without any control by the authorities. Everyone is bound only by their own feelings, their own scruples. But this order of the Prophet is considered especially sacred, and only the absolute worst individuals fail to follow through. Such charitable contributions are also never discussed, on the principle that the left shall not know what the right hand doeth. Neither father, mother, nor child may know what I have negotiated with my benevolent God. With scrupulous care, every effort is made to comply with this tithing duty down to the smallest detail in all aspects, to avoid being tormented by pangs of conscience later.

Under these circumstances, a large number of people who feign poverty, if I may say so, appears to be an indispensable part of every Islamic state. How else could this duty of self-taxation be fulfilled? These poor people are not to be compared with the pitiable, truly poor people we have here. Perhaps about half of the ones over there possess more than they actually need. Begging is their business, it has become second nature to them, and without begging they no longer feel happy. Often this trade is directly inherited, and that can lead to the following appeal: "Do you not recognize me? I am of course the daughter, son, in-law, etc. of this or that person, to whom you used to give so much while they were still alive. Now I am taking their place, and if you have alms to give, please send them to me at such and such address."

As far as religious vows, which we had opportunities to fulfill multiple times a year, hundreds of poor people would come to us from all directions to participate in the usual distribution of alms. If someone lay very ill in bed, poor people, who are quite skilled in scouting out these opportunities, would stand under the sick person's window, taking turns all day long, to be richly bestowed with gifts known as *sadka*. No Muslim would turn such a beggar away, even if it meant giving up his last coin. Perhaps this is pure altruism, perhaps it exemplifies a hope to win the Almighty's favor and obtain more of His grace, but it is, in any case, a beautiful custom.

Quite a few beggars are covered in wounds and ulcers. Some run around without noses and are horribly disfigured. They are victims of a serious disease we call *belas,* which attacks mostly the hands and feet, and the affected body parts turn white. No one wants anything to do with these sick people. They are shunned everywhere because their affliction is considered contagious. Whether this is leprosy, I cannot say. But even these lamentable poor always find ample alms, which somewhat alleviates their difficult existence.

There are no further religious celebrations in the nine or ten months that follow the small and big festivals. Life returns to its routine and is interrupted only now and again for special festivities, one of which I intend to describe in the next chapter.

We do not celebrate birthdays.

Shore scene in Zanzibar by Rosa Troemer

CHAPTER TWENTY-THREE

An Offering Festival at Chem Chem Spring

When I was fifteen, I once wore a new damask dress made of red silk for the first time. I became ill, and the next day a kind of inflammation had spread across my whole body. The older, experienced folk immediately knew with certainty that I had been bewitched, or had at least fallen victim to some jealous person's evil eye on my pretty fabric. Always somewhat skeptical of these things, I chose not to give up my new dress and wore it again at the next opportunity, despite all these notions. Whether the color contained a toxic substance, or perhaps another natural cause was at work, I became sick again and had to take to my bed. The situation was now clear. I could no longer wear the dress and, for some peace of mind, gave it to a dauntless common woman who believed in witchcraft as little as I did. Under prevailing custom, I should have subjected it to a spoken cure, or better yet burnt it, to thoroughly eradicate its bad influence.

This is just a small example of the superstitions that are so extraordinarily rampant in the Orient. I have already discussed this in previous pages, so I will present only a few additional details here, in connection with the description of a festival of sacrifice, which is entirely based on superstition.

Some springs are believed to possess especially magical powers—not the water, but the reigning spirit that resides within. If the spirit is properly handled, he will do everything for his devout follower. He can heal the sick, return missing people to their homes, bring lonely singles together in marriage, grant a baby to childless parents, cause enraged parents, spouses, and friends to reconcile and restore peace, recover missing items like gold, slaves, and cattle, or make the poor as wealthy as Croesus. This spirit is considered capable of everything.

The most popular spring on the island of Zanzibar is called Chem Chem. It lies several hours outside the city. A visit to this magical place gives the impression that its spirit is rather modest and easily satisfied even with minor offerings. A small strip about two-inches wide that waves in the wind, or even a mere eggshell, can be found there as objects left by poor and destitute believers. The spirit especially likes any kind of sweets (called *halve*), smelling powder, or incense. However, anyone who wants to be totally assured of success must offer up a blood tribute.

Many troubled souls head to Chem Chem, to bring such sacrifices, as promised in explicit vows. It is customary to apply a clever precaution to these vows by setting a specific time period within which the spirit is to fill the pending wish, for which the sacrifice would be made. If the spirit does not fulfill the wish within the stated period, then the promised vow no longer applies. So the spirit better watch out. On the other hand, people keep their word. If someone dies before fulfilling a sacred vow (*nadra*), then that person's relatives take it upon themselves to fulfill it.

As a small child, I was often taken along to such a holy spring, and those were always lovely, enjoyable days. After I was no longer called *kibibi* (little mistress), but *bibi* (mistress), which is to say at an age when I was able to observe more astutely and think more clearly, I attended only one more, indeed a very spectacular festival of sacrifice.

My unfortunately now deceased sister Chadudj was struck by a grave illness. Her concerned caretakers made a sacred vow that if this suffering could be overcome and the illness fully cured, Chadudj herself would go to Chem Chem to make an offering for her regained health. She recovered and was thus obligated to follow through on this promise that had been made on her behalf.

Festival invitations from her friends and acquaintances went out to some of her favorite sisters a full four weeks before the appointed day. Extensive preparations began at the same time. Each of us not only had to make arrangements for ourselves and perhaps a few hopeful daughters, but logistics also involved a whole regiment of slaves, both men and women, that had to be outfitted in clothing and jewelry befitting the wealth of their mistress, in addition to arranging a great number of transport animals. For such an event, where hundreds of people would be coming together, the ladies themselves were also intent on presenting their full splendor, each wishing to be marveled at and ideally outshine all the others, a desire that likely recurs for people everywhere in both hemispheres. No wonder the artists and artisans had their hands full handling all the many orders. Jewelers, who never keep a stock of finished products, but always produce on demand, were the most besieged and overburdened. On top of which, they were also tasked with inspecting and cleaning all the gold and silver ornamented harnesses, as well as all the slaves' ornate weapons adorned with precious metals. Especially the riding gear had to beam and gleam, since pilgrimages like this always travel as pageantry. Everything was mobilized, and no costs were spared, even though some of the jewelry was priced ten times the usual because of the massive demand. We paid for our vanity with all these high costs and no fewer drops of sweat. In spite of the hot and burning African sun, we wore Lyonnais velvet and other heavy, exquisitely embroidered fabrics. Pride must suffer duress!

On the day of our outing, I rode out early at five thirty to pick up my sister. It was no easy task to reach her through the huge throng of people. Once everyone was seated on their richly adorned animals, we got the sign to commence, and the shining procession rode out chatting and laughing in pairs. The ride was long and brisk, but very pleasant in the fresh morning air. We finally arrived at the enchantingly situated spring.

All the necessary preparations had been completed in advance. Today this otherwise secluded and desolate place was a magical haven that defied description. Over the past several days, a large number of slaves had busily lugged in everything and anything that might be needed from the city; plus they had cut the high grass, laid carpets for us to rest under the mighty trees, nailed mirrors to the mango trunks, placed backrest cushions against the same trunks, and set out a full assortment of useful utensils. The day before had also been spent slaughtering, cooking, and roasting for the joyful feast.

Soon after we arrived, the food was put out, and we sat down to breakfast in the shade of the trees, whose broad foliage let the deep blue sky shine through here and there. This picture imprinted itself deeply in my memory: the beautiful, brightly colored, glittering clothes and precious jewels of this radiant gathering, set in the wild, rich, and romantic vegetation of a tropical forest, alongside a lively, rippling spring in the midst of the most elemental profusion of nature. It was truly a picture that no painter's imagination could conjure, and yet, just like the fairytale descriptions in *The Arabian Nights*.

The large Omani donkeys were immediately unsaddled after the riders had dismounted, which they did by either hopping off in high spirits in one fell swoop or gingerly descending onto the backs of bent-over eunuchs to step off. The front legs of each donkey were then tied up with a short rope to impede

An Offering Festival at Chem Chem Spring

any get-away, and all were driven out to the meadow. There they stayed all day without supervision and were led back only in the afternoon.

About two hours after arrival, we got ready for the offering that had brought us to this place. Today the spirit of the spring would drink and enjoy the blood of a specially selected steer, not to mention the many sweets and vast amounts of raw eggs that had been smashed at the water's edge. We also dedicated two flags to the spirit, one in blood red, our house flag, and one in white, as a sign of peace. —

Our picnic grounds were located a few minutes from where the spring bubbled up. The entire group made its way there to witness the ceremony. One of my sister's older female slaves stepped up to the spring and gave a small speech to the spirit. She described the grave illness of her mistress and how they had had to proclaim the sacred vow as a last resort. She thanked the merciful spirit for ultimately returning her mistress back to health, so that the mistress could now personally deliver the avowed sacrifice in gratitude.

The steer was brought forward and slaughtered. The blood was carefully collected and sprinkled onto the spring and the surrounding area. Rose water was richly dispersed as well. Musk and amber were thrown onto glowing coals in silver incense burners, perfuming the air with a pleasant scent. A few prayers were said while standing in the round to conclude the ceremony.

Of the sacrificed animal, the invisible spirit got only the blood and its noble organs, heart, liver, and so on, which were cut up into small pieces and scattered around the spring. The remaining meat, according to custom, was to be distributed to the poor, and neither the person making the sacrifice, nor that person's relatives were to enjoy any of it. However, because the Chem Chem spring was so far from the city, and there were no poor people to be found anywhere nearby, a silent pact was agreed with the spirit at the time the vow was made that, in light of the distances involved, the sacrificial steer could be directly consumed, which meant the meat became part of our meal that afternoon.

During our stay at the site, we had frequent cause to note that this or that member of our group would disappear for short periods and then evade any queries about their absence. We in turn refrained from probing too much. They had sought a tranquil moment at the miracle spring to complain to the mighty, but discreet, spirit about their troubles, their physical and spiritual suffering, perhaps an unhappy love, and beseech his help. Naturally, they preferred to meet with the spirit alone, and it was always quite embarrassing when two similarly despondent individuals unexpectedly encountered each other at this peaceful place. —

Not all sacred vows were well-suited to be trumpeted out loud, if the idea was not to subject one's innermost thoughts to the reckless tongues of her dear compatriots. In cases where a strictly-held secret wish had been fulfilled, it was possible to deliver the promised sacrifice to the spring through a confidential proxy, without drawing attention, but, of course, only if this had been expressly included in the originally sworn vow. On the other hand, when it came time to thank for being cured of a serious illness, or to ask the spirit to help find a beloved someone who had gone missing—in other words, when there was nothing to hide from the world—then the sacrifice was, as a rule, celebrated as a grandiose festival with all manner of pomp.

We passed the time until four in the afternoon with food and drinks of sharbet, coconut water, and lemonade, and with walks, games, rest, and prayer. Then the horses and donkeys were brought over from the meadow to be saddled. And so another lively scene unfolded. The process of saddling the animals, specifically with women's saddles, is a special skill that perhaps only one in twenty slaves has mastered. I have often enough seen both a lady and her saddle slide under the belly of her mount within minutes and be subjected to the worst laughter. Whenever a lady has brought such a skilled person as part of her retinue, he is eagerly besieged from all sides and hard-pressed to satisfy all the enthusiastic and impatient ladies desiring his assistance.

Patience is put to the test on other fronts as well. Among their faults, Africans commonly misplace and forget the most basic things. It can take an inordinate amount of time for everything to get pulled together. Now and again, a donkey may also manage to slip out of its rope and take off, leaving its mistress in the greatest quandary. In short, there are always new grounds for anger or cause for more drama. It can easily take an hour before we are all seated in our saddles.

Mounted at last, we would settle smartly into our high saddles (woe to anyone who rode poorly, she would be mercilessly mocked and ridiculed) and shoot out towards the city in a joyful gallop, amidst the clatter and rattle of slaves and the loud cheers of a hundred voices. I have already mentioned how fast Africans can run. It was on precisely such occasions, when less familiar women joined us with their entourages, that they would really flaunt their abilities. Were I to suggest pausing for just a moment to wait for a sister or friend, so I could chat with them during the ride, my sweat-dripping speed runners would let me know their displeasure. It was a matter of honor for them to reach the goal first. As unlikely as it sounds, prior to such runs, these otherwise careless people managed for once to control their food intake and keep from overloading themselves.

An Offering Festival at Chem Chem Spring

We stopped for prayers again in Mnazi Mmoja or Ngambo, and then, after nightfall, rode together into the city to the door of my sister's house. Once again, there was a spirited mess. People dismounted to say good-bye to Chadudj, but could hardly wind their way through all the donkeys, horses, and other people to reach her. We, on the other hand, as sisters and close relatives, did not have to step down as a matter of etiquette. Once the crowd had dissipated, and we no longer feared trampling anyone with our donkeys, we simply rode over to Chadudj and also said our farewells. Thus ended a most splendid festival that remained the main topic of conversation for weeks thereafter.

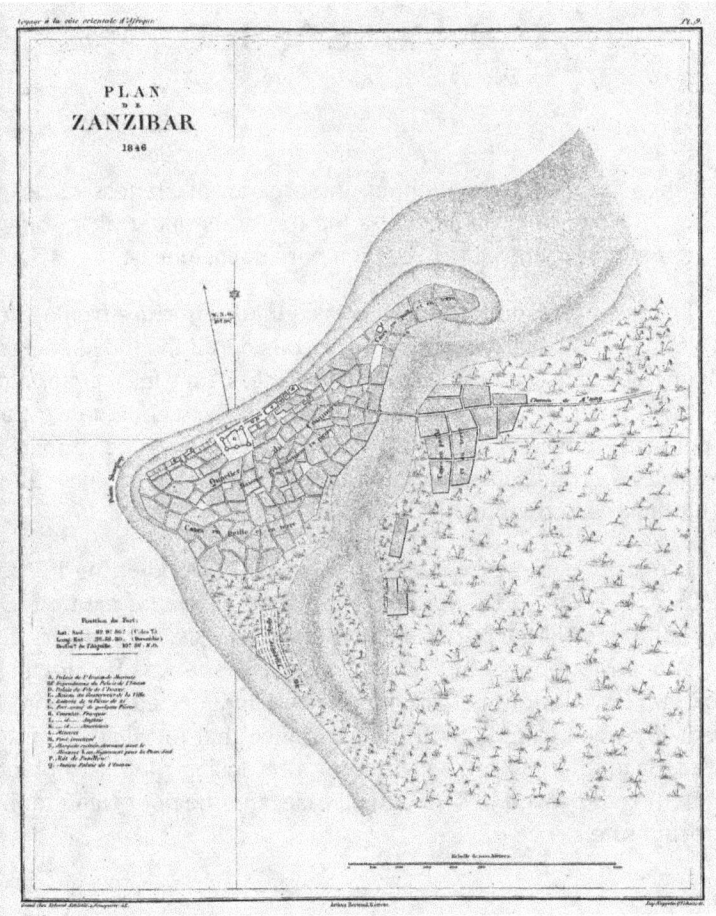

CHAPTER TWENTY-FOUR

Diseases and Medical Care; the Possessed

People in the Orient grow up without any broader awareness of health and body care. Efforts to help nature out a bit are rarely undertaken, only in the worst cases, and those measures are then pure hocus pocus.

A vile practice with a leading role in this is cupping, a torture from which only the very youngest children are spared. It is considered the universal response to all manner of aches and pains, for any illness that may arise, including smallpox and cholera. It is also used as a preventive technique for perfectly healthy people without any issues, who allow themselves to be cupped at least once a year, as was once customary in Europe. The idea is to purify the blood and strengthen the body to fight future diseases.

For people of higher rank, cupping is replaced by bloodletting in the same manner. Its application does not suffer from an excess of caution. Even to this day, I vividly recall the horrid sight of one of my sisters in a dark corridor in Bet il Mtoni. Motionless and pale as a corpse, she was being carried off by her caretakers. I let out a terrifying scream and alerted the entire house. Only gradually was I calmed by the reassurance that my sister was not, as I had feared, dead, but had only passed out after losing too much blood from the bloodletting. It proved to be a critical case, and the poor thing took a long time to recuperate.

Whether such bloodletting can occasionally be healing for the body in hot climes is something I cannot judge. Regardless, the way the technique is applied invites great danger.

Very pleasant and surely beneficial is getting one's limbs kneaded. I have already mentioned that gentle massaging is well-suited to both encouraging and ending sleep. I have also described the great skill that our female slaves display in this practice. Massaging is also a very common and popular way to relieve all sorts of ailments, especially all "body pains."

Another approach is the ugly act of vomiting. This method features a dreadful array of herbs, which are boiled together into an abhorrent brew that is supposed to be drunk. As a rule, however, the mere smell is enough to bring on the desired effect. —

When it comes to severe sickness, people turn to their faith, and as such, verses from the Koran are considered healing. A person who is widely acknowledged to be especially devout writes fitting verses on a white plate with a saffron solution. The writing is then dissolved with some water (usually rose water), and the mixture is fed to the patient. This procedure is repeated three times a day, mornings, midday, and evenings, taking extra care not to let any of this holy liquid drip onto the floor. I personally had to endure this method for a long time, as I lay in bed more than six weeks with an intense fever.

For a seriously sick female that benefited from the father's special attention, an exception might now and again be made to allow a male person, be he a real doctor or a sorcerer, to attend the patient at her bedside. I recall how my sister Chole suffered from persistent ear pain, which did not improve despite all the usual quackery, and for whom they then sent for a very famous Persian doctor (Arabic *hakim*). I was a small child back then and allowed to watch the consultation ceremony. Chole was first wrapped beyond the point of recognition in a *shele*, with only the one sick ear left visible. In this mummified state, she took her place on the *medde* that was described earlier. With her back leaning against the precious *tekje*, she sat flanked on the right by the father and on the left by my brother Chalid. My other younger brothers formed a closed circle around her, all dressed in their street outfits and loaded with weapons. The doctor was brought to the patient's room under the escort of a host of eunuchs, while other eunuchs were stationed as guards at various points around the house to signal for female inhabitants to retreat before the Persian passed through. —Naturally, the *hakim* could not speak directly to the patient, but posed his questions to the father through the brothers, who then also relayed back the responses. —

When I was later ill with typhoid and lay for several days in a delirium, and none of the Arab or Swahili treatments had done anything to help, my Aunt Aashe, the sister of my father, decided to enlist the assistance of a European doctor. Because our father was no longer alive, and I had essentially become my own master, I no longer needed the kind of ceremony Chole had received. The relevant doctor was familiar with Arab customs, but nonetheless insisted on being allowed to feel my pulse, which my concerned aunt, despite her strong misgivings, permitted. For this, a group of eunuchs was brought in after all, and I was wrapped in my *shele*, just as they had done with Chole. Since I was incoherent at the time, the incident was only later recounted to me by my aunt. When the doctor then additionally insisted on checking my tongue, he was so vociferously attacked by the chief eunuch Djohar, who refused to tolerate such an impudent request, that this disciple of Aesculapius, feeling professionally insulted, stomped out of our house in anger without completing his exam.

The underlying problem revealed by such attempted one-size-fits-all cures is, of course, always an inadequate, or indeed absent, understanding of the human body, its regular functions and related disruptions. Arabs know nothing of all this, and therefore also cannot classify sicknesses. They simply divide all internal ailments into one of two categories: body pains and head pains. Regardless of whether the stomach, liver, spleen, or abdomen is affected, it is all generally labelled "body pain." Anything affecting the head, from cerebral softening to sun stroke, is referred to as head pain. The actual cause, the basis for the affliction, cannot be ascertained. When all home remedies have failed, a eunuch is sent to a European consulate doctor to request medication. It is obvious that this doctor, who is not allowed to see the patient and receives only the vaguest description, is in a tough spot. It is equally obvious that most female patients end up with the wrong, or at best harmless, medication.

Diet likewise is not a topic. If someone with typhoid, cholera, or smallpox wants to eat something, they can freely eat anything the kitchen can deliver. Whatever nature wants is assumed to be beneficial. The strong belief in divine destiny plays into everything. This also makes Muslims blind in most cases to the possibility of contagion. No one is thinking, for example, of keeping someone with smallpox strictly quarantined from others. This deeply rooted perspective also undercuts precautionary hygiene rules. The Persian bath mentioned above, between Bet il Sahel and Bet il Tani underneath the bridge that connected the two houses, had deteriorated and become a total garbage dump. Nevertheless, as demand for living space continued to grow, these half ruins became the site of new housing, whose occupants ended up, so to speak, living on top of rubbish. It is well-known how deeply this belief in predestination obstructs all efforts toward progress and makes the *cordons sanitaires* for cholera and stricter supervision of pilgrimages appear superfluous.

I would like to highlight just a few more details about some specific diseases. Smallpox unfortunately resides permanently in Zanzibar and claims thousands of lives. The entire body of a smallpox-infected person is covered with a cream made with *djiso* (turmeric) and placed in the sun. Or the bumps are spread with coconut milk, which is always preferred to the burning *djiso*. When a body is so extensively covered with lesions that a sick person can no longer tolerate the warmth of a bed, that person is laid on a soft straw mat or a large, newly-picked banana leaf from which the hard, central rib has been carefully removed. This is all the relief provided; internal measures are not applied. Contact with water is avoided, but not with anything else.

Consumption, unfortunately another frequent guest, especially the galloping kind,[19] is left completely untreated, as we have no remedy whatsoever. And yet, this sickness is feared more than any other. It is considered contagious, and correctly so, according to European doctors. People keep their distance from anyone who has consumption, which makes that individual suffer even more. No one wants to take a seat where the poor person was sitting. No one wants to extend this person a hand or drink from a cup that has touched their lips. A very beautiful, young stepmother of mine suffered terribly from this disease. Even so, she was able to leave her bed every morning and visit the other residents in the house, until the very end. My eyes of a child did not miss how unwelcome she was to everyone. I felt incredibly sorry for her, and when she finally lay confined to her bed, I often snuck over to express one or the other kindness, in complete secrecy of course. She had only a young son, and no daughter who could have cared for her.

More than a few of my loved ones succumbed to this insidious disease, most of them in the prime of life! Their belongings are handled with the greatest caution, even after death. Clothing and bedding are washed some distance from the house on the beach. Gold and silver are heated to bring out any contagious materials.

---

19 An especially acute form of tuberculosis that almost always ended in death.

Children are afflicted by the dreaded whooping cough there as much as here. They are served large amounts of "dew water" that is gathered every morning from the giant banana leaves. A superstitious remedy is applied as well. A number of round discs the size of a one mark coin are cut from the dried rind of a type of gourd called *hawashi*, which are then strung with thick twine into a salutary necklace to be hung around the child's neck. —

A painful type of abscess is also very common. These abscesses are pasted over with the dried, brown skin of an onion, which also serves as an English-style bandage. Warm flour dough is used to get them to open and drain.

It is evident: Everywhere there are only the most basic home remedies, no medical treatment, no doctors at all. People never really know what to do. Is it any wonder that folks reach for miracle solutions or like to turn to soothsayers? These *basarin*, as they are called, are very sought after and do quite well. When someone around us got sick, we usually called on a one-eyed woman from Hadhramaut, a *shihrie*, about fifty years old. She kept her tools of the trade in a very dirty old sack, which featured quite a collection: small shells, all sorts of sea pebbles, round, bleached bones from some dead animal, various shards of porcelain and glass, rusty iron nails, crooked copper and silver coins, and more of the same. When asked in a particular case, she would pray to God that he might let her see and speak only the truth, would then untie her sack and stir the contents around before emptying them all out in front of her. Depending on where they landed, she would give her answer, whether the patient would recover and so on. Chance tended to favor this particular *basara* more than most. Of all her prophesizing that I saw, her pronouncements often came to pass, and she made a good business of it. Upfront she would get only a small amount, but if her forecast proved true, she always got a larger bonus as well.

External injuries are naturally easier to heal than internal ailments. They often respond to normal home remedies, a piece of tinder fungus to calm the blood from open wounds and the like. Broken bones are more challenging, as I discovered myself. I was still very young and not yet ready to join everyone at the table. My father had once again sent me a plate full of goodies, and I rushed down the stairs to show them all to my mother. In my happy haste, I missed a step, tumbled a long way down, and broke my forearm. My aunt, the sister of my father, and my brother Barghash bandaged my arm, but unfortunately without really straightening the bone, so that it remains somewhat crooked to this day, a reminder of my fall and the plight of my country in having no doctors.

I have yet to address a very important topic: that Mister Devil! It is well-known that practically everyone in the Orient believes in the devil incarnate, but maybe less known that he especially likes to take up residence inside humans. There is hardly a child among us that has not at some point or another been possessed by the devil. As soon as a newborn cries too much or becomes somewhat restless, no matter the reason, then it must surely be possessed, and immediate steps are taken to exorcise the evil spirit. Tiny onions and garlic cloves are strung like pearls on a string and hung in a strand around the neck and arms of the child. The technique is simple and not as foolish as it might appear. If the devil really had an olfactory organ, he could hardly withstand this attack.

Adults, too, are often possessed. Men only seldom, but many women and notably about half of the Abyssinians. The external signs are frequent bouts of cramping, lack of appetite and general apathy, a preference for solitary stints in dark rooms, and similar signs of sickness. A woman who is rumored to be possessed carries a special aura and is exceptionally respected—or feared.

To be sure, whether she is in fact possessed by a spirit requires some confirmation, and so she must undergo a special examination for this purpose. She or her family members invite only individuals who are recognized as possessed to this ceremony. These poor people form a type of secret society amongst themselves and prefer to keep all they do hidden from the eyes of the world.

They take the patient and place her in a dark room, wrapped in her *shele*, so that not even the slightest ray of light can penetrate through to her. She is then smoked, in the truest sense of the word, by putting the incense holder under her shawl directly below her nose. The group launches into strange chanting, while constantly shaking their heads back and forth. They cannot make do without an Abyssinian brew, a mixture of wheat and dates that is brought to the brink of fermentation, and not bad as far as drinks go. Subjected to all these influences, the victim begins to lapse into a kind of clairvoyance and, as reported to me, speak in very incoherent terms. Finally, she reaches full ecstasy, rampages about with a foaming mouth, and rants scattered exclamations of muddled words. Now the spirit is in her. Those present start to speak with him to ask about his intentions. This matters because there are not only evil spirits that come to afflict individuals, but also good ones that attach themselves out of love and affection because they want to safeguard and protect their hosts for life. And often two spirits, both a good one and a bad one, fight each other to possess the person, as becomes apparent when they reveal themselves during the conjuration ceremony. This can lead to horrendous scenes, and only a few valiant souls are able to witness such events all the way through. Once the ceremony concludes, the experts determine whether the subject of the examination is possessed of a good or bad spirit.

Experienced female masters of these ceremonies often succeed in exorcising an evil spirit. By contrast, a good spirit gets bound into a firm contract. Under the usual terms, the spirit may visit the victim only at prescribed times, although it can always count on a festive welcome, and it must give its darling advance notice of all that awaits him and his family members, be it good or bad.

This wicked superstitious activity is unfortunately accompanied by various other forms of crudeness. Many of the possessed do not tolerate the advance slaughter of the animals (chickens and goats) that they have selected for their secret feasts because they drink their warm blood. They also wolf down raw meat and use raw eggs by the dozen. The ones who are tested to see if a spirit really lives in them are, poor things, laid low for many days thereafter.

Here, too, I could observe how the worst examples seem to have the greatest impact on people. Although all Muslims have a strong propensity for superstition, those from Oman are far from believing such nonsense. When they visit Africa, they initially find that our conditions are heavily affected by native culture and would rather return home again immediately. And yet, in no time, they can become the most susceptible of all, internalizing exactly what they had put down. I personally knew such an Arab woman who was at first dismissive, but soon became entirely convinced that an evil spirit inside her kept making her sick, and she would need a feast to appease him.

But enough of these lamentable things!

CHAPTER TWENTY-FIVE

Slavery[20]

The subject of this chapter is controversial. I realize I will not make many friends with my views, but consider it my duty to share them. I have come across too much unawareness everywhere on this question. Even the more informed people too often overlook that this is about more than genuine humane efforts by Europeans, considering that they take place against a backdrop of hidden political interests.

I was still a child when, on the date agreed between my father and England, all resident English subjects, the Hindus and Banyans, were to release their slaves in Zanzibar. It was a very difficult time for the affected owners. There was no end to their crying and complaining. The highest-ranking ones sent their wives and daughters to us and begged for our intercession, even though this was, of course, entirely out of our hands. Some of them owned a hundred and more slaves to run their plantations. From one day to the next, all were free, and the masters ruined. Their workers were gone. Unable to cultivate their crops, they lost the whole harvest. And our lovely island had suddenly acquired the dubious good fortune of harboring several thousand loafers, vagabonds, and thieves. The freed older children took freedom to mean they no longer needed to work. They thought only of celebrating their freedom, completely unfazed that they could no longer expect lodging and upkeep from their masters. Meanwhile, the humane emissaries of the anti-slavery associations went silent. They had accomplished their goal and freed the poor victims from slavery, a status

---

20 This chapter is a product of the author's time and place. It reflects a racist perspective and acceptance of slavery that is not acceptable today, as more fully considered in "On Controversy" on pages 243–51.

unworthy of any human being. What was now to become of these slaves was no longer their concern. Or at most, their ladies, to complete the nonsense, knit wool stockings for the residents of the hot South. Let the rulers of the relevant countries figure out for themselves how to deal with these unindustrious people. As anyone who has lived for even a short time in Africa, Brazil, North America, or wherever there are Africans can attest: In addition to all their advantages, such people have a great reluctance to work and require constant supervision.

Only the English subjects, I repeat, were no longer allowed to hold slaves. England could not impose any rules directly on my father for his country. One must, however, guard against judging slavery in the Orient based on what one hears about slavery in North America or Brazil. The slaves of Muslims find themselves in an entirely different, incomparably better position.

The worst part of this institution is the slave trade, the displacement of these poor people from the interior of the continent to the coast. Countless numbers perish on these long marches from the hardships, hunger, and thirst, all conditions that, however, also affect the leader. Under these harsh conditions, it makes no sense to ascribe a special malice to the slave handlers, who often have their whole fortunes invested in such caravans. It is naturally in their own interest to get people out in the best possible condition.

Once the end destination is successfully attained, the slaves are well taken care of in every respect. They admittedly have to work without pay for their masters, but they are also free of all concerns and have the assurance of continuous upkeep, with owners that take their well-being to heart. Or should one believe that every non-Christian is totally heartless?

Africans above all love to take it easy and work only when they must. It takes strong management to get them to perform to the local standard, which constitutes a rather small workload compared to here. They are certainly not exemplary, with thieves, drunks, runaways, and arsonists among them. What to do with these? It is of course unacceptable to let them go unpunished; that would soon lead to a nice case of anarchy. Imprisonment is also no deterrent. To the contrary, they would very happily spend a few days in a cool place, interrupted only by meals, and otherwise free to daydream and sleep, in order to then resume their bad ways with new vigor. No doubt the majority of African slaves would soon be maneuvering to get such pleasant accommodations.

Under these circumstances, that leaves but one effective solution: corporal punishment. As usual, this provokes an outcry here, naturally from certain circles that are always pushing their claims while spurning any attempt to study the practical conditions. Clearly, beating is inhumane, but what alternative is there? For that matter, would it not be better for some of the thousands of inmates here to receive a beating now and again, rather than subject everyone to the same false humane treatment that lumps them all together? —

Tyranny is rightly decried everywhere, whether it affects the poor natives of Africa or, indeed, civilized people languishing in the Siberian mines. But one must take a fair and fitting approach, as not every system is just or unjust everywhere. Slavery is an ancient institution in Oriental society. Whether it can be entirely eliminated is doubtful, and it is in any case folly to want to overthrow such longstanding customs all at once. Everything takes time, and it would help to set a good example for Orientals. In my time in Zanzibar, rather many Europeans kept their own slaves and bought them when it suited their interests. Of course, this is not reported back home. Whether Arabs use slaves to work the land or in the house, or civilized Europeans use them as baggage carriers, whose workload is usually much harder and harsher, it matters not, the morality is the same. And these European slave owners are certainly not always humane enough to later free their purchased slaves, as Arabs so often do. Instead, when the slaves are no longer useful for their European master, they are simply sold again. Considerable resentment was felt among the Muslim population in Zanzibar when it became known that an Englishman, whose very government had scorned slavery with such imperious morality, had not only purchased a female slave himself, but upon leaving the island to return home, had even resold her to an Arab official, instead of freeing her. Another case was no less offensive to all Arabs. This involved the arrogant interference by a European in an Arab's domestic chastisement of an insubordinate slave. Everyone would do well to sweep in front of their own doors, and whoever keeps their own slaves should not be playing themselves up to judge the treatment by others.

It should come as no surprise, after such experiences, that Arabs harbor the greatest distrust toward Europeans. They yearn for a return to happy times when things were still stable, before the upheaval wrought by European ideas. The abolition of slavery, they reason, is intended merely to ruin them, so as to harm Islam. First and foremost, they suspect England of having all sorts of underhanded plans in store.

Some may say that I am biased, that I am unable to free myself from these views after having been raised with them, that I cannot evaluate the matter objectively. Therefore allow me to cite from a few authoritative accounts by full-blooded Europeans on the subject.

The explorer of Africa, Paul Reichard, reported in 1881 from Gonda (from *Mittheilungen der afrikanischen Gesellschaft in Deutschland*, Volume III, Folio 3, pages 171-172, Berlin 1882):

> In the night of October 12, I was woken by the screams of a woman in tears, seeking to be let in. I sought information from *askari*[21] and learned that the woman had fought with her husband and wanted to enter so she could break something of value, which would then have made her our slave according to local custom. A locally resident Arab had recently experienced three similar cases, but had accepted compensation for the damage. It is not at all uncommon for a free person who is dissatisfied with his current situation to let himself be made a slave in this manner. This is clear evidence of the exaggeration and one-sidedness of many derogatory reports about slavery that are specifically stirred up by missionaries, especially the English....
>
> As far as slavery, it is indeed the case that slaves are mistreated during transport and nearly die of starvation. When the latter fate occurs, however, we have been able to confirm that it almost always affects the relevant owner as well, since provisions easily run out at the end of longer trips.
>
> A sudden and forced end to slavery can result only in the ruin and complete upheaval of the affected countries, unless other replacement measures are immediately assured, for which the current condition of the once so prosperous island of Zanzibar may be an apt testament to my view.
>
> Once a slave is in firm hands, his lot is by no means worse, but the same or even better than in his homeland. For example, slaves brought here from under the rule of particularly cruel sultans south of [Lake] Tanganyika are loathe to return at any price.
>
> Slaves kept by Arabs are not at all overburdened with work, and only criminals are subjected to corporal punishment, since excessive strictness would require overly costly oversight. Moreover, Arabs usually free their slaves after ten to fifteen years of loyal service.

---

21 Native African soldiers in the service of a European power, especially in the African Great Lakes region.

Slaves that have children while in slavery are considered family members with their own free will. No one speaks of punishing them, but rather the opposite, since it is not unusual for violent acts of defiance against their masters to have no consequences. Others run off to the coast without their masters' permission and then return as *pagasi* (porters).

An Englishman, Mr. Joseph Thomson, assesses in his book *Expedition to the Lakes of Central Africa* (page 22) as follows:

All social classes exemplify a cheerfulness and contentment that would seem unusual anywhere else. But here life is ideal, where 4 to 6 pence a day allows for an ample lifestyle. There are no hungry or mistreated slaves to be seen anywhere. When any such cases of inhumane treatment are reported to the Sultan (of Zanzibar), he immediately frees the sufferers and protects them from abuse. This class, in fact, is in a strangely agreeable position and enjoys ten times more freedom than thousands of our servants and shop girls.

More concisely, another Englishman, who lived in the Orient many years and knows the conditions well, recently told me the anti-slavery movement with its countless meetings was simply "humbug."

To conclude, I would like to recall one more thing. This Gordon,[22] who at the time had presented himself as the most determined opponent of slavery and slave trading, commenced his second, very short-lived rule in Sudan by removing his earlier laws. He may not have been convinced of the need for slavery in Africa, but he surely understood that such a deeply rooted institution should not be eliminated all in one fell stroke, but rather only eased out gradually toward subsequent elimination.

---

22 British Major-General Charles George Gordon, 1833–1885.

CHAPTER TWENTY-SIX

My Mother's Death; a Palace Revolution

Following the death of the father, I lived, as previously described, in Bet il Tani with my mother and Chole in wonderful love and friendship. About three years had gone by when a horrific cholera epidemic spread across the city and the whole island of Zanzibar, also ravaging our house with another life expired practically every day. It was the hottest time of the year. One night, in the oppressive heat, I struggled to find sleep in my elevated bed and therefore asked my female slave to spread a soft mat on the floor, where there was just enough coolness for me to eventually doze off.

Who can describe my surprise when I awoke towards dawn to find my most cherished mother lying at my feet, writhing in pain. Shocked, I asked if her moaning meant she was sick, to which she replied only that she had been lying there since the middle of the night, fearing that cholera had taken hold of her, and wanting, if it was time, to at least die in my presence. It was a hard torment for me to watch my dearly beloved mother undergo such suffering from this vicious disease, without being able to help. She resisted its attack for all of two days before being torn from me forever.

My pain knew no bounds. I clung to the precious corpse against all admonitions, defying all warnings to protect myself from this epidemic. I wanted nothing more than for God to call me to Him and let me join my mother! And yet, the epidemic spared me. It was the will of the All-Merciful and All-Knowing; I had to yield.

My Mother's Death; a Palace Revolution

Barely fifteen, I now stood without a father or mother in this world, like a rudderless ship flailing about on a stormy sea. My mother had always guided me so adeptly and wisely, and cared for me so thoughtfully and empathetically, but now, all of a sudden, I needed to step up to adult responsibilities, both for my own well-being and that of my people. Fortunately, God knows to match new responsibilities with the strength to meet them. I was eventually able to get a handle on my situation and attend to my own affairs without requiring outside help.

But new trials came my way, and I succumbed to them. Before realizing what had happened, I suddenly found myself deep in a conspiracy against my own noble brother Madjid!

Indeed, it was as though the death of our father was meant to usher in complete discord among us, rather than have us all come together, one for all and all for one, as it should have been. Granted, it is rare to achieve complete consensus among thirty-six siblings, and so we gravitated to various groupings of three to four, drawn close by the bonds of love. To outsiders, our relationships were completely indecipherable. Even our close friends could not always penetrate our alliances, which resulted in no shortage of challenges for them and us. A loyal friend of my brother, a devoted friend of my sister, if they fell outside my inner circle, were necessarily my bitter enemies, no matter how they felt about me personally. Any neutral observer could see that no good would come from such disunity and disarray. But our eyes were clouded with passion, and we pursued each other with blind hate for basically no good reason.

Interaction among us soon stopped altogether. A great many spies, since all of us had them, served to widen the chasm as they tipped us off about every word and every intention of our opponents. Night after night, these honorable folks would show up and receive their rewards in relation to the importance or ugliness of the news they brought in. The Louis d'ors and guineas never flowed so freely. Often we did not even count the pieces, but just grabbed blindly into the linen *kis* (sack or purse), pulling out round handfuls of coins to compensate their efforts. Sometimes we were woken in the middle of the night because a mysteriously draped shape was seeking entry from the doorman, demanding to speak to us personally. Such nights were especially good for lightening our *kis*, while also making further sleep impossible and firing up the mood by another several degrees for the next while.

We were all struck by a kind of delirium. Everyone sought to outdo the others. If one of us showed interest in buying a nice horse, house, or plantation, the opponents would drive up the price four and six times higher, to the great joy of the sellers, but of course only to play tricks on the buyer. If a sister wore a new piece of jewelry, the jeweler would immediately receive orders from all sides for the same thing or, if possible, an even nicer one. The people were quick to comprehend our great weakness, and both merchants and artisans knew how to reap rich benefit from our discord.

Madjid and Chole had the best relationship at the time, which meant a great deal to me, as I loved them both dearly. They each treated me as their own child after I lost my mother. But this pleasant situation soured over time for my brother Barghash's sake, and eventually resulted in a formal rupture between Madjid and Chole. As close as I was to Chole, I still have to admit, in all honesty, that she, and not Madjid, was to blame for this break. But far be it from me to detail every circumstance that devolved into such ugly relations. We were all as if bewitched and deluded.

On a personal level, this was a time of great inner struggle. I lived with Chole in the same house, we ate and drank together and were inseparable the whole day. And then she started shunning my equally beloved Madjid more and more, for no reason, in the end even wishing him ill on everything. Initially, I hoped to stay neutral, yes, I even dared to defend my irreproachable brother, whose only fault lay in him being the reigning Sultan, not Barghash. But man knows no justice in his passion, and Chole did not let up on her resentment.

For months, I stood between two fires. I wanted the best, but could do nothing. I wavered back and forth between two beloved people, until I could no longer avoid taking a stance, and then decided for Chole. She was in the wrong, but closer to my heart, with more and more influence over me. What in this whole world do we not ultimately sacrifice for our loved ones, even if we have to fight against ourselves? In the face of their pleas and appeals, our opinions, our principles, yes, even our most sacred convictions fall like withered autumn leaves from the tree, while the healthy trunk stands helpless by.

Madjid, a truly noble man, enjoyed the heartfelt love of the people. But he was in poor health and could not engage everywhere, thus leaving much of his business to his ministers. One of these, Sleman bin Ali, knew only too well how to make himself indispensable to his master. A clever, selfish sort of man, he ultimately succeeded in making his voice the word of the land, against which the other ministers counted for practically nothing. He was presumptuous enough to act like he was the top man in charge whenever it suited. And yet, he did not even have the respected maturity of old age to justify this stature, but was instead, as we like to say here, still very green, not to mention the model of a dandy that would do anything to further his noble passions. In his

My Mother's Death; a Palace Revolution

vanity and savvy, he courted one of my stepmothers, who for her age could well have been his mother. Fatme, a Circassian, did not reject his overtures. That proved a shortsighted move, for which she paid dearly later. Sleman had been interested only in her sizeable fortune.

This evil spirit influenced Madjid in every way and surreptitiously riled the siblings against each other, all to leverage their dissonance into his personal power. Sleman succeeded in stoking trouble everywhere. Friction begot friction in our family, many individuals of rank were put down and damaged, and the situation became so fractious that people began to grumble out loud.

What a blessing that we had at least one minister holding out against him, a competent, diligent man, who always tried to soften or fix Sleman's mistakes. This was Mhamed bin Abd Allah il Shaksi, a man born into great wealth, with a generous, noble character, who was anything but self-seeking. Clearly, there could be no good relations between him and his colleague.

Meanwhile, my brother Barghash sought to take advantage of the tensions among the siblings and the discontent of the population. Because Madjid had only a daughter and no son, Barghash was next in line for the throne and generally considered Madjid's successor after our father's death. The fact that two older brothers, Muhammed and Turki, lived in Oman was not a factor; Oman lay so far away.

Unfortunately, in the Orient, successors to the throne are always in a rush to claim the reins of power. They are unaffected by assertions that others may have greater rights to the throne. They do whatever it takes and pay no heed to law and order to achieve their goals.

And so it was with Barghash. Although he had failed to become Sultan upon the death of the father, he had never given up on his plan. Ever since moving from Bet il Mtoni to the city with his proper sister Meje, he had been thinking more seriously about its implementation. The two siblings took up residence in the house directly across from Chole and me that had previously served as a secondary cavalier house for the father's second official wife, Princess Shesade (of Persia).

Thus began a most agitated time for us. Sisterly piety keeps me from sharing every minute detail, while certain activities truly do not merit much consideration. Even the great harshness with which I am still treated to this day cannot provoke me to lift the veil. Our Arab saying sticks too deeply in my mind: "All the oceans of the world are not enough to wash away my blood relations."

The brother and sister had barely moved into the area when a great friendship emerged between Barghash and Chole, and the former soon spent whole days at our place. Meje in turn felt neglected, and as she started expressing her resentment to others, a major rift developed with Chole. It got to the point that they would not even greet each other when they crossed paths. Relations continued to go downhill, and the peace in our formerly tranquil homes began to disappear forever. I was glad to have no part in the new fracture between Chole and Meje. But the two deathly enraged sisters always poured their hearts out to me in their rancor to each other, so I also got drawn in.

Sultan Barghash bin Said

Chole was in the wrong with respect to Meje. In general, she was hardly recognizable during this terrible time. Barghash was her idol, for whom she recklessly gave up everything, and I, who paid as much homage to her, followed her again and again in all she did. Privately, I truly regretted the deeply distressed Meje, who, despite her proud nature, had so much insight and measured understanding that one had to sympathize with her. She alone among us saw clearly that no good could come from these anti-Madjid partisan activities, and she constantly warned us: "You will see! You will see!"

My friendship with my two nieces, Shembua and Farshu, soon carried over to Barghash, and they joined our band. They also lived across from us, and only a small alley separated their quarters from those of Barghash. Our three houses thus constituted a very dangerous focal point for a plot.

Barghash now worked especially hard to recruit a number of chieftains and other high-ranking individuals to his side. Arabs subdivide into countless larger and smaller tribes, each with its own leader, whom they strictly obey. Every prince, therefore, has a great interest in maintaining a close friendship with one or more of such chiefs, openly or preferably in secret, to be assured of their support when the time comes. Of course, promises of influential positions and other advantages play a major role in this arena. No tribe would ever fail to support its leader, given the strong feelings of affiliation and solidarity. How far this goes is best demonstrated by the fact that anyone who has learned to write invariably adds the tribe's name to their own name. We, for example, belong to the *Lebu Saidi*, a small but courageous tribe, and my full signature must always include that reference.

Barghash entered into closer relations with these chieftains and eventually pulled together a small court, which prompted much talk on our island. The greatest scandal arose from the fact that these people, who came and went day and night, were mostly of ill-repute, quarrelsome, and looking for trouble, the kind from whom he should have decidedly kept his distance. But of course, it had to be this way. Well-disposed, law-abiding individuals simply would not have subscribed to his overthrow plans.

The more Barghash added dubious elements to his engagements, and the more his subversive plot became apparent, the more those who cared about the well-being of our family and were not enamored of adventure pulled back. Stepping into their place were the kinds of people of whom Zanzibar, indeed the world, has its share: jealous individuals that have been jilted and self-important individuals that have been slighted, who would do anything to quench their thirst for revenge against their perceived mistreatments. Dozens of these malcontents could already picture themselves as Barghash's ministers or in other higher posts. Hundreds surely counted on property and honor beyond anything they previously could have imagined. Such creatures came from far and wide to join the conspiracy, to serve Barghash, yes, but really to serve themselves. It was obvious that even the most deplorable among them would be embraced with open arms.

As the number of Barghash's adherents rapidly grew, detailed plans for the uprising became more concrete. The plan envisioned taking Madjid unawares and immediately proclaiming Barghash as Sultan. But we also had to consider the real possibility of an open fight. Meeting upon meeting was held to win over this or that additional chieftain, always in the dead of night, sometimes at eight, sometimes at four, depending on when the moon came and went, and Barghash personally presided over them all. How often we cursed the bright light of the moon that kept us from convening, while we sought to stay completely under wraps. Feverish excitement and the deepest mistrust took hold of us all. We constantly suspected being observed and overheard, and often did the work of our servants just to keep them distant and from divining our evil deeds. Among the ladies, we stopped all our visits to others and very rarely received any guests.

Barghash was increasingly on edge. Having previously participated regularly in the formal audiences under Madjid's leadership just like all the other princes, Barghash started to neglect them, showing up only once or twice a week and ultimately missing them altogether. By our standards, that signals great discontent, and such ostentatious insubordination is simply punished. Now no one could doubt Barghash's hostile plans any longer, although many had not wanted to believe them. And Barghash himself acted very unwisely in the heat of things. He tipped off his adversaries, and it became hard to see how a surprise attack could possibly succeed.

Madjid tried once more, in private, to pull me back from my misguided ways before it was too late. As he was no longer able to come to Bet il Tani under the prevailing conditions, and I similarly had avoided his house for a long time, he asked an especially beloved stepmother of mine to seek me out and convey his request that I please separate myself from the partisan activities of his enemies and not simply allow them to tow me along; I could never expect any thanks from that side or be spared the remorse of having remained loyal to this evil affair. And I would also have to accept the consequences of my actions. If it came to bombardment of my neighbor's house, he would no longer be able to make an exception for me.

My venerable brother's warning came too late. I had already pledged my word to Chole and Barghash and now considered it my sacred duty to follow through on my promise. My stepmother left me deeply distressed and crying bitter tears. She had meant so well! Later she had the sad satisfaction of reminding me of Madjid's prediction, which proved so very correct.

So as not to stir any distrust, nor incur the ugly label of "mother of two faces" for perceived double dealings, I decided to strictly avoid any connection to Madjid and his associates and instead devoted myself entirely to the conspiracy.

At this point, with such increasingly compelling suspicions, Madjid could still have easily detained this errant brother and his followers, sticking them in a fortress and locking them up long enough to return to their senses. But such decisiveness was beyond him; he was not a forceful man by nature. To the last, he continued to hope for a voluntary reversal on the part of his brother and hesitated to go after him prematurely. Indeed, nothing had yet happened between him and Barghash to justify such hostility. Above all, he hoped at all costs to spare us four women, who were so deeply enmeshed in the affair.

Madjid's forbearance lasted a long time. Only when whole throngs of figures completely covered in their *barnus* converged at Barghash's door did the government consider it advisable to monitor our three houses. But this step offered only limited success, since the guards were all Baluchi soldiers recruited from Baluchistan, who in their touching devotion to our dynasty would rather have put themselves at risk than allow any of us family members to be compromised. My skilled and savvy siblings soon figured this out and used it to their advantage. The more dangerous operations were always carried out by us directly, heedless of our customs. No one dared bother us, even as others were trailed and investigated every step of the way. Now and again some careless participant would be arrested, but that did no real harm to our party.

Our houses were like an ant colony. No one sat around, everyone worked hard to make our project a success. Our spies brought news that the government had finally decided to bring our conduct to an end, either to lock up all the suspects or expel them from the island. Our preparations were far from complete when this news came, so we had to work twice as hard. We baked great quantities of a kind of long-duration cake and brought them under cover of night to Marseille, our nieces' plantation, which was the chosen base for the insurrection.

I, the youngest female member of the conspiracy, became what was effectively the general secretary of the alliance because I was able to write and thus expected to handle all correspondence with the chieftains. To be sure, I was old enough to be tormented by bitter pangs of conscience. That the bullets, the powder, the guns I had to order were destined to kill totally innocent people weighed heavily on my soul. What should I do? Break my word and abandon my beloved sister, now of all times, with danger increasing every day? Never! I would sooner have walked through fire for her. My closeness to Chole bound me tightly to the conspiracy, far more than any devotion to my brother Barghash.

Barghash, the son of an Abyssinian, was extraordinarily gifted and exceeded us with his far superior insights and clever calculations. Proud and regal in his manner, he knew how to impress everyone. But what little love he had won was evidenced by the fact that no one in our sizeable family took his side, except us four women and one brother, twelve-year-old Abd il Aziz, and then only because he was Chole's foster child. Ever since Barghash had buried our father's corpse in secret, bereft of all ceremony, no one wanted anything to do with him. As he took the final steps to organize his coup, people all drew back from him. I recall one evening when I ran into two of my sisters on one of my rare outings, how they walked with me until about five hundred steps from my house and then hastily turned back, so as not to get near Barghash's house.

Even under extremely strict oversight, we kept up our zealous efforts. Meetings were still held despite very challenging circumstances. The date for the overthrow was set when, suddenly, several hundred soldiers surrounded Barghash's house. The soldiers had astutely waited for a time when Barghash was sure to be home. They had orders to cut off complete contact with the outside world until all the residents surrendered peacefully. Our shock was indescribable, but soon prompted a redoubling of our efforts.

Of course, we awaited the same fate for our house, and then the whole cause would have been lost. As we later learned, the ministers and other dignitaries had indeed argued in favor of simultaneously blocking all three dangerous houses. But Madjid could not be persuaded, as he wanted to spare us women from any consequences.

Within minutes of the soldiers' deployment, the six of us conspirators, two in each house, stood at our windows and consulted across the small alley about what to do. We were in a frenzied state, and Barghash refused any talk of submission or surrender.

My Mother's Death; a Palace Revolution

But our plight was severe. Virtually no house in Zanzibar has a private well, so that everyone, regardless of rank, gets their water from public wells. As a precaution over the past few days, some water had been put in reserve in Barghash's house, but with the heat, this water was no longer potable and could at most be used for washing and cooking. There was plenty of food, enough to last the besieged for several weeks, but it was water they lacked, the one thing needed most in the tropics. Under the circumstances, there was no chance of lasting more than a few days.

While the men were at a loss and devolved into talk, one woman with an inventive bent devised a fortunate solution that saved them from quick defeat. She suggested sewing a hose out of sailcloth to run water from our roof over to Barghash's roof. Someone got the cloth, several dozen hands sewed a hose in half an hour, and by the time it got dark, the captives were enjoying a deliciously cooling drink. Of course, we had to be extremely careful to avoid detection. Fortunately, the guards focused on Barghash's one seaside door, perhaps they even *preferred* not to see our rescue efforts.

With the women having already helped substantially, very substantially, it was now also up to us to keep everything going. Only our intermediation through the window enabled Barghash to maintain contact with his party. Some of the leaders were locked up with him and found themselves in a very tough position. With my sister Meje in the house, they had very limited ability to move around and were basically stuck in the gathering room on the ground floor. But the influential, hard-charging leader of the *Hurt* tribe was still free and able to recruit the soldiers.

Our whole plan had to be revised. It was decided to gather all party members at Marseille, my nieces' beautiful estate, and entrench them there. The idea was not bad. Marseille rather resembled a small fortress and could comfortably hold several hundred men. To serve as a base from which to roil the whole island, we had the arsenal and ammunition brought there and the assembled troops quartered in the area. With everyone pitching in, everything fell into place very quickly. There was no general battle kitty, but we took turns contributing what we could from our private pockets, in addition to each contributing a number of well-armed slaves.

Once we had secretly gotten everything over to Marseille, we started to consider a major maneuver. The plan was nothing less than having us women free Barghash from his house to return his leadership to the conspiracy and have him personally direct everything from Marseille. That we were undertaking a very dangerous venture was clear, but danger was no deterrent. We were determined to take the risk.

Up to this point, we had made no effort to visit our captive siblings. We had wished to avoid any spectacle that could have harmed our venture, and we feared a blow to our pride in being rebuffed by the guards. But well begun is half won! We no longer had any second thoughts and instead resolved to proceed with the removal that evening, the only way to save ourselves.

After darkness had descended on this weighty day, Chole and I left our house with a large, handpicked entourage to meet up with our nieces' retinue that had set out at the same time, and together we walked to Barghash's door. Our vanguard was held up at the sentry, without the soldiers really knowing who was in the procession. Fearless action was the only way our expedition could succeed. "Chole," I said, "let the two of us advance to the top guard and reveal ourselves, they will certainly respect us."

This suggestion transgressed all customs and norms, but in so dangerous a situation, we could not afford to be caught up in the usual concerns. Were we not already on the cusp of achieving extraordinary things? Was the whole conspiracy not already crossing all boundaries? We forgot everything in our passion.

Chole and I stepped out of the procession, walked up to the unsuspecting officers, and started to berate them forcefully. It is easy to picture their astonishment. They could never have imagined such an ambush. For quite some time, these poor men were at a loss for words, but after somewhat collecting themselves, they gave us such profuse apologies that I felt deeply ashamed in the knowledge of our bad intentions. Not a single guard could have thought us capable of such a plan, and we presented ourselves so indignantly that no hesitation betrayed us.

We had achieved our goal. We were even given an allotted time to visit our captured siblings. After entering so successfully, we hoped to exit just as successfully, together with our brother.

We found Meje and Barghash in an understandable uproar. They had watched our whole scene with the guards from above, all the while growing increasingly anxious and uneasy that we would be turned back and leave them to their fate. And now Barghash was causing new trouble. In a fit of machismo, he refused to hide under the coverings of some female attire. But we had to hurry. We could not know if the sentry had notified our visit and sought instructions on how to proceed. And the way Barghash now stood before us, no one was going to let him out of the house. The guards had strict instructions to shoot down any suspicious person on the spot, a clear indication that they could not have dreamt of our audacity, or they would have handled our situation quite differently. It felt like we were standing on a crater that was liable to crack open at any moment and swallow us whole.

Barghash finally let us dress him in a *shele*, after loading himself to the teeth with weapons, so that only his eyes were free, and Abd il Aziz was disguised the same way. Only these two brothers were to leave the palace with us. We selected the tallest women in our group to walk right beside us and shield Barghash. Before setting out, we all thought again of the Almighty and said a quiet prayer that could well have been our last.

So as not to raise any suspicion, we again had to practice the art of deceit and, despite all our excitement and racing heartbeats, had to move slowly and evenly, while appearing to chat nonchalantly. Too quick a step and that would have betrayed us. But lo and behold! The guards respectfully let us pass, allowing us to proceed undetected with our prize. Anyone who has ever found themselves in such an anxiety-ridden situation will surely understand that I will never forget this evening as long as I live, not even the smallest detail.

We had previously informed a few chieftains in writing of our plans and agreed that they should gather with their followers at a certain hour outside the city. If we did not arrive within the agreed time, that would mean our mission had failed, and they should disperse to await further news. The meeting place lay far outside the city, deep in the greenery.

After passing through the populated part of the city at our customary pace, we began to run in order to reach the gathering in time. Like a fleeing column, we raced across the field with our normally dainty feet, rushing over sticks and stones, not caring a wit for our beautiful, gold-embroidered slippers. Our servants' quiet, whispered warnings to please run more carefully, we were entering a field of thorns, fell on deaf ears. And meanwhile the night all around was dark, and we had had our lanterns extinguished as soon as we had left the city.

Dripping with sweat and completely out of breath, we finally got word from our front runner that the gathering was up ahead. This was our cue as women to act more reserved. We moved more slowly and soon heard quiet coughing and throat clearing, marks of nearby sentinels, but could not make out any individual forms in the dark of night. A muted voice inquired carefully: "Your

Highness, is that you?" and the affirmative answer evoked a broad, hushed: "Praised be the Lord!" We had made it.

Barghash, who had shown great agitation but barely spoke a word on the way, now hastily threw off his covering, called out a clipped farewell, grabbed the twelve-year-old Abd il Aziz by the hand, and immediately disappeared from view. He still had to reach Marseille by foot before the night's end.

For some time, we stood there exhausted and speechless, peering in vain at fleeting profiles vanished in the night. Meanwhile, the late-night hour pressed us to return home, and so we walked noiselessly, with trepidation, the long way back. To avoid any kind of scene, we split up as we neared the silent city and headed in small groups by detours to our homes.

Back at last, we felt utter exhaustion. We were in a pitiful state. The intense excitement of the day and the highly unusual, certainly for Arab women, long and fast march were not without consequence. There was no chance of getting any sleep, nor any sort of peace this night. Everyone was moaning and groaning. Some fainted, others convulsed into fits of crying, first here, then there. It was no surprise that the group was coming undone. The experiences of the past hours had been too much and taken too great a toll on our strength. Twice we had had to pass through rows of soldiers bearing sharply loaded guns and brandished bayonets. The slightest misstep would have sufficed to bring us down. No one could have known upfront that the rescue would be such a success, and setting out, we had had to anticipate either outcome: a completed mission or death.

Throughout the rest of the night, we fearfully registered every little noise. Weighed down by our consciences, we kept hearing horse hooves or gun shots. At any moment, we expected our enemies to close in and dole out our well-deserved punishments after discovering our role.

And yet, to our considerable astonishment, all stayed still. Looking down from above, we could see the guards the same as before, calmly pacing back and forth in front of the house where Barghash had been hostage only a few hours earlier. Finally, dawn was starting to show, and as usual, the slaves signaled the time for prayer. Normally, Chole and I prayed separately. Today, when it was as yet unclear what lay ahead, we found ourselves in the same room praying to the Highest together. And then we raised the joyful hope that at this time, about five in the morning, Barghash and his followers would have reached Marseille.

My Mother's Death; a Palace Revolution

Soon, however, we received shocking news. Around seven o'clock, we found out that our opponents knew exactly what had transpired the night before. As we had walked directly past the guards the previous evening, a Baluchi had recognized Barghash, despite his coverings. The guard chose not to sound an immediate alarm out of devotion to our late father, whom he had long and loyally served, thinking Barghash would use his freedom only to flee the country. And the guard could not bear the thought of openly compromising us women.

When the early shift of market vendors described seeing many Arabs hurrying to the area around Marseille, suspicions arose that this had to do with the conspiracy; but only this Baluchi knew what had really transpired. At this point, he realized his duty lay in sharing his discovery with the regime, rather than keeping it to himself. At the hearing, he excused himself solely by saying he would rather have given his life than put us women in a compromised position. I never found out what became of this noble man, whom we had thrown into such a deep conflict of conscience with our escapade.

The government had no choice now but to put an end to this open rebellion with open violence. Several thousand soldiers were sent to Marseille with cannons. Our partisan friends had counted on a successful overthrow and limited battle. An open fight was beyond their means. The cannon balls shattered the once charming palace of Marseille and overwhelmed the rebels, who, after putting up a brief and dogged fight, then scattered to the wind, but not without the loss of hundreds of innocent lives. —

The reader will surely wonder what happened to us women as a result of our crucial role in the insurrection, what punishment was imposed upon us. We got none! Clearly, had not the noble Madjid been at the helm, we never would have come away so easily. Our engagement had certainly deserved the strongest retribution.

We had not yet heard the outcome of the battle when we were surprised to learn one morning that Barghash, whom we assumed to be in Marseille, had arrived in his house the night before, a totally defeated fugitive. Meje filled us in on all that had happened, while Barghash, who hoped to remain undiscovered, kept away from the window. Even then, he insisted on resisting to the end, with nary a thought to surrender.

Beyond Barghash and little Abd il Aziz, who despite his youth had proved absolutely unflappable with no hint of fright or fear, a number of dignitaries and many servants had dribbled in, making the house, primarily the downstairs rooms, overcrowded once again. Barghash still hoped to implement his plan using these forces, although he had already failed once before with much more support. We, too, despite having lost so much of our assets, sacrificed such a great number of recruited soldiers and slaves on the battlefield, and forfeited the sympathies of all our siblings and relatives, we had not yet come to our senses. We were far too blinded by our passion to have registered the wretched shipwreck.

That same day, word spread throughout the entire city about Barghash's return. Everyone assumed he had come only to give himself up to his brother. Madjid himself wanted to make the surrender easy for him. Instead of soldiers, he sent his nephew, Suud bin Hilal, with the message that he was prepared to forget the past if Barghash would agree to renounce his plans forever. Suud, an extraordinarily mild and benevolent man, was to undertake this mission alone, as a sign of his peaceful intent.

At first, Barghash would not allow his significantly older nephew into the house, and instead insisted that he announce his affair from the street. Naturally, Suud firmly refused to do so. After a long wait, the front door was finally opened just enough to ensure that no one else could slip in, and he was then allowed, in the truest sense of the word, to climb the heavily barricaded stairs. Measures had been taken everywhere to make an easy target of any intruder. The top of the stairs had also been closed off with a massive, sturdy trapdoor, a mechanism that dated back to the days of our stepmother Shesade, and which had been loaded up with additional heavy chests. Madjid's envoy thus encountered a rather humiliating entry, and no less mortifying was the outcome of his mission. He left again without having accomplished anything after Barghash categorically refused to make any kind of concession.

In the face of such stubbornness, Madjid again had no option but to resort to violence, despite his great reluctance. The English Consul, with whom he consulted, finally persuaded him of the need to bring an end to the enduring offense and offered his assistance. An English cannon ship, which happened to be in the harbor and whose shallower draft was better suited than our large warships, was to anchor directly in front of Barghash's house and set up a boat blockade with its dispersed marines. If even this demonstration failed to impress, the enemy palace and all its inhabitants were to be bombarded to bits.

One morning I left my room, which faced the narrow street without an ocean view, and headed to Chole, to show the usual respect befitting an older sister and wish her a good morning. I found her visibly distressed, wringing her hands and striding back and forth in her room. "Salme, oh my dear, where have you been all this time?" she wailed, pointing to the ship and English soldiers and explaining in broken sentences what had happened.

My reproof that it never would have come to this if she and Barghash had brought things to a timely end was met with the old song that I showed so little interest in the cause. But my God, what more was I to do? Had I not compromised myself just as much as she and the others? Had I not sacrificed everything without hesitation? Had I ever spared myself whenever it mattered to serve the alliance? All of this seemed forgotten now, simply because I had called things as they were. We are never so deeply and painfully wounded by an undeserved reproach as when it comes from those we love the most and to whom we have given our whole soul!

Soon the marine soldiers started shooting at Barghash's house, at first only with guns. Several bullets broke through the windows, and one whizzed right past my brother before flattening into the massive wall behind him. The seriousness of the situation was now clear; these were no empty threats. Barghash, Meje, and Abd il Aziz, along with the other occupants, had to flee to the back of the house or face being struck by whistling bullets flying everywhere.

At the first shot, Chole broke down in wrenching tears, cursed all of Madjid, the government, and the English in a jumble of accusations, and decried them for their injustices towards us! As the shooting increased, our own house went into a panic. We lived directly behind Barghash's palace and were also at great risk. Everyone, high and low, young and old, ran aimlessly around. Here some were saying good-bye forever; there they were asking mutual forgiveness for injustices committed during happier days gone by; the steelier ones grabbed their valuables to bring them along when fleeing; others clung together crying and deploring, unable to think or act; many prayed as and where they were, in the corridors, on the stairs, in the courtyard, on the palisade-protected roof. More of us began to follow their example, so that in place of the intensive agitation a wonderfully calming awareness set in, that it is the will of God, not man, that comes to pass, that our fate is decided since the dawn of time by the All-Merciful and Almighty. Everyone had now dropped to their knees in prayer and was touching their foreheads to the ground, to show their deepest humility toward the Lord. Some in enlightened Europe may call this fanaticism, or whatever the label, but such faith certainly brings unfathomable peace to its adherents, saving them from despair in times of need, and letting the most impassable paths of our lives appear less fraught than they really are.

All the hundreds that so fervently turned to the Lord after the first shock could just as easily have fled. Our front door stood wide open, and everyone could have secured their safety. Under the circumstances, not a soul would have held it against us if we had sought refuge in broad daylight in Bet il Sahel. But no one even gave it a thought.

In the face of such danger, Chole finally got her stubborn brother to offer up his surrender. Against all rules of etiquette, she herself ran to the English consulate to relay the message and ask for hostilities to cease. One might ask, why did she not go to Madjid to arrange everything? And that was the question a great majority of Zanzibari residents also asked themselves. They could not believe that Barghash's and Chole's hatred for Madjid was so bitter that they refused to meet him under any circumstances. The two probably also felt too ashamed. It was still better to take on the humiliation (indeed a great humiliation in the eyes of all true Arabs) of turning to a foreigner for help and intervention. Back then, the English were still far from the great power in eastern Africa that they are today. They had as little place to meddle in Zanzibari domestic affairs as, say, the Turks in the German Republic. Not until 1875, thanks to English slavery politics, did relations change significantly to their benefit—and the gradual ruin of our people.

Chole did not encounter the English Consul. However, since calls of *amn! amn!* (peace, peace!) were also being shouted from Barghash's house to the soldiers, they immediately stopped firing, and doom was averted just in time. For if the cannon ship had in fact started its bombardment, then Barghash would have never become Madjid's successor, and instead, he with us women would have become victims of our reckless enterprise. By the same token, we all surely would have emerged less intact if a man less noble than Madjid had had our prospects in his hands.

To preclude the return of any such insurrection, it was decided to send Barghash to British East India, namely, to banish him to Bombay. This followed the advice of the English Consul. The English probably sought to keep him under their control, as the lawful successor to Madjid, to groom him in their interest for their later intentions. That evening we gathered at the home of Barghash and Meje to bid farewell to the departing brothers (for Abd il Aziz had volunteered to join Barghash's exile). Already the next morning they received orders to board ship. An English warship brought them to Bombay. Barghash lived there for two years, then returned peacefully to Zanzibar, and finally, in the year 1870 following Madjid's death, succeeded him to the long-coveted throne.

My Mother's Death; a Palace Revolution

Thus ended our enterprise, having begun with such high hopes. It came at a great cost to us, especially my two nieces, although they were wealthy enough to readily absorb the loss. Many of our best slaves had fallen, and others reminded us daily as disfigured invalids of the catastrophe we had created. But that was not all to come of our terrible adventure. Chole, Meje, our nieces, and I took a much heavier toll from the way all our law-abiding siblings and relatives demonstratively shunned and ignored us. I, in my heart of hearts, knew there was no begrudging their accusations.

And yet, Madjid remained a most benevolent brother all throughout. He was often criticized for letting us off so easily, since everyone knew that without our collaboration Barghash would have landed in jail long ago, and many consequences, yes, including the bloody, public fight, could have been avoided. He always responded that, yes indeed, it was all true, but that he could not bring himself to see us women punished, or even degraded, thereby showing such mercy and generosity that we did not deserve, even as some around us pegged this as weakness. To me, of course, it was incomprehensible how someone could call it weakness when a brother and uncle shows exemplary mildness to his sisters and nieces and forgives them to prevent further humiliation. Nevertheless, with all the vilifying against us, we stuck to our stance that all we had done had been right and proper. Our pride kept our heads from sinking lower; but only to the outside. On the inside, we suffered that much more.

Many people who wished us ill, or hoped to use denunciations against us to gain advantage with the government, went to great lengths to keep us in their sights. But we had nothing to fear. Our venture had failed so thoroughly that there was no rebuilding even if we had wanted. Nonetheless, the spying hurt us by dissuading any loyal friends we might have had left from engaging with us in public. Even the greedy Banyans kept their distance from us for a long time, only gradually daring under cover of darkness to slink their way back to us again to peddle their Indian treasures with their usual unscrupulousness. Our houses, which were previously like pigeon lofts and always full of guests, now stood desolate, abandoned by the outside world.

This ultimately became unbearable for me. Why stay in the city, where I encountered only hate and hostility? The litany of complaints I had to endure all day long could not improve my quality of life. And so, I finally decided to move, for an extended time, to one of my plantations.

Natives picking Cloves, Zanzibar

Zanzibar, Cloves plantation

CHAPTER TWENTY-SEVEN

Kizimbani and Bububu

Only days later, the rising sun saw me hurrying out on my little white donkey towards my plantation Kizimbani. Here I hoped to tide over the next period in peace, until the intense waves of hate and hostility toned down. Not long after, Chole, Meje, and my two nieces followed my example of forgoing the city and also retreated to the countryside.

After the death of my mother, I had seldom visited my three plantations, and then at most for one or two days. Now I appreciated the quiet country life all the more, after the restless churn of the city, compounded by my inner churn from our discord. My mother had loved to spend time in Kizimbani, and I found traces of her everywhere. I took pleasure in revisiting all the places she had gone to walk or rest. Everything reminded me of her watchful care, after she had been torn from me so early in life. All that she had handled so deftly was now mine, including all the business challenges that single Oriental women are condemned to bear in a society that excludes them from the world of men.

Under the tyranny of our customs, women are not even allowed to speak directly to our regular officials when they are free men. Orders and accounts with them must be arranged through our slaves, as virtually no high-ranking women know how to write. There are plenty of single women who have never in their lives received a written statement of accounts from their managers. If these managers fund only what the household needs and then hand over however many thousands of Maria Theresa thalers from the sale of the annual harvest, that is enough to take full care of these women. Cloves and coconuts bring in the large sums. We are too proud to sell the potatoes, yams, and other produce that come from the soil, but just use them for the household and leave the rest for the manager's own use. That explains why these individuals, who mostly come from Oman as very poor immigrants, are able to return home after but a few years with respectable gains.

During my time in the city, my Kizimbani manager, Hassun, would come to my house every week or two to report on the land and receive my instructions, all as conveyed through my slaves. Single women always set up separate rooms on the ground floor of their homes, so that their male visitors can get some rest after their long rides, with a chance to eat and drink, before heading homewards on their donkeys.

Now that I was planning a longer stay in Kizimbani, the good Hassun became a challenge. The poor man no longer knew what to do. At every moment he was having to slip in here or rush out there, just to make sure that he, as a free man, did not intentionally see us women. I therefore decided to send him to a different plantation, which had also been under his charge, and gave his original position to an Abyssinian slave named Murdjan (coral), who was very educated for his status in that he could read and write. He was also full of energy, an essential quality for someone charged with the oversight and management of several hundred plantation slaves. Abyssinians are generally very capable, and we always preferred to purchase them, instead of Africans.

Now I could walk and ride about to my heart's delight, without coming across poor Hassun bin Ali at every step. My ever-increasing number of pets gave me much joy, and I spent several hours a day tending to them. I also found great pleasure in seeking out old and sick people in their small, low-build huts and sharing the overflow from my kitchen with them through my servants. I had all the young slave children—a kind of "dividend" for their masters—come to me every morning to be washed at the draw well, using dried leaves from the Asian *rassel* tree that foam up like soap when dropped into water, and then made sure they were amply fed. These children would stay in a part of the courtyard and play under the watchful eye of a female slave until their parents returned from the fields around four in the afternoon. This way the little squirmers were in much better shape than if they had had to spend the whole day tied to the backs of their mothers in the blazing sun.

This free and unconstrained life in the countryside suited me tremendously, and my whole soul was elated to have escaped the commotions of the city for this comfort. Mothers and daughters of high-ranking families within a two-mile radius called upon me to welcome my arrival, as was proper, and soon guests were coming to the house for weeks, indeed, months.

Even complete strangers would stop by during their excursions to rest and relax in my men's room. This is completely in keeping with custom. Kizimbani lies at the intersection of two lively thoroughfares, which meant we got many such visitors.

My closest plantation neighbors were two of my sisters and a nephew. The latter was the good Fesal, Hilal's son, who, as noted, had been orphaned early on and was very kindhearted, but widely misjudged. In me, he found someone that, for the first time, understood him. He latched onto me with almost childish trust and rode over to me daily.

I similarly kept up with the city. Two alternating messengers had to set out daily, leaving early in the morning and returning with all the news in the evening. I also sent my chamber maid to my siblings and friends two or three times a week to be informed of what there was to know. And the reverse, messengers arrived daily from various others who wanted to check in on me.

This way I remained in constant contact with the city, and it was my great joy to receive only harmless visits and be rid of those evil spies.

The outrage caused by our so pathetically conducted plot eventually calmed down, but the hate and disharmony among the siblings remained. It was just one more reason to resist thoughts of returning to the city any time soon. Even a short visit was best avoided, despite needing only two or so hours to get there. On the other hand, the siblings that stuck by me came to see me quite often.

And so I was happy and content, except for one thing: I missed the sublime sea, the view of which had greeted me every day, with only very short interruptions, for as long as I had lived. All three of my plantations were in the interior of the island, but I was not used to having any unfulfilled desires, and I was still resolved to stay away from the city, so I decided to acquire a waterfront plantation. And yet, to my chagrin, that proved quite difficult, since all the desirable locations were already owned by others who had purchased with the same consideration, more for pleasure than profit. The *dellal* (broker) whom I entrusted through my slaves to undertake the search swore up and down that he would not rest until he had found a suitable plantation, but in the end had to concede that not a single one was for sale.

He had just come to Kizimbani and conveyed this unpleasant news through one of the servants when a friend stopped in for a visit and told me of a country estate that belonged to one of her cousins, complete with a lovely villa and directly by the sea. This cousin lived permanently in the city, hardly ever used the property, and might allow me to purchase or rent.

For some, my dilemma will appear incomprehensible, as most people in Germany seem to believe the whole country is the personal property of the Sultan and his family and that his subjects have neither rights nor ownership. It is presumed that if we want something, we can simply take it, without needing consent of the affected owner. But conditions in Zanzibar were not that primitive in my time. Private property was just as untouchable as here. The best example is how hard it was for me to get what I wanted, even though I was offering good money. Regrettably, however, during my recent visit to Zanzibar, I learned that the legal situation has changed considerably of late. Among other things, I was told that the English Consul's estate was a present from the Sultan, who is said to have taken it from the prior owner without any compensation.

The next morning, we rode early to Bububu, the name of the estate, to take an initial look. We found the house locked, and it was a long time before someone finally let us in. The overall estate gave the impression that no one had spent much money or effort on it, as opposed to relying only on nature's care. The villa was large, massively built, and stood on its own, connected on only one side to a spacious courtyard with a kitchen and servants' quarters off in a corner. Streaming through the courtyard was a creek, such a priceless advantage in our climate, which reminded me vividly of the beloved Mtoni. The most enchanting feature, however, was the lovely view from the second floor of the house. Countless large and small palm trees flanked the sides, and there, straight ahead, lay the wide-open sea, sending waves that frequently sprayed the walls of the villa.

I decided on the spot that I would either buy or rent Bububu. The next morning, my friend rushed back to the city to tell her cousin. After a few days, she let me know that he was not willing to sell the estate, but had gladly offered to let me live in his villa. I, of course, did not accept this offer, but instead managed after long negotiations to enter into a rental arrangement for a fixed annual sum of Maria Theresa thalers.

About a week later, after the contract was signed—for this, too, is not unknown in Zanzibar—I moved to Bububu, where I could once again behold the splendid sea, my special love my whole life long, directly in front of me.

My joy was dampened only by the farewell to my nephew Fesal. He took our separation very much to heart and complained that he would now have no one other than his aged stepmother to whom he could speak freely and openly.

All my spoiled pets had to come along. They were rather surprised to have been driven off, or packed into cages and baskets, only to re-encounter each other in a completely different courtyard in Bububu. But apparently, they were as pleased with the change as I was. They drank with delight from the creek or, in the case of the parrots, ducks, and doves, cheerfully walked right in. Meanwhile, I happily sat and watched, or ambled along the beautiful beach and observed the various ships that had to pass this way, traveling from north to south towards the city, as well as the many small fishing boats that sped past with their singing crews. Often the sea looked just like a lively street.

I had now also moved much closer to the city and could reach it easily by both land and sea. Three of my brothers, Abd il Wehab (servant of the Lord), Hamdan, and Djemshid, took great pleasure in giving me surprise visits almost every day, traveling by either horse or boat, whatever happened to be most convenient. They were just a bit older than me and always funny and merry. Our favorite pastime was to head to the beach, where we talked, ate, drank, played cards, or burned off whole baskets of fireworks, all in harmless happiness and high spirits. In the evening, when Djemshid, with his "cat eyes," rode off alone in his boat, he saluted us for a good distance with many *fetak* (fireworks). We returned his farewell gesture no less lavishly.

I had much more of a social life here than in Kizimbani. No day passed without my hosting at least one or two, and often up to ten, ladies, some of them stopping over in Bububu to rest for a few hours on their way to another destination, some staying with me for one or more days. It was a totally cheerful and carefree time.

When I think back to those lovely days of my youth, a time when I knew only the good and wonderful sides of the world, as yet unaware of the many thorns that would later threaten to block my life at every pass, I get a heavy heart. In my hours of sorrow, however, it is these sacred memories of my youth, memories of parents and siblings, of my homeland, that give me renewed vigor again and again, and I bask myself in them almost daily. I acknowledge with thanks that the good hand of the Lord is everywhere, as he, in his infinite wisdom, measures out the good and bad fortunes and always gives at least some joy to comfort the unfortunate.

As it was, my time in Bububu ended soon after. One day around noon, I peered out onto the sea as usual through the large telescope on the second floor of the house, expecting to spot one of my brothers coming up from afar. Indeed, a single boat was soon headed toward us. Abd il Wehab came alone this time, and his face betrayed immediately that he was bringing an unpleasant message.

"Abd il Wehab, what's new, my brother?" I called as he came toward the house. "Oh sister, oh Salme," he answered, "I was sent to you today with a request that I do not like at all. But guess from whom!" On my insistence, he finally began: "You know that a new English Consul recently arrived." "What do I care about this Englishman? Is he the one who sent you here?" "No!" "Then answer, tell me everything, and do not torment me any longer." "But please, don't be upset with me, oh Salme." "No! No! Just be quick and tell me!" "I am coming on behalf of—Madjid, who is sincerely imploring you, if you still care about him, to give up Bububu. The new English Consul sent him the request yesterday, asking if he could have Bububu as his residence."

This request from Madjid hit me extraordinarily hard. Anyone else, I would have bluntly turned them down. But Madjid, against whose government and perhaps even against whose life I had so wantonly conspired, how could I leave him hanging? Until then, I had not sought a rapprochement and was even convinced that he had long ago forgotten the affair. But now that the offended and aggrieved person himself was making the request, I believed I could also unload a small portion of my heavy guilt by giving him what he asked. I shared this decision with Abd il Wehab.

Madjid had included the message that he knew I would not be inclined to return to Bet il Tani, and could instead arrange a suitable place for me in the city through Abd il Wehab. I was not ready to make a quick decision about this. I asked for time to reflect.

For possibly the first time in my life, I felt deep grief about something tangible. I had been so happy in Bububu that I could not have wished for anything else. Abd il Wehab left after having eaten, but not before once again emphatically discouraging me from returning to Kizimbani. And then I was left counting down a tearful farewell in my mind to all my favorite spots. I vacillated a long time about whether to really throw myself back into the clamor of the city. I had a dark premonition that new and inevitable misunderstandings awaited me there.

The next morning, I wrote to Abd il Wehab that I would vacate Bububu within the week and leave it entirely to Madjid's disposal. I arranged everything for my return to Kizimbani, my final decision. That same afternoon, the three dear brothers appeared and called to me as they walked in the door: "Salme, drop that Kizimbani idea! If you love us, then you have to come back to the city. "Or," added our jokester Djemshid, "if you decide to hide out on your plantation, then we will ambush you in the dead of night and set your house on fire!" They also conveyed the kind requests from their mothers (all three were Circassian) that I should please again make my home in the city. It was the last time all four of us were together in wonderful Bububu. When we separated, my brothers left in triumph, as I had promised to give up the move to Kizimbani.

The author's residence in Stone Town

CHAPTER TWENTY-EIGHT

My Last Stay in Zanzibar

A few days later, I found myself on the roof of my new city home that Abd il Wehab had arranged for me. It was a moonlit night around eight o'clock, as I chatted with an earlier acquaintance who was now my neighbor, when Selim came and announced a visit from Chole.

"Oh Salme, I expected better of you!" were the first words out of her mouth. "Good evening, Chole, how have I wronged you?" I asked in surprise, while leading her to the *tekje*, the seat of honor. "What? You really think you have not wronged me? Is it nothing that you relinquished Bububu to benefit Madjid and his godless *kafer* (Englishman)? "But dear sister," I replied, perhaps somewhat offended, "that is of course my own business, and moreover, I recently explained the matter to you in my letter." "Well, you apparently wanted to curry favor with the wretch (by whom she meant Madjid), isn't that true?" "No, you are completely wrong. I have no need to curry favor with anyone, you of all people know that well." "Yes, but then why did you gratify him this way?" she persisted more vehemently. "From what I heard, he is also to blame that you chose this house rather than Bet il Tani. Is that so?" "No, he was not responsible for that, it was Abd il Wehab, Hamdan, and Djemshid who urged me to come here." "Well, well, I see now that you are against us; so be it," she exclaimed as she rose to leave and waved off the refreshments offered by the servant. "From now on, you will have to choose between Barghash and me or the vassal of the English. Adieu!" And with that, she disappeared.

After that day, I never saw Chole again, even though we lived in one and the same city for several more years. Only after my departure did she start to become more conciliatory. Time and again, I asked myself if I had not in fact intended to offend her, but I always came to the reassuring conclusion that I never knowingly gave offense, that I had no purpose in leaving Bububu other than some slight relief to my guilty conscience. But this idea that I had wanted to ingratiate myself, what an absurd accusation! Chole was so overwrought that evening as she aired her grudge that she seemed absolutely incapable of any calm consideration.

Up to that point, I had not seen either Madjid or Chadudj again and was now even more determined to avoid them at all costs, so Chole's suspicions would not appear justified after all. And yet, that is not how it went. I had been in my new apartment barely two weeks when—Madjid himself, plus a large entourage, came to visit. "Good morning, Salme," he called to me, "you see, even though I am older than you, I am still coming to you first to express my thanks for not wanting to disgrace me to the Englishman." "Oh brother, that was nothing, nothing at all," I stammered, since no one was more surprised by the visit than I. Gentle and noble as always, Madjid made no mention of the past, not a word, but instead tried to alleviate my insurmountable embarrassment with all sorts of stories.

"Of course, you'll come soon to visit Chadudj?" "Yes, of course, I'll come," was my totally natural answer. "Our Aunt Aashe as well, who is so very fond of you, now lives with us and would be happy to see you again."

Madjid lingered for about an hour, and we had reconciled by the time he left. That very same day, news of the visit became general knowledge and was reported to Chole as well.

With the much older Madjid having come to visit me first, something I had thought impossible, I had no choice—even if I had been truly unforgiving towards him, this good soul—but to return the visit to him, Chadudj, and our Aunt Aashe, the father's only sister. That this simple act of reciprocity would come at such a steep price was something I could not have surmised at the time. Even to this day, this one step is held against me as the ultimate transgression, while my participation in the fateful alliance, and everything I accomplished and suffered for it, was completely discounted in no time. Though this jealousy might appear unseemly, I came to realize, too late, that it was built into our family relations at the time. As they would have it, I was not allowed to show any kindness to my brother, much less visit my brother, sister, and aunt, and even less have any close interactions with them, without immediately being forever spurned by these other siblings!

The two parties persisted, and the intrigues continued, although more as an undercurrent, less overtly than before. It was not uncommon for an unpleasant encounter at some location to cause the oncoming guests to immediately pull back or the guests already there to leave as quickly as possible, so as not to get caught under the same roof as the enemy. And meanwhile the hostess always found herself in a most uncomfortable position, having to maintain complete neutrality and refrain from any kind of interference. What use was there that I swore never again to be drawn into politics? The calamity had occurred and could never be undone. With everyone being so public in their attitudes, the enmity between the parties was that much harder to bear.

Orientals are by nature very candid and totally incapable of dissembling in certain situations, the way people so masterfully do here. There people make no secret of an avowed enemy and adversary and do not hesitate to heap on slights with cutting looks, gestures, and words. They simply have no sense for behaving other than how they really think and feel. The conventional courtesies, consistent with polite society, are just not in their repertoire. Indeed, efforts to dissemble, which rarely succeed with our hot-blooded natures anyhow, are considered cowardly. So often since that day did I hear these words: "Why should I not express myself the way I feel? Are not all my thoughts and feelings open and apparent to the Lord, my God? Why should I make any pretense toward these lowly children of the Lord or even be afraid?" —

To the delight of many, the engagements and weddings of two sisters to two cousins brought a happy distraction into our lives, and the eternal brawling and wrangling in our family circle seemed to die down for a few months. Even though the two sisters married two brothers, they drew entirely different lots, as so often happens in life. One ended up very happy, although she did not have any children; the other experienced joyful motherhood, but was not happy in the marriage. Who does not see in this a kind of compensating higher power that so wisely and mercifully cares for every individual?

Times were hard in Oman, and our family circle was augmented by a large number of immigrating relatives. That allowed me the renewed pleasure of experiencing the full comfort of being with family.

There is one friend, in particular, that remains unforgettable to me. I may not say her name or offer any details of our relationship and separation. But I can say that this friend was loyal to the end, even as I was on the cusp of leaving my homeland forever and at great risk. She knew all my household affairs, so I could not hide my plans from her. She stuck with me nonetheless, until I finally, in the last half hour before my departure, removed her with gentle force, for her own safety. "My honor," she said at the farewell, "may the Lord of this Universe protect you. I know I will have to give up my life within the next twelve hours, but for you, that is never too much!" Her words are still ringing in my ears at this very moment, and I can exclaim with complete conviction: "Blessed are those who can rely on good and true friends!"

Anyone who wants to experience a genuine and truly selfless friendship must go to the Orient. Not that this exists only in the Orient among Orientals, but it is a fact that Arabs, once they love someone, attach themselves with such tenacity and self-sacrifice that they necessarily lose sight of every other consideration. Even though the social classes are nowhere as pronounced as in the Orient, these status distinctions have no bearing on true friendships. A prince engages as dearly with a beloved son of a poor stable master as with another friend of noble lineage, without even a trace of difference between the two. And a princess gives herself in friendship to the wives and daughters of a simple plantation manager as much as to a higher-ranking Arab woman. My sister Meje, for example, had grown very close to just such a manager's daughter and eventually invited her to move into her palace. The two of them, this poor, modest, but very bright being and my sister, shared an extraordinarily intimate connection that only death could part.

It is not uncommon for a woman of status to forge a close friendship with a slave kept by someone else, naturally not with an African, but a Circassian or Abyssinian. That can prove especially fortunate for the slave, in that she may then be purchased for five or ten times the usual price or the slave may be gifted in order to be freed by her benefactress. This release is always legalized, so that no third party can ever harm the freed friend.

If someone is thrown into jail, his friend will ask to be locked up with him for several hours every day. If someone is sent into exile, his loyalists will follow wherever his steps take him. If someone has an accident or is impoverished, his faithful friends will rally with all their resources to his side, so there is never any need to resort to public charity and the collection lists. We grow up this way and learn these attitudes from our childhood onward, so this is all commonplace and just the way we are.

Rudolph Heinrich Ruete, the author's husband

CHAPTER TWENTY-NINE

Great Transformations

In this sad and dismal time, when disagreements and discord pervaded our family, I felt fortunate to receive the attentions of a young German, who was staying in Zanzibar as the representative of a Hamburg trading company and later became my husband.[23] There have been such frequent, public mischaracterizations of the ensuing events that were of such great consequence to me that I feel the need to provide a brief overview of what happened. Under the rule of my brother Madjid, Europeans enjoyed a very privileged status. They were welcome guests in his house and on his properties and always received the most attentive hospitality. Both my sister Chole and I were also on friendly terms with the Europeans in Zanzibar, which were manifested in various small gestures, as allowed by the customs of the land. European ladies that were present in Zanzibar usually visited only Chole and me.

I got to know my husband not long after my move from Bububu. My house stood directly next to his. The flat roof of his lay just below mine, and from a window on my top floor, I was often witness to merry gatherings of men, which he had arranged to introduce me to the art of European dining. Our friendship, which in time became a deep love, soon became known in the city, and the news also traveled to my brother Madjid. Despite all the rumors, I never experienced any animosity on his part, much less imprisonment because of this.

---

23 Rudolph Heinrich Ruete, born March 10, 1839, went by the name Heinrich. He arrived in Zanzibar in 1855 as an agent for the trading company Hansing & Co. out of Hamburg, Germany, later switching to Koll & Ruete as a partner and then his own Ruete & Co.

A union with my beloved would have been impossible in my homeland, so I naturally harbored the wish to leave the island quietly. A first attempt in this direction failed. Soon, however, a better opportunity presented itself. Through the assistance of Mrs. S., a befriended wife of the English doctor and consular representative at the time, the commander of the English warship *Highflyer*, a Mr. P., picked me up one night in a boat. Once I was on deck, the ship immediately released steam and headed north. We reached our destination, Aden, in good shape. Here I was taken in by a Spanish couple that I had gotten to know in Zanzibar, and then waited patiently while my fiancé wrapped up his affairs on the island over several months until he could join me.

My baptism took place in the English chapel in Aden, where I was given the name Emily in recognition of the English friend mentioned above. Immediately after that, our wedding took place according to English rituals. And when the ceremony was over, we started our travels through Marseille to Hamburg, my husband's hometown, where we received a loving reception from his parents and relatives.

I soon adjusted to this strange setting and eagerly learned everything I needed for my new life. My unforgettable husband followed the different steps of my development with lively interest. He took special delight in observing my first impressions of European life and customs of the civilized world. I have written up these impressions in reverent memory and may find a subsequent opportunity to report on them as well.[24]

Our happy, contented, and unburdened life together was not to last. Barely three years had passed since our arrival in Hamburg when my beloved husband had the misfortune to fall as he jumped off a horse tram and was run over. After three days of intense suffering, he took his last breath. I now stood alone in this great and strange world, with three small children, of which the youngest was but three months old. For a while I considered returning to my homeland, but as fate would have it, two months after this tragedy, my unforgettable brother Madjid, who had always been so good to me, passed away as well. When I left the island, he had not laid a finger on my fiancé, but instead let him settle his affairs in Zanzibar freely. He also never held my clandestine escape against me. As a devout Muslim, he believed in divine predestination and was convinced that this alone had led me to Germany. He gave me touching proof of his enduring

---

[24] This likely refers to what became the author's *Briefe nach der Heimat*, which was found posthumously among her possessions. An English version from the translator appears in *Letters to the Homeland: An Accurate Translation of An Intimate Voice*, a companion book to this book.

brotherly sentiments shortly before he died when he sent a steamship loaded with a range of gifts to me in Hamburg. The ship was still on the way when this generous benefactor suddenly passed away. The items he sent never made it to me. I did not even know about Madjid's gallant act until much later when I learned that his intentions had been thwarted, and I had been cheated. At the time, the rumor had been spread in Hamburg that the ship was docked at the port only for repairs. Nine years later I learned from a German friend, who had inspected Madjid's ship in Gibraltar and spoken with the captain, who was also German, that the ship had contained cargo destined for me! Notwithstanding the cover-up, the dark-skinned crew of this vessel was able to locate me in my house in Hamburg. The poor fellows were overjoyed when they succeeded, and they charmed me with their most endearing affection.

I lasted in Hamburg two more years, during which time misfortune continued to pursue me. I lost a significant portion of my assets through no fault of my own and was then forced to think about taking affairs into my own hands. The prospect of staying at the site of my earlier family joy had been thoroughly spoiled, especially after failing to receive as much courtesy in some circles of this maritime city as I might have expected.

I moved to Dresden, where I experienced the warmest welcome from all circles. From there, I took a trip to London, about which I will report in some detail in the next chapter. When I later found myself wishing for a calmer setting, I withdrew to idyllic Rudolstadt for several years. Here, too, I encountered much love and friendship from the local society, including especially from the local nobility. This place also let me readily restore my health, which opened the possibility of moving to Berlin, where my children could get a good education. Here, too, I found dear friends that sought to lighten my stay. Even the very highest nobility engaged with me most graciously, which I will forever recall with love.

Sultan Barghash and his entourage

CHAPTER THIRTY

Sayyid Barghash in London

All this time, I continued to correspond with my homeland and never gave up hope of seeing it again someday. The rigid attitude of my brother Barghash had, however, made any such rapprochement impossible. His intransigence, as it were, has nothing to do with religious fanaticism, but instead came from his obstinate and hateful resentment. He simply could not forgive me for resuming friendly relations with his former enemy Madjid! The longing for my loved ones in my distant homeland, however, never abated, and I still held a silent hope that I might one day reconcile with them.

Then word spread in all the newspapers—it was the spring of 1875—with news that moved me to my core: My brother Barghash, the ruler of Zanzibar after Madjid's death, was planning a visit to London!

At first, I took no action in response to these rumors and kept any uneasiness to myself. I had already suffered far too many disappointments to be able to take courage again. Only the most insistent eloquence of my faithful friends persuaded me to take action. I finally decided to travel to London, and the foreign minister at the time, von Bülow, assured me of diplomatic support from the Ambassador, Count Münster, which unfortunately proved of little help.[25]

I used the short time before my departure to learn English, in an attempt to mitigate my significant state of helplessness at least a bit. During these six to

---

25 German Foreign Minister Bernhard Ernst von Bülow (from 1873 to 1875) and German Ambassador to the United Kingdom Georg Herbert zu Münster von Derneburg (from 1873 to 1885).

eight weeks, I consistently pored over books into the wee hours of the night, reciting one English dialog after another or learning vocabulary. Added to this was the ever-increasing concern for my three small children, from whom I would be, for the first time, separated for an unforeseeable duration.

These and similar thoughts addled my already exhausted brain, as I traveled through Ostende on my way to the giant city. Totally spent and feverishly excited, I was relieved to reach my destination, where I checked into a hotel room that had been reserved by friends of my husband. I knew no mortal soul in all of London except this couple, and even then, I had met them only once for all of an hour when they visited us, or more precisely my blessed husband, as they passed through on their honeymoon. Turning to them in my time of need proved an excellent step, as they both went to great lengths to take care of me.

I arrived in London about a week before my brother's arrival and used the time to settle into this complex, new setting. Most importantly, I paid a visit to Count Münster, who again assured me of his support.

On the fifth day after my arrival, as I sat in the hotel salon deep in dreary thoughts, my room number was suddenly called out, a sign that someone was looking for me. I was presented with the business card of Dr. P., Member of Parliament, the brother of a dear friend of mine.

Standing before him and his now deceased wife as a complete stranger, I came to know the most noble being, who did everything possible to ease my life there. They had come to lend their support and offer the very welcome suggestion that I take up residency in their home. I had to join them immediately for a leisurely ride and dinner, and then moved in completely the following day. And with that, London took a happier turn for me, and I summoned up fresh hope.

My friends in Germany had given me no peace until I made a firm promise to be as careful as I could and, in particular, engage the support of the English government for my cause. Having experienced so much heartbreak over time, and with the addition of indescribably difficult hardships because of my unfamiliarity with European languages, traditions, and customs, I had gladly concluded that one could do no better than rely on God and oneself in all challenges. I had therefore originally intended to tackle this endeavor on my own, before ultimately giving in to the urgings of my friends. As it turned out, my original fears that I would be put off with diplomatic courtesies and empty talk, and then simply have my matter relegated to the files, were way under the mark. I would find out soon enough that I had landed in a world where seeming and being completely diverged.

Not long after I had taken up residence in the heartwarming P. household, I received a visit from Sir Bartle Frere, whom I as yet knew only by name and who later became High Commissioner of South Africa. If ever my instinct was true, then on this day, on which my most fervent hopes and the future of my children were dashed and buried. I was overwhelmed with an ineffable foreboding the moment I laid eyes on this great diplomat, a man who, so to speak, had Zanzibar and my brother in his pocket.

After the usual introductory formalities, Sir Bartle began to inquire about my business and specifically the reason for my visit to London. Although he appeared fully informed about the exact details, I shared with him my full purpose. There was not much to tell, as there was but one thought: reconciliation with my family.

Who can describe my astonishment when Sir Bartle simply lobbed me a cool question in response: What did I care about most, reconciling with my family or—assuring the future of my children! Even today I feel far too weak to describe my emotions at the time. I was ready for anything but such a question. Surely no one would accuse me of lack of fortitude or consistency if I wavered at that critical moment. For me, the well-being of my children had to prevail over my personal wishes.

After overcoming my initial bewilderment at this absolutely unexpected diplomatic chess move, I asked my counterpart to clarify and explain the motivations behind his question. Sir Bartle responded decisively that, above all, the English government had no interest whatsoever in serving as an intermediary between me and my brother; they viewed him solely as a guest and did not wish to see him burdened by any inconvenience. (It is, of course, doubtful what the Sultan would have found more inconvenient, signing the slave treaties effectively under the duress of a pointed gun, thereby indirectly recognizing the English protectorate, or extending a hand to a remorseful sister.)

Elaborating positively on his proposal, he added that if I promised to refrain from any contact with my brother during his London visit, whether in writing or in person, then the English government would provide material support for the future of my children.

Sick at heart and deeply disappointed, I felt like that depleted soul who has marched for endless miles and craves a cool spring where he can take a refreshing drink as recompense for all the trials and tribulations along the way, and indeed finally comes upon such a coveted well, only to find its opening shut by a mighty hand. The choice lay before me, either operate on my own without any assistance from the English government, knowing full well they would put all manner of insurmountable obstacles in my way, for which my weak abilities would be no match, or accept the offer of the English government in the interest of my children. Mindful of the promise I had made to my motherly friend, the unforgettable Baroness von T. in Dresden, not to see my brother alone and unprepared, even though I never doubted my brother would stringently respect English law everywhere, especially in England, and even though I would have had no qualms to suddenly face him, I accepted the offer of the English government.

Even then, England's behavior engendered a degree of mistrust. When a friend of mine squarely asked Sir Bartle Frere how it was that the English government was suddenly so interested in taking care of me, this skilled diplomat presented no less than three reasons: 1. This lets us do the Sultan a favor. 2. We keep the princess at bay for a while. And 3. We preempt any subsequent ability of the Chancellor Prince of Bismarck to somehow meddle in the matter. That all sounded very plausible and reassuring.

In order to avoid a knowing encounter with my brother, whether in public buildings with paid access, or in Hyde Park and on the streets, I carefully studied the precise details of his scheduled outings in the papers every day, so I could plan accordingly. I asked my kind hostess to stop taking me on her local drives, as I preferred to stay at home and make sure I could not possibly break my promise. She responded quite firmly that I must continue to go out with her for health reasons, and she would be sure to follow only suitable routes. So we drove east when the Sultan was in the west, and the reverse. Unfortunately, this extra caution on my part was absolutely necessary. If a sudden encounter were to occur, I doubted I could control my emotions and keep my word in that critical moment. On the other hand, there was practically no risk that he might recognize me. Even my own dear mother, were she still alive, would hardly have known me in my current outfit, even less so one of my brothers, who seldom had the chance to see us without our masks on.

I would have preferred to leave the city immediately and return to my children in Germany, now that I saw my hopes and desires crushed. But I was not even afforded this relief. So distant from my children and always anxious and concerned about them, I still had to spend week after week of unspeakable torment in the very place that brought me only grief and disappointment. That is how Sir Bartle Frere wanted it, by insisting that a detailed pro memoria still needed to be prepared and submitted.

Completely unfamiliar with such business affairs and mentally so downtrodden that I was more of an automaton than a thinking person, I gladly allowed my devoted friends to prepare the note for me and had total confidence that this would surely turn out well. It was almost seven weeks before I could finally end my tortuous stay and leave England at long last to return to my children and Germany. My feelings and state of mind at that moment should not be hard to guess.

Because Zanzibar back then was already considered a certain prospect for becoming an English colony, my submission had to be routed to the Indian government, so to East India. This took a few months until one day, I was painfully surprised by a letter that arrived from London. It contained the duplicate of a document the English government had sent to Count Münster for transmission to me, and presented nothing more than a short rejection of the pro memoria Sir Bartle Frere had so insistently urged upon me. The letter gave the reason for the rejection: I had married a German, I was resident in Germany, and the German government would accordingly have a much greater interest in supporting me.

This tasteless turn of events was all the more ludicrous for my never having asked either one or the other government for any charity; I had in fact sought only moral backing, both here and there. Sir Bartle Frere himself was the father of the pro memoria, the same diplomat who had moments before elicited my promise to stay away from my brother in exchange for an assurance of my children's well-being! At the time, I had taken the need to prepare a written document as a mere formality, firmly believing that if I kept my end of the bargain, the other party would, too. Inexperienced as I was, it never occurred to me that even a helpless widow could be treated so outrageously and deceitfully in robbing her of all her hopes.

Whether such treatment of a dejected woman is worthy of such a power as England, I leave to all fair-minded people to judge. There is but one more question I would ask: Did the English government, did Sir Bartle Frere, as they approached me with their offer, not know that my husband was a German, that I accordingly also had German citizenship?[26] Was this even considered as they extracted my promise? And did I not hold to the agreement and fulfill my promise as exactingly as if I had resided in London and been called Mrs.

---

26 There would have been no mystery here, as the author became a certified citizen of the newly proclaimed German Reich when the State of Hamburg formally recognized her status in 1872 as a German widow (*Bürgerswitwe*). Emeri van Donzel, *An Arabian Princess Between Two Worlds*, plate XIX (1993).

Brown? Yes, clearly, as long as I was in a position to reach out to my brother, in whatever manner, I was not a German woman, but rather the sister of the Sultan, who could have damaged English interests. And now, long after my brother was back in our homeland and I was no longer to be feared, now it was time to play the card they had intentionally held in reserve, in order to finish me off forever. It was but a pretense to get out of an agreement that was entered into grudgingly to begin with!

Later, I came to better understand why my deeply desired reconciliation with my brother would have been especially unwelcome in London at that very moment. Since the Sultan neither speaks a European language, nor understands the subtleties of European diplomacy, the English wanted to keep him in a complete state of ignorance to ensure no last-minute trouble in getting specific treaties signed. Had I in fact made peace with him, they assumed I would have used my somewhat broader knowledge of European affairs to share various bits of information that would have benefited him and Zanzibar, but been all the more contrary to English government interests. Without suspecting a thing, I had simply become a victim of these "humane" politics.

It would, however, be a great lack of gratitude on my part if I did not sharply distinguish the English government from English society. Although I thank the former for my misery, indeed, through whose insidiousness I lost my true faith and trust in humanity, the latter showed me only kindness and caring. Empathetic interest in my fate was manifest all the way up to the highest echelons in England, and I remain immensely obliged for the rest of my life to very many people for their kindness.

The author and her children

CHAPTER THIRTY-ONE

Returning to the Homeland After Nineteen Years

When I wrote the previous chapter several years ago, I still could hardly have believed in the possibility of fulfilling a wish that had pervaded all my thoughts and feelings, indeed my whole being. The eventful period since I had last seen my beloved homeland had been filled with more storm and stress than I could have imagined. My life had undergone the most astonishing changes in that time. I had had experiences that not even the cruelest person would have wished upon his enemies. For a good while, my relatively hardy constitution had enabled me to endure the challenging life and raw climate of the North, but even that was becoming harder and harder.

One evening exactly two years ago, I said to my two daughters: "Children, I have spent some time contemplating whether now is not finally the moment to think about returning to Zanzibar." I explained my views to them in some detail. The one reminded me of the unlucky star that was always hovering over us and all our past failures, claiming that this time, too, would merely cause pointless excitement and disappointment. But the other chimed in enthusiastically: "No, Mama, you must not leave any avenue unexplored; you would blame yourself later for missing that one right moment to go." She said exactly what I was thinking.

I took the preliminary steps in confidence and was met with encouraging reactions from the relevant authorities. Even so, the matter failed to progress for a long time. After repeated disappointments, by which time it seemed the longing for my homeland would never be fulfilled, I received a request one day from the Foreign Ministry to keep myself ready to leave for Zanzibar shortly. The news moved me so profoundly that I initially failed to register my full joy at having reached this long-awaited good fortune. Beyond praise and glory for God's wonderful guidance, I first and foremost felt a deep appreciation toward our beloved, venerated Emperor William I[27] and his high Ministries, for whom I and my children will forever retain undiminished gratitude.

This is not the place to belabor all the minute details of what took place, and I can more readily bypass them because the daily newspapers reported more than enough of the concurrent political happenings.

I was to be in Port Said on July 12, 1885. On July 1, I left Berlin with my children and traveled through Breslau and Vienna to Trieste, where we arrived in good shape on July 3. My children were delighted with all the new and beautiful things they saw. I was still too drained to share in their enthusiasm.

Not until we had boarded the Lloyd steamer *Venus*, which set off to sea at one o'clock the same day, did I again find the calm that I had been so sorely missing these past weeks, and the ability to enjoy what was around us. The weather was so lovely that we were able to stay on deck practically the whole time.

The morning of July 5, we docked in Corfu. We rode around for several hours and got to know the main attractions of this charming island. Fully satisfied, we were back at the steamer by afternoon and then continued aboard past the barren island of Ithaca at the southern tip of Greece and the towering island of Kantia for an arrival in Alexandria on Wednesday, July 8.

Upon entering this city, with its palms and minarets, I was overcome with the most blissful sense of my homeland, a feeling that can only be felt and not described, sentiments that can be understood and appreciated only by those who likewise had been long separated from whence they came. For nineteen years, I had never again set foot in the actual South, and winter after winter, I had passed my time by a heated stove in Germany. Even though I resided in the North and carried the many obligations of a German housewife, my thoughts were always far, far away. There was no better entertainment or distraction for me than sitting alone and undisturbed while burrowing into a book about the South. No wonder then, when I set eyes upon Alexandria, that I was deeply moved, as in a dream, watching the throngs of people in the port!

---

27 Kaiser Wilhelm I, German emperor from 1871 to 1888, the first to lead a united Germany.

At the customs house, we were stopped to present our papers. Determined to identify myself only if absolutely necessary, I asked my travel escort to try her luck with her calling card, which thankfully proved sufficient. Boxed in by boisterous crowds, we struggled mightily to find a coach with which to escape to a hotel. With some twenty people gathered around us, all simultaneously offering their services, it took the interference of a policeman to get them to disperse. Only then could the coach make its way, and even so, someone still managed to jump up on the back to extol his skills as a translator on our drive. That I spoke Arabic myself and therefore had no need for his assistance took a while for him to comprehend.

The two days we spent in the expensive and dirty hotel flew by way too quickly for me. My favorite activity was to head to the Arabic quarter, where I did not tire of watching the colorful commotion for hours on end. Folks appeared wary at first, but as soon as I spoke Arabic with them, their faces brightened, and their eyes glowed with joy. "Mother," (meant in the general sense) they would call from all sides, "where did you learn our language so well? You have surely been in Baghdad; how long did you live there?"

Our Arab coach driver, named Muhammed, became so attached to us that he ended up begging me to take him along as a servant. He would, he assured me, remain loyal to us until the end of his days—and never touch our bottles of wine. The next morning, when his coach arrived perfectly on time to take us back to the harbor, he was visibly despondent, and I had quite a time trying to console the poor man.

And thus our very enjoyable time in Alexandria flew by. It took eighteen hours from there to reach Port Said, where the tender vessel *Adler* of the East African squadron lay docked. We boarded that same evening. Port Said is a small port town, but it offers practically everything. The shops contain a great abundance of anything one could ever want.

Here is where the sand desert begins, through which the canal also runs, where the Mediterranean Sea connects with the Red Sea and so also the Atlantic Ocean with the Indian Ocean. The travel lane is so narrow that two ships cannot pass, which is why passing locations have been inserted at several spots with signs on shore that say *Gare Limite Sud* and *Gare Limite Nord*. Ships frequently have to wait for hours until the oncoming ship has passed through. Every steamer brings a canal pilot on board at either Port Said or Suez to successfully navigate the obstacles. These pilots have a thorough understanding of the signal language that uses buoys hoisted on halyards, whose numbers and placements indicate if it is safe to proceed or how many ships are still in the queue ahead. Ships

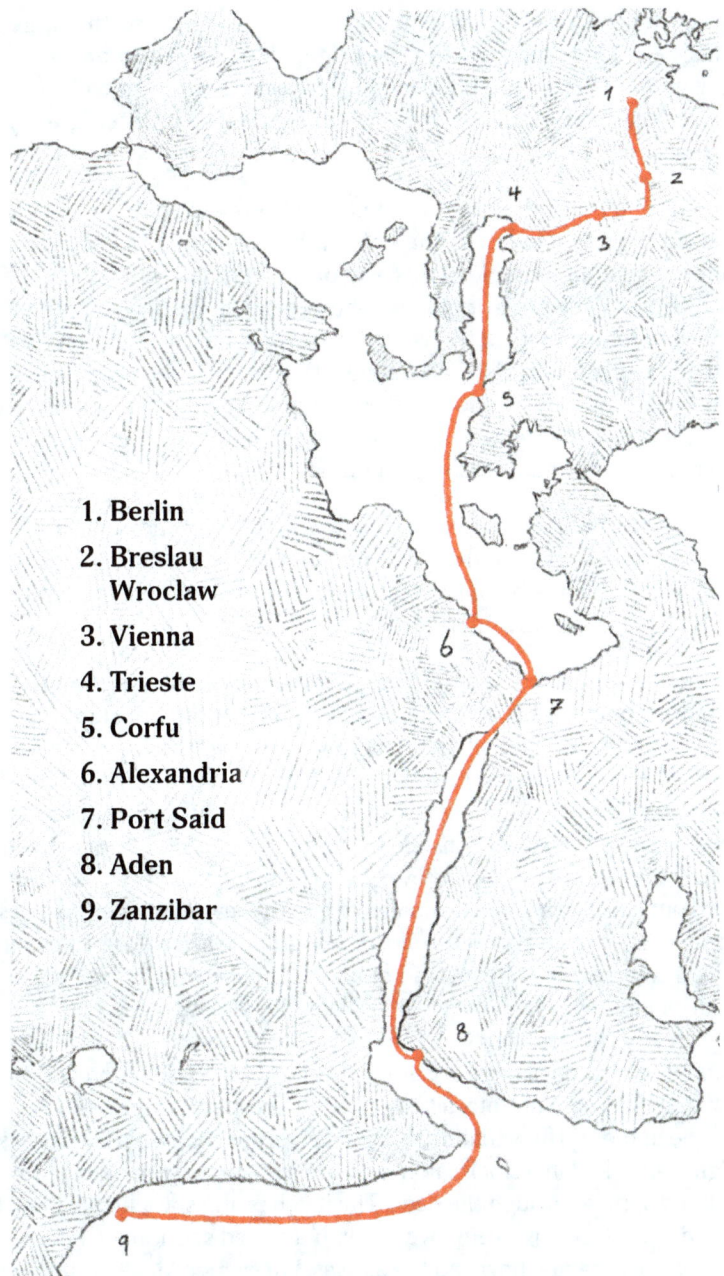

The author's trip from Berlin to Zanzibar

are not allowed to traverse the canal at full power because the large waves can damage the loose sands at the shoreline. Ships also must anchor at night. The trip is nonetheless quite entertaining, especially when individual ships get into a "race," as often happens when they enter the Great Bitter Lake. All ships naturally want to be the first to enter the narrow ship lane up ahead.

Approaching the Suez, the canal widens, and there we could finally plow "full speed ahead" into the Red Sea. The heat in the Suez Canal is very intense, but it becomes almost unbearable in this arm of the Red Sea with tall cliffs bearing in on both sides. We were dripping wet both day and night. I felt better in this familiar temperature than all the years I was away, but my children had a hard time of it and became sluggish, even sullen. Because the sea rode high, we were unable to open the side windows of our cabins. The air became increasingly oppressive until one very hot night we abandoned our cabins to sit on deck chairs in search of some refreshing slumber.

The trip to Aden took seven days, and then we kept anchor in the same heat for another five days before the *Adler* was given the command to continue its travels. Who could have been happier than me? In a week, at last, after a long separation, I would see my homeland again.

Up to Aden, the sea had been easy on us, but the rocky city was barely behind us when we found ourselves in a horrific southwest monsoon. Our ship was entering the same dangerous regions where the SMS *Augusta* had gone under a few weeks before. One morning at eight o' clock, just as we were having breakfast on deck with the officers, the first wave careened across the deck and scattered the gathered company in all directions. So much for our peaceful, comfortable times, as suddenly the worst storm I had ever experienced let loose. Day and night the sea played our ship like a pinball. Spumes of mighty waves pounded so incessantly on both smokestacks that after the storm, once all the saltwater had evaporated, they looked completely white instead of black. Anyone who has not experienced such a sea cannot really imagine what it is like. Our situation was quite dire. After suffering greatly the first day from sea sickness caused by the terrible pitching and rolling, the next days were miserable because of the agitation and sleepless nights. Water was coming into all the rooms. The berths were so wet that we could not lie in them. The situation was so dangerous that we stayed dressed for three nights and slept in a small salon near the men, often with open umbrellas to catch water dripping through the deck. The hatches and skylight had been tightly closed, and the latter was even covered with a tarred sailcloth as a tarp. It does not take much to imagine how bad the air was. We women looked utterly pathetic all this time, as we could not really wash or coif ourselves. All our clothes in the drawers had gotten wet, so we could not change our completely soaked outfits into anything dry. Our shoes were totally ruined, and with no other dry shoes on hand, I had to borrow slippers from the commanding officer, Mr. von D.

After three days, the storm finally calmed down. Even though waves still frequently crested the deck, we were able to spend a few hours in an elevated space where the commanding officer had pitched a tent for us.

Although I had been quite fearful in the beginning, the awareness that we are always in God's hands and that I was with my three children, who meant more to me than anything, allowed me to soon become calmer.

On August 2, the island of Pemba came into view. Oh! what a word that was for me. Namely, the distance from Pemba to Zanzibar is only thirty nautical miles, a trip that easily takes a mere three hours. With encroaching darkness, however, we sailed only to the northern tip of Zanzibar to avoid the multiple sandbanks that make a nighttime port entry too dangerous.

It was a wondrous convergence for me that I would see my homeland again in the same month that I had left it nineteen years ago, and on the same day in the same hour that my husband had been taken from me exactly fifteen years before. I hardly need to describe what my heart felt on this day. I turned in earlier than usual, but then slept barely a wink the whole night. I was like a volcano inside, and only the most fervently hopeful prayer now and again gave me a passing moment of calm.

During the night, our ship drifted slowly close to the lighthouse. As I walked out onto the deck the next morning, the palms of my homeland were already greeting me from afar! What else could I do upon seeing this magical sight but run quickly back into my cabin and thank the Almighty for his great goodness! The events of my life are all too varied, and they in turn have shaped my feelings and perspectives. People are in large part no more than what their lives, experiences, and given circumstances make of them: I left my homeland as a complete Arab and a good Muslim, and what am I today?

But in this moment, it seemed as if my entire youth came back to me, as if to make up for the many years of strain and sorrow. Everything, everything appeared vividly before my soul, and the cheerful pictures of my past strode forth, one after another, before my inner eye.

This first impression also appears to have had a sobering effect on my otherwise so cheerful and lively children. All three could not hug me enough on this day, and they kept gazing at me with still and earnest eyes. Deep inside, I could not thank the Lord enough for such rich recompense for all the loss.

As we neared the city, we were disappointed to discover that the German squadron had not yet arrived. Since the *Adler* was supposed to be part of the ensemble, we had no choice but to backtrack and stay adrift on the east side of the island until the squadron came in. And so, we waited an additional eleven days. Then, on August 11, shortly before four o'clock, the sailor posted on the yard announced: "Ship in sight!" We figured it was just a passenger ship and barely registered the call. Soon, however, we noticed that the ship was headed directly for us. We therefore made steam, showed our flag, and signaled our name. A short time later came the countersignal, and minutes later, we recognized the tender vessel *Ehrenfels*. It soon lay broadside to ours and let us know through signals that it had been looking for us under instructions from the Commodore since the morning, to convey orders that we come to the harbor, where the squadron had already been docked for four days. We immediately set course for the harbor, but could not enter because of lacking steam power and impending nightfall, so we had to spend yet another night near the lighthouse at the northern tip.

The next morning, we were already up and about by six o'clock. On the horizon, we glimpsed the forest of masts in the harbor. For the second time, we rode close to shore, past marvelous palm groves in which little African villages lay scattered. Through steady signaling, the flagship directed us to a berth, only to have us switch locations again half an hour later. We saw four German warships: the SMS *Stosch*, *Gneisenau*, *Elisabeth*, and *Prinz Adalbert*; two English warships; five steamships belonging to the Sultan; and various sailing ships.

Commodore Paschen initially considered it necessary to treat me as "secret cargo," a description that garnered considerable amusement among the officers of the squadron. However, as soon as Admiral Knorr arrived with the SMS *Bismarck*, things changed, and I was able to go on land as I pleased. Beyond the feelings that had overwhelmed me upon seeing my homeland again, the fact that I now walked the streets in broad daylight in the company of men, whereas before I went out only veiled and at night, made a truly remarkable impression on me. One would think that, after living in Europe for nineteen years, I would simply take this aspect in stride. Indeed, I did, in spades. But now in Zanzibar, it was the first time after so many years that I became acutely aware of the transformations I had had to undergo over the course of time. I did not have these same sensations in Egypt, where I had been twice before, only on the ground of my homeland.

Returning to the Homeland After Nineteen Years

On our first foray into the city, I thought I saw unmistakable astonishment in the eyes of the crowds that gathered around us. People pressed in from all sides, calling to me in both Arabic and Swahili: "How are you, my Mistress?" Whenever we went into stores to make purchases, vast masses of people collected in the narrow streets, but then respectfully made room as we left. Day after day, our accompanying crowds grew larger, and the welcoming spirit of the public became more affectionate. That naturally annoyed the Sultan and his advisor, the English Consul-General, more than a little. The former even had a number of those who followed us soundly whipped. He, as well as the English Consul-General, moved to lodge a complaint with the squadron chief about these increasingly heartfelt demonstrations by the population towards me. Once I heard this, I felt I had to advise the people to stop flocking to us, but they answered that, no matter the punishment, they still wanted to show me their joy. Often slaves would push their way forward with utmost caution to convey greetings from their masters. They asked me not to doubt their loyalty and devotion; they wished fervently to be allowed to visit me on board, their houses were at my disposal at any time. Even letters, which slaves that had no pockets on their clothes carried under their little caps, were discreetly slipped my way. Sometimes, when walking past the houses, I would find ladies hiding behind a door, seemingly waiting for our arrival. As soon as I walked past, they would speak to me, at times just a short greeting: "God be with you and give you good health!" My siblings, relatives, and former friends sent repeated requests that I come visit them. But I never followed up on any of the invitations, not for personal reasons, as my feelings were too strong for any personal reservations to get in the way, but because the current circumstances forced me to this level of consideration.

Whenever our rowboats came in front of the palace, or passed under the windows of the harem house, we could always see the Sultan's women at the windows, greeting us kindly. Because all our outings were undertaken with the friendly escort of Marine officers, I had to ask the men, in the interests of the women, to please refrain from responding. I, too, avoided it, so the shortsighted beauties would not become unnecessarily ruined, as I had been informed that their ruler and master would often hide himself in the house where he could watch both the sea and the street and easily discover the unsuspecting culprits, followed by cruel punishments. That is not a mere assumption. It is well-known, and Europeans in Zanzibar know to tell the story, that hardly a year ago, as the Sultan was peering out of his hiding place, he noticed how a Portuguese man passed by on the water and greeted his favorite, a beautiful Circassian, who greeted back. This custom is nothing new. Already thirty years ago, when I was still a child, we were regularly greeted by Europeans, especially the English and French Marine officers that came over to our island rather frequently, as well as the local merchants, and we would return the courteous greeting. Our male society had always accepted this and thought nothing of it. Barghash, however, saw things differently and personally whipped his Circassian with such vehemence that she succumbed a few days later. He is said to have begged forgiveness at her death bed, but to no avail. Even today, he has someone say prayers regularly at her gravesite.

On our excursions to the interior, we often encountered people riding donkeys on the backroads. To show their respect, they always dismounted, led their animals past us, and then remounted. Despite all the punishments from the Sultan, the population did not let up on demonstrating its attachment, and the loud calls, *Kuaheri, Bibi! Kuaheri, Bibi!* (All good fortune, Mistress!), that resounded almost directly under the Sultan's own windows as we returned to our ships, could not have been comfortable for him. I was told that whenever our boats came into view, someone would use an empty cookie tin as a signaling drum to alert the population.

For obvious reasons, there was no shortage of spies lurking around us, mostly Hindus, who were very annoyed that we spoke only German amongst ourselves. Even on the last evening prior to our departure, two loyal friends, who had come on board under cover of night to bid me farewell, alerted me to a dark figure, who had already frequented our ship as a visiting salesman, but was actually just a skilled tool of the exceptionally influential, namely, the former lamp cleaner and court barber, the merchant Madoldji Pera-Daudji.

This Pera-Daudji, an exceedingly cunning Hindu, had elevated himself to the role of the Sultan's general factotum. He, this erstwhile lamp cleaner, serves the ruler of Zanzibar in all things high and low. All diplomatic negotiations go through his hands, and those same hands also wait on the tables of the Sultan's guests. For this, he receives a full thirty dollars every month. I was assured that everyone in Zanzibar takes great care not to get on the wrong side of Pera-Daudji; so very much depends on him. Naturally, thirty dollars are not enough to pay for his expensive outfits, so he needs other sources of revenue. The court jeweler of the Sultan, who declined to turn over a fixed percentage of his earnings from the Sultan's orders to the lamp cleaner, lost the entire business. Pera-Daudji blessed a more amenable rival with those orders.

It just so happened that my birthday took place during these few days. For the first time ever, I celebrated it in my homeland, where birthdays are not otherwise celebrated. The gentlemen of the squadron went out of their way to make this a truly joyful day for me, and they succeeded magnificently. I cannot be grateful enough for all their kindness. One thing, however, moved me especially oddly: The dear captain of the *Adler* arranged to have a pig slaughtered to honor me, a born Muslim, in my devout Islamic homeland. Had our most reliable local soothsayers prophesied this event to me nineteen years earlier, even as superstitious as we were, I would have laughed in their faces. What unintended humor can reveal itself in the most fateful challenges of our lives!

As seen from the sea, my impression of the city of Zanzibar was the same as before, perhaps even friendlier. There are many new houses, and the lighthouse rising in front of the palace looks quite stately with its electric lighting. The officers always called it the Sultan's "Christmas tree" because of the rings of lights wrapped around it. I was less pleased with the inner city.

With my extended time in Germany, I may well have lost touch with the conditions at home. In any event, I found the inner city in a truly sad state. From house to house, rubble was piled along the narrow, dirty streets. Ruins everywhere were filled with flourishing weeds and even hosted large trees that were growing unencumbered. No one was taking care of things. Everyone walked by with the most indifferent attitude in the world, sidestepping pools of water and piles of rocks. There were no separate depots for ash and trash, since that is apparently what the open street is for. The art of organizing a city administration must not be very easy, otherwise the Sultan—who has amply experienced the comforts of walking on clean streets in Bombay, England, and France—would have addressed this long ago. Indeed, he has introduced ice manufacturing, electric lights, a so-called railroad, and who knows what else in Zanzibar, not to mention French cooks and their cuisine.

The visible deterioration of the inner city filled me with indescribable melancholy. I could not yet know what conditions awaited me in my venerable Bet il Mtoni and the back-then barely completed Bet il Ras. The first time we went to the house where I first saw the light of day, I was utterly shocked. What a sight it was! Instead of a house, I saw a completely disintegrated ruin. No sound, no noise could pull me out of the distress that coursed through me at this wholly unexpected view. For a long time, I was unable to compose myself. One staircase was missing entirely, the other was so overgrown and decayed that it was dangerous to climb. More than half of the house lay in shambles, right where it had collapsed. Virtually all roofs were missing from the beloved baths that had once been so popular and teeming with happy people. A few were but heaps of rubble, and any parts left standing had been robbed of their roofs or floors. Everything either had fallen or was falling apart!

The whole courtyard was full of every kind of grass. Nothing remained to give the unknowing observer even the slightest hint of the former splendor of this palace.

How differently this sight impacted me than the others! My own children struck me in this moment as far too cheerful. Had I had any inkling of the devastation, I would have preferred to make my first visit here alone. From every door hanging askew and about to collapse, from the decaying masses of beams lying on top of each other, yes, from the mountain-high piles of rubble, I thought I saw figures of former residents stepping forward. For a brief period, my spirit escaped the dismal present back to the wonderful years of my youth. Only the friendly comments of the officers and the voices of my children, as they combed through various sections of the ruins with alarming dexterity, woke me from my gloomy contemplations.

I have occasionally encountered the mistaken view that Arabs show devotion to the dead by letting their former homes fall apart. That is wrong. This is not a matter of religious purpose, but rather the laissez-faire attitude of Orientals. Arabs rarely renovate their houses, and thus the weather, which is notably quick to destroy the bad limestone of the island, is left to do its damage undeterred. Once a house is run down, a new one is erected, and the old ruins are just ignored. The land itself has virtually no value.

One section of the house still contained relatively intact rooms, where my nephew Ali bin Suud, the son of Zuene, had lived until his death, out of pure attachment to the family's old homestead. He had passed away just two years earlier.

Upon entering this section, we were greeted by two Arab soldiers, who had come from Oman only a few months before. They had left their families behind in order to earn more in wealthier Zanzibar, but the situation was so bad that they sincerely regretted their trip and planned to return to Muscat as soon as possible. Both complained to me about their physical ailments and begged me to cure them. One had pain in his eyes, and the other had stomach trouble.

In response to my somewhat puzzled query, why they were even living in these ruins, I learned to my astonishment that they were not alone, but part of a troop that, unbelievable as it sounds, was charged with keeping a strict watch over the place. This measure could hardly have had a military purpose. More likely, it seemed to me, was a case of evil spirits. That said, since I have been distant from all these superstitions and their adherents for nineteen years now, I may be wrong.

I took a few grasses, some leaves, and a stone from the niche where my dear father used to say his prayers, as mementos of the place.

We were leaving the house when a well-dressed, very distinguished-looking Arab came towards us and presented himself as the first officer of the troop. He stayed with us a good while and then accompanied us to our boat. On this short stretch, however, we spotted a venerable old man, who stood in the Mtoni river to wash himself before praying. As we came closer, we realized he was totally blind. Since my arrival in Zanzibar, I had strictly avoided being the first to greet anyone, so as not to cause them any trouble. Here, for this blind person, reverence led me to make an exception. Going up to the old man, I wished him a good evening in Arabic. I hesitated to do even that small gesture. His prayer preparations were surely the least appropriate time for me, as a Christian, to bother him, and I expected at most a surly response to my greeting. He must have already realized from the foreign sounds of our distant conversation that we were European.

How astonished I was when he instead stretched out both hands, took my hand to his lips, and pressed it to his face for some time. I was extremely touched, but also embarrassed to think that he might be confusing me with someone else. I asked him, "Do you actually know me?" "As if I know you!" he responded, "Oh, you are my Mistress Salme, whom I so often held on my lap years ago when you were still a child. Oh, how happy we were to hear you had returned. God bless you and protect you, our precious dear!" With these and other words, this poor, helpless blind man said farewell from the fullness of his heart. The Arab officer, who was witness to this loyal devotion, reported to me that this long-bearded old man was the *muedden* (muezzin) of the Bet il Mtoni settlement and also had the Sultan's orders to pray at the gravesite of Ali bin Suud (to whom the Sultan had shown bitter hostility during all of his lifetime).

This last comment, in particular, caught my attention. I knew exactly how harshly and also immaturely Barghash had treated Ali bin Suud and my oldest sister Raje. Raje, the proper sister of Ali's mother, was already relatively old when she moved from Muscat to Zanzibar a number of years ago, at which time the Sultan gave her a house and an appanage. Later, as Ali bin Suud, whom Barghash hated bitterly for no good reason, lay dying in Bet il Mtoni, without any wife or children to take care of him and dependent on the mere kindness of his slaves, what would have been more natural than to have his proper Aunt Raje support him? But this approach got no support from Barghash, who had absolutely no sense for Samaritan assistance or the kind of compassion that moved Raje. To let her feel his wrath, Barghash not only withdrew her appanage, but alas! also chased her, his older sister, who could well have been his mother, ruthlessly out of her designated home. He did not show up to Ali's burial, a slight that no one bestows on even their worst enemy. And now he has someone praying at his nephew's gravesite! Stranger behavior would be hard to come by.

As long as I am commenting on the head of our family in Zanzibar, I am drawn to remove the veil from yet another story of his private life. It pains me greatly to share something bad about my own blood with the world. For even after all these years of separation from my loved ones, and despite all the heartlessness and harshness that Barghash has shown me even after I put my life and livelihood on the line for him, I still harbor the feeling of everlasting unity with my own family. Sayyid Barghash is, however, not a man to spare either his subjects or his own bloodline.

It is widely known in Zanzibar that Barghash, upon ascending to the throne in 1870, threw his next younger brother Chalife,[28] suddenly and wantonly, into the dungeon. The poor man had to languish three long years in prison in heavy iron foot rings and chains. And why? No one could say. It may well have been a fear that Chalife, as next in line for the throne, would plot treasonous plans against Barghash, just as Barghash himself had once done against Madjid.

Not until a sister, whom Barghash had also aggrieved, planned a pilgrimage to Mecca, did he feel any pangs of conscience and went to ask for her forgiveness. He feared the prospect of having a curse uttered against him directly in the holy city of the Prophet. But the sister refused to forgive him unless he set the innocent Chalife free.

And even then, Barghash continued to hound Chalife and his friends. He learned that Chalife had a loyal friend who was blessed with worldly riches. Barghash was reminded of the value he himself had placed in alliances with wealthy tribal chiefs and therefore decided to do anything necessary to cut off this support to his successor to the crown.

He had Chalife's friend summoned and spoke with him briefly along the following lines: "I have heard that you intend to sell your plantations; tell me, how much you would like for them, as I would like to buy them." "That must be a misunderstanding," came the response, "I have never intended to sell my property." "But it would be to your advantage to sell them to me; now go and consider the matter."

---

28 This half-brother, otherwise known as Khalifa bin Said, became Sultan when Sultan Barghash died, for a brief reign from 1888–1890.

A while later, this unhappy individual was again summoned and received with the following words from the Sultan: "Now tell me, how much are you charging for your plantations?" "Your Honor, I have never thought of selling them." "Well, what you think does not concern me. I will pay you 50,000 dollars for them. Here is the order for the designated amount; go and let them pay you."

Deeply dismayed, the poor soul slunk away from the man who thus serves as the "father of his people." But an even more painful surprise awaited him. When he went to claim the 50,000 dollars, he learned that the sum was payable over twenty years, and he would receive annual installments of only 2,500 dollars. And so the man was ruined, which is exactly what the Sultan had intended.

I will follow with an incident whose recounting makes my face red with shame and evokes my deepest commiseration. A malicious rumor had spread that one of my sisters was in love with someone Barghash did not want as a brother-in-law. When he heard the rumor, he confronted her directly. She protested that she knew nothing more than the next person, but in vain. The gentle brother then personally caned the blood-related sister fifty times. After this brutal treatment, the poor woman was bed-ridden for more than a month and continued to suffer from the consequences for a long time thereafter. I have no doubt he will also have someone pray at her gravesite after she dies, just like at the gravesites of his wife and Ali bin Suud.

Europeans are very frequently heard to praise the kindness of the ruler of Zanzibar. Let the reality be judged in light of the foregoing. It is in any case certain that, deep down in his heart, Barghash has never hated anything as much as the mere mention of a European.

It pains me greatly to touch on another issue here, but people would be apt to misinterpret its omission. Anyone who is aware of the situation in Zanzibar knows full well that the Sultan is the ruler only in small things, whereas the English Consul-General rules everything. Even the enemies of the latter openly concede that he is one of the most adept diplomats there is. Were I still as inexperienced in the diplomatic arts and chess moves as I was ten years ago, and were I to take every friendly-sounding word at face value, then I surely would have been very happy to learn from one of the highest officers of the squadron that the English Consul-General was very sorry he could do nothing to promote my interests, that he immensely regretted not having found an opportunity to meet up with the Sultan to urge my case.

It was indeed good that I did not put any stock into such assurances. I simply would have set myself up for yet another disappointment. Not long after, I heard that the good sir had just spent several days as a guest of the Sultan on one of his plantations two weeks prior, despite the isolation of harem life. I also learned of a much-used telephone line that directly connects the English Consulate-General with the palace of the Sultan.

From what I know, Germany has a law that subjects the unauthorized opening of private letters to harsh punishment. I do not know if England also has such a law, but if so, it would apply only to the motherland, while in the heat of Africa—the postal system in Zanzibar is English—one looks the other way. Indeed, some of my letters to Zanzibar never reached their destinations. In March of 1885, I happened to come across an article in the *Berliner Tageblatt*[29] titled "Germany, England, and Zanzibar," which clarified the matter for me:

> ...Long before the advent of German colonies, the Sultan was warned and shielded against any relations of this sort; long before the black cross on a white background[30] waved over Zanzibar, the English consuls and officers on the island—since even the Army has English instructors—always had the concern about whether letters from 'Germany' were in fact reaching the royal court....

The authorities leveraged everything they could to rile the population against me. A few officers asked me to help them select and procure jewelry for their loved ones back home, and so we made several trips to a goldsmith, who, without our knowledge, happened to do work for the Sultan as well.

As soon as the Sultan found out about this through his general factotum, Pera-Daudji, whose job it is to inform him of all news, he summoned the jeweler and dumped the full measure of his wrath on him for having dared to sell something to us. This normally meek businessman calmly answered this rage by saying he would have been ashamed to turn away the sister of his ruler from his store. The Sultan was not at all pleased by this response and threatened to withdraw his very substantial patronage. Even this did not phase the goldsmith. He retorted that he was already done with Zanzibar and would prefer, as soon as possible, to return to his homeland. To steer clear of any trouble, as he also wished not to appear unkind to me, he then closed up shop for the rest of his time on the island.

---

29 Major German language newspaper that published from 1872 to 1939.
30 The flag of German warships that bore the flared, black-and-white-rimmed Iron Cross of the German Empire.

Similarly, it was thought that I would be harshly punished by a strict prohibition against donkey owners renting their animals to us. A few of my former slaves, who dared approach me out of long-standing devotion, were imprisoned for this demonstration of their loyalty.

These and similarly inane measures were not uncommon, but produced the exact opposite result. The verdict of the crowd came in their own words: *pija kana kasi ja watoto, Bibi*, meaning "he is behaving just like a little child, oh mistress!"

As I was approaching Zanzibar, I had been very unsure what reception would await me. That my brother would respect Germany's wishes, I had no doubt, and so it was. That he would hardly be kind towards me, at most putting on a good face in deference to Germany, for that I was also prepared. The ugly behavior he had shown my other siblings truly gave me no reason to expect any friendly outreach from him. But it was a different question as to how the population would react to my sudden appearance. To my greatest joy, I can simply repeat that I received the warmest reception. Arabs, Hindus, Banyans, and natives, they all pressed me over and over again to please stay in Zanzibar.

This fortified my belief anew that there was no way that religious hatred toward my person was at stake. One day, I encountered two Arabs, with whom I began to converse. When another person pointed out that they were relatives of mine—I had not recognized them—I told them, if I had known, I would never have engaged in conversation, being so unsure about how my relatives stood towards me under the current circumstances. They immediately responded that, to them, I was still my father's daughter. And when I touched upon my religion, one of them countered that this had been predestined as my fate from the beginning of time. "Yes, the God that has separated you and us from the homeland is the same God that all people praise and adore; it is through his mighty will that you returned to us, and we rejoice in it. Is that not so? Will you and your children now stay here forever?"

Such demonstrations of love and devotion have tided me over many a difficult hour, along with the blissful feeling of having seen my homeland once more. They have indeed made my trip a fount of delight for the rest of my life, and I can forever give thanks and praise to the Almighty for his goodness!

Not without great sadness in my heart did I say farewell to my homeland for a second time, and all my beloved, whom I had to leave again, felt the same.

There is no better ending for my book than to share such sentiments from my circle of friends as they appeared in an Arabic farewell letter that reached me in Europe, even if its literal translation loses much of its tenderness and originality of expression. It reads:

> You left and did not let me know;
> That tore my heart and filled me with all-consuming fire.
> Oh, that I had wrapped my arms around your neck, inseparably, when you left us!
> I would have let you sit on my head and walk on my eyes![31]
>
> You live in my heart, and in leaving,
> You have made my soul suffer like never before.
> My body is emaciated, and my tears relentless;
> One after another rolls down my cheeks like the waves of the sea.
>
> Oh, Lord of the universe! Bring us together before we die,
> If only for a single day.
> Should we live, we will come together!
> Should we die, the Immortal remains.
>
> Oh, if I were a bird, I would longingly follow you;
> But how can a bird fly, whose wings are clipped?

---

31 An Arabic expression for "I would do anything for you!"

AFTERWORD[32]

In the foregoing pages I have endeavored to draw a picture of Oriental life and its customs, especially with regard to life at Court, and the position of woman in the East. Some of the subjects contained in this book may be thought to possess less general interest, but, as part of the whole, my description would have been incomplete without them. It must be remembered that I have not been writing a novel or a tale of fiction, but the faithful recollections connected with the life of my native land in all its phases.

If I have naturally felt tempted to exalt such of our customs and institutions which, in my opinion, are deserving of commendation, I have, on the other hand, never endeavored to excuse or disguise others which, in the eyes of more highly-cultured nations at least, may justly be ridiculed or thought objectionable; and if, in drawing comparisons between foreign and Eastern customs, I have not shrunk from speaking my mind openly and candidly, and have sometimes sent home a shaft, I may aver, in justice to myself, that I have by no means spared myself, but have readily and frankly admitted the errors into which I fell.

Even in this century of railroads and rapid communication, so much ignorance still exists among European nations of the customs and institutions of their own immediate neighbors, that one can hardly wonder how little is actually known about those of races far removed. The ablest and most conscientious writer must always, to some degree, fall short of giving a perfectly precise and faithful picture of a foreign nation; and in the case of an Eastern nation, he will of course, find himself heavily handicapped out of all proportion when family and domestic life generally is so jealously guarded from the gaze of the outer world.

Having been born and bred in the East, I am in a position to set down the unvarnished reflection of my Oriental experiences—of its high life and its low life—to speak of many peculiarities, and lift the veil from things that are always hidden from profane eyes. This, I hope, will constitute the main value of my book, and my object will have been fully gained if I have been able to contribute my share, and above all, if I have succeeded in removing many misconceptions and distortions current about the East.

My task is done—and, in conclusion, it only remains for me to say farewell to my kind readers, who have followed me through these pages, and who, I trust, will always bear a friendly memory for one whose life has already gathered so rich a store of changes and vicissitudes.

---

32 The first English translation of the German *Memoiren* was published in 1888 by Ward and Downey, London. As the only English translation authorized by the author, it included this additional Afterword from her, reproduced here in the original, unedited English.

ON CONTRIBUTIONS

Zanzibar is a small island, and Oman is a small country, but they shared a remarkable nineteenth-century history, including as recorded in Sayyida Salme's writings. She is not usually counted among the explorers of the time, but nonetheless stands with those who charted new territory. In so doing, she crossed boundaries, especially boundaries wrought by systems and institutions, in ways that still speak to us. We can hear her voice as an enduring contribution—ringing out to us, recounting, questioning, probing. We can see her light shining into the twenty-first century, encouraging us to stay centered and step forward.

Undertaking this translation expanded my own exploration of her legacy. Among those who supported this journey, my gratitude goes first to Professor Emeri van Donzel, who put the map in my hand. From his base at Leiden University, he spent decades researching Sayyida Salme's past and impact. His groundbreaking book, *An Arabian Princess Between Two Worlds* (1993), has been at my side and remains the seminal academic resource for anyone wanting to know more on the subject. In this connection, too, we are beholden to the Oriental Institute and the Netherlands Institute for the Near East (NINO) in Leiden, which over the decades safeguarded materials that were provided by the family to their good friend there, Professor Christiaan Snouck Hurgronje.

On Contributions

In that tradition of friendship, I was fortunate to discover Anita Keizers, subject librarian of the Ancient Near East at the NINO. For the past decade, she has been the custodian of much of the family's *Nachlass*, including the special Sayyida Salme bookcase. As a loving caretaker and our best resource, she has also become a kind of hub for Sayyida Salme inquiries. Through her, I met Freiburg-based researcher Godwin Kornes, who not only shared his scholarship, photos, and enthusiasm, but also led us to a branch of our extended family, the von Brands, descended from Sayyida Salme's daughter Antonie.[33] Small world, they live nearby, and Alexander has graciously shared his well-preserved family treasures with us, including some of the photos in this book. And that completed the trio along with Michael Bauer and his family, who are descended from Sayyida Salme's son Rudolph and reached out to us many years ago—all three branches having found their way to the United States, now reconnected here.

I also give great thanks for pre-release reviews of the full manuscript by Kathleen Ridolfo, the director of the Sultan Qaboos Cultural Center who has done so much to build Omani community in our area and across the United States, and by Eija Pehu, a former World Bank colleague and dear friend who has always been there for my books. In addition, I am grateful for feedback from Anita Keizers, Godwin Kornes, Andrea Nour, and Inga Harting, as I finalized these pages. I am also grateful to Torrence Royer, who has collected historical materials for decades and happily shared what he had.

My deep gratitude extends as well to the tried-and-true duo that has made self-publishing such a joy. While I was focused on bringing out Sayyida Salme's voice, they gave me the tools, and their professionalism and experience, to let me realize my own vision and voice. To my copy editor, the forever upbeat Lauri Scherer of LSF Editorial, and my graphic designer, the incomparable, indefatigable Joe Bernier of Bernier Graphics—thank you both for all your help in docking this ship.

As a family project, I have my family to thank, above all. My first mate on this journey has been my mother Ursula Stumpf, with whom this effort has been a shared joy. As a wonderful partner, she has been ever ready to help, ever diligent, ever thoughtful. Being able to create this book with her direct engagement has buoyed the project from inception to completion and made it all the more meaningful. I am also ever so grateful to Max, my wonderful son. He knows what

---

[33] The research by Godwin Kornes of Antonie Brandeis is based primarily on her ethnographic Micronesia collection at the Museum Natur und Mensch in Freiburg, Germany.

it took and always gave me full space and support. This marks his third book as my inhouse illustrator, now also mapmaker, and I have loved having him join in. Max does not need this translation to read his remarkable ancestor's story, but with Salme in his name, I now also give him this edition, much as she gave her original account to her children.

Credit also goes to my father Walter Stumpf, for putting the wind in my sails. His vision got us to Zanzibar in 1998, the trip from which all else followed. At a time when tourism was just beginning, we were the first of Sayyida Salme's descendants to set foot on the island in almost seventy years. Also noteworthy is my grandfather Erich Schwinge, who embraced the Arab side of the family and took up the mantle when his wife and her sister died so early in life. To keep the legacy alive, he put everything in place for republication of the *Memoirs* in the 1970s, but then refrained in full respect for the family's preferences.

This book is dedicated to my brother Martin, who promoted and pursued Sayyida Salme's memory more than anyone in my immediate family, including by working hard on a documentary film of her life. I still use his heavily notated copy of Professor van Donzel's book. One of my last memories of Martin was the two of us handing out little handcrafted packages—more than a hundred of them—with sunflower seeds wrapped in a paper as a gesture of peace and appreciation. One of my favorite experiences of all time, it was the summer of 2005, when the Smithsonian's Folklife Festival on the Washington Mall featured Oman. This book is in all ways indebted to Martin's inspiration.

In that same spirit of peace and appreciation, and recognizing the support and rapport of her worldwide audience, I hope Sayyida Salme herself would have considered this publication to be in her honor, as I have intended.

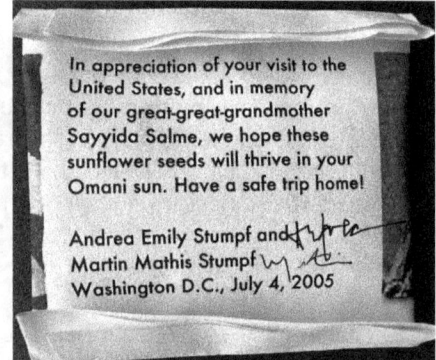

ON FAMILY

Sayyida Salme is my great-great-grandmother in a line that runs straight through the women: from her youngest daughter Rosa to Rosa's daughter Emily to Emily's daughter Ursula, who is my mother. The small percentage of Arab blood that links me to the historical Zanzibari Sultanate and the current Omani Sultanate may have limited biological significance, but is unambiguous. We are five generations over a century and a half.

Almost a dozen Omani Sultans later, the story remains interesting in part because my mother and both the late Omani Sultan Qaboos and the current Sultan Haitham are distant cousins on the extended Al Bu Said family tree. But when Sayyida Salme became Christian—taking a Christian name and a Christian husband on that memorable day in 1867 in Aden—she became an infidel. That was enough to banish her from the royal family, especially by her half-brother Sultan Barghash, who also found it politically and financially convenient to disown her.

In our particular case, the family ties were further attenuated during and after World War II. Rosa's immediate family remained in Germany, even though the Third Reich was no time to refer to non-Aryan ancestry.[34] Not long after the war, two generations of our family line passed away in less than two years, creating a generational gap. Rosa died in February 1948, preceded by her youngest daughter Berta in December 1946 and followed by her other daughter Emily in July 1948.[35] My mother was eleven at the time, too young to have learned much of the legacy. Her father preserved the special memory, some family contacts, and much-cherished original editions of the *Memoirs*, but beyond that, my mother grew up with little direct exposure to the family's unusual past.

Sayyida Salme
(1844–1924)

Rosalie (Rosa)
(1870–1948)

Emily
(1903–1948)

Ursula
(1936–)

Andrea
(1962–)

---

34 Rosa's brother Rudolph and his family, including his Jewish wife, had left Germany long before. Rosa's sister Antonie stayed in Germany, while one of her daughters moved to America with her husband in 1936. Antonie was tragically killed by the British bombing of Bad Oldesloe in 1945, near the end of the war.
35 With Antonie's death in 1945 and Rudolph's death in 1946, all the author's children died in these years.

As a result, some of our current connection to the family is more sentimental than personal. The link to Rosa's ancestry is perhaps most evident in the names. With us, the Christian Emily, as in Emily Ruete, abounds. It is also the first name of my mother's mother, my cousin, my niece, and the middle name of my mother and myself. Not until I had my own child did I appreciate the significance of naming. But rather than follow our tradition, I felt truly privileged to reach back to the original name, Salme, as a middle name for my child. To my knowledge, this has happened only once before, when Rudolph honored his mother by naming his daughter Olga Salme.[36] Perhaps more to the point, though, our current connection is also more deliberate. Like many others who have valued Sayyida Salme over the years, we too are circling back in history to get to know her.

On the subject of family, a few additional aspects are worth noting. For one, within the scope of Sayyida Salme's life, family was hard to come by. Although she grew up with dozens of half-brothers and half-sisters,[37] this was a family in the broadest sense, as she amply describes in her *Memoirs*. Telling, of course, is her reference to "the father" (*der Vater*),[38] a label that sounds more honorific than intimate. He was a father shared by scores of wives and children, not to mention the people of two countries.

More poignantly, though, Sayyida Salme went from being an orphan at age 15 to a widow at age 25. In between lay only three precious years of a partnered life with a happy, nuclear family, while the before and after were replete with challenge. Sayyida Salme not only faced the hurdles of making it on her own, especially as a girl and woman in a man's world, but did so in contexts that were unusually politicized; and, once in Germany, also completely foreign. In the time before she met her husband, she spent her teen years in the harem with no father or mother looking out for her, and with allegiances forming fast and furious around her. It has always made sense to me that she was still unmarried at the ripe old age of twenty-two, open to alternatives, possibly looking for a way out. And in the period after reaching Germany, she has given us enough clues[39] to know that her subsequent life took its toll beyond anything she could have anticipated.

---

36 In full, Olga Salme Mathilde Benvenuta Said-Ruete. Notably Rudolph's daughter was born in England outside the more restrictive German name approval process that might have disallowed Salme. Rudolph also honored his father when naming his son, Werner Heinrich Mathissen Said-Ruete.
37 As the author tells us, thirty-six sons and daughters were living when Sayyid Said died in 1856 (*Memoirs*, pages 8, 87, 89, and 171), out of a purported hundred or so that were born from seventy-five *sarari* (concubines) (*Memoirs*, page 8).
38 *Vater* is capitalized in the original publication, as is the case with all German nouns, but potentially also in a titular fashion. For this translation, I debated whether to capitalize the word in English as well, but decided to stay neutral by keeping the "father" lowercased.
39 Many details appear in her *Briefe nach der Heimat*, which she wrote after her *Memoirs*, but which remained unpublished until the 1990s. My new translation appears in *Letters to the Homeland: An Accurate Translation of an Intimate Voice* (2023).

On Family

But we can also consider Djilfidan, Sayyida Salme's mother, the little we know of her from the *Memoirs*. She, too, was orphaned, although much younger and more tragically, bereft of her entire Circassian family by rampaging Russian mercenaries. The more I understand of her origins, the more I appreciate my own link to a people that no longer has its place on a map, of which Djilfidan's extinguished family is but one of a million and more stories. Circassian women were prized for their fair-skinned beauty, and Djilfidan was apparently just old enough to be trafficked. Or maybe there was another layer. Rather than purchased by the Sultan, perhaps she was gifted to him.[40] That seems plausible, since she joined the harem at an unusually young age, still a child herself, and grew up with children of the other *sarari*. The Sultan would have been a father figure to her before he made her a mother.

We can also recall that "family" among Arab royals (perhaps all royals) could be brutal. As a rule, governing was a male enterprise, and there was only one Sultan among the many sons (or two when they split Oman and Zanzibar). Sayyid Said himself had to eliminate his usurper cousin to become Sultan. After Sayyid Said died, his son Barghash had designs on his older brother Madjid. Madjid, in claiming Zanzibar, in turn defied his older brother Tueni in Oman. Even a century later, the young Qaboos had to sideline his father Said bin Taimur to take the crown. Although Sayyida Salme was born in a prosperous and stable period, the older she got, the more fragmented and fraught the family became. Loss of the beloved patriarch led to infighting right at the time that Sayyida Salme reached the age of agency and became a player herself.

That Sayyida Salme's Zanzibari family meant a lot to her goes almost without saying. Even so, we can note that in the *Memoirs*, her shortest chapter is about her marriage union and her longest is about the family rupture.[41] She does not dwell on what it was to fall in love with her husband, but gives us page after page on how the coup attempt unfolded. Memories seared in her mind, the saga was still deeply present a decade later when she wrote that account. She does not name her husband even once in the entire book, but Barghash is named a hundred times. Seemingly, the shadow cast over her life by her original family, not just politically and existentially, but also emotionally, was as long as the one cast by what became—and became of—her new family. We might say she freed

---

40 As suggested by our friend Dr. Abdallah Daar, who provided great support on my first trip to Oman. He had researched the question in relation to his own family.
41 Sayyida Salme would have preferred good relations with all, but ended up choosing sides in the power play and then later, having extended a hand to Madjid, was accused by Chole and Barghash of having chosen. Such hard lines were clearly not conducive to family harmony, as such yet another example of that elusive middle ground: *In my opinion, the happy middle has not yet been found anywhere.* (Memoirs, *page 132*)

herself of the one to find the other, but there was no freeing herself from the memory of her original home and homeland.

On a more personal note, as far as family goes, where I see Sayyida Salme in the vanguard of feminism in her time, I see myself as a classic "sign of the times" in my own. Both of us single mothers, both shaped by our settings, we both wrote our own scripts. It was far easier for me than for her, which says something about society's progress. She chose to follow the love of her life and then had to deal with the rejection and isolation that followed. I chose a career path and still found my way into family, becoming a so-called—socially acceptable—single mother by choice. It is not lost on me that Sayyida Salme's grounding became her children, as for me with my child, despite the very different circumstances. To know my child is in her line of children, for whom she originally wrote her *Memoirs*, gives me a deeper connection to her and greater meaning to this family project.

ON FATE

I believe some readers may read the word "fate" and feel some pity towards me, or if nothing else, shrug their shoulders. But one must not forget that the author was a Muslim and raised this way. And I am of course telling the story of an Arab life, an Arab household, that is, a real Arab home, where two concepts in particular were as yet unfamiliar: the word "chance" and materialism. A Muslim not only recognizes his God as his creator and keeper, but also feels the presence of the Lord at all times. He is certain that it is not his will, but the will of the Lord that comes to pass, in all things, large and small. (Memoirs, page 14)

Fate weaves its way throughout Sayyida Salme's *Memoirs* like a red thread that appears and reappears at consequential moments. Predestined fate is at work when the tracks are shifted, as in German *die Weichen werden gestellt*, and thus becomes both the explanation and extrapolation of events. In her story, it was fate that determined their move to Bet il Watoro; fate that took father, mother, and many others, but spared her; fate that brought her to the city; but also fate that let others excuse her transgression, namely her apostasy, thus making it an act *of* the Almighty, not against Him.

Of course, in our multicultural society, fate belongs to the beholder, as does its corollary, faith. Sayyida Salme tells us that fate is part and parcel of being a Muslim, woven into everyday life. Being Ibadi, her form of Islam, meant deferring all power to Allah's omniscience and omnipotence. But even after the author becomes Christian, we continue to feel the imprint of fate on her life. It is a stark exercise to draw a line through Sayyida Salme's most fateful span of years: finding Bububu, losing Bububu, moving to the city, meeting a German merchant, falling in love, bearing a child, losing a child, bearing three more children, losing her husband, losing her assets and inheritance—incidents that laid down the tracks for what came next, with no way back. What is given and taken in each of these strokes hits high and low pitches that are octaves apart.

Fate in this story can feel not only fatalistic, but also quite fatal—especially where medicine is mystery, and fate is how people, as she says, come to grips with death. Even so, with her mother and father already gone, what a calamitous tragedy it was that Sayyida Salme's first born died less than a month after her baptism and betrothal, while they were still on their journey to Germany! This little life that precipitated her escape from the island was now gone, less than a year later. How could Sayyida Salme not have taken this as a sign from God? She never writes about it, and that is comment enough.[42]

Fast forward just a few years. What are the chances that her beloved husband, to whom Sayyida Salme had hitched her entire destiny in an entirely new place, culture, language, family, religion, and all—no way back—would die so tragically at the prime age of thirty-one? What a crazy fluke of an accident! It was not the first time Sayyida Salme felt the helpless despair that beckons thoughts of fate. She lost both her mother and husband by watching them disintegrate, painfully, unfathomably in a matter of days, with nothing she could do, even told to stay away as they succumbed. By the time Sayyida Salme starts writing her *Memoirs* several years later, her three children have become her one and all. And yet, as she alludes in her Preface, and as she has learned all too well, nothing is assured, not even her chance to tell them her story unless she writes it while she can.

Indeed, Sayyida Salme describes an early incident that almost cost her her life, when she rode straight into a twisted, bent-over palm while horse racing her brother, but—as if by a miracle—threw herself backwards in the last seconds. Such fate! And then on the very next page, we read about her mother's story, how her mother's parents were murdered by marauding mercenaries, who then rode off with her brother and sister, never to be seen again, while she lived on. More fate! What let Djilfidan escape death at that perilous moment and live a long and comfortable life thereafter? Could one even say she had a better life for being forced into servitude as a child? The question may test our understanding of slavery and society, especially because we can never prove counterfactuals. We might more readily conclude that none of this, these *Memoirs*, your attention, and least of all me, would have happened if she and her daughter had not been spared by this hand of fate.

When fate determines life's events, and things are pre-ordained, then everything is what it is, beyond us. In this way, fate is the foil of free will. But this letting go to the Lord may also prompt believers to look for signs that validate their

---

[42] Not until the death certificate of their infant Heinrich was discovered by Heinz Schneppen in a Hamburg archive (*Staatsarchiv*) did the puzzle piece fall into place. Schneppen served as German Ambassador to Tanzania from 1993 to 1996 and published the first German edition of Sayyida Salme's/Emily Ruete's *Briefe nach der Heimat* in 1999. My new English translation appears in *Letters to the Homeland: An Accurate Translation of an Intimate Voice* (2023).

On Fate

circumstances and choices. Like, perhaps, the very devout Djilfidan more readily accepting her lot as part of the harem—and accepting it all the more when bestowed with a free and royal child. Or like the intensely pious Barghash believing narcissistically in his own destiny as Sultan—and believing it all the more once he finally got there. It is etymologically significant that in the German phrase for "it is fate"—per the *Memoirs, es ist bestimmt*—the word *bestimmt* has a double meaning as "it is certain." And so, invoking fate lets us move forward with more certainty, indeed, more confidence, less confusion, less concern.

For Sayyida Salme, whether fate or free will, she also bore a free heart.[43] At first blush, this is an early multicultural tale of what we do for love, long before such crossovers were accepted, much less in vogue. But sometimes we are propelled by forces beyond our choosing. Perhaps it was just such a love that led Sayyida Salme to leave home, where, in her words, a union with her beloved was impossible. And then it became a love for her budding child and even love of self, to escape for their lives. But there are also early clues that Sayyida Salme was headstrong and independent. As a child, she learned gun shooting and cock fighting, becoming "half an Amazon." She was not much interested in needlework and lace making, and she was a prankster. And somewhere along the way, she probably pined for a life beyond the narrow and rigid confines of cloistered royalty and sequestered womanhood.

To me, the fact that she secretly taught herself to write is the most important clue. She was ambitious and capable and non-conformist. She knew writing for girls was taboo, but that did not stop her. "When word got out, I was denounced in the strongest terms, but not much bothered" is one of the most telling sentences in the *Memoirs*. And then come to find out, this special skill was in demand; it even elevated her to an indispensable role. For a young teen, it must have been quite the flattering headrush to become the scribe for such an important intrigue, whether she liked the plan or not.

One could say, though, that it all began with Sayyida Salme's birth into royalty. This quirk of fate was all the more significant with her coming from both royalty and slavery. Unlike the Americas, Arab society privileged this combination with full ranking, full royalty, full rights of inheritance (and even subsequent freedom for her mother). And so, she woke up in the harem household every day knowing she was at the top of the hierarchy, not for anything she did— just by fate—surrounded by second class eunuchs and supported by third class servers and slaves. But what did it all mean anyhow? Moving across extremes,

---

43 Notably, one of Sayyida Salme's themes is to let us "not forget the heart for the head." (*Memoirs*, page 60)

from lowest to highest, it is strange to see what fate wrought. Her mother, a slave, ultimately lived a life of comfort, but she, a princess, found a life of strain.

We start the story in a time and place of fairy tales—once upon a time long ago, there lived a princess. . . . Coming from such a world, Sayyida Salme can feel almost mystical to us today. But in confounding such a world, she becomes inspirational. It is a real life, whose fate, like history, may not repeat, but can give us rhymes. She, as author and narrator, primarily worked off of contrasts— East to West, Muslim to Christian, women to men—in other words, what is different? We, as readers, instinctively seek meaning in her life and writings. Coming many generations later, when differences are the default, we seek the parallels—what is the same? For all that has changed between then and now, it is surprisingly easy to find rhyming couplets between her time and ours.

It is perhaps my fate—the red thread that lets me connect the dots—that I am here, reaching back to give voice to her life through mine. Should these pages also resonate with rhyme for you, dear Reader, perhaps you feel your fate here, too.

ON CONTROVERSY

The subject of this chapter is controversial. I realize I will not make many friends with my views, but consider it my duty to share them. I have come across too much unawareness everywhere on this question. Even the more informed people too often overlook that this is about more than genuine humane efforts by Europeans, considering that they take place against a backdrop of hidden political interests. (Memoirs, page 165)

Sayyida Salme says it herself, in the opening words of her chapter on Slavery. She knows she is treading on fraught ground with her views, but is nonetheless compelled to add to the conversation, rather than stay silent. I believe that is to her credit. She knew she had an unusual, indeed unique, perspective. Writing to a European public, her lens and pen drew from the local slave society she had personally experienced. Clearly, that personal connection colored her views, for better or worse, but also came from a place of genuine concern about her community. And, in contrast to the prevalent, colonial, missionary, West-over-East attitudes of the time, that voice arguably deserved to be heard.

We can see Sayyida Salme and her *Memoirs* as part of a difficult contemporary conversation about societal transformation, while still today flatly rejecting some of her views. We can even call her racist, while still appreciating that she chose to use her voice. There is always more nuance to the matter, and Sayyida Salme was not afraid to go there. She prods her audience to become more aware. She makes us consider that multiple truths can co-exist.

This is not to excuse or defend Sayyida Salme's views, particularly on race and slaves, only to put them in context. Rather than cherry-pick controversial statements to discredit her wholesale—what some have done and what others may call cancel culture—I suggest that both she and her story are more complex and layered. Indeed, there is much to study here, as the flourishing scholarship that draws from the *Memoirs* would indicate.[44]

---

[44] As one indicator, according to Google Scholar, citations of "Memoirs of an Arabian Princess" more than doubled each decade from 1971 to 2020 (2, 6, 29, 58, 128). A Google search of the title when these *Memoirs* were originally published brought up over 12,000 results.

Exactly this position was taken by the expert opinion recently commissioned by the Free and Hanseatic City of Hamburg, where Sayyida Salme spent her first years in Germany. In 2019, the city elected to name one of its open spaces in honor of Emily Ruete, Sayyida Salme's Christian name. After the street sign went up, some individuals filed a complaint on account of her racist beliefs and writings. The sign was taken down, but an expert opinion was also sought to evaluate the complaint and give the matter a full and fair hearing. Hamburg has been exemplary in running this process openly and transparently, with the expert opinion readily and globally available online. Reading the opinion, city government may have realized that Sayyida Salme cannot be boxed into one category, and for now, the matter remains under consideration:

> In the Salme/Ruete biography, the categories of gender, class, and race overlap in various combinations. Her [cross-continental] migrations add to the other different, above-referenced roles of a woman, who, as a princess and migrant, author, single mother, and anti-black racist, that was cosmopolitan and excluded, exoticized and privileged, was also—as a self-determining subject of her own rights—a feminist.
>
> The description of Salme/Ruete is complicated by the effort to situate her in the international colonial (today North-South) relationships, the various contexts, and the racialized black-white hierarchy in which she lived.
>
> .... The censure cops of the global North that decide, rightly or wrongly, how people like Salme/Ruete should be remembered risk serving a Eurocentric point of view. A decision to rename [the location] is no invitation to dialogue and exchange, but rather an imposition of a final judgment that does not allow for nuance with respect to the forced category of race and instead reduces Salme/Ruete's identity to her racist statements.
>
> Salme/Ruete's works are, by contrast, the first documented non-white female voice from the global South that addresses Germany (Europe) and Zanzibar (Africa). She could be remembered as such, with all her ambiguities and ambivalences, in that her writings are read as a window into German colonialism, a display of racism, and a report of the challenging, even impossible, integration into nineteenth-century German society.[45]

---

45 „*Gutachten: Ambivalente Identitäten—Salme/Ruete, koloniales und kolonialisiertes Subjekt zugleich*," pages 14, 22, by Tania Mancheno at the University of Hamburg (2021) (the above translation of the excerpted text was approved by Dr. Mancheno).

Sayyida Salme was no stranger to controversy. She acted controversially and spoke on controversial subjects, even as what counts as "controversial" has shifted over time. Views that were mainstream then, in both East and West, like racial hierarchies, are unacceptable now. But other views that were unacceptable then, like choosing to reject Islam, are currently accepted, even validated as religious freedom. Clearly, society is not done working out complex topics.

Conversion to Christianity

For all her striking behavior, Sayyida Salme's most controversial act was her apostasy, when she became a Christian to marry her husband. The most severe and sustained consequences came from her Sultan brother Barghash. Despite Sayyida Salme's many efforts and entreaties, both directly and through others, he never forgave her infidelity and never allowed a reconciliation. Surely she was crestfallen when her brother Barghash replaced her Sultan brother Madjid, who died at age thirty-six shortly after her own husband, both deaths so early and untimely. It was another blow to her connections to home. Whereas Sultan Madjid had reached out with gifts (unbeknownst to her at the time), Sultan Barghash proved implacable.

Not only did Sultan Barghash reject Sayyida Salme out of hand, but his recalcitrance abnegated the unwavering loyalty she had shown him and his cause during the failed coup attempt. She had been an indispensable figure in his aggrandizing venture—as scribe, financier, plotter, rescuer, and more, putting her relations, reputation, even life at great risk. But Islam was both his conviction and cover. Sultan Barghash seemed so personally offended by her rapprochement with his archenemy Madjid, the Sultan he had sought to depose, that he could not get beyond his own emotions. Her reconciliation with Madjid seemed to offend Barghash as much as her conversion to Christianity. Later, Barghash's dogged piety was also in stark contrast to the overwhelmingly enthusiastic reception she received from the island population upon her return at long last after nineteen years. He could not stand the outpouring and instead cracked down on his people. And yet, as she reports, the throngs were not to be deterred, even at pain of punishment.

Sayyida Salme was perhaps her own harshest critic. Caught in her circumstances, she remained unsettled: "I left my homeland as a complete Arab and good Muslim, and what am I today?" With her heart on her sleeve, she started to answer—her famous answer: "A poor Christian and somewhat more than half a German!"—but then deleted it.⁴⁶ We can speculate about why she struck that response in her edits, but we can also feel the anguish in her conflicted soul.

Faith was no less important to her than it was to Barghash. Originally an unquestioning Muslim, and then persisting as a Christian despite encouragement and even financial inducements from her Zanzibari family and friends, she spent a lifetime close to her Lord, seeking Him as much after the conversion as she did before. She never lost her faith, no matter how much the circumstances changed.

But having transgressed, Sayyida Salme was no longer considered part of the family.⁴⁷ For some, it remains a point of sensitivity. For others, views may be softening. The Omani/Zanzibari Sultanate has historically shown great tolerance for different religions and is a strong proponent of religious freedom today.⁴⁸

We can see that for someone like Sayyida Salme, religion was not an open, inconsequential choice at the time, nor was marriage. Clearly, Sayyida Salme broke two cardinal rules, knowingly and boldly, when she chose her husband and thus her religion. But just as clearly, today we can see that those rules deserve more criticism than her behavior.

Views on Slavery and Africans

In our present day, the greater controversy is about Sayyida Salme's racism. Today she is criticized for her acceptance of slavery and her denigration of black Africans. Both aspects merit a closer look.

In the years since Sayyida Salme left Zanzibar, the anti-slavery movement had continued to build in Europe. To a shocking degree, the interior of East Africa

---

46 The translated version in this book reflects the author's latest views by including all edits that appeared in her handmarked copy of the original German publication. The Leiden University Libraries has made a digitized version available at NINO SR 613 a-b.

47 Rudolph Said-Ruete tried to engage the British on behalf of his mother starting in 1914, but not until 1923, less than a year before she died, was she finally granted a small annuity by the Zanzibari Sultanate. In 1932, Sultan Khalifa also recognized Rudolph as the grandson of Sultan Said bin Sultan and a member of the royal family, conferring on him the title "Sayyid" at his request. Nevertheless, Sultan Khalifa later declined to invite him to the bicentennial of the Al Bu Said dynasty in 1941, explaining to the acting British resident that "the elopement of Mr. Ruete's mother was and still is regarded by the Arabs as a shameful affair and they prefer not to be reminded of it." Emeri van Donzel, *An Arabian Princess Between Two Worlds*, pp. 105, 119, 125, 131 (1993).

48 The majority of Omanis and many Zanzibaris follow the Ibadi strain of Islam, which is distinct from Sunni and Shia Islam and is known to promote social harmony and tolerance. On a web page entitled "Religious Freedom," Oman's Foreign Ministry assures "the freedom of religious belief, worship and education" under the Basic Statute of the State, naming Christians among the protected citizens and referring to Oman's "long history as a multicultural society."

was being increasingly raided and ravaged. The East African slave trade, which Sayyida Salme rightly criticized, grew to horrifying dimensions. However, far from simply being "Arab" slavery, as some made it seem, it involved a wide network of players, in large measure by Africans upon Africans, and was propelled by market forces that fed profiteering financiers, Zanzibari coffers, labor-needy plantations, and European appetites for grains, spices, ivory, and other commodities.[49]

Ironically, and tragically, British anti-slavery efforts appear to have spurred, not deterred, increased slave trade in Zanzibar. At first, as demand for labor increased, prices of slaves went up, which fueled more caravans into the hinterlands, which in turn fueled the export slave market. But when the British tamped down on slave exports with the treaty of 1845, under which Sayyid Said agreed to limit legal slave trade to routes between East Africa and Zanzibar,[50] the slave movement was concentrated and prices in Zanzibar fell. At the same time, to keep the Sultanate from complete demise, Britain pushed for the export slave trade to be replaced by "legitimate commerce," which included cloves, rubber, and copal, all export products that required extensive slave labor, and—helped by the cheap cost of slaves—the sale of slaves surged again. Trade in domestic slaves eventually exceeded export slave trade, as the rise of Africa-sourced farm commodities turned more Africans into commodities.[51]

Despite this broad web of complicity, it was easy, even trendy, for British, German, and other anti-slavery crusaders to criticize from West to East, enlightened to backward, and assume a certain superiority. Zanzibaris had grounds to look skeptically at European imperial agendas, and British anti-

---

[49] To underscore how intertwined these forces were, 1834 was both the year the British Slavery Abolition Act ended slave trade in the Indian Ocean and the year Sayyid Said bin Sultan entered into a commercial treaty with the United States. To offset British pressure to end slavery in Zanzibar, the U.S. treaty brought in major quantities of cotton produced by African slaves in America, whose currency was used in East Africa to purchase more slaves. Clifford Pereira, "'Naturalists,' 'Explorers,' and Imperialists: German Ambitions in the Horn of Africa and the Anti-Slavery Movement," p. 9, on www.academia.edu; Steven Feierman, "A Century of Ironies in East Africa (c. 1780–1890)," in P. Curtin, S. Feierman, L. Thompson, and J. Vansina, *African History: From Earliest Times to Independence*, p. 357 (1995).

[50] Given Zanzibar's pivotal role in the slave trade, some even recognized Sayyid Said as an exemplary figure in the anti-slavery crusade. "His stalwart and fearless personality prompted him, at great moral and practical inconvenience, and even danger to himself, to identify himself openly with Great Britain (who enjoyed no co-operation from other western powers at that time) in her determined efforts for the suppression of the African slave trade...." Foreword by Major-General Sir Percy Cox (p. ix) in Rudolph Said-Ruete's *Said bin Sultan (1791–1856)—Ruler of Oman and Zanzibar: His Place in the History of Arabia and East Africa* (1929).

[51] Cosmo Rana-Iozzi, "Why did slave trading intensify in the nineteenth century, and with what consequences for East African society?," on www.academia.edu; Steven Feierman, see footnote 49, pp. 352–76.

slavery treaties, in particular. This vulnerability bore itself out over time, as Germany and Britain struck inland deals, and Zanzibar increasingly came under British debt and control. Indeed, there are those who cite a continuing history of British repression of Arab culture, who also think those forces were hard at work in efforts to tarnish Arabs, and antagonize Africans against them, leading up to the rampaging Zanzibar revolution in 1964 and its aftermath.[52]

Without the benefit of such hindsight, Sayyida Salme certainly had her own reasons to attribute ill will to colonial powers, starting with Great Britain. It was, admittedly, the British who originally helped her escape the island, but also the British who kept her from her Sultan brother, callously strung her along, and then pathetically reneged. Although she is full of praise for the very kind couple that hosted her during her interminable London nightmare, it is hard not to speculate that this was all calculated design. Out of the hotel and into their house for the entire time, she was conveniently under constant supervision, always directed away from her brother on daily outings, and ever so grateful that they were only too happy to draft Sir Bartle Frere's pro memoria for her. A bit too perfect, no?

More to the point, rightly or wrongly, Sayyida Salme was speaking up for Zanzibari society as a Zanzibari, whereas others sitting a continent away had no problem disaggregating slavery from the rest of society. We can more easily draw a bright line—zero tolerance—today than at a time when slave societies, like Zanzibar, still existed. Back then, when class and race defined every relationship in Zanzibari society, meaning the entire social strata, it was natural to consider the topic for its effects across all of society.[53] Without condoning her positions, can we blame her for flagging that an abrupt end to slavery would precipitate calamitous consequences for slaves and slavers alike in a society where an estimated two-thirds of the population were slaves?[54] Should one perhaps blame others for not having dealt with the question of transition

---

52 Nasser Abdulla Al-Riyami, *Zanzibar Personalities and Events (1828–1972)* (2014); Anne Chappel, "Zanzibar: A Question of History, a Question of Slavery" (July 2010), on www.afrikacalismalarimerkezi.com. As Chappel points out, Zanzibari slavery was weaponized in the politics around independence and is now being commercialized for tourists. In her view, fabricated slave sites not only feed tourism, but also perpetuate racial splits and stereotypes that continue to stoke island tensions today.

53 To bear this out, Zanzibar became a British protectorate in 1890, but slavery was not completely outlawed there until 1897, and even then concubinage, as a form of "privileged slavery," was still allowed until 1909. As we can see here, even the British, once they were in control, felt the need to transition slowly to maintain social stability. Elke Stockreiter, "British Perceptions of Concubinage and the Patriarchal Arab Household: The Reluctant Abolition of Slavery in Zanzibar, 1890s–1900s," p. 6, in *Slavery & Abolition* (2015).

54 Thomas Vernet, "East Africa: Slave Migrations," p. 3, in *The Encyclopedia of Global Human Migration*, ed. Immanuel Ness (2013).

more holistically? Zanzibar is not the only country where a precipitous end to a slave society created so much social upheaval that the turmoil is still being played out today. In any case, the end of slavery pushed Zanzibar straight into Western colonial hands, presumably according to plan.

And meanwhile, Europe was less inclined to look critically at itself and its own social and class dynamics, as Sayyida Salme was asking her readers to do. She challenged her audience to think about the condition of all lower classes, even suggesting—based on her direct empirical observations—that many Zanzibari slaves had better conditions than many Western workers who were subjected to the dehumanizing pressures of industrialization and capitalism. That is no doubt debatable, but in comparison to other slave states, she knew that Arab society in general, and Zanzibar in particular, had a more nuanced approach, one that rested on Islamic tenets, legal rights, and social conventions. Here slavery existed alongside a complex array of other forms of dependence and covered a spectrum of arrangements, including many slaves who were held primarily for prestige, where productivity was less important than total numbers and personal attachment.[55]

Lest we forget, even Sayyida Salme's mother had slave status as a concubine (*surie,* pl. *sarari*).[56] In another slave society, Sayyida Salme herself would have been born a slave. Instead, as a princess, she was given slaves as her own personal servants and surrounded by caretaking slaves from infancy onward. She even became the owner of her own retinue of slaves, with full responsibility, when she was declared of age at barely twelve. Sayyida Salme grew up amidst an extensive stratification of slaves—including eunuchs, *sarari,* house servants, and plantation workers—who were further stratified amongst themselves. This extreme juxtaposition of slavery and royalty,[57] numbering up to a thousand in the same household, and the intimacy of this day-to-day experience, necessarily gave Sayyida Salme a different view of slavery than the one presented to members of German or British anti-slavery societies or experienced by inland explorers, like the abolitionist crusader David Livingstone.

---

55 Ibid.
56 Abdul Sheriff, "*Suria*: Concubine or Secondary Slave Wife? The Case of Zanzibar in the Nineteenth Century," in G. Campbell and E. Elbourne, *Sex, Power, and Slavery* (2014). Sayyida Salme's mother Djilfidan was torn from her Circassian homeland as part of a century of Russian invasions that eliminated and dispersed up to 90 percent of the indigenous population. Stephen Shenfield, "The Circassians—A Forgotten Genocide?" from *The Massacre in History*, ed. Mark Leven and Penny Roberts (2006).
57 This tendency to separate classes and recognize noble status was hardly limited to Oman and Zanzibar. We can keep in mind that Europe also had its share of royalty at the time. Sayyida Salme was able to connect into this echelon of society through her own royal status.

The more intractable point is that most of this slavery, certainly the East African trade, rested on hierarchical concepts of race. Race—and especially blackness—was the salient marker of social status and human value. Sayyida Salme was hardly alone in taking this view. This was not a matter of West over East in a hierarchy of international relations—putting Arab and Zanzibari society down—but a matter of social relations, putting blacks and natives down. To say it clearly, the anti-slavery movement was not seeking to elevate the status of black Africans as equals to enlightened Europeans. Scholars have noted, for example, that foreign missionaries took slavery to be a "natural phenomenon for the African *Naturvölker*," which fed right into the colonial ideology of the time. Explorers were entering the "dark continent," and freed Africans were prized as candidates for evangelizing and enlightening, even to the point of keeping younger ones from their families.[58] Moreover, the British view, as documented explicitly, considered white slavery far more "revolting" than black slavery, indicating that even purported anti-slavers harbored racist views that debased Africans.[59]

The places in the *Memoirs* where Sayyida Salme treats Africans as less capable and less worthy were the most difficult to translate because they are so uncomfortable, so dismaying to take in. She was otherwise open to and appreciative of different races and origins, making it all the more striking how much she deprecated indigenous blacks. But she wrote about the behavior she saw around her, and to see her, and many others, jump from such observations to wholesale determinations of inferiority and a license to pre-judge challenges us to realize how blinkered we can be. How easy it is to confuse cause and effect, with no apparent awareness that the conditions of slavery, limited access to resources, and disparaging attitudes of society would give rise to such behavior, rather than reflect a natural state of being. In the same way that Sayyida Salme sought to open the eyes of the European public, our eyes have been opened through greater exposure and understanding over the decades. Sayyida Salme is, of course, not in a position to take her words back today, but I think she would if she could.

Today the international community understands human rights differently and rejects all human bondage and racist hierarchies. We would like to believe that we have a different understanding of humanity now, and that we also

---

58 Clifford Pereira, see footnote 49, p. 9.
59 Quoting British Consul Sir John Kirk, who began consular duties the year Sayyida Salme left Zanzibar, after five years accompanying explorer David Livingstone as his physician and naturalist, as cited by Jeremy Prestholdt in his chapter titled "Symbolic Subjection and Social Rebirth: Objectification in Urban Zanzibar," in *Domesticating the World: African Consumerism and the Genealogies of Globalization*, p. 129 (2008).

would not have "othered" Sayyida Salme in the same way that she herself experienced at the time.⁶⁰ The *Memoirs* are part of a rich tapestry of complex, at times contradictory and counterintuitive, dynamics of history that deserve a nuanced, holistic, intersectional view of the world. As my friend SB Rawz says: "Acknowledging the complexity of humans, our history, and our institutions cannot erase their value, unless we trade one kind of oversimplification for another."⁶¹ In this era of soundbites and stereotypes, cancel culture and caricatures, it is all the more important to listen fully, lest we miss some of what is really going on.

Certainly, the assessment is a personal one. Each of us can decide individually whether Sayyida Salme's racist statements overshadow the rest of her writing. If we take up the challenge, though, we can both reject some of what she had to say and recognize what she may have to teach us—about her life and times, but also what she reflects back to us about our own lives and times. And with that, I would let Sayyida Salme have the last word from her *Memoirs*, as she was the first to admit:

> *The events of my life are all too varied, and they in turn have shaped my feelings and perspectives. People are in large part no more than what their lives, experiences, and given circumstances make of them.* (Memoirs, *page 217*)

---

60 Sayyida Salme describes this stereotyping and caricaturing more fully in her *Briefe nach der Heimat*, which I have newly translated in a companion book, *Letters to the Homeland: An Accurate Translation of an Intimate Voice* (2023).
61 Rawzcoaching.com (June 28, 2021).

ON TRANSLATING

When I first embarked on this translation more than twenty years ago, it was me and my little Langenscheidt to take my German that extra mile. I got through one-third of the original *Memoirs*[62] and then set the project aside. A career, a child, a couple of professional books, and considerable time and events later, I found the neglected file deep in my storage drive and decided to pick up where I had left off, literally with the next paragraph. The pandemic was still rocking the world, and as we hunkered down, I was finding room for other things.

It began as a desire to get to know my esteemed ancestor better, to literally get inside her words. She had taken care to leave this record behind; I had the privilege to explore its import. As I delved in, I found real pleasure in revealing her meaning. To make sure I could find my voice in response to hers, I translated the first run cold, without any comparison to other texts.

When I used round two to cross-check against the two early English translations,[63] I was stunned by their sloppiness (what else to call it when whole words, sentences, paragraphs, even chapters, simply go missing?). One translation had some lovely renditions, but must have been done in haste. The other translation took such license that the translator's discretion at times seemed to morph into his own flights of fancy. Perhaps notions of authenticity have changed over the years,[64] but in neither case was I truly reading the author's own story. Seeing these reconstructed versions of her tale, I was no longer just intrigued for myself. I felt compelled to translate for others.

Also compelling was that I have had my mother as a partner. Although the translation is mine, she has given it her meticulous review and quality control, along with much sensitivity and thoughtfulness. What better way to continue the family legacy than by combining generational forces in the effort. It appears that mother and daughter had already collaborated once before

---

62 *Memoiren einer arabischen Prinzessin* made its German debut as two volumes in 1886, which are reproduced as a composite publication here. Public interest was so great that four editions were sold that same year.
63 The first English translation came out in London by Ward and Downey in 1888 as *Memoirs of an Arabian Princess* and also appeared in New York through D. Appleton and Co. that same year, with no translator named. A decade later, in 1907, a new—apparently unauthorized—translation was presented in New York by Lionel Strachey with Doubleday, Page and Co.
64 Almost ironically, the Lionel Strachey edition included a front section titled "Authenticity of these Memoirs," in which the translator informed his readers that his book, having to do with "the Black Continent and its peoples," presented "so romantic a supposal seeming to require confirmation," which he then delivered.

when Rosa, Sayyida Salme's youngest and my direct ancestor, helped hone the original manuscript. Perhaps this translation, too, will become part of the greater family story.

One need not look far in the marketplace of books and ideas to appreciate the mutable form that Sayyida Salme's legacy has taken and will continue to take, whether in the service of scholarship, social or political agendas, or commerce. This publication, too, is inevitably new and different, but sets itself apart from the readily available translations and other variations[65] by hewing as closely as possible to the original German.[66]

We are all born into our circumstances. For my great-great-grandmother, that meant a fantastical combination of royalty and slavery out of which her extraordinary life unfolded and to which she gave voice in her *Memoirs*. For me, born German and raised American, and for my mother, raised in Germany and then raising her children in the United States, we bring both languages from both sides of the ocean. It feels like we have been perfectly placed these generations later to restore and revive Sayyida Salme's voice. Rather than speak for her (as in the perfect German word *bevormunden*, to "put in front of the mouth"), our project strives to reinforce her story in her own words, as much as a translation can. This book is meant to free her voice, to have her speak directly from her time to ours by both rebooting back to the original and refreshing for today.

Our two watchwords have been *accuracy*, saying what she says, and *authenticity*, portraying what she presents. My mother and I have been mindful of Sayyida Salme's writing, word-for-word, along with her context, while staying attuned to her wit, irony, passion, nuance, and even silence, all of which emerge from her pages. I have kept her exact volume, chapter, and paragraph structure, even virtually all of the same sentence structure (although changing many semi-colons to periods), as well as the one-off dashes she so characteristically inserted. But the goal was also accessibility and readability for modern eyes and

---

[65] In addition to the two original English translations, G.S.P. Freeman-Grenville published an annotated and somewhat corrected version of the 1888 London edition almost a century later, in 1981. Since then, with open season on copyright, both the 1888 and 1907 translations have become available in multiple guises, some more packaged than others. Of note as well, Annegret Nippa took the significant step of resurfacing the original German work in 1989, also a century later, with her lightly edited *Leben im Sultanspalast*.

[66] One other more recent English translation also stands apart for its commitment to accuracy. Anyone interested in the full historical context will be grateful for Professor Emeri van Donzel's remarkably comprehensive and thoroughly researched book, *An Arabian Princess Between Two Worlds* (1993). Containing his own translations of the *Memoirs*, *Letters Home*, and other writings, this scholarly work has been an important resource for us and others seeking to learn more about Sayyida Salme's life and legacy.

ears, a matter of adjusting Victorian recounting to contemporary resonance—keeping her tone and style, while speaking plainly. For it must be said: The original *Memoirs* are quite fluid in their German narrative and deserve an easy, lucid reading in English, with some elegance as well.

It has felt like the right time and place for me to do this—perhaps you know the feeling. I am not a professional translator, but I am a trained wordsmith. I have played with words all my life. My early years as a transactional lawyer spilled into poetry to offset the rigors of legal memo writing. As I eased into my metier over time, I developed the deep conviction that you can always find some combination of words to make things work. I have practiced the written form as a skill; I have published about the power of shared articulation. The joy of words, both to convey understanding and ground common understandings, has given me much professional and personal fulfillment over the years. And so it has been a joy here, the ultimate word game. Like an extended crossword puzzle, I have sought that exact word, that exact turn of phrase, to match the meaning and suit the setting. Like a game of pick-up sticks, I have tried to take that layered, interwoven German and give the whole just enough daylight to flow into neatly unpacked English.

Along the way, I also had a choice to make.[67] To be true to Sayyida Salme's intentions, I opted to incorporate edits she had left behind.[68] In her additions and deletions, she brought forth helpful clarifications and better judgments several years after publication. With so much preparatory work already done, why was this edited version never published? Whatever the case, the decision to honor her subsequently annotated version became a further justification for an updated translation.

For my own process, what a difference two decades can make. The technology boost since my first foray in 2001 has been remarkable, something I envisioned little more at the turn of my century than Sayyida Salme could have anticipated at the turn of hers. Now, in the internet, smartphone, and app age, the

---

67 There were other choices to be made as well regarding the spelling of Arabic words and names in English. I am aligned with Professor van Donzel in mostly following the author's original spellings "for historical and linguistic reasons" (ibid. at p. x), with a few adjustments, like ungermanizing "sch" to "sh." I also appreciate the author's son's approach in the biography of his grandfather "to follow my own judgment in the matter," after noting five accepted English spellings of the capital of Oman. "In the circumstances I hope my arbitrary decision will be accepted with forbearance." From the Introduction to Rudolph Said-Ruete, *Said bin Sultan (1791–1856)—Ruler of Oman and Zanzibar: His Place in the History of Arabia and East Africa*, p. xviii (1929).
68 Her book with handwritten annotations is available digitally in the Leiden University Libraries Special Collections at NINO SR 613 a-b. Professor van Donzel also reflected Sayyida Salme's subsequent edits in his book (ibid.), in a rigorous presentation that clearly identifies deletions and additions for direct comparison.

translator's arsenal is vast: multiple tabs for various German-English dictionary sites (and immediate visibility of dozens of possible translations), tabs for searches in actual translated texts (turning phrases into scores of sample paragraphs), tabs for synonyms (and synonyms of synonyms), and, of course, general Google searches. Translating has always been a skill, but what used to be mostly in the head has acquired such abundant supporting resources that it is now more like a mix-and-match puzzle of invigorating proportions.

That brings me to our other watchword: *respect*. In this translation, I have sought to reflect Sayyida Salme's own words and style, but go no further. Within this safe harbor, I could provide a faithful reproduction without trying to tease out the unspoken, fill in the interstices, or add manufactured details. Unlike those who have fictionalized her tale, as more than a few have done, I dared not trespass and write the story for her. Instead, this translation let me work within my comfort zone, a chance to get closer—respectfully—without overstepping.

But even translators have a tremendous responsibility to the authors of the works they translate. Inserting myself in this role, I have felt that calling perhaps more than most. How interesting, on the one hand, that the original English translator for the London publication was not named—no accountability there. But equally interesting, on the other hand, is that the subsequent English translator in the United States named himself prominently on the title page, perhaps more accountable to his own work than her original. I have meant to position myself differently, both named and accountable, but as a conduit, a bridge, to Sayyida Salme herself.

May the spotlight on this story shine back on her, in her full intensity and complexity. It is with all due deference that I seek only to illuminate her own words for all of us, to turn her German into English with utmost fidelity, in both senses of the word.

LIST OF IMAGES

[iv] Indian Ocean showing the relationship between Oman and Zanzibar, two countries that were conveniently connected through monsoon trade winds that blew downward from the cool, dry northeast during December to March and then reversed to blow upward from the warm, wet southwest from May to October, while also connecting to India to complete the trade triangle; by Max S. Stumpf, © 2022.

[v] Map of the island of Zanzibar, showing select nineteenth-century destinations, most of which are mentioned in the *Memoirs*; by Max S. Stumpf, © 2022.

[xi] Book announcement pasted into a scrapbook that belonged to the author's son, Rudolph Said-Ruete, including the following text: "Sensational novelty! An important contribution to the cultural history of the Orient. The author is the sister of Sultan Said Barghash [sic] of Zanzibar. The first work of an Oriental woman about the Orient and its social and societal conditions. Fourth edition, September 18, 1886. Publishing company of Friedrich Luckhardt in Berlin"; located in the Leiden University Libraries at Or. 27.135 C1.

[xiii] Hard cover of an edition of Volume 1 of *Memoiren einer arabischen Prinzessin* from 1886; from the collection of Alexander von Brand, great-grandson of Antonie Brandeis, oldest daughter of the author; here rimmed in blue, as compared to the translator's family copy rimmed in brown.

[xiv & xv] End paper and title page of the third edition of Volume 1 of *Memoiren einer arabischen Prinzessin* from 1886; from the translator's family collection.

[xvi] Bookplate of Emily Troemer, granddaughter of the author through Rosa Troemer and grandmother of the translator; appearing in Emily Troemer's books in the translator's family collection.

[xviii] Studio portrait of the author taken by photographer H.F. Plate in Hamburg, Germany around 1867, not long after her arrival, and used as the frontispiece for her 1886 publication of the *Memoiren*.

[2] Drawing of Bet il Mtoni in Zanzibar of unknown origin; provided by Torrence Royer, curator of www.zanzibarhistory.com.

[4] "Vue de M'Tony, Résidence de Campagne du Sultan, prise de la pièce d'eau"; from C. Guillain, *Voyage á la Côte Orientale d'Afrique, exécuté pendant les*

List of Images

années 1846, 1847, and 1848 (1856), in the Leiden University Libraries at NINO SR 190a-c.

[10] "Vue de M'Tony"; ibid.

[13] "Ruined Palace of Syed Saaid ben Sultan at Mtony," by Celia L. Weeks, who travelled with her American husband and captain to Zanzibar in 1869; provided by Torrence Royer, creator of www.zanzibarhistory.com.

[28] A rare portrait of Sayyid Said bin Sultan, Sultan of Oman and ruler of Zanzibar from 1806 to 1856. It was used by Rudolph Said-Ruete, the author's son, as the frontispiece for the biography of his grandfather, with likely attribution to Lieutenant Henry Blosse Lynch, who was in Muscat in the early 1830s; presented to the Peabody Museum in Salem, Massachusetts, in 1906 by the wife of Michael W. Shepard, who traded in Zanzibar from 1837 to 1852. R. Said-Ruete, *Said bin Sultan (1791-1856): Ruler of Oman and Zanzibar—His Place in the History of Arabia and East Africa (1929).*

[29] A colored replica of the original portrait by Amy Clive Edwards and presented by the Peabody Essex Museum to Rudolph Said-Ruete, the author's son, in 1929; now in the Leiden University Libraries at Or. 27.135 D15.

[36] Top: The author's signature in tunghra-style calligraphic Arabic, translating roughly from bottom to top "Salme bint Said Sultan," as it appeared on the title page of her *Memoiren* in 1886. Bottom: Handwritten version of the author's signature. There may be some question about how to properly anglicize the author's name, as the Arabic shows variations, and spellings vary in the secondary literature. However, the author and her family consistently wrote "Salme" in both German and English contexts (see, for example, the great bookcase from her son and her own use in the original *Memoirs* (pages 232 and 9 here)), so there should be no doubt that this is the preferred spelling.

[45] Coffee servers as part of the image captioned "Some Presents from Zanzibar" in *Three Journeys* by Viscountess Cave (Anne Estella Sarah Penford Matthews Cave) published in 1928; in the Leiden University Libraries at NINO SR 135.

[46] "Vue de la Ville de Zanzibar (Prise du Mouillage)"; also from C. Guillain's *Voyage á la Côte Orientale d'Afrique.*

[54] Painting of Stone Town's coastline signed and dated "Rosa Ruete 1886" by the author's youngest daughter; from the translator's family collection.

[65] Painting by Rosa Troemer with "Bet il Ras—Zanzibar 1888" written on the back, likely from her second trip to Zanzibar with her mother; from the translator's family collection. Construction of the palace was started by Rosa's grandfather, Sayyid Said bin Sultan, in 1847, but never completed.

[72] "Muscat from the Harbour," from R. Temple, *Sixteen Views of Places in the Persian Gulph, taken in the years 1809-1810* (1813); located in the Leiden University Libraries at Or. 27.135 J17.

[79] Top: "Muscat Harbour from the Fisher-men's Rock"; ibid. Bottom: "A View of Mutra from the East," ibid.

[83] "Altes arabisches Kriegschiff" (an old Arab warship) handwritten by Rudolph Said-Ruete, the author's son, under a photo in the album he gave as part of his collection to Professor Christiaan Snouck Hurgronje in 1929; now in the Leiden University Libraries at Or. 27.135 H.

[88] Two images of Madjid bin Said, Sultan of Zanzibar from 1856 to 1870. Top: Colored lithograph; located in the Leiden University Libraries at Or. 27.135 D18. Bottom: Image provided by Torrence Royer, creator of www.zanzibarhistory.com.

[116 & 117] Two of four studio portraits of the author by photographer H.F. Plate, taken in Hamburg in 1867; from the Leiden University Libraries at Or. 27.135 D1.

[118 & 119] End paper and title page of the third edition of Volume 2 of *Memoiren einer arabischen Prinzessin* from 1886; from the translator's family collection.

[120] Bookplate of Rudolph Said-Ruete, the author's son, with calligraphy stating "Rudolph Said Ruete, son of Salima bint Said Sultan, ruler of Oman and Zanzibar"; appearing in various books in the special bookcase located in the Netherlands Institute of the Near East (NINO) in Leiden.

[122] Drawing of Stone Town viewed from the sea with the following handwritten notation at the bottom: " —sibar 18? Handzeichnung v. Heinrich Ruete für seine Eltern in Hamburg" ([Zan]zibar 18–? Sketch by Heinrich Ruete for his parents in Hamburg); from the translator's family collection. Rudolph Heinrich Ruete, who went by Heinrich, was the author's husband.

[136] "Zanzibar from the Sea" included by Richard F. Burton in Volume 1 of his book *Zanzibar: City, Island, and Coast* (1872); located in the Leiden University Libraries at NINO SR 115a-b.

List of Images

[151] A Zanzibari shore scene by Rosa Troemer, the author's youngest daughter, likely from 1888 during her second trip to Zanzibar with her mother; from the translator's family collection.

[157] "Plan de Zanzibar" from 1846 with a map of Stone Town before the lagoon was filled in, noting A through D on the coastline as buildings of the royal family; also from C. Guillain's *Voyage á la Côte Orientale d'Afrique*. Ngambo is the area east of the bridge.

[174] Image of Barghash bin Said, Sultan of Zanzibar from 1870 to 1888, taken during his visit to London in 1875, when the author had hoped to meet him; provided by Alexander von Brand from his family collection.

[188] Horizontal: "Zanzibar, Cloves plantation"; from Photo Artist A.R.P de Lord of Zanzibar, showing one of many clove plantations that were introduced during Sayyid Said bin Sultan's reign and helped the island prosper. Vertical: "Natives picking Cloves, Zanzibar"; from A.C. Gomes & Son of Zanzibar. Both part of the Torrence Royer and Pamela Washington Collection of Zanzibar Images and Archives at the Sultan Qaboos Cultural Center in Washington, DC.

[195] View of Stone Town with the following notation on the back: "Haus von Bibi Salme, Sansibar 1867" (House of Mistress Salme, Zanzibar 1867); provided by Alexander von Brand from his family collection. According to Professor van Donzel, "[T]he four lower barred windows belonged to the house. The upper storey was later added when the Hansing firm acquired the house." Emeri van Donzel, *An Arabian Princess Between Two Worlds*, page 15 (1993).

[200] Image of Heinrich Ruete, the author's husband, with the following notation on the back: "Für Tony" (referring to Antonie Brandeis, the author's oldest child) and "Mein Vater, geb. 1839, gest. 1870, Rudolph Heinrich Ruete" (My father, born 1839, died 1870, Rudolph Heinrich Ruete); provided by Alexander von Brand from his family collection.

[204] Image from a glass plate of Sultan Barghash, together with his traveling entourage in London in 1875; located in the Leiden University Libraries at Or. 27-135 D37-13.

[211] Image of the author with her children (from the left): Antonie (Tony, Thawka) Brandeis, Rudolph Said Ruete (later Rudolph Said-Ruete), and Rosalie (Rosa, Ghuza) Troemer; from the translator's family collection.

[215] Itinerary of the author's travels from her hometown, Berlin, to the island of Zanzibar in 1885; by Max S. Stumpf, © 2022.

[230] Image of the author's husband, Heinrich Ruete, with an imprint of "E. Bieber, Hamburg" and handwritten "1863" on the back; provided by Alexander von Brand from his family collection.

[231] Image of the author in Germany; provided by Alexander von Brand from his family collection.

[232] Original bookcase with the golden header "Seyyidah Salme (Emily Ruete)," designed by the author's son Rudolph to house the "Said-Ruete Library," as the collection became known, that he presented to the Oriental Institute (Oosters Instituut) founded by family friend Professor Christiaan Snouck Hurgronje; currently located in the Netherlands Institute for the Near East (NINO) in Leiden.

[234] Front and back of one of more than a hundred small, handcrafted packets containing sunflower seeds that were handed out by the translator and her brother Martin to Omani participants and other visitors on the last day of the 2005 Smithsonian Folklife Festival on the National Mall in Washington, DC, which featured four programs: Oman, USDA Forest Service, Food Culture USA, and Latino Music.

[260] Seaside view of the port of Stone Town, Zanzibar, signed on the front side and dated "W. Rice. Ship River Krishna. 12.12.70"; located in the Leiden University Libraries at Or. 27.135 D16.

[Back cover] Top: One of four studio portraits of the author by photographer H.F. Plate, taken in Hamburg in 1867; with the Leiden University Libraries at Or. 27.135 D1. Bottom: The translator in front of the special "family" bookcase in the NINO on her first visit to Leiden in 2014.

View of Stone Town, Zanzibar

Letters to the Homeland
An Accurate Translation of an Intimate Voice

———•———

By Andrea Emily Stumpf

Translating the original turn-of-the-century
Briefe nach der Heimat
from her great-great-grandmother,

Emily Ruete,
born Sayyida Salme bint Said bin Sultan Al Bu Said,
Princess of Oman and Zanzibar

Copyright © 2023 Andrea E. Stumpf
First edition; published in the United States, 2023
Cover design: Andrea E. Stumpf
Copy Editor: Lauri Scherer, LSF Editorial
Graphic Designer: Joe Bernier, Bernier Graphics

Andrea E. Stumpf has asserted her right as copyright owner of this publication, including under the Copyright, Designs and Patents Act of 1988, to be identified as the author of this work, including as translator of the translated text contained herein. Max S. Stumpf is the copyright owner of the illustrations appearing on pages 3, 15, 28, 53, 87, 97, and 121.

The original text that has been translated for this publication comes from handwritten documents from Sayyida Salme/Emily Ruete, along with a later typed version, entitled *Briefe nach der Heimat*. Compiled as part of the *Literarischer Nachlass* (literary estate) of Sayyida Salme/Emily Ruete, her son Rudolph Said-Ruete granted the documents to the Oriental Institute in Leiden in 1937, along with his own collected books and materials. This special collection was then moved as a permanent loan to the Netherlands Institute for the Near East (NINO) in 1977 and became part of the Leiden University Libraries in 2018 as the Said Ruete Archive, Or. 27.135.

All rights reserved. No part of this book may be reproduced, translated, or transmitted in any form or by any means, electronic or hard copy, including photocopying, recording, by any storage or retrieval system, or otherwise, without prior written permission of the author, translator, and copyright owner. For permission, send a request with complete information to andrea@sayyidasalme.com.

www.sayyidasalme.com; www.emilyruete.com

ISBN 978-1-7323975-5-2

Dedicated to my dearest, devoted mother,

Ursula Emily Stumpf.

———·•·———

When mothers and daughters collaborate,

I hear history rhyme.

This book is presented as a sequel to *Memoirs of an Arabian Princess: An Accurate Translation of Her Authentic Voice*, also by Andrea Emily Stumpf, the author's great-great-granddaughter. All references to the *"Memoirs"* in footnotes and elsewhere in this book are to this version of the *Memoirs*.

CONTENTS

Introduction:

About Sayyida Salme vi

About the Manuscript xx

Letters to the Homeland

— translated from the original German —

pages 1 to 120

From the translator:

Map of Places Lived... 121

On Collaboration... 126

On Freedom 129

On Fear 135

On Inspiration 140

List of Abbreviations... 152

Timeline.. 153

List of Images... 160

v

ABOUT SAYYIDA SALME

Because she wrote her own story, there is less for me to say. Sayyida Salme, who later became Emily Ruete, published *Memoiren einer arabischen Prinzessin* in 1886, which I newly translated in 2022 as *Memoirs of an Arabian Princess: An Accurate Translation of Her Authentic Voice*. She also wrote *Briefe nach der Heimat* in subsequent years, which you now have here, newly translated in 2023 as *Letters to the Homeland: An Accurate Translation of an Intimate Voice*.

Sayyida Salme began her life in Zanzibar, born into the Omani Sultanate that ruled the island. Her father was the Sultan, and her mother was a *surie* from the Circassian diaspora. So much of that remarkable time and place would have faded into the past were it not for the generous details Sayyida Salme shared with us in her *Memoirs*. And now with her *Letters*, she gives us a whole new perspective, a deeper, more dismal view of her life in the West. In the aftermath of her fateful decision—if it was fate—we realize that she never really left the island, or at least, the island never left her. We also see that she never really settled into her new home, with much to unsettle her along the way. Geographically, socially, spiritually, at every level, she found herself straddling two worlds, but secure in neither.

If I dare sum up her long life in two points, it was her learning to write at the end of her first decade and her choice of husband at the end of her second decade that defined her the most, even into the present. Already inclined to bump up against the sides of the box, in these two points she breached the confines, by learning a taboo skill and choosing a taboo husband. With the latter, at the same time that explorers from the West were "discovering" the East, including East Africa, she uniquely became the reverse: a probing and insightful explorer from the East (including as an Arab) of the West. With the former, through her writing, she acquired the tools to record her remote setting, reveal spaces hidden from view, share thoughts and critiques, stay in touch with her homeland, and most importantly, capture words on a page for us to study, enjoy, criticize, and contemplate—notably, as the first Arab woman to publish a book.

About Sayyida Salme

Although she used the name Emily Ruete for most of her life, I choose to refer to her as Sayyida Salme.[1] I do not know if she would approve, since she took the name Ruete out of lasting love and devotion to her husband, and she was endeared to her namesake Emily Seward, the British consul's wife who helped her flee. Then again, she included her Arabic name on the cover of her *Memoirs*, and her family added this appellation to the cover page of her *Letters*. What motivates me above all, however, are the circumstances of her name change. When she gave up her name, she gained her husband, but also had to give up so much more. I see her Western name as yet another coercive element that she had to accept in her chosen life, in which so many choices were met with so much lack of choice. I reach back to her original name, wanting to connect with her deep down inside, and feel grateful for how much more choice we have today.

Whatever moved her to write, we are the beneficiaries. She left a legacy of recollection and remembrance that still speaks to us. The world is her audience, and the relevance of her life and writing still resonates.

Andrea Emily Stumpf,
her great-great-granddaughter

---

[1] "Sayyida" has a particular meaning in Oman, not to be confused with the usual Islamic reference to a descendant of the prophet Muhammed. "Sayyida" for Princess, and "Sayyid" for Prince or Sultan, denotes a member of the Al Bu Said royal family, a hereditary honorific through paternal lineage without religious connotation. The author's father preferred the title "Sayyid" and expressly set aside the religious title "Imam" of his forebears to which he and his family were entitled. Omani Ibadism allowed for this separation between Imamate and Sultanate. As for his full name, Sayyid Said bin Sultan, Sayyid is equivalent to "Sultan," whereas Sultan was, in fact, the first name of his father, Sayyid Sultan bin Ahmed.

The author, Hamburg, ca. 1867.

The author, Hamburg, ca. 1867.

The author, Hamburg, ca. 1867.

The author, Hamburg, ca. 1867.

The author, Hamburg, ca. 1868.

The author, Hamburg, ca. 1868.

The author, Berlin, 1888.

The author, Berlin, 1888.

The author, 1908.

The author, 1908.

The author, Beirut, between 1892–1914.

The author, Bromberg (now Bydgoszcz), 1914.

ABOUT THE MANUSCRIPT

Briefe nach der Heimat, literally translated "Letters to the Homeland," is the title that Emily Ruete, born Sayyida Salme, gave her own manuscript. Whether the contents came from actual letters is unclear. Perhaps the text was transcribed from individual letters and melded into a single, end-to-end account. Perhaps letters, as such, were never meant to be sent, but rather served as a literary device to unleash her recollections. We have only her handwritten manuscript, without any documented history of its provenance, no original letters or prior drafts. In its pages, we do not in fact see letters. To pick up the original is to see one long rendition, without to and from and dates, without even paragraphs or indentations—merely the occasional stroke of a line to separate topics, as if to take a quick breath before rushing on.

Even so, the label "letters" rings true. The tone of Sayyida Salme's account is familiar, interspersed with frequent references to "you" that speak directly to someone in Zanzibar.[2] The presentation is knowing and personal, addressed to someone close to her, someone who grew up with her and drew from common experiences, who knew her jewelry, her moods, her values. It feels like the author is writing a kindred spirit, an intimate soulmate—this someone who owned a plantation, journeyed to Mecca, and was jealous of a pretty white cat. Across from the author, we sense someone expecting to hear from her, awaiting her news, and sharing in return.

In this literary work, the passages seemingly pour out of her—*in einem Guß*, in one flow, as we say in German. The visual effect is stunning, with long cursive lines that course across page after page. The author gives us an unbroken stream of scenes and stories of her painfully broken life, as if to play on her lifelong theme of perseverance. She fills three volumes of black on white handwriting, both front and back on thin paper, traversing more than six hundred pages in all. This is the trail of a long run, an uphill climb, an exhausting marathon—a narrative that marks one excruciating, extenuating episode after another. So much to say, to recount, to fathom, even as we know details are being left out, and the end leaves us hanging.[3]

---

2 This starts with the very first sentence, which calls out a *geliebte Freundin*, a dear female friend. Sayyida Salme also tells us that she corresponded with "loyal friends" she left behind in Zanzibar, although there is no known record of these letters, either coming or going. See A.E. Stumpf, *Memoirs of an Arabian Princess: An Accurate Translation of Her Authentic Voice*, p. 36 (2022) (hereinafter *Memoirs*).

3 We can still find ample meaning in her closing words, as I do in my essay "On Fear" on pages 135–39 below.

About the Manuscript

As lengthy as the work is, and as searing the detail, Sayyida Salme kept it to herself. Even the author's three children were seemingly unaware of this heart-wrenching account until she died. Their discovery of the manuscript among her belongings after she passed away on February 29, 1924, was surely shocking. No matter that the family had been so close, no matter how much the children thought they knew their mother, this found text presented a new level of intimacy and anguish. As one daughter wrote to her brother: "Her martyrdom was hard—it is shattering to read through her literary legacy."[4]

What to do with them, these three volumes marked only I, II, and III? Tony, Said, and Rosa[5] (the latter being my direct ancestor) immediately registered their importance. As the first Arab woman to have published a book, to great interest and popular acclaim, who had also written another piece in close collaboration with her children,[6] the author's voice was already out there, her intention to share more of her struggles had been clear, and here was another dimension of her life that was hard to ignore. To make this part of her public legacy or not—that was the question. The children exchanged differing views amongst themselves, but in the end, the view that this substantial text deserved to be shared with the world apparently prevailed. Tucked in at page 16 of the family's copy of Lionel Strachey's unauthorized[7] translation of the *Memoiren* are several letters dated 1925, documenting overtures that were

---

4 *Ihr Martyrium war schwer—beim Durchlesen ihres Nachlasses ist man erschüttert.* Rosa Troemer writing to her brother Rudolph Said-Ruete on June 15, 1924. Leiden University Libraries Or. 27.135 C5(2).

5 Tony is what Antonie (also Thawka) was called; Said was called by his second name (men in the Ruete family appear to have been called by their second names), until he later chose to be called by his first name, Rudolph; and Rosa is what Rosalie (also Ghuza) was called.

6 Evidencing this interaction, the *Nachtrag zu meinen Memoiren* (Addendum to My Memoirs), primarily about the circumstances of the author's 1888 trip to Zanzibar, consists of two notebooks of draft text that are preserved in the Leiden University Libraries: one in the author's hand, with handwritten edits primarily by her daughter Rosa (Or. 27.135 A1), and one in Rosa's hand, with handwritten edits likely by the author's son Rudolph (Or. 27.135 A2).

7 It seems clear that Lionel Strachey took it upon himself to issue a translation of the *Memoiren* without consulting or collaborating with the author or her family, based on two pieces of evidence, in particular. First, his edition is a significant misrepresentation of the original, in which Strachey took great license in revising the author's original text, including adding his own subheaders, merging and dropping chapters, and inserting misleading photographic images. The continuing popularity of this inaccurate and abridged distortion of her original publication is a major reason I decided to publish my version of the *Memoiren*, which I had translated as accurately as possible, as much as a translation can be. Second, one can readily deduce that the family itself had concerns about Strachey's edition from the fact that Rudolph had loosely inserted a clipped article from the London *Times* dated March 31, 1928, at the title page of Strachey's book (Leiden University Libraries SR 618). Entitled "America and the Law of Copyright," it discussed copyright rules in the United States after Congress failed to pass much-needed legislation. According to the article, "The difficulty which has principally confronted both English and American authors ... has not in fact been actual piracy ... so much as the willful inconveniences of the present system." Against this backdrop, there was apparently little the family could do to remedy the situation and redirect attention to the family-authorized edition that had been collaboratively produced with London's Ward & Downey in 1888.

made to two English publishers, but turned down.⁸ One can perhaps surmise that unsuccessful overtures were also made to one or more German publishing houses. Even in the years after that, some of the children, and later some of their descendants, vacillated between leaving history alone and drawing attention to this remarkable story.⁹

It was not until Professor Emeri van Donzel published his impressive 1993 compilation of the author's literary works, which included his newly translated "Letters Home," that an English version of this text saw the light of day.¹⁰ Not long after, Heinz Schneppen, the German Ambassador to Tanzania from 1993 to 1996, was the first to publish the *Briefe nach der Heimat* in the original German.¹¹ With an English version of the *Letters* nestled in an academic volume that is superb but pricey, and with the original German version offered in another book that has long been out of print, it is not clear how much currency this illuminating document has received to date, but it deserves more.

As to my own work, as Sayyida Salme's great-great-granddaughter, this new translation you have in your hands, or on your screen, or in your ears, is the sequel to my newly translated *Memoirs of an Arabian Princess*. The two books make a meaningful pair, one primarily about the author's early life in Zanzibar, the other primarily about her later life in Germany. But that is too neatly stated. The push-and-pull of her straddled existence is evident in both texts. She writes from an emerging German perspective when recounting her life in Zanzibar. She addresses her thoughts via a Zanzibari perspective when detailing her life in Germany. This ability to hold the two in one hand is a gift to us, but was, in so many ways, raw agony for her.

---

8   Both William Heinemann Limited of London and Doubleday, Page and Company of New York reviewed the *Briefe nach der Heimat* manuscript provided by the author's son Rudolph, but declined to publish. See letters placed by Rudolph in the book located at Leiden University Libraries SR 618.
9   Rosa, who had a close working relationship with her mother, took the latter view: "The main thing is to preserve the memory of someone of mother's importance." (*Das Wesentliche ist, eine Persönlichkeit von Mutters Ausmaß dem Gedächtnis zu erhalten.*) Rosa writing to her brother Rudolph in January 1928, according to H. Schneppen, *Emily Ruete geb. Prinzessin Salme von Oman und Sansibar: Briefe nach der Heimat*, p. 7 (1999) (hereinafter H. Schneppen, *Briefe*).
10 E. van Donzel, *An Arabian Princess Between Two Worlds: Memoirs, Letters, Sequels to the Memoirs, Syrian Customs and Usages*, pp. 407–510 (1993) (hereinafter E. van Donzel). As Professor van Donzel explained to me, he had initially intended to publish the original German texts, but was unexpectedly preempted by Professor Annegret Nippa, who had published the *Memoiren* in German a few years before, thus causing him to shift to English. Ibid., Preface at p. ix, referring to A. Nippa, *Leben im Sultanspalast* (1989).
11 H. Schneppen, *Briefe*.

About the Manuscript

From a timing perspective, these two accounts, the *Memoirs* and the *Letters*, are, roughly speaking, her BE and AE, the before and after elopement and self-exile. Only the tail end of her *Memoirs* takes place after Sayyida Salme left Zanzibar, and none of the *Letters* takes place before she left. The two were also written sequentially. The *Memoirs* were started in the mid-1870s,[12] and the *Letters* were started only after the *Memoirs* came out in 1886.[13] In the *Memoirs*, we are simply given a short, two-page, rather positive AE picture of the first dozen or so years in Germany, with merely a hint of difficulty.[14] The *Letters* then lift the lid and let loose her truth.

Indeed, it is almost jaw-dropping to realize that Sayyida Salme was living much of the agonizing period described in her *Letters* at the same time she was writing the *Memoirs*. During those years, in her early thirties, she was so critically at the end of her rope that it seems almost implausible for her to have been writing on the side. But she admits in the *Memoirs* that she felt time-bound and needed to write about her past while she could.[15] She also tantalizingly tells us in the *Memoirs* that she may share more about her "first impressions of European life and customs of the civilized world."[16] This may well refer to what later became the *Letters*. For the reverse, however, nothing in the *Letters* mentions the *Memoirs* that she was creating during the years she describes.

---

12 It makes sense that Sayyida Salme would have felt the urge to hold onto her history after the children, in their first days of public schooling in 1877, became aware of her unusual ancestry (below at page 98). Or she may have started writing the *Memoirs* earlier, after failing to reconnect with Sultan Barghash in London in 1875, which is the year cited by Professor van Donzel. E. van Donzel, p. 1.

13 As to when the author wrote her *Letters*, the exact dates are unknown. The opening line indicates that she is finally responding after a long silence, looking back years later. Extrapolating from her mention of Sultan Barghash's death in 1888 (below at page 71), the manuscript may well have originated after the author's second trip to Zanzibar that same year, during her time in Jaffa (now part of Tel Aviv) (1888–1892) or Beirut (1892–1914). By then, her children were of age, and she presumably had more time and space of mind to put her memories and thoughts to paper. But it was likely also completed before she wrote her original last will and testament in 1910. There she addresses both her *Memoirs* and "the as-yet unpublished manuscripts that describe my life in Europe," the latter possibly, at least in part, a reference to the *Letters* manuscript.

14 "[M]isfortune continued to pursue me." *Memoirs*, p. 203.

15 "Physically and emotionally spent, I did not expect to last long enough to see them into adulthood to then tell them about my fateful journey and childhood memories. I therefore decided to write up my experiences and undertook the project with great love and dedication, knowing it was for my dear children, whose tenderness had comforted me during long and troubled years, and whose deep empathy has sustained me through my trying times." *Memoirs*, Preface, p. 1

16 "I have written up these impressions in reverent memory [of my late husband] and may find a subsequent opportunity to report on them as well." *Memoirs*, p. 202.

Readers of the *Memoirs* may be surprised by the *Letters*; it is not what you would expect. The *Memoirs* are as light in tone and style as the *Letters* are dark. How could she have been living under such trauma and duress without letting that permeate her writing of the *Memoirs*? It surely took focus and discipline to convey the special, happy, carefree childhood she had had on the island, without dwelling on the present—or maybe it was some degree of disassociation. Writing a book for children, her own children for them to remember her by, would have been reason enough to hold back on her sentiments. And then later, it may have been all the more necessary to channel her dire truth, to unload her part two. With the *Memoirs*, she may not have wanted to burden her children right away, but with the *Letters*, she knew they would, one day, read the rest of her story.

In developing this new translation, I was able to draw from three sources of the author's *Briefe nach der Heimat*. First is the original text I described above, of which you can get a sense in the photographs right after this essay. While beautiful in its flow, the handwritten use of the old Sütterlin script makes it challenging to read (unless you are my mother). Second is a carefully preserved, typewritten manuscript of 181 pages as part of the historical collection kept by Antonie's branch of the family, to which I was given gracious access by my third cousin, Alexander von Brand. It turns out he lives near us in the Washington, DC, area, as did his grandmother, who knew and interacted with my German grandfather, although that connection got lost and was only recently rekindled (with thanks to Anita Keizers and Godwin Kornes).

Third is a subsequently typewritten manuscript of 177 pages that resides at the Leiden University Libraries Or. 6281. It was formally presented by the author's son Rudolph to the Oriental Institute in Leiden in 1929,[17] shortly after the Institute was founded by Professor Christiaan Snouck Hurgronje, a close friend of the family.[18] Perhaps showing some sensitivity for the nature

---

17 Copies of this typewritten text were also formally sent to the Zanzibar Museum in Stone Town, the British Museum in London, the Staats- and Universitätsbibliothek in Hamburg, and the Preussische Staatsbibliothek in Berlin, per correspondence at Leiden University Libraries Or. 25.137 C8.
18 Professor Hurgronje also welcomed Rudolph's subsequent interest in providing his extensive private library to the Oriental Institute. Over six hundred books and other documents relating to the history of Oman and Zanzibar, Middle Eastern politics (especially the question of Palestine), and much of his mother's legacy, including letters, photographs, and other personal documents, made their way to Leiden in 1937, one year after Professor Hurgronje died.

About the Manuscript

of the narrative, or maybe just to keep control, Rudolph stipulated that his mother's *Briefe nach der Heimat* could not be published before 1940. This third copy corrects a number of grammatical and other minor errors in the prior typewritten copy, but otherwise leaves the tract intact. I used primarily this third copy for my translation, cross-checking with the two earlier versions as needed.

Since the original manuscript was a posthumous find, the children had no opportunity to work with their mother to get her text in good shape for a book. And so it remains, one or more drafts shy of a polished publication, unlike the *Memoirs*. To my mind, that makes the *Letters* more poignant, more unabashed. What may feel like repetition actually reflects the tenacity of certain topics. What comes across as a lack of structure is, in fact, true to the endless stream of life. I appreciate this unvarnished account as the unedited real deal.

In translating, I have hewn to the original as much as possible, barring a few added subdividers and lots of paragraph breaks, all marked, to help pace the reader. The footnotes and accompanying essays are all mine. For these, my work has benefited from many other documents, including those assembled and annotated over the years by Rudolph for his private collection. The special bookcase he provided to house this collection is no longer filled,[19] since its varied contents now rest more comfortably in climate-controlled vaults. But even now, these materials remain a treasure trove for anyone who wishes to delve deeper and discover more.[20]

Andrea Emily Stumpf
September 2023

---

19 *Memoirs*, "On Contributions," p. 232.
20 We are grateful that Leiden University and the Netherlands Institute for the Near East (NINO) continue to safeguard these materials, while also making them available to the public. A useful description of this history and itemization of some of the collection appears in the Leiden University Libraries' collection guide (at ubl649) of the Sayyida Salme (Emily Ruete) and Rudolph Said-Ruete archive from 2018 that was excellently prepared by Hans van de Velde and Arnoud Vrolijk.

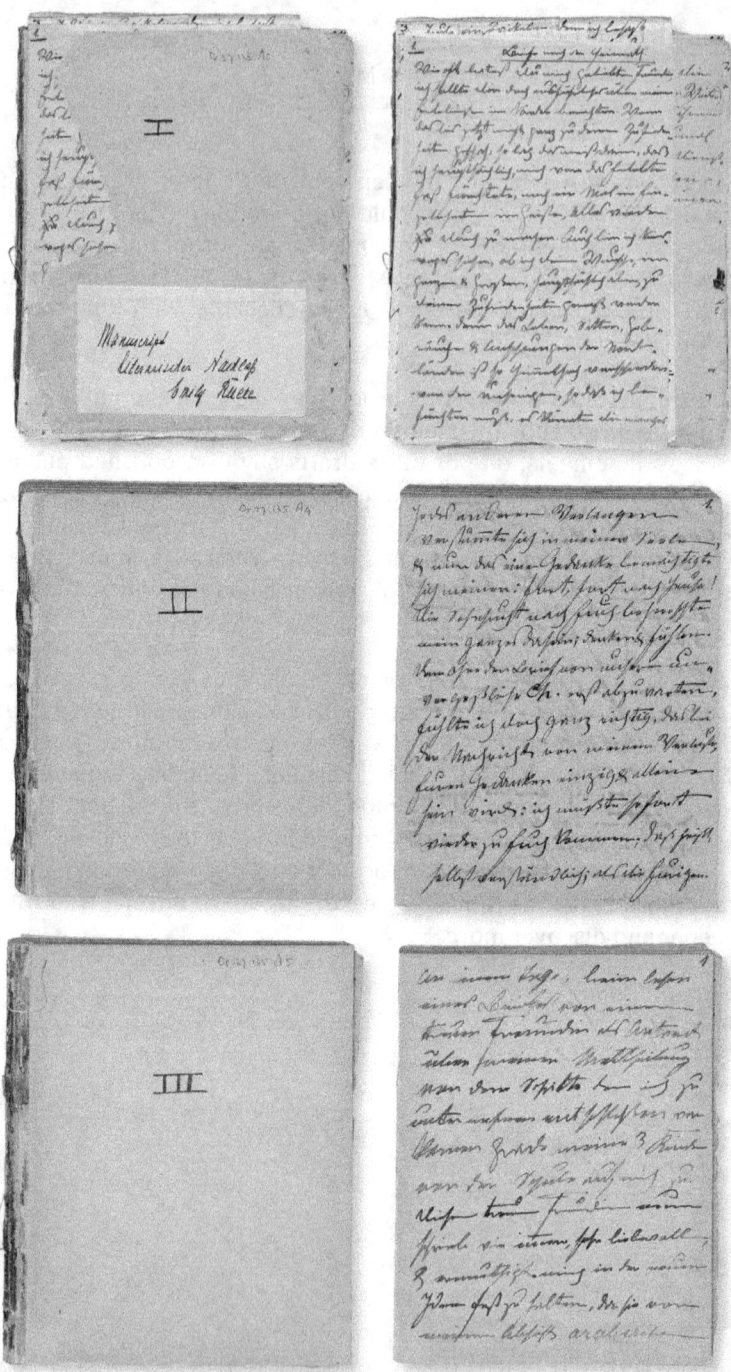

The author's handwritten manuscript, three filled notebooks.

Cover page followed by pages 1, 2, and 3 of each notebook.

BRIEFE NACH DER HEIMAT.

Wie oft batest Du mich geliebte Freundin, ich sollte Dir doch ausfurliches ueber meine Erlebnisse im Norden berichten. Wenn das bis jetzt nicht ganz zu Deiner Zufriedenheit geschah, so lag das meist daran, dass ich hauptsaechlich mich vor dem Erlebten fast fuertete, noch einmal in Einzelheiten im Geiste alles wieder durchzumacen. Auch bin ich keineswegs sicher, ob ich Deinem Wunsche im Ganzen und Grossen, hauptsaechlich aber zu Deiner Zufriedenheit gerecht werden kann. Denn das Leben, Sitten, Gebrauche und Anschauungen der Nordlander sind so himmelhoch verschieden vo den unsereigen dass ich befurchten muss, es konnte Dir manches ubertrieben, ja selbst vielleicht unmoglich erscheinen. Ging es denn mir selbst von Anfang auch aders, wo ich doch lebhaftig in deren Mitten versetzt wurde? Jahre brauchte ich, um aus der stillen Verwunderung heraus zu kommen, von all dem was mich umgab und was ich im Laufe der Zeit zu sehen und zu horen bekam. Denn die Erfindungsgabe der Menschen hier im Durchschnitt ist ganz erstaunlich. Sie stehen jedenfalls in ihrere Geistigen Leistung oben an. Dagegen sind sie aber auch - fur unsere - etwas gar zu prosaisch, so dass unser einem nicht leicht wird, sich in ihre Anschauungen hineinzu dnken. Dem Fremdling gegenuber sind sie im allgemeinem zuvorkommend; iher Antipoden vor

First typewritten version of the author's manuscript.

BRIEFE NACH DER HEIMAT.
==

Wie oft batest Du mich, geliebte Freundin, ich sollte Dir doch Ausführliches über meine Erlebnisse im Norden berichten. Wenn das bis jetzt nicht ganz zu Deiner Zufriedenheit geschah, so lag das meist daran, dass ich hauptsächlich mich vor dem Erlebten fast fürchtete, noch einmal in Einzelheiten im Geiste alles wieder durchzumachen. Auch bin ich keineswegs sicher, ob ich Deinem Wunsche im grossen und ganzen, hauptsächlich aber zu Deiner Zufriedenheit gerecht werden kann, denn das Leben, die Sitten, Gebräuche und Anschauungen der Nordländer sind so himmelhoch verschieden von den unsrigen, dass ich befürchten muss, es könnte Dir manches übertrieben, ja selbst vielleicht unmöglich erscheinen. Ging es denn mir selbst im Anfang anders, wo ich doch leibhaftig in deren Mitte versetzt wurde ? Jahre brauchte ich, um aus der stillen Verwunderung herauszukommen von all dem, was mich umgab und was ich im Laufe der Zeit zu sehen und zu hören bekam. Denn die Erfindungsgabe der Menschen hier im Durchschnitt ist ganz erstaunlich. Sie stehen jedenfalls in ihrer geistigen Leistung obenan. Dagegen sind sie aber auch - für unsere Begriffe - etwas gar zu prosaisch, so dass es unser einem nicht leicht wird, sich in ihre Anschauungen hineinzudenken. Dem Fremdling gegenüber sind sie im allgemeinen zuvorkommend; ihre Antipoden vor allem erfreuen sich stets ihrer Aufmerksamkeit und Teilnahme. Demgegenüber tritt aber dem Neuling überall der vorherrschende Realismus so mächtig entgegen, dass er unwillkürlich und aus Mangel an Verständnis die Zuflucht nur in sich

Second typewritten version of the author's manuscript.

Literarischer Nachlass

von

EMILY RUETE

(Seyyidah Salme bint Said bin Sultan)

geb. 30.August 1844 in Zansibar,

gest. 29.Februar 1924 in Jena.

In Ergänzung

der

"Memoiren einer Arabischen Prinzessin."

Berlin 1886.

Translated:

Literary Estate of *EMILY RUETE* (Seyyidah Salme bint Said bin Sultan), born August 30, 1844, in Zanzibar, died February 29, 1924, in Jena.

As a supplement to the "Memoirs of an Arabian Princess," Berlin 1886.

All footnotes in the following pages were added by the translator.

Letters to the Homeland

How often have you implored me, dear friend,[21] to tell you more about my experiences in the North.[22] Any failure by now to meet your full satisfaction on this score lies primarily in my reluctance to drag myself anew through all the details of my past. I also highly doubt that I could fully respond, enough to do justice to your request, since the life, rituals, customs, and attitudes of Northerners are so diametrically different from ours that I must fear you would find some of it exaggerated, yes, perhaps even improbable. Was it any different for me in the beginning, when I was physically dropped into their midst? It took me years to find my way out of my inner astonishment at everything around me and all that I saw and heard.

/[23]The ingenuity of the people here[24] is, in general, quite remarkable. They excel, at any rate, in their mental abilities. And yet, they are also—for our way

---

21 The identity of this female friend is not known, nor even if it was an actual person or various people to whom the author wrote. See the preceding translator's essay "About the Manuscript" on page xx above.
22 The author places Germany, and Europe more broadly, in the North relative to her homeland Zanzibar, as well as her patriarchal country of origin, Oman, in the South, and similarly refers to the Occident relative to the Orient and the West relative to the East.
23 The author's original manuscript featured long, continuous sections, many of which carried over multiple pages. The translator has divided these extended pieces into multiple paragraphs for greater readability, in each case denoted by a "/" to indicate a paragraph or section break added by the translator.
24 "Here" being Germany, where the author lived from 1867 to 1888, after leaving Zanzibar, and then again from 1914 until her death in 1924. See the "Timeline" on pages 153–57 below.

of being—rather too prosaic, so that from our perspective it is hard to get into their mindset. Generally welcoming toward strangers, they especially delight in giving special attention and care to people who are their opposites. By contrast, the imposing reality hits the newcomer with such heft that he cannot, for lack of any understanding, help but seek refuge only in himself. People here may well be shaped by an excess of culture; there is hardly any other explanation. Then, too, this culture seems to breed conceit and, for some, goes hand-in-hand with arrogance. Both are certainly very ugly traits, and such people are best avoided. Overall, this is a place where weaklings will go under if they cannot sufficiently counter the endless moral blows that are seemingly part and parcel of this civilization. How often did I catch myself over time in this less than consoling thought: Are you, truly, awake or asleep?

/But why get ahead of the facts?[25]

---

25 This "beautiful but elusive" opening passage is perhaps best understood in retrospect, as suggested by my third cousin, Alexander von Brand, who is also descended from Sayyida Salme. He recommends returning to this first section after completing the *Letters*, and optimally also the *Memoirs*. In this way, readers, too, will not "get ahead of the facts," but rather let the account speak for itself in substantiating the author's trenchant introductory observations.

1[26]

Our journey on the Red Sea[27] was indescribably hot. Around midday, no one dared spend time under the awning, and all passengers had to stay in the salon until the sun dipped more to the West. Sitting down to eat with so many completely unknown gentlemen and ladies made me very uncomfortable, and I was always happy when mealtimes came to an end, all the more because I suspected the presence of pork or lard in every dish. I thus passed on anything that I sensed contained pig and instead lived off only biscuits, boiled eggs, tea, and fruit during those early days. My false pride kept me from telling my husband about my fear of these unclean, and for us strictly forbidden, animals, knowing that Christians have no restrictions and make no distinction between "clean" and "unclean." I therefore mostly feigned lack of appetite and put my hope in the future, which so often works wonders.

/If there was anything that seemed to mock my past seclusion from the world of men, then it was these few nights here onboard the ship. Already for several nights now, all first-class passengers—male and female—had been sleeping on their mattresses all together in the salon. I was no fan of this new kind of freedom but, aspiring to be civilized, had to join in. For when I explained to my husband that I would rather sleep in the suffocatingly hot cabin, instead of going up to the salon as he suggested, he turned to a very amiable Madame C.[28] from Mauritius, of French birth. This lady gave me absolutely no rest until she had extracted my firm promise to sleep upstairs together with the other passengers. In recognition of my concession, she promised to sleep by my side the whole time. And the best part was the display the next morning when everyone awoke! The gentlemen all in nightshirts with thin, white night trousers, and nothing more. The ladies all in long English nightgowns under thin, white slips. And of course, no one wore stockings. Indeed, only a few individuals had woolen blankets for cover. As soon as anyone awoke, they immediately made themselves scarce, that no one might see them in their scant attire.

---

26 All subdivisions are included as they appear in the author's original manuscript, except in the few cases preceded by /. The subdivision numeration has been added by the translator for ease of reference.

27 The author took this trip with her new husband, Rudolph Heinrich Ruete (known as Heinrich), who had just rejoined her nine months after she fled Zanzibar. They left Aden, Yemen, on May 30, 1867, and traveled by sea and train to Hamburg, Germany, her husband's city of origin. This short travel description complements the author's "Great Transformations" (*Grosse Wandlungen*) chapter in her *Memoiren einer arabischen Prinzessin* (1886). *Memoirs*, pp. 201–03.

28 As with many of the abbreviated names in the author's account, the identity of this lady is unknown. See the "List of Abbreviations" on page 152.

2

The first European city I ever saw was Marseille. Although we arrived in the month of June, I nonetheless froze to such a degree that dear Madame C. was kind enough to wrap me in her shawl. I possessed no warm clothes of my own, and my outfit was only suited for the Tropics, in no way for the Northern Hemisphere. Thus freezing, we arrived at customs, where the numerous customs officials immediately descended upon our various travel effects. Soon matters became somewhat uncomfortable for my husband, as the gesticulations and loud words of the officials increased, from what I was able to observe from the corner where I sat. Since I could comprehend nothing of what was being said, I pressed my way over to my husband to discover the cause of these exchanges. And so I learned what all the fuss was about. Upon opening our hand luggage, the officials had come upon my Arab jewelry, which they then wanted to tax in the belief that these were commercial goods being imported for sale. Whereupon my husband explained that these were all personal items belonging to his wife and anything but commercial. This was the cause of the dispute, for these dutiful officials had never before, so it seemed, come across the precious jewelry of an Oriental woman. When my husband's assurances that the entire collection belonged to his wife appeared to have no effect, he, too, lost his patience and finally told the officials my birth name. Thus ensued deep bows on the part of the officials, nor could they keep from staring at me with bald curiosity. Enough, my things were finally released to me untaxed, and we could at last make our way to a hotel. Upon arrival, I was so cold, I had to go straight to bed.

/We naturally planned the very next day to look up Madame M.[29] and her niece, whom you of course got to know and love in Zanzibar not all too long ago. Both ladies spoke such good Swahili, and the husband such good Arabic, that it was a true pleasure for me,[30] not to mention that we had so much of the past to talk about. At this time, they lived in the upscale part of Marseille, in a truly lovely villa with a large garden, where they welcomed us with utmost hospitality. On the drive from the hotel to their place, I saw a large house that greatly caught my attention. I inquired about it and learned this was an orphanage, where young children without parents were tended to and cared for until they were old enough to take care of themselves. This straightforward explanation made

---

29 Madame Mass was the wife of Bonaventura Mass. The author first got to know the Spanish couple in Zanzibar and then stayed with them during part of her sojourn in Aden, before re-encountering them in Marseille. E. van Donzel, p. 19; *Memoirs*, p. 202.
30 The author grew up speaking Swahili, the indigenous language of Zanzibar where she lived, and Arabic, the language of the Omani Sultanate into which she was born. Her father, the Sultan, expected the family to speak only Arabic—which was also the language in which the author was taught to read and then secretly taught herself to write—but other languages filled the house when he was not around. *Memoirs*, pp. 26, 36, 55–56.

a huge impression on me, and I found such an institution to be extraordinarily praiseworthy and humane.

/We stayed in beautiful Marseille about a week, and the thought of continuing our travels to northern Germany filled me daily with an ever increasing, totally indescribable trepidation. It was not the climate conditions, which were indeed practically without parallel to ours; no, it was the unknown! At least here in Marseille I had the incredibly dear M. family, who spoke my language and loved my homeland so much. The M. couple, who were originally from Spain, treated us as lovingly as parents would their own children. How comfortable, oh how comfortable they made me feel! The thought of leaving them enveloped me with a melancholy beyond words. Our good friends must have been struck by the same feeling, for when we were ready to reembark on our travels, we received only a letter from them admitting their weakness, that there was simply no way they could take their personal leave of us. Such dear people! Before we left Marseille, Madame M. had pulled together a small trousseau of clothes for me, suited for the Northern clime, at my husband's request.

As we drove from our hotel to the train station, I was gripped by such an unfamiliar fear that I would have preferred to scream out loud. I had the feeling as though, from this moment on, my homeland was being pulled ever further from me, and all the bridges were crashing in behind me. The cry of my soul for you turned into a thousand voices from my beloved island, all seemingly calling to me in unison: "Do not go any further, better to return again!" I fought a terrible fight within myself. Like an automaton, I stepped into the train that would now seek to take me, as quickly as possible, to an unknown land, to total strangers, as if I was in the greatest hurry to reach my future destination. And so we kept on riding toward the North.

It was an afternoon, just as the sun was going down, that we arrived in Hamburg, my husband's hometown. As a carriage took us through the busy streets, my husband called to me and pointed to a person passing by, wearing very short sleeves and a white cap on the head. She seemed to be carrying something bulky under her arm, which she kept covered with a cloth. "Did you see that person, Bibi?"[31] he asked. Then he explained that this was a servant girl, wearing the same outfit as virtually all servant girls in Hamburg. Until now, I had never seen so many fair-skinned and blond people, which naturally struck me as very odd, and the same with the long strides and hurried pace that practically everyone on the street seemed to have.

---

31 "Bibi" can mean wife in Swahili and is also associated with *habibi* meaning "my love" in Arabic, as a term of both endearment and high respect (see also Bibi Azze, the author's stepmother and Sultan's principal wife in the *Memoirs*, p. 8).

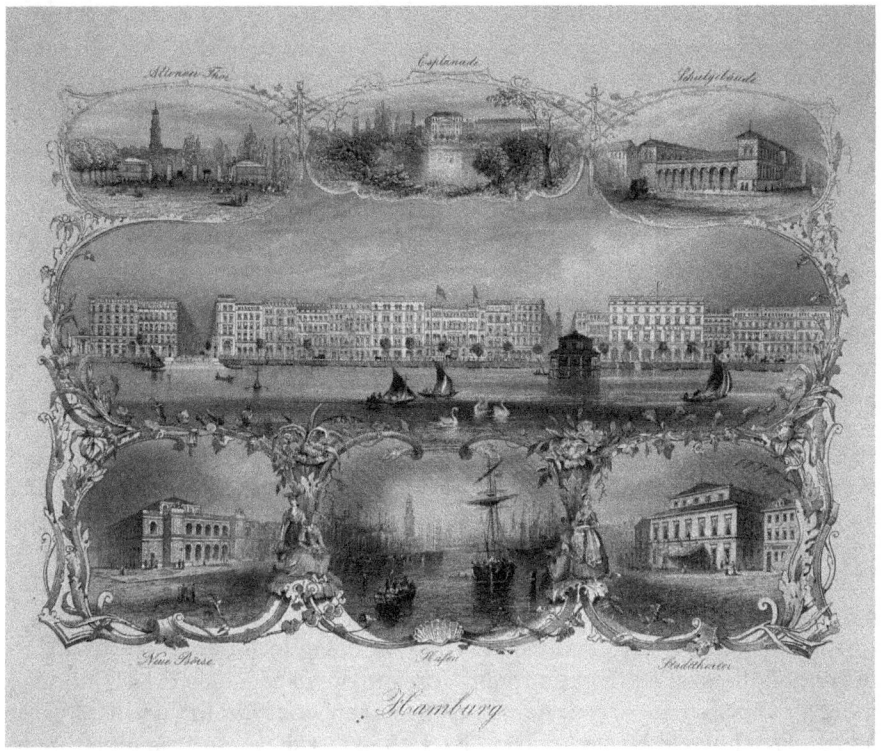

Steel engraving of Hamburg, mid-1800s.

3

You will, of course, also want to know what I thought and felt in those early days on European soil, am I right? Yes, I was wholly and completely overcome by the strangest of sensations. All in all—and I admit this freely—I constantly felt anxious, and it was only in the presence of my husband that I could free myself from this excruciating feeling that tormented me both day and night. Everything was so foreign, so very different, from what I had known and been accustomed to before. Only one voice still rang out within my soul—since I was unable to comprehend anything else—as it pitched a constant refrain: "And this is where you want to spend the rest of your days?"[32] I would have sooner given up my life before I could have answered this horrid question with an honest "yes."

/On top of that, to be called Christian, even though I was as much a Muslim inside as you yourself. Through and through, I felt so despicable that I should appear different from what I actually was. I will tell you this in unvarnished frankness: Beware of changing your religion without complete conviction! Conviction? Yes, from whom and what should I have gained any conviction? No one, as it was, cared one whit about my true faith.[33] It was apparently enough for the pastor at my baptism and ensuing wedding to hear me say "yes"[34] to everything he said to me in a totally foreign language, since clearly nothing more was needed. As of that moment, I had been won over to Christianity; for all the rest, I would be on my own. Back then, I truly knew little more about being a Christian than you. And the consequences did not fail to take their course.

/Divorced from my old beliefs, and attached to the new in name only, I began a time for which I have no words. Never in my whole life—neither before nor after—did I feel so morally bereft, robbed of every support, as right after my

---

[32] The final typewritten manuscript inserts a handwritten superscript number 1 at this point, signaling a possible footnote. Similar superscripts appear throughout this manuscript at several dozen locations, especially next to abbreviated names. These superscripts are not part of the original handwritten manuscript and were all added posthumously. Unfortunately, the intended contents of any footnotes have been lost to time, and the markings have accordingly been omitted here.

[33] The original handwritten manuscript contains an insertion labeled "10A" here, with content that does not fit the narration. Since the pagination at this point also jumps from page 5 to page 11, something appears to have gone awry, and some text may have gotten lost. Insertion 10A reads: "Here I made my first acquaintance with the so very superfluous gloves (except in winter). I could not fathom their utility, considering as well that the eager salesman in the store took, as it seemed to me, all too much time and effort with my hands."

[34] The word "yes" appears in the handwritten German original, meaning the author responded to the pastor with her wedding vows in English.

baptism. Had you been witness to my inner struggles back then, that would have sufficed for you to soften your stances against me. My expectation that *every* follower of Christ would take me, lead me, and guide me in matters of the Lord, to induct me into religious ways and thus build my inner faith as one of them, unfortunately proved a complete deception. Soon I also came to see the power of religion as the most powerful of all when it comes to affecting our inner lives and well-being. I felt so despicably false to be considered a Christian when I had absolutely no clear idea *how and what* Christianity even means. I knew only what stood in the Koran, nothing more. As for my inner peace, it would have been far better had I at least stayed true to my old faith at the start. For there is no doubt that it is a thousand times better to be a Muslim than to be neither Christian (meaning from the heart) nor Muslim. And it was with this largest possible chasm inside me that I entered Europe and its hallowed civilization. I fought internally with myself, no one surmising how much I suffered in silence. Not even to my own beloved husband could I openly admit that our views differed on this point.

Oh, I will never ever forget the day during our short stopover in Cairo on our way to Europe. Here we visited the famous Muhammad Ali Mosque on the Citadel, where we had to pull felt slippers over our shoes before entering. I was unaware of what this requirement meant, but then found out that entry into the mosque without overshoes is strictly forbidden of all non-Muslims. This is when I realized what I had in fact become. In my eyes, there is no greater sacrifice than changing religion; neither rank, riches, nor the highest worldly status can feel as irreplaceable to us as our sacred faith. To console you, I can also let you know that, in the initial years after my baptism, I instinctively recited my old prayer to myself whenever I was alone.

Soon I drew inward and became reticent, and always deflected my husband's anxious questions if something was wrong by simply pretending homesickness. Why discuss something when the views are so diametric? When we are younger, we can hardly imagine how much people stay attached to their upbringings throughout their lifetimes, no matter how much the circumstances may change over time.

4

I lived through this initial period in Europe as in a dream. Instead of two eyes and two ears, I wished for ten of each to take in all the new and incredible things around me. The wildest fantasies a person could ever invent and imagine will suddenly and abruptly confront you here all at once. Although I am no weakling by nature, I felt on edge in a way I could not shake. In a word, it was almost eerie. Everything, but everything is different here: houses, streets, clothes, food—yes, even the air and the people! There was no end to what I had to absorb and process all at once. With all the languages, manners, and customs completely foreign to me, my position was hardly optimal, all the more because immediately upon arriving in Hamburg, we had to go straight into the obligatory round of visits to my husband's family and friends. Nothing is more dreadful than the so-called courtesy calls that they do here. And then to have the bad luck of being Arab—not speaking a word of German. No, I was close to despair.—The physiognomy of the people, with names that were impossible for me to pronounce, speaking a language I could not remotely understand, full of sounds like s, sch, t, tz, that were practically lively bird twitter to my ears, left me very confused. No wonder that I almost felt bewitched.

/One curious trait struck me right from the start, namely the way these people perpetually smile. It matters not what time of day you might show up, your host will always be smiling, except of course when you come to convey condolences. Privately, I referred to the Germans as simply a "happy nation," but my husband soon set me straight. This perpetual smiling, he told me, was in no way to be taken at face value; it was just customary good manners, with no particular meaning. Some may have a rather cheerful mien, but both inside and in reality, they are anything but cheerful. You can surely imagine how surprised I was by this. Your natural demeanor would not be all too well-received here, and rather than the customary cloth mask, which is not the norm here, you would have to sport a natural mask, as much as your facial muscles would allow. There is no point in protesting against such ingrained habits, since sooner or later, you must succumb to the usual practice. These and similar things are resolutely required and demanded by this exacting dame that we call Civilization.

/I also have to share with you the masterful way people are able to shape their thoughts and speech here. Oh, there is so much to learn in this place, an endless amount. At first, it all felt so strange. To be exclusively around white people, and so many with blond hair! It took a long time before I got used to that. I even found it hard to distinguish people from each other; to my unpracticed eye, they all looked so very much alike. My greatest difficulty, however, lay in the often totally unpronounceable names of the locals. Once I managed to get over that hurdle, I then often ran into issues with the customary forms of address. Despite endless explanations, I could not initially grasp the difference between the words "Sie" and "Du," so that I often enough mixed them up, saying "Du" to strangers and "Sie" to my husband's relatives. Meanwhile, I would catch the bemused smiles of strangers, notably the gentlemen, which soon prompted me to pay more attention to my use of "Sie" and "Du." My inability to speak a single European language, in particular German, took such a major toll on me early on that I resolved I would not rest until I had learned the native tongue.

/Just imagine you are situated in a household without being able to speak to your servants. You must pay visits to strangers and your entire conversations consist exclusively of handshakes. The same thing repeats when they undertake the unavoidable return visits to you. You are invited to a large social gathering, where all eyes are on you, whose gazes reveal nothing but nosiness. Ladies and gentlemen stare at you from head to foot for so long that you, as a matter of decorum, are forced to lower your astonished eyes. You need something and would like to have it, but there is no way to obtain it without your husband nearby, since he must translate all your occasional wishes and needs to the servants. Every day, except Sunday, I was completely unable to speak and remained consistently mute from nine-thirty to four while my husband was in his office. All this, as you can see, was of more than trivial consequence for me. And so I had no alternative but to learn the local language.

/With life made so unbearable, I promised myself, as mentioned, to put all my energy into learning this language, indeed for two reasons: first, to address the helplessness of my situation, as I have described, and second, for fear of you at home, knowing that people here could easily interpret my personal incompetence as generally characteristic of "Arabs." I was determined to do all I could to learn the customs and habits of the land where I now lived as quickly as possible, in order to keep what many perceived as our primitive upbringing from also being stamped an object of general pity.

/Upon my inquiry, my husband engaged an expert lady, who spent every afternoon from one to three teaching me, with admirable patience, first the names of household items and then reading and writing. Truly, it must have been more than boring for my teacher back then to wander with me from room to room, even down to the basement kitchen and up to the attic, to show me individual objects that were unfamiliar to me, but also could not be readily brought to me.

Letters to the Homeland

/I also had great difficulty with writing at the time. Instead of writing from right to left as before, I now needed to take my pen from left to right. It also took some time for me to understand why there were big and small letters. Of course, I had to learn the ABC's just like a five-year-old child. Except for a few letters, such as Ö, Ü, Ä, I fortunately soon knew these basic building blocks by heart. After eleven months of tutoring, I could even dare to join in with a word here or there. From this point on, it did not take long before I was able to keep the household book myself, understandably to the annoyance of our, until then, self-governing servants. What is a household book? Something that you naturally do not even know by name. Whereas in your home, you are used to depositing your annual income into a cashbox, counted of course, while your expenditures are then taken out again uncounted, matters here are handled altogether differently. The assets and liabilities of every individual play a much greater role than you might at first be able to comprehend.

/In the practical ways of the North, everything is done systematically, and the sense of order is admirable. Precise accounting is expected from everyone across the board, and woe to anyone who carries on mindlessly into the day. Even the Ministers, the actual government of every country, must account for every penny they spend to maintain the whole. Children toward their parents and wives to their husbands must answer for the funds they receive, if so requested. When young children start going to school, even they are taught this method with the allowances they get, so they can later maintain their own households. As you can see, this place is based on such an excellent system that it can only be praised. People here are raised with a feeling of responsibility, and this aspect of society cannot be overly appreciated. Motivated by what I observed from others, I, too, as mentioned, soon started to maintain our household accounts and write up all our expenditures.

5 House[35]

Having arrived in Hamburg mid-summer, we moved into a little villa on the beautiful Alster, with the later intention of buying a small house. From the start, I thoroughly disliked the tiny rooms that are typical of the houses here, whose narrow and low-ceilinged spaces were so cramped and anxiety-inducing. I was always relieved when I could breathe in the fresh and free air. People, it seems to me, care more about the number of rooms than their size. Space in the rooms is even further constrained by placing useful and useless furniture right in the middle and in all the corners, often making it difficult to navigate between all the "essential" items. Here, doors to the rooms are even kept shut by day, something that very much struck me, since I had never encountered that before. It took a long time before I could get used to this rather uncomfortable necessity. Outside doors to the houses are also closed the whole day, for there are no doormen to keep watch day and night as with us, except in hotels.

/You have absolutely no idea what all it takes to furnish a European household. As we were setting up our living quarters, there was no end to the incoming stream of hundreds of things. I was above all astonished by the sight of the vast quantities of kitchen utensils that are required here. I could not help but think of the mass feedings in our house, where at least ten kinds of baked goods and other kinds of sweets had to be prepared daily, and yet it was all done with so few instruments.

/The tight and disquieting feeling in our house was accentuated even more by the sight of thick, ribbed curtains, which threatened to obscure my view of the beloved sun, whose appearance was already so limited. Having to sit exclusively on chairs left me quite miserable in the beginning, and I harbored no small jealousy toward your comfortable "meddes" and "tekjes"! (The former being a kind of low, very soft divan; the latter, padded cushions about three feet square.) But outfitted with corset and crinoline, as I now was, and feeling caught in a vise the whole long day, I would have been very challenged to sit on a medde.

In the beginning, too, I was extremely loathe to bathe in a bathtub, but even this, as with so much else, was something I had to get used to over time. It seemed so unclean to have to wash our bodies in stagnant water, instead of what we were accustomed to at home. In response to my question as to why the same

---

35 This is the only subdivision title provided by the author. All subdivision headers provided by Heinz Schneppen in his publication of the original German are, as he noted, not part of the author's original manuscript, including a modified version of this header. H. Schneppen, *Briefe*, p. 9.

simple drain arrangement was not possible here, I was told the climate was too cold. I very much liked how the water pipes and gas lighting were set up. The degree to which European households maintain order and keep things clean is exemplary and even quite exaggerated in some of the houses.

/People are generally not very enamored of bathing, even though it is, in my opinion, far more essential than keeping the floors clean. Young children are bathed daily only up to a certain age, and thereafter only once a week. For older ages, it is best not to ask. When T.[36] was born, she was given a nanny who seriously needed a bath, something we had to tell her before we could entrust her with the child. It was not easy to persuade this genuine farm woman to undergo the salubrious act. Only after a lengthy back-and-forth did she begrudgingly step into the tub.

/Among other things, we purchased an English four-poster canopy bed, which we both liked very much and whose size reminded me of our Indian-style beds. But how can I describe my surprise when the bed was all made up with its heavy curtains, and inside lay two massive feather beds. When I asked what was the meaning of these monstrosities—up to this point, I had seen only quilts and flannel blankets - I was informed of their indispensable nature. Nevertheless, in the lowliness of my uncivilized state, I considered it a major imposition to have to cover myself with these appalling chicken feathers (as was translated to me at the time), and I refused.

The food here, I felt, was cooked much too blandly, and early on, it was quite hard for me to get used to what was served. Most of all, the thought of pork simply horrified me. It took me forever, and only after extensive cajoling, before I could agree to eat the meat of these less than appetizing creatures. Cooking, an activity where we, as children, used to bring our resident kitchen staff to despair, served me very well here. At times when I could not bring myself to consume what we would have considered just a bunch of trifles, I simply went into the kitchen and cooked myself some curry and pilaf. Anything else would have needed tools that were lacking and mostly do not exist here. The first time I got sick and lost my appetite, the doctor recommended that I eat oysters. Of course, I did not understand what he said at the time, but when my husband translated the word into Swahili, I was indignant.[37] As you know, none of us eats oysters back home, except possibly the absolute wildest native Africans.

---

36 This refers to the author's eldest daughter Tony, who was born Antonie (Arabic "Thawka") Ruete on March 25, 1868.
37 Swahili was the common language between the author and her husband, who had learned the language as a German merchant trading on the island of Zanzibar, where they met. (*Memoirs*, pp. 201–03).

That early period was truly terrible for me, especially after the contract with the English woman we had brought with us came to an end, and she accordingly had to return to her husband. I spoke Hindustani[38] with her and could converse some while my husband was away, usually from nine-thirty to four. And so it was that, after she left for England, I barely spoke a word for seven, pensive hours of every day. I had absolutely nothing to do, of course, nor anything to read, since I had already read all the Arab books my husband had ordered for me from Alexandria at least ten times over and knew them practically by heart. I did not yet know how to do European needlework, and so I found secret joy, crazy as it may seem, in welcoming every new hole in our stockings that I could set about darning. And yet, this peculiar pleasure occurred only rarely, since I had but recently forced my freedom-loving feet into stockings and owned only new ones.

To kill some time in these lonely hours, when I was quite literally speechless, my Arab articles of jewelry and clothing were imposed upon. With them, I could silently share my thoughts, no words needed. Were these not the only items I had to remind me of you and my beloved homeland? As childish as it may sound, I openly admit that I sometimes hugged and kissed these lifeless things during this exercise, but only behind closed doors. Quite often my husband would enter when the whole room was still strewn about with unpacked items and would then help me pack them up again. Now—upon seeing my husband and my familiar things all around me—I could again dare to doubt the power of sorcery, even though a belief in real bewitching so often crept over me.

---

38 Hindustani, a hybridized lingua franca derived primarily from Hindi and Urdu, was the language of "Hindustan," the Persian variant for Land of the Indus, or northern India (including what is now Pakistan). Zanzibar drew many traders, financiers, artisans, and others, along with their families, from the area.

/You will consider it ridiculous that I, who as a child was the wildest among you, without any trepidation or terror, would become so anxious in this new environment, in a way you can hardly imagine. Every time my husband left the house to go to his office, I would tremble with fear. My dread would fill me and shatter my nerves so much that I would often burst into tears. In a word, it felt beyond petrifying to have to exist in the midst of all that was so new.

/No wonder then that I would await my husband's arrival every day already starting at three in the afternoon, when I knew full well that he could not come before four. He rarely arrived with empty pockets, which he usually took care to fill with southern fruits. One day he brought me fresh pomegranates. I took one look and could not hold back the tears, as these were the first I had seen in Europe, with all the many old memories they evoked.

My first "white" cook was called Lene, and I naturally did my best to communicate with her through pantomime. One day, on a Sunday when my husband's relatives usually came over for lunch, I was headed to the basement to get something when I came across our worthy Lene as she was preparing the coffee. I personally stayed away from this wonderful drink for more than two years after my arrival in Europe for the simple reason that what people here call coffee does not even begin to deserve the label. But had I indulged in European coffee at the time of this incident, it would have undoubtedly killed my appetite for coffee henceforth. Namely, there she stood, diligently dripping coffee through an old stocking. In response to my gesticulated query about how she could possibly do such a thing, she came back with a naïve enough answer: "But Madam, the stockings are of course freshly washed!" Straight to the point, I took the instrument out of her hand and threw it into the fire.

/When we first moved into the house, I asked my husband how many cooks we would actually need, which made him burst out at me in hearty laughter. He then replied, to my great consternation, that Europeans, even very rich ones, tended to keep only one cook per household. Of course, I was thinking of our conditions back home, where people take the slightest opportunity to say they are sick, causing us to always have a second and sometimes even third person available to step in. But I also realized soon enough that a stout German maidservant could achieve ten times more than a native African.

The unusually long summer days made a big impression on me here, since every day for you has only twelve hours, regardless if summer or winter. How good of Mother Nature to have so wisely arranged this time frame to suit practicing Muslims with their annual, sun-up to sundown, thirty days of continuous fasting, during which any kind of food or drink is prohibited, as opposed to destining the residents of Greenland or Siberia to these daytime restrictions.

6

The consequence of our visits was unavoidable; we were in turn courteously invited back by all. Hamburg dinner parties are famous far and wide in Germany, and that is justified, as no one prizes a well-appointed table as much as here. For my part, these dinners were simply excruciating. Seeing as how I usually had the honor of being led by the gentlemen of the house to the table, they apparently also took it as their personal duty to fill my plate with delicacies and encourage me to eat them all. It is also not uncommon to stay seated from six to ten, a full four hours by the clock, with ten to twelve glasses arrayed at one's place. Added to that, people are so loud and talkative that my head would often spin. For certain, all this talk at mealtimes is a European peculiarity that we Arabs do not share.

/Because grace is very rarely said at mealtimes in Germany, everyone apparently has to take care of thanking the Giver of all earthly things in private. At least so I thought at the time, until I was informed that this was simply not customary. Table prayers are not said even in the closest family circles, or at most only among the very devout. Of course, this was completely alien to me, since I had up to that point assumed that all people, whether pious or not, rich or poor, high or low, owe thanks for their existence and well-being, yes, in fact, for everything, entirely to the good Lord.

My untrained eye often took great offense at the deep décolletés of the ladies. And truly, it makes no sense to me even to this day why one would choose to expose so much to hundreds of individuals of both sexes, when on other occasions that appear much less consequential, one is then demure. Even so, it is rather peculiar that people feel less shame when they see a native African woman, who often wears only an animal-hide apron, than when they see a white lady in her low-cut dress.

The first ball, where I went as an observer, had a very strange effect on me, for the many people and all their incessant swirling actually made me dizzy. As I watched the way people engaged in animated conversation and saw the gentlemen lead the ladies with their demonstrative low cuts to the dance floor, it was obvious to me that long years of friendship had created close and intertwined bonds among all who were assembled here. But I was then informed, no matter how unbelievable it sounded to me, that many on the dance floor had met and spoken here for the very first time! That is when I really grasped the extent to which I was still a stranger here. People also frequently asked me on those occasions whether we, too, danced back home. When I explained that we did not dance ourselves, but instead let others dance for us, people considered this all too droll.

Heinrich Ruete, the author's husband

The author, likely around 1868.

Invitations often arrived four weeks in advance, which left plenty of time to live and die in the meantime. The idea that people would stay at a party so late into the night, thereby getting to bed only at three or four in the morning, was new to me. I was always happy when we were finally headed back home again. Since there were so few exotic individuals to be seen in Germany at the time—relative to England and France—I suffered immensely during those first years. At parties, in theatres and concerts, I felt like I was under constant surveillance, which I found extremely vexing. My husband and I were taking a walk one day when some ladies drove by in a carriage. It was not enough for them to blatantly stare at us as they passed, but when I happened to turn around, I saw them both kneeling on the back seat to get a closer look. I later learned these ladies belonged to Hamburg's "high-life." Through experiences like this, I became so reluctant to be among people that I almost always rode in a closed carriage and turned down invitations whenever I could.

/Having usually worn the full rainbow of colors, I found European outfits all too dreary. Tastes have, however, shifted considerably over the past few years. In some circles where people are wedded to fashion, they now simply seek to outdo the Orientals. I was especially struck by all the little children whose totally white outfits made them look like ghosts, as compared to our children, who are already clothed in bright clothing from birth.

With regard to the theory of "human equality" that is so widely extolled by its proponents in the North, I had a very tangible experience. One day we were walking along a relatively narrow street. A servant girl carrying a large handbasket was coming in our direction, but rather than move to the side, she chose to bump into me with her basket, thus causing considerable damage to my new, pearl-decorated, silken mantilla. So this, I thought to myself, is a demonstrative test by a republican[39] servant girl in the push for freedom. This type of person, by which I mean European servants, as hard-working and useful as they are, often behaves so boldly and brashly that I was at times tempted to stroke their characteristically red cheeks in a less than delicate manner. But my husband let me know that a slap in the face is subject to a ten thaler penalty. I naturally preferred to withhold my ten thalers from both the police and the obstinate girl in question, and instead behave, as much as possible, in a "civilized" fashion.

/People already had more than enough outlandish tales to tell about the Arab lady. To wit, I was as fat as a barrel, even though at the time I looked more like a

---

39 "Republican" here refers to someone favoring a republic form of German government, in contrast to a royalist.

beanpole. I had the hair and complexion of a native black African. My feet were as small as those of a Chinese woman, which naturally meant I could not walk. These good folk probably had no idea that this purported Chinese woman went on walking tours from Reinbeck to Bergedorf and all around the Alster.[40] I still remember when a gentleman acquaintance came to visit us for the first time, how he could not hide his surprise at finding me as the Lord had made me, rather than the product of all these fantasies. My husband was often enough at pains to make the simple-minded Northerners understand that there is a big difference between Arabs and native Africans, and that other peoples besides native Africans also lived in greater Africa. I even had to put up with a very naïve lady who engrossed herself in my supposedly African hair and then took the strange liberty of touching it! This was but the second time I had met her.

I cannot describe how I froze that first summer, and in July and August, I was often seen moving about the house wrapped in a flannel blanket. One of my pleasures was working in the garden and watering the lawn with the rubber hose. The pretty white cat, which cousin H. had brought to Zanzibar from Mecca and later gave to me—the one that made you so jealous—was unfortunately stolen from us here. This loss made me very sad, for she was a living emblem of the homeland and very dear to me. As a replacement, my husband soon gave me two pet dogs, a poodle and a greyhound, who often reminded me of your ingrained aversion to these very devoted creatures. I also received a singing canary and a milk-bearing goat, and so I found my daily joy in this little menagerie. The same way we used to love to milk the cows and goats on the plantations, to the dismay of our female attendants, I now also milked our goat with my own hands.

The environment around Hamburg is absolutely delightful, especially the area along the Elbe, where I always loved to go. We accordingly spent the entire Sunday there virtually every second or third week. I had a very special fondness for the port, where I saw the ships that sailed to you, and now and again Africans that come here as sailors. How very comical they looked in their European clothes, and the poor souls usually appeared to be frozen and miserable.

I often experienced the downsides of not knowing the native language. Here is a funny example of one such trial: One day, I lost my way downtown and could not figure out how to get back. By chance, I happened upon the street where our shoemaker lives. I went in and could do no better than the English phrase: show me. Whereupon the shoemaker had nothing more urgent to do than to

---

40 Distances of approximately five kilometers and seven and a half kilometers, respectively.

pull up a chair for me, grab my foot, and start to take measurements to fit a pair of boots. Astonished by this act, I wrested my foot from between his hands. Totally baffled, he went out and got someone who better understood my "show me" and pointed me in the right direction. The good man had taken the English words to indicate a desire for a pair of shoes.

The need to always close the door upon entering or leaving a room or other space—even the house door, which for you only happens at night—made no sense to me. I habitually left the doors open, even in the winter. I also could not fathom why, despite rooms that were usually so small, and then even in the summer, doors and windows had to be kept shut. Accustomed to living with open windows, year in, year out, day and night, I initially did not do well with the used-up air that was so offensive to the nose. Any time I found myself in a room with too little ventilation, I got a headache. Just consider how my love of fresh air unwittingly made me the laughingstock of the neighborhood, only because I frequently opened the windows for long periods even in the winter. The word was that I was also heating the streets.

7

The first snow I ever saw struck me as simply too bizarre. Even today, I can recall the exact hour that I watched the first flakes swirl down from the sky. I sat as usual, idle and alone, in the anteroom awaiting my husband's return from the city. The lonelier I felt in my new surroundings, the quicker my thoughts rushed to you, so that, in effect, I was living two lives: one in my mind, bathed in the eternal blue sky and teeming with all your dear figures, full of high spirits and mischief; the other in the reality of my destiny. It appeared all too odd to me that anyone up in the sky would try to spread lots of white wadding onto this dirty earth, a rather pointless exercise it seemed, since at first the flakes simply would not stay on the ground. At that moment, I could not yet explain this display and instead became uncomfortable. I awaited my husband's return with even more impatience than usual, so that he would solve this Northern puzzle for me.

/This was also the time that my dear husband, in his concern for my well-being, could not dress me warmly enough. I was very displeased by all this, since I thoroughly disliked how much attire the rough climate here requires. You cannot imagine what all I had to layer on, all at the same time. Not infrequently, my dear husband would come rushing after me with some item of clothing in his hands, calling: *Bibi! Wewe umasahaw[41] kitu!* (My wife, you have forgotten something.) To which my response was always the same: *Siku sahaw lakini sipendi.* (I have not forgotten anything; I just do not like it.)

/I found it awful when I was supposed to wrap a heavy scarf around my neck; it felt like someone wanted to choke me. I also soon realized that people can rarely afford to leave the house without an umbrella. Men, women, and children head out day and night armed with this completely indispensable item, which at first sight would also very likely make you suspect some danger in the vicinity. Is that not so? Very different from how it is for us at home, where people live and die without ever having called a single umbrella their own. Actually, the Northern winter is one of

---

41 The last letter of this Swahili word is unclear in the typewritten original (Leiden University Libraries Or. 6281), but the author's handwritten original clearly shows a "w" at the end of "umasaha-" (Or. 27.135 A3). More generally, the Swahili phrases in this translation are shown as they appear in the author's manuscripts, while her German translations of the Swahili have been replaced with English translations. Professor van Donzel has footnoted alternate Swahili spellings, perhaps to clarify meanings or make corrections, citing to G.S.P. Freeman-Grenville's heavily-researched and well-annotated edition of *Memoirs of an Arabian Princess* from 1981. Nevertheless, the author's spellings may reflect the local Zanzibari dialect of her time and may also represent a more phonetic transliteration, since the author learned as a native without being schooled in Swahili.

the greatest wonders of the world, to the unending astonishment of the Tropics. Can you believe that people and creatures all start steaming when the temperature reaches certain levels in the winter? How amazed I was to see the horses on the street letting off steam at the same time I saw so much steam coming out of my own mouth.

/Once on a winter drive in a closed carriage, I saw through the glass pane how the coachman repeatedly pounded his chest with both arms. Alarmed by this remarkable demonstration, my first thought was that the poor man had suddenly lost his senses. I naturally wanted to leave the carriage as quickly as possible, but my husband broke out in hearty laughter and tried to calm me, while also explaining that the poor coachman needed this motion to keep himself warm. Did you ever consider—not in a dream, but in real life—that one could cross a river, on foot or in a heavy coach, without getting even the slightest bit wet? Indeed, this is an annual spectacle under conditions that often last two to three months here. You can shake your head as much as you want, it is simply so. In light of all these odd occurrences, which I would have considered completely out of the question only a short time before, should I not have believed this to be some kind of magic?

Two instruments, called barometer and thermometer, are of great importance here. People frequently look to the first one with avid anticipation because its readings rather often determine the dispositions of individuals, although with no impact on their moods. The second one by contrast, to the extent it is found in a closed room, registers very randomly in the winter. With some people it is high, with others it is low, such that I, too, soon started paying attention to this house friend and advisor. Oh, across the board, I never, ever seemed to get out of learning mode, for the list of things to learn here can hardly be enumerated. What little children are able to absorb and learn slowly and successively over time, from the crib onward, all came crowding quickly and completely unmediated into my poor brain, so that I, as I said, could not get past learning.

The onset of this dreary winter also ushers in the so-called social season. For a good six months, people are stuck in their four walls, while the period for sitting outdoors, as in the summer when trees and bushes beguile the hearts and eyes, belongs to the past. Thus begins a time when countless folks, the ones who find cozy familial togetherness much too boring, embark on an existence that is not unlike a frenzied hunt. Such people apparently cannot be happy without, for example, spending the day with A. at breakfast, B. for lunch, and C. for dinner. I personally knew a very sickly lady, who spent most of the day in bed, but just "had" to go out in the evening. Of course, as happened every time, whenever she had to go out, as she herself put it, she would down several glasses of champagne shortly before leaving the house to sustain her weak health. On such occasions, the poor stomach is often subjected to much too much excess. But no harm done when there is still ample socializing and fun to be had, since that is why people simply head to Karlsbad[42] the following spring. It is astounding how little sleep people need to survive here during winter nights; certainly, another triumph of civilization.

Every once in a while, we would also go to the Circus Renz, where I took great delight in the magnificent horses. I was very interested in all the feats the animals performed there. But I was less enamored of the wonderful appearance of the ladies, who seemed to come up short with their attire. What people referred to as outfits in this case were in fact hardly worthy of the name. It was also beyond me how people could enjoy and even cheer for the often quite insipid pantomimes.

/Although I as yet had not the slightest sense for European music, the plan was for me to attend a major concert. For this purpose, I was advised to throw on my red shawl entwined with gold, which, you may recall, was a present from my dear brother M.[43] from his East India trip, and let it hang like a burnoose. But oh, how I regretted that act, for we had hardly entered the great concert hall overflowing with people, when all eyes and opera glasses turned to my unfortunate person. I had no idea that this shawl would serve as a billboard, or I never in my life would have worn it across my shoulders. You can surely imagine how glad I was to finally leave.

After a while, I was told it would also be good if I visited a theatre. "Theatre," I asked my husband, "what is that?" "Yes," he answered, "the theatre is a large house where various plays are performed. Today, for example," he continued, "there is a play that will remind you of your homeland. It is called: The African Woman."[44] We drove there—I was full of anticipation. The commotion from the many people rushing about the theatre brought forth uncomfortable memories of the concert evening with my red burnoose, so I hesitated somewhat going in, especially because I had followed my husband's request and again put on something Oriental, namely a loose jacket with gold embroidery. So that I could see everything better, we took parquet seats near the orchestra. Never in my

---
42 Now Karlovy Vary in the Czech Republic, a renowned spa town with an abundance of large and small hot springs.
43 Possibly the author's half-brother Madjid, who became Sultan of Zanzibar upon their father's death and reigned from 1856 until 1870.
44 "L'Africaine," by Giacomo Meyerbeer (1791–1864), a popular French grand opera that debuted in 1865.

life had I sat so close to European instrumental music, and my unmusical head was battered about quite badly that evening.

/Finally, the curtain was raised, and I now had a very good view of the actors. Since I could not understand a single word of what was being said, I was left to observe the fantastical outfits and rather expressive gestures of the players. Everything seemed so new and peculiar, but hardly natural, and I had next to no sense of the whole thing. When my husband asked if I was enjoying the play, I could only answer "no." I then asked him whether the players were—crazy. "Oh, not at all," he laughingly responded. "But then why are they acting like it, if they are not supposed to be crazy?" was my totally uneducated question. "Of course, this is how the people want to imitate life in Africa." And what was I to say in response to that? Nothing at all!

/Africa is well-known to be very large, but the European imagination seemed to me larger yet. The late Meyerbeer was perhaps happily spared the experience during his lifetime of having such a real African woman in the audience of his play with, as it were, so little appreciation for his art. Most certainly his spirit looked down with great disappointment upon my lack of refinement, and he would have found it even less edifying to see me head home already at nine o' clock. After this first foray into the House of Thalia, there was, predictably for me, little hope that I would fill in my lacking knowledge, despite the considerable subsequent encouragement.

/These theatre performances have nowhere near the effect on Orientals that they have on Europeans; we are apparently missing the necessary understanding for the so widely-admired artistic achievements here. As an example: I later spoke with an Arab, who had also been in a European theatre. I asked: "What did you like the most about the piece you saw?" To which he responded so naturally and simply: "The sunset, Bibi, for it looked exactly the same as in Zanzibar!" My unrefined taste for theatre performances changed little over time; quite so, when I saw in some piece how priests were so disrespectfully satirized. When my neighbor noticed my displeasure, she said totally laconically: "But you are Protestant, are you not? What do you care about Catholic priests?" My only retort was to ask if Catholic priests were not "servants of God" just as much as any Protestant pastor. In my humble opinion, basically anything having to do with religion is a very poor fit for the stage, and that is especially true when presented as caricature. Given the nascent state of my Christianity, what I saw and heard was so disheartening that I went home more aggrieved than pleased.

/The thought that kept me so preoccupied put my poor soul into great conflict. I found so few good examples of devout Christians that I personally felt I was neither fish nor fowl. Separated from my former beliefs, I had nonetheless found no real replacement. How was I, as a Mohammedan, supposed to feel attracted to the new faith, when even the people who were born and bred Christian were so disdainful toward their own religion? Your kind heart would certainly have suffered, had you been able to see into my tormented soul. I judiciously wrote nothing of it. Not even my dearest beloved Ch.[45] was privy to this sore subject. I knew, of course, that she would only repeat her urgent plea that I return as one of yours to the old homeland. More on this later.

---

[45] The author's half-sister Chole, who features prominently in the *Memoirs*.

8

After we had made the rounds on all the numerous invitations to dinners, lunches, and suppers, the time came for us to return the favor. That was a hefty shock for me, as this meant I would, for the first time in my domesticity, have to play the hostess for a large gathering. What this job entails, you have no idea. The gathering was expedited through an occurrence that at the time helped me get through the lonely hours. It so happened that two weeks before we decided to undertake the soiree, a mighty tortoise reached us on a sailing ship directly from Zanzibar. The tortoise took up residence in the bathtub, although we used the latter multiple times a week. It was a lot of work for the servants to heave the big beast out and back in every time. I could sit in the bathroom by the tortoise for hours on end, and my thoughts would be hundreds and hundreds of miles from the place where fate had driven us both out—the tortoise and me. And the most nostalgic thoughts would then course through my soul upon seeing the animal sit so still and motionless in the water. I had the illusion that my silent companion must have divined and understood my thoughts and feelings. Ever since the animal's arrival, I had been feeling less lonely and was therefore very saddened when she ultimately, unequivocally, had to be killed. Her meat was namely destined for the mock turtle soup.[46]

---

46 The original manuscript says "Mock-Turtle-Suppe," although technically this was to be real turtle (i.e., tortoise) soup.

For this purpose, we also brought on board a special female cook and two hired servants in tails. Starting early in the morning, I would run up and down the stairs the entire day to supervise our supporting cast, which had since grown to six heads, and lend a direct hand where I thought necessary. In the kitchen, I helped with cleaning the vegetables, drying off plates and glasses, and setting the table for the hired servants in the afternoon. Since some of our expected guests had also been in the South, I prepared an extra curry for them, to the astonishment of my cook, who, it seemed to me, found this unfamiliar dish rather too spicy.

/An indescribable anxiety took hold of me as the time for the guests to arrive came closer. I was absolutely convinced I would be subjected to the utmost criticism and thus sought to put forward whatever I could manage, so as not to suffer a fiasco right from the start. A most apropos saying now came to mind, which translates roughly like this: "If you open your door, then behave accordingly, with dignity; otherwise close your door and hide yourself." And so I thought to myself: Well, if the criticism that will surely come is directed only at me, that would not be so bad; but people may go further and take my own incompetence as a reflection of the ineptness of our race. This worry plagued me the most, as I considered how easily I could botch European manners and customs, without the faintest notion of having done so. At that moment, my situation was truly not to be envied.

/Soon enough, the doors were opened to receive the first guests, followed shortly by the rest. I now had to do the honors as the hostess, however it might go. To be able to introduce the ladies to each other, I had spent several days beforehand practicing the correct pronunciations of their names. The unfamiliar sounds made the task quite difficult, and I constantly mixed up the names in the beginning. When the soup was announced, the gentlemen came and offered their arms to each of the ladies, even though they were, of course, complete strangers. The usual practice for such events was to alternate the seating of ladies and gentlemen at the table. With such a divergent, yes, even diametrically opposed way of life, relative to what I was used to, I felt—quite naturally, of course—your disapproval every time. And you can believe me that it put my soul in turmoil every time.

/But what could someone in my position do differently? And so, I just had to "howl with the wolves." For if I had wanted to act otherwise, who knows how that would have been received, and I was sure to become a very uncomfortable half of the marriage for my husband. In front of every lady's plate stood a small bouquet in a glass, which I had placed there myself an hour before. Who can describe my feelings when the servant asked me: "Madam, bouillon or mock turtle soup?"—That was too cruel! How could I have had the heart to enjoy the meat of my silent companion? Of course, I chose the bouillon.

If there is something I find especially disagreeable about these social gatherings, then I will name two things: First, how much and how loud people talk while eating, often making it hard to hear what your neighbor is saying, and then—how much they drink. You cannot even imagine the totality of what people drink here. Often enough, the matter has left me simply disgusted. How amazing people are with their countless customs; in the Tropics, they first consume their meals completely and then drink some water afterwards. In the North, by contrast, it seems to me that people drink more than they eat. It struck me as very unnatural to have to drink so much wine, without really being thirsty. No wonder that people get all too loud and seek to override each other in conversation. Here this condition is called an "animated gathering," although I very much doubt you can fully grasp this description.

People very much liked my curry, at least those who had been in the Orient and were familiar with the dish. Happily, I was able to converse a considerable amount on this day in Hindustani as well as Swahili, since some of our guests understood those languages.

Now it was time for the unavoidable toasts. You would surely like to know what this word means, would you not? I was no wiser than you initially about the importance of this practice, that at virtually every meal a gentleman suddenly taps on his glass before standing up and embarking on a long speech, while all the guests listen with rapt attention. On such occasions, the speaker loftily intones the virtues of the hosts, whether justified or not, something listeners are, as a rule, left to decide for themselves. The end of the speech typically results in a scene that a foreigner, such as me, is hard-pressed to describe. Chairs are pushed back, and the whole group appears to rise up, as if on command, to clink each other's wine glasses. This ritual is usually conducted rather noisily, so much so that I hardly knew what to make of the scene the first time I experienced it. Having been so richly praised and flattered, the host must then naturally respond in kind, as described above, to express his thanks. My head would start spinning so much on these occasions that I was always happy when people left the table and went into another room.

After our guests left, and my husband informed me that they had apparently spoken very appreciatively of our gathering, I was somewhat relieved that we had not embarrassed ourselves all too much, despite my private fears for days on end. And so I was truly happy to have successfully survived my opening debut in my own house in this quite highbrow Hamburg. I had to tell myself that if there are but a few people in the world who might refrain from criticizing others, then even they would be least likely to overlook the mistakes of someone they considered a totally uncultivated Arab woman.

You have no idea how difficult and complex European life was for me in the beginning, the thousand cliffs that confronted me everywhere, under conditions that were primed to cause my untrained feet to stumble. That Europeans come to us, to a setting where they are always able to maintain their lifestyles, struck me as child's play in comparison to my situation. Here, they constantly put obstacles in my way, which I had to tacitly work around, so as not to appear too helpless in the eyes of others. In a state of mind that still felt like I was barely awake, I was bombarded with never-ending impressions that hit me so quickly, one after another, that I felt like I was caught in a dream. There were just too many things that needed to be grasped and managed as quickly as possible if I hoped to make my life halfway tolerable in this completely strange setting. The prevailing conditions gave me no indulgence and no mercy; I had no choice but to cope and make do. Everything initially seemed so impossibly difficult, especially considering that so much went against my grain, and yet I still had to conform.

/Oh, how often did I wish we could have stayed in lovely Marseille, where I had felt so secure in the company of Madame M. and her niece. Nothing is harder to bear than to have to fight with oneself. And yet, it is good not to reveal all the apprehensions and doubts of our beleaguered souls every day, for this cold world seldom has a proper appreciation for what we feel and perceive most deeply. Only our true friends care about our personal joys and cares, not the alien world. At that point in time, all my friends, my husband being the sole exception, were basically antipodally distant from me.

/Had I, for example, been born and raised in Constantinople or Cairo, where European culture made inroads long ago, I may not have found such a stark contrast between Occident and Orient. In both cities, it was already long-established good form to engage European governesses to raise growing daughters, who were cultivated with various European languages, as well as music. Food there is also served forthrightly *à la franca*, meaning at a table with knives and forks. And as far as outfits and upkeep in the palaces, there is hardly any difference left to be found between Mohammedan and Parisian ladies. Should fate ever destine another Mohammedan from Constantinople or Cairo to be transplanted to Europe under the same circumstances as me, she would not even remotely be subjected to the same upheaval I have had to undergo. Had I not, until then, still been wearing the clothes of my great-ancestors from a thousand years ago and used my five fingers as natural knives and forks.

/The very slow progress of my German left me impatient. Things would get much easier, I had to tell myself, once I gained some ability to communicate with others. Most of all, I envied the people who went to Sunday church with their hymnals in the summer, while we took off on another outing. I had this deep desire to finally get to know how Christians pray to their God, and so I asked my husband to go to church with me. One Sunday we then went, but as I stood at the door, ready to go in, I had the feeling I was about to do something wrong. I had no choice now but to enter, though, if I did not want to disgrace myself toward my husband.

/Having taken my place on a pew between other congregants, I was overcome with an indescribable feeling of trepidation, which continued to worsen as I realized that the church service kept on going. I naturally could not understand a word of what was being sung and said. But the sense that I was in the holiest of holies soon calmed me. More than anything, though, I disliked the images in the church, first because it is strictly prohibited for us to pray in a room with any kind of picture, and second because I found they distracted me from my devotion, which I considered sinful. The fact that the worshippers showed no outward sign of humility toward the Almighty, by which I mean they did not prostrate themselves, struck me as very strange and arrogant; I found it very off-putting. Moreover, when I saw that money was being collected in the middle of prayer, my sensibilities, albeit completely uncultured from a Western perspective, registered nothing but desecration. I must openly admit that I consider it truly profane to call for money in a church and during a church service. One would think that, as soon as someone enters the house of the Lord, naught but a single thought would prevail, that every soul would give itself over totally and devoutly to God, and not that this place, of all places, would become a reminder of this worldly Mammon. Praying in the midst of several hundred people was also completely new for me.

/9

The first winter in the North did me no favors. I came down with a cough that refused to leave me for half a year. As a result, I learned the value of handkerchiefs, which everyone in these parts carries—like our talismans—everywhere they go. The time for Christmas was gradually getting closer, and these often foggy, sun-starved days put me in an indescribably despondent mood. To this day, even after so many years, the weather still has a great effect on my well-being. Whenever there was one of those rare sunny days in the winter, I would feel so much better. Later I also completely understood why the English suffer—as is said of them—from the "spleen" precisely in November and December. A dreary, foggy day could make me so melancholy that I often just wanted to cry.[47]

/The way people rushed about on the streets with their countless packages, the closer Christmas came, made such an impression on me that I pestered my husband with questions. For one, it was completely new to me that people would ask each other what gifts they wanted. As an example: "Friedrich, my son, what would you like for Christmas?" or also "Dear Anna, is there anything I can give you as a present?" and more of the same. I was therefore quite surprised when my husband asked me one day what I might in fact desire and what I most wanted to have. Of course, I had absolutely no specific wishes, since I had everything I might need. We now often went into town to make purchases for my husband's relatives and our servants. In general, I really enjoyed the way everyone, from the highest to the lowest, could make their own purchases. This struck me as much better and more comfortable than our way of doing it, which makes us so dependent on the taste and intelligence of our slaves.

/Until now, I was used to buying things only together with my husband, so I found it very difficult to get something for him for Christmas without his knowledge. How could it have been otherwise, since I still did not understand German, much less speak it. I wanted to give him a golden pocket watch, since his no longer worked very well. One day I gathered enough courage to go into town alone at a time when I knew he would be busy in his office and could not easily run into me on the street. After I had studied the lovely shops on

---

[47] In historical understandings of the human body, melancholia (from the Greek for "black" and "bile") was one of the four temperaments that matched the four humors, each tied to a human organ. If the spleen produced too much black bile, that was said to create an imbalance with blood, phlegm, and yellow bile that would lead to a melancholic temperament. Under humorism, black bile corresponded to the cold and dry conditions of autumn.

the Jungfernstieg and Neuer Wall[48] from the outside for a while, not without a heavily beating heart, I slipped into a watch store and found myself standing somewhat helplessly in front of the storekeeper. He bowed politely and began to speak to me, which of course was beyond my comprehension. My only response was to point to the pretty watches he kept in his case. This poor watchmaker looked at me quizzically, apparently not quite knowing what to do with me. He shook his head and proceeded to simply seat himself again. This impolite treatment did not suit me at all and so I persisted with my pointing. Finally, he conceded and opened the case for me. I then began to canvass my options, all the while feeling how this man kept a sharp eye on me. Who knows if he did not at that moment consider me a store thief.

/Having now found a watch that I liked, we encountered major problems with the payment. It proved impossible to reach an understanding, at which point I lost my patience and grabbed this startled man by the arm, rubbed my thumb and pointer finger together, our way of signifying payment, and simultaneously pointed to the door. Nearby I knew a very famous jeweler, who I hoped could help me out of this dilemma. I spoke the jeweler's name to the watchmaker, and lo and behold, his face lit up, despite having previously looked at me so skeptically. And thus we actually walked out the door, the watchmaker bearing my chosen watch, to the jeweler in question with whom I had good credit, to ask him to enable the transaction with the watchmaker. Later, this jeweler could not get enough of telling my husband the tale of this very funny situation we had found ourselves in. Quietly triumphant, I headed back home, although not before buying a couple of *berloques*[49] for the watch from the jeweler, my rescuer in time of need. The whole way home I was beset with concern that I might still happen to run into my husband on the street and spill my secret in an untimely fashion. It would have been too easy for him to figure me out, since I never liked to go out without him.

/On Christmas Eve, after our servants had gotten their presents, we drove off in a carriage to my husband's parents with their presents, to spend the evening there. It was my first Christmas celebration ever, and to this point, I had absolutely no idea how Christians celebrate their festivals. I was acutely interested in finding out what this Occidental ritual was like. I had seen pictures in the church, but without knowing their meaning and purpose, and not having

---

48 The author refers to two perpendicular streets in Hamburg: first, the beautiful waterfront avenue that lines the Binnenalster and second, a major avenue that remains one of Europe's top luxury shopping streets. Reconstructed after the great fire of 1842, the Jungfernstieg and adjoining area acquired a horse tram line in 1867, just as the Ruete newlyweds moved in on the other side of the Außenalster.

49 From the French, meaning small trinket or charm, usually worn on a chain or bracelet.

wanted to ask my husband about them—on the one hand, out of consideration for his feelings toward his religion (for what did I know back then of the countless ways to profess one's Christianity?), and on the other hand—and that was the main thing for me—to avoid discovering that the Christian religion was in fact, as some tended to believe in our parts, idol worship. Exactly that would have been contrary to my convictions. For these reasons, I steered clear of any questions pertaining to the upcoming celebration.

/On our drive, we passed one of the busiest streets in the city, with people whose rushed pace could hardly be described as walking. The whole world seemed to be in such an inexplicable hurry. I will never forget the scene of a man, tightly gripping a pendulum clock with both arms, who rushed along with such speed that everyone scurried out of his way. When the carriage stopped, I could see an array of heads looking down at us from the second floor. My husband's younger brothers came out and helped us carry the presents into the house. Once we had reached the upstairs, I found everything so secretive, and there was no end to the whispering. I was strictly forbidden to enter the dining room, which heightened my curiosity even more. And then we heard a bell ringing out from that mysterious room, whereupon the younger generation jubilantly ran in. "Bibi!" my husband called, "Emily!" the others called, and so we all went in.

/There I stood, in front of a tree filled with so many burning lights and draped with all sorts of sweets. Now I was led to a table on which all sorts of things had been stacked for me. But I completely missed the main present, until my dear husband said to me: "Bibi, this is also for you." Only then did I take a closer look. It was a large velvet coat, lined with fur and trimmed from top to bottom, including the sleeves, with ermine. You can imagine my amazement when I saw what was from a European point of view the most precious of coats. Really—I thought to myself—of all things, I am to wear fur here, which only the wildest of our native Africans would ever wear? No, for my husband to expect that of me would be too extreme. I could not help but say to him in Swahili: "Is it possible that I am actually supposed to wear this thing, and that you, of all people, would give it to me?" "Please, Bibi," came the answer, "this is something especially fine. The outer fur is called ermine and is usually worn only by royals." "Royals, you say, wear this? But why? Are the princes and princesses here so poor, as poor as our native Africans in Zanzibar?" "Oh no, surely not," he responded with laughter. "Indeed, ermine is the height of luxury here." I must confess that it took me a long time before I could accustom myself to this cloak of European royalty. Back then, the only value this ermine fur had for me was exactly the same as—the fur of a cat.

Shall I now tell you what I thought of this first Christmas celebration? Well, it is a tricky matter to comment on the customs and traditions of other peoples without now and again offending the latter, even if unintended. I only want to tell you my personal impressions, as I perceived them, but nothing more. For although I had previously considered the Protestant religion to be one of the most easygoing, and personally would have preferred somewhat greater formality, I found to my disappointment that the whole point of the Christmas Eve celebration was entirely overlooked. It astonished me to hear that the birth of Christ was being celebrated without even a single thought of prayer. Can you even imagine that? Surely not easy, and yet it is so. I was, as I said, very disappointed and would gladly have had fewer presents in exchange for a short religious ceremony. Of course, at the time I would have understood next to nothing, but even just the sight of a devotional would have sufficed for me to turn to prayer in my own way. From that time on, it became quite clear to me that being Christian was a relative term. Accordingly, my inner struggle grew more and more excruciating every day. I thought of our festivals, and my thoughts shot like arrows over to you—as if I could seek what I was missing amongst you!

/The next morning, on the 25th of December, my husband was surprised to see me coming down the stairs from the bedroom already at ten o' clock in my full regalia. He shouted something to me like: "My God, Bibi, what has happened, where on earth do you plan to go?" I first swooshed calmly down the stairs with my long train and then asked if he had not himself said to me that today and tomorrow were holidays. "As you see, that is why I got so dressed up." "Yes, Bibi, that is customary for you, but not here with us." Strange people, these Northerners, I thought to myself, and went back upstairs to change into my normal clothing. The way we prepare very special meals and cakes for festivals, they do the same.

So as not to offend my husband, I followed his wishes and had to wear this monstrous fur coat on our next outing. How that made me feel you can tell yourself without difficulty. And if a thief had conveniently thought to come to our house to steal this coat, I would surely have let him conduct his business without interfering in any way.

On New Year's Eve, I had a pretty shock when confronted with a totally drunk servant girl. According to the usual German custom, my husband had prepared the indispensable New Year's punch for himself and his brothers, of which our servants each received a glassful. For my part, the first sip did nothing for me, as with all strong drinks, so I completely refrained. When I wanted to head to bed as usual at ten o' clock, I rang for the servant girl, for her to light the upstairs. She let me wait an unusually long time, so I went into the corridor to call her up from the basement. At long last, she dragged her way up the stairs and slurred several times: "Madam, Madam!" Only a few more stairs to reach me—and this punch-indulging character collapsed into a heap. Since I had thus far fortunately never had such direct exposure to a drunkard and only heard talk of such godless people, which is what we call them, I let out a noteworthy scream, causing my husband to rush out of the dining room to me. From then on, I took note of how much punch every servant girl could bear on New Year's Eve, having learned from this experience. What do you think about such a thirst and even more, such a throat?

Early on, I found the sight of thousands of people ice skating on the frozen river truly magical. I could not get enough of watching the people, who seemed equipped with some sort of invisible wings, from our front yard. An extraordinarily talented young girl among our acquaintances seemed to me just like a sailing ship tacking against wind and weather. Great efforts were also made to teach me how to skate, but sadly to no avail, since my clumsy feet, which move very awkwardly on icy surfaces even to this day, could not master the challenge. Much later, I had a gentleman tell me when he noticed my inability in this art: "Ah, Madam, you are not so easily led onto the ice?"[50] How witty this man must have thought himself in making this joke!

Summer finally arrived. Although the warmth was not quite exhilarating, it was a much better fit for the never-ending hustle and bustle on the part of all of humanity here in this land, as compared to an excessively hot season. I was filled with childish joy by the first leaves on the trees, which had looked like broomsticks for almost six months, giving newcomers the impression that they had all suddenly dried out and were waiting to be cut down. I was so happy to be able to sit in the yard again, or generally outdoors, for after months of sitting in heated rooms, and only occasionally letting in the fresh air, I had really had more than enough. In these rooms, I frequently felt so pinned in and pent up that I often stretched my whole head out of the window, even in the biting cold, just to breathe in some air. But I could tolerate this sport only a few minutes at a time, since the indescribably cold air quickly propelled me back in again. Often enough, this craving for fresh air left me feeling quite sick.

This was also the time when everyone asked each other, "And what are your summer plans?" We, or more specifically my husband, also faced these questions. When he translated for me, I was quite surprised to hear that

---

50 The German expression cited by the author—*aufs Eis führen*—is idiomatic for duping someone.

everyone—of course, only if they had the necessary funds—made it a point to leave the city for several months. When I asked him if we also had to travel, I was very happy to hear the comforting answer from my kindhearted and always accommodating husband that, if I preferred not to go anywhere, he would be happy to stay at home. Surely you also want to know why people leave the city in the summer and where they go. In the big European cities, there are houses and apartments that have absolutely no trees or bushes in their vicinity. Indeed, there are even living spaces, the so-called inner court and cellar apartments, where the residents—pity them!—barely see any sky. And precisely those people are so impoverished and in such need that fate condemns them to live and die there.

/ So the well-to-do class goes to the countryside or to the coast to indulge in some of summer and, as people also like to say here, recover from the winter. Later I also had the chance to participate in these so-called recuperation trips. Traveling when schools are on vacation is the worst, worse than you can possibly imagine. Both coming and going, it is a relief not to simply be crushed in the railway compartments, and it is best not to elaborate on the frequently prevailing atmosphere. During these travel periods, there is such a hustle and bustle at the train stations that it often feels like Judgment Day is coming, as taught to us in the Koran.

After eleven months of instruction for two hours every day, I finally began to understand some German, enough that I soon thereafter ended my lessons. Grammar, however, seemed to pose such insurmountable obstacles for me that I was happy to leave it to my devoted teacher. The German language is tougher than most, and its grammar is a hard nut for the novice to crack, one that takes so much time to overcome. Given my ignorance of the usual arrangements, language, and more, it was to be expected that our good servants would do their utmost to enrich themselves at our expense. We were in essence completely in their hands for almost two years and lived in our own house during that time much like in a hotel. We seldom knew exactly what we would be served. Not until seated at the table did we get to see what they deemed adequate for us to eat.

/As bad behavior seldom prospers, it eventually became clear how much these people had taken advantage of us. Once I became aware, I considered it my duty to look after things, as much as I could. The first thing I did was send all the old servants away. They had demonstrated their disloyalty more than enough and naturally could not be retained, not a one, so as not to set a bad example for the new domestics. From then on, I kept the household book, in German of course, but please do not ask me "how"! That it was filled with countless errors, and the script was of dubious legibility, you can well imagine. I took charge of the household funds, handled all expenditures, ordered the necessary provisions, and made up the daily grocery list myself. As I undertook my new task, my abilities gradually grew. Less than half a year after taking up this new position, I received my husband's praise, for by then we were eating no worse than before, but living at about half the cost of what it took when our servants still ruled.

In the third summer of our time in Hamburg, my husband proposed that we take a trip to Copenhagen. The plan was to travel without our two children, which did not suit me at all. The idea of leaving one's small children behind, for no reason, with the youngest being only four months old,[51] was completely incomprehensible to me. And yet, it was to be a pleasure trip. It is, I suppose, rather naïve of me to admit that I actually spent the night before this "pleasure trip" sleepless and in tears. We were meant to be away from the children for only two weeks, and yet, that seemed far too long for me. The thought of leaving the children behind, just for me to have a little fun, struck me as so heartless. When I asked, what on earth was the point of going to Copenhagen, I received an answer that I did not well understand. I could not be with the children forever, so I might as well start getting used to that. Does that make any sense to you? Certainly not to me. Not even when my dear husband told me about a Mrs. C., who had only recently left with her husband for China, and for several years at that, while calmly leaving her children back in Hamburg.

/I could see that resistance was futile, especially as my husband appeared to take such stock in having me come along. On this occasion, he jokingly claimed that I loved the children more than him, which was of course not true. And so, we arrived happily in Copenhagen, and the first thing we visited was the Museum of Thorwaldsen. I saw so many beautiful things here for the first time, but they left no impression on me. Even the concert in Clamlenburg, where the royal family was in attendance, had no effect on me, as my thoughts were constantly with my children. And in the end, rather than stay the entire two weeks as planned, we hurried home after just a week. I believe no living soul was happier than I was that day when I could once again press my young children to my heart.

My first reading material in the German language was newspaper advertisements. I was quite proud of this accomplishment, especially as I had initially been quite sure that learning this language would be impossible for me.

---

51 Her youngest at the time was her son Said, later called Rudolph. Rosa, her youngest daughter and last child, was born the next year.

Time passed without any noteworthy events for me. Only once did I experience a small shock, which fortunately passed quite quickly. Namely, we came close to moving to Valparaiso. My ability to stay in touch with you all would have been significantly challenged from America. Plus for now, I had had more than enough with my transition to Germany, even if the Chilean climate would have suited me much better. So we stayed in Germany.

/In the spring of 1870, it turned out that my husband needed to travel to England for a couple of weeks on business. Our youngest child at the time was barely six weeks old, so I naturally needed to stay at home. But that was easier said than done, for the mere thought of having to rely entirely on myself in this foreign setting, even for just a short while, put me into such a state of anxiety that I begged my husband to take me and the children along. "No, Bibi, that really is not possible," was his answer, "because I need to visit many towns in England, and you cannot join me everywhere. But you will see that I will be back in two weeks, at most three!" My husband did what he could to assuage my inexplicable, even to me, fear of staying in Hamburg alone without him.

I expect you may be asking yourself why it took so long for me to get used to my new environment. Please do not judge me too rashly, and believe me, adapting to a people that is so very different is more easily contemplated than practiced. On the outside, I gave as little cause as possible for anyone to think I was challenged, but on the inside, I never stopped feeling lonely and vulnerable when my husband was gone. A sign of how much you all still occupied my thoughts during this time—when I was still unencumbered and fortunate that my husband treated me with such love and devotion—is evident from the fact that I dreamt exclusively of you all, night after night. Oh, how often did my husband tease me when I was ready to turn in somewhat earlier, for he would say: "Aha, Bibi, do you want to travel to Zanzibar so soon today? Then please give my best to our friends there." The three weeks passed by very slowly, and I was happy when my husband returned back home.

10

A few weeks later, the great war between Germany and France broke out,[52] which caused tremendous excitement for everyone. We were assigned soldiers to be quartered in our home for a short time, but opted to avoid the related inconvenience by lodging them in a simple inn. Now began a war between the two nations that you, on your peaceful island, cannot fathom. Hundreds upon hundreds of thousands of people were sacrificed on both sides. Somewhat in the manner that the devout Muslims, during their annual pilgrimage, sacrifice countless sheep on Mount Arafat, where it is said our father Adam and our mother Eve met again after being expelled from Paradise.[53] When the war erupted, people here were as if electrified, for all the talk was of the war and nothing else. One has to marvel at the patriotism of the Germans, since their sacrifice of blood and goods was virtually unlimited at the time. What offerings of men and money such a war consumes mocks any description. To undertake such a war of attrition—nota bene: Christians against Christians—Europeans start to train their male youth already at a very early age for this purpose.

/All European states suffer more or less from the same very bad malady, namely jealousy. No one grants the others anything, and every state always strives to be ahead of every other state, no matter the cost. Every state, even the very smallest, has its own host of spies, who are tasked with reconnoitering their dear neighbors. And naturally, all the statesmen are constantly striving to assure each other that they are not aware of the existence of any such individuals. Efforts are made across the board to invent the most terrible instruments of mass murder, in order to take the first opportunity to duly impress one's own power upon the neighbor, without diminishing the lovely-sounding words by which the statesmen mutually assure each other of the sincerity of their goodwill.

/Woe to any nation that has the misfortune today of losing a war. On top of all its material losses, the ruthless imposition of taxes poses an added threat, as a screw that gets turned ever tighter, depending on how great the need or desire. Under these circumstances, it has always seemed to me that the so-called humanitarian principles in Europe were mainly studied and applied to free the

---

52 The author is referring to the Franco-Prussian War from July 1870, when France declared war, to January 1871, when France surrendered, followed by the Treaty of Frankfurt in May 1871.
53 Mount Arafat is also known as the Mount of Mercy because, as some Muslims believe, the Lord forgave Adam and Eve when they reunited and repented there. He then also promised to forgive any of their offspring who subsequently appeared there on the same day, the day before the Big Festival or Great Bayram. *Memoirs*, p. 148.

slaves. But what does it mean for one African state to fight and raid another when compared to a single war in the North! The view here is that when a nation loses a war, its wings must also be clipped, to create a crippling effect that will endure a minimum of many years hence. And what an outcry there is here about the slaves we keep, even though these slaves are far better off than some of the people here. As you know, we are not remotely social democrats, and yet I have often had to consider whether it would be more appropriate if the individual European governments were to spend their countless millions on their own impoverished populations, who suffer such privation, especially in the winter, instead of using the money for the so-called "liberation" of Africans. But all this is mostly decided at the usual green table,[54] which is to say by people who know just about as much about Africans, their temperaments, and their needs as you and I know about the inhabitants of other planets.

/Nowhere does the contrast between the haves and have nots appear greater than right here in the cold North, where one finds, on the one hand, such opulence and luxury, and on the other, such heart-rending poverty. I once saw such poverty in the case of an unemployed coach driver's family, who had absolutely nothing but a number of freezing and hungry children! When I saw this misery, for which I unfortunately had no means of providing a durable remedy, and could only provide momentary relief, I was so seized by this plight the entire day that I could hardly eat. I could not help but think that out of a hundred of our slaves, not even two would want to exchange their lot with this kind of freedom.

/And what indeed is the military draft if not a type of slavery, a system that, with the exception of England, is highly nurtured across all of Europe. As a result, when war breaks out in a country where this system of obligatory military service prevails, the male population from 17 to 45 years of age is, as needed, pulled into the field. This arrangement also signifies great justice, with no distinction made between rich and poor, or the son of a prince and the son of a cobbler. Even Jews must go to war, just like Christians. With this constant preparation and the ongoing new procurements for the military, the State takes on expenditures that completely exceed your ability to comprehend. For entirely impartial outsiders, meaning people who have no association with Christianity and know of the peaceful, love-thy-neighbor teachings of Jesus only through books and stories, it must appear totally incongruous to watch

---

54 The German expression used by the author—*etwas am gruenen Tisch entscheiden*—refers to people sitting at the classic leather- or cloth-covered green table (picture today's billiard tables) and making out-of-touch decisions in the official, bureaucratic meeting room.

how its adherents seek to outdo each other in who can invent the deadliest and most *en gros* annihilating weapon. But this is called progress here. You, however, in your simplicity, if you were to consider all these arts that they call progress here, were you to see all of it and everything that goes with it, I am entirely sure you would call them—simply satanic.

Stereograph entitled "Red fields of slaughter sloping down to ruin's black abyss"

11

In this tumultuous time of war between Germany and France, I was struck, as you know, by the greatest tragedy of my life. During this period, I was just beginning to gradually get used to the climate, the people, the food, and the until-then completely unfamiliar conditions, when fate delivered me such a powerful blow. The way we usually feel safe from any storm under a clear and cloudless sky, that is how I felt shortly before my misfortune. I happened to be lying in bed with a fever, where I needed to be given cold compresses for my head to combat the heat resulting from weaning my youngest child. Beyond that, there was no sign of what was to come.

On this day, I felt somewhat better, and so my husband opted to set out on a visit to his sick father, who was staying in his summer cottage and could be reached only by horse-drawn rail. He returned from the office as usual at four o' clock and then left me to go downstairs at half past four to eat his lunch alone. Shortly thereafter, he left the house, and I fell into a deep sleep. When I awoke, it was already completely dark. The nanny brought the children to my bed to say good night. Until nine o' clock, I lay there peacefully, without any concern, knowing to expect my husband's return during that time. But from then on, I was gripped by a totally inexplicable fear, which also grew from minute to minute. I was too spoiled by his exemplary punctuality, in addition to the fact that he almost never went out for supper, unlike so many others. I listened with strained breathing to the regular call of the steamboats in the Alster, which passed right by our front yard, and each time, I imagined that he might have gone into town with the horse tram and then continued by steamboat out to us.

/But all remained still, and no one pulled at the doorbell, so as to calm my heart perhaps for just an instant, while it pounded with such foreboding. Around eleven, I succumbed to a cold fever and lay there shivering, barely able to exchange even a sound with the nanny. Midnight struck, and my husband still had not returned. A thousand thoughts coursed through my head in my already agitated feverish state, and one scary scene chased another. I suspected some calamity by now all too clearly, and my fever-exacerbated fantasy drew up the most horrid images, for I knew my husband only too well, that he would never intentionally cause me to be afraid, especially now when I was sick. Every instant, I wanted to get up and at least walk up and down our street in case I might run into him. But each time, I forced myself, with effort, to give up the thought. This night remains forever unforgettable, as it counts for years of my life.

Then finally—the quiet sound of the doorbell being pulled. Thanks be to the Lord! evoked my soul, for here he has now finally come. Naturally he pulled softly on the bell, so as not to wake me from my sleep, I thought to myself, and waited with tense nerves for his familiar footsteps. Five minutes passed, seemingly an eternity, and yet I heard nothing. This, too, struck me as so strange, so peculiar, since it was his usual custom, as soon as he got home and deposited his hat and coat in the wardrobe, to immediately seek me out in one room after another until he found me. At this time, he would have come straight up to the bedroom, so late at night—or so I calculated.

/When, however, everything continued in silence, I felt such an indescribable fear and dread arise anew that I suddenly sprang out of my bed, just as I was. Without pulling anything more on, only in my long English nightgown, I ran down the corridor and loudly began calling my husband. I took the opportunity to bend deeply over the banister for him to hear me more clearly, when I suddenly felt myself being grabbed tightly by the servant girl, who had come leaping up the stairs. "Where is the master, where is my husband, Anna, where is my husband?" I called to the girl, who was very flush in the face. I wanted to free myself from her and rush down the stairs, for now it appeared all too clear that something had happened to him. This foreboding at first seemed to practically rob me of my sanity, and so I exerted extra-human effort to try to pull myself away to reach the stairs, as the nanny and cook, who had also rushed over, sought to remove me from the banister. Meanwhile one of them tried to comfort me with words that gave me little relief: "Madam, calm yourself, the master is still alive, but he is very sick!" That was too much for my fever-impacted body, and I apparently collapsed. My otherwise robust nerves gave out for just a short while, though, and when I opened my eyes again, still dazed, I saw a male stranger standing before me.

/"Madam," began the gentleman with emotion rising in his voice, "take courage, your husband still lives, for he is the one who sent me here." "Where is my husband? I want to see him!" I repeatedly pressed my question, as yet unaware how great my misfortune was. "Madam, do you recognize me? I am of course R., your neighbor's house doctor." And yet he still hesitated to answer my question, even as I posed it again and again. His hesitation signified only disaster, and so I implored him, as much as I could in German, to tell me everything quickly and truthfully. Whereupon he shared enough detail that I could see how very dire the disaster was.

/For this is what happened: My husband was on the way home, returning from his sick father, on the horse tram. When he got to the end of the line, which was still a ways from our home, he jumped, as is unfortunately the habit of all gentlemen here, from the open platform in the front and fell with such disadvantage that he was gripped by the still-moving tram and—overrun! And even though he was fatally injured, he did not lose his powerful strength right away, as he went on his own by foot to a nearby carriage stop, had the carriage call on Doctor R., who happened to live in the area, and then rode with the same to the next hospital. Upon arrival, he was given emergency care. He then bade Doctor R. to ride to me, so as to let me know of the events in the gentlest way possible. And thus it was midnight before I learned of the accident. How badly my husband was injured and how dangerous his injuries were, of that the Doctor naturally said nothing. But from his tone and compassionate manner with which he tried to comfort me, I could feel and guess the magnitude of the damage enough.

/Against all reason and overcome by an indescribable fear, I demanded on the spot, in the very form I had left my bed, to go to my husband. "No, Madam, that is not possible. They would never even let you into the hospital so late at night!" That was the Doctor's answer. I responded, however, that if he was not willing to take me in his carriage to my husband, I would go the whole long

One of the first horse-drawn trams in Hamburg, late 1860s.

distance on foot. And if then the people at the hospital were so hardhearted as to keep me from seeing my husband, I would rather spend the night under the open sky at the hospital door than stay here in this house. When the sympathetic Doctor now realized that I would not be held back, he finally said: "Well, Madam, at the very least you must get yourself properly dressed, or you may otherwise end up freezing to death." After having hurriedly added the minimal clothing, I ran more than walked down the stairs and drove with the Doctor and the nanny to the hospital.

/Oh, my God, what a ride! Everything seemed to progress so slowly, the horse, the carriage, even the driver seemed half asleep to me. My mind had already reached the hospital long before, and my sick fantasy mercilessly painted the absolute worst images before my eyes. I cannot conjure up the right words to adequately describe my state of being, since there are pains that can only be experienced, where words do not suffice. May the good Lord preserve everyone from such a trip.

/Finally, after barely half an hour, the carriage reached its destination. Dear Doctor R. led me in and then looked for the supervisor. The latter arrived, but seemed very ill-disposed that I had come. When I noticed that, I went down on my knee and begged: "Oh, Mr. Supervisor, please take compassion and let me go to my poor husband." "That is not allowed," he answered, "and patients can be visited only on certain days during certain hours." "What?" I said, "I may not see my husband any time soon?" Oh my God, how hard and unfeeling people are here. What an imposition, that total strangers would suddenly take the power upon themselves to stand between me and my husband, callously uncaring about my unspeakable despair.

/Permission and policy! How I could have cared less for those two words in that instant, for I found myself in such desperation that law, authority, and the whole world seemed entirely non-existent. I was not far from losing my sanity altogether that night. Later my female companion told me how I had run along the endless hospital corridors, back and forth, from one end to the other, exclaiming my misery in a foreign language, of which I subsequently had no memory. I was now no longer willing to let myself be sent off without first having seen my husband again, even if only briefly. For who could know, other than the Almighty himself, if I would ever, subject to all these complete strangers and their countless rules, see him alive again. They would have had to carry me out the door to make me leave the hospital, since I certainly would not have gone on my own.

/One needs to have been born and raised in Europe to be able to subordinate oneself to the thousand limitations that so frequently infringe on personal liberties and simply turn the individual person into a number. Such compulsion does not fit us primitive peoples, since we mostly put our hearts first and then apply cold calculations.

Finally, the supervisor showed some mercy and promised his willingness to take me to my husband on the condition that I stay at most a quarter hour and generally keep my composure. Were I to follow his terms, I could come again to visit my husband tomorrow. Even so, I had to wait a very long time until the hospital surgeon, Doctor C., arrived to properly diagnose and bind the countless deadly wounds. The humane supervisor tried to comfort me in the meantime, which was apparently not easy for him, since he had a kind, soft heart, and I often saw how he surreptitiously tried to dry his moist eyes.

/When Doctor C. had finally finished with the poor patient, what seemed an eternity to me, the supervisor returned and led me to the sick room. It was kept largely in darkness, and as I entered with trembling limbs, I almost lost my breath. In this moment, I could not have emitted a single sound, even if it had cost my whole being. With difficulty, I approached his bed, from which I heard an eternally unforgettable voice: "*Bibi, roho jangu!*" (Bibi, my soul, my life, my breath), before I could catch myself. "You still came so late, be brave, my life, and do not cry so!" I could muster but a few words in response: "Are you in great pain?" "Yes, very much!" "Where?" "On my chest." "What happened?" "*Amury ja mungu!*" (By God's will.) I barely dared speak any more, much less ask more questions, for I saw how difficult it was for him. So I sat in the half-darkened room and had to very much strain my eyes to make out the beloved features. One of his hands held mine tightly, without my suspecting that the other arm, which lay under the blanket, was completely shattered. I would learn more the next day.

/It took about half an hour before the supervisor returned to pick me up, so that the patient could try to get some sleep. I cannot rightly express in words what feelings I had as I took my leave. We exchanged our "*jacu onana!*" (good-bye!), without much convincing energy from at least one of us, and I slunk more than walked out of the room on the arm of the supervisor. Outside in the corridor, the friendly supervisor let me know that I could stay with my husband from tomorrow onwards and that he would hold an adjoining room for me. Hearing these words with unspeakable gratitude, I simply threw my arms around the neck of this good old man.

I was so physically diminished that it took considerable effort for me to move. In the end, my strength completely left me, and I was half carried, half dragged by the nanny and the supervisor back to the carriage. The rest of the night I spent on the balcony in the open, since I could not tolerate my small room where I felt suffocated. Even though it was summer, the night was still so bitter cold. Wrapped in a thick throw, I sat there deep in my misery until the glittering stars, one after another, faded away to make room for the breaking dawn of the new day. Then I crept back into my room and waited for the children, one by one, to wake up. Upon seeing them, I became so unutterably sad that I broke down in uncomprehending tears, for a deep premonition told me only too clearly how soon they stood to lose the blessing of having a father.

/After assisting the nanny with bathing the children and their breakfast, I left for the hospital already at nine o' clock. Here I had to wait again for almost another hour in the supervisor's room, until the chief surgeon came to replace the patient's bandages. I approached the door of the sick room with a pounding heart and had to stand there for a long time before I found the courage to enter. Finally, I entered the room. There I found my husband still without fever and possessed with a clear understanding. But, oh how he looked! For now, in the bright light of a July day,[55] I could see immediately what had been obscured the night before. A large gash covered the length of his forehead, the nose was damaged, the back of his head revealed an even larger and more dangerous wound. One ear was completely gone. The fatal wound, however, lay on his chest, which along with his arm was thoroughly crushed. One leg was also very significantly damaged. I had to pull myself together to hide the shock and pain I was feeling. I would not have thought such deformity possible in such a short time! It seemed to me that he himself did not clearly understand the hopelessness of his situation, as he went on about all sorts of trivial things, which amazed me. And so I only too gladly allowed myself to be lightly deluded by his calm state and clear mind, and accordingly soon took heart again. Since it was late July, and the day was quite hot, I had brought along a handheld fan, which he himself had given to me in my homeland, to keep the flies off him. That brought us to recalling past days and events, with our thoughts drifting far off to the Equator.

---

55 This daytime visit appears to have been on July 30, 1870, based on the hospital intake report of the Allgemeine Krankenhaus St. Georg (General Hospital of St. Georg) from the prior day, discovered and kindly shared by Fridjof Gutendorf, as part of his extensive research in various Hamburg archives.

View of Zanzibar

I sat by his bedside, for the moment almost happy, until about two o' clock in the afternoon, when he suddenly became feverish and toward evening also began to fantasize. Under the circumstances, the doctors considered it better that I spend the night at home, as I also felt somewhat unwell, and then return the next morning. Although with a heavy heart, I followed their advice, if only to retain my hard-won advantages, as opposed to being able to see my patient only twice a week for short periods, as otherwise dictated by the harsh rules. I also longed to see the children again. When I arrived at home, all three were already in their beds and long asleep, which left me sitting at their bedsides where I could be persuaded of their healthy, regular breathing. The house seemed so barren and desolate. I felt like I was in someone else's home and could not sit still anywhere. In the end, I found my refuge in the children's room and stayed there.

The next morning, I returned to the hospital and arrived just as the church service was beginning (it happened to be a Sunday). I encountered many recovering patients on their way to the chapel. Oh, how full my heart was at that moment, all my feelings culminating in but a single thought, whether my husband would ever be granted the privilege of thanking the Lord in this same chapel for his own convalescence! Later, it was indeed a great comfort for me to have been together with him in church shortly before his accident. For even though I had barely understood the sermon, simply the thought of being in the Lord's house has always given me fulfillment and kept me from becoming discouraged.

/Today the kind supervisor greeted me with a glowing smile, as he told me that my husband had slept quite well and also asked for something to eat. And so it was; I found him not only without any fever, but also in good spirits. He had almost no pain, which struck me as very odd. He also hoped to be up and about again very soon. Encouraged by this positive turn of events, I asked the two assigned doctors to allow my husband to be transported to our house, since the transport itself could not do him much harm. I had noticed that a canal of the Alster flowed directly to the hospital, so that a boat ride right up to our front yard could be handled quite easily without much exertion by the patient. But the doctors categorically rejected my suggestion, saying "Absolutely not, your husband is not transportable." Nor did the doctors allow my suggestion that the patient's full beard, which was covered with blood and seemed to bother him greatly, should be shaved. "A few more days, Madam, and then it will happen." That was their answer. Toward evening, his condition again shifted so very rapidly that I could only leave him with growing concern, to return the next morning.

When I came back the next day, I found him very sick, as he had been feverish and delirious the entire night, and still was. On this day, I wore a white embroidered blouse, as was the fashion at the time. When my husband saw me coming, he indeed recognized me right away, but soon asked seriously, almost imploring, if I had gotten dressed so nicely to take him on a walk. And then he repeated these words several times: "*Ngodje kidogo, Bibi, mimi ntakuischa kuwa nguo sangu karidu!*" (Wait a moment, Bibi, I am almost done getting dressed!) His state deteriorated visibly, and three strong hospital staff had difficulty keeping him in bed, since he kept wanting to jump out.

/My heart bled indescribably as I watched him fight so wildly with these men, without my being able to help him. If it had been up to me, I surely would have left him alone, since the unnatural exertion was bound to cause him more harm than if he had been free to move around the room with sufficient oversight, as was the case here, until he would have ultimately tired himself out. I could see that the arm, which had been run over, and the leg as well, had turned a dark blue, but had no idea this was something bad. It was, in fact, a sign of gangrene, the name of this condition, something I had never previously heard of. No one made any effort to cure me of my ignorance, and I could hope as much as I pleased.

/For whom did I have that could have gradually prepared me for all that was to come? Absolutely no one. Small wonder then that I took no particular note of the increasingly blue appearance of the damaged limbs, with no inkling of the hopeless state the patient was in. This afternoon I begged the doctors to please grant me permission to spend the night with my patient, as it was impossible for me to find any peace, much less sleep, in my home and distant from him. But it was all for naught, since the smart doctors mostly show neither heart nor compassion.

With feelings I cannot describe, and deeply distressed, I again had to leave the hospital for the night. On the street, my carriage was stopped by an unfamiliar gentleman, even though the carriage was closed, and I sat deep in the back. The friendly old man inquired so empathetically about my husband, and as he closed the carriage door, I saw the bright tears flowing down his cheeks.

That night, my soul had all the feelings in the world for this hospital system and its leaders, except any good wishes! And since then, I have retained such an aversion to anything having to do with hospitals that it took me years to get over myself and enter one. Although in the evening, our house doctor, Doctor G., still stopped by, apparently to share some news, since I had not called for him, and he never simply came on his own. He was coming directly from my husband. This otherwise so worldly gentleman, who loved to tell jokes, was rather awkward today. He seemed to be avoiding my gaze and did not want to dwell on my questions about my husband. This all instilled in me an ever-increasing disquiet. When I pressed him to please tell me the absolute truth about my husband's condition and his own views of it, he visibly overcame his hesitation to say these few words: "Be strong, Madam, for there is no hope left!" Oh, that was enough for me. The doctor took his leave with sincere sympathy, and I was left alone with my misery.

/I must have sat there for hours without realizing that it was already late at night. When I finally came to my senses, my first impulse was to get down on my knees and plead fervently with the Almighty that if what the doctor had said was true, that there was now no hope left, that he accelerate my husband's demise, so as to free him from his anguish as quickly as possible. This time my wish was granted very soon.

/When I arrived at the hospital the next morning, the change was so great that the end was but a matter of hours. And although he momentarily recognized me, in that he spoke to me with these words: "*Heli gaeni, Bibi?*" (How are you, Bibi?), he soon reverted to an unconscious state. Around midday, his consciousness briefly returned, when he recognized me and asked for some fresh cherries. There were none to be had at this hour in the entire hospital, and by the time some were brought in from a store, it was sadly already much too late, since those had been his last conscious moments in this world. From that time on, I needed some years before I could again eat this fruit, which I had previously enjoyed so much. But in those early years, I gave the first cherries to the poor annually, exactly in the way, as you know, that we treat the favorite dishes of our dead. Oh, what I would have given in that hour for a handful of cherries! With pleasure, I would have offered up a few years of my life, and that certainly would not have been too much for me.

For hours I sat at the bedside and tried to cool the burning forehead of my husband with the eau de cologne I had brought along. Exactly at five thirty in the evening, the Lord delivered my poor husband from his severe suffering.

I would rather stay silent about this hour of my life because I have no words and not enough strength to recount what I suffered. At times, I abruptly lost my mental equilibrium, the only state in which I could have abandoned the almighty Creator. Bitterly, I accused him of allowing this untold misery to occur. I lost everything with my husband, yes everything—even the thought of my three children was not enough to comfort me. I suddenly stood there, forsaken and without a foundation, a wide chasm opening before my seeing eyes, seemingly pulling me in with all its might. Although I had prayed for an imminent release of my husband from his hardship, the hour came far too early for me. All preparations suddenly vanished, and the blow left me fully unprepared. Heaven and earth no longer existed for me then, and my soul was caught in an impenetrable desolation. Oh, what comfort I would have found at that moment in death! For what is a real death in relation to the boundless pain and suffering within ourselves! Nothing, absolutely nothing!

In the hospital, no one was interested in my desire to stay by the corpse until the burial. This struck me as beyond heartless. More dazed than awake, I drove back home where I experienced the bitter loss even more. Here at the stairs, I saw his sticks, his overcoat, his hats still hanging in the wardrobe, no one as yet having thought to remove them. I apparently also went through the whole house in a delirium, searching high and low, calling loudly for my husband. That he was dead, torn from me, never to be seen again, seemed more than I could comprehend or believe in my bottomless anguish. I was plagued by doubts that he was in fact gone. A secret voice kept saying to me: "Go on back to the hospital and get your husband; he is still alive!" "No, it cannot be true that he would have left you forever in this foreign land, hurry on over, hurry!" Oh, what insanity, what agony! I believed with complete certainty that all the doctors in the hospital had made a mistake and that my husband only appeared to be dead. And what now, if he were to come to his senses again and no one would be there with him? Would he not be aggrieved by my lack of loyalty, to have abandoned him precisely in such a moment? Oh, I could not bear it!

/I spent that night obsessively wandering the balcony and returned to the room only when I could no longer control myself, to hide my loud sobbing. Up in the firmament of the Eternal One, I furtively sought a sign, a miracle, to give my poor, struggling soul some small comfort. The nighttime calm and quiet, and the rustling leaves in the garden, even the stars shining in the sky, proved quite troubling to me that night. Nothing had changed outdoors, all of nature continued on as before; the only change was within me. I hoped for a calamity that would snatch me and my children away, to put an end to us as well. Just the thought of having to live alone with my small children in a foreign land, and without my husband, threatened to simply rob me of my sanity! Oh, and what that really meant! In all of Germany, yes, in all of Europe, I had not a single soul I could have leaned on for support, on top of my deficient German. The loss I had only recently suffered, of homeland, extended family, and possessions, and the youthful resilience with which I had borne it, only now revealed its true impact and reach. For at no point had my homesickness burned as severely as now. I could feel how, in an instant, I went to having no homeland and no relatives. Inconsolable thoughts took over my spirit, plaguing me day and night.

The burial was set for the third day after death, and so, on the appointed day, the corpse was brought early to our residence, already nailed shut in the coffin, so the usual ceremony could take place from here. It pained me deeply that they had unilaterally chosen to close the coffin in the hospital, so that I could no longer see the corpse. I wanted to come along to the burial, but was told that was not customary in Hamburg. What did I care at that moment about the customs and courtesies of Hamburg! Not in the least. My pain was too intense for me to give any deference to hollow and contrived formalities. Nothing around me mattered; I was indifferent to the whole world. No one moved to order a carriage for me, and by now, little time was left to make new arrangements. I therefore decided to follow alongside the hearse on foot. But when the amiable Pastor T. heard about my desire, he kindly offered me a seat in his carriage, which I accepted with sincere thanks. And thus we commenced our sad trip, accompanied by some acquaintances.

/Although it was early August, the weather was rainy and dreary. There was not a ray of sunshine to be seen, and nature was all cloaked in grey. On this day, perhaps for the first time in my life, I did not mind forgoing the glorious, all-animating sun. Today the gloom of nature fit my mood better than a cheerful day. Allow me to skip the details of the next hour, for which words fail me. When the usual ceremonies were over, and I saw how people got ready to lower my all into the grave, I was gripped by one single wish, to belong to the caste that condemns wives to step onto the funeral pyre and thereby also follow the husband directly into death. What is the act of being burnt alive and the short suffering as compared to the constant and indescribable pain of a poor mortal soul. "These thoughts are heathen," you will surely be thinking. And so they certainly are, for they fit neither Islam, nor Christianity. Are the many torments we must undergo on this earth not much worse than a short death by fire?

I am told I gripped the coffin so vehemently that people could barely wrest me from it. Did it not contain everything I possessed?! My children? Oh yes, but at this moment, they gave me no solace. To the contrary, I even believed I could bear my misery more easily without them, as I felt so abandoned and alone. And perhaps this is exactly why I saw no comfort in my children, because without them I would have made my way from the burial grounds straight to the train and from there onward to you. And what else might have shackled me to this place? Absolutely nothing!

We started our way back home, while I sat in silence wishing the trip would never end. I simply dreaded returning to the quotidian cast of people, the house, the furniture, and such. Upon entering the house, my three children were brought to me. According to local custom, they were for the first time dressed in half-mourning, which I found to be a melancholy sight. Everything, everything in the house seemed to remind me of my loss. The house felt devoid of life, even though only one person was missing. No place gave me peace, and I wandered from one room to another as though driven by ghosts. I resented my fate and eternal providence. I felt spurned by my Creator and was thus totally unmoored. Although prayer would have been the one avenue to bring me some solace, for the first time in my life, alas, I could not do it. My soul was in a kind of revolution and now had to fight its way through. When I finally found the conviction to pray as I had, of course, been taught from youth onward: "Nothing shall ever happen to us but what the Lord has decreed for us, so praise be unto him forever, Amen!"[56], I began to feel somewhat better inside.

But the barrenness within me grew more and more intense.—

---

56 From the Koran, Surah at Tawbah 9:51.

The author's husband in Hamburg.

Also Hamburg, either 1869 or 1870.

12

All other desires in my soul shut down, except the one thought that took over: Leave, leave, go home! The longing for you ruled my whole being, all thoughts and all feelings. Even without awaiting the letter from our unforgettable Ch., I indeed believed entirely correctly that with the news of my loss, your thoughts would be one and the same: I must immediately return to you, naturally as one of yours. Without the mighty oceans of the world between us, and with confirmation that I was free from every moral duty, even if I had had to traverse the distance to you on foot, I would not have hesitated a single second to say yes.

My husband died without leaving a will, without ever having spoken even one word about the future of me and the children, much less about how to raise them. Outwardly, I was, of course, free to go wherever I wanted, since my children were still so young and not yet subject to the usual school or military requirements. I had to undergo a huge struggle within myself—one that lasted years—to come to a decision. My whole existence was attached to you and the homeland that was paradise on earth.

/But between the two now lay the memory of my husband, which I had to honor. With a bleeding heart, I renounced the prospect of a reunion and determined, in the memory of my husband, to raise his children in his country, as he surely would have wished it. I had to acknowledge for myself that if the situation had been the reverse, I certainly would have wanted my children to have an Arab upbringing. And thus, I followed simply and solely the voice of piety, regardless of all the nice concepts here like education and civilization. For still to this day, I am not a great fan of such forcibly imposed schooling, especially if it neglects the true development of the heart. I would have made the same choice whether my husband had been Chinese or Japanese, instead of German. In so saying, I simply wanted to prove to you that what I did back then was done only out of love for the deceased and no other motive. I was too much one of you to let myself be guided by any motives other than those described above.

Back then I had decided to raise my children in their father's homeland without thinking in the least about myself. If I had been more astute in my thinking, I might have concluded otherwise, since the children naturally took on the customs and habits of the land in which they grew up, while

I naturally remained an Arab through and through. On the outside, I may appear totally "à la franca," but inside, I did not change and was also not that easy to reform. Not without some apprehension, I had to admit to myself that the path I was choosing carried rather too much risk. But it is enough for me that I acted in good faith to fulfill what I believed to be my moral duty to the deceased. Now you can also understand why giving up the thought of returning to you became so unspeakably difficult for me, since that was so very much what my heart longed for.

Had I been able to foresee the dismal years that still lay ahead of me here, I doubt I would have had the necessary courage to carry out my intentions. The loneliness inside, and the boundless emptiness in the house grated unceasingly on my soul. I often just felt absent and had to exert great effort to pay attention to what was being said to me. My husband's smoking room, where I had a view of the garden and the Alster, became my constant abode. Already three weeks had passed since my hard fate had befallen me. As usual, I sat there, disconsolate in my thoughts, staring blankly ahead of me, when suddenly I jumped up and hurried to the front door to open it, as I had previously done so frequently when my husband came home. Completely crestfallen, I went back, once I realized my mistake. My young son, who was hardly one and a half years old, called for his father all day long, which always threatened to break my heart. My eldest daughter, all of two and a half years old, noticed this so much that she whispered to her little brother, do not call Papa or else Mama will cry. And then she would regularly traipse over to me with her tiny handkerchief and wipe away my tears.

In the meantime, it was October. On that day, as best I can recall, it was very damp, cold, and dreary. Around five in the afternoon, lunch was announced, and I remember going to the table. Shortly thereafter, however, I apparently got up abruptly, without having touched the food, left the house just as I was, neither coat nor hat, and headed rapidly down the street. Not until the Walhalla steamboat station did people catch up with me and bring me back home again. During this time, I suffered from severe headaches that plagued me day and night. I had this constant feeling of ants crawling under the skin of my head. The doctor thought it was the nerves on my head that caused these complaints.

In this ailing state, I received the completely devastating news that my noble brother M.[57] had died, a last blow suited to crush my soul. You know, of course, what I lost in him. I deeply mourned the loss of this kindhearted brother, who had been especially forbearing and loving toward me, who was uniquely qualified, like no other, to replace our noble and justice-seeking father. It also reflects tellingly on M.'s magnanimity that when B.[58] took the reign after him, the latter is said to have on some occasion called out to the notables in the land: "My father was your father, and M. was your brother, but I am your ruler and master!" You will recall how much bad blood these words evoked among the people.

Because of the poor postal connections between Zanzibar and Germany at the time, I had no inkling of M.'s sickness, and so the news of his passing caught me totally unprepared. This sad dispatch only served to heighten my longing for my beloved homeland. I now felt doubly disconnected, as I had not a single soul here with whom I could have discoursed at length about you all and our circumstances. Oh, you have no idea how much this sentiment oppressed me and left me feeling like a complete stranger. If the children had been even just a bit older, perhaps I would not have had to feel quite so mentally forlorn. That very headstrong Salme of but a few years ago would have been unrecognizable if you had seen her now in an unguarded hour. It is indeed remarkable how quickly humans can change under certain conditions.

/Because of the circumstances in these first months of my mourning, I became so very indifferent toward even my beloved children that neither their presence nor absence had any effect on me. The inner upheaval was so overpowering that I needed considerable time to restore my lost equilibrium, even only minimally. The worst was that I did not have sufficient confidence in my ability to achieve the path I had chosen to honor my husband. My whole being, as well as the future, seemed shrouded in an impenetrable fog. Indeed, I initially had no idea how I was supposed to find my way forward. Only my old trust in the Almighty held me upright and kept my courage, at that moment, from sinking all too much.

As we say here, misfortune rarely comes alone. This also seemed to apply in my case. Even as I was still oppressed by my mental stupor, I was confronted with the bleak news that the export business between Hamburg and Zanzibar

---

57 Referring to the author's half-brother Madjid, who became Sultan of Zanzibar in 1856, when the father died.
58 Referring to the author's half-brother Barghash, who was Sultan of Zanzibar from 1870 to his death in 1888.

was in dire straits as a consequence of the German-French war, and we could expect great losses. On top of that, my husband's agent in Zanzibar, a friend from his youth and the son of a senior pastor in Hamburg, had shown a very deficient understanding of "mine and thine," and so I had to anticipate the worst. This disloyal agent tried to enrich himself as quickly as possible at the expense of the widow and fatherless children of his deceased friend, against which the Hamburg-based liquidator of my husband's business was unable to exercise any effective control.

/Given this situation, the view was that I needed to be prepared to significantly limit my expenditures from now on, and that I would be unable to continue our previous lifestyle. This news had anything but an uplifting effect on me. Even though my soul needed no wealth, luxury, and all the rest, and was instead more than content with an average lifestyle, and could never thank the Giver of all earthly things enough for our daily bread, I could not possibly remain indifferent to these bad tidings. As such, I could not help but be reminded of our Arab saying that privation, hardship, or need is nowhere and under no circumstances felt as oppressively as in a foreign land! Yes, in a land that truly felt so very foreign to me. Oh my God, I could have been knocked to the moon or some other celestial body and my loneliness and helplessness would have been the same.

/We need a certain amount to survive everywhere in the world, but the exact quantity always depends on the location. You may have heard how expensive life is in Europe, compared to our blessed homeland. Amounts that are in excess there would cover only the most necessary items here, and perhaps not even suffice for that. You cannot imagine what kinds of sums are consumed by a decent European household. You cannot even dream how much the countless needs grow from year to year.

I was filled with anxious foreboding, for what should I do now, and where should I even begin? The first thing that needed to happen, of course, was to terminate the villa, where we had been living, and move into a cheaper residence. I also let go of the chambermaid, to whom I had gotten very accustomed, thereafter retaining only one servant girl across-the-board and one nanny. Until then, we had sent out all our loads of laundry, but now I hired a wash lady to come once a week to wash the clothes in our home, which somewhat reduced our weekly expenditures. And I decided henceforth, once and for all, not to make any purchases that I could not immediately pay in cash. Back then in Hamburg, it was customary to let all purchases accrue on credit until the new year—excluding the grocer, baker, butcher, milkman, etc. that are paid weekly. Given

The author's half-brother, Sultan Madjid.

The author's half-brother, Sultan Barghash.

my math incompetence at the time, I could hardly have kept proper track of our debits and credits any other way.

/Worst of all for me was the fact that I had absolutely no idea how much money we had and what I could afford to spend. This rather disconcerting situation unfortunately lasted more than three full years. Against this backdrop, feeling totally powerless and fully dependent on the grace and mercy of strangers, I suffered terribly. Do not ever let yourself be persuaded by the fairy tale that widows and orphans generally fare better in Europe than with you. Perhaps excluding the orphanages, which have become necessary for the enormous populations in European cities. For them, however, the people here pay immense taxes, which are unknown to you.

Never a fan of Northern winters, and always happy when summer returned, I found this winter even more unbearable than usual. The foggy, dreary weather of November and December weighed so heavily on me that I have no words to describe it. Spiritual emptiness and loneliness, plus the early darkness of the winter days, conspired to oppress me. No rays of hope anywhere, neither outside, nor within my soul. In addition, I was overcome by an inexplicable, but excruciating, sense of fear that plagued me day and night. I was often stalked by the notion that the lives of me and my children were no longer entirely safe in this alien environment after the death of my husband. I therefore rather frequently gathered my unsuspecting small children and locked myself up with them in my room for several hours.

/All these feelings and beliefs I had to keep to myself, so as not to be misunderstood or even wrongly judged. Truly, did I have anyone who could fully understand me and grasp my situation? No one, absolutely no one. To avoid revealing my weakness to the cold, indifferent world, or even making myself a laughing stock, I made sure not to show any of this to the outside. Certainly, it would have been hard for anyone without similar experiences to comprehend my state. Fortunately, there are, I believe, not many who have gotten to know the full spectrum of misery as much as I have.

/Certainly, now and again there were people who meant well with me and tried to comfort me in their way. I say, in their way, because after I once called out in utter despair: "Oh, if I knew not that this was my God's will, I could never find peace!", the response was to try to reeducate me. I was asked if I really believed that God in fact takes care of our fates and everything we encounter on this earth. I need not describe to you how innerly appalled I was at this profane question. It seems to me that but a very few, select Christians are familiar with the complete Holy Scripture, which clearly enough tells us that the Lord knows the number of our hairs and that no sparrow falls off the roof without His will.[59] On such occasions, I could not thank the Lord enough for letting me enter this world as a Muslim.

/It was always hard not to compare how little Muslims are taught about their own religion and yet exhibit such solid faith—in contrast to Christian children, who are so painstakingly instructed in school. I had the impression that religion is taught here more as mere science, to be forgotten again at the first opportunity or even oft-criticized, as I regrettably had to observe several times. How else would there be so many tragic suicides if people believed in God and his purposes! In the face of whatever misfortune, be it a death in the family, business losses, often completely unintentional slights, and many other trivial matters, people here turn straight to suicide. Yes, even half-grown youngsters, when they are expecting a well-deserved punishment at home, prefer to take their lives than face parental punishments. Would they do all this if they had even some minimal religion in their soul? Surely never!

---

59 Here the author is paraphrasing from the Bible, Matthew 10:29–30.

/13

Your warship, the *Ilmedjidi*, came to Hamburg in the most severe cold of that same winter, purportedly to be repaired. The Hamburg company to which this ship was sent was an avowed enemy of my husband, for the simplest of reasons, namely: He did business in Zanzibar as well. I had many opportunities to experience this inexcusable fault, as the widow of this deceased competitor. Of course, you know that this company flew the German, which is to say at that time the Hamburg, consular flag, which also carried the moral duty to intervene on behalf of the estates of all decedents under their protection. In my case, they completely failed their obligation. Even after I personally went to their Hamburg bureau to request support in dealing with the liquidation of my husband's business in Zanzibar, nothing happened.

/With this example, you can see how much you all were mistaken if you thought that I, having married a German and a Christian, would never lack for aid or assistance. Oh, what a fallacy! Believe me, that was nothing more than pure illusion on your parts. That an Arab would marry a German, and a Muslim would become Christian, is so inconsequential that no one pays any attention to it. You are too far away from the European arena to be able to assess the true conditions. What governs here is always the same: Every man for himself! And if you happen not to be a man, then the mere nationality of your husband will do little to help you. As far as our country and its customs more generally, the English nationality is preferable by far. Because of their experience with the Indian colonies, the English are better able to deal with Orientals, especially with Arabs.

While the *Ilmedjidi* lay in the harbor, our unforgettable M. had long since left the land of the living, and his successor had exclusive rights over the ship. As always in this world, here, too, the weak ones lose out. Back then, my own fate was keeping me busy, and I gave little thought to the ship. One day, as I headed into town along one of the main streets for an errand, I saw, from afar, at least a hundred people gathered ahead of me. Not suspecting anything, I tried to make my way through the crowd until I suddenly stood stock still in front of a group of people. What did I see? Across from me, completely unexpected, was a group of our sailors, of whom I believed to even recognize a few. My feelings cannot be described. At first, I wanted to walk over to the sailors and talk to them, but then my thoughts turned to the dear public that surrounded us and surely would have recognized me on this occasion and then treated me with the usual curiosity. And what fodder that would have been for the local section of the newspapers, naturally embellished with plenty of fantasy. Taking into account all of these factors, I decided, with much emotional tumult, to step into a coach and let myself be driven back to my home.

/If I had had any inkling of this encounter, I would have opted to stay home. My extreme longing for you all was stoked anew by this experience, and the thought that had never fully left me—leave, leave, go home!—was revived. It was only your slaves that I saw this day, and yet, the sight of them once again awakened a world of memories.

/In my current attire, there was no chance the sailors would ever recognize me, so I was safe that way. I speculated that the men would very probably ask about me and try to find me. And so it was. About two weeks after my street encounter, I was alone in my room, consumed by melancholy thoughts of the past and fearful thoughts of our future. The servant girl came in and told me that about twenty African men wanted to see me. It was not hard to guess who my guests were, and I therefore let them come in. You should have seen the scene that now followed. We had barely exchanged our Arabic greetings when the men all threw themselves at my feet, reverently kissed the floor, and broke out in hefty tears. I would be lying if I were to insist that my eyes stayed dry at this moment. How could that have been possible! Taking this all in, my traditional sense of social hierarchy disappeared, and I saw in this group only one thing, that they came from Zanzibar—and from all of you. I will tell you quite openly that a visit from a hundred strangers with crowns on their heads would not have moved me as much as the presence of these plain people. As if in unison, these men called out in Arabic: "Thanks be to the Lord our God that we found you! *O Bibi tua*! (Our Mistress!) How long we have searched for you!"

The Zanzibari warship Ilmedjidi, *here as the former Confederate raider CSS* Shenandoah

/Those were the first words of these good and simple men. Our touching reunion must have been very moving, since I found both of my German servant girls, who of course understood not a single word of what we were speaking, sobbing loudly at the door. Not all the men were African, as the servant girl had announced, but about half were Arab. Under no circumstances did they want to sit on chairs, and so they seated themselves cross-legged on my rug, just as we are used to doing at home, gathering all around me. When I asked how they had managed to find me, they told me the following:

/As soon as we arrived in Hamburg, we asked every European in English—the sailors did not understand German—that came to us on the ship to tell us where you live, but no one was willing or able to answer. Most of the fine gentlemen who came to see the *Ilmedjidi* simply shrugged their shoulders at our questions and said they did not know your whereabouts. But finally yesterday, when two of us wanted to buy some smoking tobacco, they went into a store and also tried to use this opportunity to find out your address. The tobacco salesman then said to them that he had lately seen frequent stories about me in the paper and wanted to look for my address in a big book (presumably the address book). Then he wrote something on a piece of paper, which we naturally could not read. With this paper in your hand, he told us, you will indeed find your Mistress, and so it was. These two comrades shared their experience and successful venture with us. Practically all of us wanted to come find you immediately, but not everyone could get permission. Now we want to take turns to visit you, so we can all see you.—With this slip of paper in hand, asking on the street all along the way, people finally led us to your door, for which we cannot thank the Lord enough.

Although the poor sailors were dressed in thick European outfits, the harsh winter made them so freezing cold that they were truly to be pitied. In the course of the conversation, after many greetings from home had been extended, and I, as you can surely imagine, had no shortage of questions, several of them suddenly called out: *"Bibi, unawesage kukandan ja inchi kana hiji?"* (Bibi, how can you live in such a land?) *"Tafasali rudi kuwetu, watu wote wanakutamani ssana!"* (Please come back to us, all the people are yearning for you!) These words almost broke my heart, and I could only shake my head and wistfully respond, *"ssissassa, ssissassa!"* (not now, not now!). *"Lakini lini tena, Bibi?"* (But when, Bibi?) *"Wakiwa Watoto wakuba kidodo."* (When the children are somewhat older.)

/That I would have gladly followed their advice, I need not reaffirm for you. But the duty to the deceased to raise his children as he would have wanted and in his fatherland, to the extent possible, exerted all its power on me to keep me here.

Your reproach that I did not love you enough to leave Germany and hurry straight to you after the death of my husband, was all too cruel. Have I not, in my difficult position, unceasingly asked the dear God for help and support, since I always remained discontented inside, indeed utterly miserable. I must reiterate for you that what I did back then occurred only because I wanted to show my last love to the deceased; as to all else, I knew myself to be free of any other considerations.

From this point on until their departure, the sailors, coming mostly in smaller groups, were my daily guests. Some of them played with the children and often took them on walks. Naturally, they favored S.[60] because I had named him after my noble father. They loved to pull the extra-large stroller, built expressly to fit all three children, through the garden. On such occasions, a large group of people would usually gather in front of our yard, enough to constitute a crowd. I had them served coffee in the usual European cups, since I no longer had enough of the little Arab ones, and they apparently found it very strange to find that missing in my house. They called the Occidental coffee cups simply "*bakuli kuba*" (big *Kummen*[61] or even bowls). The first time I had them served something to eat, they long hesitated to enjoy what had been offered, and I had to repeatedly urge them to dig in or the food would very soon get cold. To which one of the Arabs asked a question that surely was not easy for him to ask: "Bibi, the servant girl has not put pork in the food, that is true, is it not?" Only after I had clearly assured them that they could, in my house, at all times, rest easy on this point, did they decide to partake.

/Often enough I had to act as their paymaster as well because I, as they said, was not only their Bibi, but also their father, mother, and sole relative in Hamburg. Some of them implored me almost daily to let them stay and take care of the children until we could travel back together. That I would have loved only too much to keep them here, you can surely imagine. But to want and to be able are obviously two very different things, and only the most privileged mortals can master both at once. Coming exactly at this moment, when circumstances were forcing me to let one servant girl go and generally scale back my lifestyle, this request felt like an irony of fate, these people suggesting unawares that I should keep several of them with me as servants. To educate them on this point would have been futile, since they would have had no sense for, much less any understanding of, the high cost of living in Europe, especially Hamburg, in comparison to our plentiful island.

---

60 S. refers to the author's son and middle child, who was born Rudolph Said Ruete and initially went by "Said." He later changed his name to Rudolph Said-Ruete (a hyphenated combination of his middle and last names) when, in 1906, the city of Hamburg finally granted his request to preserve his Sultan grandfather's name as part of his last name (perhaps corresponding to the customary Arabic "bin Said").
61 A regional German word used by the author for cups.

/As the time drew near for the *Ilmedjidi* to return home, and the ones who absolutely wanted to stay with me shared their serious intent to desert their posts, I considered it my duty to notify the ship commander with enough time for him to keep the sailors on board. As you know, the *Ilmedjidi*, together with its entire crew, totally foundered a few years later. These poor people!

The author's father, Sayyid Said bin Sultan.

/14

The following spring my children and I moved into a different, cheap and simple, residence. Because the new home was much smaller than the villa we had been living in, it was with a heavy heart that I had to sell some of the furniture. Leaving our old home hit me very hard, oh so hard, in a way I cannot even explain. Not only was I bound to this house by countless memories that exacerbated my departure, in whose walls I had experienced both fortune and tragic misfortune, but I also had to fight another feeling. With this move, I also felt, for the first time in my life, the stinging sense of an initial descent into poverty. This change had, however, become so necessary that I could no longer, in good conscience, postpone the inevitable. Without any idea of what it takes to be a competent *Hausfrau* here, I did my best within my ability to live as economically as possible. Numb to everything else, I lived exclusively for the rapidly, oh so rapidly vanished past and for the care of my children.

With my spirit in upheaval, and feeling helpless and defenseless, it made me so happy back then when I now and again received news from you. M.[62] wrote me a heartfelt letter with the urgent plea that I should take the trip home with my children at the first opportunity. All would be good again, once I resolved to return, etc., etc. This awareness, that you had my back, gave me huge joy, and I would very often say to myself that if, over time, my self-imposed goal indeed proved too difficult a task for my strength, I would in any case return back home. But until then, I would spare nothing to try to finish what I had begun.

/This refusal, as you well know, brought upon me the unrelenting anger of B., and he never chose to forgive me until his dying day. All subsequent efforts to have him pay out even just a small portion of my inheritance were categorically rejected.[63] This much became clear to me over time, that had I been an English subject, I would have come out much better. B. was completely in English hands and had to do whatever the English required. And so, inherently, he had greater sympathy for England than any other country. Later, it was, in fact, his greatest wish to put Zanzibar under English protection, except that support from the relevant English circles was lacking at the time, so nothing changed. My English friends had advised me urgently to change my residence from

---

62 Of unknown identity, although possibly the author's half-sister Meje (*Memoirs*, p. 199) or, as Professor van Donzel speculates, the author's half-sister Mettle. E. van Donzel, p. 465.

63 The usual approach was for all living siblings to receive portions of a deceased sibling's estate. The author maintained that she had a right to this inheritance, despite her status as an infidel after her conversion to Christianity and marriage to a Christian in 1867.

Germany to England in 1875,[64] which, for all the reasons you know, reasons that of course also kept me from you, I could not do.

/Did I make the right choice in this regard? I must admit openly to you that I have asked myself this question so many times. Overall, I believe I handled the situation far too idealistically. Every year more than a hundred thousand people leave Germany, some to become American subjects, some English. And these are even full-blooded Germans, meaning pure Germans, more German than my children. From a purely materialistic point of view, I did not approach things carefully enough back then, and instead gave exaggerated importance to ideals that I pursued with such effort and the greatest sacrifice.

It is its own special exercise to have to shift from living in a place where everything shortly before appeared practically in excess to suddenly being subjected to the greatest limitations. Not that I would have been enamored of all the trifles and glitter that are just for show—no, that fortunately was not my style. But the need to anxiously guard this vile Mammon, to make sure we had enough of it, was for me so oppressive and at the same time so humiliating that I can hardly describe it to you. The deck was especially stacked against me because Hamburg, of all places, turns almost exclusively on the role of money, and it was here of all places that my lucky boat ran aground. All too frequently, I was cuttingly reminded of my dismal situation.

/That I would, in keeping with my intentions, prefer to allow my children to grow up in their father's hometown is, of course, natural, even though the climate of this foggy town was hardly to my liking. But the present circumstances dictated that I begin a completely new life, to meet the new conditions, if I wanted to find enough room under a blanket that had shrunk too short. It was clear that I could not easily follow through on this in Hamburg. From our youngest days, we are accustomed to showing true humility before the Highest, indeed, we are effectively raised in it. And even so, there is nothing my people are more sensitive about than being humiliated.

/Yet, the totally different life I was going to have to live was one I had never even dreamt of. In the past, whenever I had undertaken something here or there in the household simply to pass the time, or engaged with the children too much, I was sure to hear reproaches from my dear husband, who never liked to see me working. He was always saying: "Bibi, you are not supposed

---

64 This was the year the author went to London to try to see Sultan Barghash during his State visit (*Memoirs*, pp. 205–10). Professor van Donzel also gives this as the year the author began writing her *Memoirs*, which were then published in 1886. E. van Donzel, p. 1.

to work!" Or also: "Do not always carry the children on your arm, take a seat instead, we have enough people to take care of the children!" And the like. Oh, what would he have said, if he had seen me a couple of years later in the ice-cold winter without any help at all, doing everything, yes, everything by myself, often spending half an hour beside the cold oven, bitter tears streaming down my face, before I was finally able to get the fire burning! And meanwhile, two of my children lay ill with serious cases of scarlet fever. If my husband had gone bankrupt in his lifetime, and we had lost everything that way, I would most certainly have been at his side to perform the most difficult and, if needed, also most demeaning work for him and the children.

/The thought of continuing to live in this, for me, so incredibly complicated European setting, and the memory of my irreplaceable loss, often robbed me of my courage to go on. Above all, I was pursued by a constant feeling of abandonment that threatened to break my heart throughout every day. Under these circumstances, everything became so very difficult for me, and over time, I started to lose my resolve. "Strength, oh Lord, strength and steadfast perseverance!" remained my constant prayer for years.

/Alone the fact that I, nonetheless, managed to keep all five of my senses shows the great mercy of the Lord. I can tell you openly that I was close to losing my mind. The doctor wanted me to go out frequently, to get more movement. My headaches became increasingly severe, and the feeling that thousands of ants were crawling under the skin of my head made me very nervous. No medication proved helpful. And taking aimless walks, always completely alone because my children were still much too young to join me, was truly dreadful. I therefore decided, in order to follow the doctor's orders, to take lessons from a writing teacher far off in the city, so I would have a practical destination for my outings. Twice a week, rain or shine, I would go there and back by foot, from Blücherstrasse up to near the Thalia Theatre,[65] where the teacher lived.

In the meantime, I was seriously considering leaving Hamburg in the not-too-distant future and seeking another cheaper residence, as it became increasingly clear that staying in Hamburg was out of the question in the long run. Or should I first wait for my children to go to school, where they would be confronted with all the other children that were raised in luxury in this city and then feel disadvantaged by fate? No, I hoped to spare them and myself precisely that. But where should I point my feet to find what I was looking for? That constituted a serious problem for me.

---

65 About an hour's walk each way. According to meticulous research by Fridjof Gutendorf, she was headed to J.G. Herbst's lessons in "Schön- und Schnellschreiben" at Raboisen 74.

/My deliberations were met with very little understanding within the narrow circles I frequented, which left me feeling quite uncomfortable. Once again, I had to deal with strangers who somehow imagine they can better ascertain other people's circumstances, yes, even their feelings and perceptions, than the people themselves. I was cited hundreds of examples of other women and widows who were able to live their lives in Hamburg with even more limited means than mine, and more of the same. But such lecturers apparently did not get that these women and widows were Hamburg born and bred, for whom it would be natural to stay in their homeland, whereby I, in contrast, as a non-German, with nothing to anchor me to Hamburg, could just as well choose to take up residence anywhere. It also seemed to me, over and over again, that most people, despite having written the word "freedom" on their flags, are hardly inclined to give others the same degree of freedom. It is, above all, rather rare to find that people are treated on an individual basis, rather than generically, across-the-board, as is so often the case.

Finally, I found an unbiased lady, who came from Middle Germany and advised me to travel to Darmstadt, to have a look at that town. If I liked it, I could readily move there, since the climate would be somewhat warmer and the cost of living somewhat cheaper than here in Hamburg. My decision to travel there without another living soul and spend time there with complete strangers did not come easily. And yet, I had no choice but to strike out on my own, no matter the personal cost to me. Or was I to simply sit passively by and watch our pecuniary circumstances continue to go downhill, thus exposing myself to countless disagreeable experiences that could hardly be avoided and would be far harder to bear than might first appear? No, that would have been completely contrary to my nature. And so, I pulled myself together and set a date for my trip to Darmstadt.

/The train I planned to take left at six in the morning, so I ordered a coach to take me there at five, in view of the distance to the station. By the time the clock showed quarter after five, however, and the coach was still nowhere to be seen, the servant girl and I hoisted the leather suitcase and travel bag and headed to the home of the driver in question, who lived not all too far from us. Upon arrival, I was very surprised to find everything deathly quiet and the driver still needing to be awakened from his deep sleep. After much loud calling, he finally came to the window, only half awake and in his shirt sleeves. At which point, as later recounted by my servant girl, I apparently called to the driver, "Mr. Hinrichs, should I help you dress the horse?" Oh, what did I know about terms like harnessing and hitching, as they refer to it here.

/The courtyard where the coach stood, was set back quite some distance, a good stretch from the road. While the driver began to put on the driving harness with the help of the servant girl, I started pulling the coach toward the street all by myself, in an effort to expedite our already extremely late trip to the train. It really was high time for us to get going, and then we rode wildly toward the station. Once arrived, the guileless Hinrich called after me multiple times: "Hurry, Madam, if you still want to catch the train!" As if pursued, I dashed to the box office, got my ticket, and then half-ran all the way to the car. Barely had I set my foot in the door than the train was in motion.

/As I sat, still completely drained from this unaccustomed mad dash, my environment mercilessly confronted me with the reality of my life. The bare walls, the unupholstered seats, stared me in the face with such pity, such questions, that I broke down and erupted in hot tears. For a long time already, I had felt my strength ebbing, yet had no choice under the given circumstances but to undertake the trip, despite the terrible headaches, which had been plaguing me for more than a year. For the first time in my life, I found myself in a third-class carriage. Fortunately, I sat alone and unobserved in the railcar and could give my emotions free rein.

/This was one of the many bitter pills I was often made to swallow. I of course had to live frugally to make ends meet. Nevertheless, there were people who called themselves "friends" who felt the need to weigh in on every little purchase I made. For example, when I had to start wearing a pince-nez, as prescribed by the eye doctor to address the stress on my eyes, I undertook something completely unacceptable by procuring one with a golden rim, for which my "friends" resented me. On this occasion, I first learned the meaning of the local saying: "Lord, protect me from my friends, for I can handle my enemies on my own!"

/I took the third-class ticket this time, traveling on my own, to carry the humility alone and then planned to take my children along only once I had withstood this trial. Even though my children were still so young that they had no real grasp of life, much less the different train compartments, I did not want to expose them right away to the ugly third class. Such are the cares of a mother, who had to learn step-by-step that she would have to bow deeply in order not to break.

The trip took quite a while, and it was already late when the train arrived in Darmstadt. I had a driver take me to a simple hotel, where I stayed in my room until the next morning. I then got up early to quickly gather information about housing, grocery prices, and similar aspects, without which I would have had no real basis for comparison. The caretaker of the hotel was my only source of information, since I knew no one in the area. However, this unsophisticated attendant treated me with totally blatant curiosity, no doubt unaccustomed to encountering someone like my lowly self, born near the Equator and a relatively brown complexion. Instead of answering my questions, as much as I cared about getting answers, she took it upon herself to interrogate me, like, for example, what country I came from (here I used a white lie and named a South American region in response), and if I also had a husband and children. When I responded that I was a widow with small children, she started to take pity on me. Following her advice, I took a coach to see some of the housing. But, how unfortunate! Everywhere the same questions: Where are you from, my lady, do you have acquaintances here who can vouch for you, and so on. Not a very encouraging welcome for a stranger, to be sure. These and similar questions were so disheartening for my already alienated and downtrodden soul that I gave up the idea of moving to the area and accordingly embarked on my return to Hamburg the very next morning.

/This type of mistrust against anyone who was not a full-blooded German is something I subsequently came across many times in Germany. And I was often forced to consider how offensive it must be for someone to be confronted with such mistrust right from the start (as my case in Darmstadt had sufficiently demonstrated). Later, a Hungarian woman in Dresden complained about the exact same treatment, and likewise a Russian woman. How so very different it is for you, where every European, if there was no reason to think otherwise, is accorded complete trust, whether this person was an upstanding citizen or a crook in his homeland. It is just too unkind to give non-Germans such dubious treatment when there is no reason to be wary of them.

I arrived back in Hamburg rather disappointed. On the return, I remembered a lady, who had told me much about Dresden, where she lived, when I had made her brief acquaintance. I decided to turn to this woman and inquire further about the conditions there. I wrote the letter myself, although do not ask me how. In any case, the sweet lady managed to decipher my letter, for she answered my various questions in great detail. Thereupon I decided to travel to Dresden myself, potentially to rent a place while there. I had the impression that life in Dresden was significantly less expensive than in Hamburg. I also hoped to live as peacefully and reclusively as possible, so that I might devote myself entirely to the care of my children.

/Dresden immediately made a good impression on me, also helped by the fact that the family of this lady (an officer's family from Hanover) gave me the warmest welcome. Thus the two of us, my new friend and I, went apartment hunting. Up the stairs, down the stairs, fortunately we were both still young, or we might not have had the stamina. Since this friend was a very determined lady and did not readily take an X for a Y, I hardly had to talk to any of the many landlords myself. I was indeed grateful not to have to listen to the insipid questioning again this time: Where do you come from, my lady? and all that. If my German had been any better at the time, I would have gladly told those good people in Darmstadt: I am from the moon, dear folks! The people in the interior of Germany back then had as little sense of Zanzibar as you to this day have of Siberia and the endless snowfields. It would have taken an extended discourse to educate them about the existence of our dear island, and even then, I doubt they would have believed me. I have often been reminded of our very apt saying, roughly translated as "Those who do not know you also cannot assess you."[66]

A little house with a bit of garden, to live separately as I would have preferred, was not to be found at a price I could afford. On the other hand, the thought of living in a big house on one floor together with other people was extremely unpleasant for me, so that I entertained my companion's very practical suggestions only with reluctance. One of the options was for me to rent the attractive ground floor on ____ Street that was too expensive for me, but then rent out a few furnished rooms. At first, I found the idea thoroughly appalling. From now on, I would not only have to live like a bird in a cage on a single floor, but also need to rent out a few rooms to offset the high rent, if I wanted a spacious home in a healthy location. I had come to Dresden at a very inopportune time, since it was after the usual period when apartments change hands, and it was not easy to find something fitting. I ultimately chose the place on ____ Street after all, with the intention of subletting two furnished rooms, and then traveled back to Hamburg to arrange the move.

/The relocation of a well-equipped European household by train is one of the most unpleasant things, one that you would be hard-pressed to imagine, if only because you do not even know the names of the many useful and less-than-useful items. Your home arrangements that have continued unchanged for hundreds of years are no grounds for comparison, in that here every generation has its own very specific fashion and taste. We often see how the parents and grandparents are satisfied with basic furnishings, while their offspring want

---

66 *Asiyejua kitu, hawezi kujua thamani yake*, translated as "A person who does not know an object cannot know its value," according to "Swahili Proverbs: Methali Za Kiswahili," posted by the Center for African Studies at the University of Illinois at Champaign-Urbana.

only the absolute newest and ever more elegant things. Our household was not overdone, but still expansive enough for me to have to consider whether all these things were truly necessary. The packing of the furniture proceeded, and about two weeks later, we, my children, a nanny and I, sat in the train on the way to the capital of Saxony.

During these last days in Hamburg, I frequently visited my dear gravesite, as the only place where my soul could confess all its suffering. Is it just an illusion when the losses we suffer make us feel even more strongly that our loved ones only give the appearance of being dead, and that they instead are as aware of all our earthly woes as we are? Oh, can anyone unravel this puzzle other than the Almighty alone?! Regardless, this idea gave me great comfort in my bereavement.

15

In Germany, France, and most other European countries, custom requires that newcomers make the first visits after their arrival. In addition, anyone who leaves must make farewell visits, just the opposite of what we are used to. In this regard, the English are an exception, in that they visit the new arrivals first, just as we do. They reason that it is kinder to welcome unfamiliar strangers to new locations and help them, if possible. But, if I did not want to come across as too backwards, I had to make the rounds of all the Hamburg ladies who were my friends and acquaintances to take my leave. More limited is the practice of giving gifts to someone who is departing, if only a trifle, as a sign of love; only true Orientals still engage in this custom.

It is only too understandable that I could not leave a city, in which I had spent the bleakest hours of my life, without inner agitation.

Steel engraving of Dresden, mid-1800s.

16

As fate would have it, my landlady in Dresden turned out to be from Hamburg and had, as she said, already heard much about me. I was therefore spared the question: "Where do you come from?" On the second day of our move, when everything on our floor still lay in complete disarray, and I had on a large working apron while helping the movers with the unpacking and arranging—as the servant girl had the difficult task of keeping my three young and very lively children away from the chaos in the apartment—I received an invitation from my landlady to a coffee. I was invited at three o' clock and was supposed to go down at four, as my landlady lived on the ground floor, while I was one floor up. I would have much preferred to decline the invitation, since I was more than occupied, but went anyhow, so as not to insult anyone. Who can describe my surprise when I arrived and did not see the lady of the house anywhere, even after the coffee was carried in, but rather found myself alone with the man of the house.

/Although providence in no way determined to make me a shy person—a trait that would not have let me overcome all the steep and anything but rose-bestrewn paths of my life—I nonetheless felt quite ill at ease sitting together with a completely unknown gentleman. But the riddle was soon solved, for I had taken but a few sips of the rather weak coffee when my counterpart began to clear his throat and said approximately the following to me: "Madam, tomorrow I am traveling to the trade fair in Leipzig, ahem, ahem—and I am in need of funds, so may I not receive the rent from you immediately?"—"Yes, certainly, Mr. X, with the whole move, I overlooked the need to get the rent to you in advance, please accept my apology." A quarter hour later, I sent the money down with my servant girl, who soon returned with the receipt. Just as I had thought, it was in fact, for I later found out that the wife had kept her distance, so as not to be witness to her husband—nota bene, the happy owner of more than a million—when he admonished me about the rent. Had this rich landlord considered that the rent I just paid constituted nearly all of my cash? Hardly! But so it was, and that only increased my motivation to get the apartment in place as quickly as possible, so I could rent out the two furnished rooms. Soon I succeeded in finding a couple, which had lived in Brazil many years and had a black servant, that wanted the rental for two months.

/Who was happier on this day than I! For let me tell you that worries about one's daily bread bear down on everything and crush the courage to live. What that means—N.B. for a miserable Arab woman, such as myself—to care for children and household, often without knowing where the small sums needed for the next day should come from, can be understood only by someone who has been in the same situation as I have. And all that because widows and orphans here are especially cared for.

/After the death of my husband, I was designated the sole heir, namely for so long as I stayed a widow and did not remarry. This was determined according to Hamburg law, under which my assets were not divided between me and my children. The court named me the guardian of my children—without my fully suspecting or understanding what that in fact involved—along with the additional caveat that I was strictly obligated to designate two men as my "assistants." Until then, the word assistant was completely unknown to me, much less any inkling of what this position and its related duties entailed. So I had to ask what was meant by this term and how I was expected to behave towards them. Whether I understood or not did not trouble the court. The fact that I had been born in faraway Africa, and not on the shores of the Elbe, or that I had little sense of European ways, appeared to be outside the concern of the law.

/I asked two gentlemen from my circle to take on this position of assistant, which they did. They proceeded to invest my money in Russian and American bonds, Hungarian railway stocks, and mortgages. The concept of bonds and railway stocks was completely alien to me back then, and it took a long time before I could understand and appreciate their nature. Shortly before my move to Dresden, both gentlemen resigned from their positions, which left me having to find two others. One was our reliable, older house doctor, whom I had come to appreciate highly; the other was a very well-known lawyer. The house doctor accepted the position only nominally because, as he explained, he did not much understand these things and also had a very demanding practice. That left me to deal solely with the lawyer when it came to financial matters.

/It turned out this lawyer was entirely capricious and unaccountable in his treatment of my affairs, often causing me to suffer to the point of destitution. Even after three years of being a widow, I still had no idea how much yearly interest was at my disposal! It took great effort and multiple admonitions before I got my regular allowance, and then he would again leave me without a penny, no matter how much I pleaded. As a result, my daily life became so indescribably difficult. I was left completely in the dark and all my queries remained unanswered, such that I had no idea how much annual budget I had available.

/Under all this extreme duress, I survived many a day with barely a thaler in my possession. Of course, I could have borrowed some money to manage my immediate needs and feed my children something other than exclusively soup meat, while contenting myself with a dry slice of dark bread and a glass of milk to still my evening hunger. I always hated borrowing, and so I could not, even in the direst of circumstances, allow this evil enemy to enter my life.

/Dismal, such dismal times were upon me, and I had to rally all my remaining strength to avoid succumbing to the bitter hours of my life. Even the children's little piggybank had to give up its contents of crown thalers, so we could procure the absolute essentials. And when once again all the pleading and admonishing to this Mr. Assistant that he send some funds remained unanswered, and the few thalers in the piggybank had been used up, there I stood one day without any cash available at all. Picture my situation when the servant girl came to me as usual to get the money for the market, which was cheaper than the store— and I simply had no penny. In my thoughts, I had long seen this day coming and also considered the necessary recourse. But the prospect of this very step weighed on me more and more, from one day to the next, until finally I could no longer evade it. I was, in fact, thinking of selling my jewelry, so I could confront the penury staring me in the face. And yet, I held onto these things tightly, out of piety for the days gone by, while dreading the inevitable trip to the jeweler.

/I told the servant girl that I had no small bills or coins in the house, but would bring some with me upon returning from the city. All I said was true, except I withheld that I not only had no small bills—but actually none. Then I opened my cabinet and took out a pair of earrings that you know from before, which I had had adjusted at the start of my stay in Hamburg. I quickly deposited the earrings in my purse when I heard the steps of my children coming to the door, inseparable from me as always, since I simply shied away from their innocent questions. Despite their youth, they were extraordinarily alert and sharply observant. Indeed, how could I have answered their query: "Mother dear, what are you going to do with those earrings?" I had no courage to tell them the bitter truth, but they were also not used to hearing me spout some other kind of story.

/And thus I went with a troubled heart to a jeweler in the old part of the city. It seemed like I had stolen the earrings from someone, rather than being their rightful owner, and I felt so insecure along the way, as though I had committed a crime. I stood in front of the jeweler's expensive shop window for a long time before being able to take heart and go in. Finally, I stepped inside, and a young, somewhat Jewish-looking gentleman, dressed in the latest fashion, bowed to me and asked in French what had brought me here. Timidly, I pulled out my little box and asked him in German if he wanted to purchase the earrings. In this moment, my existence seemed so miserable and worthless that I would have welcomed a sudden death for me and my children as the best recourse for this wretchedness. I do not wish to say much about the haggling and depreciating valuations of the jeweler, except that I finally succeeded after endless efforts to sell the earrings for an amount far under their actual value and then rushed home with the proceeds to my children ....

/I remember very well that I was unable to eat anything that day. We say back home that the cow worshippers, the Banyans, are the worst cutthroats. That may be true, but they are not the only ones, for people like that can be found everywhere and surely not least in Europe. Much later, I had a similar experience, which was unfortunately even far less heartening. You will probably remember that golden clasp, which I had commissioned out of solid gold and modeled to look like the English Marines. When it came time to dispose of this piece as well, I took it to a famous jeweler and asked him to give me an estimate, as I wanted to sell it. The gentleman in question gave me an amused look of pity, since he evidently saw me as naïve and confused. Without giving the clasp any attention, he gave it back to me and said very kindly: "We only work with gold and silver!" I did not, however, allow this to put me off, but rather told him he should please make the effort to test the clasp on a touchstone. On the inside, I was indignant that this person could believe I had brought in a worthless item, perhaps of brass, when the clasp in fact consisted of eighteen carat gold. The unerring stone thus proved the correctness of my assertion and revealed the jeweler's mistrust as completely without basis. Slowly and guardedly, he had to admit that the solid wrought clasp was indeed eighteen carat gold. And then it was time for the usual perceptive questioning: "You are in fact a foreigner, not a German, are you not?" "Well, do I look German?" I retorted, whereupon the jeweler simply answered no. Having been rather irritated by the jeweler's behavior, I started to wrap up the clasp and said to him: "If you knew I was a foreigner and not a German, why did you ask?" I then went into a simpler shop, where I sold the clasp by the weight of the gold and fewer words. Later I learned that the same was converted to coinage in the mint. Who knows if it may not someday find its way back to you as coins!

The extra room rental unfortunately did not work out well, since our place lay rather far from the city that foreigners tended to prefer. I soon had to accept that I could no longer stay on this expensive floor. When my one-year contract came to an end, we transferred to another cheaper residence. Before I moved out, however, the landlady visited me to invite me to coffee the following day. I told her that if she was planning to invite other guests as well, I would thank her but decline the kind invitation, as I preferred to avoid social gatherings. However, if the invitation was only with her, I would gladly come. She confessed, not without some embarrassment, that another older lady, the Baroness von Such-and-Such,[67] would also be present, having expressed the wish to make my acquaintance and asked my landlady to facilitate the encounter. Whereupon I declined even more decisively with the explanation that I did not enjoy meeting such inquisitive people, in addition to not wishing to make any new acquaintances. My landlady then launched into such begging and pleading that I not disappoint this honorable lady of high standing, who although a stranger had a fondness for me. You know, of course, that I have always appreciated older people and hold them in some degree of piety. With this in mind, I finally let my landlady persuade me and agreed to the visit.

/When I arrived the next day at the appointed time, the guest in question was already there. We were introduced to each other, and after the usual empty formalities of a first encounter, I felt myself very drawn to this older lady. She was so motherly and heartwarming that I felt an immediate, soothing effect. There was not a trace of the vulgar curiosity that I so often had to endure, just the calming presence of a motherly friend. What had started as an unwelcome meeting soon revealed itself as one of the happiest hours I have ever experienced in Germany. As I extended my hand to say farewell to this honorable old lady, who could easily have been my grandmother, I was as yet unaware that the good Lord was mercifully offering me this stranger as a moral support for my inner isolation. A few weeks later, I was very surprised by a visit from the lady in question, something I had not anticipated after my landlady had explained that she was unable to climb stairs. It was indeed touching to see how she tried to ascend them with the help of a cane. I could see how happy she was with my children, in whom she also subsequently found great pleasure. Upon departing, I led her by the arm down the stairs. When saying good-bye, she looked me straight in the eye and said: "My dear, I think we understand each other!" Oh yes, we did indeed have an understanding between us. From then on, I felt a gradual improvement in my state of mind.

/Through my new motherly friend, I was able to find the first true Christian, someone I had been seeking, unfortunately without success, all this time. Noble in her very being and devout through and through, she possessed a clear mind, which helped her see everything in sharp relief, while also allowing her to judge fairly and objectively. From then on, she called me "my precious dear" and that is how I soon felt about her. Still today and surely until the end of my life, I will bless the hour that I first saw her. She understood everything

---

67 Louise Friederike Ottilie Freifrau von Tettau, according to H. Schneppen, *Briefe*, p. 159, n. 34.

about me, as only a devoted mother can understand her child. I soon had such confidence in her that my thoughts and actions were like an open book before her.

/Oh, how often did my heavy heart lead me to her, since I could always be sure of her empathy and understanding. How often, oh how often, did I return home after being comforted and strengthened by her, able to continue the terribly difficult road in life. I could not thank the merciful Lord enough for his care. My path was truly too steep for me, and the ever-increasing barriers often threatened to block my way. The unquenchable longing for my beloved homeland that stirred in me was overpowering. Although my motherly friend and I were so far apart in age, we were nonetheless so unified in our thinking and feeling that I could always count on her being fully there for me. Quite frequently, I would sit on a stool next to her, at her request, and taking my head between her hands, she would caress me like a loving mother. "You are like a transplanted palm," she once said to me, "which, instead of being nurtured in a warm and well-kept greenhouse, has to freeze outdoors in the wind and weather. But do not give up, my precious dear, and stay confident that the Lord will be there for you." Such words of comfort did wonders for my soul, especially since my assistant, the lawyer, left much to be desired in the administration of my finances, and I went from one worry to another.

It was around fall in the second year of my time in Dresden, as I was playing with the children in the small arbor that belonged to our floor, when two elegantly attired gentlemen addressed me along the following lines: "Excuse us, does the Princess of Zanzibar perhaps live here?" And when I responded, I was the one and what could I do for them, the older of the two explained that they were planning to travel to Zanzibar, as lawyers, and would be happy to convey any message to you all. Both men appeared so mysterious to me that I thanked them for the offer, with unmistakable brevity. These same purported lawyers then wanted to speak to me again the next morning, but I let them know through my servant girl that I did not receive gentlemen who did not come recommended to me by acquaintances. What do you make of that?

/17

My normally healthy constitution gradually began to give way, and over time, I became so nervous and irritable that my doctor prescribed a change of air as soon as possible. This was easier said than done. To take such a trip with three little children in the middle of winter to southern Europe, where everything was so expensive, went beyond my means. I had no choice but to simply stay at home. Even the smallest noise caused me to start, such that the children and servant girl always had to wear felt slippers around the house. My health the following winter left much to be desired as well, and so I had to come up with a way to spend the summer away from Dresden. I considered renting my furnished residence as a whole during the summer months, perhaps to a family that wanted to spend the summer in the city. With the countless boarding houses and furnished rooms in Dresden, there was hardly any prospect of realizing my plan. But before I simply gave up and accepted the inevitable, I wanted to try everything I could. I advertised numerous times in the papers, unfortunately to no avail. Finally, I went to a real estate agent in Victoria Street and had my residence noted just in case someone came along. Not long after, I was happily able to rent the whole floor to a Romanian princess with her children, who were planning to spend the summer in Dresden.

/This way I was now able to travel with the children to the Sächsische Schweiz.[68] Here I got to know a professor, to whom I later became much indebted. One day, the nanny brought me two calling cards: one from a lady of Russian nobility, whom I had briefly gotten to know in Dresden and who was now asking me to please assist the professor, and the second from the professor himself, who was waiting outside. I hardly wanted to believe the girl when she told me that the gentleman in question had arrived in tails, top hat, white tie, and white gloves. This ceremonious outfit surely could not have been easy for this famous academic, since I learned later through a closer acquaintance that he abhorred such formalities, and even more considering he had taken the train the whole way from Dresden.

/The purpose of his visit was to ask if I might help decipher a celestial globe, which, if I am not mistaken, was said to be more than six hundred years old. The script on the globe was in old Kufic characters,[69] with which I had only

---

[68] The "Switzerland" of Saxony, a German national park southeast of Dresden that features a sandstone mountain range with stunning rock formations.
[69] Kufic script, developed in Al-Kufa in Iraq, is one of the earliest handwriting styles used to record the Koran. Its calligraphic style accentuates short vertical and elongated horizontal strokes that are well-suited for inscriptions.

little familiarity. I openly admitted my lack of knowledge about this type of script that deviated significantly from ours, but let him know I was happy to try to help him in any way I could. He asked if he might return the following week, and I agreed. When he arrived the next time in the same formal attire, I considered it necessary to free him from such superfluous convention and told him: "Please, Professor, from now on come in your usual clothes." Usefully, this also allowed me to gain some knowledge about astronomy, since I had until then still relied on our understanding that the sun turns around the earth, not the other way around. That said, this dear scholar had to exert great effort to convince me of this, since our perspective made more sense to me.

/Later, after we were done deciphering and translating the text on the globe, the professor made me an extraordinarily welcome proposal, which I immediately accepted: I should give him Arabic lessons in exchange for science lessons from him. Thereafter he visited me in Dresden twice a week for us to teach each other. Such a good man! I must have handed him quite a chore to introduce me to the mysteries of science, for I did not simply accept whatever he taught me. Instead, I constantly had questions about how this or that came to be and always wanted proof. I could not have asked for a better teacher, and if I did not learn more, that was not his fault. Often I would point out that it was getting late and we should start the Arabic lesson, since he would get so caught up in his eagerness to teach me that the Arabic got short shrift. He then often answered: "No, no, your questions interest me too much, since you are like a jungle that must first be plowed to produce the lushest vegetation." From then on, I was able to read German books and papers with more understanding, and even attend scientific lectures now and again. Soon he introduced me to his wife and daughter, and I could be truly happy about their harmonious family life. And when I traveled to England, what an effort he made to teach me English history.

I must once again return to my assistant, the lawyer in Hamburg, to report on his unscrupulous behavior, which continued to cause me abject poverty. Because the wonderful jurisprudence of the City of Hamburg required that our entire capital had to reside in his hands, I was completely powerless and entirely subject to his mercy. After untold efforts, I would now and again get some money from him, but always much less than the interest accrued from our capital. I could never get him to provide an accounting, since he was always making one excuse after another, forever leaving me in the lurch. As a result, I had to resort to my jewelry far too often, as my one and only refuge, and one piece followed the next.

/One day, when it was winter and I was already in a very melancholy mood because of the dreary weather, I received a letter from a friend in Hamburg, who informed me that, as widely known in the city, the financial situation of my assistant, the lawyer, was very bad. In addition, he was said to be very dangerously sick at this moment, and the letter went on to say that if he were to die now, chances were that my children and I would just be reduced to beggars. You cannot fathom my situation then, what fate was handing me. Shocked to the highest degree by this alarming news, I stood there helpless. What should I do to avoid this looming peril? As the widow of a Hamburg citizen, I had no choice but to subordinate myself to the local laws, which is to say that as long as I did not remarry, my husband's estate and its administration remained with me. But the effective power had been put in the hands of judicially-ordered assistants, as amply demonstrated by this case. A few months before receiving the warning, I had been in Hamburg on a visit. When I asked the lawyer where he kept our papers, I received the laconic answer: "Madam, that depends entirely, for sometimes they are with a banker, sometimes they are with me." From this, it is evident that the law leaves the management of widow and orphan funds in the full and unlimited discretion of the relevant assistant.

/In my plight, I sought out the professor mentioned earlier, who gave me the good advice to turn directly to the Royal Saxon Court Office, Department of Guardianship Matters, with the request (now that I lived in Dresden) that they take up the administration of my assets. I was immediately informed that the Guardianship Office only managed money for guardianship purposes, meaning that if my application were to be accepted, it would first necessitate a division of capital between me and my children. Did I want that? Oh yes, I did want that; it was only for the children that I sought to salvage whatever could still be salvaged. My own person was the least of my thoughts. Beyond anything else, I was focused on the future of my children. Physically and mentally, I was so rundown that, more than anything, I increasingly expected my own early demise.

/The Court Office in Dresden took up my application and straightaway engaged in the necessary steps to have the Hamburg Guardianship Agency transfer our assets to the Dresden Court Office without delay. In this unsettled time, I was beset with worry and sleepless nights, and I had to take significant amounts of chloral,[70] as prescribed by the doctor, to engineer any sleep. Moreover, one of the children suffered from a perpetual throat infection, one of the bad sicknesses that holds sway in the North and made me ever fearful. You have no idea how depressing a sick room here looks in the winter. Windows and doors are shut, and felt and moss are even used to seal the windows. Meanwhile, the dense fog acts so oppressively on temperaments that there is room for nothing more than melancholic thoughts. How often, oh how often did my thoughts then fly over to our dear island, and I envied you for the constant blue sky and your simple lifestyle, which is still free of all the complications that people here characterize as achievements of civilization and emblems of the harried human spirit.

It soon became clear that my worries about our Hamburg-administered assets were not entirely unfounded. When the Guardianship Office demanded from the assistant Dr. K. that he provide the commercial papers he had received, he was not able to produce them right away; in other words, the assets entrusted to him were not all in hand. Consequently, it took a long time before he was able to replace the missing documents. I cannot describe how I suffered during this time. No matter what the Guardianship Office reported to me or wanted to determine, I simply said yes, since I was unable to have any opinions or take any decisions back then. Putting all my trust in the God of my fathers, who alone knew my true internal state of being, I gave everything over to his care, all that, in my ignorance of these new conditions, I was unable to even remotely understand.

---

70 Administered as chloral hydrate, this pharmaceutical sedative was widely used to counter insomnia, starting in the latter part of the nineteenth century. It was first formulated and promoted in Germany and found a ready market as an inexpensive, easy-to-use drug, despite its addictive properties and overdose risks (with no effective reversal agent), in addition to potential for abuse (also known today as knockout drops and the date rape drug). See, for example, E. Shorter, *Before Prozac: The Troubled History of Mood Disorders in Psychiatry* (2008).

/One day I was called to the Guardianship Office. They informed me that the commercial papers that had been received from Hamburg included the obligations of the Hungarian Northeastern Railway, which, in light of their uncertain value, could not be accepted as guardianship funds, but would instead need to be sold. I was, however, further informed that the value of this particular railway was no longer anywhere near the price at which they had been bought and that this sale was expected to result in a significant loss. With this news, I decided to take these papers as my widow's portion, so as to spare my children from this unavoidable loss.

/Only now, after years of begging and pleading, was I finally able to have an overview of the annual income I could expect to receive. Even if the amount was only modest in comparison to the needs of daily life, I was still relieved to have a clear picture of my situation. My inherited portion, consisting of the Hungarian papers and a small fraction of the other papers, was now paid out. The agents, as explained, were there only to manage the underage guardianship funds, and may the widow take care of herself. All German widows were covered by this merciless, one-size-fits-all statute, whether they were born near the Elbe or next to the Indian Ocean. Who cared if I, coming from a foreign land, did not immediately grasp and understand the intricate conditions? No one but myself.

/I was most kindly advised to bring my commercial papers to a bank for safekeeping. This I did. After some time, I took the usual trip to the bank in question to withdraw the interest accrued. But instead of the money I expected came rather shocking news. I was given the following terse message: The stock of the Hungarian Northeastern Railway had gone down significantly in value in the past days, and bankruptcy was feared. Do you actually understand what these few words meant for me? Effectively, if the railway company did in fact become bankrupt, I would go down with it, or rather because of it, and I would lose virtually my whole fortune. The bank advised me to sell the papers as quickly as possible. I was not ready to make that decision on the spot and promised to return the next day. With a heavy heart, I went back home. Instead of sleep that night, I had plenty of time to reflect on the actual value of my current assets.

/I was unable to come to any conclusion other than the position advised by the bank, since I understood absolutely nothing about these things. The next morning I was again advised to sell the papers, which then resulted in a loss of more than thirty percent. Just be happy that you are a fortunate owner of a plantation and have nothing to do with all these government and industry investments. Your plantation ownership is more secure than when you are compelled to invest your wealth in papers, whose creditworthiness is often cloaked in an impenetrable fog. You will not have a sufficient basis for comprehending these things, and how could it be otherwise! I was not much better off, despite having already spent a number of years living in the midst of such progress. And you will likely comprehend even less when I tell you that investing wealth in papers is incredibly risky. It depends on such an array of circumstances, like for example, crop failures, the frequent encounters of the various monarchs, the persistently recurring speeches of politicians, and many other serendipitous events. They can all cause the value of these papers to rise or fall, meaning one must always anticipate random chance.

/Although now safe from the arbitrariness of an assistant, I was entering a troubling period that required my precise calculation if I did not wish to fall victim to prevailing circumstances. My children's assets had been converted by the Guardianship Office to government securities, which are known not to produce much interest. When the amount owned is insignificant, the greatest frugality is required, if liabilities are not to exceed assets at the end of each calendar year. All my efforts went into applying this theory, but I often had to struggle mightily with the execution. You must not think, however, that I lived a life of unnecessary luxury and excess, not at all, but rather had a lifestyle that is considered middle class here. Despite all my computations and considerations, I could not do much to improve my situation. And meanwhile, the time was drawing closer when my children, according to the law of the land, needed to be sent off to school, in part because I was in no position to have them taught at home, as I would have loved to do. The private schools in Dresden are quite expensive, and with my limited resources, there was no chance of having my three children go to such schools. And so, I had no choice but to come up with means and ways—without an adequate grasp of their ramifications—to find a solution.

As happens frequently in life, I found myself in a situation where I resolutely closed my ears to reason and made room for my heart to rule. My mind frequently gravitated to the thought that told me it was pure obsession for me to keep holding onto my plan to give my children a German education. And yet, is the point not only and exclusively a matter of love toward the deceased? So spoke my heart. Whereupon my mind returned fire by repeating a hundred times that my poor husband, in his great love for me, never would have allowed me to lead a life under circumstances that required me to mobilize all my moral and physical strength to fight each step of the way. And my mind admonished me further: Now the time has come when you can move to a southern location with a clear conscience, where you have neither a harsh winter with all its demands, nor a duty to attend school. You cannot stay in Dresden over the long run, you can see that yourself, and what will you do then? Keep on trying, I thought to myself, as long as I still can.

Zittau or Weimar were suggested to me as places where the cost of living was lower. But I did not know anyone in either city, so I found it hard to come to a decision. Then someone suggested Rudolstadt, where I knew a Swiss woman and her family from my time in Hamburg. Through this family, I now gathered details about Rudolstadt, on rents, grocery prices, taxes, tuition, etc., all the things that make a difference when one does not have full pockets to transact costs.

/My first step was to discuss all this with my motherly friend, the old Baroness, who also encouraged me in this direction, even though it would be indescribably hard for both me and her. However, she feared I would feel isolated in little Rudolstadt, especially mentally. "My precious dear," she said to me, "the circumstances dictate that you need to move to a small town, where everything is cheaper than here in Dresden, but someone of your nature and manner will hardly feel comfortable in such a constrained environment over the long term. The views of small-town folk are very parochial, and even Germans who only know the big city rarely become enamored of small-town conditions." I told her I saw no other option and wanted to at least give it a try. "I do not need to tell you that I will miss you very much, but one should not be egoistic." Those were her words, and yet, I would be the one to miss her so much more because she was simply irreplaceable—and so remained.

Whereupon I terminated the rental, and let go the nanny, and tried to sell as much of the excess furniture as possible. From now on, I wanted to live in a smaller space and make do with only one girl to help with everything. Do you know what the phrase "girl for everything" means"? Let me teach you! The girl for everything must cook (that is, if she can), get groceries, wash laundry, iron, clean, heat in the winter, open the door when the bell rings, and about a dozen more tasks. Hence, correctly, "girl for everything."

Steel engraving of Rudolstadt, mid-1800s.

/18

I traveled to Rudolstadt first and rented an apartment. Soon thereafter the furniture was packed and sent. Then I followed with my children and the servant girl. I had adjusted very well to Dresden and enjoyed life there, including my limited circle of acquaintances that was nonetheless far better than in Hamburg. The few families I had gotten to know over time were almost exclusively from Hanover or Prussia. I spent many a pleasant hour in their midst and received many signs of their love and friendship. I therefore bid very reluctant farewells to my loyal friends, but above all my unforgettable, motherly friend, the Baroness T. My heart practically broke as I said good-bye to her. She held onto me so tightly, until her son separated us, kindly but firmly, in consideration of her poor health. As he led her to her chamber, she waited a bit longer while I bid farewell to her children. Then she returned once more to draw me one last time to her noble, loyal heart!

/Did she perhaps sense that this would in fact be our last time on this earth together? Who knows? After this day, I never again looked into her wise and trusted eyes, never again heard the voice that had given me such courage and comfort so many countless times. Dejected and pursued by thoughts of our earthly condition, I returned home that evening to a sleepless night. It is good, and we can never thank the Highest enough, if we are allowed to stay of sound mind to the last, and yet, there are moments in life, when people would be decidedly happier if they, at least temporarily, did not need to think and feel so much. But the ways of the Lord are not ours, and no mortal has thus far been able to fathom exactly why fate decides when to favor us and when not. It is a problem that mankind pursues in vain.

The next day, I traveled with my children and the servant girl to Rudolstadt, with its most lovely location, and we put up in a simple hotel until our furniture arrived from Dresden. Later I happened to ask my acquaintance from Hamburg if there had been anything special going on in town the day we arrived, since there were unusually many people at the train station. With a hearty laugh, she let me know that it was all because of unsuspecting me. It is true that the landlord, from whom I had rented the place many weeks earlier, had not posed the question to which I was so accustomed: "Where are you from, my lady?", and had instead agreed to rent on the spot, presumably because he knew my friend's family well, the ones who had looked at the apartment with me. But after I had left, this worthy Thuringian apparently did not rest until he had figured out the nationality of his new renter. In any case, my arrival was duly featured in the Rudolstadt newspaper, which had piqued the town's curiosity.

Not that we looked very Oriental upon our arrival, with me wrapped in nothing less than a modern Scottish coat, and my children wearing their basic winter coats. This news was anything but pleasant for me, though, since I now had to fear that this would make my goal, to live as simply and withdrawn as possible, extremely difficult.

Initially, I had firmly intended not to make any social connections, nor even visit anyone. Was I not plenty busy simply raising and caring for my three children? I should say. But this intention was thwarted by the kindness of a friend from Dresden. This lady made it a point to introduce me to a local family. In addition, more than I wanted to know, I now also learned that all newcomers to town, in order for them to be considered part of respectable Rudolstadt society, had to visit all the local *Honorationen*. To be honest, I considered this last point somewhat childish, all the more because I put little stock in respectable society. But I acquiesced to the unavoidable and decided to seek out these honorable people.

/What, in fact, led me to take this step? That would be you, which is to say, my remembrance of you. I had to tell myself that people would not easily forgive a faux pas and could instead feel justified in accusing me—naturally from their vantage point—of a lack of good breeding. As it was, I had already come across the most wondrous ideas all over Germany about our lifestyle and upbringing, often to my utter astonishment. Apparently, we are viewed merely, to put it mildly, as primitive folk, devoid of any refinement. Aside from my own preference against having a large circle of acquaintances, which does little for the heart and instead promotes that much more unnecessary gossip about others, I did not want to give these dear people any unnecessary grounds to spend time deliberating the dearth of Arab decency at their coffee parties.

/I had the most important names of the relevant families given to me, with the intention of visiting them over the next few days. The list turned out to be quite long, but could not be much shortened, as I would have liked, because of all the family relations among the locals. I naturally started my excursion with the prince's family in the palace[71] and was able to conclude my visits after several days. You cannot imagine how boring these visits are, since conversations must always be so forced to keep up the appearances of mutual pleasantry. It felt bizarre to have to go from house to house to visit complete strangers with whom I had absolutely no connection. And everywhere I had to listen to

---

71 The stately baroque Heidecksburg in Rudolstadt, Thuringia, where Prince Georg Albert, born 1838, was regent at the time. Although he may have had some interest in the Princess from Oman and Zanzibar, nothing materialized. He died unexpectedly of pneumonia in 1890, unwed and without direct descendants.

the same conversations and answer the same questions. It was a clear stroke of luck for me to have seen the first light of the world on our beloved island—because I do not know what else these good people would have discussed with me. Everywhere I had to report faithfully on Zanzibar, the great fecundity of the land, the heat, and so on. Once, when a lady somewhat naïvely asked me about slavery and I gave her a factual answer, she was honest enough to acknowledge that our slaves were far better off than many of the poor Europeans, who must often struggle in anonymity to eke out an existence.

/The degree of cliquishness here struck me as greater than anywhere else I had been. This makes it very uncomfortable for the newly arrived stranger, especially someone who has social ambitions and is unhappy without a busy social life and large circle of acquaintances. I soon indicated to all that I intended to live a quiet and withdrawn life and therefore preferred not to attend any social gatherings. But that did me absolutely no good, as I still had to decline many invitations to avoid the frequent and fascinating afternoon gatherings.

Here I sent my children to school for the first time, in fact, all of them on the same day. I was quite unhappy on this day and constantly battled my gloomy thoughts. Oh, how much I would have wanted the children to be educated at home, if only the circumstances would have allowed it. Until then, I had looked after my children myself, day and night, even hour by hour, and watched over them like the apple of my eye. From now on, however, I needed to entrust them *nolens volens* to total strangers, if I did not want to get in trouble with the law of the land.

Wistfully, I embraced all three tightly the first morning they went to school, and it felt to me like they were about to embark on a trip around the world. They were all very animated that morning, full of anticipation of things and settings they had until now only heard about. On this day, the house felt deserted. I could not get comfortable anywhere and missed the incessantly bubbly bunch everywhere. From one of the windows, I could see quite far into the distance where the children had to return from school. And so I sat there, already half an hour before their arrival time, in order to spot them from afar. With quick strides, they rushed home, and when I met them at the front door, there was a rousing reunion. The previously still and barren house resounded anew with the voices of their lively company. The four hours of their absence struck me as endlessly long, and I thanked God when they were back around me. At that moment, I forgot all the bitter hours of my existence that were forever making my life so difficult. Today, their chatter never stopped. The names of the teachers and classmates swirled in my head for days, since it was impossible to talk to them about anything other than school and everything about it.

With this new chapter in the life of my children, a new period began for me as well. Accustomed to having the children around me, life between us had developed to the point that I often did not register their ages and instead discussed every happening in the house, all the practical things, yes, even our income and expenditures—as though they were adults. Their ability to quickly grasp what I shared with them always warmed my heart, and I was entirely fulfilled by them. Now that they had to be absent many hours a day, I often felt an oppressive loneliness that frequently also overwhelmed me with melancholy. In addition, I was not spared the less than encouraging feeling of how ill-equipped, in fact, an Arab mother is here, despite all her efforts, to be a mother of school-bound and fatherless children.

/In this country, it is apparently not enough for children to learn while at school, so they are also given a sizeable amount of homework, meaning they can never free themselves from learning. And then I was frequently expected to help my crying children do their work in subjects about which I, too, often had no clue. It also made me very sad to hear the children say—especially in the later years—that their classmates did better at their schoolwork because they always got help from home. I could not monitor the homework, nor was I in a position to bring someone on board for that purpose, so I often had to listen to the children's complaints without being able to do anything about them. As you can see, life is very complicated here, and an Arab woman does not come out unscathed if she chooses to follow her sense of piety.

/It was, however, only this feeling of piety that got me back on track the many times my spirit sunk, like a carriage seeking to stay upright in the thunder and storm, to keep its balance and remain firmly grounded. And yet, I was often so close to being overwhelmed, at any moment, and cast into ruins. Or did I have any attachment at the time to Western education? Heavens no, absolutely not, for I did not even know back then how to understand what all this education meant.[72] Perhaps I was not yet sufficiently Europeanized to be able to render homage to the prevailing approach here, that children are supposed to strive for better positions, better standing, etc. later in life than was bestowed upon their ancestors. Namely, this is the method that epitomizes the much beloved word "progress." Since we back home are still in baby shoes, so to speak, as far as fully appreciating this characterization, nothing was further from my mind than this specific intention. Our practice, which has existed across centuries until now, and by which the children, especially the sons, are proud to become what their parents and grandparents were before them, has no currency here, and such a viewpoint is considered long passé. The label "conservative" no longer has the meaning it once had.

My children had been in school only a few days when they stormed into the house terribly excited and overheated, surprising me with the totally unexpected question: "Mama, is it true that you are really a princess, please, please, tell us!" How should I have answered? I could only draw them into a deep embrace. Apparently affected by my reaction, they began to sob heartbreakingly, and even their midday meal did little to cheer them up. When I asked who had told them, S. responded that a classmate, an officer's son, had said it to him, and

---

[72] The author uses the word *Bildung*, a word that means something more than education and can be said to include a socialized upbringing, refined acculturation, and broadly acquired knowledge of the arts, humanities, and sciences—a Western notion based on Western perspectives and principles.

he had then told his sisters on the way home. Their childish ways prevailed, as they acted rather strangely toward me that day, and I could see how they kept watching me. They were apparently thinking of fairy tale descriptions the nanny used to read to them. Soon, however, this strangeness dissipated, and I was once again nothing more in their eyes than their loving mother, and they were as always my beloved little children.

As you can imagine, on this day my thoughts were largely with you, as was usually the case when my soul was heavy. With their innocent question, the children had evoked many wistful memories that did little to ease my current task. I also feared their childish lack of understanding and would much rather have kept them unknowing until they were somewhat more mature. For a time, I was besieged by legions of questions to be answered, arising from their childish imaginations. Only now did the things I had brought with me from the homeland start to take on meaning, with constant calls of: "Come! Come! Mama is going to open the big wardrobe, and we can take a quick look at her Arab things."

/19

Winter arrived, and so did the many dangerous illnesses for children. In November, S. got such a dire case of acute diphtheria that it was a miracle he survived. The doctor who was treating him had completely given up on him one evening. Despairing, I stayed alone in the sick room with my son, who had already become stiff. My soul wrangled with the Lord to save my child, who barely continued to breathe. Perhaps an hour or so after the doctor had taken my last hope, a hefty stream of blood suddenly gushed from the mouth of my motionless child, and this release also brought rescue. The child opened his eyes and recognized me. I forgot the doctor's urgent warning to keep my face away from his, to avoid contagion, and kissed this child whom the Lord had restored to me in his grace.

/Getting someone to help with caretaking was out of the question. Our only servant girl had to stay isolated with the two small girls and was not allowed to come into the sick room. Outside assistance was absolutely unthinkable. There were no deaconesses in the area back then, and the residents were so petrified about catching the disease that when my two girls walked out on the street, women walking towards them would detour to the other side. You can best tell how tremendously arduous the care was by the fact that I stayed on my feet day and night for the first week and never changed out of my clothes. My feet became so swollen that I could no longer fit into my shoes and instead had to walk in stockings, despite the fierce cold in the sick room, whose windows had to stay open under the doctor's orders. Even though the oven fire in the next room over stayed on the whole time, I never managed to get the temperature above 5° Réaumur.[73] Barely was S. starting to regain his health when I, too, apparently as a result of all the anxiety and excitement I had experienced, ended up spending six weeks in bed and then another three months taking quinine[74] to fight the weakness and chills. I do not know what is customary across Germany, but in our case the doctor who handled the diphtheria took a double payment because, as explicitly stated in the invoice, the disease was contagious.

Spring had just begun when the two girls simultaneously got scarlet fever. S. had to be isolated, while I was so preoccupied with their care that I was

---

73 Under the Réaumur temperature scale with water freezing at 0 degrees and boiling at 80 degrees, this is the equivalent of 6.25°C and 43.25°F.
74 According to Professor of History Andrew Goss in "A History of Quinine Drug Hype Since the 19th Century," quinine was discovered as an effective anti-malarial drug extracted from the bark of the cinchona tree, but was also experimentally and incorrectly promoted in the nineteenth century as a cure for a variety of other ailments.

unable to attend to him at all. I therefore had him lodge with a teacher. At that point in time, I had a very bad servant girl, who hardly wanted to work and just took it easy. No surprise, of course, that she needed to do more now because of the sick children, which suited her even less. Indeed, lo and behold the emancipation of European servant girls! One day, as I wanted to get supper for the children from the kitchen, I found neither soup, nor servant girl. Since the apartment was not very large, it did not take long to conclude that the servant girl had, without saying a word, up and left. As if this were not enough, I soon also discovered that she had locked the door shut and taken the key. Now just imagine my situation. Locked in with two children beset with scarlet fever, and no one at all there to help, truly this could have been conceived and enacted only by the greatest perfidy. The fear that something might happen to the sick children overnight, when I would have no way to get care, disconcerted me so much that I yelled out the window for help. Because the house had a front yard and lay somewhat distant from the isolated street, there was no hope of getting help right away. At long last, someone heard me, and it took about another two hours before the door could be opened.

/There is hardly any way for you to comprehend what my life was like in the period that followed. How can you understand when I tell you that I had to survive for six weeks on end with two sick children and absolutely no help. I had to take care of every bit of work in the house myself, since I found no new servant girl for fear of contagion. Our fatalism is often mocked here, but I honestly do not know if their degree of trepidation is not worthy of pity. Even the disloyal servant girl later cited her dread of contagion as her excuse. I was completely helpless and abandoned by everyone. Initially, I saw no one but the doctor, a different one from the one we had when S. was sick. This new one was so humane that he helped with errands outside the house and even later assisted with the children's baths. An old seamstress, who had said she would occasionally come for an hour or two to help out in the kitchen or run errands, one day explained quite downcast that she was sorry, she could no longer assist me if she did not want to lose her other clients. What do you think about this kind of humanity? Better to do as I have done and put no stock in such vaunted terms, absolutely none. I have found that people generally are charitable only when it suits them. Even the heathens are persuaded and stand by this lesson.

/I became, as I said, the sick nurse and servant girl for everything. The doorbell almost never rang to disrupt my work, since it is apparently not the custom here, as it is by us, to call on the sick around us. Perhaps the fault also lay with the great fear of contagion. During this period, I lived through days that I will not forget as long as I live! In order to meet S. on the street or buy what was missing in the household, I had to lock my sick children up in the house, oh horror. I cannot describe to you in words how that made me feel. Perhaps the closest I can come to conveying it is how disgusted I felt to be alive.

/The hardest task for me was and remained getting the fire to start in the stove and the oven. Often I was still unsuccessful even after half an hour of trying. I know you too well to fear that you would laugh at me if I admit that I frequently cried bitter tears of complete despair. One day, it was so frigid, oh so bitterly frigid. I was crouched down by the cold and depleted oven, trying and trying to light the fire, when I was suddenly completely startled by the doorbell. I found the baker's boy with his goods at the front door. Seeing him there, I jumped at the thought that I could perhaps ask this boy to get the oven going in the living room. No sooner said than done. And look, how quickly the fire sprang into being with his practiced hands.

/I now had to head out to the promenade twice a day to meet S. and comfort him because the poor boy was suffering so much from homesickness. Meanwhile, the two sick children simply had to stay locked up in the house. Oh, how I hurried home afterwards to confirm that my children were still alive or had not somehow, as my extremely frayed nerves led me to fear, died from a house fire. During the day, I almost forgot how to sit, except at mealtimes, and not until evening could I take a bedside seat by the sick children and read them stories from Hoffmann and Nieritz for their entertainment. That was my only hour of rest every day, for once the children were asleep, I went into the small sitting room to mend old sheets and clothes.

Given these circumstances, the prospect of continuing to live in Rudolstadt was greatly spoiled, even though it was so pleasantly situated, and I consequently felt very unhappy here. Life in a German city is not advisable for strangers from distant shores for the simple reason that they will feel isolated in their perceptions and perspectives. The impulsive Southerner, who is averse to all affectations, has no sense for the countless ceremonies and formalities that the people here subscribe to so minutely. By the same token, more straightforward, natural individuals are then often labeled as naïve. And meanwhile, the views of people here are often so narrow that their interests typically do not extend beyond a ten-mile circumference. No, especially the ladies amongst themselves take virtually no interest in larger topics, and instead all the more in—their neighbors.

/With these and similar conditions, I regrettably did not find the life I sought, such that I could live quietly and unnoticed within my means. As unbelievable as it may seem, the good people here really knew exactly when I had bought a new hat, how long I wore my clothes, when I had last gotten a new ribbon, who came to visit me, and even more: what we had cooked for dinner! You are constantly being observed, and it feels like living in a glasshouse. At first, I ignored it all, but over time I really had my fill with all the pettiness. One day I received a visit from a complete stranger, a traveler to Africa, who was sent to me by a well-known family in L.[75] He had just returned from Zanzibar and wanted to show me the latest photographs from there. Since this gentleman was very tan from the tropical sun and sported a very black beard, these characteristics were enough for the staid Germans to stamp him as one of my brothers. And within twenty-four hours, pretty much everyone had something to say about it.

I eventually came to understand that a small German town is not quite the place where a foreigner from overseas will feel comfortable. In a big city, individuals are less watched and controlled and can much more easily blend in. One day I received correspondence from the Head of Guardianship in Dresden, to which a response from me in German was no easy chore, given my minimal understanding of bureaucratic and legal terms. I was rather troubled and discouraged, pondering the best way to formulate a response that would avoid any possible misunderstanding. My eight-year-old youngest daughter found me in this state when she came home. Since the age of three, she had called me "my child," and so she ran over to me and said in her childish way: "Child, do you have a fate again?" Namely, the word fate for her represented troubles, since she could not yet express herself any better. When I explained to her my situation, what I was thinking and how hard it was for me to draft the letter for the Guardianship Office, she called out: "You poor child, can I not help you? Tell me what you want to answer, and I will make a draft for you that you can just copy." And that is how it went. I told her what I was intending to write, and she, this eight-year-old, crafted the sentences better and more clearly than I could have done at the time.[76]

For more than a year, I was caught up in a particular thought that caused me countless sleepless nights, until I was finally able to come to terms with myself. The source of my struggle was no less the idea that I might try to give lessons in my mother tongue—or rather in my case, more like my father tongue—so

---

75 It is not known what location the author is referring to here.
76 Rosa's support, which began so early, continued in the later editing support of her mother's *Memoiren* and other writings. See more about this mother-daughter relationship in the translator's essay "On Collaboration" on page 126 below.

as to meet the growing needs of my children over time. My thoughts would always rush to you, and as a result, I always wavered, again and again. Which then led me to start my wrangling anew, as it seemed to me the only way to stave off poverty from my beloved children. The powerful traditions of our upbringing are not easy to simply shake off. We are conditioned to stay true to them, even if this fidelity can very often become uncomfortable, as in what I was experiencing at the time. But the love for my children ultimately proved victorious, and gradually over time, the decision ripened within me.

/In this mental battle, I amply felt that even my dear German friends would have little deeper understanding for my deliberations, if only because people here have a completely different concept of working women than we do at home. The view here is that work is ennobling. Where such attitudes govern, my perspectives would certainly have come across as backwards and even bizarre in their eyes. But for someone who was not raised with this philosophy of life from youth onward, and who is then induced to accept its message through cold and rigid necessity, taking such a step is certainly no trifle. Orientals are often enough criticized for being lazy and indolent. When seen from an Occidental lens, that may be true, except that this too often overlooks how contented Southerners are in general, which definitely cannot be said of civilized Europeans. In addition, the Northern cold makes a necessity of a thousand things, of which those who live in the South simply have no concept. The natural consequence is that people take virtually no pleasure in undertaking arduous tasks.

/In any case, I found myself still too beholden to my upbringing to be enthralled by the thought of necessity-driven employment. Since the death of my husband, I often had to work hard, indeed, often more than a servant girl would have done. I doubt such a one would have repaired her torn shoes, except in rare cases, whereas I at times achieved a certain virtuosity therein by improving my children's shoes with the remnants of old and worn kid gloves. But that work could all be done in private, without anyone needing to bear witness. And I did the work knowing I was not trying to earn any money, just wanting to hold things together. This constituted, for me at least, a significant difference. As I said, it was only after a long internal struggle that I came up with a plan, since I saw no other way out.

20

One day, my children came home from school just as I was reading a letter from one of my loyal friends, who was responding to my news about the step I had determined to take. This true friend as always wrote very affectionately and encouraged me to hold onto this idea, as she felt my intention to give Arabic lessons in Berlin held much promise. She also acknowledged with sensitive empathy the soulful struggle I had gone through to make this decision, so that when the children entered, I was in a somewhat emotional state.

/"Mama, what has happened, did H.[77] perhaps write something sad, please tell us about it!" Those were their first words. And when I explained the situation to them and shared the contents of the letter, they all let loose a hefty stream of tears and showered me with their caresses. After hearing the reason for my dejection, they all asked in their childish way what they could do, so that I, in their words, "need not do any lessons."

/The feeling that we must care for our loved ones, above all to be able to protect and preserve them from all the rigors of the world and their consequences, often gives us a totally unimagined strength, which succeeds in overriding all obstacles. In this way, we see our tradition: Pride and all the similar words gradually disappear, like ice under the hot rays of the sun. Here in this country, people very much love to praise what children are on the outside—in my view, much too much—in being bright and well-behaved, etc., yes, often enough as non-pedagogically as possible in the presence of the children themselves. These attributes mostly left me cold. By contrast, I felt indescribably happy to have the love of my children, which, coupled with the feeling that I would fulfill my duties to them as much as my strength would allow, helped me over many a hurdle.

My choice of Berlin did not reflect my inner conviction for a successful venture, since there was little interest in Oriental languages to be found there at the time, in any case not nearly as much as, say, in London, Paris, and Vienna. Had I been able to decide to direct my feet toward one of these three worldly cities, I might have, most likely, succeeded in my endeavor. But thoughts of my dear husband precluded any other choice. Whether I did the right thing, though, by following this feeling, in light of my situation, struck me later as very doubtful.

---

[77] Professor van Donzel suggests that this may refer to Hermann Ruete, who apparently handled some financial matters for the family. E. van Donzel, p. 496. According to the Ruete family tree shared with us by Ursula Luther, a direct descendant of the Ruete family, this would be Heinrich's younger brother, Andreas Hermann Ruete, who was born in 1850 to Heinrich's stepmother.

/In short, I took a few days that winter to travel to the German capital to find a place to rent, leaving my children behind in Rudolstadt, as hard as that was for me, in the sole care of our servant girl. The matter was, however, not as easy as I had thought, since looking for a modest apartment in Berlin is no small feat. The number of stairs I had to climb as a child was negligibly small compared to the many I had to mount during those few days of my search.[78] After I had gotten a newspaper, in which the available rentals were advertised, and studied them carefully, marking the ones that appeared suitable, I embarked on my still unforgettable expedition. Oh, it was so bitter cold, and the streets seemed paved with ice. At one point, before I knew it, I had slipped on the Leipzigerstrasse, directly in front of a little sentry box. But this disciple of Mars, standing at his post, just calmly watched me, as my repeated attempts to get up on my own proved unsuccessful. Finally, a humane civilian helped me get on my feet and order a coach. After minimally pulling myself together again, I continued my journey, up and down the stairs.

Not that I desired a rental on the second floor, oh no, I no longer dared to aim for this craving, after prices had thwarted that option. It is well-known that the second floor is only for the favored few. And since I was not part of that group, it was not hard for me to quickly comprehend the situation. I still very well recall how you described your pilgrimage to Mecca and the trials you suffered. It is of course to be expected that a trip in the desert would bring many discomforts, but I would counsel you to never undertake a journey like mine, to look for an apartment in Berlin as a complete stranger and completely alone in the very cold month of January. Finally, after much walking back and forth, I was able to rent a ground floor space with four small rooms, but, of course, situated so that the two back rooms had practically no view of the sky, much less the dear, enlivening sun, while the two front rooms looked onto an imposing wall of multi-story apartment buildings. And for a residence like this, people demand a rent that borders on disbelief.

As part of my move to Berlin, I let the Thuringian servant girl go and thus embarked on the trip with my children alone. Already on the train, the eldest began a heavy fever, and once in Berlin, came down with chickenpox. We stayed in a simple hotel the first few days, until the furniture arrived, and I was able to hire a servant girl. With the latter, it was not long before I made a very bad discovery, when she ended up so drunk one day that she had to be removed from the house with help from the police. On top of that, this episode even landed me in front of the court. Would you have thought something like this possible? I

---

78 The author's childhood home, Bet il Mtoni, was known for its extensive stairs (*Memoirs*, p. 5).

certainly least of all! For us, all of mankind stands equal before God but nowhere else, whereas here, this so-called enlightenment, which levels everything off, makes everyone equal. In short, I had to appear before the judge to testify against the woman because she had assaulted a policeman. I was quite surprised to find a long article in the morning paper a few days later about my humble self. Much was rehashed about me in this piece, and even my plain attire was described. How else would they fill the long-winded columns of the paper, without resorting to such trivialities. If only the correspondents and reporters could stick to the truth, then that would even be acceptable, but—but!

I was deeply touched to discover that the ladies of Berlin follow English and Arabic custom by initially welcoming strangers to their city. In this way, strangers soon feel at home, especially when they, as in my case, are fortunate to meet high-minded, selfless people. Oddly enough, Berlin is the only city in Germany where I felt somewhat at home, even though I appreciate the calm and peaceful life in the countryside more than the endless commotion of the big city.

Steel engraving of Berlin, mid-1800s.

Letters to the Homeland

/Now I began to think seriously about the purpose that had brought me here: giving lessons. According to the advice of my newly-won friends, I should "simply" advertise in the paper. The first advertisement I placed for Arabic lessons was anything but "simple" for me, as it felt to my disheartened soul like an epitaph for my own tombstone. Heavy-hearted, I was nevertheless very grateful to the gentlemen of the *Kreuzzeitung* and *Norddeutsche Allgemeine Zeitung*[79] for their generosity. The gentlemen would not accept any payment for the advertisements, and the latter even printed theirs in especially large letters. My first pupil reached me, however, not through the newspapers, but through the kind recommendation of one of my acquaintances, which was a great relief. This way I could rest assured that the pupil in question was a respectable person, whereas that cannot always be so clearly ascertained with an advertisement. Spare me any further description of the first lesson I ever gave in my life, as it was the first time I had to earn my keep by the sweat of my brow.

/Later other pupils followed. I often had to repeat a single word five to seven times until they were able to pronounce it more or less correctly. You cannot imagine how much difficulty Europeans have with the rich vocabulary of our language. It is not like any European language, and our guttural sounds just leave some in complete despair. In response to my advertisement, I was soon getting requests from America, England, Holland, and Austria to provide instruction through correspondence. What do you make of this idea? One can conclude only that the letter writers had had no previous encounter with the Arabic language, otherwise they could hardly have come up with this suggestion. Unfortunately, I so often had reason to feel that this teaching profession, to which I had resigned myself after so much inner effort, was not made easy for me. It was impossible for me to ascertain upfront whether I would be dealing with an avid student or a hollow dandy. But nothing did more to dampen my ardor for giving lessons than the unsavory behavior of a Jewish couple. As an Arab, I myself am Semitic, so one cannot refer to me as anti-Semitic in the European sense. That Arabs generally disdain Jews and consider them unclean is, of course, widely known.[80]

In the meantime, I had swapped my ground floor apartment with a similar one on the fourth floor. Here I became very ill and had to take great care of myself.

---

79 Founded as the *Neue Preussiche Zeitung*, the *Kreuzzeitung* became known as the "Cross Newspaper" because of its Germanic Iron Cross in the banner and lasted until 1939. The *Norddeutsche Allgemeine Zeitung* had its roots in the *Leipziger Allgemeine Zeitung* that was founded and run by Heinrich and then Eduard Brockhaus. It later became the *Deutsche Allgemeine Zeitung* and lasted until 1945. See Wikipedia for "Deutsche Allgemeine Zeitung."

80 It may be noted that the author's son Rudolph married into a Jewish family and spent much of his later life seeking to mediate between Jewish and Palestinian interests in the period leading up to the creation of Israel.

Letters to the Homeland

Upon returning from a short walk with my children one day, I found a letter in which I was being asked to provide Arabic lessons in the home of the sender. This lady belonged to one of Berlin's richest banker families, and her princely residence was situated on the upscale Alsenstrasse. She explained in her letter that she was ailing and therefore could not climb my three flights of stairs. I intended to decline the request, but when I told one of the ladies I knew, she advised me for material reasons not to simply reject the offer. She argued that I should think of my children. Oh my God, as if I would not have jumped through fire had that been necessary for my children! So I wavered in my decision, all the more because this friend offered to go to this lady for me and speak with her, before I went myself. I learned that this lady was preparing for a trip to Africa with her husband and therefore wanted to learn Arabic. The plan was for two hours a week. I decided to swallow even this pill, since the feeling that I should not miss any opportunity for my children was once again the driving impetus for my actions.

/Unfortunately, my acquaintance had not discussed the hourly rate, and so I asked her to write my pupil that I would charge 10 Marks. Although I normally charged 5 Marks in my home, the long way, for which I would occasionally need to take a coach, in addition to the extra travel time, would justify the extra amount. Now guess what answer I received! You are unlikely to get it right because your thoughts are no doubt influenced by "noblesse oblige." And yet, such people have no sense for this "noblesse oblige," but operate instead on the basis of their slogan, namely that friendship stops where finance starts. In this case, there was no friendship to bring to an end because it had never begun, but rather the urge to learn Arabic. The response I received from this Jewish lady consisted of payment for the lessons provided to date—and a thank you for the remainder!

There was, sadly, little demand for Arabic lessons, presumably because at that time Germans had, as yet, little interest in the Orient. Later, I also gave lessons in Swahili, a language that is much easier for Europeans to learn. Often, I had to give lecture-style sessions to my students about all sorts of things, like the local inhabitants, the animal and plant world, climate conditions, food, religion, and similar questions. The main topic, however, was usually the question of slavery. It typically provoked wide-eyed amazement on the part of these good people when I answered their question, whether I myself had had many slaves, with a completely natural yes. When I was once asked how many slaves I had owned altogether, and I answered that I did not know the precise number because we did not keep records of such things, although the number surely would have reached many hundreds, the amazement took no end.

/It is rather astonishing how little objectivity Europeans bring to their judgments about slavery. There is a tendency to sentimentalize, often to an unbelievable degree, in ways, it seems to me, that practically equate slavery with cannibalism. These views are often so shortsighted that one cannot help but be reminded of the Biblical story of the splinter and the beam.[81] As if our field and house slaves had to work even half as much as the so-called free people that are doing the mining and factory work in Europe. And one should not forget the general military draft that applies in all of Europe, except England, where there is certainly not much to be said about any special freedom. One is forced to conclude that slavery exists here as there: here whites, there blacks. So everywhere the same. Just that people try to outdo each other in their assimilation, habits, and not least in their imaginations. As far as the practice of caning slaves, it is possible to have differing viewpoints. But even reasonable Europeans do not dare to completely reject this approach. Humanitarianism is a noble trait, and yet, its application with respect to each individual, as every person can attest from their own experience, is not always easy. The highly cultivated infatuation with humanitarianism here in the North differs from the limited drawing power such cultish behavior has on more sober, practically-minded Orientals. And who knows, in light of the shocking brutalities that are so rampant here, enlightened Europe may in the end be forced to take up caning after all, despite all its humanitarian efforts!

---

81 Matthew 7:3: "Why do you look at the splinter in your brother's eye, but don't notice the beam of wood in your own eye?"; Luke 6:42: "Or how can you say to your brother, 'Brother, let me take out the splinter that is in your eye,' when you yourself don't see the beam of wood in your eye? Hypocrite! First take the beam of wood out of your eye, and then you will see clearly to take out the splinter in your brother's eye." (Christian Standard Bible)

21

The increasing sickliness of S. caused him to miss a lot of school and fall far behind in his learning. You will surely want to know, what does the latter actually mean? The point is that everything in this country turns on the words "to learn." Whoever has learned a lot is, in the eyes of the people, already a made man—or a made woman. Woe, however, to anyone whom nature has not favored with such talent and who has learned little besides. This species of person—especially if he has the added misfortune of being allocated an empty sack—might as well be buried alive. Should he, however, wish to compensate for this inexcusable defect through his awe of God, his reverence for old age and sustained life, as well as his devotion to truth and honesty, he could easily become an object of the greatest pity. For such traits are no longer among the most desirable and are long since outdated. Everywhere there is talk of cases where one or the other person is to be pitied because they did not learn anything and therefore cannot become anything. For myself, as I said, I was completely unfit to be a mother of Germanic children, for various reasons. First, I was—according to German criteria—far from able to consider myself sufficiently educated, and accordingly also unable to fully appreciate the school's targeted results as the children's one-and-only task that would lead them to bliss. Second, I had no way to support my children in their schooling because I was unable to give them any help with their schoolwork, as German mothers are wont to do. As a result, the boy made only laborious progress in school.

Already back in Dresden, well-meaning friends had recommended to me that the boy be sent to the cadet corps,[82] not least because they believed this would be a great relief regarding the costs of education. But I could find no pleasure in this thought. As far as costs, I would have preferred to eke out a living with my children, even if that meant eating dry bread together, rather than carrying on a light and breezy lifestyle without them. Oh no, what would be the point of an easy life on my own when they were my whole being! And as for what ultimately mattered for their upbringing, I trusted myself to work that out as well, as long as God gave them a good, God-fearing nature. Were we not also raised by our mothers and teachers, and do we not ultimately owe it to their principles and perspectives that we have become who we are? Humility,

---

82 The *Königlich Preussische Kadettenkorps* was the German military academy for young boys from 1859 to 1892. Bensberg was one of the *Voranstalten*, or preparatory schools, where cadets received seven or more years of education before being routed into the regiments. John F. Morris, "Crucibles of Virtue and Vice: The Acculturation of Transatlantic Army Officers, 1815–1945," pp. 120–21 (Columbia Academic Commons, 2020).

tact, interactions with others, and setting a moral example, in other words everything the inner person needs, can be influenced more, in my opinion, by the parents' home than in a large institution that does less justice to each child's disposition. Then, too, such institutions present many, and often very bad, examples that are easily taken as role models by children who are not self-sufficient or fully developed, which in many cases wreck the later adult. Often enough I spoke with officers who strongly counseled against an upbringing in the cadet corps. Putting a child in such a massive establishment, which many of my good friends were encouraging me for the above cited reasons to do, ran completely counter to my nature as well.

/Oh, it was very bitter, so very bitter for me, to have to swallow this cold pill of civilization after all. Or should I now stop the journey, still only midway, and throw in the towel before the laborious work was done? Yes, had it been on my account only, I would have taken that step long ago, but the reasons you know so well called on me even now to persevere. Countless sleepless nights, which severely afflicted my already frayed nerves, dragged me so far down both physically and mentally that I finally rallied my courage and took the first step. Namely, I wrote to the noble and benevolent Emperor William I[83] and requested that my son be admitted to the cadet corps. As I wrote the letter, I comforted myself with the thought that I might well be declined, since I had asked for a full stipend, or, in the best case, be made to wait a year or more, while the child could still stay with me. I readied myself for this latter possibility by accordingly, shortly thereafter, extending my rental contract another year.

/This time, though, I miscalculated. A mere three weeks later brought the answer that the noble Emperor William I had arranged for S. to be taken up by the cadet corps. Privately, I had already been informed that the Emperor had immediately approved my request and that S. was to enter the cadet academy in Bensberg on October 1. Such a prompt resolution of my inquiry caught me completely off-guard, and the rapid enlistment did not fill me with joy, exactly the opposite. It was already September, meaning we would be separated very soon. This imminent enlistment also had a very dispiriting effect on the child, who had until then been very enamored of soldiers, the way practically all German lads are. He got quieter and quieter by the day and completely lost his robust appetite, although he was not sick. This circumstance made me even sadder, until I could not bear to watch it any longer.

/One day, I asked him if he would like us to move to Cologne, so that he could at least visit us every other week. Oh, how his face glowed when I said that.

---

[83] Kaiser Wilhelm I, German emperor from 1871 to 1888, the first to lead a united Germany.

He was full of joy, and called out repeatedly: "Please, please, do come to the Rhine!"[84] What should I do now? Follow the heart or the head? I was cleft in two, since it was obvious that moving to the Rhine right now, just after I had extended the rental contract for another year and was still picking up new pupils for lessons now and again, would be unreasonable. But the shift in the boy's disposition, on the one hand, with the certainty that he would soon leave home, and his indescribable happiness, on the other hand, that I could perhaps be nearby, haunted me day and night and left me no peace. I could not even think of a potential move, unless the landlord allowed me to sublet the apartment at my own risk, but I resolved to at least give a try.

/The landlord, who was a very kind and accommodating man—not a common occurrence in Berlin—obliged my request, for which I was very grateful. I put an advertisement in the paper, and among those who came to assess the place was a lady who appeared to suffer from some haughtiness. After having given the rooms for rental a close examination, she also wanted to examine me. Specifically, she noted that I was having to get rid of the apartment as quickly as possible, even below value. When she asked why, I told her I was hoping to leave Berlin in two weeks' time, to live at the Rhine near my son, who would be joining the cadet corps on October 1. "So, your son will be joining the cadet corps in October?," she asked in astonishment, "how is that possible, when did you apply?" I told her that it had happened just a few weeks prior. Oh my! That really got her riled: "Is your husband perhaps a senior officer?" When I responded no, she informed me that she was an officer's widow and had been waiting for one and a half years for her son to be placed in the cadet corps. And she was even more amazed, considering that admissions usually happen only in the spring.

Happily, I managed to sublet the apartment at cost. Having been notified that S. would be transferred to Potsdam as soon as a spot there became available, I thought it best to leave the furniture in Berlin and settle with the two girls in a simple furnished room in Cologne. Through the great kindness of a family we knew as friends, I left the furniture with them for free, which gave me some significant relief.

During this time, I was plagued by persistent rheumatism that I had picked up in a humid summer house. Ever since the death of my husband, I additionally suffered from a nervousness that endlessly threatened to undermine what little will to live I still possessed, and what I tried to maintain for the well-being of my children. The

---

84 The Kadettenanstalt Bensberg was housed in Schloss Bensberg, now in a suburb of Bergisch Gladbach, which lies just east of Cologne and the Rhine River.

upcoming change in our humble existence, which was forced by conditions that positioned my son in a career that was so contrary to my preference, impacted my health so negatively that it took the most strenuous effort for me to take care of even the most basic needs. The list of things to be done to dissolve the household was endless, and with only a single servant girl left, I had to handle more than my health could sustain. Even past midnight, I would sit and mend the already defective curtains and the many clothes of the children, to the point where my painful, rheumatic hands and fingers often became stiff.—

/To top it all off, this was exactly the time I lost my beloved, motherly friend in Dresden. How deeply this loss affected me, I have no way of expressing to you. My heart was pulled in the strongest way to Dresden, to accompany my most unforgettable friend to her last resting spot. But with our departure so imminent, I was deeply saddened to accept the inevitable and forgo the mere twenty-four hours needed for a trip to Dresden. With her, I lost much, so very much that was—irreplaceable! Where could I now find the great love and understanding with which this rare woman had blessed me for ten years, as she helped me lighten my load? Who else would now understand me so fully, as she did from the very first moment we met? Or stand by me, with the love and comfort of a second mother, through all the hard struggles and conflicts? Surely no one, and so her passing left me feeling immensely lonely.

/Undeservedly, and thanks only to the great mercy of the Lord, I never lacked for good friends. And yet, among them all, no one could have taken her place in my heart. Many years have passed since her death, and still to this day, I have this special feeling whenever something joyful happens. I always recall her words that she made sure to say to me so often: "Up there, darling, I will pray for you and plead for you."

Thus I remained beset with sadness for the loss of my motherly friend as I traveled at the end of September from Berlin to Cologne with my three children in a third-class railcar. Through one lady's kind recommendation, we found a temporary stay for a small sum with an officer's widow in Deutz, instead of having to go straight to a hotel. The first of October, the date on which I was to deliver S. to the Bensberger cadet corps, came much too quickly for us all. Early that morning, I rode there with him on the train, leaving both girls behind with the landlady in Deutz. The short trip progressed in silence, for each of us knew only too well how meaningful these next hours would be for us. We still had a considerable stretch to the institute on foot before we could reach our destination. With every step we took, my heart beat almost to bursting from an indescribable inner excitation. It would not have taken much for me to simply turn around with my child and go back.

/We finally reached a gate and had to wait a while, until an officer called by a soldier came to us. He was a friendly, amiable man and also offered to show me around. We followed him everywhere, me in my distracted thoughts, only barely able to follow his descriptions. On another occasion, I might have listened with more interest to all that he was so kindly showing and telling us. Today, however, nothing would have been more welcome than to have the whole academy hurled to the South Pole, out of reach for me and my child.

/Now I was told that I should go to the nearby guest house and wait for the results of the examination, which S. had to undergo before the cadets would take him in. After a while, he came to the guest house to let me know that—thank God!—he had been deemed healthy and was expected to join the line-up at a set time the very same day. Quietly and without much delight, we had our simple meal together in the hotel before returning to the academy. Once there, I handed the boy to the relevant company chief, in whose division he was to stay.

The farewell was excruciatingly difficult for both of us. Even to this day, I cannot forget the last look S. gave me. In it, I could read so much pain that he was trying not to show. My child seemed to me like a sacrifice on the altar of loyalty—to my deceased husband, his father—that I had placed there.

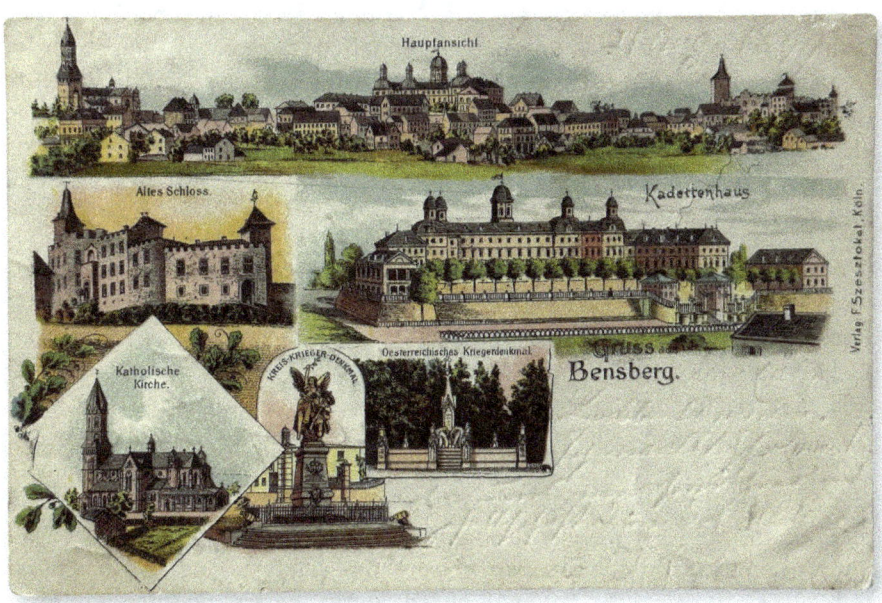

Colored postcard lithograph of Bensberg, late 1800s.

/Oh, how often had I wished to distance myself from the complicated European approach to life, where the individuality of each person only rarely finds room for its freedom of expression. Everything goes by templates here, and the individual numbers nothing more than one among millions. Out of a hundred residents, 95% are go-getters, and woe to any that take a different course, since they will simply be drowned. Everyone has to learn a certain amount to be considered capable overall, regardless of whether it is something they like or can do. Everyone is subordinated to the law and sharply monitored. Every nation here is like a big institution, and its citizens are just the wards, naturally without them realizing it. And meanwhile, the word "freedom" is in the mouth of every child. All those who do not want to stay a newspaper carrier, street sweeper, or quarry worker for their entire lives must properly equip themselves to count for something. There is no statutory or social exception for the children of an Arab mother. They must step up to the same level as the other children of true Germanic parents and traditions.

Feeling utterly dejected, I returned to Deutz to my two girls. It was now time to seek out an apartment in Cologne and let both girls go to school. As a widow of a German and living in Germany, the law obligates me to send my children to school up to a certain age. A popular girls high school that was led by an evangelical minister was recommended to me. So I went there and registered my girls for the winter semester. After extensive searching, with much back and forth on the rough cobblestone streets of Cologne, I finally succeeded in finding an inn in the old part of town, under the condition, however, that we did not have to eat in the restaurant area, but could sit in our own rooms.

/We were given two very small rooms with a view onto a narrow courtyard, so-called back rooms, to which the blessings of the sun had apparently been denied. As a result, the rooms were sullen, even on sunny days. It was one of the many gloomy days when we moved in, and I was overcome with the feeling—I do not know how—as if I had stepped into a grave that was above ground, where I would have to stay for the time being. I had no taste for the hotel rooms with better furnishings, that lay on the somewhat sunnier side, because for me they were simply—sour grapes! On the other hand, the landlord and landlady were both so good and kind, and tried to ease my way as much as they could. After two weeks, on a Sunday, S. came to Cologne on his leave to spend the day with us. Of course, he arrived in his uniform, which seemed much too large for him. My heart was truly in pain, as I saw him there in his altered attire, and since then, I can no longer stand the look of any soldier's uniform.[85]

The days I spent in Cologne in the two sun-starved rooms were often very bleak. I always counted the hours until my girls came home from school, since the two narrow rooms felt so cramped, oh so very cramped, to the point of suffocation. Only in their presence could I forget some of my misery. Every morning when they went to school, I was overcome with a wave of indescribable loneliness and isolation, often making me feel like I was in a prison. Under these conditions, it was also inevitable that my health would increasingly deteriorate, although my nerves suffered the most. The doctor I sought out for advice urgently recommended a change of air. That was easy to say, but where was I to go in the cold winter, especially when the children had to be in school? What could not be handled by quinine and bromide,[86] of which I had to take unbelievably large quantities, would simply have to go unaddressed.

At some point during the winter, we were invited to Bensberg for an evening presentation by the cadets. I went with the girls, and we were happy to see S. again, since he was allowed to visit us only a few hours every two weeks. On this evening, though, I felt especially sorry for the boy. I did not see much of him during the opening presentation, which he was required to participate in, but later noticed how quiet and listless he was about everything. I could tell that he suffered greatly from homesickness and still had not gotten used to life in the corps. But there was nothing to be done at that moment, despite my deepest regret. It was simply something to get through.

If there was anything to console me while here in Cologne in my dank back rooms, then it was the warm attention of a couple I had the joy of getting to know through a recommendation. As had already so often been my fate, in a life that was anything but roses strewn on my path, here, too, I found good and noble souls that sought to ease my way as best they could. I owe this family much gratitude for so much good, including the comfortable hours that I spent in their house, which distracted me from my own pondering and brooding. Alas, there is nothing harder than being far, far away from your own when having to endure the blows of fate that come from on high and sometimes also from the hands of men. It is only in foreign lands that one discovers what one has lost in the homeland.

---

85 Likely around the time this was being written, probably around the turn of the century, the author's daughter Rosa became engaged to Captain Martin Gottlob Reinhold Troemer, who as her husband continued his military career to become a Major and then Major General.

86 See footnote 74 above on quinine. Bromide was also a popular sedative in the nineteenth century, until its use as a calming agent was discontinued because of its long-term toxic effects.

/Because I felt so extremely unhappy, and because I could only write what I thought and felt, my letter correspondence became harder and harder, which led to steady complaints from my friends and acquaintances. I therefore burrowed into myself and often let months go by before I could get myself to respond to even one letter. A prisoner could not have yearned for freedom more than I did here, although I was completely free like all others to move around as I wished. My thoughts became darker and darker, and life seemed to become less and less bearable by the day. Death alone could have freed me from my agony, and yet I never feared it more than when I thought of my small children, who would have ended up with strangers. And this fear, fed by my bad health, often persisted for days and nights. In this state, it seemed that winter would never end.

/When spring came, I followed my doctor's advice and went to the mountains near the Rhine. This stay in the countryside initially seemed to do me some good, but unfortunately, it did not take long before I felt myself getting weaker and weaker until I could no longer move. Oh, I will never forget what impression this condition made on my two little girls. The summoned doctor was no longer able to feel a pulse at my wrist, and only a weak one at my neck. I was told that I absolutely needed to go to an invigorating seaside resort to overcome this abnormal weakness. But these doctor's orders were very problematic for me because it meant a totally unanticipated and unwelcome expenditure. My greatest worry was that I had no hope of taking all three children on this prescribed seaside trip, since the boy, who had looked so very emaciated and wretched in the corps, was due home just then to join us for his summer vacation. Of all three children, he was in the greatest need of recuperation, so that, bearing a heavy heart, I decided to take only him and left the two girls as boarders with a family we knew.

For obvious reasons, because I wanted to live and move about normally, I always, as a rule, withheld my birth name when registering in hotels, so I could live in peace and be spared the often very irksome gaze of the public. But such times unfortunately did not last long, since a carelessly addressed letter already sufficed to make my situation uncomfortable. Normally, I asked my friends and acquaintances to leave my birth name off the address, so that I could move around undetected in the summer season, for at least a short while. Here, in this remote area near the Rhine, a letter addressed to my birth name proved a bit costly. We had been in the hotel already two to three weeks when a letter arrived with the afternoon post, whose address contained the telltale word from my birth name. Because the innkeeper always delivered the mail to me personally, he would naturally have read the address. That same evening—shortly after supper—I was already made to feel the consequences. The innkeeper wrote me a very polite letter and quite simply informed me that he would from then on be kindly raising the hotel rate to such-and-such amount. This heavy-handed form of extortion was rather too blatant, especially considering that the hotel was still mostly empty, aside from the occasional Sunday visits, since the season was too early for the usual summer guests.

When the prescribed resort trip was over, I returned to Berlin, and S. returned to the cadet academy. Upon my arrival in the German capital, I was legally required to register myself anew with the regimented police. I did so, but who can describe my indignation when a policeman stood in front of my door one morning, wishing to speak to me personally. "Are you the princess from Zanzibar?" he began. Totally surprised, I responded positively, and he continued didactically, "You have three children, is that not correct? Two girls and a boy?" When I again responded positively to these additional, still inexplicable questions, he pressed further: "Well, why did you register only your two daughters and not your son with the police, and where is your son?" Imagine that!

/Now I could really see how far this lauded freedom actually goes. The police simply give themselves the right, without any solicitation, to meddle in family affairs. The fact that I bridled at such patronizing interference may well be due to my uncivilized nature, considering that, to my astonishment, the locals do not find this type of intervention to be anything of note. For us, such a question could at most be posed to a female slave, but never to a free person. From then on, I would not have been at all surprised if a policeman had come into our home from time to time to gather information about our food, clothes, activities, and social circles, to also exert some control over these things. I could not help but feel that I was in a strictly regulated institution, rather than a great nation state. Everything is so rigidly organized and maintained off a fixed template that even the very smallest deviation deserves punishment. Everything and anything is governed by statute, and the sections of the latter are as numerous as the grains of sand on the shore.

Our new apartment in Berlin was on Potsdamer Street, not far from the Botanical Garden. It had four tiny rooms, one of which had two windows, the others only one each. The doors were all tight and narrow, but the place was otherwise bright and cheery. We had sun in the mornings and afternoons, which was delightful for me. Life reverted to its usual routine. The two girls returned to their former school, and I took care of all the household matters, such as cooking, filling the lamps, dusting the furniture, and sewing and mending, with only the help of a so-called morning woman that often came in for a few hours before noon. If we wanted to take a walk in the afternoon after school, we locked the front door and took the key. When we got back home, I would always be ill at ease and check under the beds and sofas to make sure no uninvited guest had slipped into the empty apartment while we were away, which is not a rare event in a big city like Berlin.

/Quietly and withdrawn, I lived entirely for the children, as I never felt comfortable anywhere without them. We were always invited together because people knew I did not like to go out on my own. And to let them go out alone made me much too scared, since for me, the crosswalks in the lively streets were forever a source of enduring fear.[87]

---

[87] Consider the manner in which the author's husband died. See the translator's essay "On Fear" on pages 135–39 below.

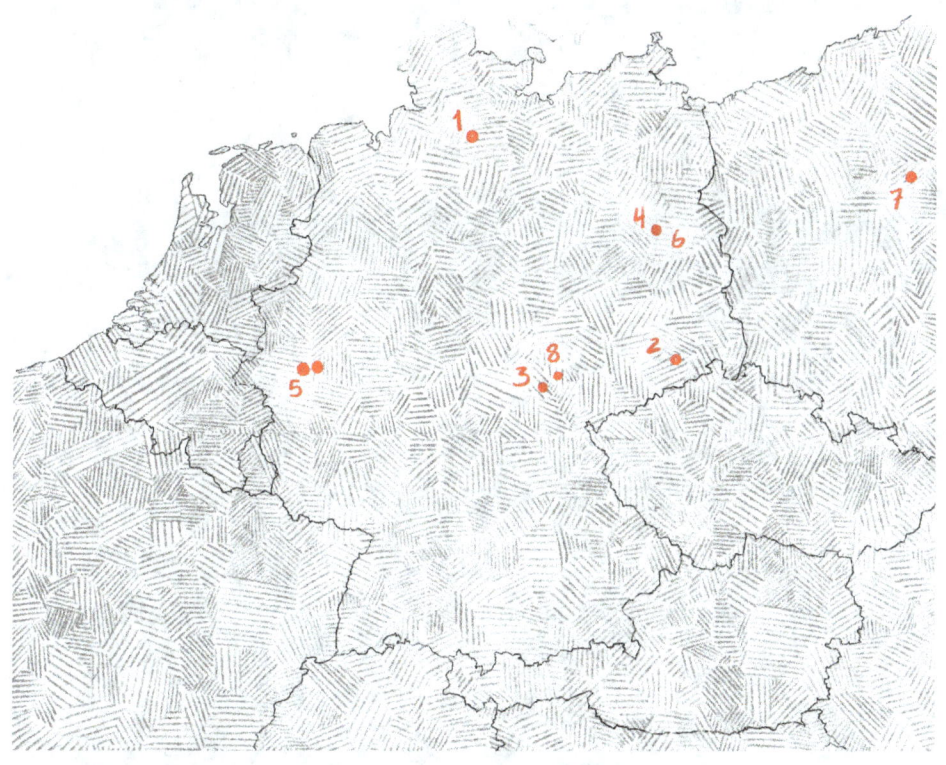

1. Hamburg 1867–1872
2. Dresden 1873–1877
3. Rudolstadt 1877–1879
4. Berlin 1879–1881
5. Cologne/Bensberg 1881–1882
6. Berlin 1882–1888
7. Bromberg (Bydgoszcz) 1914–1920
8. Jena 1920–1924

Map of places in Germany where the author lived (showing current borders).

The author with daughter Antonie and her husband with son Said in 1870.

The author around 1871 alone with her three children, Said, Rosa, and Antonie.

The author in fall 1884 with Rosa, Said, and Antonie.

The author sometime after 1885 with Antonie, Said, and Rosa.

ON COLLABORATION

Sayyida Salme was never schooled to write, and yet, she published a two-volume book totaling 400 pages of beautiful, animated prose in a language, alphabet, and script she did not learn until her mid-twenties. How was that possible? Some reviewers at the time speculated that the *Memoiren* had been ghostwritten, doubting the author could have come up with such an elegant and extensive account by herself. But we can now see from the historical record, from her handwritten edits of the *Memoiren* and especially from the hundreds of handwritten pages of the *Letters*, that this is very much hers. These documents are proof positive of her original authorship. They not only showcase her language ability after two decades in Germany, but also reveal the insightful and artful writing style as her own.

As a descendant of Rosa, her youngest daughter, I also take delight in knowing that Sayyida Salme had support within the family. Not to take anything away from the author's creation and imprimatur, we can see that Rosa and her mother worked together. It is lovely to recognize Rosa's even script alongside her mother's energetic strokes, as witness to this mother-daughter collaboration. Although we do not have early drafts of the *Memoiren*, the subsequent hand-marked edited version[88] and especially the two drafts of the *Nachtrag*[89] show the family interaction. The *Letters*, on the other hand, are different. With the posthumous discovery of the original manuscript, there was no opportunity for direct collaboration, but the children nonetheless made sure a typewritten, grammatically upgraded version would be available to us today.[90]

Studying this record has been both inspiring and validating for me. How special that I have been able to undertake this project with my own mother! In our shared endeavor of publishing first the *Memoirs*, and now the *Letters*, our roles are reversed. The writing is mine, but I have greatly benefited from

---

[88] Leiden University Libraries Digital Collection at NINO SR 613 a-b. For reasons I explain, these edits were brought into my newly translated version of the *Memoirs*. See my essay "On Translating," *Memoirs*, p. 254.
[89] The *Nachtrag zu meinen Memoiren* manuscript exists in three versions in the Leiden University Libraries: first, Sayyida Salme's original handwritten draft (Or. 27.135 A1); second, Rosa's original handwritten rewrite (Or. 27.135 A2); and third, a final typewritten version appearing right behind *Briefe nach der Heimat* (Or. 6281). The *Nachtrag* (meaning addendum) was intended to supplement the already-published *Memoiren*, presumably as an add-on for a re-publication that, however, never occurred. An English version is available in E. van Donzel, pp. 511–22.
[90] As noted, Leiden University Libraries Or. 6281.

On Collaboration

my mother's fastidious and tireless review of my translations, comparing every word and phrase to the original German over many drafts, along with her ability to decipher the old German script, while also sharing her highly nuanced comments regarding meaning, placement, tone—all contributing to what we have jointly sought to make a most authentic rendering of Sayyida Salme's voice. Here we are, repeating the intense ritual of mother-daughter literary bonding with just a generation in between. I could not be more grateful.

Others have contributed to this book as well. The staff at the Leiden University Libraries, especially the front desk of the Special Collections room, gave us great support on multiple visits. They were very exacting on the rules, as custodians of these irreplaceable archives, something we truly appreciate. Also in Leiden, Anita Keizers, subject librarian of the Ancient Near East and our friend at the Netherlands Institute for the Near East (NINO), has been particularly generous in sharing her interest, expertise, and enthusiasm over the years. Extended family has played a meaningful role as well, above all Antonie's branch through Alexander von Brand, as well as Sarah Maria (née Ruete) Rothenbücher's branch through Ursula Luther, both of whom have warmly supported the effort with their family collections and memories. I also appreciate the support provided by B.K. Atrostic, Lark Bergwin-Anderson, Eija Pehu, Kathleen Ridolfo, and Alexander von Brand with their pre-publication reviews of this book.

We know ourselves to be part of a larger, international community of individuals who have supported and respected the memory of Sayyida Salme over the years. I can take this opportunity to thank all those who have come to appreciate her extraordinary life. That includes, among many in a long list, the Sultan Qaboos Cultural Center in Washington, DC, particularly under the leadership of Kathleen Ridolfo; Said el-Gheithy with his groundbreaking "Behind the Veil" exhibit in London in 2001 and his Princess Salme Museum in Zanzibar today; the Arabia Felix team in München led by Georg Popp; the German-Omani Association led by Wolfgang Zimmerman; Godwin Kornes, whose research focuses on Antonie Brandeis; Hielke van der Wijk, the creator and collector behind the remarkable www.omanisilver.com; Nasser Alrashdi, in Beijing's Oman Embassy, who gave me a copy of his booklet of selected Sayyida Salme quotes; and Michael Bauer and his family, who are related to us through Rudolph Said-Ruete and reached out to us many years ago in their own ancestral quest.

Of great importance is the tremendous work done by Professor Emeri van Donzel, who spent much of his lifetime exploring and preserving Sayyida Salme's life and writings, culminating in his remarkably comprehensive book, *An Arabian Princess Between Two Worlds*. Also of immense value is the extensive work done by Ambassador Heinz Schneppen, reflected in his German publication of *Briefe nach der Heimat*, which has similarly enriched our understanding of the contours and context of Sayyida Salme's legacy. We can also be grateful for two other books that revived the story after a century and set the stage: Professor Annegret Nippa's seminal contribution in 1989 when she reached back and took the bold and consequential step of republishing the German *Memoiren* with her thoughtful commentary in *Leben im Sultanspalast*, along with G.S.P. Freeman-Grenville's well-researched and thoroughly annotated reissuance of the original English translation in 1981.

In addition to all this, I am very happy again to give great thanks to my steadfast book publishing team, which has seen me through every book I have written so far and somehow always manages to make time for me: for copyediting, Lauri Scherer, and for proofreading, Bob Anderson, of LSF Editorial, and for graphic design, Joe Bernier of Bernier Graphics. Ever responsive to everything I send them, they have been excellent companions on this splendid journey.

And finally, I embrace my dear son Max, to whom I, like Sayyida Salme, give my "thousand love." He has been witness to my efforts every step of the way, as my companion and cheerleader, my source of second opinions and illustrations. He is my ultimate inspiration to create for the next generation.

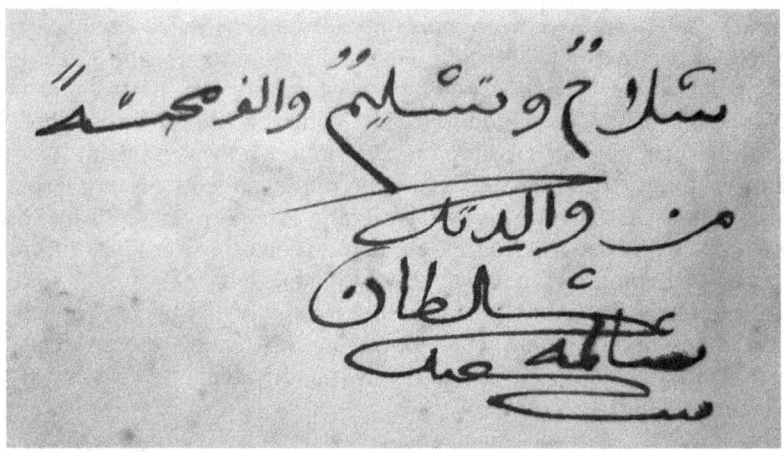

To her son: "Peace and a thousand love from your mother."

ON FREEDOM

It is tempting to read Sayyida Salme's story with a modern lens and see an arc of freedom. This Arabian princess, tied down by patriarchal culture and religious mores, unshackled herself by riding a Christian marriage into Western enlightenment and opportunity—or so this story goes. It is a narrative her *Memoirs* seem to set up, and there may be some truth to it.[91] There are, however, counternarratives that also ring true, and wrinkles that undercut such a facile, pro-Western view. With *Letters to the Homeland*, we get a different lens.

That the life of an Omani princess in Zanzibar was strictly regimented, severely limited, and heavily supervised is clear. Sayyida Salme lets us know, with some envy, that life at the top of the hierarchy was far more constrained for women than life at the bottom. Princesses could not show themselves to outside men without full covering, while common women were, by contrast, remarkably free.[92] The Sayyidas had all the privileges of being royal, but at a price, with almost complete sequestration from the male world and subjugation to the confining palace rules.

I have always thought it understandable that a free spirit like Sayyida Salme, who as a child enjoyed gun shooting and cock fighting (becoming "half an Amazon"), ran with the boys, and pranked with the best of them,[93] would find it difficult to simply become the demure wife of a designated husband relegated to a woman's world of bobbins and lace. Where to channel all that energy, intelligence, and self-confidence? Zanzibar seemed to afford her some latitude even after she became a young lady, especially out in the countryside where she could roam free(r) on her plantation and by the seashore, beyond the watchful eye of the harem and broader society. That is, until she was called back into the city, where her expansive spirit and society's tightening expectations were bound to collide.

Without a father or mother to channel their daughter into a straight and respectable lane, by encouraging a suitable husband and smoothing out the edges, Sayyida Salme had probably become a loose cog in a tightly wound

---

91 Some have even likened this story to recent attempts by other Arab princesses, like Sheikha Latifa bint Mohammed Al Maktoum, to escape their families, but those comparisons fall short. Sayyida Salme never sought to leave her family and was, in fact, devastated by having to lose her family.
92 "[S]ince such coverings are so unpleasant and disfiguring, high-ranking women avoid going out by day and frequently enough envy the Bedouin women who forsake such requirements. If such a Bedouin woman is asked whether she is embarrassed to go out without the required coverings, she will respond: 'Such rules are only for the rich, they were not created for poor women!'" *Memoirs*, pp. 108–09.
93 *Memoirs*, pp. 19, 30–31.

society. She normally should have been screwed back into place and married off before the age of twenty-two. It did not help that the family rift, and her landing on the wrong side of the divide, put a wrench into once functioning machinery. What a remarkably smooth ride the family, indeed the whole island and two countries, had had under their great patriarch, Sayyid Said bin Sultan.

Not that any of what became of our protagonist was inevitable.[94] Sayyida Salme made choices—she exercised her free will and took deliberate steps[95]—in opting to exit her clearly defined box and engage with a European man. That is, of course, the point. She allowed herself the luxury of self-expression beyond the point that society could bear.[96]

Part of a 1928 letter sent by the author's son to correct the record.[97]

---

94 Unless you put it all up to fate, a topic I consider in my "On Fate" essay in the *Memoirs*, pp. 239–42.
95 We can marvel at how deliberate her moves were once she decided to follow her love. In addition to sending many of her belongings to Germany on one of Heinrich's ships (E. van Donzel, p. 16), Sayyida Salme sold her property. I was stunned when Thomas "Dodie" McDow showed me one of his research finds: an official deed of sale from Sayyida Salme to her husband-to-be, in which she transferred her plantation estate, recorded by the clerk as "Kyajeenee," to Heinrich for $12,600 Maria Theresa thalers in late June 1866, not long after confirming her pregnancy and two months before leaving the island. Dodie's hard work in the Zanzibar and other archives resulted in his excellent book, *Buying Time: Debt and Mobility in the Western Indian Ocean* (2018).
96 That Zanzibari society could bear at least some transgressions seems enticingly clear from a phrase that Zanzibaris themselves told us came from David Livingstone: In Zanzibar "nothing is as it seems."
97 Quoting: "October 14th 1928, Sir Arthur Hardinge, Travellers' Club: My attention was called to your book A DIPLOMATIST in the EAST. On page 88 you mention my mother Emily Ruete. May I point out that she was not "carried off" by my father to Europe. She left Zanzibar on her own will on board H.M.S. "Highflyer" for Aden, was joined there several months later by my father, where they were married in the English Chapel, my mother being converted to Christian faith before...."

In theory, then, she ripped through the chains of misogyny and spread her wings, buoyed by love, for a life of free-to-be-me. But we are missing the punchline if we stop there and fail to read beyond the *Memoirs*. The *Letters* crucially continue the story. In this German sequel to her Zanzibar upbringing, scene after scene unspools a life in the West that proved anything but free. The German cultural norms were not only unfamiliar, but even anathema to her deep-seated values—and thus all the more constricting.

It is a tormented account. How to truly express herself when language—not just the words, but even the meanings behind them—proved such a barrier? How to freely interact when the weight of being the mascot and measure for all Arab society bore down on her shoulders? How to step up to her best self when she was constantly objectified, sexualized, mocked, and othered? This is often the immigrant's lament, but in her day and age it was especially acute, and in her case especially extreme, both in her face and behind her back. Sayyida Salme lets us know that the demands to fit in were oppressively incessant—and of course, she wanted to please her husband and fit in. But where she could not or would not adapt, especially after her buffer and protector was gone, she was either left out or sought refuge within. Both cases left her more and more withdrawn and alone. In some ways, apparently, the best way for her to fit in was to opt out.[98]

How tempting to imagine where her life might have gone had she been free to break into the Omani patriarchy. At the end of her first volume of the *Memoirs*, she tells the wonderful story of her great aunt who governed Oman at a crucial time, although Sayyida Moza never made it into the official narrative or family tree.[99] Thank goodness we have this written account! For her own part, Sayyida Salme came as close as she could when she served as scribe, financier, and co-plotter of the aborted coup. But even if the coup had succeeded, there is little chance that a promotion to a government posting would have followed.

---

98 This disconnect pursued Sayyida Salme as she moved from place to place in Germany, five towns in ten years, mostly driven by economics, but also social dynamics. Tellingly, after she finally dead-ended in Zanzibar in 1888, and no longer needed to shepherd her children in Germany, her next move was to a liminal space in the Middle East. There she stayed more than twenty years, a few years in Jaffa and the rest in Beirut, this cosmopolitan, mixed-culture, mixed-religion city—more of a "both/and" than "either/or" kind of place, where she could more readily be her composite, not conflicted, self.

99 *Memoirs*, p. 106. Sayyida Moza bint Ahmed was a daughter of the original Al Bu Said ruler, Ahmed bin Said, and her own daughter, Sayyida Azze bint Seif, became the first principal wife of the underage nephew she brought to power, Sayyid Said bin Sultan. Little is written about Sayyida Moza, but another good description appears in P.J. Ochs II, *Maverick Guide to Oman*, pp. 111–13 (2000). See also the family tree created by the author's son Rudolph, Leiden University Libraries Or. 27.135 E1, and the online Royal Ark compilation at Oman, Tab 3.

In this counternarrative of "freedom" gone foul, we might ask: What does it mean to be free? The hills and valleys of the United States, where I live, ring out with chants and rants of freedom. We are the "land of the free," and being free is a litmus test for being American. But the real test is recognizing that freedom does not operate in isolation. It is always embedded within society, and almost always a trade-off. Indeed, since time immemorial, one man's freedom has been another woman's yoke. Across the country, there is no counting the many ways freedom here creates or perpetuates limits—free to restrict abortions, free to ban books, free to deny medical care, free to impose religious practices. Even as America's exceptional freedom is exalted, restrictions rise.[100]

Now I am speaking *my* peace, so to speak—contributing my piece, the way Sayyida Salme was emboldened to do.[101] In this context, I would be remiss not to pick up the topic of slavery, where she took the freedom to express her views—her local concerns, drawn from direct experience—and for which she has been amply criticized. Even where this criticism is justified,[102] she also asserted what we can understand today: Freedom from bondage is only part of what we owe humanity.[103] Sayyida Salme called upon her audience—if it would listen—to consider the conditions of European factory workers, baggage carriers, stone cutters, and Siberian miners, or the fate of young conscripts being led off to war, all of whom were in bonded conditions, often much worse off than slaves living under Arab social tenets in Zanzibar.[104]

Taking a closer look, where did Sayyida Salme's leap into freedom leave her? This is where, I think, the *Letters* are the most instructive for us today.

---

100 Could the author have been more prescient? "It also seemed to me, over and over again, that most people, despite having written the word "freedom" on their flags, are hardly inclined to give others the same degree of freedom." (above at page 74)

101 "Having been born and bred in the East, I am in a position to set down the unvarnished reflection of my Oriental experiences—of its high life and its low life—to speak of many peculiarities, and lift the veil from things that are always hidden from profane eyes. This, I hope, will constitute the main value of my book, and my object will have been fully gained if I have been able to contribute my share, and above all, if I have succeeded in removing many misconceptions and distortions current about the East." *Memoirs*, Afterword, p. 229.

102 See my essay "On Controversy" in the *Memoirs*, pp. 243–51.

103 I am struck by Sayyida Salme's biting humor when she recounts what happened after the British-held slaves on Zanzibar were freed: "Meanwhile, the humane emissaries of the anti-slavery associations went silent. They had accomplished their goal and freed the poor victims from slavery, a status unworthy of any human being. What was now to become of these slaves was no longer their concern. Or at most, their ladies, to complete the nonsense, knit wool stockings for the residents of the hot South." *Memoirs*, pp. 165–66.

104 On the wide variety of slave experiences in East Africa, see Thomas Vernet, "East Africa: Slave Migrations," in *The Encyclopedia of Global Human Migration*, ed. Immanuel Ness (2013). Said a Captain Mignan of Oman in 1825: "My residence in Arabia has convinced me that a slave may be perfectly happy; and I feel persuaded that his condition, when compared with most of the peasantry of Europe, is in every respect the more fortunate of the two." Excerpted in R. Said-Ruete, *Said bin Sultan (1791–1856)—Ruler of Oman and Zanzibar: His Place in the History of Arabia and East Africa*, p. 158 (1929).

On Freedom

Her choice of husband, her willingness to transgress, her resolve to keep going and not turn back—these became reinforcing layers in direct decisions she made over and over again, at her moments of greatest distress when the harsh reality bore down on her. The answer is, page after page if we can absorb it all: It left her in a deeper sinkhole than she could ever have imagined.[105]

Who knows, if her husband had survived and the two had thrived, if an unimaginable tragedy had not followed her unthinkable travesty, what counterfactual she might have had? Or if she had never even met her Heinrich? I will let someone else write the thesis of the many ways nineteenth-century women in the East had more agency, room, and opportunity than their peers in the West, a topic Sayyida Salme herself raised. Someone else may well consider the many ways Sayyida Salme escaped one set of limits only to land in another set of constraints that kept her from being free—in relation to society, her God, and herself.

The challenge is apparent. In the enlightened West, we like to think of freedom as quintessential to self-expression and success. But in Sayyida Salme's trajectory, especially when compared with her slave mother Djilfidan, we see that freedom is no free-for-all, no panacea. It takes at least some sense of security to be our best selves. The great flourishing of societies in history comes during periods of great stability. How else to understand the amazing Omani story under a Sultanate that has lasted longer than the American republic and yet is a monarchy, under much benevolent leadership over the generations, but not a freedom-loving democracy?

As I read our author's story, it took only one generation to transition from slavery to royalty, from *surie* Djilfidan to princess Salme, under the generous rules of progeny within Omani-Arab society. This leap from deep down on the totem pole up to the very top, from being a slave to owning slaves, hundreds if not a thousand slaves, pivoted on a single birth. But as we turn the page and move from the *Memoirs* to the *Letters*, it also becomes clear that it took less than a generation to go from the height of security and well-being to deep poverty and privation. Compared to her mother, social status went way up for Sayyida Salme, but then freedom intervened, and her social welfare went way down.

---

105 In her own words: "A prisoner could not have yearned for freedom more than I did here, although I was completely free like all others to move around as I wished. My thoughts became darker and darker, and life seemed to become less and less bearable by the day." (above at page 118)

We need not caricature this as an East-to-West fable. Clearly, a host of specific circumstances converged in the case of Sayyida Salme. But even so, it is hard not to see this descent from stable security to insecure freedom as emblematic of the closed cocoon of the harem (already a privileged place, even for the enslaved *sarari*)[106] vs. the brutal openness of the nineteenth-century Western industrialist, capitalist, consumerist revolution. There was not much of a German safety net back then,[107] and German society did not much know what to do with a far-flung princess, an Arab turned Christian, an exotic. It is perhaps just an isolated case, as opposed to a parable for her or our times, but still incredible to see how Sayyida Salme lost almost everything by exerting her freedom—everything but her dear children, a trace of royalty, and whatever she managed to salvage and build.

I suggested in my essay "On Fate" accompanying the *Memoirs* that fate is the foil of free will.[108] Here I will ask if freedom is the foil of security. The more choices Sayyida Salme took on, choosing even the unthinkable and unpardonable, the less stable and secure her position became—indeed, the more vulnerable she became to the vagaries of life, the machinations of detractors, the whims of custodians, the heft of government bureaucracies (a "pawn" on the colonial chessboard), and the insensitivities of the insensitive. Hers is an especially stark story, spanning the extremes from royal privilege to roiling poverty, but may still contain a kernel of recognition for all of us. Who has not seen that greater agency can bestow power, but standing alone can be disempowering? Maybe we are as strong as our connectedness. Maybe the allure of freedom is best tamed by the advantages of community.

Or maybe the lesson is also more direct. No one should have to self-exile to self-express. If someone seeks to act freely to be themselves, that need not imperil our own sense of self and security and provoke a negating response. We can strive to be more tolerant than that. Today, mostly we do, but only mostly.

---

106 Notably, the Arab harem afforded both protection and eventual freedom, in that Djilfidan became free upon Sayyid Said's death. But even then, she continued to benefit from the comfort of the harem and was amply provided for with the plantations and funds inherited by her royal daughter.

107 Germany did not even become a unified republic until 1871, after Sayyida Salme had arrived in Hamburg. Because her husband died in 1870, he was never a German citizen, only a citizen of the Free Hanseatic City of Hamburg. When Emily Ruete took the official step as a *Bürgerwitwe* (resident widow) in 1872, she was named a citizen of both the State of Hamburg and the German Reich.

108 *Memoirs*, p. 240. Simply put, what is ordained by fate is not a result of free will; what is decided by free will is not due to fate.

ON FEAR

After reading *Letters to the Homeland*, one might hypothesize that freedom is correlated to fear. The more Sayyida Salme loosed her moorings, the more vulnerable she became, the less secure, the more she had to fear. Perhaps this is too speculative of me, as I tread on the thin ice of conjecture. The clues I find are liable to crack under the weight of my presumptions, and I do not mean to distract from her own voice or descend into fictional musings. But I cannot resist saying a few empathetic words about fear, her fear.

I start with the last line of the *Letters*, which grips me, especially her last word: fear. And thus her long discourse ends abruptly—wasn't there more to recount as her struggles continued? But as I sit with her last thought, I find it circles back, and back again, and could not be more poignant.

When she finished, did she simply run out of time, ink, or interest? She does not put a stamp on it and say "I have concluded, here is a nice little bow to wrap it all up, now you have my story." No, there is no finishing touch, no rounded edge; the ink ends, her pen lifts, and she is done. This is the end of her long run, her uphill climb, her marathon. She gave us what she had, and then maybe, just maybe, a rush of emotions, a flood of memories wiped her pen clear off the page. I am done.

At first glance, she takes her leave with a quotidian thought—watch out at crosswalks—that she could have buried somewhere in her long account that has no chapters, paragraphs, or even indentations. But it was her last thought. And I think, if we connect the dots, she did leave us with something more meaningful:

> Quietly and withdrawn, I lived entirely for the *children*, as I never felt comfortable anywhere without them. We were always invited together because people knew I did not like to go out on my own. And to let them go out *alone* made me much too scared, since for me, the crosswalks in the *lively streets* were forever a source of *enduring* fear. (above at page 120, emphasis added)

Thus ends the story, and it is perhaps a bit odd that crosswalks would be so scary, even if she feared nothing more than harm to her children,[109] or was projecting her own fears onto them. But now let us consider her words—specifically, the four italicized keywords—more closely:

Keyword *alone.*

Sayyida Salme refers to her children, but she could just as well be referring to herself, as she says "on my own." For this is what she had become—quiet and withdrawn—a different form of sequestration than the one in which she had grown up. So many forces had compounded to make her alone; being alone was both a result of and remedy for a treacherous world. We might ask, for example, in all her dire scenarios, where were her in-laws? Where were her good friends? I do not have the answers, but perhaps it was some combination of her not knowing what to do with them, and them not knowing what to do with her. Sayyida Salme gives us cascades of examples where she was othered or ogled, as an object of fascination, even titillation—verily, a victim of the Oriental stereotypes she wrote her *Memoirs* to dispel. Others may have supported her up to a point, but she was probably socially shunned, at least by wives who did not need an attractive, exotic, single woman floating around. Even today, couples invite couples. It was hard enough when her husband was still alive, but how could she have felt at ease on her own without the social currency—language, culture, custom—of a Western upbringing? Exposing herself in public invited danger for herself and others. Keeping to herself afforded security for herself and her children.

Keyword *enduring.*

Unabated, exacerbated, this was her journey without respite. Some things cannot be undone, and consequences may take their endless toll. In her case, we see that self-expression beyond the bounds of social acceptance did not go unpunished, and exile was not for the faint of heart. Indeed, there is hardly a more moving passage than Sayyida Salme's anguished inner lament as she and her husband headed to the train in Marseille. It was just the beginning of her physical and metaphysical journey from East to West, Orient to Occident,

---

[109] This greatest fear even kept her alive: "Death alone could have freed me from my agony, and yet I never feared it more than when I thought of my small children, who would have ended up with strangers. And this fear, fed by my bad health, often persisted for days and nights. In this state, it seemed the winter would never end." (above at page 118)

South to North, the first steps that led to all the rest. Fearful and conflicted, she nonetheless persisted and endured:

> As we drove from our hotel to the train station, I was gripped by such an unfamiliar fear that I would have preferred to scream out loud. I had the feeling as though, from this moment on, my homeland was being pulled ever further from me, and all the bridges were crashing in behind me. The cry of my soul for you turned into a thousand voices from my beloved island, all seemingly calling to me in unison: "Do not go any further, better to return again!" I fought a terrible fight within myself. Like an automaton, I stepped into the train that would now seek to take me, as quickly as possible, to an unknown land, to total strangers, as if I was in the greatest hurry to reach my future destination. And so we kept on riding toward the North. (above at page 6)

Keyword *lively streets*.

And here is the kicker. We could take her last lines as an unremarkable concern of a typical mother of young children, or we could look just below the surface and recall how the author lost her husband. This is not just any crosswalk, nor simply the bustling streets of a hustling city; this is a deep and searing memory, one that today would likely be diagnosed as PTSD. It is the trauma of seeing her husband lie there with a crushed body and delirious mind, the last wisp of life draining from him. He was her all. The year was 1870. She had hardly begun to settle—and the latest traffic innovation, the horse tram riding on rails, was new and exciting. Hamburg, as part of the vanguard, had inaugurated this form of transport only a few years earlier in 1867. Sprightly young men, including Heinrich at 31, had no reason to fear as they sprung lightly off the moving platform into the streets to reach their destinations ....

Keyword *children*.

Even in the *Memoirs*, Sayyida Salme tells us how devoted Arab mothers are to their children. She also had a good role model in her own mother, Djilfidan, who lost her first daughter early on and clearly loved Salme above all. This closeness was intensified, if possible, when Sayyida Salme had her own children. If there was one thing that never wavered, one thing that was her truth and purpose on earth, it was her responsibility to and love for her children. I, like many mothers, know what it feels like to be grounded and centered in this miracle of creation. And yet, my single motherhood has no comparison to the circumstances and complications that made Sayyida Salme devoted beyond measure. For her, it is like a current that circles around and around, that never lets loose, but surfaces over and over again in her discourse—her fear of not making it, of not being able to follow through—in this deliberate and defiant, even delusional, choice to raise her family in Germany in her husband's memory and honor. Does she define it, or does it define her? She is anchored to this precept even when the sea feels bottomless. As though she has no agency or identity left, but for her children, the only tie that still binds.

Such maximal attachment might be enough to instill an almost obsessive fear of loss, but there is more. Her husband was not the only loss that rocked her world. She also carried an earlier loss, a private loss, a devastation she apparently never spoke of, much less wrote about—that most unnatural loss of a parent losing a child. When she despaired about crashing bridges, she was mere hours from this calamity. Her first son, little Heinrich, born in December of the prior year, died en route, somewhere between Lyon and Paris. Retribution for sin, opprobrium for audacity, the wrath of God?—what all she might have felt. It was surely a defining moment in the life of a new wife and new mother, too painful, too taboo, too unspeakable. As far as we know, not even her children ever knew of this sibling they had lost. With the passing of her husband, the only one who knew the trauma of her sacrifice, even the shared memory was lost. Today we know the truth.[110] Once the reader becomes aware, the silence is deafening.

———•·———

What we may fear the most is the loss of what we love the most, what defines us. To lose the core of one's being is to face an abyss, enough to turn on the Almighty, as Sayyida Salme admits to doing in her darkest moment (above at page 55). With her losses, she also had plenty to fear in a world that left little room for being different. As she says of life in the West, "[W]oe to any that take a different course, since they will simply be drowned" (above at page 116). But if we care to read deeper, her last sentence reveals her essence. Here is a proxy for her daily triage to overcome her traumas, to find and make her way on the crosswalks of those all too lively streets.

---

110 Heinz Schneppen, who served as German Ambassador to Tanzania from 1993 to 1996, retrieved a record of the infant Heinrich's death from the Hamburg *Staatsarchiv*, while doing research for his 1999 publication of the author's *Briefe nach der Heimat*. H. Schneppen, *Briefe*, p. 174.

On Fear

I choose to read her last sentence as an acknowledgment of fear that is in fact an affirmation of love. If we know the back story, it tells us that her losses—of her homeland, her family and friends, her firstborn, her husband—would not prevail. She would find her way, alone, on her own, with and for her children, determined to protect and persevere—as she did. She ends on a note of fear, but in a paragraph that starts with love. In all her writing, I hear her say that fear is no match for love. Not from the shores of Zanzibar, nor on the seas of life.

ON INSPIRATION

Why should writings by someone who came from circumstances beyond our imagining, who grew up in a distant thousand-and-one-nights setting more than a century ago, whose original publication appeared in an old and outdated German script—why should the *Memoirs* and now also the *Letters* be of any interest, much less inspiration, today? Why, indeed, has there even been an uptick of interest in the last decades? I will not provide the catalogue of reasons here, but just offer a smattering of thoughts, like a trail of crumbs to entice further travel, as we journey with Sayyida Salme's writings toward greater awareness and understanding.

It is often said that Sayyida Salme was ahead of her time, and being the first Arab woman to ever publish a book already puts her in that category. People remark on her proclivity to do the unthinkable, and also her ability to question social constructs and challenge common tropes. She had her own notions and tested limits, not necessarily because she wanted to, but often because of what she had become: an infidel, a single mother, a pawn, a caricature. But what made her so prescient, I would say, is her uncanny and uniquely situated ability—through the life she led and the piquant observations she made—to tap into currents and questions that still dog us today.

Having been deep in these translations over the past several years while preparing my two books, I am particularly prone to finding her relevance wherever I look. But really, I can hardly scan the headlines without finding some news story or commentary that echoes her life and concerns. My pile of "relevance" topics runneth over—from the writings of 2021 Nobel Prize-winner Abdulrazak Gurnah (whose modern fiction is an amazing overlay to Sayyida Salme's time and place); to the Taliban's push to train female doctors (something Sayyida Salme advocated in her time) as a small exception to (and necessitated by) their appalling subjugation of women; to the proliferating examples of backlash against minorities and the politically-motivated "cancel culture" responses (including Hamburg's rejection of its previously-designated Emily-Ruete-Platz); to royals that choose to give up their royal stations (Princess Martha Louise of Norway, Prince Harry of England); to reports of PEN America's Manifesto on Literary Translation (espousing principles that were sorely lacking in Sayyida Salme's time); and much more. The range of her experiences and the precious detail of her accounts refract one theme after another that still pertains.

On Inspiration

As a writer myself, I cannot consider the story of Sayyida Salme without being struck by the power of the pen. It began with some combination of intelligence and audacity, guts and gumption, perhaps even a drive to compete with the boys, when she secretly taught herself to write in Arabic using homemade ink on a camel shoulder blade. If she was testing limits, making trouble, or subverting authority, at least she was writing holy verses from the Koran. How subversive can that be? Or perhaps she was just indulging in creative exploration, since she could already read and recite much of the Koran, and how do you undo the learning once it is learned? Even though she stunned those around her and got into passing trouble when it came out, the act of making literacy part of her identity enabled a degree of self-expression and empowerment that shaped the rest of her life.

I try to picture a teenager, having first been scolded for writing, but then validated and encouraged, even expected, to write one letter after another to serve the cause. In supporting Barghash with his coup attempt, Sayyida Salme weaponized her pen at age 15 before she learned to write for herself and reveal her own sense of the world. As she tells us in her Preface and Afterword, writing the *Memoirs* for her children was an act of love, and publishing the *Memoirs* for an international audience was an act of truth-telling. But her *Letters*, did she write them to remember, for the record, or perhaps even to soothe her soul? We do not know, but as we read her words now, her voice is clear, her tone is pronounced, and her self is amply expressed. Coming fresh off the success of her *Memoirs*, she must have known she had more to write. And in so doing, this literary legacy has not only let her "contribute my share,"[111] but also illuminates the importance, across the ages, of words and writing as a way both to be oneself and to reveal oneself.

Such tools of liberation have heightened importance in societies where voices are tamped down and expression is caged in. Women, in particular, keep bumping up against the bars of the cage, of which Sayyida Salme gives us so many examples in her time, both in Zanzibar and Germany. We can dwell, for example, on that awful moment when she was first turned away from the hospital where her husband lay dying, or less obviously when no one moved to help her get to his burial—as the cultural tropes go, better keep the

---

111 *Memoirs*, Afterword, p. 229. Given the author's explicit mission, including her goal of "above all, … removing many misconceptions and distortions current about the East," it is more than ironic that the author's original German has been so mistranslated. My new translations, written to be as accurate and consistent with her originals as possible, seek to rectify the distortions from historical translations. For comparisons to make the point, see www.sayyidasalme.com.

women away, they are too emotional, too hysterical, too embarrassing, too uncontrollable, whatever the thinking.

We also see who built the cage. Whether imposed as the virtual mummification women had to endure to protect men in Zanzibar or disclosed in low décolletés that flaunted bodies to entertain men in Hamburg, social mores were typically designed from a male point of view.[112] Indeed, if we look closely enough, this difference in attire readily maps onto the difference between the Western monogamy and Eastern polygamy that Sayyida Salme so bitingly describes: "I am tempted to say that the only difference between an Oriental wife and a European wife appears to be that the first has knowledge of the number, as well as the nature and character, of her rivals, while the other is kept in loving ignorance."[113] Whether the women were massively or scantily dressed, both the Zanzibari Sultanate and the Hamburg elite were patriarchal societies that had their private codes, their conservative principles, their closed circles, and their need to keep up appearances—where a dangerously errant or exotically vagrant princess had little room.

A society that likes its order, this is how we do it, and a patriarchy that likes male hierarchy, this is how *we* do it, are apt to respect—and fear and other—women to the point of abnegation. In her day, Sayyida Salme had to advocate, persuade, and persist, but as an act of resistance, she could also write—and thus let us feel her pain, contemplate the cost, and consider our own experiences. How striking that this early transgression became a lifelong lifeline: "Oh, how grateful I have been over the years for a decision that enabled me, however imperfectly, to correspond directly with my loyal friends in my distant homeland!"[114] Thank goodness she could and did reach for her pen.

This commentary is perhaps a bit unfair in that we have only her writings, not those of her husband, Heinrich. He surely had views, but did not share the literary craft, and his life was cut so short. The mind wanders, and we can wonder, what on earth was he thinking? Sayyida Salme's unwavering respect, appreciation, and love for him stand as a pillar across all her pages, and that I would take at face value, as genuine as the rest of what she writes. But there are clues that he, too, did not quite fit in. He was his father's first child, born to a mother who died when he had just turned four. When his father remarried

---

112 My thanks to Anita Keizers at the NINO (Netherlands Institute for the Near East) in Leiden for our stimulating conversation, in which she also shared this thought.
113 *Memoirs*, p. 110.
114 *Memoirs*, p. 36.

two years later, and started a second family with five more children,[115] Heinrich may have been the odd one out.

Having grown up in a great port city, Heinrich was still a teenager when he apprenticed with Hansing & Co. and all of 18 when he became one of their agents in Zanzibar.[116] There he lived a trader's life for almost a decade before he met his wife. Who was there to teach him "proper" behavior, if he had in fact wanted to learn? From a Hamburg perspective, being part of elite society, but not so high up that he could easily break the rules, he was surely expected to marry a respectable local. From a Zanzibari perspective, laying a hand on a royal daughter was the height of insolence, not to mention endangering her life more than his. Even after Heinrich's perceived transgressions toward the Sultan's sister, and clear indications from the Sultan that this German was no longer welcome, Heinrich still insisted that he had violated no rules and demanded, all the way up to Chancellor Bismarck, his right to engage in Zanzibari trade. The stand-off was resolved when both Heinrich and Sultan Madjid died tragically young in the same year.[117] Would that we had more details of Heinrich's life, seemingly another fish out of water.

Yet, this is what happens when people move. This is the confusion and collision of cultures when people leave their homelands. The lines were starker and the contrasts greater in the mid-nineteenth century, before the homogenizing forces of our flattening world. Still today, though, the immigrant experience challenges both the people on the move and the people they are moving to. It is not hard to foresee a future where climate change, social upheaval, and forces beyond our imagining will propel more movement, and mixing and matching, that put a premium on our ability to be open, tolerant, and humane. It is not hard to see history rhyme.

All of which reminds me why I do the professional work I do, my many years as a lawyer helping build international partnerships at the World Bank and beyond. It lets me be part of the international community's effort to find a better balance between developed and developing countries.[118] The tendency throughout history has been so vertical—as with colonialism, autocracy, royalty, slavery,

---

115 We are fortunate to be friends with Ursula Luther, a kindred spirit and namesake of my mother Ursula, and a direct descendant of one of Sayyida Salme's in-laws, Heinrich's half-sister Sarah Maria (Ruete) Rothenbücher. She provided some of these details, along with a detailed Ruete family tree.
116 Heinz Schneppen, "Jena: Emily Ruete, eine Prinzessin aus Sansibar," in *Kolonialismus hierzulande. Eine Spurensuche in Deutschland*, p. 222 (U. van der Heyden, J. Zeller 2008). But see E. van Donzel, p. 12, which states that Heinrich was in Zanzibar already at age 16.
117 H. Schneppen, *Briefe*, p. 151–52.
118 This distinction between "developed" and "developing" countries still largely tracks the old Oriental-Occidental/East-West/South-North divide of Sayyida Salme's time.

war,[119] and plunder—and the world is still young in trying to organize itself horizontally. Whether, for example, through more democracy within countries or more consensus-based platforms across countries, the ability to engage peer-to-peer as citizens and as sovereign nations remains a work in progress.[120]

In her Omani father and Circassian mother, Sayyida Salme herself embodied a remarkable alignment between the heft of Omani colonialism and the effect of Russian genocidal incursion. Although she ended up at the top of the vertical, she could just as easily have ended up at the bottom (witness slavery in the American South). But vertical it was, and vertical it stayed, albeit with a twist. Even though she came from a great Omani dynasty, arguably as prosperous as any European nation of the time, the trip from South to North flipped her status from princess and privilege to exotic and primitive.[121] We may ponder some of Sayyida Salme's descriptions, and rightfully criticize some of her statements, but ideally not before we appreciate her views as an exposition and defense of her own highly-developed society and culture with legitimate local interests.

Her title, *Letters to the Homeland*, reminds us that she came from both a home and a land: a place, a people, a culture, a society.[122] What a different life she would have had with less hierarchy in the harem and less verticality in the international arena. It is not a question of being equals—Sayyida Salme was unlikely ever to fully conform, nor should anyone have to—but it is a question of more equivalent footing, of being horizontal more than vertical in relation to each other, whether as individuals or countries. And that is one more way in which we might be inspired.

> Let history surprise you, let her story inspire you—
> let her authentic voice speak to you.

---

119 Having come from a warring culture, including a father who killed to succeed his father and was venerated for his military accomplishments, Sayyida Salme was remarkably anti-war: "For . . . people who have no association with Christianity and know of the peaceful, love-thy-neighbor teachings of Jesus only through books and stories, it must appear totally incongruous to watch how its adherents seek to outdo each other in who can invent the deadliest and most *en gros* annihilating weapon. . . . [Y]ou, however, in your simplicity, if you were to consider all these arts that they call progress here, were you to see all of it and everything that goes with it, I am entirely sure you would call them—simply satanic." (above at pages 42–43)

120 A favorite example of such a horizontal effort is the 2005 Paris Declaration on Aid Effectiveness, which espouses principles like developing country ownership based on country priorities, corresponding alignment by donor countries of their support, and mutual accountability for results.

121 Anyone who studies Sayyida Salme's life immediately recognizes the contradiction of someone who was both a subject and object of the racism that was so widespread at the time.

122 The inscription on Sayyida Salme's gravestone is a fitting verse from Theodor Fontane's 1854 "Archibald Douglas," about an exiled soul who found his way back home: *Der ist in tiefster Seele treu, wer die Heimat liebt wie Du.* (Whosoever loves his homeland as you do, is loyal to the core.) Although Sayyida Salme never returned for good, she was laid to rest with a small sack of sand from Zanzibar that was found among her belongings.

From her pen to mine,

her voice to mine,

this quest to self-express:

· • ·

words that echo over time,

pain to prose in lines that rhyme,

from her to me to you to us.

Andrea Emily Stumpf
September 14, 2023

The children, Rosa, Said, and Antonie, in Dresden probably around 1873.

The children, Said, Antonie, and Rosa, in Dresden in 1875.

The children, Antonie, Said, and Rosa, in Berlin in 1879.

The author's son Said, who usually also got special solo poses.

The son Said in traditional attire in 1875.

The daughter Antonie in traditional attire in the mid-1880s.

LIST OF ABBREVIATIONS

Abbreviations		Pages
B.	half-brother Sultan Barghash	60, 71
Doctor C.	unknown identity	48
Madame C.	unknown identity	5
Ch.	half-sister Chole	27, 58
Doctor G.	unknown identity	52
H.	likely brother-in-law Hermann Ruete	105
Cousin H.	unknown identity	21
Dr. K.	unknown identity	89
L.	unknown location	103
M.	half-brother Sultan Madjid	25, 60, 66,
M.	possibly half-sister Mettle or Meje	71
M.	couple Mr. and Mrs. Bonaventura Mass	6
Madame M.	Mrs. Bonaventura Mass	5, 6, 31
Doctor R.	unknown identity	46, 47
S.	son Said (later Rudolph Said-Ruete)	98–102, 111–119
T.	daughter Tony (Antonie)	14
Baroness T.	Baroness von Tettau	94
Pastor T.	unknown identity	54

TIMELINE

These dates have been collected from various sources, some more substantiated than others. This list is meant to provide an approximate overview and should not be considered a fully verified historical record.

1698	The Omanis defeat the Portuguese on the island of Zanzibar
1806	Sayyid Said becomes Sultan of Oman
1822	Sayyid Said signs the Moresby Treaty with Britain to end the export of East African slaves to Christian colonies
1834	British Slavery Abolition Act frees all slaves held by British subjects (including from India) on Zanzibar and elsewhere
1837	Sayyid Said defeats the Portuguese in Mombasa
March 10, 1839	Rudolph Heinrich Ruete (called Heinrich) is born in Hamburg
1840	Sayyid Said moves his primary residence from Muscat to Zanzibar
August 30, 1844	Sayyida Salme is born in Bet il Mtoni in Zanzibar
1845	Sayyid Said signs the Hamerton Treaty with the British limiting slave trading to routes between Zanzibar and East Africa
1851	Sayyida Salme and her mother move to Bet il Wataro
1853	Sayyida Salme and her mother move to Bet il Tani
1853	Hansing & Co. of Hamburg opens shop in Zanzibar
1856	Sayyid Said dies; Madjid steps in as Sultan of Zanzibar

1856	Sayyida Salme is declared of age and inherits her portion of the estate
1857	Heinrich Ruete moves to Zanzibar as an agent of Hansing & Co., later becoming a partner in Koll & Ruete and then his own Ruete & Co.
1859	Sayyida Salme's mother dies in a cholera outbreak
1859	Barghash attempts his coup to replace Sultan Madjid
1860 ~	Sayyida Salme moves to her plantation Kisimbani
April 1861	Under arbitration by British Lord Canning, Zanzibar and Oman formally settle claims and divide rule
1862/3 ~	Sayyida Salme rents Bububu and moves to the seashore
1864/5 ~	Sayyida Salme moves to Stone Town because Madjid asks to give Bububu to the new British Consul
1865	Sayyida Salme meets Heinrich Ruete as a neighbor in Stone Town
August 9, 1866	Sayyida Salme makes an unsuccessful attempt to leave Zanzibar
August 24/25, 1866	Sayyida Salme escapes Zanzibar on the HMS *Highflyer* to Aden, the night before *Siku ya Mwaka*, the Swahili New Year
December 7, 1866	Sayyida Salme's firstborn Heinrich is born in Aden
April 1, 1867	The infant Heinrich is baptized in the Anglican Church in Aden
May 30, 1867	Heinrich Ruete arrives in Aden from the Seychelles; Sayyida Salme becomes Christian and is baptized Emily; Sayyida Salme marries Heinrich Ruete; the new couple and their son leave Aden for Hamburg via the Red Sea and Marseille-Lyon-Paris
June 24, 1867	The infant Heinrich dies on the train between Lyon and Paris, as certified in Paris by the child's father on June 25 and again by the child's grandfather in Hamburg on June 30 (thank you to Fridjof Gutendorf)

Timeline

June 24, 1867	The young couple arrives in Hamburg and takes up residence at Schöne Aussicht 29, Uhlenhorst
March 25, 1868	Antonie (Tony or Thawka) Ruete is born (who later became Antonie Brandeis)
April 13, 1869	Rudolph Said Ruete is born (who later changed his name to Rudolph Said-Ruete)
Summer 1869	Sayyida Salme and her husband travel briefly to Copenhagen
April 16, 1870	Rosalie (Rosa or Ghuza) Ruete is born (who later became Rosalie Troemer)
1870	Sultan Madjid sends gifts by steamer to Sayyida Salme, which are never received
July 1870	The Franco-Prussian War begins and lasts into 1871
August 6, 1870	Heinrich Ruete dies a few days after a tragic tram accident
October 7, 1870	Sultan Madjid dies in Zanzibar; Barghash becomes Sultan
Winter 1870/71	The Zanzibari warship *Ilmedjidi* docks in Hamburg
Spring 1871	Sayyida Salme moves to a cheaper Hamburg residence, Blücherstrasse 11 (now Heinrich-Hertz-Strasse 112) (per Fridjof Gutendorf)
1871	The German Reich under Bismarck is established
May 1, 1872	Sayyida Salme becomes a citizen of Hamburg and thus Germany
1872/3	Sayyida Salme moves with the children from Hamburg to Dresden
June 5, 1873	Sultan Barghash signs a treaty with the British to end all slave trading
1873	Sayyida Salme finally gets full visibility of her deteriorated finances

1874	Sayyida Salme moves to a cheaper residence in Dresden
Summer 1875	Sayyida Salme travels to London to meet with Sultan Barghash, without success
1875/77 ~	Sayyida Salme begins writing her *Memoirs*
1877	Sayyida Salme moves again, this time from Dresden to Rudolstadt
1877	The children find out at school that their mother is a princess
1879	Sayyida Salme moves from Rudolstadt to Berlin, Genthiner Strasse
October 1881	Sayyida Salme's son Said joins the Bensberg Cadet Academy; Sayyida Salme and her children move temporarily to nearby Cologne
1882	Sayyida Salme returns with her daughters to Berlin and takes up residence at Potsdamer Strasse 70a
1883	Sayyida Salme writes Sultan Barghash directly to reconcile
Summer/fall 1885	Sayyida Salme returns to Zanzibar with her three children under German military escort
October 1885	Sultan Barghash provides a small sum to settle claims that Sayyida Salme declines to accept
May 1886	*Memoiren einer arabischen Prinzessin* is published in Germany; four editions that year
Spring 1888	Sayyida Salme returns to Zanzibar, this time with Rosa only
1888	The authorized English translation of the *Memoiren* appears in London
1888	A bootleg copy of the English translation appears in New York City

Timeline

November 1888	Sayyida Salme leaves Zanzibar on a down note
December 1888	Sayyida Salme settles in Jaffa (now southern Tel Aviv)
1890	Sayyida Salme visits Berlin
1892	Sayyida Salme moves to Beirut
1897	Sayyida Salme visits Berlin
April 30, 1898	Antonie marries Eugen Brandeis and moves to the Marshall Islands, where he was appointed governor of the German protectorate
1900	Sayyida Salme visits Said in Cairo
September 16, 1901	Said's wedding to Maria Theresa Mathias of the Mond family in Berlin; Sayyida Salme attends
September 17, 1902	Rosa marries Captain Martin Gottlob Reinhold Troemer (later Major, then Major General)
1905	A French translation of the *Memoiren* appears in Paris
1907	An unauthorized English translation of the *Memoiren* by Lionel Strachey appears in New York City
1914	Sayyida Salme leaves Beirut to move in with Rosa and her husband at Bülowstrasse 17, Bromberg (now Bydgoszcz in Poland)
1920	Sayyida Salme moves with Rosa and now retired Major General Troemer to Gartenstrasse 4, Jena
February 29, 1924	Sayyida Salme dies in Jena, in Rosa's home, of double pneumonia
1924	Sayyida Salme is buried on the Ruete family plot, next to her husband, in the Ohlsdorf Cemetery in Hamburg

1866. Abreise von Zanzibar nach
       Aden
1867. Abreise von Aden nach Suez,
       Cairo, Alexandrien
       Marseille & Hamburg 24 Juni.
1872. Reise von Hamburg nach Berlin
       zu Staatssekr. von Bülow.
1873. Umzug von Hamburg
       nach Dresden.
1875. Reise nach London
1877. Umzug nach Rudolstadt.
1879. Umzug von Rudolstadt nach
       Berlin (Genthiner Str.)
1882. Nach Cöln (wegen Said)
1885. Reise mit dem Reichs Kommissar
       nach Zanzibar.
1888. Zweite Reise nach Zanzibar,
       Cypern, Jaffa ...
       ... Horn Str. 8.

Handwritten timeline from the author.

1890. Reise nach Berlin, Calais etc.

1892. Reise nach Mailand, Genua, Port Said, Cairo & Beirut.

1897. Reise nach Berlin (b. Schreier) & zurück nach Beirut mit Tany.

1898. Im April Rosa & E. nach Beirut.

1898. Im Herbst Port Said nach Beirut.

1900. Reise ich allein p. Said nach Cairo.

1901. Reise ich mit Rosa p. Said, Jaffa nach Berlin.

1901. Juli, August, kam Tany mit Gretchen nach Deutschland.

1902. Reise ich im Januar von Berlin nach Beirut zurück.

Tucked away by her son in one of his collected books.

LIST OF IMAGES

Special thanks are due to Alexander von Brand and his family for the extraordinary gift of preserving and sharing many of the family photographs appearing for the first time in public in these pages. They tell a story in and of themselves, and it has been a joy to lay them out in their full succession here.

[Front cover] Same photograph as [xiv] below.

[iv] Front cover of *Memoirs of an Arabian Princess: An Accurate Translation of Her Authentic Voice* (2022), by Andrea Emily Stumpf, ISBN 978-1-732397-3-8.

[viii–xi] Four studio photographs of the author in traditional Omani/Zanzibari attire by photographer H.F. Plate, taken in Hamburg in 1867, not long after her arrival in Germany; from the Leiden University Libraries at Or. 27.135 D1.

[xii–xiii] Two studio photographs of the author in German attire by photographer W. Breuning, taken in Hamburg around 1868; from the Leiden University Libraries at Or. 27.135 D2(3) and D2(2).

[xiv] Studio photograph of the author by photographer J.C. Schaarwächter, taken in Berlin in March 1888, according to the handwritten notation; from the Leiden University Libraries at Or. 27.135 D5.

[xv] Studio photograph of the author by photographer J.C. Schaarwächter, undated but presumably from the same 1888 studio session as the prior photograph; provided by Alexander von Brand from his family collection.

[xvi] Studio photograph of the author dated December 1908, according to a handwritten notation ("XII/1908"); the same photograph in duplicate is accompanied by a photograph of the author's son Rudolph Said-Ruete and a handwritten dedication dated October 1924 from Rudolph to Professor Christiaan Snouck Hurgronje ("Herrn Professor Dr. C. Snouck Hurgronje das Bild meiner ihm in aufrichtiger Wertschätzung verbunden gewesenen Mutter, Frau Emily Ruete/Prinzessin von Oman und Zanzibar, freundschaftlich zugeeignet – RSaidRuete"), apparently presented as a gift following her death; from the Leiden University Libraries at Or. 27.135 D7.

List of Images

[xvii] Studio photograph of the author, undated and unattributed, but presumably from the same 1908 studio session as the prior photograph; provided by Alexander von Brand from his family collection.

[xviii] Photograph of the author, undated but presumably taken during the period from 1892 to 1914 when the author lived in Lebanon; the handwritten name on the photograph is misspelled (it should be Ruete, not Reute), while "Libanon" is the German spelling of Lebanon; provided by Alexander von Brand from his family collection.

[xix] Photograph of the author, dated July 1914, the year she left Beirut to return to Germany, and taken in Bromberg (now Bydgoszcz, since 1920 under the Treaty of Versailles), where she moved in with her daughter Rosa and husband Major General Martin Troemer; from an album compiled by the author's son Rudolph Said-Ruete in the Leiden University Libraries at Or. 27.135 H5.

[xxvi–xxvii] Excerpts from the author's three handwritten notebooks (I, II, and III) containing her original "Briefe nach der Heimat" totaling over six hundred pages, in each case showing the cover page plus the first three pages; from the Leiden University Libraries at Or. 27.135 A3–5. These notebooks will soon become available for public access as digital copies, in part to safeguard the very fragile originals. A useful additional reference point is the collection guide and inventory located at ubl649, which provides historical background and itemizes the materials in the "Sayyida Salma [sic] (Emily Ruete) and Rudolph Said Ruete" archive.

[xxviii] First page of an early typewritten copy of the author's "Briefe nach der Heimat;" provided by Alexander von Brand from his family collection.

[xxix] First page of an upgraded typewritten copy of the author's "Briefe nach der Heimat" that is part of the compilation described under [1] below; from the Leiden University Libraries at Or. 6281.

[xxx] Studio photograph of the author taken by photographer H.F. Plate in Hamburg around 1867, not long after her arrival in Germany, and used as the frontispiece for her 1886 publication of the *Memoiren einer arabischen Prinzessin*; from the translator's family collection.

[1] Cover page of a compilation of the author's legacy writings prepared as typed manuscripts by the family after the author's death in 1924 and formally presented as her "Literarischer Nachlass" (Literary Estate) to various institutions by the author's son Rudolph, including to Professor Christiaan Snouck Hurgronje and his Leiden-based Oriental Institute in 1928–29; the

compilation consists of the "Nachtrag zu den Memoiren" (Addendum to the Memoirs) and "Syrische Sitten und Gebräuche" (Syrian Customs and Conventions), in addition to the "Briefe nach der Heimat"; located in the Leiden University Libraries at Or. 6281.

[3] Illustration by Max S. Stumpf, © 2023.

[7] Steel engraving of Hamburg from the mid-1880s, including in the center the Jungfernstieg; published by A.H. Payne Dresden & Leipzig.

[15] Illustration by Max S. Stumpf, © 2023.

[18] Studio photograph of the author's husband Heinrich Ruete, with an imprint of "E. Bieber, Hamburg" and handwritten "1863" on the back; this date is somewhat in doubt, since Heinrich was in Zanzibar during most of this time; see also regarding the photograph described under page [56] below; provided by Alexander von Brand from his family collection.

[19] Studio photograph of the author in Germany that was paired with the prior photograph; undated and unlabeled, but likely taken around 1868; provided by Alexander von Brand from his family collection; a second copy of this same photograph taken by photographer H.F. Plate, likely the original photographer, is located in the Leiden University Libraries at Or. 27.135 D2(1).

[28] Illustration by Max S. Stumpf, © 2023.

[43] Stereograph of a French battlefield entitled "Red fields of slaughter sloping down to ruin's black abyss," taken during World War I between 1914 and 1918 and published in 1923 by the Keystone View Company; from the Library of Congress Prints and Photograph Division, call number Lot 14008, no. 175 [P&P].

[46] Horse-drawn tram in Hamburg from the late 1860s; photograph featured in an article by Matthias Schmoock, "So fuhr die erste Strassenbahn in Hamburg" (This is How the First Streetcar in Hamburg Ran), August 13, 2016, in the *Hamburger Abendblatt* (photograph credit Hochbahn).

[50] "Ansicht von Sansibar" (View of Zanzibar) on page 3 of the article "Sansibar und Bagamoyo" in the January 1874 edition of the *Illustrierte Monatschrift* (Illustrated Monthly) of the Catholic Mission; with thanks to Hans van de Velde for generously sharing.

List of Images

[53] Illustration by Max S. Stumpf, © 2023.

[56] Undated studio photograph of Heinrich Ruete from photographer W. Breuning in Hamburg; this may be a set with the W. Breuning photographs of the author on pages xii and xiii above, but also appears to be from the same studio session as the photograph on page 18 above taken by E. Bieber; because a handwritten "Copie" appears on the back of this photograph, it may be that E. Bieber was the original photographer and W. Breuning reissued the photograph in connection with the author's subsequent studio session; from Leiden University Libraries at Or. 27.135 D3.

[57] Studio photograph of the author's husband Heinrich Ruete, taken by photographer E. Bieber in Hamburg sometime in 1869–1870 (undated, but noting exhibits attended in 1865, 1868, and 1869); with the notation "Für Tony" (For Tony) on the back; provided by Alexander von Brand from his family collection.

[62] Undated colored lithograph of Sayyid Madjid bin Said, Sultan of Zanzibar from 1856–1870; from Leiden University Libraries at Or. 27.135 D18.

[63] Undated colored lithograph of Sayyid Barghash bin Said, Sultan of Zanzibar from 1870–1888; from Leiden University Libraries at Or. 27.135 D21.

[67] Painting of the ship that became the *Ilmedjidi* or "El Majidi," taken from J.L. Carvel, *Stephen of Linthouse: A Record of Two Hundred Years of Shipbuilding 1750–1950*, pp. 40–41 (1950), and fortuitously provided by Thomas Theye, Bremen, who contacted me during his research and alerted me to this ship's fascinating twists and turns. The formidable vessel with its characteristic smokestack was built in Glasgow and began life in 1863 as the tea clipper *Sea King* before taking on a second life in the American Civil War as the feared Confederate raider CSS *Shenandoah* that demolished Yankee whaling fleets wherever it could find them. After the war ended, the ship was surrendered in Liverpool and later sold to Sultan Madjid, who turned it into a Zanzibari warship. Wrecked in the April 1872 cyclone that devastated Zanzibar, the ship was soon headed to Bombay for repairs when it started to leak and then sank. Officers and crew dispersed in several boats, but many perished, according to a letter from Lieutenant Arthur Philpotts, HM Ship Briton at Zanzibar on December 18, 1872, a copy of which resides in the Hamburg City Archives at 111–1_46996, Annex 2, again helpfully provided by Theye. Theye also reveals the even more astonishing story of how photographs taken by Carl Dammann in 1870 of the *Ilmedjidi*'s crew were heralded, sold, and scrutinized as racial specimens. See Thomas Theye, "Im Spinnennetz: Karl Ernst von Baer und Otto Buchner, Adolf

Bastian und Rudolf Virchow, Carl Dammann und die 'Photographiesammlung' der Berliner Gesellschaft für Anthropologie, Ethnologie und Urgeschichte," in *Mitteilungen der Berliner Gesellschaft für Anthropologie, Ethnologie und Urgeschichte*, Vol. 43, pp. 102–08 (2022).

[70] Sketched portrait of the author's father, Sayyid Said, Sultan of Oman and ruler of Zanzibar from 1806–1856, with a handwritten notation from the author's son Rudolph Said-Ruete; the image was glued by Rudolph into W.H. Ingram's "Said bin Sultan: An Appreciation" from 1926, which Rudolph had inserted into his copy of Shaik Mansur's *History of Seyd Said, Sultan of Muscat* (1819); this type of careful compilation of annotated materials is typical of Rudolph's 600+ book collection that he gave to the Oriental Institute in Leiden; located in Leiden University Libraries at SR 432.

[79] Steel engraving from the mid-1800s of Dresden scenes; published by A.H. Payne Dresden & Leipzig.

[87] Illustration by Max S. Stumpf, © 2023.

[93] Steel engraving from the mid-1800s of Rudolstadt; as printed on the bottom, "Aus der Kunstanst. d. Bibliogr. Inst. in Hildbh." (Hildburghausen).

[97] Illustration by Max S. Stumpf, © 2023.

[107] Steel engraving from the mid-1800s of Berlin scenes; published by A.H. Payne Dresden & Leipzig.

[115] Colored lithograph of Bensberg, including the cadet academy to which the author's son was assigned; used as a postcard for correspondence within Germany in 1899.

[121] Locations where Sayyida Salme lived in Germany (including one in what is now Poland); by Max S. Stumpf, © 2023.

[122] The only photograph of the author and her husband together with their children, in this case Antonie and Said, by photographer W. Breuning in Hamburg; with 1870 on the background cardstock handwritten by the author's son (this was likely taken before April 1870, when the author was pregnant with Rosa); from Leiden University Libraries at Or. 27.135 D4.

[123] Unlabeled studio photograph of the author and her three children, Said (in the chair), Rosa (on the lap), and Antonie; taken after the author's husband died, probably in the first half of 1871; provided by Alexander von Brand from his family collection.

List of Images

[124] Studio photograph of the author and her children, Rosa (14), Said (15), and Antonie (16), by photographer J.C. Schaarwächter; with "Herbst 1884" (fall 1884) written on the background cardstock; provided by Alexander von Brand from his family collection.

[125] Studio photograph of the author and her children, Antonie, Said, and Rosa, taken by photographer W. Höffert; although undated, it appears that Ernst Friedrich Wilhelm Hugo Höffert had studios in Berlin from 1885 to 1900; the four coats of arms reflect his various appointments as court photographer; from the translator's family collection.

[128] The author's signed dedication to her son in a copy of her 1886 *Memoiren einer arabischen Prinzessin*; from www.omanisilver.com by permission of Hielke van der Wijk, whose significant collection of artifacts from and related to Oman is accompanied by thoughtfully researched descriptions.

[130] Excerpt from a carbon copy of a letter dated October 14, 1928, from the author's son Rudolph Said-Ruete, in which he protests Sir Arthur H. Hardinge's characterization of the author in his book *A Diplomatist in the East* (1928), this example being just one of many errors about the author that appeared in the book; Hardinge died before the publisher took responsibility, and no corrections were made as no further editions were published; this is one of several letters placed by Rudolph in the referenced book that is part of his bestowed collection, located at Leiden University Libraries at SR 289.

[146] Studio photograph of the author's children Rosa, Said, and Antonie, undated but probably around 1873 after the family moved to Dresden; taken by photographer Wilhelm Hoffmann in Dresden; provided by Alexander von Brand from his family collection.

[147] Studio photograph of the author's children Said, Antonie, and Rosa taken by photographer Carl Arazim from Dresden in 1875; provided by Alexander von Brand from his family collection.

[148] Studio photograph of the author's children Antonie (11), Said (10), and Rosa (9) taken by photographer J. van Ronzelen from Berlin with a handwritten date of October 1879 on the background cardstock; provided by Alexander von Brand from his family collection.

[149] Four studio photographs of the author's son Said, posing alone: (i) taken during the same studio session as page 146 above (top left), (ii) studio photograph with a handwritten date of November 1875 on the background cardstock (bottom left), (iii) taken during the same studio session as page 124

above (top right), and (iv) taken by photographer L. Haase & Co. from Berlin, undated; most family studio sessions appear to have included solo poses by the son, but not the daughters; provided by Alexander von Brand from his family collection.

[150] Studio photograph of the author's son Said in traditional Omani/Zanzibari attire, including an Omani kummah cap typically worn by men, taken during the same studio session as page 147 above; provided by Alexander von Brand from his family collection.

[151] Studio photograph of the author's eldest daughter in traditional attire, including the same Omani kummah cap that Said wore in the prior photograph about ten years earlier; taken by photographer L.A. Vassel (Gustav Leon Alfred Vassel) from Berlin and undated, but probably in the mid-1880s, around the time of the family's 1885 trip to Zanzibar; provided by Alexander von Brand from his family collection.

[158–59] Timeline handwritten by the author and enclosed by her son Rudolph Said-Ruete inside E. Sachau, *Über eine arabische Chronik aus Zanzibar* (1898), one of the books that is part of Rudolph's bestowed collection, located at Leiden University Libraries at SR 631.

[166] Image imprinted on the cover of an album of family photographs compiled by Rudolph Said-Ruete and preserved as part of his special collection; located at Leiden University Libraries Or. 27.135 H5.

[Back cover] Left: Same photograph as [xi] above. Right: Studio photograph of the author by photographer Progress-Photographie, with a handwritten February 1, 1915 date on the framing cardstock; provided by Alexander von Brand from his family collection.

The Centennial Collection
More of Emily Ruete, born Sayyida Salme, Princess of Oman and Zanzibar

By Andrea Emily Stumpf

Copyright © 2024 Andrea E. Stumpf
First edition; published in the United States, 2024
Cover design: Andrea E. Stumpf
Copy Editor: Lauri Scherer, LSF Editorial
Graphic Designer: Joe Bernier, Bernier Graphics

Huge appreciation to my book publishing team, Lauri, Bob, and Joe. Let it be said: There is no better partner on graphic design than Joe Bernier. Thank you!

Andrea E. Stumpf has asserted her right as copyright owner of this publication, including under the Copyright, Designs and Patents Act of 1988, to be identified as the author of this work, including as translator of the translated texts contained herein.

The original texts that were translated for *The Centennial Collection* come from handwritten documents from Emily Ruete, born Sayyida Salme, Princess of Oman and Zanzibar, and her children. They were subsequently typed and included as part of her *Literarischer Nachlass* (literary estate) that was granted to the Oriental Institute in Leiden in 1937, along with a number of other collected materials. This special collection was moved as a permanent loan to the Netherlands Institute for the Near East (NINO) in 1977 and became part of the Leiden University Libraries in 2018 as the Said-Ruete Archive, Or. 27.135.

All rights reserved. No part of this book may be reproduced, translated, or transmitted in any form or by any means, electronic or hard copy, including by photocopying, recording, any storage or retrieval system, or otherwise, without prior written permission of the author, translator, and copyright owner. For permission, send a request with complete information to andrea@sayyidasalme.com.

www.sayyidasalme.com; www.emilyruete.com

ISBN 978-1-7323975-7-6

Lest we forget those who slaved and served,

this book is dedicated to

Djilfidan.

1924–2024

To commemorate the centennial anniversary of Sayyida Salme's death in 1924, this book is presented in 2024 as a collection of writings and images that complement two previously published companion books. It is the third in a series after:

Memoirs of an Arabian Princess:
An Accurate Translation of Her Authentic Voice (2022)

Letters to the Homeland:
An Accurate Translation of an Intimate Voice (2023)

All references to the *Memoirs* and *Letters* that appear in footnotes and elsewhere in this *Centennial Collection* are to these books. All three books also appear as a combined set in *The Centennial Compilation: All of Emily Ruete, born Sayyida Salme, Princess of Oman and Zanzibar* (2024).

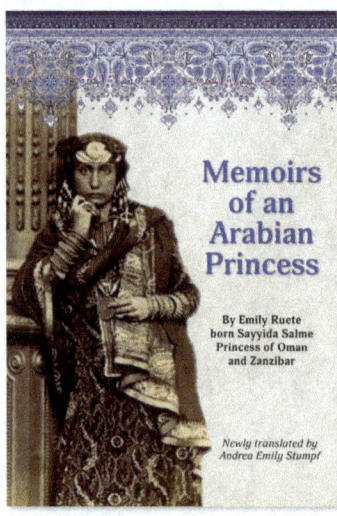

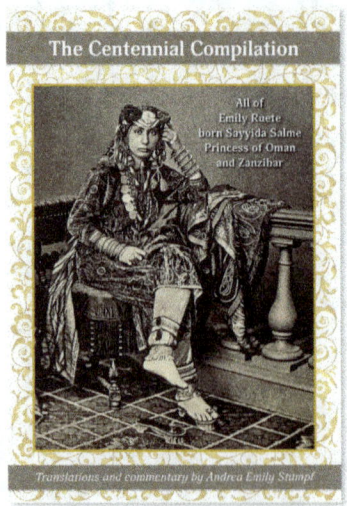

CONTENTS

Introduction	On Transits 6
	Addendum to My Memoirs
	About the Addendum 12
Translations	*Addendum to My Memoirs* 22
	Syrian Customs and Conventions
	About Syrian Customs and Conventions 36
	Syrian Customs and Conventions 46
	On Faith.. 54
Remembrance	On Legacy 76
	In Memoriam.. 80
	Salam 108

List of Images.. 109

ON TRANSITS

Being "trans" has a specific meaning nowadays, but it is a condition we have all felt to some degree or another. Some of us have had relatively simple lives with fewer transits. Many of us, however—more than in Sayyida Salme's time, and more and more as the world changes and the ground keeps shifting—have journeyed across borders and boundaries, and transcended limits, both in the wider world and in our own minds. Often, change comes to us, both subtle and seismic. The question then is what we make of the change, how we choose to respond when things happen beyond our control. But whether we are responding to change or making our own, it is a good thing to have room to move and maneuver. It is essential to our self-preservation and self-expression that each of us, in our own way, can create and claim our own space, to reach for better, more authentic, more fitting and fulfilling lives. It is a good thing when we have choice.

Sayyida Salme had all the instinct to reach, but only minimal room to choose. Living a hemmed-in life was perhaps typical for her time, and it was certainly part of her place in society. As a Muslim, a woman, a princess, each identity drew an ever tighter concentric circle around her being. I just want to breathe, she might have said at some point. And then she opened a window, which became a door, and then a vista beyond anything she had ever known.

Sometimes we step off the ledge into the unknown, trusting in ourselves, in God, or simply finding ourselves compelled to move forward. Have you been there? And once we have tasted the fruit, or learned what we did not know, then what has transpired cannot be undone. In Sayyida Salme's day, so many forces conspired to keep her in a narrow lane, and once she transgressed, those same forces closed ranks to deny her return.

Transgressed. Society lets us know when we have transgressed. We do not need a scarlet A to be shunned, and we are perhaps more likely to conform than clash anyhow. I admire those who raise the stakes to be themselves. As we see with Sayyida Salme and so many others, it is not easy. It has consequences. It can cut to the core. A single transgressive choice can cast a shadow for life. And if transgressive enough, it can trigger so much more lack of choice. Sayyida Salme took a step out of the box that became a slippery slope that moved across oceans and hemispheres, cultures and civilizations. She kept transiting as the bridges crashed in behind her. And she kept persisting, as she transformed into something much bigger than her transgression.

Sayyida Salme escaped on the British Highflyer *in 1866*

Transformed. Her shortest chapter in the *Memoirs* is called "Great Transformations"[1]—that is the translation I chose for her German *Grosse Wandlungen*—while the *Letters* then fill in the details. Her transition that started with love was more than mere change; it was a total reverberation, a metamorphosis, an unmasking and unspooling into a new self. And it did not happen in an instant. It drew definition over time, as she kept defining her own world, transcribing her own thoughts, and making her own mark. All the while, she grounded herself in her beliefs and values and sense of self. This, I believe, is how she steadied herself over all the challenging terrain that she traversed.

Translated. I have had the great privilege of transiting Sayyida Salme's words from her original German into our modern lingua franca. I have also had the audacity to make that choice, to allow myself to substitute my words for hers, even as I have tried (together with my dear mother) to be as accurate and authentically true to her as possible. But playing with words is just one way to translate; we translate our experience into perspectives and choices every day. We translate ourselves to others, so they might better understand us, and they reflect those translations back to us, so we might better understand them.

---

[1] Her other very short chapter is about another transition, the move with her mother to Bet il Tani. This was the last of three childhood moves, having come from Bet il Mtoni, where she was born, and then moving to Bet il Watoro, where her mother—still a slave—supported her half-brother Madjid's family. Sayyida Salme moved thrice more before leaving Zanzibar, first to her plantation Kizimbani, then to Bububu on the coast, and finally to that fateful home in Stone Town. In that last move, she did as then-Sultan Madjid asked, even though she knew the city spelled trouble: "I had a dark premonition that new and inevitable misunderstandings awaited me there." (*Memoirs*, p. 194) These many relocations on the island previewed her many moves in Germany—five towns in ten years, each time to elude poverty, and then two more after she returned from Beirut at age 70. See the map of Germany in the *Letters* (p. 121; also footnote 199, p. 131).

To be sure, words often fail. And there is much that Sayyida Salme did not write. We cannot be fully transparent even to ourselves. What we say, what we convey—and how others translate that into their understanding—is never really straightforward. But we can still be grateful for the incredible range and depth of detail that Sayyida Salme left us of a time and place that would otherwise have disappeared from view. Now we are left to translate that into the world today, to find the relevance that shows us how history rhymes and teaches us about ourselves. I hope my translations of her writings[2] will enable many others to learn more about the past, reflect on the present, and take inspiration for the future.

———·•·———

I will bring this opening essay to a close with the very last words Sayyida Salme published in her own name—her last sentence at the end of the "Afterword" to her *Memoirs*, a text that was originally written in English as an addition to the official 1888 English translation:

> *My task is done—and, in conclusion, it only remains for me to say farewell to my kind readers, who have followed me through these pages, and who, I trust, will always bear a friendly memory for one whose life has already gathered so rich a store of changes and vicissitudes.* (Memoirs, p. 229)

Changes and vicissitudes. Thus ending the English version of her *Memoirs*, she gave us an apt, if understated, summation of what her life had been to date. We can put the emphasis on *vicissitudes*—a word that sounds like slithering sand sucked into time—to capture not just the mutability of it all, but also our exposure and vulnerability to external forces as we are whisked through our lives.

> vicissitude • \vuh-SISS-uh-tood\ • noun. 1: the quality or state of being changeable: mutability; 2a: a favorable or unfavorable event or situation that occurs by chance: a fluctuation of state or condition; 2b: a difficulty or hardship usually beyond one's control. Example: "The vicissitudes of life strike us all."[3]

---

2 All of these translations have been combined in a separate book, *The Centennial Compilation: Writings from Emily Ruete, born Sayyida Salme, Princess of Oman and Zanzibar* (2024), which bundles the three companion books: the *Memoirs* (2022), the *Letters* (2023), and this *Centennial Collection* (2024).
3 From the online Merriam-Webster Word of the Day for November 28, 2016.

Sayyida Salme certainly felt the vicissitudes of life. We can read and feel that in what she left us. Those writings are, for now, enduring markers in the sand, as they harken back to an almost unimaginable past—taking us from her fantastical childhood to a drastic turning point to the tragic and transformative sequel. She gave us the bright and dark, the mundane and undaunted. These writings not only entertain, but also enlighten. Indeed, the latter was her mission, to "contribute my share . . . in removing many misconceptions and distortions." (*Memoirs*, p. 229) Her task is now mine in a new time and place, as I help transport[4] her words about the many changes and vicissitudes across languages and generations.

Many of the borders and boundaries that shaped Sayyida Salme's struggles are not the barriers they once were. Not to be taken for granted, we have more range to choose our transits and chart our transitions today. And yet, her bold and steadfast way may still speak to us. Even as the world gives us never-ending changes and vicissitudes, Sayyida Salme shows us what it means to believe in our own choices.

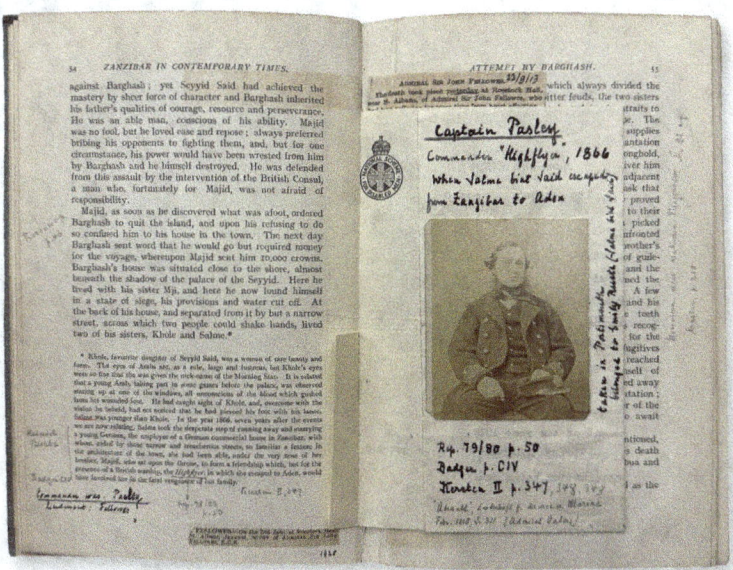

Captain Thomas Pasley took Sayyida Salme from Zanzibar to Aden

---

4 That totals ten trans words. Did you catch them all?

Literarischer Nachlass

von

EMILY RUETE

(Seyyidah Salme bint Said bin Sultan)

geb. 30. August 1844 in Zansibar,

gest. 29. Februar 1924 in Jena.

In Ergänzung

der

"Memoiren einer Arabischen Prinzessin."

Berlin 1886.

Translated:

Literary Estate of *EMILY RUETE* (Seyyidah Salme bint Said bin Sultan), born August 30, 1844, in Zanzibar, died February 29, 1924, in Jena.

As a supplement to the "Memoirs of an Arabian Princess," Berlin 1886.

ABOUT THE ADDENDUM

After twenty years in Germany, Sayyida Salme returned to Zanzibar in 1885 with excitement and hope, but left disappointed. She returned three years later in 1888, hopeful again, but ended up disappointed again—and jaded and bitter. For all the joy in seeing her homeland, and all the love and acceptance she was shown by the people, she failed to reconcile with her Sultan siblings, Sayyid Barghash on the first trip and Sayyid Chalife on the second.[5] That also meant she failed to secure any of the inheritance she believed she was entitled to. As she repeatedly stated, her pursuit of these claims was tied to the well-being of her children, for them more than for herself. Her impoverished circumstances animated her quest in a way that would not have been necessary had her husband survived.

Sultan Chalife (1888–1890)

With her conversion to Christianity, becoming an apostate seemed an obvious disqualifier for any claims to the family estate. Sayyida Salme, however, persisted over the decades in wide-ranging efforts to obtain her fractional portion from, as she calculated in 1888, the twenty-one siblings who had since died.[6] She had already received her full portion of the father's estate outright at the unusually young age of 12. This consisted primarily of a large sum of money and several plantations and was expected to support both her and her mother.[7] Once in Germany, she had also been sent a gift by her late brother, Sayyid Madjid, although it mysteriously never reached her.[8] But Sayyid Barghash was not to be swayed; he showed not one iota of empathy or filial attachment. To the contrary, her repeated efforts, including through direct correspondence, and any sporadic German and British diplomatic inquiries, seemed only to irritate his already irascible stance. Sadly, whatever relief and excitement Sayyida Salme felt when Sayyid Chalife took the mantle also became a painful exercise in futility and humiliation.

---

5 Sayyid Barghash bin Said reigned from 1870 to 1888; Sayyid Chalife (Khalifa) bin Said from 1888 to 1890.
6 E. van Donzel, *An Arabian Princess Between Two Worlds: Memoirs, Letters, Sequels to the Memoirs, Syrian Customs and Usages*, pp. 74–81 (1993) (hereinafter E. van Donzel).
7 *Memoirs*, p. 87. As per Arab custom, her *surie* mother gained her freedom upon Sayyid Said's death, but did not inherit assets.
8 *Memoirs*, p. 202–3. The cargo was on the *Ilmedjidi*, also the subject of an endearing chapter in the *Letters*, pp. 66–70.

About the Addendum

The story of her first trip had made it into the *Memoirs*, when publication was delayed so that the travel account could be added as the last chapter. But her second trip came after publication, so an "addendum" (*Nachtrag*) for a reissued *Memoirs* made sense. What would have been contemporary history at the time is now almost a petty detail, but we can tell from her writing that the manner in which she was treated left her smarting for a good long while.[9] For all the official British and German accounts and opinions, I am glad we also have her side of the story.

———•———

Unlike other writings in this collection, I think we can safely call the *Addendum* a family project. We have not only Sayyida Salme's original draft, but also subsequent iterations. In fact, we have four versions, two from during her lifetime, both handwritten, and two from her children after she died, both typed, with photos of each on the next pages.[10]

In the original notebook, Sayyida Salme's bold, black strokes in the old German script course across the pages with an energy that matches the intensity of her memories and opinions. Added to her text is an overlay of edits, in pencil likely from her son Rudolph and in a fine pen from her daughter Rosa, as they honed their mother's writing. This harkens back to Rosa's earliest school days when she offered to draft a letter for her mother, whose German was still relatively new.[11] It is perhaps a familiar immigrant story, where the younger generation leapfrogs into the new language, while the older generation provides continuity with the old.

What we see next is a second notebook, this time in Rosa's even hand, with another overlay of edits, also presumed to be from her brother Rudolph. The young adults were still at it. This was an important piece of writing, the sequel to the saga, particularly regarding finances and inheritance. It was a chance to set the record straight, what with all the speculation, rumors, false reporting, and innuendo out there. Sensitive topics, lots of details—they clearly wanted to get it just right.

---

9 I cannot help but note that the German word "Nachtrag" has the same root as *nachtragen*, literally "to carry after." Among other definitions, the word is used to refer to someone who bears a grudge against someone else.
10 The handwritten notebooks are in the Leiden University Libraries at Or. 27.135 A1–2. The first typed version is in Alexander von Brand's private collection. See footnote 16 below for the second typed version.
11 "I told her what I was intending to write, and she, this eight-year-old, crafted the sentences better and more clearly than I could have done at the time." (*Letters*, p. 103)

The *Addendum* was, however, never published during Sayyida Salme's lifetime.[12] The family was unable to find anyone willing to reissue the *Memoirs*, to which the *Addendum* would have been appended. Interest in the Oriental princess had perhaps waned; times had moved on. In 1890, Germany had ceded its interest in Zanzibar and much of East Africa to the British in exchange for Heligoland (German *Helgoland*). Neither Sayyida Salme's marked edits in her copy of the 1886 *Memoirs*,[13] nor the complementary *Addendum* account with details from her 1888 trip, made it to the public.

Instead, after Sayyida Salme died in 1924, when more writings were found, her children first debated and then agreed to share the unpublished materials.[14] In addition to the *Addendum*, this consisted primarily of the surprise *Letters to the Homeland* manuscript, as well as a short piece on her time in Beirut.[15] The handwritten texts were all typed up, first in a version that is still well-preserved in the possession of my third cousin from Antonie's branch of the family, Alexander von Brand, and then in a somewhat cleaned-up version that the children used to solicit interest. Once again, however, no publisher was forthcoming. In the end, Rudolph sent the final package to numerous institutions, where it was left for later generations to discover.[16]

---

12 In fact, the *Addendum* was not published for another hundred years. The only publication before this one came as part of Professor van Donzel's English-language compilation under the translated title "Sequels to My Memoirs." E. van Donzel, pp. 511–22. The *Nachtrag* has never yet been published in German.
13 This copy resides in the Leiden University Libraries at NINO SR 613 a–b. These later edits are reflected in my translation of the *Memoirs*. See also "On Translating." (*Memoirs*, p. 254)
14 See *Letters*, page xxi.
15 See *Syrian Customs and Conventions* on pages 46–50 below.
16 This was the "Literary Estate" (see *Letters*, pp. 1 and 161–62), of which one set was presented to Christiaan Snouck Hurgronje, a family friend who founded the Oriental Institute in Leiden, now in the Leiden University Libraries at Or. 6281. Correspondence regarding distribution of the other sets to the Zanzibar and British Museums and the major Hamburg and Berlin public libraries, can be found at Or. 27.135 C8. Rudolph's large collection of books and other materials that he gave to the Oriental Institute in 1937 is now preserved as the Said-Ruete Archive at the Leiden University Libraries.

```
                                    Postmark 21 Mei '45
Rudolph S a i d - R u e t e      27, Kensington Court
                                 WES 3664    LONDON  W.8

       I should be very much obliged  to hear
   if the LIBRARY has survived the war or what
   has become of same.  I ask this as I intend to
   let you have a substantial amiunt of more books.
              Anticipated thanks.
                                        RSR
ontvangen 7 Juni '45
en beantw.
```

An inquiry by Sayyida Salme's son about his collection a year before he died

Custom-made bookcase to house the Rudolph Said-Ruete collection

Pages from Sayyida Salme's original handwritten text, with edits by her children

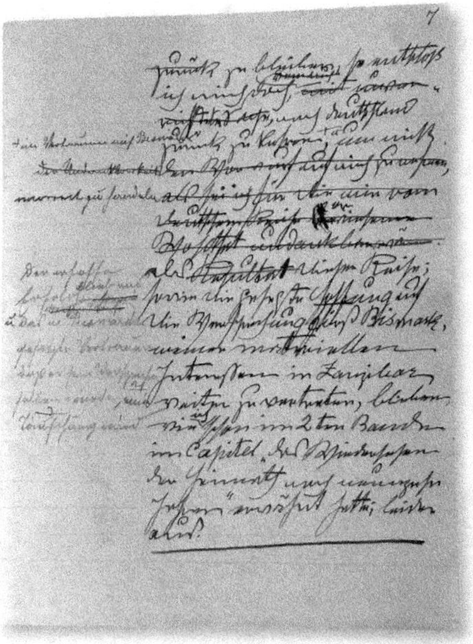

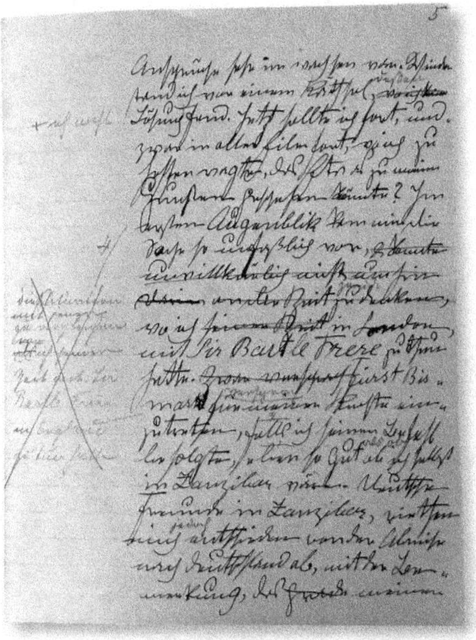

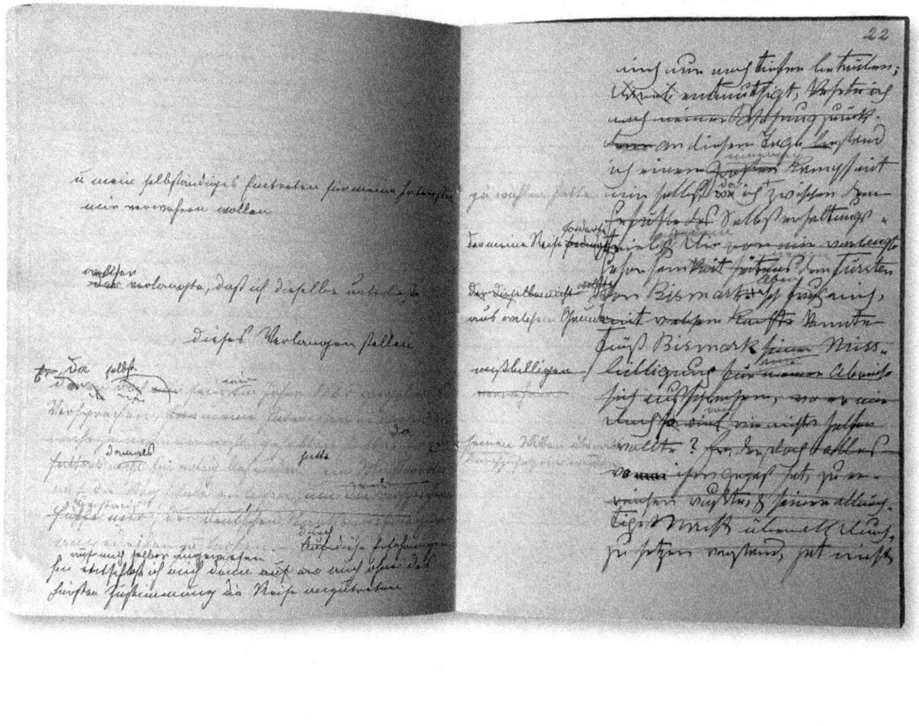

Pages from Sayyida Salme's text, after edits, as rewritten by her daughter Rosa

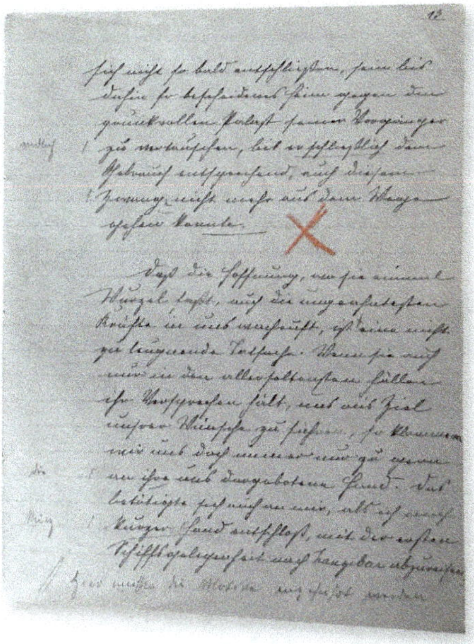

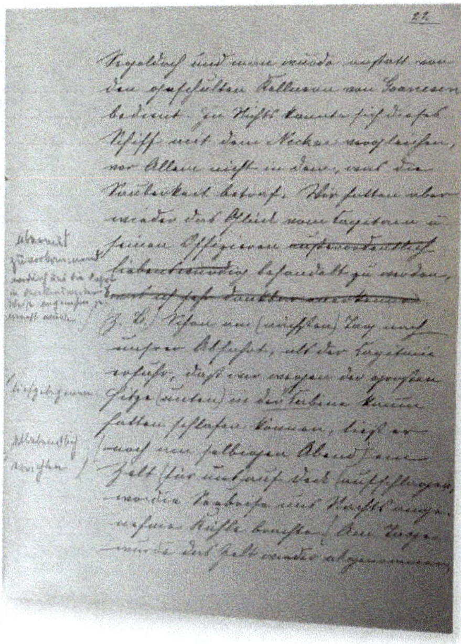

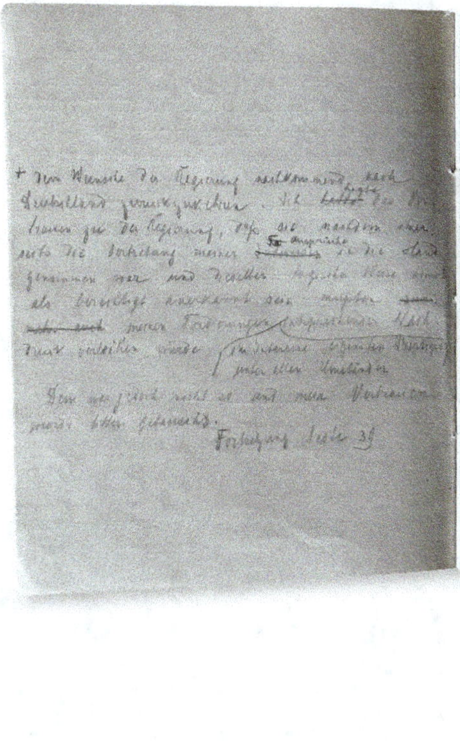

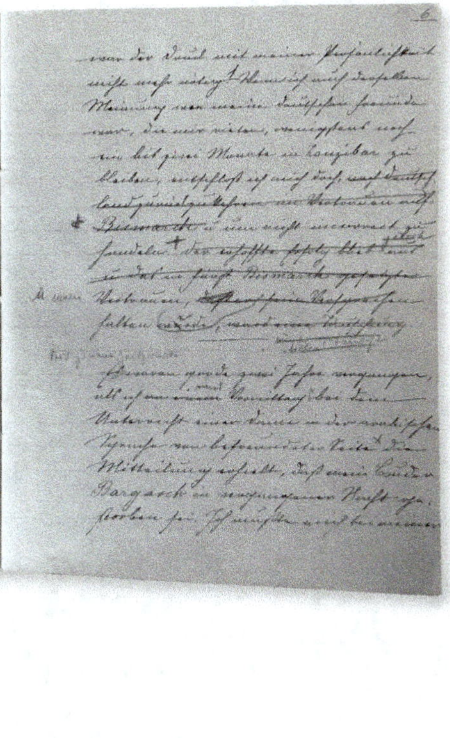

-:-
-----122-----

Nachtrag Zu Meinen Memoiren.

Mit einem Gedicht, das meine geliebte Schwester mir zugesandt hatte schloss ich die Memoiren da sie, wie so viele bei uns, nur des Lesens aber nicht des Schreibens kundig war, liess sie mir dasselbe von einer gemeinsamen Freundin niederschreiben. Der klagende Ton in den einfachen Zeilen hatte seinen Zweck nicht verfehlt, denn er schlug auch bei mir tief empfundene Saiten an. Betruebt wie sie selber bei meiner so ploetzlich beschlossenen Abreise war, ahnte sie nicht, wie viel mehr ich unter derselben litt. Auch konnte und durfte ich sie nicht mit den meiner Abreise bedingenden Umstaenden bekannt machen. Die Situation war so verwickelt, dass sie dieselbe kaum begriffen haben wuerde; auch waere ich Gefahr gelaufen mich in ihrer Auffasung herab zu setzen. Ich empfand eine Art Scham ueber meinen von Berlin aus befohlenen Rueckzug und vermied gern jegliche Mitteilung ueber denselben : denn sowohl die Meinen als auch die Bevoelkerung von Zansibar glaubten, dass die Ankunft des Geschwaders zu dem Zwecke erfolgt sei mich - die Deutsche Untertanin - bei der Geltendmachung ihrer Ansprueche zu unterstuetzen. Die Naturvoelker, denen es an Vestaendnis fuer die so meisterhaft geschulte Diplomatie des Abendlandes und ihrer Schachzuege mangelt, nahmen dies diese Erzaehlung fuer bare Muenze. Weshalb kam ich denn auch auf einen Regierungsdampfer in Begleitung des Geschwaders nach

First typewritten version of Sayyida Salme's manuscript

Nachtrag zu meinen Memoiren.

Mit einem Gedicht, das meine geliebte Schwester mir zugesandt hatte, schloss ich die Memoiren; da sie, wie so viele bei uns, nur des Lesens, aber nicht des Schreibens kundig war, liess sie mir dasselbe von einer gemeinsamen Freundin niederschreiben. Der klagende Ton in den einfachen Zeilen hatte seinen Zweck nicht verfehlt, denn er schlug auch bei mir tief empfundene Saiten an. Betrübt wie sie selber bei meiner so plötzlich beschlossenen Abreise war, ahnte sie nicht, wie viel mehr ich unter derselben litt. Auch konnte und durfte ich sie nicht mit den meine Abreise bedingenden Umständen bekannt machen. Die Situation war so verwickelt, dass sie dieselbe kaum begriffen haben würde, auch wäre ich Gefahr gelaufen, mich in ihrer Auffassung herabzusetzen. Ich empfand eine Art Scham über meinen von Berlin aus befohlenen Rückzug und vermied gern jegliche Mitteilung über denselben; denn sowohl die Meinen als auch die Bevölkerung von Zansibar glaubten, dass die Ankunft des Geschwaders zu dem Zwecke erfolgt sei, mich - die deutsche Untertanin - bei der Geltendmachung ihrer Ansprüche zu unterstützen. Die Naturvölker, denen es an Verständnis für die so meisterhaft geschulte Diplomatie des Abendlandes und ihrer Schachzüge mangelt, nahmen diese Erzählung für bare Münze. Weshalb kam ich denn auch auf einem Regierungsdampfer in Begleitung des Geschwaders nach Zansibar ? Man konnte nichts anderes glauben, als dass die Deutschen den Arabern zeigen wollten, dass sie gekommen waren, um ihrer Untertanin zu ihrem Rechte zu verhelfen. Diese Annahme fand seinerzeit nicht nur in meiner Heimat, sondern selbst in

Second typewritten version of Sayyida Salme's manuscript

Addendum to My Memoirs

I closed my memoirs with a poem that my beloved sister had sent me. Since she, like so many others back home, could only read and not write, she had had a common friend write it up for me. The plaintive tone in its simple lines did not miss their mark, for they struck deep chords in me as well. Distressed as she was by my abrupt decision to depart, she could not have divined how much more it made me suffer. Nor was I able or allowed to let her know the circumstances that compelled my exit. The situation was so convoluted that it would have been hard for her to comprehend, added to which I would have risked denigrating myself to her.

/[17] I felt a degree of shame about Berlin's command that I pull out and preferred to avoid any mention of it.[18] My loved ones, and all the Zanzibari population, believed that the arrival of the fleet of warships had been intended to support me—as a German subject—in asserting my claims. The indigenous people, who lack the capacity to understand the masterfully schooled diplomacy of the Occident and all its chess moves, accepted this tale at face value. Why else would I be traveling to Zanzibar on a government steamer under the escort of warships? There could be no reason other than the Germans wanting to show the Arabs that they were here to enforce the rights of their subject.

/This assumption prevailed not only in my homeland, but even in Germany, where many of my friends were filled with hope for my future. I will always gratefully recall their selfless love and concern for me. Because of this erroneous

---

17 The translator has inserted a number of paragraph breaks for greater readability, in each case denoted by "/."
18 Sayyida Salme is referring to the end of her first return trip to Zanzibar in 1885, when she visited the island under escort of a German naval fleet, as more fully described in the last chapter of her *Memoirs* (pp. 212–28).

Addendum to My Memoirs

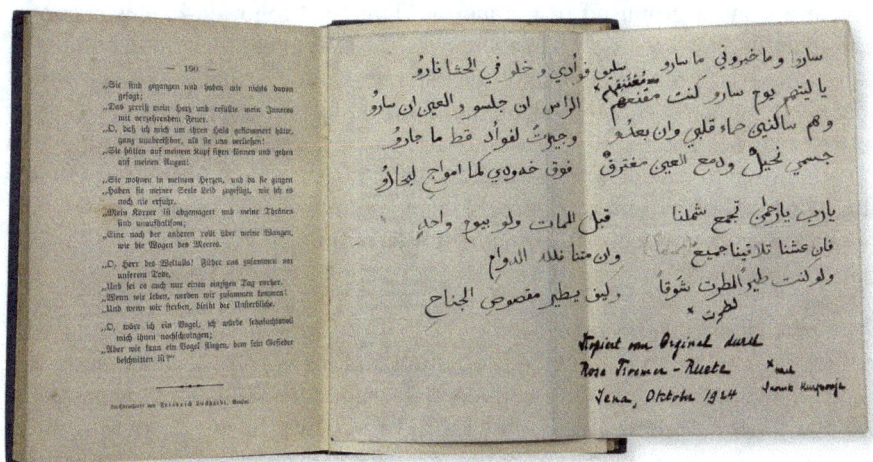

Arabic version of the poem at the end of the Memoirs, *handwritten by Rosa*

perception about the unfolding display of German power in the harbor of Zanzibar—presumed to represent my interests—I received numerous inquiries from my Arab acquaintances about applying to become part of the German Reich. It did not take long, however, for these gullible people to realize that their enthusiasm had been somewhat premature.

Prince Bismarck[19] had apparently deemed it prudent to call me back to Germany in view of the superior political maneuverings of the English toward Zanzibar. His instructions came completely out of the blue, just at a time when the prospects for realizing my material claims were very much on the upswing. I thus faced a conundrum I could not crack. I was to leave now, without delay, at the very moment that I finally dared hope things would shift in my favor. At first, I found the turn of events utterly incomprehensible, and I was sorely reminded of the disgraceful experiences I had been subjected to in England, courtesy of Sir Bartle Frere at the time.[20]

---

19 Otto Eduard Leopold von Bismarck (1815–98) was Chancellor of Germany at the time. He had received the title Prince in recognition of the victory over France in 1871 and then oversaw Germany's unification to become its first Chancellor, a position he held until 1890.

20 Sayyida Salme describes this English manipulation in her chapter "Sayyid Barghash in London" (*Memoirs*, pp. 205–10; and my commentary on p. 248). While seeking to exercise what she perceived as her rights, Sayyida Salme became a "pawn" in the colonial maneuverings of the time, both used and abused by the great powers. No country—neither Zanzibar, Germany, nor England—stepped in to treat her as a legitimate subject or showed her a worthy degree of responsibility. As she put it herself: "Every nation here is like a big institution, and its citizens are just the wards, naturally without them realizing it." (*Letters*, p. 116)

Prince Bismarck promised to pursue my rights, if I followed his instructions, as vigilantly as if I were in Zanzibar myself. Nevertheless, German friends in Zanzibar advised me emphatically against a return to Germany. They observed that my presence at exactly this moment portended success, in that the Sultan, as well as the English Consul General, had reached the conclusion that it would be preferable to placate me sooner than later. I had become uncomfortable for them through what appeared to be a validated interest on the part of my new homeland's government, which had even led to interpellations in the English parliament.

With my dismissal, it became clear to me that the German side had simply used me as a means to an end. Once the Sultan had met Germany's demands and seemed inclined to conclude a commercial treaty, the pressure of my presence was no longer needed. Although I shared the views of my German friends, who advised me to stay in Zanzibar at least another month or two, I ultimately decided to appease the government and return to Germany. I put my trust in the government, which, after having agreed to pursue my entitlements, must have logically considered them valid. I trusted that it would in any event give my claims due emphasis in the interest of its own prestige. And yet, this proved not the case, and my trust was bitterly betrayed.

/At the time, the newspapers spread the falsehood that I had returned to Germany in full possession of my inheritance, consisting of a bounty of no less than twenty-eight houses. That is completely false. Although five of my brothers, five sisters, my Aunt Aasche, three nieces, a nephew, and a very well-off stepmother have died in the time since Barghash became Sultan, and I am permitted to assert my claims to a portion of their estates, I have not received a penny. And my claims, which by now amount to several hundred thousand Marks, and which even the English Consul General declared legitimate—and that is certainly not insignificant—remain unanswered to this day.

/This fact remains the case, despite my brother's offer, as disclosed to me by the Foreign Ministry several months after my departure, to settle the aggregate of my claims with a one-time payment of 6,000 Rupees (approximately 9,800 Marks). Such a resolution of the efforts on my behalf has done nothing to demonstrate Germany's political strength at the start of its colonial endeavors. To the contrary: Today, after twenty years, even the insiders of the colonial movement have no doubt that our politics regarding Zanzibar, including the initial, deceitful saber rattling, reflect a record of exceptional ineptness. Prince Bismarck, after having already left the political stage a number of years earlier and reached the "dismal Treaty of Helgoland"—as he himself described it to my son during a visit to Friedrichsruh[21]—was apparently also convinced that our engagement in East Africa was severely lacking in purposeful energy and vision.

/I immediately declined the amount offered to me by my rich brother, which represented but a small fraction of the lavish gifts with which he sent the representatives entrusted with German interests on their way. As such, I believed to have made my brother aware that, despite all the vagaries of life, my pride was still intact. And yet, sometime later, I coincidentally discovered that my intention had rested on a false assumption, for the sum in question had been inexplicably deposited in the Foreign Ministry's general account. By this time, my brother had died. Rather humiliating for me, he will have departed from this life with the impression that my claims had been satisfied with this scant sum. There was no way to rectify this misimpression, and since I had no reason after all these experiences to allow the slush fund of Germany's foreign affairs to accrue new amounts in such an odd and uncontested manner, I reclaimed the amount on behalf of my children, which was then promptly put at my disposal, together with interest on the interest.

Two years had just passed after my return to Berlin when I was giving Arabic lessons to a lady and received word from a friend that my brother Barghash had passed away in the night. I had to excuse myself to my student and cut the lesson short. How could I have continued teaching under those circumstances! That was completely out of the question, heavily affected as I was by the news that had reached me. In this moment, any bitterness toward the deceased disappeared. Before my soul stood only the picture of the merry companion of my youth, this hot-blooded youngster, and next to him, the picture of my unforgettable sister Chole, as she pleaded with me at the time, with her tearful, soulful eyes, that I not desert her so very beloved brother in his distress, but rather stand by him in his difficult position. These and similar thoughts of my youth overtook me completely, and even though it was impossible for me to suddenly forget all that I had had to endure in the past eighteen years, the harshest of all from Barghash, I nonetheless forgave my dead brother everything in that moment.

/I gave my spirit wings that day and hurried far over the seas to the beloved shores of the homeland, where today the earthly shell of the ruler of Zanzibar was being laid to rest, among the very mixed feelings of the relatives and

---

21 Friedrichsruh became Chancellor Bismarck's residence as a gift from Emperor William I following Germany's victory over France and unification in 1871.

population. Even there it will be said: Le Roi est mort, vive le Roi!²²

/How many people will have seen their secret hopes irrevocably dashed, and yet, how many others will have seen their quietly harbored desires suddenly sprout? Such is the way of the world. The camarilla that Barghash had so favored—and are they not everywhere?—will naturally complain, while the poor downtrodden in their unseen quarters will sing songs of praise in their souls. Who could blame them? It is, of course, human! Even the otherwise humane and very beloved ex-Minister Abdalla il Shachsi, for example, had felt himself compelled on this day, against all customs and conventions, to hoist a flag at his home, as a sign of—his joy.

/Our house rules always call for the oldest male member of the family to be the successor to the deceased Sultan. As such, a son may rise to the throne only if no older brothers or nephews of the Sultan are still alive. In this case, Chalife was the legally determined successor to Barghash as his oldest brother, and not Barghash's son Chalid.²³ Nothing in this whole wide world could have been more undesirable to Chalife, this poor, much plagued and much pursued, man, than to have to step up to this legacy. Worn out in body and soul, nothing lay further from his mind than to covet this honor (compare Volume 2, page 179).²⁴

I learned later that my brother Barghash had returned deathly ill on a trip from Oman to Zanzibar at six o'clock in the evening and had then died the very same night at one o'clock in the morning. He had had high hopes of improving his health on this trip, but must nonetheless have felt the end nearing, as he bade the captain to push full speed ahead back to Zanzibar, so that he could die amidst his family. And so he did arrive in Zanzibar just hours before his death. Immediately after he died, the news was rushed to Chalife to inform him of the event.

/Chalife was on one of his plantations at the time and unaware that Barghash had returned at sunset, much less was no longer among the living. When the messenger reached him toward morning—it was still very dark—and had him

---

22 Written in French in the original, this means "The king is dead; [long] live the king!"
23 Chalid later attempted to take his turn at being Sultan, but, courtesy of the British, it did not go well. See, e.g., "Sayyida Khalid Bin Barghash, Britain and the Throne of Zanzibar" by B. Saud Turki, in *Anaquel de Estudios Árabes*, Vol. 21, pp. 35-53 (2021).
24 This page reference is to the second volume of the original *Memoiren*, at the end of the book, where Sayyida Salme describes how the newly ascended Sultan Barghash threw his next-in-line Chalife into the dungeon—for no known reason—where he lay in chains for three years. (*Memoirs*, p. 224)

Addendum to My Memoirs

woken to present the news, Chalife refused to believe the message, thinking this was instead some underhanded trick. Abused by much unfair treatment in the past, the poor, skittish man did not trust this nighttime visit and at first kept the messenger from coming forward. Once, however, he was finally convinced of the verity of the matter, he is said to have called out that he had no wish to become Sultan, that this honor should go to his younger brother. When in the end he had no choice but to take on this designated role, which he also later always considered a burden, he had a hard time making the switch to the pompous palace of his predecessors in lieu of his until-then so humble home. But ultimately, he conformed to custom when he could no longer avoid the obligation.

It is an undeniable fact that hope, once it takes root, also awakens in us the most unexpected strength. Even if it keeps its promise only in the rarest cases to lead us to our desired goal, we still love to cling to its outstretched hand. That was confirmed in my case as well, when I decided on the spot to leave for Zanzibar on the first ship to sail. I firmly believed that, with the death of my hostile brother, I would encounter no difficulties reconnecting with my relatives and receiving my inheritance for the benefit of my children. I had no time to spare if I wanted to catch the next ship due into Aden, which, coming from Bombay, headed to Zanzibar every four weeks. And so, the next days were filled with very much to do, very much to consider. Above all, we had to sell some stocks to free up the travel cash.—

/I felt I should inform the Foreign Ministry of my travel plans to avoid later misinterpretations, thus also using the opportunity to request the good will of the German government. I believed Germany would now have an easier time supporting my pecuniary claims than was the case three years earlier during the naval display towards Zanzibar. Back then, it was Barghash who, in his diplomatic calculations, had put obstacles in the way. Now that he was no longer living, there should be little impediment to recognizing my modest inheritance claims. Added to that, here I was, the widow of a German, who, in the eighteen years since the death of my husband, had fought my way through all the heartaches and hardship of life with my three children. I considered this request to be self-evident and justified.

/My interest in speaking with the Foreign Secretary at the time, Count Herbert Bismarck, was not granted. To the contrary, I received notice that Prince Bismarck did not condone my trip to Zanzibar, naturally without giving any rhyme or reason why. This rejection, so categorical and without any clarification, only served to heighten my grief. Deeply disheartened, I fought a great fight within myself during these days, with the choice between my own survival instinct that called for travel and my obedience to Prince Bismarck that commanded me to let it go. But, I now asked myself, on what basis could he make this demand and deny me the ability to independently stand up for my own interests? It had been him, who knew only too well how to exert his power, that had considered it unnecessary in 1885 to tip the balance and assert his will in order to give me, a German citizen, the support that had been firmly pledged.

/Recalling that experience, and left to rely only on myself, I opted to move ahead with the trip without the Prince's endorsement. I would have liked my son to come along, so he could support and help me on the long trip. As a cadet who was just about to enter the army, my son was back then already at an age when he could not leave his fatherland without permission of the authorities. I therefore returned to the Foreign Ministry and requested that he be given some leave, with the commitment that he would return to Germany within six months. But this request, too, was categorically denied. Rather than assistance, I once again encountered only repudiation and hard-heartedness. And so, it was clear to me that Germany, in which I had previously placed my trust, was leaving me helplessly to my fate.

/With all this, I could not help but feel skeptical about the word "humanity," a word so widely used in Germany. I told myself that, although the theory was mostly admirable, the practice was anything but. The same applies to much-lauded freedom. In my case, too, it was just "yes, commoner, that is something completely different!" The broad stroke that was hitting me at that moment looked rather much like an act of despotism. Three years ago, when Prince Bismarck considered it useful to have my person present in Zanzibar, he had allowed my son to come along. But why not now? Did they perhaps fear my relatives were so simple-minded that they would attribute political motives to me about my son? There could be no greater error, since my relatives are nowhere near so dumb as to have a completely unauthorized ruler forced upon them, especially considering they have so many of their own pretenders in their midst.

/During my stay in London in 1875, when I sought support from the English government vis-à-vis the Sultan, they referred me to Germany as my second homeland, and not without justification. We can see, however, how far that got me. Germany left me on my own, as did England at the time.

Addendum to My Memoirs

It was the spring of 1888 when I left Berlin for Genoa, with my youngest daughter[25] instead of my son, to meet up with a ship of the Norddeutscher Lloyd[26] that would take us to Aden. Once on board, we ran into German acquaintances who were also headed for Zanzibar and proved most engaging and agreeable. The captain and his officers were also exceptionally kind to us, so that we were very well cared for. The trip progressed splendidly. We reached Aden in the late evening and then had to be shipped out to continue our travels on the steamer due in from Bombay. The captain had the ship's band perform a farewell tune for us. Even after we had gone a long distance, a very long distance towards shore, we could still see the white handkerchiefs waving us on our way. We were really very sad to leave the hospitable *Neckar*.

/We spent several days in Aden before the steamer from the British-India Company finally appeared, and we immediately made our way to the ship. What we found was completely different from the *Neckar*. Meals were eaten on deck under a tarp because of the heat and were served by Goans, instead of polished waiters. Nothing on this ship could live up to the *Neckar*, least of all its cleanliness. Then again, we were fortunate that the captain and his officers completely catered to our needs, which thankfully made the trip quite comfortable. Already the day after we took off, when the captain heard that we had hardly slept because of the great heat in our low-lying cabins, he had a tent pitched on the deck every evening, where we enjoyed the cooling sea breeze.

/Upon arriving in Mombasa, the friendly captain brought us to shore in his boat. As it happened to be Sunday, we went to church. I was surprised to hear a local African pastor give such an impressive sermon in Swahili. Everything here looked neat and clean under the caring administration of the English. There is absolutely no denying that wherever the English get a foothold, they spare neither effort nor cost to lift up the country in every respect. One need not look far for proof; just consider Egypt. In colonial matters, the English are a nation that—in contrast to its many rivals and thus accounting for its dominant position—engages in healthy, purposeful politics.

---

25 This was Rosalie, also known as Rosa, the translator's great-grandmother.
26 The Norddeutscher Lloyd, known as the Bremen Line, was founded in 1857 and grew rapidly with the increase of transatlantic trade and migrant flows after the U.S. Civil War. The carrier began traveling east in mid-1886 under a contract with the German government to serve as a mail line to China and Australia. According to records posted by Norway-Heritage Hands Across the Sea, the *Neckar* traveled from Bremen to Hong Kong, where it arrived on May 18, 1888. In subsequent years, the company lost its entire seafaring fleet at the end of World War I, and again during World War II, before merging with the Hamburg-America Line in 1970 to become HAPAG-Lloyd, currently the fourth biggest shipping line in the world—which Norddeutscher Lloyd had also become by its 25th anniversary in 1882.

The ship that took Sayyida Salme and her daughter Rosa to Aden in 1888

We also put in a call at Lamu[27] and took a short excursion onto the island. When we wanted to return to deck, we found the ocean completely changed. The tide had set in with such force that massive waves were pounding the shore. With utmost effort and delay, we finally reached the ship as the last to arrive, and it immediately powered up to head out. Since it is not customary to wait for tardy passengers, and ships are meticulous in maintaining their departure times, I apologized to the captain for our involuntary lateness. And yet, he was kind enough to respond in his simple manner that he would have waited for us in any case.

From Lamu, we continued directly to Zanzibar. The joy of seeing my beloved homeland again was not as straightforward this time. I was aware that, in pursuing my goal, some hurdles would lie in my way. I nonetheless considered it my duty to spare no effort in championing my rightful portion of the inheritance from the estates of my deceased relatives. Not that I even remotely indulged any sanguine hopes; that was dispelled by all my many dismal experiences of the past. There is no contesting the fact that in the

---

27 Lamu became a UNESCO World Heritage Site in 2001 as "the oldest and best-preserved Swahili settlement in East Africa," which also features much Arab, Persian, Indian, and European influence. The period under Omani protection, when Sayyid Said bin Sultan, Sayyida Salme's father, answered Lamu's appeal to fend off the Mazrui rebels from the Kenyan coast, is considered Lamu's golden age. Meanwhile, a report from 2010 found that Lamu was one of a dozen worldwide sites most "on the verge . . . [of] irreparable loss and damage" (out of 500 surveyed). "Saving Our Vanishing Heritage: Safeguarding Endangered Cultural Heritage Sites in the Developing World," Global Heritage Foundation (2010).

Orient, and even more so in the Occident, questions of money are among the most uncomfortable topics that one could even contemplate. This fact may not, however, mislead those who have been harmed to remain passive in the pursuit of their legal claims. Only after the battle has been lost may one lay down arms, not before.

We had only just arrived in Zanzibar when I had to take note that the local German Consul displayed a less than obliging attitude towards me. The gentleman in question was a complete stranger to me, such that his animosity could not have been personal, but had to be of a much more political nature. I mention this explicitly to indicate the state of relations. I had traveled to my homeland fully cognizant of my status as a German subject, and I presented myself as such.

/From my inner circle, I learned that my brother, Sultan Chalife, who spent most of his time outside of the city, was very favorably disposed towards me and also often took my side among his other relatives. This news emboldened me to try to reach a reconciliation with my loved ones. Meanwhile, it must have become very obvious to everyone the degree to which the German Consul, upon whose goodwill I depended for reaching my objective, not only avoided us on every occasion, but apparently even slighted us relative to all other Germans.

/This behavior left my relatives completely baffled. They believed the German Consul must have his reasons for being so dismissive of me. To my mind, however, the matter was clear. I knew to a certainty that I had become subject to Bismarck's caprice. Having embarked on my travels without his consent, I was to be ignored by the representative of the German Reich. What that meant for me, he surely would have known. All my relatives concurred: Let the German Consul step in for you and take up your cause, for only then can something be undertaken for a German subject. They were right, and my desolation became doubly palpable.

/Ashamed on the outside and deeply wounded on the inside, I believed I had one last step to take before giving up hope forever. I decided to write to the German Emperor[28] and bid him to relieve the cause of my distress with a

---

28 By then, it was Kaiser Wilhelm II (1859–1941), the last German Emperor and King of Prussia. He had only recently stepped up to this role in June 1888 at the age of 29, after succeeding his father's 99-day reign. In March 1890, he effectively dismissed the much older Chancellor Bismarck and then ruled directly until abdicating with the loss of World War I in 1918.

merciful word. I also wrote Prince Bismarck at the same time, in which I implored him yet again not to withhold his benevolence, if only to preserve Germany's reputation among my fellow countrymen. I found myself in a situation that truly was not to be envied. As I extended this request to the Prince, I convinced myself that it would be all but impossible for such a great man as Bismarck to avenge himself in such a petty manner by continuing to deny a helpless lady her rightful protection.

/In the meantime, there was no end to the questions from my friends about why the German government was so clearly deserting me. Yes, why?! As the weeks and months passed with no response to my letters, my hopes of achieving anything through Germany died off forever. Denied any closure, I had no choice but to leave.

Whether this undeserved treatment that was bestowed on me was well-suited to elevating Germany's prestige in Zanzibar is something I cannot judge. It occurred at a time, while I was there, when Germany began to introduce various reforms in East Africa and expanded the tax system. Every coconut palm was to be taxed one Mark per year, which led to loud grumbling on the part of local Arabs. Many came to seek my advice. When I explained that I had nothing to do with these things, and they would better seek out the German Consul, they responded: Who can help and understand us better than you, who knows our customs and conventions better than all the Germans in East Africa put together, since you also speak their language and are well-versed in their affairs unlike any of us.—The following years have, of course, shown how little the people in German East Africa were able to befriend the one-sided military regiment.

Before now leaving my homeland forever, I entered once more into a period that was very amply filled with inner conflict. My siblings and relatives felt great compassion for me, and they beseeched me to become theirs again, to return to the old faith of my fathers and turn my back on the Germans. "Come, be ours again, for you belong to us! Do not go back to those strangers, but stay here with your family. You have our sacred promise that you will have a good life with us. But as long as you turn away from us and attach yourself to other people and their faith, we will never be in a position to freely support you."

Addendum to My Memoirs

/For weeks, yes months, I was forced to listen to these and similar words with a torn heart. Most gripping of all was when my sister Z.,[29] since passed away, begged me to give in and stay with them. How I fought within myself to hear her words, only my God knows. I openly admit that I was often at the edge of my resolve, and naught but the thought of my children, who had been born and raised in the European way, kept me from succumbing to their pleas and staying with them in the beloved homeland. I valued the wellbeing of my children above my own happiness. Under no circumstances, not even for the most shining prospects, was I willing to sacrifice the emotional equilibrium of my children.

In the fall, we set off to depart, but there was no way for me to return to Germany after having been so aggrieved. We chose Palestine as our next destination. For proper appearances, we traveled from Zanzibar to Port Said in first class, but since low tide had set into my cashbox with a vengeance, I considered it necessary to travel second class with my daughter along the Syrian coast, where no one would know me. In Port Said, we embarked on a ship of the Messageries Maritime[30] headed for Jaffa. The next morning, as we were strolling back and forth on deck, the captain came to us and began to converse. It did not take long for him to pose the less than delicate question of why we were not traveling first class. I looked with surprise at this good man, whom I had until now never before seen. He took note of my astonishment and hurried to explain that he had learned of my identity, probably from the ship agent in Port Said. He was a former officer of the French Marine and had thus gotten to know Oman and Zanzibar, also knew my nephew, the Sultan of Oman, and my brother, the Sultan of Zanzibar, from whom he had received various tokens.—Such encounters were least desirable at this time, but fate unfortunately does not care much about our feelings. The captain was kind enough to invite us to tea with him in the first class, but I thanked him and declined.

About a year later, I received a visit in Jaffa from the former physician of my brother Barghash, a highly educated, amiable gentleman, who spoke

---

[29] We have no record of which sister this was, but it may have been Zemzem, who had grown close to Sayyida Salme when they both lived on their plantations in the countryside. (*Memoirs*, p. 98)
[30] This French shipping company, also known as MesMar, thrived on the Mediterranean Sea during this time, with ports of call from Marseille to Malta, across to Alexandria, and up to Constantinople.

practically all the cultured languages perfectly. He told me that when my *Memoirs* appeared in 1886, and my brother learned about the book, Barghash had ordered him to translate it word for word. When I asked if he had also dared to translate the chapter "Said [sic]³¹ Barghash in London" (Volume II, page 146), he confirmed that he had had to do this as well, and indeed, this chapter had interested Barghash the most. This gentleman also assured me that my brother had even voiced a good bit of praise about the *Memoirs*. That took me very much by surprise, for I must admit, I had rather expected the opposite.

/What must Barghash have felt when taking up my *Memoirs*, to see such a book written by his sister, of which he was unable to decipher a single word beyond my Arabic signature. Did he think back to the time when I, in my youth, took up my Arabic pen in his service?³² Very possibly! And since then? What all has happened between then and now! For me, beyond measure!

---

31 This is an error in the typed manuscript. The chapter title in the original German is "Sejjd Bargasch in London," referring to his appellation "Sayyid" as Sultan. Sayyida Salme used the same title for the father as "Sejjid Saîd" in the first chapter of her *Memoiren*. The "Said" error noted here confuses the proper name with the title, probably because they sound the same. "Sejjid" means Sultan and "Saîd" is the first name of the father, not of Barghash. To add to the confusion, Barghash's father's full name was Sayyid Said bin Sultan, where Sultan was, in fact, the first name of his father, Sayyid Sultan bin Ahmed. "Bin" means "son of." In sum, Barghash was a Sayyid, but was not named Said, even though his father was both. Barghash's full name was Sayyid Barghash bin Said. Got it?

32 Acting in support of Barghash's attempted coup, "I, the youngest female member of the conspiracy, became what was effectively the general secretary of the alliance because I was able to write and thus expected to handle all correspondence with the chieftains." *Memoirs*, p. 178.

Shoreline view of Stonetown in 1847, with the Zanzibari red flag waving

Beach view of the Adler, *the German ship that took Sayyida Salme to Zanzibar*

ABOUT SYRIAN CUSTOMS AND CONVENTIONS

Sayyida Salme left only a few tantalizing pages about a place where she lived much of her life, and we could wish for more. We do not know exactly when she wrote these pages, except that it must have been after 1892,[33] when she took up residence in Beirut. It is also not clear whether the children knew about this handwritten text before she died, but likely not, since the wide left margin, ready for edits, is blank.[34] Fortunately, however, the contents of this black notebook made their way into the collected writings that the children had typed up after her death, as part of her "literary estate."[35] It gives me an excuse to say a few things about this third chapter of her life.

From 1889 to 1914, the eastern shore of the Mediterranean Sea, first Jaffa, then Beirut, was her home.[36] That was a quarter century, close to a third of her life, even though Sayyida Salme is almost always associated with Zanzibar and Germany. Of course, we mostly know her through her own writings, the *Memoirs* that describe her young life in Zanzibar, and the *Letters* that describe her early days in Germany. There is no equivalent third book to publish about her older, wiser years, the denouement after the plot twists.

As she had done with Zanzibar and Germany in two prior manuscripts, it appears that Sayyida Salme still had the same instinct to describe the time, place, and people in her new location. With her customary bold strokes, she started to lend her ethnographic lens to Syrian society, but then got no further. It is a pity for us that she did not keep going, but I would like to think that it was good for her. To me, it means she had a busy and fulfilled life in Beirut, without the need to dig around in her experiences. It may signal that she was more content in her new setting, no longer feeling the need to dispel misconceptions or rectify the record. It may be that the fervor to recount had receded. For the first time, she was no longer the outsider looking in, but comfortably becoming an insider. With respect to Beirut, it may have made that distancing, scrutinizing lens harder to position.

---

33 The Leiden University Libraries guide for the Said-Ruete collection (ubl649) suggests circa 1895.
34 Compare this to the intensive editing by Rosa and Rudolph of the *Addendum* (pages 16–19 above).
35 Now located at the Leiden University Libraries Or. 27.135 A6.
36 Sayyida Salme left Zanzibar in November 1888 and was so done with both Zanzibar and Germany that she headed straight to Jaffa, where there was a strong German presence. In 1892, she made the move to Beirut, both of her daughters still with her. E. van Donzel, pp. 95–97. Beirut was the capital of a Syrian province (*vilayet*) at the time and did not become part of Lebanon until after World War I.

About Syrian Customs and Conventions

Her second trip to Zanzibar in 1888 had also left her spent.[37] She may have needed the years that followed to regroup and re-energize. In the relative comfort of her new life, she now also had time and space to delve into her past. These were presumably the years when she filled the three notebooks, more than 600 pages, that she called *Briefe nach der Heimat*—the *Letters* I mention above. Harkening back to such a hard time was no doubt also hard to do. Even if it was cathartic, it surely also took an emotional toll. Her third *Briefe* notebook ends rather abruptly, like running out of steam after all those pages.[38] Her Syrian reflections appear to have had a similar fate after only a few pages.

As far as my own translations of her work, it would have been easy enough to leave out this fragment of an essay. Like a sketch on a napkin, it does not seem to be a serious piece of anything. She might have edited one or the other passage if she had gone back to hone her thinking or sought to create a more coherent narrative. So why include it here?

I think of these pages as a placeholder, a proxy for all that she did not write. In pointing to a portion of her life that was not captured by her pen, the message is in the silence. On the one hand, we can appreciate what she did write all the more. It is simply not normal for someone in her place to have written hundreds and hundreds of pages. On the other hand, the fact that she stayed in Beirut as long as she did, leaving only when age and circumstances meant it was time, speaks for itself.

So what might she be saying with the blank rest of the notebook that never got written? What made Beirut such a comfortable place? I can just feel the relief in her silence. She had found a liminal space, finally a place where she was not forced to be "either/or," but could be "and."[39] Oriental in heart, Occidental in mind; Muslim in sensibility, Christian in belief; not a Zanzibari, Omani, or German as much as an amalgamation—a cosmopolitan citizen of the world. When she found Beirut, the city was becoming the new Constantinople.[40]

---

37 This seems evident in what Rosa wrote her brother Rudolph after the trip: "Mama is no longer the person she was when she left Berlin last April, the robust nature that could until then defy all storms. Our dear mother has suffered severely from the latest events, and her health has become more delicate." Ibid., p. 95.
38 See the essay "On Fear." (*Letters*, pp. 135–39)
39 See more in my very first blog post, "The Liminal In-Between," at www.sayyidasalme.com/blog.
40 As she says: "Had I, for example, been born and raised in Constantinople or Cairo, where European culture made inroads long ago, I may not have found such a stark contrast between Occident and Orient.... Should fate ever destine another Mohammedan from Constantinople or Cairo to be transplanted to Europe under the same circumstances as me, she would not even remotely be subjected to the same upheaval I have had to undergo. Had I not, until then, still been wearing the clothes of my great-ancestors from a thousand years ago and used my five fingers as natural knives and forks." (*Letters*, pp. 31–32)

And perhaps best of all, here she could live a rather normal life, without the extremes, neither in royalty, nor poverty.

———·•·———

Sayyida Salme spent her time in Beirut during a pocket of prosperity—a sweet spot when Beirut was thriving as a vibrant port city, a nexus between Europe and Arabia. Its bustling trade and mix of commerce, culture, and complexions must have felt very familiar to her, reminiscent of Zanzibar's heyday in her youth. Under the stable and savvy reign of her father, the great Sayyid Said bin Sultan, from 1806 to 1856, Zanzibar had become everyone's portal to and from East Africa. No one, it was said, went to the interior without passing through Stone Town—for money, supplies, the latest news, and whatever else. As much as we rightly recognize and criticize that this boom was built on the backs and lives of slaves, the rest of the world was in on it, seeking the spoils and making out hand over fist. As with Zanzibar, though, in Beirut the prosperity also ate itself and did not last.

Before jumping to her departure, we can hold onto what made a place like Beirut at the turn of the century so special, especially for someone like Sayyida Salme. Living as a single woman was still unconventional, but Beirut flourished as an intellectual hub that began to see the promotion of basic women's rights, like respect and autonomy, that was also trending in the West and other cosmopolitan centers.[41] She would have had one foot firmly in the traditional Arab culture, especially with her native Arabic as the dominant local language, and another foot among the Western-influenced, educated elite. And she was even well-practiced in straddling the two.

Beirut offered a dynamic cultural scene that surely appealed to someone like her, who had been so interested in science[42] and was, by then, an acclaimed author. As her daughter Rosa wrote, she was appreciated for her beautiful Arabic script.[43] She likely participated in educational offerings. We can even imagine that she was an excellent role model for others trying to meld Eastern

---

41 An apropos example is the literary magazine *The Woman's World*, begun in 1886 and edited by Oscar Wilde part-time from 1887–1889 (after he had the name changed from *The Lady's World*). It included Wilde's review of the 1888 Ward & Downey translation of the *Memoirs*, in which he noted: "No one who is interested in the social position of women in the East should fail to read these pleasantly-written memoirs. The Princess is herself a woman of high culture, and the story of her life is as instructive as history, and as fascinating as fiction" (pp. 229–31, 1888). Available online from the University of Minnesota.
42 *Letters*, pp. 87–88.
43 E. van Donzel, p. 97.

About Syrian Customs and Conventions

and Western influences. And yet, she probably did not stick out like a sore thumb. Unlike Rudolstadt, where the gossip had reveled in her every detail, or Stone Town, where she had become a larger-than-life personality, Beirut was both too large to care and small enough to give her a community that did.[44]

This carried over into Beirut's religious mix as well, where Muslims, Christians, Druze, and Jews all had their place. For someone whose faith remained essential to her being,[45] Sayyida Salme found access to a ready-made religious community. As she settled into Jaffa and Beirut, two and three decades after first setting foot in the West, it seems Christianity had matured to become a part of her. She was no longer a "poor Christian,"[46] but had evolved in her relationship to God and the church. The road had not been easy, and it corresponded to an evolution on many fronts. Already when she was writing her *Memoirs*, a decade or so after her arrival in Hamburg, we sense some distancing from her cultural groundings; she is seeing the sacrificial rituals and soothsaying spectacles in a different way.

With the tide lifting all boats, Christians in Beirut did well back then, increasing both their wealth and social standing. Protestants were in the minority compared to Catholics, but had a prominent presence in intellectual, educational, and social circles. Sayyida Salme found her community in the *Evangelische Kirche* (the German Protestant church) that was started in 1856. She also found two very close Christian friends in Paul Schröder, who was the German Consul in Beirut from 1896 to 1909, and his wife. The two families continued to be close friends into the next generation, when they all ended up back in Germany.[47] That Sayyida Salme was an integral part of the church community is also reflected in Rudolph's sponsorship of an altar at the *Evangelische Kirche* in his mother's memory.[48]

Not until 1914 did Sayyida Salme return to Germany, when she moved in with her youngest daughter Rosa, my great-grandmother. Many others were leaving Beirut at the time. Although we know few specifics about Sayyida Salme's life

---

44 Citizenship was also no issue, as the Ottoman Empire gave special privileges to many Europeans, including Germans, in negotiated "capitulations" that put them under consular jurisdiction. Her son Rudolph was even posted to the German consulate in Syria for a year in 1894. Because Germany had good relations with the Ottoman Empire, German nationals also faced less scrutiny than other nationals, especially as World War I neared.
45 See the translator's essay "On Faith" at pages 54–75 below.
46 This description of herself was later crossed out in her marked copy of the *Memoirs*. See pages 58–59 below.
47 See the photo on page 92 below. One of the Schröder daughters, Hedi, became the godmother of one of my aunts, and a Schröder granddaughter got to know my parents around 2000 when they lived for a time in Brazil.
48 See footnote 85 below.

in the Levant, nor what specifically motivated her to leave, history records what was going on around her. The end of the nineteenth century was a time of both ferment and volatility. The prosperity that brought in Western influence, that let Beirut blossom into a worldly city, also became a source of agitation. As businesses grew their heft and countries jockeyed for influence, the power balance started shifting. With the Young Turk revolution in 1908, Turkification increasingly clashed with Arab nationalism, and the Empire clamped down with martial law, arrests, executions, and other militarization. By now, the power balance was destabilizing. Local Christians made common cause with Muslim activists in a shared quest for autonomy, as Western influence continued to shape ideas of national identity and reform. The discontent with outside Ottoman rule turned even more toxic after the Empire aligned with Germany and Austria at the start of World War I. And politics were only part of it. The spring of 1915 brought an onslaught of locusts. Coming at the same time as the Allied maritime blockade at the start of World War I, the result was an absolutely debilitating famine.[49]

Whatever prompted Sayyida Salme to leave Beirut in 1914, it was a good time to be gone. By then, she was seventy years old, having lived a longer life than most of her half-siblings who had been born into the Sultan's harem, a time and place that must have seemed worlds away and an eternity ago. Times had greatly changed in those seventy years. As her end drew nearer, and the world grew madder, Sayyida Salme no doubt saw the benefits of having family around. No matter where in the world, the next years promised to be dark and difficult.

———•———

So now I have written even more than the Syrian text that she wrote. I hope only to amplify her words.

---

[49] The tragedy of these and other conflating factors is exhumed in detail in M. Tanielian's 2012 dissertation, "The War of Famine: Everyday Life in Wartime Beirut and Mount Lebanon (1914–1918)."

Rosa (Ghuza), Sayyida Salme's youngest daughter, in traditional attire

Notebook containing Sayyida Salme's handwritten essay on her time in Syria

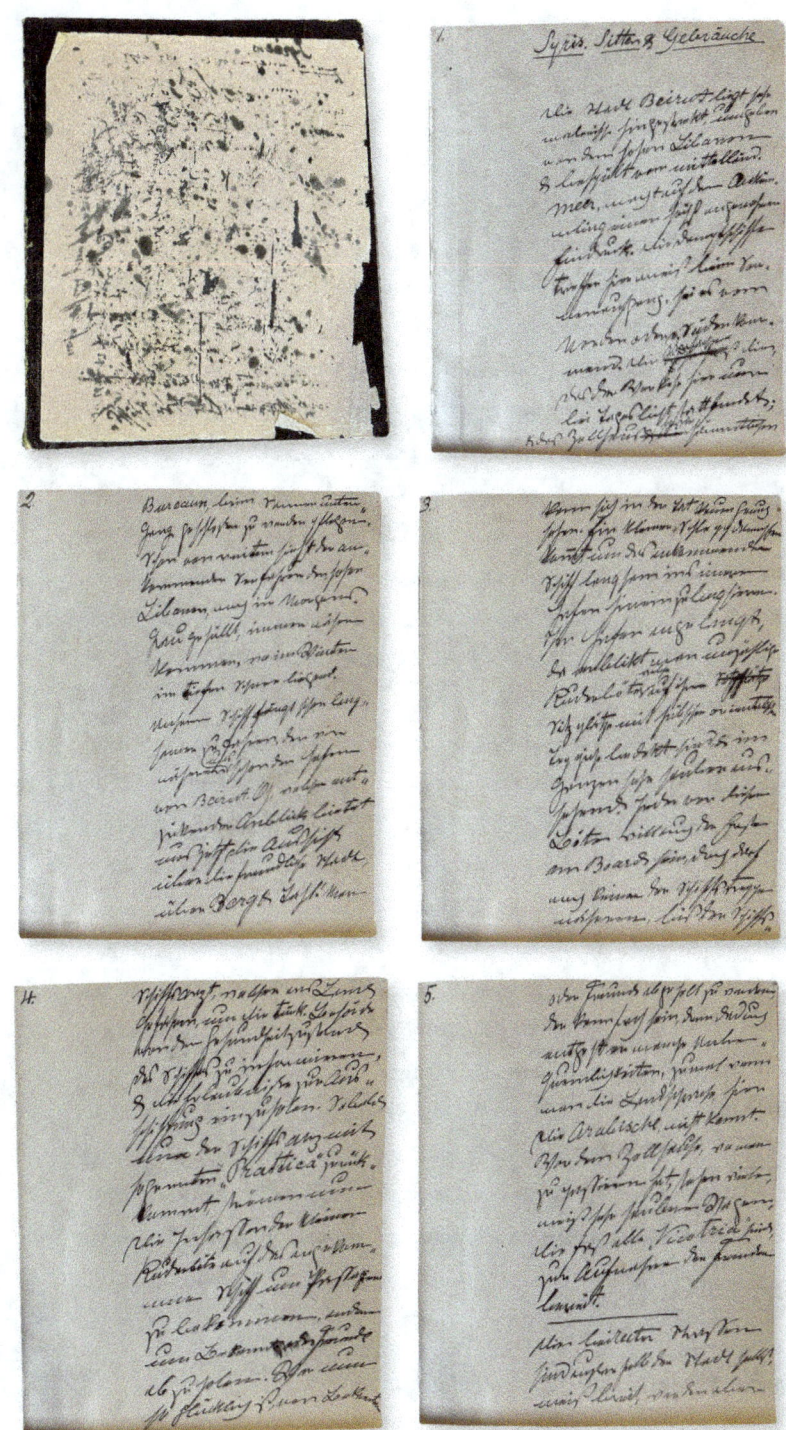

Syrische Sitten und Gebraeuche.

Die Stadt Beyrut liegt sehr mahlerisch hingestreckt; umgeben von dem hohen Libanon und bespuelt vom Mittel-Laendischen Meer macht sie auf den Ankoemmling einen hoechst angenehmen Eindruck. Die vom Norden oder Sueden kommenden Schiffe treffen hier meist beim Sonnenaufgang ein. Die Ursache hierfuer ist, dass der Verkehr hier bei Tageslicht nur statt findet, da das Zoll - Haus so wie saemmtliche Bureaus beim Sonnen Untergang geschlossen zu werden pflegen. Schon von weiten sieht der ankommende Seefahrer den im Morgengrau gehuellten hohen Libanon, auf dem im Winter bis tief hinab der Schnee lagert.

Unser Schiff faengt schon an die Fahrt zu verlangsamen, da wir uns der Hafeneinfahrt naehern. Oh, welch entzueckenden Anblick bietet uns jetzt die Aussicht ueber die freundliche Stadt, ueber Berg und Tal! Man kann sich in der Tat kaum genug sehen. Ein kleiner Schlappdampfer kommte entgegen gefahre um das ankommende Schiff langsam in den inneren Hafen hinein zu buchsieren. Im Hafen angelangt, erblickt man unzaehlige Ruderboete, deren Sitzplaetze mit huebschen orientalischen Teppichen bedeckt sind u nd im ganzen sehr sauber aussehen. Jedes von diesen Boeten will das Erste an der Schiffstreppe sein, doch darf sich keines derselben naehern, bis der Schiffsartzt, der an Land gefahren ist, um die tuerkische Behoerde ueber den Gesundheitszustand an Bord zu berichten die Erlaubniss zur Aus - schiffung eingeholt hat. Sobald nun dieser mit der sogennanten

First typewritten version of Sayyida Salme's manuscript

Syrische Sitten und Gebräuche.

Die Stadt Beyrut liegt sehr malerisch hingestreckt; umgeben von dem hohen Libanon und bespült vom mittelländischen Meer macht sie auf den Ankömmling einen höchst angenehmen Eindruck. Die von Norden oder Süden kommenden Schiffe treffen hier meist beim Sonnenaufgang ein. Die Ursache hier ist, dass der Verkehr hier nur bei Tageslicht stattfindet, da das Zollhaus sowie sämtliche Bureaux beim Sonnenuntergang geschlossen zu werden pflegen. Schon von weitem sieht der ankommende Seefahrer den im Morgengrau gehüllten hohen Libanon, auf dem im Winter bis tief hinab der Schnee lagert.

Unser Schiff fängt schon an die Fahrt zu verlangsamen, da wir uns der Hafeneinfahrt nähern. Oh, welch entzückenden Anblick bietet uns jetzt die Aussicht über die freundliche Stadt, über Berg und Tal ! Man kann sich in der Tat kaum satt sehen. Ein kleiner Schleppdampfer kommt uns entgegen gefahren, um das ankommende Schiff langsam in den inneren Hafen hinein zu bugsieren. Im Hafen angelangt, erblickt man unzählige Ruderboote, deren Sitzplätze mit hübschen orientalischen Teppichen bedeckt sind und im ganzen sehr sauber aussehen. Jedes von diesen Booten will das erste an der Schiffstreppe sein, doch darf sich keines derselben nähern, bis der Schiffsarzt, der an Land gefahren ist, um die türkische Behörde über den Gesundheitszustand an Bord zu berichten, die Erlaubnis zur Ausschiffung eingeholt hat. Sobald nun dieser mit der sogenannten prattica zurückkommt, strömen die Insassen der kleinen Ruderboote an Bord des Schiffes, um sich der

Second typewritten version of Sayyida Salme's manuscript

Syrian Customs and Conventions

The city of Beirut has a most picturesque layout. Surrounded by the highlands of Lebanon and bathed by the Mediterranean Sea, it makes a most pleasant first impression on visitors. Ships coming from the North or South usually arrive as the sun rises. It is a fact that traffic here happens only during the daytime, since the customs building, and all the various offices, are wont to close by sunset. Arriving sailors can see the Lebanese heights already from afar, shrouded in the fog of dawn, and in the winter covered deep down the slopes with snow.

Our ship is already starting to slow down, as we near the entrance to the harbor. Oh, what a lovely sight lies before us, across the welcoming city, across mountains and valley! There is, in point of fact, no getting one's fill from this view. A small tugboat approaches us to tow the arriving ship slowly into the inner port. Once in the port, the sight is full of countless rowboats, whose seats are covered with beautiful Oriental rugs and look very clean overall. Every one of these boats wants to be first in line at the ship's stairs, and yet none may come near until the ship's doctor, who has traveled to shore to report on the health conditions on board, has received permission from the Turkish authorities to disembark. As soon as this doctor returns with the so-called *prattica*, the occupants of these little rowboats swarm on board the ship to confirm their passengers, or to pick up friends or acquaintances. Whoever is lucky enough to be picked up by friends or acquaintances can be glad to avoid various inconveniences, particularly if the native tongue—in this case, Arabic— is unfamiliar. Usually there are many, mostly very clean carriages, almost all of which are Victorias, standing in front of the customs house that one has to pass through, ready to pick up any foreigners.

———·•·———

The streets of Beirut even on the outskirts of the city are mostly wide, but very poorly maintained, as the honorable municipality prefers to let the communal taxes disappear into its own pockets, instead of, as it should be, using them for the benefit of the community. And therefore, the summer dust and winter mire are permanent guests on the streets. As soon as one steps into one of the invariably very airy and massively built houses, those dirty streets that were just traversed are quickly forgotten.

/Everything here is nice and neat, even in the very poorest homes. The finer houses are completely laid out with marble floors; polished red tiles are now and again selected for the bedrooms. The manner of constructing houses is very simple, but suited to the climate and very comfortable. One usually enters directly into a very large hallway, completely covered with marble and about eleven meters long and seven meters wide. From there, any number of doors lead into rooms on the east, south, and west. A high window and a door that opens onto a balcony finish off the house on the north. This northern-facing room usually serves as the living room and stays cool throughout the summer, since it has no direct exposure to the sun. The best rooms in the house lie in the west, from whence a refreshing breeze is usually blowing, which makes these rooms particularly well-suited for bedrooms.

Beirut has a water pipeline, as well as gas lighting. The water travels down from Lebanon and is simply unmatched in quality. The fact that Beirut has seldom experienced a harmful epidemic is attributed to the good characteristics of the water. There were times when cholera was spreading in Egypt, Jaffa, Damascus, and neighboring Tripoli, while Beirut was completely spared. Food and rent is very cheap here; one can see that the people—by which I naturally mean the local population—are well-nourished.

The Residents

Syrians consistently come across as very intelligent. Their faces and figures are attractive; the coal-black eyes, and also the hair, notably of the youth, but above all of the women, may be called very beautiful. The men possess undeniable business skills worth marveling at; they are all, so-to-speak, born businessmen. With demonstrative talent in making money, even very simple folk often become rich so quickly that they are soon multi-millionaires (calculated in Franks). They love to imitate all things European, which frequently does them no favors, especially in their attire, as, for example, with their handsome head coverings. Their red fez looks much better on them than the European hats.

One particular major evil passion rules the population, namely the harmful game of hazard.[50] Rich people are said to play uninterrupted all day and night, whether in the club or their own homes. When they have trouble finding a partner, they entice their cooks, servants, or coachmen to play until someone else fills in. This passion has also taken hold of the women, who in this respect concede little to their men. Of course, there are also many exceptions, who strongly denounce their fellow citizens.

The population here is divided into two groups: Muslim and Christian. Although the first are fewer in number, they dominate to a much greater extent. Not because the state government is Muslim, but because the weaker group receives more government protection. This is generally how Turkish rule operates;[51] the weaker ones get more protection than the stronger ones. Whether Christian or Muslim, it is the same, as evidenced by the situation in Jaffa. There the Christians are in the minority and find consideration in every respect, as acknowledged by those affected. These state politics have, however, had a somewhat dispiriting effect on the Christian population in Beirut, despite it being in the majority over other religions. Accordingly, these Christians are also, as is commonly known, not exactly heroes. But in their defense, there is the fact that they, as Christians, are never drafted into the military and thus never get to experience the tough and very disciplined life in the service.

Foreigners are somewhat taken aback to discover that Syrians have practically no patriotic feelings! Syrians just want to know that the country is in the hands of one of the great European powers, according to their liking, of course, ideally with either England or France as their ruler. Beyond that, they have no shortage of personal pride. Both adults and adolescents possess sufficient self-esteem.

There are also many Jews who pursue their livelihoods as workers or merchants. They can mostly be seen on Saturday afternoons, with the women

---

50 A two-dice betting game that dates back to the Middle Ages, often likened to craps.
51 Syria was part of the Ottoman Empire and was governed by Turkish rulers until the Empire's collapse in 1918.

Syrian Customs and Conventions

and girls looking their finest, as they walk in droves on the beach. The devout women in the group wear wigs or headscarves, still very much in the old style. By contrast, the young generation is in very modern dress. Since only those who believe in the Mohammedan religion are drafted into the military, all other believers are free of the draft.

Syrians are very hospitable, and the more guests to care for, the happier they are. In conversation, they often address total strangers with "oh, my uncle" or "oh, my aunt," which sounds rather droll. Even small children are often referred to this way. In general, their behavior is very courteous, and they are polite beyond reproach. The one thing where they go a bit overboard is in the many compliments they make, even though they are truly masterful in this. Their character cannot always be described as open, and they are a bit veiled, for they are quite skilled in concealing their true opinion behind a deluge of meaningless words. Whenever they wish to skirt a question that might not be all that comfortable, they respond with a counterquestion to circumvent the answer.

What distinguishes Syrians, in their favor, from so many other cultures is their love of cleanliness. Even the simplest folk put great stock in keeping things clean, which makes a very favorable impression.

The well-to-do folk live totally *à la franca*, which is to say, according to European custom. They eat with knives and forks at set tables, sleep on European beds, and use whatever is needed for their comfort. This makes for great contrasts in that these same people, who are often surrounded by every conceivable convenience, also frequently have parents, siblings, and near relations that still live the way it was done a thousand years before, with no sense at all for using beds or table settings. It appears quite odd when a Syrian lady, dressed in the absolute latest Paris fashion from head to foot, rushes by in her equipage, while the mother or aunt sits beside her still wearing her traditional attire, with a black, silken mantilla on her head, rather than an imposing Parisian hat. The same applies to modern gentlemen, who sport European hats, while their relatives have kept the old headdress.

/The contrasts between the old and new generations can often have a strange effect on observers. There they are, the honorable old men, sitting on their divan, drinking black coffee, and smoking their *nargile* (hookah pipe), as in time immemorial, mindful and thoughtful, while their offspring sit beside them on modern, European seating, dressed in the latest Parisian look and speaking French amongst themselves. The latter is spoken as fine and accent-free as possible. Indeed, on the subject of learning foreign languages, the Syrians are masterfully predisposed. People who speak four or six foreign languages are not unusual. This race is very intelligent, very teachable, and hard working.

/As an example: There are a great number of wholesale merchants, bankers, and commissioners who work primarily with Europeans and who take their rising sons directly from school into their own shops to teach them on the spot. These inexperienced, half-grown boys are then soon so skilled in their trade that they quickly become the mainstay of their fathers. The people also possess a most astonishing ability to grasp things. A seamstress, for example, who can neither read nor write, nor even owns the otherwise indispensable measuring tape, sits on a mat on the floor and, following a picture she has been shown in a fashion magazine, produces the very finest high society and ball outfits.

Antonie's 1898 wedding in the Hotel Bassoul in Beirut

Sayyida Salme standing in the front yard of her 1909 Beirut home

At the front entrance of the same home, from Rudolph's album

From Rudolph's album, Sayyida Salme's first residence in Beirut

Ground floor, Sayyida Salme's daughter Rosa seated on the right

ON FAITH

There is no way to understand Sayyida Salme's life without considering her faith—by probing both her own beliefs and the religions that framed them.[52] Faith was her ultimate touchstone and throughline. Sayyida Salme's connection to God is the backdrop to all of her writings, as is the impact of religious dictates on her life. Throughout her formative years in Zanzibar and her transformative years in Germany, faith posed a duality that was profoundly personal and excruciatingly public. It embodied her spiritual connection as a social construct in ways that both stabilized and destabilized her.

Who am I to speak about her faith? Spiritual beliefs are intensely personal. I hold this question of faith in my hand—pen poised—and hardly dare go there. But there is plenty to say, even beyond the many things she said herself, about this—what is the word?—penumbra, essence, omnipresence—by which she defined her world, which in turn defined her. This essay can do no more than tap at the edges, knowing the topic is broader and deeper than any pen can consider. What faith meant to her can only be answered by what she said and believed. In writing this essay, my thoughts are but a distant prism to refract some light onto her life and writings.

Sayyida Salme had three principal phases in her life, with three geographies that also framed her faith: Zanzibar where she grew up as a Muslim until the age of twenty-two; Germany where she lived as a Christian until the age of forty-four; and the Middle East, principally Beirut, where she found her liminal space and stayed until the age of seventy.[53] Her pivot from Zanzibar to Germany came when she fell in love with a German merchant, Heinrich Ruete, and chose him as her husband. It was a choice that cascaded her into much lack of choice, including her conversion to Christianity.

In this long life of almost eighty years, there is one compelling truth: Faith was the source of both her anguish and relief. It tied her to her homeland in the

---

[52] At the outset, it is important to note the difference between faith and religion. In simple terms, faith comes from the inside, religion from the outside. At the nexus, faith is the translation of an established belief system into personal beliefs. It is also the connection of personal beliefs into a community of practice.

[53] See my first blog entry, "The Liminal In-Between," at www.sayyidasalme.com/blog. Her last ten years were spent back in Germany with her youngest daughter, until she died in Jena on February 29, 1924.

East and unsettled her when she moved to the West. It divided her into the before and after, here and there. Faith came from her core, as her source of meaning and purpose in life, but was shaped by others, by religious mores, rules, laws, the Koran and the Bible, as directed by authorities and society—with a violence that cut her to the core.

No bloodied Omani khanjar split her skin, and yet her conversion did no less damage when it dissected her soul. Like an amputation, the cut left her exposed and flailing:

> Divorced from my old beliefs, and attached to the new in name only, I began a time for which I have no words. Never in my whole life—neither before nor after—did I feel so morally bereft, robbed of every support, as right after my baptism. . . . [T]here is no doubt that it is a thousand times better to be a Muslim than to be neither Christian (meaning from the heart) nor Muslim. And it was with this largest possible chasm inside me that I entered Europe and its hallowed civilization. I fought internally with myself, no one surmising how much I suffered in silence. Not even to my own beloved husband could I openly admit that our views differed on this point. (*Letters*, pp. 8–9)

To add to this agony, can anyone even imagine what she felt when—literally days later—her infant son, whose budding life in her womb had precipitated her escape, died on the train as they travelled between Lyon and Paris on the way to Hamburg? What she thought of herself, and what she thought the Lord was saying to her, we will never know, as she never wrote a single word about it.

In time, she found some healing, but the scars barely masked the inner conflict. As she confronted one obstacle after another, and life descended into poverty, her distress continued to echo in the void. "Soon I also came to see the power of religion as the most powerful of all when it comes to affecting our inner lives and well-being." (*Letters*, p. 9) "Spiritual emptiness and loneliness, plus the early darkness of the winter days, conspired to oppress me." (*Letters*, p. 64)

Yet, where religion cleft her asunder, she managed to find footing in her underlying faith. To take one example, the first time she was in a German church, she still felt her God:

> Having taken my place on a pew between other congregants, I was overcome with an indescribable feeling of trepidation, which continued to worsen as I realized that the church service kept on going. I naturally could not understand a word of what was being sung and said. But the

sense that I was in the holiest sanctuary soon calmed me. (*Letters*, p. 32) Later [after Heinrich's death], it was indeed a great comfort for me to have been together with him in church shortly before his accident. For even though I had barely understood the sermon, simply the thought of being in the Lord's house has always given me fulfillment and kept me from becoming discouraged. (*Letters*, p. 50)

And again, after she learned of her brother Sultan Madjid's death: "Only my old trust in the Almighty held me upright and kept my courage, at that moment, from sinking all too much." (*Letters*, p. 60)

With this enduring devotion to God, it is tempting to suggest that the difference between Islam and Christianity did not need to create such a chasm in Sayyida Salme's life. It was, after all, the same Abrahamic God.[54] In those last months in Zanzibar, perhaps she had a naïve sense that crossing over to Christianity would be eased by this continuity. Or maybe, looking up to her husband, looking up to the West, she might have trusted that the "enlightened" ways held great promise. Then again, maybe she just trusted herself to find her way, as she had all along. For what did she know about the brave new world she was about to enter, or any world beyond her limited confines? She surely had no inkling of how little would carry over, how disappointed, even despairing, she would become. Realistically, she probably had no real room or means to think about it at all.

Whatever the case, it was all irrelevant once she chose her husband—and let me put "chose" in quotes, since we may fall in love more than we scan and select. Occam's Razor would point us to the simplest truth: Love conquers all. After that, there was no further choice in the matter. Conversion was the step she had to take.

We can thus trace her transgressive choice of husband to the severe consequences that followed. A Christian husband meant a Christian marriage, which for her meant a Christian baptism, both of which took place back-to-back in Aden on the very same day—May 30, 1867—only shortly after she saw Heinrich for the first time in nine months since fleeing the island and first introduced him to their infant son. This was the day her identity changed from princess in the royal family to wife of a German merchant, when her name changed from Sayyida Salme to Emily Ruete. It was also the day they left for Europe, when she was catapulted from East to West across a newly risen wall of religion that stood as a boundary with no way back.

---

54 Muslims view Jews and Christians as "people of the book," reflecting a recognition of shared early scripts and a shared, monotheistic belief in but one, true God.

Emily's baptism recorded on the Archdeaconry and Diocese of Bombay's form

To be clear, her conversion was the issue, the gravest sin under *Sharia* Islamic law, not her contact with a German man, nor even the pregnancy, though those were bad enough. It was the rejection of Islam that was considered inexcusable. No matter that she did not reject religion altogether, but stayed fully committed to a belief in God. No matter that the conversion was not a choice per se, just a pre-condition for her marriage. Devout as she was, she might well have stayed Muslim, had that been allowed. But no, Christianity was her only option. And this was the travesty, the treason. Death, or at the very least imprisonment, was at the time—and in some cases remains today—the expected punishment for voluntary rejection of Islam.

It is plausible that the Ibadi Islam of the Omani Sultanate, with its tradition of moderation and tolerance, might have put less emphasis on official retribution, and instead put the onus on the defector's accountability to God, but no one gave Sayyida Salme a free pass. When word came around that she would be "sent to Mecca"[55]—and everyone knew what that meant—it was a clear invitation for her to leave the island. Whether she chose to do so of her own free will may still be debated. Yes, there should be no doubt that she chose her

---

55 Said to be "tantamount to a death sentence." E. van Donzel, p. 14.

husband,[56] but did all the sequelae of her need to flee the island and her need to answer "yes" to the pastor[57] meet the criterion that she voluntarily rejected Islam, as Islamic doctrine requires? [58] On that August evening as she set foot in the Indian Ocean, and on that May day in Aden when she took her Christian name, how voluntary was it?

We hear her cry for help as they left Marseille, headed for Hamburg:

> As we drove from our hotel to the train station, I was gripped by such an unfamiliar fear that I would have preferred to scream out loud. I had the feeling as though, from this moment on, my homeland was being pulled ever further from me, and all the bridges were crashing in behind me. The cry of my soul for you turned into a thousand voices from my beloved island, all seemingly calling to me in unison: "Do not go any further, better to return again!" I fought a terrible fight within myself. Like an automaton, I stepped into the train that would now seek to take me, as quickly as possible, to an unknown land, to total strangers, as if I was in the greatest hurry to reach my future destination. And so we kept on riding toward the North. (*Letters*, p. 6)

For most of us today, the consequences of choosing our partners, married or not, are nowhere near as stark. In Sayyida Salme's time and place, however, this was a hard border, an either/or and no in-between. In choosing Heinrich, she lost almost everything—her homeland, family, close friends, possessions, properties, and past; everything familiar was brutally wrenched from her. And when even her religion was exchanged, she lost an integral piece of herself that was replaced by something that at first meant nothing. The only foothold she had left was in herself, in Heinrich, and in what she could make of her faith.

Years later, she asked herself the question: "I left my homeland as a complete Arab and a good Muslim, and what am I today?" (*Memoirs*, p. 217) She then responded: "A poor Christian and somewhat more than half a German." It is a favorite and oft-cited quote. Yet, what typical readers of the *Memoirs* do not know is that she later struck that answer when she marked up her *Memoiren* for

---

56 See the excerpt from her son Rudolph's letter that I describe in my essay "On Freedom." (*Letters*, p. 130)
57 See my footnote on her affirmation in English. (*Letters*, footnote 34, p.8)
58 Notably, traditional Islam did not support forced conversions. Modern interpretations go further and accept freedom of belief in quoting from the Koran that "there is no compulsion in religion." (Surah Al-Baqarah 2:256)

subsequent publication.[59] It speaks volumes that she originally responded as she did, but it speaks even more loudly that she then crossed it out. It tells us that, over time, she became more certain of her Christianity and claimed it for her own. We do her wrong to tether her to an unevolving sense of her own spirituality.

The early years were, however, no less agonizing. The problem was not just the switch from one religion to another, but also the straddle that left her hanging between religions, not knowing what to make of herself or the new religion. Worse than being neither-nor was being a fraud. It was a condition that plagued her from page to page:

> On top of that, to be called Christian, even though I was as much a Muslim inside as you yourself. Through and through, I felt so despicable that I should appear different from what I actually was. I will tell you this in unvarnished frankness: Beware of changing your religion without complete conviction! Conviction? Yes, from whom and what should I have gained any conviction? No one, as it was, cared one whit about my true faith. . . . I felt so despicably false to be considered a Christian when I had absolutely no clear idea *how and what* Christianity even means. (*Letters*, pp. 8–9)

> The thought that kept me so preoccupied put my poor soul into great conflict. I found so few good examples of devout Christians that I personally felt I was neither fish nor fowl. Separated from my former beliefs, I had nonetheless found no real replacement. How was I, as a Mohammedan, supposed to feel attracted to the new faith, when even the people who were born and bred Christian were so disdainful toward their own religion? Your kind heart would certainly have suffered, had you been able to see into my tormented soul. (*Letters*, pp. 26–27)

> [I]t became quite clear to me that being Christian was a relative term. Accordingly, my inner struggle grew more and more excruciating every day. (*Letters*, p. 36)

Her spirituality was terribly unsettled in those early years. It was an immense struggle to find herself and her God within the religions that defined him. Understandably, she kept reverting back to the God of her childhood when

---

59 Although there was no subsequent publication—the family was apparently unable to find a willing publisher—her intention to delete is clear. My new *Memoirs* translation incorporates all her edits from her hand-marked edition, found in the Leiden University Libraries Special Collections at NINO SR 613 a-b. For more on this, see my essay "On Translating" in the *Memoirs* (specifically p. 254).

Christianity failed to replace the ingrained rituals and threatened to strain the relationship between her and the Almighty. As she wrote to her counterpart in Zanzibar: "To console you, I can also let you know that, in the initial years after my baptism, I instinctively recited my old prayer to myself whenever I was alone" (*Letters*, p. 9)—all the while consoling herself.

———•———

If we consider the essential differences between Islam and Christianity, doctrinally and practically, it seems that Sayyida Salme's upbringing persisted beyond her Christian conversion. Even after she gave herself up to her new religion, her reliance on an undifferentiated God appears to continue. There is no sense of the trinity. We never hear her address Christ or Jesus, the son of God, directly. Instead, her account of the early years in Germany is filled with appeals only to God, the Lord. "Have I not, in my difficult position, unceasingly asked the dear God for help and support, since I always remained discontented inside, indeed utterly miserable." (*Letters*, p. 69)

For Sayyida Salme, it seems that God the Almighty was still the maker and mover of all.[60] There is but one moment after her husband's death when she lost that certainty and could not pray—"I felt spurned by my Creator and was thus totally unmoored"—until she finally caught herself again in the prayer of her youth: "Nothing shall ever happen to us but what the Lord has decreed for us, so praise be unto him forever, Amen!" (*Letters*, p. 55) And yet, she knew that this Islamic belief in destiny did not translate well into Christianity. She seems to have held back on her views to others, so as not to come across as ignorant, or humiliate herself, or discover what she did not want to know.[61] But in a telling passage, we hear her resisting with reproof:

> Certainly, now and again there were people who meant well with me and tried to comfort me in their way. I say, in their way, because after I once called out in utter despair: "Oh, if I knew not that this was

---

[60] This reflected the Islam in which she was raised: "A Muslim not only recognizes his God as his creator and keeper, but also feels the presence of the Lord at all times. He is certain that it is not his will, but the will of the Lord that comes to pass, in all things, large and small." (*Memoirs*, p. 14)

[61] She was, for example, "acutely interested" in her first Christmas experience, "not having wanted to ask my husband about [Christian festivals]—on the one hand, out of consideration for his feelings toward his religion (for what did I know back then of the countless ways to profess one's Christianity?), and on the other hand—and that was the main thing for me—to avoid discovering that the Christian religion was in fact, as some tended to believe in our parts, idol worship. Exactly that would have been contrary to my convictions. For these reasons, I steered clear of any questions pertaining to the upcoming celebration." (*Letters*, pp. 34–35)

On Faith

my God's will, I could never find peace!", the response was to try to reeducate me. I was asked if I really believed that God in fact takes care of our fates and everything we encounter on this earth. I need not describe to you how innerly appalled I was at this profane question. It seems to me that but a very few, select Christians are familiar with the complete Holy Scripture, which clearly enough tells us that the Lord knows the number of our hairs and that no sparrow falls off the roof without His will. On such occasions, I could not thank the Lord enough for letting me enter this world as a Muslim. (*Letters*, pp. 64–65)

As she describes in the *Memoirs*, her life growing up in Zanzibar had few distractions and even fewer obligations. She had time and space to amply live out her faith, not only to pray five times a day, but also to register virtually every act from a faith-based perspective. This was in the nature of the Muslim experience, where social rituals are particularly pronounced, where religion is often described as a lifestyle. Indeed, the *Memoirs* offer a rare ethnological insight into the totality of the Muslim experience in the harem and royal household. It is an excellent primer on how Islam's code of conduct structured all hours of the day, especially in the absence of other structure. As Sayyida Salme says: "In our house, with its hundreds of residents, fixed rules were elusive, since everyone could and did follow their own tastes and convenience. Only the two main meals and regularly recurring prayers forced the community to live according to a specific, more established order." The ensuing pages lay out the course of the full day. (*Memoirs*, pp. 39-42) It is no surprise then, when she gets to describing her later life in Germany, that the *Letters* painfully witness Sayyida Salme's grasping search for a Christian equivalent.

The shock of switching religions also came with the overwhelming inundation of everything new and incredible, often incomprehensible, in the West. In effect, Sayyida Salme moved from a life where her faith could be central and practical to a life where it was intangible and elusive. Rather than living a religion that was patterned into the daily rituals, her European communing with God was all but crowded out—first, by all the new, but even over time, by a much busier life, especially as a bereft, impoverished widow with three small children. Is this a fair statement: Her reaching for God took far more effort and extra intention right at the time when she needed him most? She does not talk about it this way, but this crowding out feels palpable. With her change in setting, her changed lifestyle became more existential than spiritual. And yet, the spiritual remained as existential as ever to who she was.

Not for lack of trying, it was all about the struggle. Poor Christian and half a German? We can ask ourselves why Sayyida Salme chose to delete those words, but the rest of her words tell us that they were, in any case, too simplistic, too categorical a description for what she was made to endure. Arab society, however—at least the patriarchal dynasty—saw none of the nuance and refused to forgive. It left no room for any residual attachment or deeper connection. In an instant, she was reduced to an insurmountable label: infidel, apostate, heretic. All else, it seemed, might somehow be absolved, but not her rejection of Islam.

Why was her conversion so threatening to society that it merited death? That she would be so dangerous as to be disappeared? Was it about religion, sex, purity of the blood line, social cohesion, all of the above? It did not help that Sayyida Salme was subjecting herself to an encroaching colonial power, an abandonment of Islam with greater political bite. It also did not help that she was a princess, not just anyone, but representative of the royal house. Failure to rein her in would make the Sultan look weak, no matter how sympathetic he might have been to her cause.[62]

From a modern lens, it seems apparent that this was also about guarding and controlling women. In the hierarchy of the patriarchy, it was acceptable for Muslim men to marry non-Muslims, notably Christian and Jewish women "of the book"[63]—but not the other way around. Why? Because it was assumed that men would be in charge of the home. Wives would presumably accept the husband's religion, but whether converted or not, the main point was the fate of the children. If the man was in charge, the children would be raised under Islam. Socially speaking, it seems, men's eyes could roam as long as Islam ruled the home. By contrast, Islam typically considered matrimony between a Muslim woman and a Christian man invalid. Not only was the marriage rejected, but social rejection would follow as well.[64]

In Germany, too, interfaith marriage was frowned upon, if not forbidden. In this specific case, Heinrich was a Lutheran from the outwardly positioned,

---

[62] Her half-brother Madjid, who was Sultan at the time she fled, was indeed very supportive of his errant half-sister, even after she participated in the coup against him. The two had reconciled before she left the island, and it is clear that he wished her no harm. (*Memoirs*, pp. 201–3)

[63] See footnote 54 above.

[64] In the Arab world, gender differences around marriage are still remarkably pronounced today. See, for example, "An Insta Triple Talaq" on my blog at www.sayyidasalme.com/blog. From speaking to Omani women, I hear that social pressures also keep women constrained even where rules and laws have changed, perhaps even more than in Sayyida Salme's time. Comparisons can be made with her chapters "Arab Matrimony" and "Arab Visits Among the Ladies." (*Memoirs*, pp. 123–32)

trade-oriented port city of Hamburg. But even though Protestants were less rigid than Catholics, and even though this autonomous city-state was more cosmopolitan than other parts of Germany, social codes and proper behavior in Sayyida Salme's new setting left little room for exotic entanglements.

To be sure, Sayyida Salme's conversion was both a religious betrayal and a social violation. This is even evident in the institutional response. In Sayyida Salme's case, it apparently did not matter that both Christianity and Islam were happy to gain new believers. Christianity preaches conversion as a pathway to salvation, and Muslims believe in the universality of Islam; both are called to bring others into their religious folds for the betterment of humanity. In all its missionary zeal of the time, including in East Africa, did the Protestant church appreciate that Sayyida Salme had found her way to Jesus? Did it at least recognize and nurture her intense effort to crack the code of Christianity? Not that the record shows. The brunt that she bore for leaving Islam, it seems, was not compensated by much of any affirmation by the Christian church. It may not be farfetched to think that many Christians could not see past her Oriental exoticism to embrace Sayyida Salme as one of them.[65]

Notably, the couple was not married in either Zanzibar or Germany. They could not wed in Zanzibar, where the union was out of the question,[66] and they could not travel and arrive respectably in Hamburg as a couple with a child without already being married. Instead, they tied the knot in Aden, apparently another one of those liminal spaces, in the Anglican Christ Church[67] with an English minister.[68] And that had its consequences, too. This riveting act of mixed-faith, mixed-race matrimony not only cost Sayyida Salme her religious and royal identities, but, unbeknownst to Heinrich, also cost him his national identity. Only later did he discover that he was no longer a citizen of Hamburg—he had apparently become stateless. Fortunately for him, he was

---

[65] This was also the time that Christian missionaries in East Africa engaged in mass conversions to bring enlightenment and salvation to local "primitives"; academic endeavors to document "scientific racism" were flourishing; and the gawking public was drawn in masses to popular human zoos, which started, of all places, in Hamburg. See my blog post "Who remembers human zoos?" at www.sayyidasalme.com/blog.
[66] As Sayyida Salme herself succinctly says: "A union with my beloved would have been impossible in my homeland, so I naturally harbored the wish to leave the island quietly." (*Memoirs*, p. 202)
[67] See G.S.P. Freeman-Grenville's annotated reprint of the 1888 Ward & Downey *Memoirs of an Arabian Princess*, p. 319 (1981) (hereinafter G.S.P. Freeman-Grenville).
[68] "My baptism took place in the English chapel in Aden . . . Immediately after that, our wedding took place according to English rituals." (*Memoirs*, p. 202) Notably, when preparing her marked copy for republication, Sayyida Salme deleted the accompanying statement that she had received prior religious instruction.

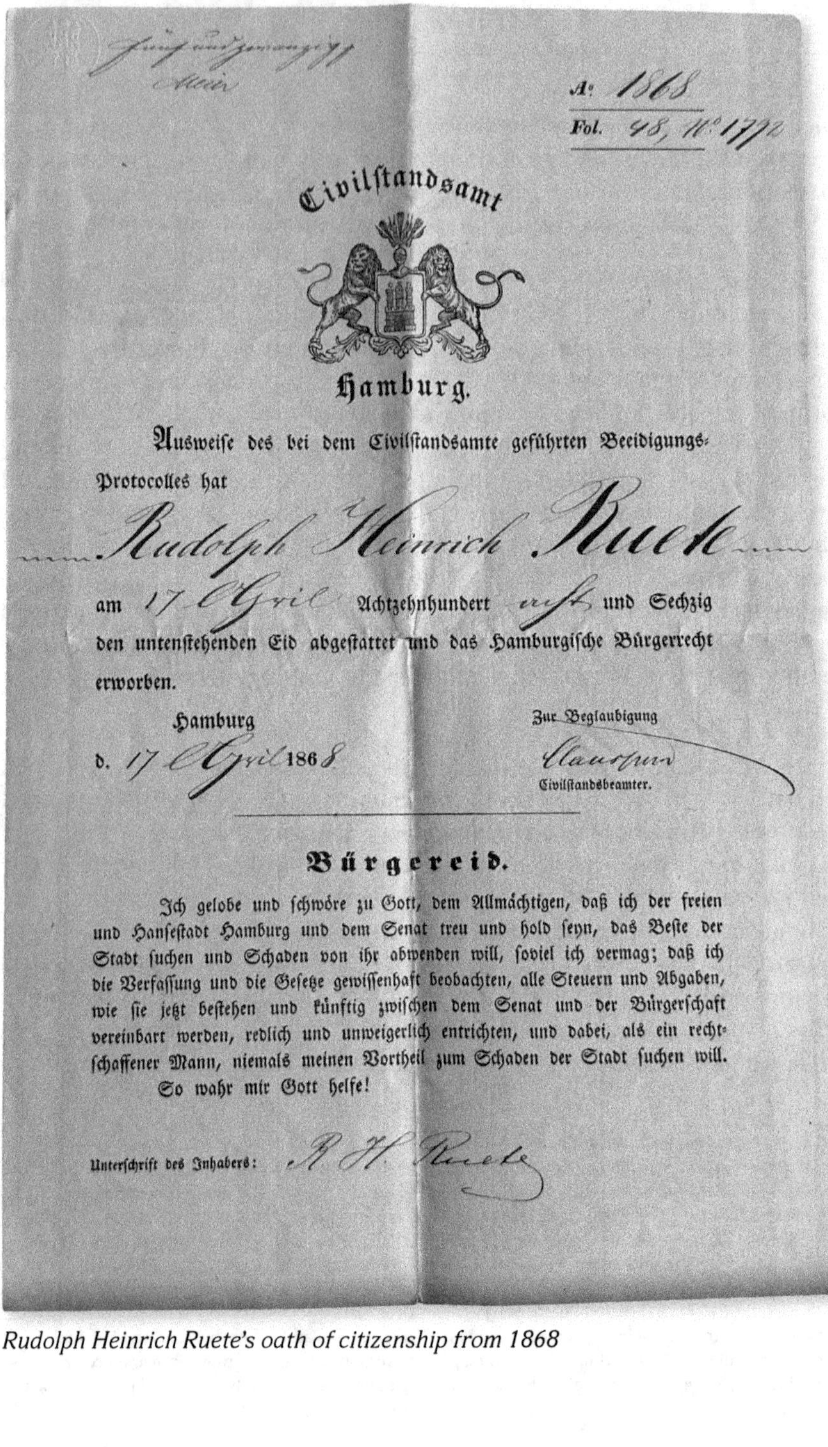

Civilstandsamt

Hamburg.

Ausweise des bei dem Civilstandsamte geführten Beeidigungs-Protocolles hat

Rudolph Heinrich Ruete

am 17 April Achtzehnhundert acht und Sechzig den untenstehenden Eid abgestattet und das Hamburgische Bürgerrecht erworben.

Hamburg
d. 17 April 1868

Zur Beglaubigung

Clausnitz
Civilstandsbeamter.

Bürgereid.

Ich gelobe und schwöre zu Gott, dem Allmächtigen, daß ich der freien und Hansestadt Hamburg und dem Senat treu und hold seyn, das Beste der Stadt suchen und Schaden von ihr abwenden will, soviel ich vermag; daß ich die Verfassung und die Gesetze gewissenhaft beobachten, alle Steuern und Abgaben, wie sie jetzt bestehen und künftig zwischen dem Senat und der Bürgerschaft vereinbart werden, redlich und unweigerlich entrichten, und dabei, als ein rechtschaffener Mann, niemals meinen Vortheil zum Schaden der Stadt suchen will. So wahr mir Gott helfe!

Unterschrift des Inhabers: *R. H. Ruete*

Rudolph Heinrich Ruete's oath of citizenship from 1868

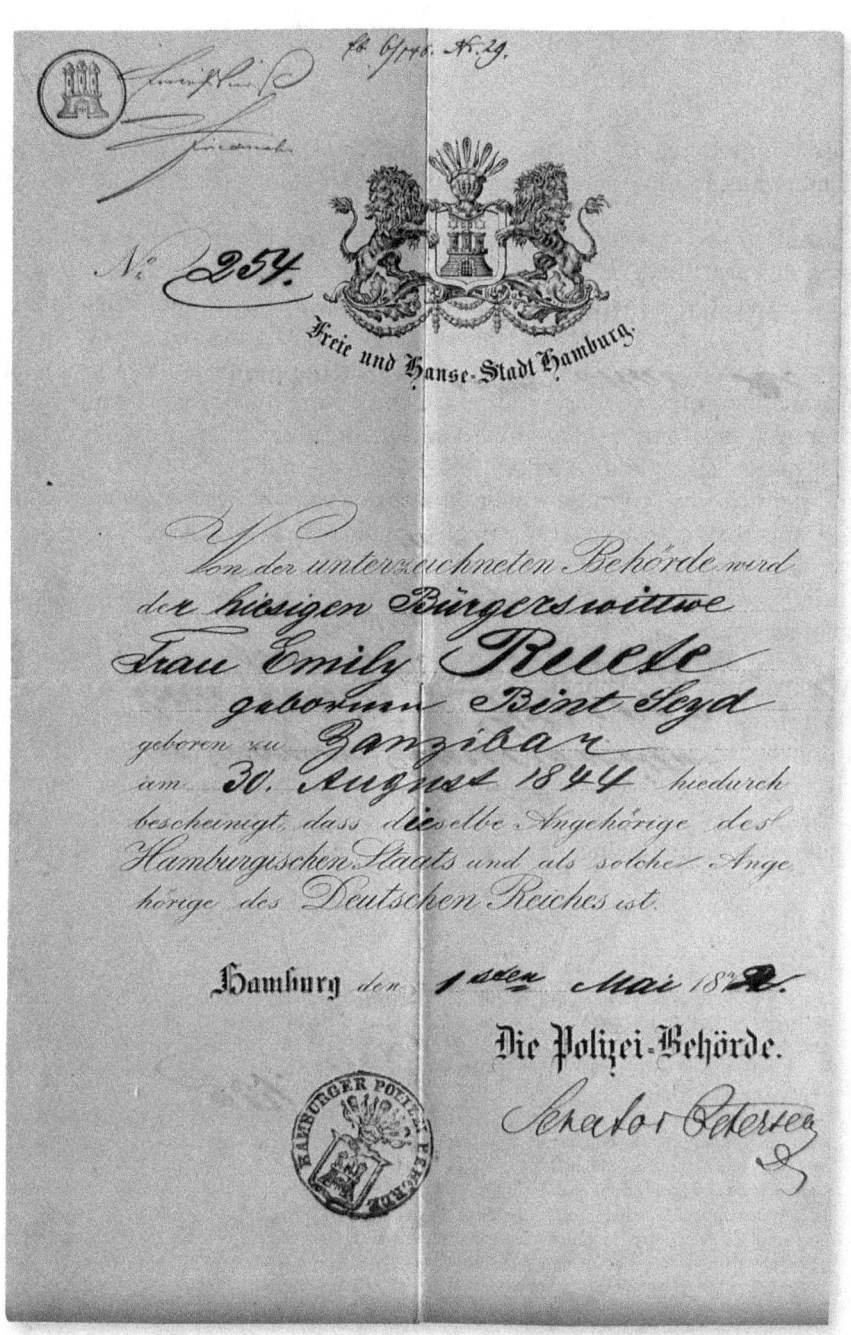

Emily Ruete's certification of citizenship from 1872

quickly able to regain his status.[69] Sayyida Salme, in turn, became a citizen of Hamburg as a widow some years later.[70]

This unforeseen loss of citizenship was not a fluke, but the norm. It reflected geopolitical attitudes at a time when dual loyalty and dual citizenship were not recognized. The act of marrying abroad essentially meant subjecting oneself to another country's regime, thereby signaling diminished loyalty to the state. In this respect, Sayyida Salme's conversion from Islam to Christianity also mapped onto the larger Oriental-Occidental divide, in which religious identity was largely conflated with social and national identity. The choice of Islam or Christianity was not just a religious marker, but also a cultural and political one, through which boundaries were set and on which public cohesion rested. Crossover marriages not only bucked the established order, but also threatened political primacy, particularly at a time when Muslim societies were loath to give any further influence and dominance to Western colonial powers.

At some level, lighter touchpoints through trade and exploration were fine,[71] even crossovers through slavery and *sarari* (concubines) were fine, but losing a princess to a foreign marriage was not. With stability resting on East-West divisions, the different religions played their parts in creating recognizable borders. That Sayyida Salme was seen by the British as a wild card that could undermine their cunning diplomacy,[72] that her status as a German citizen was

---

69 We know this from records that Fridjof Gutendorf found deep in the Hamburg archives—our thanks to him for his extensive efforts. As the records show, a proverbially diligent bureaucrat came across the discrepancy when handling the birth certificate of Antonie, the couple's first child born in Hamburg. Issuance of the birth certificate was delayed until the matter was resolved. Since Heinrich came from a well-established, upstanding family, the whole procedure, from application to Hamburg Senate confirmation, took little more than a week.
70 At the same time, Sayyida Salme acquired German citizenship as an automatic add-on, following German unification in 1871. It is an odd history that Heinrich, who died in 1870, never became a German citizen, while his Omani/Zanzibari wife did.
71 Indeed, it was basically business as usual when Heinrich was allowed to continue his commercial activities in Zanzibar without restraint or repercussion in the months after the scandal became known.
72 As part of her "education" in the West, Sayyida Salme eventually became wise to the games that countries play: "Later, I came to better understand why my deeply desired reconciliation with my brother would have been especially unwelcome in London at that very moment. Since the Sultan neither speaks a European language, nor understands the subtleties of European diplomacy, the English wanted to keep him in a complete state of ignorance to ensure no last-minute trouble in getting specific treaties signed. Had I in fact made peace with him, they assumed I would have used my somewhat broader knowledge of European affairs to share various bits of information that would have benefited him and Zanzibar, but been all the more contrary to English government interests. Without suspecting a thing, I had simply become a victim of these 'humane' politics." (*Memoirs*, p. 210)

later put into play against her Sultan brother Barghash,[73] and that she herself confidentially wrote to Sultan Barghash that she could "be useful to you with all the arts of Europe,"[74] went straight to the point.

The controversy around Sayyida Salme's conversion also signaled the primacy of the church. Even though her father had dropped the Imam part of his title, preferring to use only Sayyid as the Omani equivalent for Sultan,[75] he was the picture of piety, signaling to the Omani and Zanzibari people over which he ruled that Allah ruled above all. There was no discernible daylight between his reign and his religion. Sayyid Madjid, who succeeded his father, was also entirely devout, and the subsequent Sayyid Barghash even more so. Barghash, feeling justified by her travesty against the Almighty, persisted to his dying day with his refusal to reconcile, claiming "I have no sister, she died many years ago."[76]

In Germany, on the other hand, a little daylight between church and state appeared with the dawn of the *Kulturkampf* (literally translated "culture war") under Chancellor Otto von Bismarck. It is a quirk of fate that the German Civil Marriage Act[77] was passed only a few years after Sayyida Salme found the love of her life. Until then, marriage had been entirely controlled by the church, but suddenly the state was stepping in. As of 1875, German marriages could be officially recognized only through administrative acts, which had to happen first. This opened the door to unions outside of Catholicism and Protestantism, at least theoretically. Surprising as it may be, a Hamburg administrator could have legally married a Christian Heinrich and a Muslim Sayyida Salme, if only

---

73 See E. van Donzel, pp. 63–70; see also page 23 in the *Addendum* above and G.S.P. Freeman-Grenville at pp. 329–30.
74 Citing Sir John Kirk's translation of her handwritten letter to Sultan Barghash in 1883, as provided in E. van Donzel, p. 53.
75 G.S.P. Freeman-Grenville at p. 308; see also *Memoirs*, p. 6.
76 From Colonel J.W.C. Kirk's summary of his father Sir John Kirk's files, appearing as an annex in G.S.P. Freeman-Grenville at p. 330. This is also corroborated in correspondence from Sayyida Salme's son Rudolph to his sister Antonie dated January 17, 1926, that was kept in the family of my second cousin, Alexander von Brand. This letter states that Barghash said the same to Sir Lloyd William Mathews, the English military leader (known as the "strongman of Zanzibar") during most of Barghash's reign, as recorded by Sir Rennell Rodd in 1893. Rudolph writes this in the context of his thoughts about potentially publishing his mother's writings.
77 As one of a series of policies enacted during this time, the *Gesetz über die Beurkundung des Personenstands und die Eheschliessung* marked an important shift from church-controlled marriages to state-controlled marriages that was largely aimed at the Catholic church, following the papal infallibility declaration as part of its *Pastor Aeternus* in 1870 and the rise of its *Zentrumspartei* (Center Party). Considering that this step towards marital freedom was decried at the time as an attack on religious freedom, it seems that not much in the playbook has changed 150 years later.

their timeline had been slightly delayed. But whether this emerging power struggle between church and state would have made a difference for them is unlikely. In their tightly wound, nineteenth-century society, this requisite civil marriage was still no substitute for church marriage.

Despite the progress in modern times, however, conversion from Islam is still seen to violate religious norms and remains controversial in some Muslim circles today. Even in Oman, the effort to balance tradition and modernity has reinforced some conservative strands. Religions are free to worship in certain areas, for example, but active proselytizing of Muslims is prohibited.[78] Despite Oman's showcased support of religious freedom that developed under Sultan Qaboos bin Said's reign (1970–2020),[79] residual concerns about someone like Sayyida Salme may linger. Over the years, I have wondered to what extent the Omani Sultanate would be ready to fully embrace a family member who is a great literary figure as the first Arab woman to publish a book,[80] and who is better known worldwide than any of her sibling Sultans, with arguably more name recognition than even her illustrious father—despite her conversion. Some may say that she received this visibility for all the wrong reasons, but I sense a different mood emerging. That many Omanis appreciate and love Sayyida Salme is something I feel unequivocally whenever someone from Oman finds out how I got my middle name.[81]

---

78 See the "2022 Report on International Religious Freedom: Oman" published by the United States Department of State through its Office of International Religious Freedom.

79 According to the Foreign Ministry of Oman's website on its Religious Freedom page: "Freedom of belief is guaranteed under the Basic Statute of the State.... The Omani Penal law stipulates that all the Abrahamic faiths (not just Islam) shall be protected from offence." www.fm.gov.om/about-oman/state/religious-freedom (2024) Oman also showcased its approach in a very successful traveling show that lasted a decade, from April 2010 through June 2019. Entitled "Tolerance, Understanding, Coexistence: Oman's Message of Islam," 125 exhibitions in 37 countries were sponsored by Oman's Ministry of Awqaf and Religious Affairs, under the project guidance of Mohammed Said Al-Mamari, now Minister since 2022, in collaboration with Arabia Felix Synform under Georg Popp. The 2019 status report notes that "[t]he success of this Omani-German venture demonstrates that constructive cooperation between East and West is, contrary to widespread opinion, quite possible even today ... [as it] helps raise awareness and reduce misunderstandings about Islam, contributes to a public dialogue, and substantiates the positive image of the Sultanate of Oman." www.islam-in-oman.com

80 Others may assess to what extent the multiple Arabic translations of the *Memoiren*, both government-sponsored and privately published, have remained true to her original text, as opposed to leaving out religiously sensitive parts.

81 In case there is any question, no one in my branch of the family, from Rosa on downwards, has any current status within the royal family, nor, to my knowledge, has anyone in my branch actively sought reconciliation. This is in contrast to Rosa's brother Rudolph, who made it his mission to return to royal status. He was finally granted recognition in 1932 as a member of the royal family by Sultan Khalifa bin Harub, who reigned from 1911 to 1960. E. van Donzel, p. 125.

Holiday card fashioned after a stamp that was issued to commemorate the Sultanate of Zanzibar's independence (uhuru) from the United Kingdom, just a month before the Jamhuri 1964 revolution that deposed the Sultan

The situation seems much the same in Zanzibar. While conversion from Islam has some constitutional protections, it remains largely taboo and socially unacceptable. However, this is also a country that has a long history of religious tolerance, dating back to Sayyid Said's multicultural flourishing of society in the mid-nineteenth century that included active mosques, churches, and temples in Stone Town.[82] And far from disparaged, Sayyida Salme features heavily in the island's bid for tourists, notably these days with the Princess Salme Museum and Princess Salme Spice Tours. As far back as 1998 when my family first visited the island, Sayyida Salme even had her own room in the Palace Museum. Unfortunately, the building, which is the original Bet il Sahel described in the *Memoirs,* is now closed due to disrepair.

When I step back, I am especially saddened to think it all stemmed from love. The conversion, the calumny, the casting out, the inner conflict—all because she expressed her physical, emotional, and spiritual self in her love for Heinrich and her love of God. How can such love be the root of such tragedy and agony? Precisely because she was true to her love—and that, I would suggest, was also rooted in her ability to love herself, to see her own value, to embrace her creative, inspired, and even boundary-breaking being. Later, it also reflected love for her children, when everything she did was ultimately for them. "It was only for the children that I sought to salvage whatever could still be salvaged. My own person was the least of my thoughts." (*Letters*, p. 89)

---

[82] The influential and internationally respected Zanzibari historian, Professor Abdul Sheriff, penned an impassioned portrayal of this history in his essay titled "The Zanzibar Riots, the Union & Religious Tolerance" (2012).

In the raw repetition of her lived experience, the *Letters* keep returning to the question:

> Did I make the right choice in this regard? I must admit openly to you that I have asked myself this question so many times. Overall, I believe I handled the situation far too idealistically. . . . I did not approach things carefully enough back then, and instead gave exaggerated importance to ideals that I pursued with such effort and the greatest sacrifice. . . . The thought of continuing to live in this, for me, so incredibly complicated European setting, and the memory of my irreplaceable loss, often robbed me of my courage to go on. Above all, I was pursued by a constant feeling of abandonment that threatened to break my heart throughout every day. Under these circumstances, everything became so very difficult for me, and over time, I started to lose my resolve. "Strength, oh Lord, strength and steadfast perseverance!" remained my constant prayer for years. (*Letters*, pp. 72-73)

It was a constant prayer. And while her faith was rooted in her love of God, it was also rooted in her community. Her connection to God was in many ways how Sayyida Salme drew close to others, particularly in Zanzibar, where the beloved connections she had to give up were embedded in Muslim rituals. The memories recounted in the *Memoirs* feature the praying, fasting, major festivals, sacrificial offerings, marriage ceremonies, funeral rites, all described with deep attachment, all about her community. It was a matter of belonging. Being connected through Allah meant belonging to the tribe. As she described at the end of her second visit to Zanzibar in 1888:

> My siblings and relatives felt great compassion for me, and they beseeched me to become theirs again, to return to the old faith of my fathers and turn my back on the Germans. "Come, be ours again, for you belong to us! Do not go back to those strangers, but stay here with your family. We give you a sacred promise that you will have a good life with us." (*Addendum* at page 32 above)

This closeness, however, points to a disconnect. Sayyida Salme never writes about what it meant to abjure the faith of her parents, both of whom had been so devout. Surely, this also stung. It is not hard to wonder if she would/could have chosen Heinrich had her mother or father still been living, had it required a direct choice against them. But they were gone, her father having died in 1856 and her mother in 1859. Sayyida Salme, barely a teenager, says that she initially drifted "like a rudderless ship flailing about on a stormy sea" (*Memoirs*, p. 171). The ensuing post-coup rift in the extended family then intensified the sense of abandonment, leaving even more room for Sayyida Salme's community to shift. In the vacuum of her orphaned and shunned state, as her harem family pulled away, her chosen family became all the more important on this earth.[83]

And yet, her choice of Heinrich is another disconnect. Did she realize early on that he was not as full of faith as she? Soon enough, it seems, she came to understand that his connection to God was more superficial. For many in the secularized Hamburg where he was raised, Christianity was more of a social and cerebral experience, perhaps more head over heart, or as Sayyida Salme put it, more taught and less lived:

> It was always hard not to compare how little Muslims are taught about their own religion and yet exhibit such solid faith—in contrast to Christian children, who are so painstakingly instructed in school. I had the impression that religion is taught here more as mere science, to be forgotten again at the first opportunity or even oft-criticized, as I regrettably had to observe several times. (*Letters*, p. 65)

Although Sayyida Salme affectionately portrays Heinrich as a dear and devoted husband, and never disparages him in any way, in this area, she lacked his support. Not only did his devotion to God fall short of hers, but it also seems that he was unaware of the intensity of the gap, in part because she proved deferential to his nature and chose not to insist. She also seemed afraid to validate a difference that she knew was there, but preferred not to confront. I have wondered, if Heinrich had not died so soon, whether this fundamental asymmetry would have pulled at the harmonious balance between them over time. As it was, it proved one less dilemma she had to face.

After Sayyida Salme arrived in Germany, the whole context let her down and left her hanging. As important as faith was to her social fabric in Zanzibar, the initial lack of faith connection in Germany may have been a major reason for her separation from Hamburg society, including, it seems, the extended

---

83 One could say the same of her mother, Djilfidan, who was orphaned at age five or six, when Turkish mercenaries from Russian incursions raided her family farm, killed both parents, and rode off with her two siblings, never to be seen again. Sold into slavery, however, hers was not a chosen family. Even so, as a child and then *surie* in the harem, she found safety and solace. We do not know whether her original family was Christian or Muslim, although by the start of the 17th century, most Circassians had converted from Orthodox Christianity to Islam.

Ruete family.[84] This became more extreme after Heinrich died. She had no social currency without her husband, no cultural bridge to tide her over, and no active religious life to tie her in. Not until she met the Baroness von Tettau in Dresden, with whom she could finally learn and live her new religion, could she at last—seven years after arriving in Germany—speak of a meaningful Christian connection and a dearest, deepest faith friend once again.

> Through my new motherly friend, I was able to find the first true Christian, someone I had been seeking, unfortunately without success, all this time. . . . Oh, how often did my heavy heart lead me to her, since I could always be sure of her empathy and understanding. How often, oh how often, did I return home after being comforted and strengthened by her, able to continue the terribly difficult road in life. I could not thank the merciful Lord enough for his care. (*Letters*, pp. 84–85)

What was it about the Baroness that made such a difference? Even after Sayyida Salme moved to a new town, they kept close through correspondence. Von Tettau had originally sought her out, perhaps as a charity case, but they grew to appreciate each other in their mutual embrace of the Lord. Long after the Baroness passed away, Sayyida Salme kept her in heart and soul—never forgetting this crucial pillar at a crucial time. Indeed, mother figures played a prominent role in much of Sayyida Salme's life. Whether in the confines of the harem or the tumult of the West, Sayyida Salme thrived under the protective wings of older women around her—her mother, of course, but also her half-sister Chole, even as she led her astray, and the sisters Zeyane and ZemZem, in addition to the beloved Baroness who called her "my dear precious thing." I can see how they might have helped calm and guide Sayyida Salme's flapping wings.

What ultimately sustained Sayyida Salme, however, was how she communed with God. In the shifting spiritual terrain that underpinned her community on earth, God, it seems, was always with her. For all the breaches and brokenness, she was never alone.

And once she crossed over, she never crossed back. Sayyida Salme remained a Christian to the end of her days. It is meaningful that she never returned to

---

84 It is hard to know whether this distance from the Ruetes stemmed from her or her husband's family. The record, including her writing, is noticeably silent on this score. Not even Ruete descendants I have spoken with were able to shed light on why there was so little apparent interaction between Sayyida Salme and her husband's extended family over the years.

On Faith

Islam, even after she gave up on Germany, even after her children had grown, even after she returned to Arab lands. There were surely many factors, not least her attachment to her children, whom she had deliberately and diligently raised as Christians. She felt tied to Christianity through them:

> I openly admit that I was often at the edge of my resolve, and naught but the thought of my children, who had been born and raised in the European way, kept me from succumbing to [the Zanzibari] pleas and staying with them in the beloved homeland. I valued the wellbeing of my children above my own happiness. Under no circumstances, not even for the most shining prospects, was I willing to sacrifice the emotional equilibrium of my children. (*Addendum* at page 33 above)

But perhaps she had also found peace with her Christian God. It is hard to know, but in a significant gesture, her son Rudolph sponsored an altar piece at the Protestant Church in Beirut in 1930 in memory of his mother.[85] When I think about it, though, one more thing may have been at play. At the deepest level, I can imagine that the painful memories of her conversion had so drastically seared her soul that the residual scars were simply too raw to be reopened. Despite all the cajoling of her Zanzibari fans—just come back, we promise you a happy life—she could not take it lightly. This, too, the all-encompassing gravity of her religious identity, was in the nature of her faith.[86]

As I reach the end of this essay, I can do no better than quote primarily from her. While I have relied mostly on the *Letters* to explore her conversion experience, it is the very last encounter in her *Memoirs* that makes me sit up and ponder the conundrum of it all:

> As I was approaching Zanzibar, I had been very unsure what reception would await me. That my brother would respect Germany's wishes, I had no doubt, and so it was. That he would hardly be kind towards me, at most putting on a good face in deference to Germany, for that I was also prepared. The ugly behavior he had shown my other siblings truly gave me no reason to expect any friendly outreach from him. But it was a different question as to how the population would react to

---

[85] See correspondence with the *Evangelische Kirche* in Beirut at the Leiden University Libraries Or. 27.135 C9.

[86] It seems fair to say that, as her views evolved, the border she crossed between religions proved more intractable than any border between nation-states. In her disappointment as a German citizen, she eventually saw the benefits of being a British citizen and second-guessed her own insistence on staying in Germany. (*Letters*, pp. 71–72) Her identity therefore did not appear to rest on her national status. Religion was the greater tie, the root cause of her trauma, even at a time when state and religion were so interdefined and intertwined.

my sudden appearance. To my greatest joy, I can simply repeat that I received the warmest reception. Arabs, Hindus, Banyans, and natives, they all pressed me over and over again to please stay in Zanzibar. This fortified my belief anew that there was no way that religious hatred toward my person was at stake. . . . Such demonstrations of love and devotion have tided me over many a difficult hour, along with the blissful feeling of having seen my homeland once more. They have indeed made my trip a fount of delight for the rest of my life, and I can forever give thanks and praise to the Almighty for his goodness! (*Memoirs*, p. 227)

What a critical moment after all her hardship, what an important revelation this must have been for her! All the religious rules and social opprobrium that had taken so much from her were still no match for the human spirit. Two decades later, Sayyida Salme's enduring love of her homeland was reciprocated in the love of the people, who would not let religion stand in the way. What the church and the state condemned with their levers of hate still found refuge in the hearts of the local folk. Sayyida Salme's faith could transcend religion to find love and humanity. Her story is enough to give hope for today.

But look further at what I left out in the ellipses above, as it comes full circle:

> One day, I encountered two Arabs, with whom I began to converse. When another person pointed out that they were relatives of mine—I had not recognized them—I told them, if I had known, I would never have engaged in conversation, being so unsure about how my relatives stood towards me under the current circumstances. They immediately responded that, to them, I was still my father's daughter. And when I touched upon my religion, one of them countered that this had been predestined as my fate from the beginning of time. "Yes, the God that has separated you and us from the homeland is the same God that all people praise and adore; it is through his mighty will that you returned to us, and we rejoice in it. Is that not so? Will you and your children now stay here forever?" (*Memoirs*, p. 227)

History also records that even Sultan Madjid understood Sayyida Salme's behavior to be a manifestation of God's will.[87] Say what?! If her conversion and escape to Europe was in fact part of the Almighty's plan, how did she deserve to be so castigated and cast out?

---

87 Succinctly put by Sayyida Salme herself: "As a devout Muslim, he believed in divine predestination and was convinced that this alone had led me to Germany." (*Memoirs*, p. 202)

This, to me, is the strangest twist of all. Can it be that all the denigration, rejection, and danger, all her sacrifice, doubts and depression, inner conflict and pain, amounted to but a simple explanation that proved a complete excuse? True to Islamic principle, it was her fate. Her conversion was a betrayal, but it was also her destiny. That still implied a choice—that she could choose to revert—but it also anticipated the reverse. Today, if we are more sensitized to the balance of power, we can see that her original conversion was a form of coercion. But if even Islam, the religion that spurned her, answers that it was all foreordained anyhow, what was the offense of it all?

———•———

I have written a number of essays for these books on key topics—on family, freedom, fear, controversy, inspiration, and more—but faith is the one I absolutely knew I had to write. And yet, I knew it would be the hardest to unpack. Faith is so profoundly present in her writings, and yet, for me, it felt too deep to reach, too sacred to touch. But now I have ventured forth nonetheless, in this centennial collection, and hope to have succeeded in my effort to illuminate, not obfuscate. I hope she would allow that I dared to tread so close. I hope she would approve of what I have had to say. It is now for you, those of you with faith and those of you without, to consider the meaning in it all and carry her touchstones to a throughline for today.

ON LEGACY

Sayyida Salme gave us her own legacy. It is one hundred years since she left this world and one hundred and eighty years since she entered it. In between, she lived a life that was remarkable in its contours, and all the more remarkable for what she wrote about it. Remarkable because she was the first Arab woman to publish a book, remarkable because she taught herself to write when it was taboo, and remarkable because so much of what she lived and recorded remains present and prescient for today. There is much to remark upon, and my various essays scattered throughout my three companion books[88]—including on family, fate, controversy, freedom, fear, inspiration, transits, faith, and now legacy—provide some of the cues and seek your reflections in return. The real legacy of Sayyida Salme lies in what we make of it.

That is how legacy works. We can leave behind as much as we want, but it has meaning only to the extent that those who come later pick it up. For this reason, I embrace the privilege and responsibility of sharing my great-great-grandmother's writings all these generations later in a worldwide language, a modern cadence, an attractive layout, and various formats (paperback, ebook, and audiobook), all to ease access to words that might make us ponder. Through her colorful, thoughtful, and soulful voice, we can allow some of the past into the present and aim for a better future.

We are all part of a continuum of time where the world that has been matters as much as where it is going. Anyone who has even a mild sense of history realizes that we are prone to revisit our foibles and failings again and again. Hard-won peace and prosperity become increasingly at risk the more time that passes since the last manmade calamity. We can feel it right now, and it becomes even more essential that we summon our better angels. Looking probingly into the past can remind us of what is at stake and where we went astray.

Sayyida Salme is just one life and one voice among multitudes to teach us. But it is in diversity that we can see most clearly. What other female voices do we have of the time, what other female Arab voices, what other female Arab Muslim-to-Christian voices? The value in paying attention to what Sayyida Salme wrote lies not only in her keen eye, witty spirit, bold assertions, and intimate

---

88 The *Memoirs* (2022), the *Letters* (2023), and this *Centennial Collection* (2024), which are also available as a combined set in the *Centennial Compilation* (2024).

detail, but also in her convergence of perspective. Not only is her journey worth recounting, but it is the very source of her trenchant observations and penetrating insights—this overlay of Orient and Occident, this passage from Islam to Christianity, this descent from royalty to poverty. She lived a complex life that pitched external forces against internal fortitude. Her story gives us a prism to illuminate struggles we all face. In her self-expression, as she lived her life and as she wrote it down, she prods us to express ourselves.

And here, I am doing just that. In adding my voice to hers, I offer a stepping stone from her past that, in the words of my late brother, who deeply appreciated Sayyida Salme, may help us find our way forward:

> the stepping stones—
> which we skip *On*,
> crossing the universal pond
> make them part of the
>   going-from
> one thing
> to the next thing
> in our being
> and becoming[89]

---

*Let history surprise you, let her story inspire you—
let her authentic voice speak to you.*

---

[89] Martin Mathis Stumpf, August 15, 1963—August 18, 2005. Excerpt from a poem dated May 11, 2005.

In Memoriam

Emily Ruete,
born Sayyida Salme,
Princess of Oman and Zanzibar

* August 30, 1844
+ February 29, 1924

Death Certificate, Nr. 129, Jena, February 29, 1924

After a brief illness, our unforgettable mother, mother-in-law, and grandmother gently passed away in Jena on February 29, 1924, in her eightieth year.

Frau Emily Ruete
born Princess of Oman and Zanzibar

Antonie Brandeis, born Ruete, Hamburg
Rudolph Said-Ruete and Mrs. Therese,
born Mathias, London W8
Rosa Troemer, born Ruete, Jena
Martin Troemer, Retired Major General
and six grandchildren.

The private burial took place in Jena.

Theater der Stadt Jena

Aufführung der literar. Arbeitsgemeinschaft
an der Universität

Wiederholung

Montag, den 3. März, abends ½8 Uhr

„Was ihr wollt"

Von Shakespeare

Karten bei Raßmann und Volksbuchhandlung

Familien-Nachrichten

Nach kurzem Krankenlager entschlief sanft am 29. Februar im 80. Lebensjahre unsere unvergeßliche Mutter, Schwiegermutter und Großmutter

Frau Emily Ruete

Antonie Brandeis geb. Ruete, Hamburg
Rudolph Said-Ruete und Frau Therese
geb. Mathias, London
Rosa Croemer geb. Ruete
Martin Croemer, Generalmajor a. D.
und 6 Enkelkinder.

Die Beisetzung findet in aller Stille in Jena statt.
Es wird gebeten, von Beileidsbesuchen abzusehen.

Sayyida Salme in 1908

Sayyida Salme in 1908

Sayyida Salme, back in Germany, in 1915

Sayyida Salme, in Berlin, in 1916

New Year's greeting card for 1922 with Sayyida Salme's face inserted

Signed photo from Rudolph gifted to Professor Christiaan Snouck Hurgronje in 1924

The family with Sayyida Salme's first grandchild from her daughter Antonie in 1901

The family with two grandchildren, from Rudolph (on lap) and Antonie in 1902

Some of Sayyida Salme's family with the Schröder family in Jena in 1919

Rosa's family at the baptism of her second grandchild in 1934

IV 18/25.   *Abschrift*

Beirut, den 14. Dezember 1910.

Mein letzter Wille.

Ich unterzeichnete Emily Ruete, geborene Prinzessin von Oman & Zanzibar, bestimme ich hierdurch wie folgt.
Nach meinem Ableben vermache ich hierdurch die Hälfte meines Vermögens bestehend aus Wertpapieren, welche in der Reichs-Hauptbank zu Berlin, teilweise auch bei der Centrale der Deutschen Bank zu Berlin niedergelgt sind, sowie auch mein gesamten Hausstand bestehend: aus Möbel, Silbersachen, Teppiche, Bücher, Kleidungsstücke, Wäsche, Bilder, Schmucksachen, sowie Alles, was ich im Hause besitze, meiner Tochter Rosalie Troemer, geborene Ruete.

2, Die verbleibende Hälfte meines Vermögens fällt zur Hälfte an meine Tochter Antonie Brandeis geb. Ruete & die andere Hälfte an meinen Sohn Rudolf Said-Ruete.

3, Tritt der Fall ein, dass meine Tochter Rosalie Troemer vor mit stirbt, so fällt das ihr von mir bestimmte Erbschaft vollinhaltlich nach Abschnitt 1 den Kindern zu, sie sollen Alles bekommen: was ich für ihre Mutter bestimmt habe.

4, Das Recht über die „Memorien einer arab. Prinzessin " sowie über die noch ungedrukte Manuscripte, meine europ. Leben beschreibend, sollmeinen drei Kindern Antonie, Said & Rosalie & ihren Kindeskindern zu gleichen Teilen angehören.
Eigenhändig geschrieben.

Emily Ruete, geborene Prinzessin von Oman & Zanzibar.
Beirut, Syrien, den 14. Dezember 1910.
++++++++++++

Initial Last Will and Testament from December 14, 1910, in Beirut

Transcription

Beirut, December 14, 1910.

My last will and testament.

I, the undersigned, Emily Ruete, born Princess of Oman and Zanzibar, set forth the following:

After my death, I hereby bequeath half of my estate, consisting of securities deposited in the National Bank main office in Berlin, in part also in the German Bank central office in Berlin, as well as my entire household consisting of furniture, silverware, rugs, books, clothing, linens, pictures, jewelry, as well as everything I own in the house, to my daughter Rosalie Troemer, born Ruete.

2. The remaining half of my estate shall go half to my daughter Antonie Brandeis, born Ruete, and half to my son Rudolph Said-Ruete.

3. In the event that my daughter Rosalie Troemer dies before me, then the inheritance set forth under point 1 shall go in full to the children; they shall receive everything that I have bestowed to their mother.

4. The rights to the "Memoiren einer arabischen Prinzessin," as well as the as-yet unpublished manuscripts that describe my European life, shall belong to my three children, Antonie, Said & Rosalie & their children in equal parts.

Written in the author's own hand.

Emily Ruete, born Princess of Oman and Zanzibar.

Beirut, Syria, December 14, 1910.

Last Will and Testament of Mrs. Emily Ruete, born Princess of Oman and Zanzibar.

In the year 1912, I drew up a will that was deposited in the local court of Spandau. Deviating from this will, I hereby set forth the following:

1. All my personal property, consisting of furniture, art, jewelry, linens, rugs, clothing, silverware, and the like, shall go to my two daughters, namely:

    (1) Mrs. Antonie Brandeis, born Ruete in Kl. Niendorf near Segeberg in Holstein.

    (2) Mrs. Rosalie Troemer, born Ruete in Jena.

    I wish for them to agree amicably on the division.

    As the only exception to this, I now order that my son, Mr. Rudolph Said-Ruete in Lucerne, be the one to receive all the items that come from Zanzibar.

2. My capital assets shall be divided equally among my three children, provided that if one of my children dies before me, such child's children shall stand in such child's stead.

3. In such event, my grandchildren shall not receive their shares before they reach the age of 25. Naturally, the children may already have use of the assets before reaching the age of 25. Until the age of 25, the administration of this estate shall reside in the hands of:

    (1) Mr. Rudolph Said-Ruete, or if he has died,

    (2) My son-in-law General Troemer, or if he has died,

    (3) My daughters, in order of age.

4. I name my son Said-Ruete as executor of my will, in the first instance, or if he should die, my son-in-law, General Troemer.

Jena, September 30, 1920.

Emily Ruete, born Princess of Oman and Zanzibar.

Final Last Will and Testament from September 30, 1920, in Jena

Translated on page 93 above

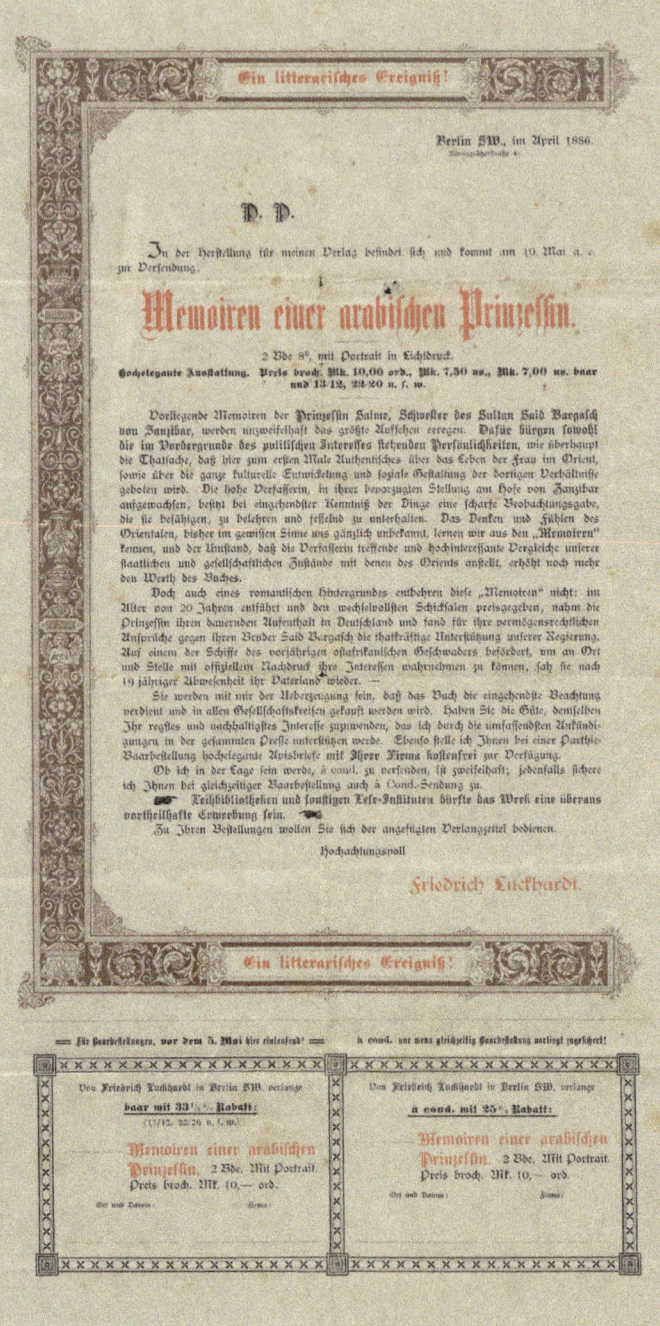

A literary event!

Among the publications for my publishing house, the following will be available for distribution on May 10 of this year [1886]:

Memoirs of an Arabian Princess

----

2 Vols., 8°, with a collotype portrait.

Very elegant arrangement. Regular price per book 10 Marks, ordered in advance 7.50 Marks, ordered in advance and paid in cash 7 Marks; and 13/12, 22/20, and so on.

The present Memoirs of Princess Salme, sister of Sultan Said [sic][90] Barghash of Zanzibar, will without a doubt evoke the greatest interest. This is assured not only by the prominence of politically important individuals, but also the general fact that authentic details about the lives of Oriental women, as well as the overall cultural development and social organization of local conditions, are presented for the first time. The distinguished author, who grew up in a privileged position in the royal court of Zanzibar, possesses a deep knowledge and a talent for keen observation that enable her to instruct you and keep you captivated. In the "Memoirs," we learn about the thoughts and feelings of Orientals, heretofore in certain ways completely unknown to us. That the author additionally provides fitting and fascinating comparisons between our national and social conditions and those of the Orient further heightens the value of this book.

These "Memoirs" are also not lacking in romantic content. Having eloped at the age of 20 and subjected to the most turbulent fortunes, the Princess took up permanent residence in Germany and received vigorous support from our government for her inheritance claims against her brother Said Barghash. Traveling on one of the ships of last year's African squadron, which allowed her to pursue her interests with official pressure, she saw her homeland again for the first time in nineteen years.

You will share my conviction that this book deserves the most avid attention and will be purchased by all levels of society. Kindly give it your most energized and sustained interest, which I will support through widely distributed announcements to the entire press. In addition, if you undertake a partial-cash order, I will offer you very elegant publication notices with your company name at no extra cost.

Whether I will be in a position to send books à condition is unlikely; in any case, I ensure you à condition shipment for a simultaneous cash order.

This would be an exceptionally advantageous acquisition for borrowing libraries and other reading institutions.

Please use the order form provided below for your purchases.

Respectfully,

Friedrich Luckhardt

A literary event!

---

90 See footnote 31 above.

In the press: "she is described by all who meet her not only as energetic, but also highly-educated/cultured"

Translation of a paragraph which was published in the
"MOKATTAM" of Thursday 27th 1924 No.10771

DEATH OF AN ARABIAN PRINCESS.

News from Berlin announced these days the death of Mrs. Emily Ruete a Princess of Zanzibar of the Barghash dynasty, sister of Sultan Saïd late Sultan of Zanzibar. She was eighty years of age when she died. This is the history of this Princess: She met a German merchant of Zanzibar, she loved him, she did her best to talk to him and succeeded. He married her and took her back to his country from fear of her relatives. He had from her one boy and two girls and he died very young. Some time after, the boy entered the service of the German Army and the writer of these lines made his acquaintance and that of his family when he was Military Attaché to the German Consulate General at Beyrouth. After that he became Manager of the German Oriental Bank at Cairo. His name is Said Ruete. This name, Said, was the name of the Sultan his uncle. [grandfather]

The Princess, Mrs. Ruete was well acquainted with the Arabic language and was able to speak it gramatically and always with a loud and clear voice in a way that surprised all those who heard her for the first time speaking arabic when wearing a european dress and hat. She was a farsighted and very intelligent lady. The daughters inherited the intelligence of their mother and one of them is well acquainted with Arabic, German, English, French and Italian and learned by heart in English the famous verses of Homer's Iliad and Milton's poem "PARADISE LOST" also in English and both are the longest poems known up to our time; she is also clever in music and singing.

The Sultans of Zanzibar come originally from Yemen and still have relations with Hadramaut.

Cairo-based Al Muqattam article translation sent from the British consulate

To the Memory

of my Mother

the

SEYYIDAH SALME

(*Emily Ruete*)

Daughter of SAID BIN SULTAN

who

born at Zanzibar on August 30th, 1844, and having fulfilled a great mission by a life that proved to the West the noble qualities of the Womanhood of the East,

died at Jena on February 29th, 1924.

Rudolph's dedication to his mother in the biography of his grandfather

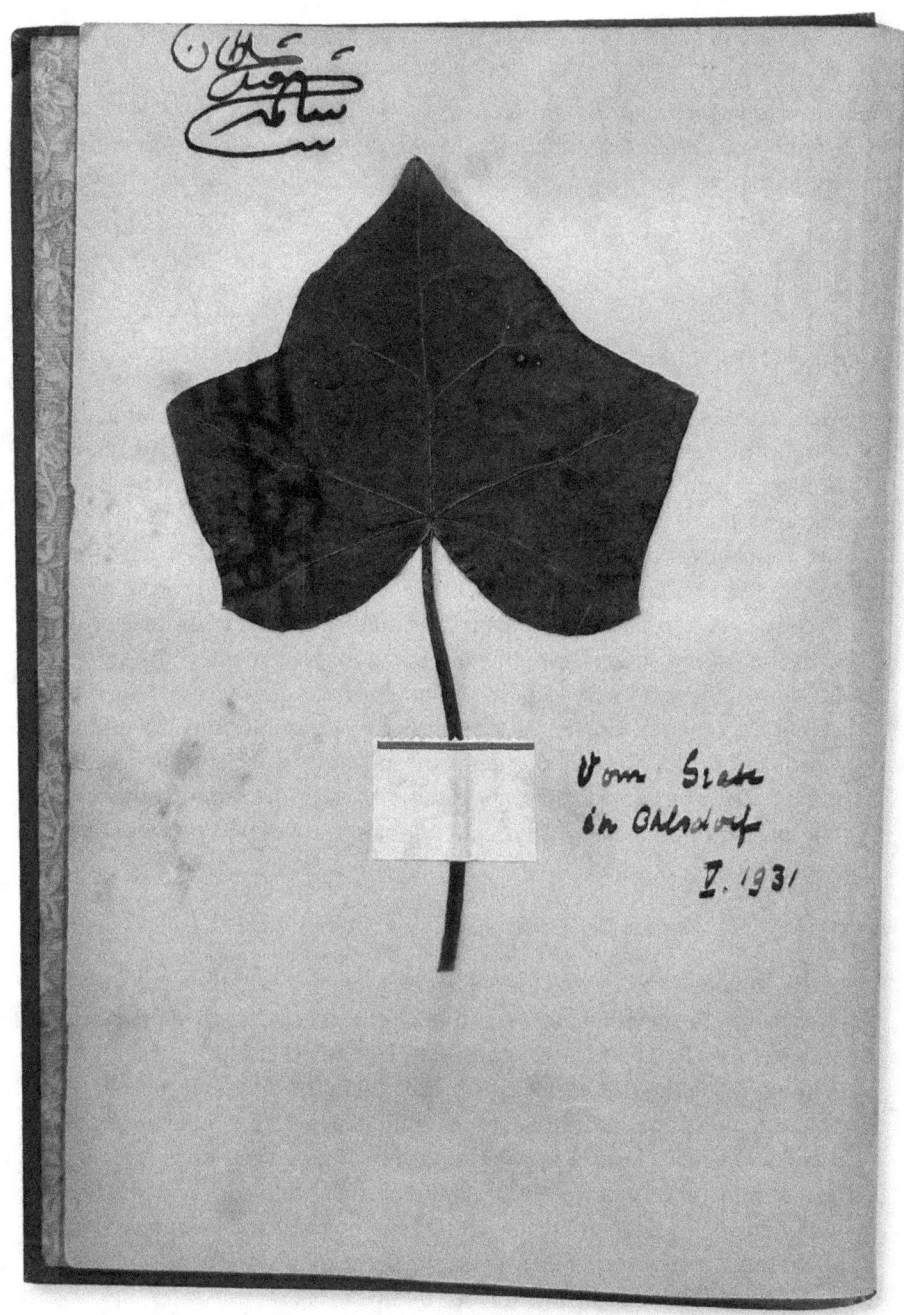

Ivy leaf from the Ohlsdorf gravesite placed in Sayyida Salme's copy of the Memoirs

The cremated remains of Emily Ruete, born Sayyida Salme, were buried next to Heinrich Ruete, her husband, in the family plot at the Ohlsdorf Cemetery in Hamburg on June 14, 1924. The plot consists of multiple gravesites located at U27, Nos. 78–89.

From a letter by Antonie to her brother Rudolph on June 15, 1924:

> Many thanks for your letter from the 6th of this month. The burial of our mother's urn took place yesterday. Several days earlier, [we] had brought a palm tree, as you had requested.... I laid out the black cloth in the stone container, then came the soldered Memoirs, followed by the metal covering, and on top of that the sand from Zanzibar. After the cemetery official was satisfied that everything was done according to the regulations, and the name on the metal covering was consistent with the formal submission, the Witte employee cemented the stone lid shut and cemented [on] the number that was recorded in the cemetery register. Cornelius Jacobs then said some very beautiful words about the life and character of our mother, which touched all our hearts. The official then shoveled dirt onto the stone container and placed upon it the pretty wreaths that relatives and [others] had brought....

From a letter by Rosa to her brother Rudolph on June 15, 1924:

> ... We placed the ashes, the soldered Memoirs and the sand from Zanzibar in the cement container that already lay in the ground, which was then walled shut (after inspection by the official) ... Toni and I had already gone there the day before and had a deep impression of this solemn space, a wonderful spot on the forest floor. I gave special thanks to Uncle Hermann that Mama could find such a lovely resting place; we would have had nothing comparable to offer. Now she lies there, in such a peaceful place, with the appeasing and calming effect of nature's presence in this beautiful time of year. We had placed benches at the location and stayed for a while....

The Ruete family gravesite at Ohlsdorf Cemetery in Hamburg, Germany

Family Ruete

		Dorothea Ruete née Schuer 1890-1962	
Lizzie Altrock née Ruete 1888-1919	Adolf Hermann Ruete 1884-1943		Ulrich Ruete 1927-1984

| Andr Hermann Ruete 1850-1926 | Charlotte Ruete née Pfister 1860-1935 | Kurt Alex Ruete 1886-1970 | Tilla Ruete 1900-1980 | Wolfgang Ruete 1922-1988 |

| Dora Ruete née Rothenbücher 1856-1923 | Johann Gustav Adolph Ruete 1848-1923 | H. Adolph Ruete 1889-1945 | Henning Ruete 1926-1988 | Ute Ruete 1938-2003 |

| Johanna Juliana Ruete née Wrigge 1816-1907 | Andreas Hermann Ruete 1892-1951 | Anneliese Ruete-Johann 1927-2001 |

| Emily Ruete 1844-1924 | Alix Spindler-Biermann née Ruete 1880-1962 |

| Rudolph Heinrich Ruete 1839-1870 | Antonie Brandeis née Ruete 1868-1945 | Johanna Botz née Brandeis 1904-1990 |

Map of the Ruete family's gravesite at the Ohlsdorf Cemetery in Hamburg

Emily Ruete
Widow of Rudolph Heinrich Ruete

born August 30, 1844, in Zanzibar,
died February 29, 1924, in Jena.

Whosoever loves his homeland as you do,
is loyal to the core.

SALAM

It might be odd to close this book with a "hello"—salam to all who have perused these pages! But in the typical richness of Arabic, this ubiquitous little word goes both deep and wide.[91] It has within it a promise of peace and protection, no aggression, no offense, no evil. It signals safety, allowing surrender and submission. Its root appears in Islam, meaning submission to God, and salamah, meaning peace and security. In As-Salam, it is one of God's ninety-nine names. In the phrase Dar As Salam, it is paradise.

Salam is also the root of Salme, the name Djilfidan gave her second daughter, after the first one died very young.[92] What hopes this mother would have had for her child, that it might survive and thrive! In Djilfidan's status as a *surie*,[93] this precious newborn was a gift to the Sultan, a step-up in status as the mother of royalty, and a pass to freedom upon the Sultan's death—but also, naturally, far more than that. After Djilfidan's early loss of father, mother, sister, and brother, with no other direct family known to her, this little girl had a special status. I would like to think she completed Djilfidan's world and made her whole in a way that nothing else could. I can imagine that Djilfidan chose the name Salme for all its deeply comforting and connecting meanings, grateful to have found such comfort and connection for herself, within a larger family and toward God, and wishing all the same for her beloved child. I do believe this chosen name reflects a wish for the wholeness of self we all seek.

---

91 It also goes far, as a greeting and word for peace, safety, and well-being in Swahili as well.
92 *Memoirs*, p. 7. Note that this detail was left out of both historical English translations, the ones from 1888 and 1907. See my comments at www.sayyidasalme.com/translation.
93 Plural *sarari*. This refers to the "secondary wife" type of concubine in the Omani harem. (*Memoirs*, p. 249)

Sayyida Salme's writings tell us how well *that* went—even to the point of effacing her name. But throughout all the transitions, despite all the hardship, she maintained a remarkably strong core of confidence and steady connection to her maker.

Although she became Emily Ruete, I still refer to her as Salme in recognition of her deepest self, that inner strength at the root of her salam. As she speaks to us today, she is still Sayyida Salme to me, and I will trace my own roots to her mother in recognition of my own mother. My mother and I are two steps in this cascading history, and with her, I have had the privilege of this shared endeavor. For all three books in this series, I am ever so grateful for my mother's gracious and generous support, her careful review, insightful contributions, unending stamina, and complete devotion to the project. This has been a wonderfully grounding and fulfilling collaboration, very much in the spirit of salam.

And with that, I can now also say ma'a salama to say good-bye—in the greater sense of the proverbial "God be with you"—with wishes of goodness and wholeness for all.

LIST OF IMAGES

[Front cover] See [85] and [89] below.

[7] Lithograph of the British sailing ship *HMS Highflyer*, said to be from 1861, artist unknown. This twenty-one gun, corvette class warship of the Royal Navy was launched in 1852 and participated in the 1854 Crimean War on the Black Sea and then the Second Opium War, before transitioning to African shores in the mid-1860s. It appears that the *Highflyer* was patrolling the waters around Zanzibar for illegal slave trade and rescued 152 slaves from an Arabian ship in August 1866, just days before Sayyida Salme came on board to be taken to Aden, Yemen. One of them was a young African boy, who eventually took the name Thomas Malcolm Sabine Highflyer after the Royal Navy captain of the ship, Thomas Malcolm Sabine Pasley. This boy worked on the ship for two years before he was adopted by a family in Brighton, but then died in 1870 from tuberculosis and dropsy. "New grave for freed slave Thomas Highflyer who lived in Brighton," by Jack Arscott, January 21, 2018, *The Argus*. Young Thomas may well have been on the ship with Sayyida Salme. The *Highflyer* completed its sailing days in August 1868. www.pdavis.nl under Royal Navy Vessels.

[9] Photograph and notes about Captain Thomas Malcolm Sabine Pasley, a British Navy captain who picked up Sayyida Salme from the open water on a late August night in 1866, first heading south and then north to Aden, thus enabling her secret departure from her homeland. The clippings were pasted by Sayyida Salme's son Rudolph into a book that is part of the collection he provided to the Oriental Institute, namely R.N. Lyne, *Zanzibar in contemporary times: a short history of the southern east in the nineteenth century* (1905), at the Leiden University Libraries in the Said-Ruete Collection under SR423.

[10] Studio portrait of Sayyida Salme taken by photographer H.F. Plate in Hamburg around 1868, not long after her arrival in Germany, and used as the frontispiece for her 1886 publication of *Memoiren einer arabischen Prinzessin*. From the translator's family collection.

[11] Cover page of a compilation of Sayyida Salme's legacy writings prepared as typed manuscripts by the family after Sayyida Salme's death in 1924 and formally presented as her *Literarischer Nachlass* (Literary Estate) to various institutions by Sayyida Salme's son Rudolph. This compilation includes the two

List of Images

texts that are translated in this collection: *Nachtrag zu den Memoiren* (see "Addendum to My Memoirs") and *Syrische Sitten und Gebräuche* (see "Syrian Customs and Conventions"), in addition to *Briefe nach der Heimat* (published in a separate companion book as "Letters to the Homeland"). The *Literarischer Nachlass* is located in the Leiden University Libraries at Or. 6281.

[12] One of six of Sayyida Salme's half-brothers that reigned over Zanzibar as the Sultan, following their father's death in 1856. Sayyid Khalifa bin Said became Sultan in 1888, when Sultan Barghash died, and continued until his own death in February 1890. A mounted engraving can be found in the Leiden University Libraries at Or. 27.135 D28.

[15] Top: Note to the Oosters Instituut (Oriental Institute) included in correspondence related to the Institute's acquisition of books and materials donated by Rudolph Said-Ruete; located in the Leiden University Libraries at Or. 127.35 J1. Bottom: The bookcase made to house the donated collection.

[16–17] Original pages of the *Nachtrag zu den Memoiren*, appearing in a single notebook, handwritten by Sayyida Salme, with edits from her son Rudolph and daughter Rosa; in the Leiden University Libraries at Or. 27.135 A1.

[18–19] Revised pages of the *Nachtrag zu den Memoiren*, appearing in a single notebook, handwritten by the author's daughter Rosa, with edits from her brother Rudolph; in the Leiden University Libraries at Or. 27.135 A2.

[20] First page of an early typewritten copy of Sayyida Salme's *Nachtrag zu den Memoiren*; provided by Alexander von Brand from his family collection.

[21] First page of an upgraded typewritten copy of Sayyida Salme's *Nachtrag zu den Memoiren* that is part of the compilation described under [11] above; from the Leiden University Libraries at Or. 6281.

[23] This handwritten copy of the original Arabic poem received by Sayyida Salme after her second departure from Zanzibar in 1885 was produced by her daughter, Rosa. The author of the poem was a half-sister from the harem, but her exact identity is not known. Rosa's brother, Rudolph, pasted Rosa's copy into a family edition of the *Memoiren*, with the notation that it was "copied from the original by Rosa Troemer-Ruete; Jena, October 1924," half a year after Sayyida Salme's death. It was also marked with two corrections by the family friend, Professor Christiaan Snouck Hurgronje. This copy of the *Memoiren* is located in the Leiden University Libraries at SR 614b.

[30] The two-masted *SS Neckar*, with screw propulsion at a service speed of fourteen knots. It sailed for the Norddeutscher Lloyd shipping line from 1874 to 1895, first transatlantic and then in the Far East service as of 1886. www.ggarchives/oceantravel/immigrantships. Image credit to the Peabody Museum of Salem (the Peabody Essex Museum).

[35] Watercolor and drawing from the "Album von Zanzibar von William O'Swald & Co." O'Swald is likely the competitor company that Sayyida Salme referred to disparagingly in the *Letters* (p. 66). These are two of more than thirty photographs and paintings in the album, which was compiled in 1899 to commemorate fifty years of the company's presence in Zanzibar. Image credit to the Northwestern University Libraries through their digital collection at www.dc.library.northwestern.edu.

[41] Photograph of Rosalie Ruete, known as Rosa, the translator's great-grandmother. She was Sayyida Salme's youngest and a mere four months old when her father tragically died. From what we know, Rosa was particularly close to her mother, including as the only child that accompanied her on the second trip to Zanzibar in 1888. Her even script is also particularly visible in marked copies of her mother's writings on which they collaborated. Rosa was gifted in languages and studied art with Max Rabe. At age 32, on September 17, 1902, she married Captain Martin Gottlob Reinhold Troemer, who later became Major, then Major General. She had two daughters, Emily (1903) and Berta (1904), both of whom received PhDs (in law and chemistry, respectively), which was unusual for women at the time. Rosa took care of her mother, first in Bromberg and then Jena, from the time her mother left Beirut in 1914 until she passed away in 1924. Rosa died in Kronberg(Taunus) in 1948. Much appreciation to Ursula Luther, a descendant of Heinrich Ruete's sister Sarah (née Ruete) Rothenbücher, for sharing this image from her private collection.

[42–43] Pages from the original *Syrische Sitten und Gebräuche*, appearing in a single, mostly empty notebook, handwritten by Sayyida Salme, with a cover entitled "Beirut;" in the Leiden University Libraries at Or. 27.135 A6.

[44] First page of an early typewritten copy of Sayyida Salme's *Syrische Sitten und Gebräuche*; provided by Alexander von Brand from his family collection.

[45] First page of an upgraded typewritten copy of Sayyida Salme's *Syrische Sitten und Gebräuche* that is part of the compilation described under [11] above; from the Leiden University Libraries at Or. 6281.

List of Images

[50] Photograph of the first wedding of Sayyida Salme's children, when her eldest, Antonie, married Eugen Brandeis in Beirut in 1898; generously provided by Alexander von Brand, a descendant of Antonie, from his private family collection. Shown is the celebration at the Hotel Bassoul, with the bride and groom in the center. Sayyida Salme is standing behind the groom and Rosa is left of Antonie. Antonie was 30 at the time, and Eugen Brandeis was 22 years her senior in his second marriage. Immediately after the wedding, the couple moved to Jaluit in the Marshall Islands, where he served as the imperial governor of the German protectorate from 1898 to 1906. Antonie gave birth to two daughters (Margarethe in 1900 and Johanna in 1904). The couple divorced in 1913. A detailed account of Antonie's remarkable work as one of very few female ethnographers at the time and her support of German colonialism appears in the thoroughly-researched final project report from Godwin Kornes for the Museum Natur und Mensch in Freiburg titled "Provenienzforschung Ozeaniensammlung Eugen und Antonie Brandeis (Ethnologische Sammlung)" (2022). See also his brief essay titled "The Ambivalence of Gender" at boasblogs.org (2022). Godwin Kornes contacted us in connection with this research. I am immensely grateful to him for his support of my work on Sayyida Salme and our family's reconnection through him to Antonie's branch of the family through her great-grandson Alexander von Brand.

[51] Top: Photograph of one of Sayyida Salme's later residences in Beirut starting in 1909, as part of a series of photographs included in an album compiled by her son Rudolph and included in the materials he gave to the Oriental Institute in Leiden in 1937; located in the Leiden University Libraries at Or. 27.135 H5. Bottom: Photograph of the same house from the same series; also at Or. 27.135 H5. Rudolph added the red x's to mark his mother.

[52–53] Two photographs of the interior of Sayyida Salme's home in Beirut from an album of photographs that was included in Rudolph Said-Ruete's collection of books and materials he granted to the Oriental Institute in Leiden; the album now resides in the Leiden University Libraries at Or. 27.135 H5.

[57] Certification of Sayyida Salme's baptism under the "Christian Name Emily" on May 30, 1867, as an extract from the official Register of Baptisms at Aden, Yemen, signed by the "Chaplain for Aden." More than a name change, this act constituted her conversion from Islam to Christianity that sealed her self-exile. It immediately preceded her wedding vows to Heinrich Ruete in the same church on the same day. The form incorrectly notes her age as 30; she was still 22. The certificate is included in Rudolph's collection in the Leiden University Libraries at Or. 27.135 C4.

[64] Rudolph Heinrich Ruete's signed oath of citizenship for the independent city of Hamburg (*Freie und Hansestadt Hamburg*) dated April 17, 1868. Born in Hamburg of German parents, Heinrich had been a German citizen all his life, including during his decade as a German merchant based in Zanzibar—until he married Sayyida Salme. Unbeknownst to him at the time, this foreign marriage was considered an act of disloyalty. Heinrich's effort to reinstate his citizenship status proved relatively minor, but quite significant, not least because it paved the way for his wife to acquire Hamburg and German citizenship even after his death. Leiden University Libraries at Or. 27.135 C4.

[65] Certification of Emily Ruete's status, in her position of widow, as a citizen of the State of Hamburg and thus also the newly-constituted German Reich dated May 1, 1872. Unlike her husband's citizenship declaration above, no oath of loyalty or signature was required. The only signature appearing here is of the relevant agent of the issuing Hamburg police authority. Leiden University Libraries at Or. 27.135 C4.

[69] Holiday greeting card to the Stumpf family from Said El-Gheithy, received in the early 2000s. We first got to know Said El-Gheithy in connection with his 2001 exhibit "Princess Salme—Behind the Veil: The Life and Writings of Sayyida Salme, Writer and Teacher (1844–1924)" at the Brunei Gallery of the SOAS University of London and maintained some contact with him thereafter. From the Stumpf family's private collection.

[81] Death certificate of Emily Ruete, who died of double pneumonia on February 29, 1924, at the age of 79 in the home of her daughter Rosa at Gartenstrasse 4, Jena, in eastern Germany. Not long after World War II, Rosa left the house in Jena when she received permission to move from the Russian zone to the American zone to join her two daughters in Kronberg (Taunus) near Frankfurt. This permission was granted on the basis of an attestation of support from Friedrich Oechsner, who was then living in Washington, DC, with his wife Olga. Olga Salme (née Said-Ruete) was Rudolph's daughter and thus Rosa's niece. The family's copy of the death certificate is in the Leiden University Libraries at Or. 27.135 C4.

[82] Death notice pasted into an album prepared by Sayyida Salme's son Rudolph and titled "Zum Tode von Emily Ruete" (Relating to the Death of Emily Ruete). Located in the Leiden University Libraries at Or. 27.135 C2.

[83] Death notice published in a local newspaper under the header "Family News" along with other notices of the day for theater, opera, and cinema

performances. Much appreciation to my uncle Helmuth Schwinge, a great-grandson of Sayyida Salme, who provided this copy.

[84] Framed studio photograph of Sayyida Salme, undated and unattributed, but presumably from the same 1908 studio session as [85]; the framed portrait stands in the Schwinge home and was photographed by my cousin Emily Schwinge.

[85] Framed studio photograph of Sayyida Salme dated December 1908, according to a handwritten notation ("XII/1908") on the same photograph in the Leiden University Libraries at Or. 27.135 D7; the framed portrait was provided by Alexander von Brand from his family collection.

[86] Studio photograph of Sayyida Salme taken by Progress-Photographie, with handwritten date of February 1, 1915, a year after Sayyida Salme returned to Germany, on the framing cardstock that is somewhat damaged by liquid below; provided by Alexander von Brand from his family collection.

[87] Studio photograph of Sayyida Salme taken by A. Wertheim in Berlin, with a handwritten date of 1916 on the back along with a notation in Arabic that reads "many greetings" (*salam kathir*); located in the Leiden University Libraries at Or. 27.135 D6.

[88] Handmade holiday card wishing a happy new year for 1922, with a figurine cut-out body in a fur coat and a face of Sayyida Salme pasted in from an actual photograph. For some blog-inspired thoughts, see my short piece 101 years later at www.sayyidasalme.com/post/prosit-neujahr. The card is part of Rudolph's collection in the Leiden University Libraries at Or. 27.135 D8.

[89] The same studio photograph as in [85] above, in this case accompanied by a photograph of Sayyida Salme's son Rudolph and his handwritten dedication dated October 1924 to Professor Christiaan Snouck Hurgronje ("Herrn Professor Dr. C. Snouck Hurgronje das Bild meiner ihm in aufrichtiger Wertschätzung verbunden gewesenen Mutter, Frau Emily Ruete/Prinzessin von Oman und Zanzibar, freundschaftlichst zugeeignet—RSaidRuete"), apparently presented as a gift following her death; from the Leiden University Libraries at Or. 27.135 D7.

[90] Top: Studio photograph taken by E. Bieber on December 8, 1901. Shown from left to right: Rudolph Said-Ruete and his British Jewish wife Theresa (née Mond); Sayyida Salme; Antonie Brandeis (née Ruete); Antonie's young daughter Margarethe; and Rosa Troemer (née Ruete); provided by Alexander von Brand from his family collection.

[90] Bottom: Studio photograph taken by W. Höffert on September 15, 1902. Back from left to right: Rudolph Said-Ruete; Rosa (née Ruete) Troemer; Rosa's husband, General Martin Troemer; Antonie (née Ruete) Brandeis, and Antonie's husband, Eugen Brandeis. Front from left to right: Theresa (née Mond) Said-Ruete; Rudolph's young son Werner; Sayyida Salme; and Antonie's young daughter Margarethe. Provided by Alexander von Brand from his family collection.

[91] Top: Photograph taken in Jena at Beethovenstrasse 15 on June 22, 1919, of Sayyida Salme's family with the Schröder family, close friends that she first met in Beirut, with a continued friendship back in Germany. Paul Schröder was the same age as Sayyida Salme and served as German consul (1882–1885) and then consul general (1888–1909) in Beirut during the time Sayyida Salme lived there. The names on the cardstock were written in by a member of the Schröder family and are noted here in italics. Back from left: *Herr Troemer* (Martin Troemer), *Mama* (Lucie Schröder), *Frau Ruete* (Sayyida Salme), *Lukki* (a Schröder daughter), and *Frau Troemer* (Rosa Troemer). Front from left: unclear (possibly another Schröder daughter, although probably not Hedwig "Hedi"), *Emily Troemer* (the translator's grandmother), *Otto* (a Schröder son), and *Berta Troemer* (another Troemer daughter).

[91] Bottom: Adding the next generation beyond Sayyida Salme in a photograph taken at the baptism of Rosa's second grandchild, with the following handwritten notation on the back: In remembrance of the baptism of Renate Schwinge in Halle on April 22, 1934. Back from left: Berta (née Troemer) Prausnitzer, and two unknown gentlemen. Front from left: Martin Troemer, infant Renate Schwinge, Emily (née Troemer) Schwinge, Emily's husband Erich Schwinge, and Rosa Troemer. From the translator's family collection.

[92] First last will and testament from Emily Ruete recorded in Beirut, Syria, on December 14, 1910, with a date notation at the top left of April 18, 1925 (perhaps the date it was typed up), with a handwritten notation "Abschrift" (transcription) at the top center (perhaps to denote the carbon copy of an original typed page). This will is part of the family collection in the Leiden University Libraries at Or. 27.135 C6(1), but was superseded by later wills, the last of which is also part of the collection (see next item).

[94–95] Third and final last will and testament from Emily Ruete recorded in Jena, Germany, on September 30, 1920. This will refers to a second will from 1912, which is missing from the family collection, but may conceivably still be preserved in the referenced *Amtsgericht* of Spandau. This final will resides in the Leiden University Libraries at Or. 27.135 C6(2).

List of Images

[96] Printed flyer by publisher Friedrich Luckhardt in Berlin announcing the upcoming publication of Sayyida Salme's *Memoiren einer arabischen Prinzessin* in 1886. To great acclaim, a total of four editions of the *Memoiren* were published that same year. The flyer is in the Leiden University Libraries at Or. 27.135 A7.

[98] Two published drawings that appear amidst dozens of clippings from newspapers and periodicals that were placed in a scrapbook kept by Sayyida Salme's son Rudolph. Top: This drawing appears above an article titled "Sister of the Sultan from Zanzibar" with the handwritten note "Illustrierte-Zeitung—1884," presumably referring to the popular weekly *Illustrirte Zeitung* (1843–1944). Bottom: This drawing appears alongside a response to a question from a reader in Milan with the handwritten note "Schorers Familienblatt [Schorers Family Paper] No. 31. 1886." Located in the Leiden University Libraries at Or. 27.135 C1.

[99] Translation of an extract titled "Death of an Arabian Princess" from the Mokattam newspaper on March or April 27, 1924, conveyed to Rudolph Said-Ruete from someone in the British Consulate in Cairo by letter dated May 12, 1924. The copy includes some fine pencil markings correcting the text. Located in the Leiden University Libraries at Or. 27.135 C3.

[100] Dedication at the front of Rudolph Said-Ruete's biography of his grandfather, Sayyid Said bin Sultan, who governed Oman and Zanzibar from 1806 to 1856. Rudolph Said-Ruete, *Said bin Sultan (1791–1856)—Ruler of Oman and Zanzibar: His Place in the History of Arabia and East Africa* (1929).

[101] Ivy leaf from the Ruete family's gravesite at the Ohlsdorf Cemetery in Hamburg that was taped into Sayyida Salme's copy of the *Memoiren*, with a handwritten notation likely from her son Rudolph dated May 1931. Sayyida Salme's own signature in Arabic appears at the top left. This is the same copy of the *Memoiren* that contains the handwritten Arabic poem described in [23–25] above. Part of the Said-Ruete special collection of the Leiden University Libraries at SR 614a.

[103] From the Ruete family gravesite at the Ohlsdorf Cemetery in Hamburg. Photograph taken in October 2020 and generously provided by Godwin Kornes. The name Emily Ruete is one of several etched into the *Erinnerungsspirale* in the *Garten der Frauen* at the Ohlsdorf Cemetery. She is also included in R. Bake and B. Reimers, *Stadt der toten Frauen: Frauenportraits und Lebensbilder vom Friedhof Hamburg Ohlsdorf*, pp. 205–8 (1997).

[104] Two photographs taken almost a century apart of the Ruete family gravesite at the Ohlsdorf Cemetery in Hamburg. Top: Mounted and undated photograph in the family collection; located in the Leiden University Libraries at Or. 127.35 D14. Note the palm tree planted between the headstones of Heinrich and Emily Ruete that was added at Rudolph's request per a letter to him from his sister Antonie on June 15, 2024 at Or. 127.35 C4(6). Bottom: Photograph taken in October 2020 and provided by Godwin Kornes.

[105] Schematic of the Ruete family gravesite prepared by the translator.

[106–7] Three photographs from October 2020 by Godwin Kornes.

[108] Photograph from August 2023 of the translator and her mother, Andrea and Ursula Stumpf, working on the *Letters* translation, with a thank you to the translator's sister, Silva Stumpf, for spotting us.

[118] Photomontage presented by Rudolph to the Zanzibar Museum in 1927; much appreciation to Torrence Royer, curator of www.zanzibarhistory.com.

[Back cover] Top: See [10]. Bottom: Sayyida Salme's signature on the left, see [101]; on the right, as printed on the title page of her published *Memoiren*.

www.ingramcontent.com/pod-product-compliance
Lightning Source LLC
Chambersburg PA
CBHW052129070526
44585CB00017B/1751